RISK MANAGEMENT, LIABILITY INSURANCE, and ASSET PROTECTION STRATEGIES for DOCTORS and ADVISORS

Best Practices from Leading Consultants and Certified Medical Planners™

RISK MANAGEMENT, LIABILITY INSURANCE, and ASSET PROTECTION STRATEGIES for DOCTORS and ADVISORS

Best Practices from Leading Consultants and Certified Medical Planners™

Edited by
Dr. David E. Marcinko MBA CMP™
Prof. Hope R. Hetico RN MHA CMP™

Foreword by J. Wesley Boyd MD PhD MA

CRC Press
Taylor & Francis Group
Boca Raton London New York

CRC Press is an imprint of the
Taylor & Francis Group, an **informa** business
A PRODUCTIVITY PRESS BOOK

First published in paperback 2024

First published 2016 by CRC Press
2385 NW Executive Center Drive, Suite 320, Boca Raton FL 33431

and by CRC Press
4 Park Square, Milton Park, Abingdon, Oxon, OX14 4RN

First issued in hardback 2019

CRC Press is an imprint of Taylor & Francis Group, LLC

Publisher's Note
The publisher has gone to great lengths to ensure the quality of this reprint but points out that some imperfections in the original copies may be apparent.

Library of Congress Cataloging-in-Publication Data

Risk management, liability insurance, and asset protection strategies for doctors and advisors : best practices from leading consultants and certified medical planners / editors, David Edward Marcinko and Hope Rachel Hetico.
p. ; cm.
Includes bibliographical references and index.
ISBN 978-1-4987-2598-9 (alk. paper)
I. Marcinko, David E. (David Edward), editor. II. Hetico, Hope R., editor.
[DNLM: 1. Risk Management--United States. 2. Insurance, Liability--United States. 3. Interprofessional Relations--United States. 4. Practice Management--United States. W 80]

R728
610.68--dc23 2015021739

ISBN: 978-1-4987-2598-9 (hbk)
ISBN: 978-1-03-291763-4 (pbk)
ISBN: 978-0-429-25794-0 (ebk)

DOI: 10.1201/b19692

Visit the Taylor & Francis Web site at
http://www.taylorandfrancis.com

and the CRC Press Web site at
http://www.crcpress.com

Contents

Foreword

Life is full of risks, especially for physicians. Some are known and likely to manifest themselves, whereas others are known but unlikely to ever materialize. There are probably far more risks that are unknown to us and, if we are lucky, remain that way. Fortunately, many of the known risks of practicing medicine are outlined in *Risk Management, Liability Insurance, and Asset Protection Strategies for Doctors and Advisors: Best Practices from Leading Consultants and Certified Medical Planners*™. It is a comprehensive textbook edited by nationally known authority David Edward Marcinko and his experienced team from the Institute of Medical Business Advisors Inc., Atlanta, Georgia.

Given this reality, how do we face both the known and unknown risks? Risk tolerance is probably partially inborn. Some of us are born more anxious than others and more prone to worry about possible eventualities; while others much less so. Inborn anxiety is likely genetically based but may also be related to prenatal environment. Others who might not have an inherent predisposition to anxiety and risk aversion, but who experience trauma or significant loss in their lives, often become conditioned to fear risk.

These observations are important when considering the many topics presented herein because if doctors are less anxious, they might be willing to take on more risk without covering themselves by way of vigilance and various insurance products. By contrast, colleagues who are generally more anxious probably do worry more, anticipate disaster more, and plan for it by insuring themselves.

For example, any time we purchase noncompulsory insurance, we have implicitly or otherwise decided that we are not wasting our money by over-insuring ourselves. Others who might be more carefree and less prone to worry often conclude the opposite and might inadvertently take on a dramatic amount of risk, in terms of financial payout, professional scrutiny, public ignominy, or otherwise. No matter our natural disposition to worry, if we have experienced an adverse outcome in the past, we will almost definitely prepare differently in the future, given that we are often fighting last battles. Thus, if a physician has previously faced a malpractice lawsuit, s/he will almost definitely err on the side of overprotection in various ways, including purchasing more insurance than might be otherwise indicated, spending much greater time writing office notes, and proceeding with extra caution in clinical encounters.

Of course, there are obvious downsides to this overabundance of caution. One might spend more than necessary on insurance policies, be less likely to innovate or experiment when treating patients, and be much more cautious in professional or personal interactions as they may believe every encounter is a potential lawsuit in the making. By contrast, someone not otherwise prone to anxiety, or who has never been sued, might err in the opposite direction. Either course of action carries potential costs, and *Risk Management, Liability Insurance, and Asset Protection Strategies for Doctors and Advisors* illuminates all sides of these issues across a broad spectrum of traditional and ever evolving risks faced in the modern era.

Just consider one of the most fundamental issues in health care—documenting the clinical encounter. The old adage is that if something is not recorded in the medical record, it did not happen. Failure to document any aspect of a medical encounter opens one up to being charged with not performing some action. Given this reality, each time we document a patient encounter we ask ourselves the fundamental question of how much should we write, dictate, or electronically scribe? If we chose to document every aspect of the encounter, our notes would presumably work well in court if sued. However, the time spent on creating *the perfect note* takes a toll in various ways, including requiring extra office time, less time with family, or less attention to basic self-health needs. Whether we are consciously aware of this decision, it is one calculus among many that is at play every time a physician meets a patient or has a professional encounter.

Another issue most of us face daily is that of how we interact with coworkers. How friendly should we be? How much should we let anyone know if we find a coworker attractive? Where is the border between friendly engagement and sexual harassment? The fact is not so clear given the rule of thumb that harassment is in the eyes of the receiver. The upshot of this rule is that if offended in some way, one could legitimately register a sexual harassment complaint. Given this reality, how much personal interaction is too much? What if someone tells his coworker he likes her scarf? Is it ever permissible to compliment a colleague on how she looks? Or ask a colleague on a date? How one answers these questions in part depends on personal psychological makeup in addition to past experiences. The fact is that one should *never* ask for a date in the office setting. One lawyer I knew advised clients that before they did so—or before they even entertained the question—they should self-guarantee that the person being asked will be the last one with whom they ever sleep. The reason is that formal complaints are unlikely in the beginning. However, relationships go sour—and that's when complaints are filed.

Of course, how such scenarios affect marital harmony, assets, and net worth is unique to each case, but the topic is humanely considered in the chapter on divorce mediation. And, what about the increasing problem of medical workplace violence? How are potential perpetrators identified, diagnosed, and treated? What about the victims and economic costs? The lurid topic is also bravely tackled herein.

Another aspect of professional practice danger discussed in *Risk Management, Liability Insurance, and Asset Protection Strategies for Doctors and Advisors* is that of licensure and licensing boards. Most of us don't even consider the nature of licensing boards or how they wield such considerable authority and power. But, for those referred to the board for questionable behavior, medical professionals quickly realize that they are disempowered and totally at the mercy of their board. For those suspected of having substance use disorders or behavioral health issues, if a licensing board refers them to a physician health program, they are generally told that they need to comply with all recommendations made by the physician health program in order to continue practicing. Contributors who understand the power of state medical boards highlight some of the potential abuses meted out and provide information to allow them to stay below the radar screen.

Nevertheless, no matter how well informed we are about potential problems or pitfalls in any of the arenas of practice life—no matter how well insured we are against personal or professional liability, and no matter how excellent our educations are in our fields—unforeseen events will happen. We will make mistakes at times. We will commit errors. Unfortunately, even when we do everything right and adhere to acceptable clinical standards of care, some outcomes will be bad. So, even as doctors tend to be risk averse, the reality is that we can never prevent all bad outcomes or eliminate all risks. And, even though we cannot eliminate them, understanding the risks we face is invaluable in protecting us psychologically, if not financially, across many risk elements.

So, we are fortunate that *Risk Management, Liability Insurance, and Asset Protection Strategies for Doctors and Advisors: Best Practices from Leading Consultants and Certified Medical Planners*™ is available to alert us of danger as it fulfills its promise as a peerless tool for doctors seeking to make good decisions about the risks they face. It is also ideal for financial advisors, insurance agents, attorneys, accountants, psychologists, and consultants who advise medical professionals and wish to add deeper value to their client relationships.

With time at a premium, and so much information packed into one well-organized resource, this comprehensive text should be on the desk of everyone serving in the health-care and medical ecosystem. The time you spend reading this frank and compelling book will be richly rewarded.

J. Wesley Boyd, MD, PhD, MA
Harvard Medical School
Assistant Clinical Professor of Psychiatry
Cambridge Health Alliance
Boston Children's Hospital
Staff Psychiatrist
Yale University

Preface

Insurance and the need to protect assets is an important part of all our lives, but it is just one component of modern medical risk management activity. This is also true for the financial advisors, attorneys, accountants, actuaries, IT specialists, and risk managers who serve physicians and allied medical professionals.

For example, it is not uncommon for a practicing physician to have more than a dozen separate insurance policies associated with the practice of medicine as a physician-executive and family man/woman. Yet, most doctors understand very little about their policies other than that somebody at some point told them that every single one was needed, and that each made sense when purchased: STILL doubts linger, as the doctor wonders:

- Am I over-insured and thus wasting money?
- Am I under-insured and thus at risk for a liability disaster?

Most never really had the means of answering these questions, until now! *Risk Management, Liability Insurance, and Asset Protection Strategies for Doctors and Advisors: Best Practices from Leading Consultants and Certified Medical Planners*™ is an essential textbook because it explains to physicians and insurance professionals the background, theory, and practicalities of medical risk management, asset protection methods, and insurance planning. The insurance haze is lifted by our team of contributing authors and leading experts.

Now, doctors, like most people, tend to experience losses more intensely than gains and evaluate risks in isolation. So it's no surprise that goaded physicians might prefer vehicles like the guaranteed minimum death benefit of variable annuities, or the assurance that comes with disability or long-term-care insurance, or traditional cash value life insurance policies, despite their decidedly higher costs and commissions.

Similarly, physicians may enter denial mode and eschew the potential business impact of divorce, practice dissolution, or Balanced Budget Act risks; self-referral risks; OSHA, DEA, EPA, OCR, P&C or managed care risks; managed care contract capitulation risks; employee, expert witness, peer review and on-call risks; and even educational debt load risks, among so many others. Not to mention, HIPAA, EHRs, CPOEs, the PP-CA and HI-TECH, meaningful use and the impact of social media on practice, today.

For ethical and informed insurance professionals on the other hand, this is an exciting time to be practicing their craft, because there is much research and creative enlightenment occurring in academic and practitioner communities. But, one must be willing to abandon ancient thoughts and remain open to new ideas that identify and provide solutions to the contemporaneous problems of physicians.

As an example of this epiphany, Christian Gollier, PhD, professor of economics at the University of Toulouse, revisits the *raison d'être* of insurance, by asking: should one even buy insurance since the industry itself is so skilled at exploiting human foibles? Although this emerging work is descriptive, it is not yet time tested since some of it aspires to be normative, as developing modern models of savings and consumption hint that insurance may deserve a smaller role in personal risk management than previously believed.

In another intuitive insight, private, state and federal health reform initiatives are increasing, and professional malaise and discouragement is expanding, so medical providers may be facing the ultimate personal contingent liability by selecting the wrong profession, as suggested by Yale University economist Robert J. Shiller, PhD. In his popular book, *The New Financial Order: Risk in the 21st Century*, Shiller states that a new risk-sharing paradigm to protect us from "gratuitous random and painful inequality" is required. The solution? Livelihood insurance, framed as a risk management contract!

OR, consider this provocative thought on medical licensing:

> Licensing has served to channel the development of health care services by granting an exclusive privilege and high status to practitioners relying on a particular approach to health care, a disease-oriented intrusive approach rather than a preventive approach. … By granting a monopoly to a particular approach to health care, the licensing laws may serve to assure an ineffective health care system.
>
> **Lori B. Andrews**
> *Professor of Law*
> *Chicago-Kent College*

Reassuringly, the risks and perils identified in this textbook are not quite as thought provoking as Gollier's, Shiller's or Andrews ideas, although they are equally compelling. They are more pragmatic however, and we are certain that *Risk Management, Liability, Insurance and Asset Protection Strategies for Doctors and Advisors: Best Practices from Leading Consultants and Certified Medical Planners*™ is of acute value to all doctors, providers and related consultants. And, it will help readers recognize and reduce personal and medical practice risks; but only if appreciated, integrated and executed with a trusted and knowledgeable risk manager, insurance agent, counselor, attorney, actuary or financial advisor.

WHY NOW?

A simple question with a complex ever evolving answer!

Today, medical practice risk management, insurance liability and asset protection strategies must include the recognition, reduction and measurement of an ever expanding tsunami of personal and business perils in a contentious and litigious atmosphere. And, modern medical risk management is not just about professional liability and medical malpractice issues anymore. There are many other issues, as well. Colloquially, for us, they are amassed into two compendium-like chapters known as the "A" thru "Z" List of Health 2.0 Risks (TNTC). So, with full implementation of the PP-ACA in 2016, now is the perfect time for *Risk Management, Liability Insurance: and Asset Protection Strategies for Doctors and Advisors: Best Practices from Leading Consultants and Certified Medical Planners*™ to be released.

Presciently, Dr. O. Kent Mercado Esq., a physician-attorney in Chicago, Illinois, states:

> Risk management and medical practice peril monitoring is a process light years beyond mere professional liability and medical malpractice issues. If doctors, medical providers and clinics view it as this ancient singularity—in isolation, or an informal ad-hoc basis—it just won't succeed. Moreover, as risks in healthcare get more significant and complex, vigilant monitoring must be a highly deliberate

process requiring oversight by a cross-functional team of risk managers, insurance agents, doctors, IT consultants and attorneys within all medical practices, offices, clinics and related health entities.

Of course, we can never eliminate all risks, but physicians and medical providers must account for new risks or potential perils to gain an understanding of where they stand and that requires vigilance and buy-in from team members at all levels.

For example, doctors have to communicate with their patients and monitor their progress to determine the effectiveness of treatment plans. Some primary care practices do this through established HIPAA compliant private electronic patient communication channels and portals, e-mail monitoring systems, and/or pro-active medical plans. This includes contacting patients by phone and sending ancillary aides to patients' homes to check on them to make sure they understand and are abiding by treatment and follow-up instructions. And, medical practices can use tele-health and technology to efficiently identify what represents high risk and establish metrics to determine whether risk is accelerating, declining, or being mitigated. Yet, onsite disclosures, business associate and cloud date security breaches abound but are not wholly noted in the popular media.

Now, we can't speak for the entire industry but studies and our own consulting experiences indicate that doctors are finally understanding and reacting. It's just a question of to what extent, how structured, and how consistently risk is proactively appreciated, and strategically avoided. The ramifications of failing to manage medical risk can be profound. Physicians and independent health-care practices are going to fall on financially hard times and close down, or be consolidated into super-groups and hospitals, unless they deal with modern risks and develop a unique competitive advantage and value proposition. The key is learning from data and developing predictive skills and strategies that reduce and eliminate future crises.

To measure the effectiveness of such risk monitoring practices and tools, doctors must ascertain how far they've progressed in the monitoring process and compare their performance to other facilities. Then, an updated compliance plan is developed and executed. Our contributing authors are experienced and knowledgeable experts in this arena. They have prepared a textbook that excels in its content and organization. It is organized in a logically progressive way that is highly useful for a busy medical practitioner regardless of specialty. Topics are introduced without the overuse of jargon and adequately explained. There are numerous subheadings and bulleted lists to assist the reader with moving through the text or highlighting a particular topic. Case models and examples provide the reader with an applied knowledge that complements the didactic sections. The book is well referenced for more in-depth reading on a particular topic with materials from both the written and electronic media links.

And so, we trust *Risk Management, Liability Insurance, and Asset Protection Strategies for Doctors and Advisors: Best Practices from Leading Consultants and Certified Medical Planners*™ will fulfill its promise as a peerless tool for physicians wanting to make good decisions about the contemporary risks they face. It is also ideal for their related personal and business advisors wishing to re-educate and help doctors by adding lasting value to their client relationships.

With time at a premium for all, and so much information packed into one well-organized resource, this book should be on the desk of every physician, or financial advisor serving the health-care space.

Simply stated, if you read this compelling text with a mind focused on the future, the time you spend will be amply rewarded. In short, the time for this textbook is indeed right now!

Fraternally,

Dr. David Edward Marcinko, MBA CMP™ MBBS (Hon)
Editor-in-Chief

ABOUT THE INSTITUTE OF MEDICAL BUSINESS ADVISORS INC.

iMBA Inc. is a leading physician executive, medical practice, hospital and health-care institutional educator; risk management and insurance advisor; economics and medical valuation consulting firm; and focused provider of financial planning textbooks, CD-ROMs, handbooks, templates, tools, dictionaries, and on-site and distance learning for the health care space. iMBA Inc. leverages opportunity, seeks change, and helps clients maximize revenue, increase profits, reduce risks, and protect assets. Client projects are completed under Non-Disclosure or Non-Circumvention Agreements. We protect the confidentiality of clients, their projects, our recommendations, and their future ongoing competitive plans.

Recently, iMBA Inc. released three other related textbooks under the CRC Press (Productivity Press) imprimatur:

- *Hospitals and Healthcare Organizations: Management Strategies, Operational Techniques, Tools, Templates and Case Studies*
- *Financial Management Strategies for Hospitals and Healthcare Organizations: Tools, Techniques, Checklists and Case Studies*
- *Comprehensive Financial Planning Strategies for Doctors and Advisors: Best Practices from Leading Consultants and Certified Medical Planners™*

So, this text represents the next iMBA initiative into the personal and business risk management arena for all health-care professionals. The firm serves as a national resource center and referral alliance providing managerial peace-of-mind to struggling physician clients. As competition increases, iMBA Inc. is positioned to meet the collaborative needs of medical colleagues and clients, today and well into the perilous participatory ecosystem of the future.

iMBA INC. CORPORATE COMMUNICATION SUBSIDIARIES:

Advisors: www.CertifiedMedicalPlanner.org
iMBA Inc.: www.MedicalBusinessAdvisors.com
Physicians: http://www.crcpress.com/product/isbn/9781482240283
Practices: www.SpringerPub.com
Hospitals: http://www.crcpress.com/product/isbn/9781466558731
Clinics: http://www.crcpress.com/product/isbn/9781439879900
Blog: www.MedicalExecutivePost.com

Notices

DISCLAIMER NOTICE

The information presented in *Risk Management, Liability Insurance, and Asset Protection Strategies for Doctors and Advisors: Best Practices from Leading Consultants and Certified Medical Planners*™ is presented for general information and education use only. Prior to engaging in the type of activities described, you should receive independent counsel from a qualified relevant professional. Care has been taken to confirm the accuracy of the information presented, but we offer no warranties, expressed or implied, regarding its currency and are not responsible for errors or omissions or for any consequences from the application of this information. Examples are generally descriptive and do not purport to be accurate in every regard. They are blinded and not all-inclusive. The health-care industry is evolving rapidly, and all information should be considered time sensitive.

Although sponsored by the Institute of Medical Business Advisors Inc., we maintain an arm's-length relationship with the independent authors and firms who carried out research and prepared the book. The goal of iMBA Inc. is to be unbiased to the extent possible, and to promote protean professional perspectives and opinions.

HOLD-HARMLESS NOTICE

This publication is designed to provide information in regard to the subject matter covered. It is not intended to constitute insurance, technology, legal, practice or risk management, asset protection, business, or any other actuarial advice. It is sold with the understanding that the editors, authors, reviewers, and publishers are held harmless in these matters. Examples are generally descriptive and do not purport to be accurate in every regard. The health-care risk management, IT, insurance, asset protection, and security planning space is evolving rapidly and all information should be considered time sensitive. If advice or other assistance is required, the services of a competent professional should be sought.

Modified from a *Declaration of Principles* jointly adopted by

- Committee of the American Bar Association
- Committee of Publishers and Associations

FAIR USE NOTICE

Risk Management, Liability Insurance, and Asset Protection Strategies for Doctors and Advisors: Best Practices from Leading Consultants and Certified Medical Planners™ contains URLs, blog snippets, links, and brief excerpts of material obtained from the Internet or public domain, the use of which has not always been specifically authorized by the copyright owner. We are also making such material from our own other books available to advance the understanding of related issues, and for the general purpose of reporting and educating. Moreover, we use modern crowd-sourcing methods as well as contributions from our blog forum: www.MedicalExecutivePost.com. We believe this constitutes a "fair use" of any copyrighted material as provided by Section 107 of U.S. Copyright Law. In accordance with Title 17 U.S.C. Section 107, the material is distributed to those who have expressed an interest in text purchase. Moreover, all register®, trade™, service (SM) and copyright© marks are the intangible intellectual property of their respective owners. Mention of any specific product, service, website domain, or company does not constitute endorsement. No compensation was obtained for including same.

ABOUT INTERNET CITATIONS

Risk Management, Liability Insurance, and Asset Protection Strategies for Doctors and Advisors: Best Practices from Leading Consultants and Certified Medical Planners™ uses Uniform Resource Locators (URLs) to direct readers to useful Internet sites with additional references. However, host entities frequently reorganize and update sites, so URLs can change rapidly. Citations for this text are therefore "live" when published, but we cannot guarantee how long they will remain so, despite our best efforts to keep them current.

Acknowledgments

It is an incredible privilege to edit *Risk Management, Liability Insurance, and Asset Protection Strategies for Doctors and Advisors: Best Practices from Leading Consultants and Certified Medical Planners*™. One of the most rewarding aspects of my career has been the professional growth acquired from interacting with medical colleagues, risk management, HIT, legal, accounting, and insurance services professionals of all stripes. The mutual sharing and exchange of ideas stimulate the mind and foster advancement at many levels.

Of course, creating this text was a significant effort that involved all members of our firm. Over the past year, we interfaced with various public resources such as state governments, the federal government, Federal Register (FR), the Centers for Medicare and Medicaid Services (CMS), the Centers of Disease Control and Prevention (CDC), and the U.S. Department of Health and Human Services (DHHS), as well as numerous private firms, professionals, and our Internet blog readers to discuss its contents. And, although impossible to list every person or company who played a role in its production, there are several other people we wish to thank for their support and encouragement: Kristine Mednansky—senior editor, business improvement (healthcare management); Karen Schober—editorial assistant; Kari Budyk—senior project coordinator; Laurie Oknowsky—project coordinator, editorial project development; and Richard O'Hanley—CRC Press (Taylor & Francis Group).

Finally, we acknowledge that this text would not have been possible without the support of our families whose daily advocacy encouraged all of us to completion. It is also dedicated to our clients and the contributing authors and peer reviewers who crashed the development life cycle in order to produce time-sensitive material in an expedient manner. The satisfaction we enjoyed from working with them is immeasurable.

Any accolades are because of them.... All defects are our own.

Thank you for purchasing, referring, promoting and using *Risk Management, Liability Insurance, and Asset Protection Strategies for Doctors and Advisors: Best Practices from Leading Consultants and Certified Medical Planners*™, and helping to make it a success!

David Edward Marcinko
Hope Rachel Hetico
Mackenzie Hope Marcinko
Ann Marie Miller

Institute of Medical Business Advisors Inc.—
Corporate Headquarters
Norcross, Georgia
www.MedicalBusinessAdvisors.com

iMBA Medical Business Advisors, Inc.
where learning is a +

ABOUT THE BOOK COVER

Our cover image is a colorful vector-graphic silhouette of a large stethoscope with medical providers seeking risk management, liability protection, and insurance advice from informed fiduciary consultants and Certified Medical Planners.

IMAGES

Black and white silhouette images placed throughout the book are courtesy of *SplitShire*.

Editors

Dr. David Edward Marcinko, editor-in-chief, is a next-generation apostle of Nobel Laureate Kenneth Joseph Arrow, PhD, as a health-care economist, insurance advisor, financial advisor, risk manager, and board-certified surgeon from Temple University in Philadelphia. In the past, he edited eight practice-management books, three medical textbooks and manuals in four languages, five financial planning yearbooks, dozens of interactive CD-ROMs, and three comprehensive health-care administration dictionaries. Internationally recognized for his clinical work, he is a distinguished visiting professor of surgery and a recipient of an honorary Bachelor of Medicine–Bachelor of Surgery (MBBS) degree from Marien Hospital in Aachen, Germany. He provides litigation support and expert witness testimony in state and federal court, with medical publications archived in the Library of Congress and the Library of Medicine at the National Institutes of Health. His thought leadership essays have been cited in journals such as *Managed Care Executives, Healthcare Informatics, Medical Interface, Plastic Surgery Products, Teaching and Learning in Medicine, Orthodontics Today, Chiropractic Products, Journal of the American Medical Association, Podiatry Today, Investment Advisor Magazine, Registered Representative, Financial Advisor Magazine, CFP® Biz (Journal of Financial Planning), Journal of the American Medical Association* (JAMA.ama-assn.org), *The Business Journal for Physicians*, and *Physician's Money Digest* and by companies and professional organizations such as the Medical Group Management Association (MGMA), American College of Medical Practice Executives (ACMPE), American College of Physician Executives (ACPE), American College of Emergency Room Physicians (ACEP), Health Care Management Associates (HMA), and PhysiciansPractice.com, and by academic institutions including the UCLA School of Medicine, Northern University College of Business, Creighton University, Medical College of Wisconsin, University of North Texas Health Science Center, Washington University School of Medicine, Emory University School of Medicine and the Goizueta School of Business at Emory University, University of Pennsylvania Medical and Dental Libraries, Southern Illinois College of Medicine, University at Buffalo Health Sciences Library, University of Michigan Dental Library, and the University of Medicine and Dentistry of New Jersey, among many others. Dr. Marcinko also has numerous primary and secondary editorial and reviewing roles to his credit.

Dr. Marcinko earned his undergraduate degree from Loyola University, Maryland, completed his internship and residency at the Atlanta Hospital and Medical Center, is a fellow of the American College of Foot and Ankle Surgeons, and earned his business degree from the Keller Graduate School of Management (Chicago) and his financial planning diploma from Oglethorpe University (Atlanta). He was a licensee of the Certified Financial Planner Board of Standards for a decade and holds the Certified Medical Planner (CMP) designation. He earned Series #7 (general securities), Series #63 (uniform securities state law), and Series #65 (investment advisory) licenses from the National Association of Securities Dealers (NASD) and Financial Industry Regulatory Authority (FINRA). He received his life, health, disability, variable annuity, and property-casualty license from the state of Georgia. Dr. Marcinko was also a cofounder of an ambulatory surgery center that was sold to a public company. He has been a Certified Physician in Healthcare Quality (CPHQ); a certified American Board of Quality Assurance and Utilization Review Physician (ABQAURP); a medical-staff vice president of a general acute care hospital; an assistant residency director; a founder of a computer-based testing firm for doctors; and the president of a regional physician practice-management corporation in the Midwest. Dr. Marcinko was a member of the American Health Information Management Association (AHIMA) and the Healthcare Information and Management Systems Society (HIMSS); a member of the Microsoft Professional Accountant's Network (MPAN); a website engineer and beta tester for Microsoft Office Live Essentials program; a member of the Microsoft Health User's Group (MS-HUG); and a registered member of the U.S. Microsoft Partners Program (MPP). And, as the president of a privately held physician practice-management corporation in 1999, he consolidated 95 solo medical practices with $150 million in revenues for a pre-IPO listing. In 2011, he joined the Physician Nexus Medical Advisory Board and was a nominated finalist for the Fourth Annual WEGO Health Activist Awards in 2015.

Currently, Dr. Marcinko is the chief executive officer for the Institute of Medical Business Advisors Inc. (iMBA). The firm is headquartered in Atlanta and works with a diverse list of individual and corporate clients. It sponsors the professional Certified Medical Planner charter designation program and counsels maverick physicians transitioning into alternate careers. As a nationally recognized educational resource center and referral alliance, iMBA and its network of independent professionals provide solutions and managerial peace of mind to physicians, health-care organizations, and their consulting business advisors. He also helped develop medical, business, graduate, and undergraduate school curriculum content for the ACPE, MGMA, and the American College of Healthcare Executives (ACHE). A favorite on the lecture circuit, Dr. Marcinko is often quoted in the media and frequently speaks on related topics throughout this country and Europe in an entertaining and witty fashion. He is a popular authority on transformational business strategies across a pantheon of related industries. He is also a social media pioneer and publisher of the *Medical Executive Post*, an influential syndicated Health 2.0 interactive blog forum.

As an award-winning journalist, media broadcaster, speaker, and public health advocate and consultant, Dr. Marcinko is available to colleagues, clients, and the press at his corporate office in Atlanta, Georgia.

Hope Rachel Hetico, managing editor, earned her bachelor's degree in nursing (BSN) from Valpariso University and her Master of Science in health-care administration (MHA) from the University of St. Francis, in Joliette, Illinois. She is an author's editor of a dozen major textbooks and is a nationally known expert in managed medical care, medical reimbursement, case management, health insurance, utilization review, National Association of Healthcare Quality (NAHQ), Health Education Data Information Set (HEDIS), and The Joint Commission (TJC) Clinical Quality Measures (CQMs) and regulations.

Prior to joining the Institute of Medical Business Advisors as the chief operating officer, Professor Hetico was a hospital executive, financial advisor, licensed insurance agent, Certified Professional in Healthcare Quality (CPHQ), and distinguished visiting assistant professor of health-care administration for the University of Phoenix, Graduate School of Business and Management in Atlanta. She was also the national corporate director for Medical Quality Improvement at Abbey, and then Apria Healthcare, a public company in Costa Mesa, California.

A devotee of health information technology and heutagogy, Hetico is responsible for leading the website http://www.certifiedmedicalplanner.org to the top of the exploding adult educational marketplace, expanding the online and on-ground Certified Medical Planner charter designation program, and nurturing the company's rapidly growing list of medical colleagues and financial services industry clients.

Professor Hetico recently completed successful consulting engagements as an ACO clinical integration coordinator for Resurrection Health Care Preferred in Chicago, and a performance improvement manager for Emory University and Saint Joseph's Hospital in Atlanta. She is currently on assignment for Presence Health Partners, the largest Catholic health system in Illinois.

Mackenzie Hope Marcinko, project manager, is a linguistic, computer science, and business management major from the University of Pittsburgh. Founded in 1787, the university is a health-care informatics and technology pioneer, and one of the nation's most distinguished members of the Association of American Universities. It perennially ranks as one of the top public universities in total sponsored research funding and is among the top 10 recipients of funding from the National Institutes of Health. Ms. Marcinko is the most recent Slavic, East European and Near Eastern Summer Language Institute's scholarship award winner matriculating at the Moscow State University.

Ann Marie Miller, RN, MHA, is the executive director for the Institute of Medical Business Advisors Inc. and the Certified Medical Planner online professional education and certification designation program in Norcross, Georgia.

Eugene Schmuckler, PhD, MEd, MBA, CTS, academic dean, is a senior educator, psychometrist, and chief academic officer (CAO) for the Institute of Medical Business Advisors Inc. and the Certified Medical Planner online professional education and certification designation program in Norcross, Georgia. He is also the course curriculum and table-of-contents developer for related iMBA Inc. textbooks and whitepapers.

Richard J. Mata, MD, MS, MI-CIS, CMP (Hon), chief health-care informaticist, attended Johns Hopkins University in Baltimore, Maryland, and earned his medical degree from the University of Texas, Southwestern Medical College. He earned a master's degree in medical informatics (MI) and computer information systems (CIS), and is a member of the Software Programmers Guild affiliated with the IEEE and the Project Management Institute. He is also a member of the Security Health Care Accreditation and Certification Workgroup of URAC, based in Washington, District of Columbia, and the Medical Records Institute (MRI) in Boston, Massachusetts.

Rachel Pentin-Maki, RN, MHA, CMP (Hon), North American ambassador, is a former intensive care unit and telemetry unit manager, nursing school instructor, and Finnish Rest Home BOD member in Lantana, Florida.

Keung Chi (Kenneth) Yeung, MBA, CMP, international ambassador, is a hospital administrator and financial consultant for the Tseung Kwan O Hospital, Hong Kong, who speaks English, Cantonese, Mandarin, and Chinese.

Contributors

Gary L. Bode, MD, was chief executive officer of Comprehensive Practice Accounting Inc., a firm specializing in providing tax solutions to medical professionals. Originally, he was a board certified podiatrist and managing partner of a multi-office medical practice for a decade before earning his Master of Science degree in accounting from the University of North Carolina. He then served as chief financial officer (CFO) for a private mental health-care facility. Today, Dr. Bode is a nationally known certified public accountant, financial author, educator, and speaker. His areas of expertise include producing customized managerial accounting reports, practice appraisals and valuations, restructurings, and innovative financial accounting as well as proactive tax positioning and tax return preparation for health-care facilities. He has been quoted in *Newsweek*.

Dr. Gary L. Bode, MSA, CPA, CMP™ (Hon) PC
Leland, North Carolina
https://cpawilmingtonnc.org
http://garybodecpa.com/

Vicki L. Buba was an attorney at the Oldfather Law Firm who now works part time on special projects and serves as client-intake coordinator. She is a 1988 graduate of Indiana University Southeast and a 1995 *cum laude* graduate of the University of Louisville School of Law.

Vicki L. Buba, JD
Oldfather Law Firm
Special Projects
Louisville, Kentucky

Robert James Cimasi is chief executive officer of Health Capital Consultants (HCC), a nationally recognized health-care financial and economic consulting firm headquartered in St. Louis, Missouri, serving clients in 49 states since 1993. He has over thirty years of experience in serving clients, with a professional focus on the financial and economic aspects of health-care service sector entities including valuation consulting and capital formation services; health-care industry transactions, including joint ventures, mergers, acquisitions, and divestitures; litigation support and expert testimony; and certificate-of-need and other regulatory and policy planning consulting.

Cimasi holds a Masters in health administration from the University of Maryland, as well as several professional designations including Accredited Senior Appraiser (ASA—American Society of Appraisers); Fellow Royal Institution of Chartered Surveyors (FRICS—Royal Institute of Chartered Surveyors); Master Certified Business Appraiser (MCBA—Institute of Business Appraisers); Certified Valuation Analyst (CVA—National Association of Certified Valuators and Analysts); and, Certified Merger & Acquisition Advisor (CM&AA—Alliance of Merger & Acquisition Advisors). He has served as an expert witness on cases in numerous courts, and has provided testimony before federal and state legislative committees. He is a nationally known speaker on health-care industry topics, the author of several books, the latest of which include *Accountable Care*

Organizations: Value Metrics and Capital Formation (2013—CRC Press, a division of Taylor & Francis), *The Adviser's Guide to Healthcare*—Vols. I, II & III (2010—AICPA), and, *The U.S. Healthcare Certificate of Need Sourcebook* (2005—Beard Books). His most recent book, entitled *Healthcare Valuation: The Financial Appraisal of Enterprises, Assets, and Services* was published by John Wiley & Sons in 2014.

Cimasi is the author of numerous additional chapters in anthologies, books, and legal treatises; published articles in peer reviewed and industry trade journals; research papers and case studies; and, is often quoted by health-care industry press. In 2006, Cimasi was honored with the prestigious Shannon Pratt Award in Business Valuation conferred by the Institute of Business Appraisers. He serves on the editorial board of the Business Appraisals Practice of the Institute of Business Appraisers, of which he is a member of the College of Fellows; as vice president of the American Health Lawyers Association (AHLA) Accountable Care Organizations (ACO) Task Force; and, as Chair Emeritus of the American Society of Appraisers Healthcare Special Interest Group (ASA HSIG). In 2011, he was named a fellow of the Royal Institution of Chartered Surveyors (RICS).

Robert James Cimasi, MHA, ASA, FRICS, MCBA, AVA, CM&AA, CMP™
Founder and CEO
Health Capital Consultants, LLC
St. Louis, Missouri
www.HealthCapital.com

Gary A. Cook, EJD, earned a degree in mathematics from the Indiana University of Pennsylvania and his Master of Science degree in financial services from the American College in Bryn Mawr, Pennsylvania, as well as Chartered Life Underwriter® and Registered Health Underwriter. As an accredited estate planner, he taught courses in that discipline, as well as insurance, business and finance planning; and is past president of the Chester Country Estate Planning Council. He received his Executive Juris Doctorate from Concord Law School of Kaplan University and is a professional author, sought after public speaker and television guest for the Insurance Broadcast System, Inc. He is also a member of the Society of Financial Service Professionals, the Financial Planning Association, and the Association for Advanced Life Underwriting. Formerly, Dr. Cook was an assistant vice president, advanced market support, for AIG Life Insurance Companies (USA). He was also content manager for COSS Development Corporation. Today, he is product manager and advanced sales specialist for Internet Pipeline, Inc of Charlotte, North Carolina. Dr. Cook has presented at financial and medical associations throughout the region, and has contributed several book chapters for the Institute of Medical Business Advisors Inc.

Gary A. Cook, EJD, MSFS, CLU®, RHU, ChFC, CFP®, CMP™ (Hon)
Bethlehem, Pennsylvania

Perry D'Alessio has twenty years' experience in public accounting. He specializes in the taxation of closely held businesses and their owners, as well as high wealth individuals. He has a broad range of experience that includes individual, corporate, partnership, fiduciary, estate, and gift taxation. Business development has also been a focus. Particularly in the healthcare and fitness industry, he worked with successful entities whose emphasis was on growth through development of strategic relationships and unit building. D'Alessio earned his bachelor of business administration degree in accounting from Baruch College. He is a Certified Public Accountant in New York, and is a member of the American Institute of Certified Public Accountants (AICPA), the New York State Society of Certified Public Accountants (NYSSCPA). He served on several New York State Society tax committees including PCAOB and HealthCare. D'Alessio presents at financial and medical associations throughout the region, and has authored chapters in the books *Financial Management Strategies for Hospitals and Healthcare Organizations* and *Comprehensive Financial Planning Strategies for Doctors and Advisors: Best Practices from Leading Consultants and Certified Medical Planners*™, for the Institute of Medical Business Advisors Inc.

Perry D'Alessio, CPA
D'Alessio Tocci & Pell LLP
Certified Public Accountants and Business Advisors
New York
www.DaleCPA.com

Render S. Davis was a certified healthcare executive, now retired from Crawford Long Hospital at Emory University in Atlanta, Georgia. He served as assistant administrator for General Services, Policy Development, and Regulatory Affairs from 1977–95. He is a founding board member of the Health Care Ethics Consortium of Georgia and served on the consortium's Executive Committee, Advisory Board, Futility Task Force, Strategic Planning Committee, and chaired the Annual Conference Planning Committee, for many years.

Render S. Davis, MHA, CHE
Institute of Medical Business Advisors, Inc.
Norcross, Georgia

Ike Devji is Of-Counsel with Lodmell & Lodmell PC and is the firm's former managing attorney. He is the executive vice-president of the Wealthy 100™, a Phoenix, Arizona based wealth management and wealth strategy firm with a network of advisors across the United States. Devji selectively consults and provides asset protection services to high-net worth, high liability clients nationwide. He has spoken to literally thousands of physicians, allied medical professionals and other high-net worth clients across the country. He provides continuing legal education on this subject to other attorneys and regularly lectures at the request of leading medical practice management and investment management groups, including most recently MultiFinancial Securities, Greenbook Financial, ING, ING TRUST, Comprehensive Wealth Management, CFO Advisors, numerous banks, and both Lorman and the National Business Institute, among others.

Ike Devji, JD
Of-Counsel
Lodmell & Lodmell, PC
Phoenix, Arizona

Eric A. Dover, MD, is a board certified family practice and primary care physician in Portland, Oregon. He is a graduate of the University of California at Los Angeles (UCLA) School of Medicine.

Eric A. Dover, MD
Portland, Oregon

Charles F. Fenton III, MD, is a board certified surgeon from Temple University, who received his law degree as class valedictorian from Georgia State University, and practices in Atlanta, Georgia. His clients include physicians involved in audits and recoupment actions, as well as disputes with insurance or managed care companies. He is a contributing author to many books on health-care law and medical practice, as well as many other medico-legal publications for physicians and the Bar. Currently, he is chief legal officer for the Institute of Medical Business Advisors Inc.

Dr. Charles F. Fenton III, FACFAS, JD, CMP™ (Hon)
Law Offices
Kennesaw, Georgia

Jay S. Grife, MD, JD, is a doctor-attorney admitted to practice law in the State of Florida. His focus is medical malpractice and health law topics, while working with counsel of other States. He earned a Master of Arts Degree in legal history from the University of Florida, and a Juris Doctor degree from the University of Florida, College of Law. He is an assistant professor of law studies at the University of North Florida, and adjunct professor of history and political science from the University North Florida. His professional affiliations include the ABA, Florida Bar Association, Association of Trial Lawyers of America, and American College of Legal Medicine.

Jay S. Grife, JD, MS
Malpractice Consultants, LLC
Jacksonville, Florida

Anju D. Jessani founded Divorce with Dignity Mediation Services in 1997, following a career in financial services that included positions as vice president at JP Morgan and manager of consulting services with Price Waterhouse. She has offices in Hoboken and Clinton, New Jersey. She served on the board of the New Jersey Association Professional Mediators from 2000 to 2010, including as president of the association from 2005–2007. In 2007, Anju received special recognition from the New Jersey State Bar Association's Board of Trustees for her work on the New Jersey irreconcilable differences divorce bill. Anju is an Accredited Professional Mediator by the New Jersey Association of Professional Mediators (NJAPM), and an Advanced Practitioner Member of the Association for Conflict Resolution (ACR). She is an instructor for both NJAPM's and the New Jersey Institute for Continuing Legal

Education's divorce mediation training programs. She is editor of NJAPM's publication, *Mediation News*. In addition, she is a frequent contributor to professional journals including the *American Journal of Family Law, CPA Journal* and *New Jersey Law Journal*. She earned an MBA from The Wharton School, and a BA from Rutgers University.

Anju D. Jessani, MBA APM®
Accredited Professional Mediator
Divorce with Dignity Mediation Services
Hoboken, New Jersey

Frederick William LaCava, JD, PhD, also known as "Duffy," earned his BA from Emory University, Atlanta; a doctorate in English from The University of North Carolina, Chapel Hill; and a JD from Indiana University School of Law, Bloomington. Now retired, he practiced health law for many years in Indianapolis, Indiana.

Frederick William LaCava, JD, PhD
Institute of Medical Business Advisors, Inc.
Norcross, Georgia

Carol S. Miller has an extensive health-care background in operations, business development and capture in both the public and private sector. Over the last 10 years she has provided management support to projects in the Department of Health and Human Services, Veterans Affairs, and Department of Defense medical programs. In most recent years, Carol has served as vice president and senior account executive for NCI Information Systems, Inc., assistant vice president at SAIC, and program manager at MITRE. She has led the successful capture of large IDIQ/GWAC programs, managed the operations of multiple government contracts, interacted with many government key executives, and increased the new account portfolios for each firm she supported. She earned her MBA from Marymount University; BS in business from Saint Joseph's College, and BS in nursing from the University of Pittsburgh. She is a Certified PMI Project Management Professional (PMP) (PMI PMP) and a Certified HIPAA Professional (CHP), with Top Secret Security clearance issued by the DoD in 2006, and is also a HIMSS Fellow.

Carol S. Miller, BSN, MBA, PMP
ACT IAC Executive Committee Vice Chairwoman at-Large
HIMSS NCA Board Member
President—Miller Consulting Group
McLean, Virginia

J. Christopher Miller, JD, is an estate planning and business law attorney in Alpharetta, Georgia. He frequently conducts seminars on the formation of limited liability companies and trusts addressing special needs issues. He earned both his bachelor's degree and his Juris Doctor from Emory University. He was admitted to the State Bar of Georgia in 2000, and is a member of the Atlanta Bar Association's Section of Estate Planning and Probate.

J. Christopher Miller, JD
Law Offices of J. Christopher Miller, PC
Alpharetta, Georgia
www.NorthFultonWills.com

Thomas A. Muldowney has 35 years experience in the banking, investment, insurance and financial services industries. He taught at Rock Valley and Sauk Valley Community Colleges and served as a contributing author for the "Elder Law Portfolio Series" published by the Law and Business Division of Wolters and Kluwer through Aspen Publishers. His topics included "Financial Planning for the Elderly" and "Postmortem Estate Planning." Muldowney earned a Bachelor of Arts degree from Rockford College and a Masters Degree in Financial Services (MSFS) from American College. He is a Chartered Life Underwriter® (CLU®), Chartered Financial Consultant® (ChFC®), Certified Retirement Counselor® (CRC®), Certified Financial Planner® (CFP®), Certified Medical Planner™ (CMP™) and an Accredited Investment Fiduciary® (AIF®). Muldowney is an active member of the National Association of Personal Financial Advisors (NAPFA), the Financial Planning Association (FPA) and the Society of Financial Service Professionals (FSP). Since 2004, he has represented Savant on *Medical Economics* magazine's list of "Top 150 Best Financial Advisers for Doctors." He has presented at financial and medical associations and authored several publications for the Institute of Medical Business Advisors Inc. Muldowney is also on the TD Ameritrade Advisory Panel and a board member of the Discovery Center Museum, chair of the finance committee and board member for the St. Anthony Medical Center Foundation, chair of the investment committee and treasurer of the Boylan Education Foundation Board of Directors, and is on the board of trustees for Rockford College.

Thomas A. Muldowney, MSFS, ChFC®, CFP®, CLU®, AIF® CMP™
Chairman of the Board and Principal
Savant Capital Management
Rockford, Illinois
www.SavantCapital.com

Eugene Schmuckler, PhD, was coordinator of behavioral science at the Georgia Public Safety Training Center and a licensed psychologist. He is on the board of directors of the Association of Traumatic Stress Specialists and is a certified trauma specialist. Dr. Schmuckler is an international speaker and author, with publications translated into Dutch and Russian. He is a consulting psychologist and director of behavioral finance, for the Institute of Medical Business Advisors Inc; and academic dean for the Certified Medical Planner™ online designation and professional certification program. He frequently writes for the Institute of Medical Business Advisors Inc. Dr. Schmuckler earned his MBA and PhD from the Louisiana State University.

Eugene Schmuckler, PhD, MEd, MBA, CTS®
Institute of Medical Business Advisors, Inc.
Academic Dean and Consulting Psychologist
Certified Medical Planner™ Online Education Program
Norcross, Georgia
www.MedicalBusinessAdvisors.com
www.CertifiedMedicalPlanner.org

Shahid N. Shah is an internationally recognized health-care thought-leader across the Internet. He is a consultant to various federal agencies on technology matters and winner of Federal Computer Week's coveted "Fed 100" Award in 2009. Over a twenty-year career, he built multiple clinical solutions and helped design–deploy an electronic health record solution for the American Red Cross and two Web-based eMRs used by hundreds of physicians with many large groupware and collaboration sites. As ex-CTO for a billion dollar division of CardinalHealth, he helped design advanced clinical interfaces for medical devices and hospitals. Shah is senior technology strategy advisor to NIH's SBIR/STTR program helping small businesses commercialize health-care applications. He runs four successful blogs: at http://shahid.shah.org he writes about architecture issues; at http://www.healthcareguy.com he provides valuable insights on applying technology in health care; at http://www.federalarchitect.com he advises senior federal technologists; and at http://www.hitsphere.com he gives a glimpse of HIT as an aggregator. Shah is a Microsoft MVP (Solutions Architect) Award Winner for 2007, and a Microsoft MVP (Solutions Architect) Award Winner for 2006. He also served as a HIMSS Enterprise IT committee member. Shah earned a BS in computer science from The Pennsylvania State University and MS in technology management from the University of Maryland.

Shahid N. Shah, MS
Silver Spring, Maryland
www.shahidshah.com

Todd A. Zigrang is president of Health Capital Consultants (HCC), where he focuses on the areas of valuation and financial analysis for hospitals, physician practices, and other health-care enterprises. Zigrang has over 20 years of experience providing valuation, financial, transaction and strategic advisory services nationwide in over 1000 transactions and joint ventures involving acute care hospitals and health systems; physician practices; ambulatory surgery centers; diagnostic imaging centers; accountable care organizations, managed care organizations, and other third-party payors; dialysis centers; home health agencies; long-term care facilities; and, numerous other ancillary health-care service businesses. Zigrang is also considered an expert in the field of health-care compensation for physicians, executives and other professionals.

Zigrang is the author of *Adviser's Guide to Healthcare—2nd Edition* (AICPA, 2014), numerous chapters in legal treatises and anthologies, and peer-reviewed and industry articles such as *The Accountant's Business Manual* (AICPA); *Valuing Professional Practices and Licenses* (Aspen Publishers); *Valuation Strategies*; *Business Appraisal Practice*; and, *NACVA QuickRead*. Additionally, he has served as faculty before professional and trade associations such as the American Society of Appraisers (ASA), the National Association of Certified Valuators and Analysts (NACVA), the Physician Hospitals of America (PHA), the Institute of Business Appraisers (IBA), the Healthcare Financial Management Association (HFMA), and the CPA Leadership Institute.

Zigrang earned a Master of Science in health administration (MHA) and a Master of Business Administration (MBA) from the University of Missouri at Columbia. He is a fellow of the American College of Healthcare Executives (FACHE) and holds the Accredited Senior Appraiser (ASA) designation from the American Society of Appraisers, where he has served as president of the St. Louis Chapter, and is chair of the American Society of Appraisers Healthcare Special Interest Group (ASA HSIG).

Todd A. Zigrang, MBA, MHA, ASA, FACHE
President
Health Capital Consultants, LLC
St. Louis, Missouri
www.HealthCapital.com

Exordium

Certified Medical Planner©
CMP
Chartered 2000

Risk Management, Liability Insurance, and Asset Protection Strategies for Doctors and Advisors: Best Practices from Leading Consultants and Certified Medical Planners™ will shape the medical office, clinical practice, and health-care provider risk management, liability reduction, asset protection, and insurance planning landscape for the next generation of doctors, nurses, and allied professionals by following these seven principles.

HOW ARE WE DIFFERENT?

First, we have assembled a world-class editorial advisory board and independent team of contributors and reviewers and asked them to draw on their experiences in contemporaneous health-care risk management, insurance planning, and asset protection for the modern era. Like many of their physician and institutional clients, each struggles mightily with the same concerns. Yet, their practical experience and physician-focused education, knowledge, and vision are a source of objective information, informed opinion, and crucial information to all consultants working with doctors and health-care entities in the expanding real and virtual risk management ecosystem.

Second, our writing style allows us to condense a great deal of information into one practical volume. We integrate bullet points and tables, and pithy language, prose, and specialty perspectives with real-world examples, checklists, and case models. The result is an oeuvre of integrated principles vital to all modern medical professionals and their consulting advisors.

Third, this is a peer-reviewed styled book as we seek to follow traditional medical research and journal publishing guidelines for best practices. Yet, we still present differing viewpoints, divergent and opposing stakeholder perspectives, and informed personal and professional opinions. Each chapter has been reviewed by one to three outside independent reviewers and critical thinkers. We include references and citations, and although we cannot rule out all biases, we do strive to make them transparent to the extent possible.

Fourth, our perspective is decidedly from the physician–client side of the equation. More specifically, as consultants to our medical professional colleagues, we champion the medical practitioner and health-care entity over their risk managers, insurance agents, attorneys, or consulting advisors. And, to the extent that both sides ethically succeed, we hope all concerned *do well—by doing good*. This is unique in the risk management consulting, insurance and actuarial planning, health law, and financial services industry, where hidden fees and commissions abound. Much like the emerging patient-centered care initiatives in medicine, we call it physician-centered transparent advice.

Fifth, it is important to note that deep specificity and niche knowledge are needed when advising physicians, medical providers, nurses, and health-care entities. And so, we present information directly from the health-care industrial complex, and not by indirect example from other industries as is the unfortunate norm. Blinded case models, tools, templates, real-life examples, and anecdotal insights are also included as risk management, asset protection, and insurance information for health care is our core and only focus.

Sixth, we include a glossary of terms and acronyms specific to the text, and industry, and a list of comprehensive risk management, legal, and insurance consulting resources.

Finally, as editors, we prefer engaged readers who demand compelling content. According to conventional wisdom, printed texts like this one should be a relic of the past: from an era before e-mails, instant messaging, and high-speed connectivity. Our experience shows just the opposite. Applied literature from informed sources is woefully sparse, just as a plethora of generalized insurance product sales information makes that material less valuable to doctors and medical clients.

A SEMINAL WORK

Rest assured that *Risk Management, Liability Insurance, and Asset Protection Strategies for Doctors and Advisors: Best Practices from Leading Consultants and Certified Medical Planners* will become a seminal book in this niche ecosystem. In the years ahead, we trust that these principles will enhance utility and add value to your copy. Most importantly, we hope to increase your return on investment by some small increment. It is the ideal companion textbook to our recently released text: *Comprehensive Financial Planning Strategies for Doctors and Advisors: Best Practices from Leading Consultants and Certified Medical Planners™*.

If you have any comments or would like to contribute material or suggest topics for future editions, please contact us.

Professor Hope Rachel Hetico
Managing Editor

TARGET MARKET AND IDEAL READERS

Risk Management, Liability Insurance, and Asset Protection Strategies for Doctors and Advisors: Best Practices from Leading Consultants and Certified Medical Planners should be in the hands of all.

*Allopathic (MD), osteopathic (DO), and podiatric physicians (DPMs); dentists (DDS and DMD); nurses (RNs–LPNs), advanced nurse practitioners (ANPs) and physician assistants (PAs); physical therapists (PTs), doctors of chiropractic (DCs); CRNAs and DVMs; occupational therapists (OTs), physical and speech therapists, and related assistants; and allied health-care providers.

*Hospitals, health-care organizations, medical and surgical clinics, private practices, outpatient facilities, and ambulatory care centers, along with their related risk managers and insurance consultants.

*Medical school, law, graduate and nursing school students, interns, residents, and fellows, as well as new, midlife, and mature allied health-care practitioners of all types

*Financial advisors (FAs), Certified Divorce Planners and Certified Financial Planners (CFPs), Certified Medical Planners (CMP), chartered life underwriters (CLUs), bankers, health attorneys, certified public accountants (CPAs) and enrolled agents (EAs), and all

other risk managers, insurance agents, actuaries, and financial intermediaries and consultants of all stripes, degrees, and general designations.

*Fraternal financial services organizations like the American College of Financial Services in Bryn Mawr, Pennsylvania; Certified Financial Planner Board of Standards (CFP-BOD) in Washington, District of Columbia; the College for Financial Planning (CFP) in Centennial, Colorado; the Financial Planning Association (FPS) and the National Association of Personal Financial Advisors (NAPFA) in Arlington Heights, Illinois; as well as all U.S. state insurance commissioner offices, etc.

*Fraternal medical associations like the American Medical Association (AMA), American Osteopathic Association (AOA), American Podiatric Medical Association (APMA), American Dental Association (ADA), American Chiropratic Association (ACA), American Nursing Association (ANA), etc.

*All undergraduate, graduate, and business schools and universities with related health administration certification conferring education programs and insurance, risk management or related diplomas, adult learning, and CEU programs.

Section I

Humanitarian Wisdom in Patient Care as a Moral Imperative and Risk-Management Tool

MEDICAL PRACTITIONER PERSONAL ISSUES

(It's Not Just about Professional Liability Anymore)

Traditionally, the physician protected his family with whole-life, home, umbrella, and automobile insurance and perhaps an annuity plan and some disability and long-term-care insurance. As the physician executive of a private practice, he or she also protected it with malpractice liability and business interruption insurance. Then, he or she threw in a few stocks, bonds, mutual funds, and ETFs for longer-term financial goals.

Thereafter, perhaps the doctor would take some continuing education courses on risk identification, avoidance, transference, and mitigation, as well as litigation support, malpractice trial conduct, and review, if sponsored by an insurance company. Later, as financial success expanded, s/he might seek to self-learn some budgeting, debt reduction, financial planning, and personal creditor and asset protection principles, as well as attend refresher courses on medical records preparation and charting as a medical risk management and modern malpractice liability reduction strategy in the era of electronic medical records. Maintenance of certification (MOC) for board-certified doctors was an every decade event, as was annual license registration and the attainment of an appropriate number of continuing education units (CEUs). Medicare documentation, compliance, and recoupment issues soon became another emerging concern as well. Of course, one of the growing threats to family and personal financial security was that of amorous patient relationships, sexual harassment, and divorce, as evidenced by the rise of prenuptial, intranuptial, and postnuptial agreements in the legal space.

Appropriately, physician risk reduction became a continuing career education need that sought answers to questions like, What is behind the medical malpractice crisis? What legal reforms would alleviate the crisis? What can be done to prevent/reduce litigation, should we apologize for mistakes or adverse outcomes, and what should we do when sued? Doctors sought alternatives to the traditional legal system and wondered how the medical malpractice insurance and legal industry really functions, from day 1 of civil lawsuit service to the discovery and deposition process and ultimately case settlement or trial and/or jury verdict. Of course, procedural billing, evaluation and management (EM), Current Procedural Terminology (CPT) coding, ICD-10, telehealth, and meaningful use of MU implementations through third-party payer issues became a cottage industry in the last several years.

Accordingly, the integration of all these fundamental personal issues and risks is no longer an academic luxury for modern practitioners, but a pragmatic survival imperative long recognized by the Institute of Medical Business Advisors Inc. (iMBA Inc.) and presented in Section I of this textbook.

In Section I on medical practitioner personal risk-management issues, let us all recall the Canadian physician Sir William Osler, MD, one of the founders of Johns Hopkins Hospital in my hometown of Baltimore, Maryland, where I played stickball in the parking lot as a kid. He left a sizeable body of wisdom that has guided many physicians in the practice of medicine. So, allow me to share with you some of that accumulated wisdom and the quotes that have served me well over the years.

From Dr. Osler, I learned the art of putting myself in the patient's shoes. "The motto of each of you as you undertake the examination and treatment of a case should be 'put yourself in his place.' Realize, so far as you can, the mental state of the patient, enter into his feelings." Osler further stresses that we should "scan gently (the patient's) faults" and offer the "kindly word, the cheerful greeting, the sympathetic look."[1]

"In some of us, the ceaseless panorama of suffering tends to dull that fine edge of sympathy with which we started," writes Osler in his famous essay "Aequanimitas."[2] "Against this benumbing influence, we physicians and nurses, the immediate agents of the Trust, have but one enduring corrective—the practice towards patients of the Golden Rule of Humanity as announced by Confucius: 'What you do not like when done to yourself, do not do to others.'"

Medicine can be both art and science, as many physicians have discovered. As Osler tells us, "Errors in judgment must occur in the practice of an art which consists largely of balancing probabilities."[2] Osler notes that "medicine is a science of uncertainty and an art of probability" and also weighs in with the idea that "the practice of medicine is an art, based on science."[3,4]

Osler emphasized that excellence in medicine is not an inheritance and is more fully realized with the seasoning of experience. "The art of the practice of medicine is to be learned only by experience," says Osler. "Learn to see, learn to hear, learn to feel, learn to smell, and know that by practice alone can you become expert."[5]

Finally, some timeless wisdom on patient care came from Osler in an address to St. Mary's Hospital Medical School in London in 1907: "Gain the confidence of a patient and inspire him with hope, and the battle is half won."[6]

Osler has also imparted plenty of advice on the business of medicine. In "Aequanimitas," Osler says there are only two types of doctors: "those who practice with their brains, and those who practice with their tongues."[7]

In a valedictory address to medical school graduates at McGill University, Osler suggested treating money as a side consideration in a medical career.[8] "You have of course entered the profession of medicine with a view of obtaining a livelihood; but in dealing with your patients let this always be a secondary consideration."

"You are in this profession as a calling, not as a business: as a calling which exacts from you at every turn self-sacrifice, devotion, love and tenderness to your fellow man," explains Osler in the address to St. Mary's Hospital Medical School.[6] "Once you get down to a purely business level, your influence is gone and the true light of your life is dimmed. You must work in the missionary spirit, with a breadth of charity that raises you far above the petty jealousies of life."

It is not easy for doctors to combine a passion for patient care, a knowledge of science, and the maintenance of business, according to Osler in the *British Medical Journal*.[9] "In the three great professions, the lawyer has to consider only his head and pocket, the parson the head and heart, while with us the head, heart, and pocket are all engaged."

While some aspects of practice may fall short or be devoid of appropriate financial remuneration, the giving of one's time, expertise, and experience in improving patient outcomes and the quality of their lives may be the greatest gift. "The 'good debts' of practice, as I prefer to call them...amount to a generous sum by the end of each year," says Osler.[9]

And so, as you read and reflect on the chapters of Section I, always remember the words and wisdom of Dr. William Osler, and keep patient welfare as your first priority.[10]

Dr. David Edward Marcinko, FACFAS, MBA, MBBS (Hon.), CMP™
Chief executive officer, iMBA Inc., Norcross, GA

REFERENCES

1. Penfield W. Neurology in Canada and the Osler centennial. *Can Med Assoc J.* 1949; 61(1): 69–73.
2. Osler W. *Aequanimitas.* Chapter 9, P. Blakiston's Son and Co., Philadelphia, PA, 1925, p. 159.
3. Bean WB. *William Osler: Aphorisms.* CC Thomas, Springfield, IL, p. 129.
4. Osler W. *Aequanimitas.* Chapter 3, P. Blakiston's Son and Co., Philadelphia, PA, 1925, p. 34.
5. Thayer WS. Osler the teacher. In: *Osler and Other Papers.* Johns Hopkins Press, Baltimore, MD, 1931, p. 1.
6. Osler W. The reserves of life. *St. Mary's Hosp Gaz.* 1907; 13(1): 95–8.
7. Osler W. *Aequanimitas.* Chapter 7, P. Blakiston's Son and Co., Philadelphia, PA, 1925, p. 124.
8. Osler W. Valedictory address to the graduates in medicine and surgery, McGill University. *Can Med Surg J.* 1874; 3: 433–42.
9. Osler W. Remarks on organization in the profession. *Brit Med J.* 1911; 1(2614): 237–39.
10. Jacobs AM. First Do No Harm. *PMNews*, March 25, 2015.

1 Physician-Executive Leadership and Risk Management

Human Nature, Medical Ethics, and Modern Principles

David Edward Marcinko, Render S. Davis, Hope Rachel Hetico, and Gary A. Cook

CONTENTS

In any textbook of *gravitas* on medical risk management, asset protection, and insurance planning, a chapter on human nature is usually placed at the end of the book, or as an appendix, or an afterthought, if included at all. However, we elected to prominently place this material as the premier chapter of our textbook.

Why? In the end, the success of any risk-management endeavor ultimately comes down to changing human behavior—helping doctors/nurses/technicians alter whatever they were doing toward something that will better allow them to avoid errors and pursue quality care and practice management goals. Yet, there is still remarkably little education or training for medical professionals focused directly on motivation or change theory, in any related area, except psychiatry/psychology or perhaps professional liability. Instead, doctors are increasingly turning to professional consultants to learn best practices on how to help them actually make the behavioral changes necessary to achieve their quality improvement and risk-reduction goals, as we attempt to answer these questions:

- Are you and your medical, or clinical, practice ready for change?
- How will you transition from (traditional) solo practitioner B-models to modern forms?
- What are leadership, management, and governance?
- In group practices, how is leadership shared?
- What issues need to be considered when hiring a practice administrator or clinic CEO?
- What are medical ethics and munificence? Why are they needed? How do they work?
- What are the types of risk?
- How are risks managed in the medical practice space?

In addition, medical practitioners need to strive to avoid what Zenger and Folkman describe as the 10 most common leadership shortcomings based on a survey of 11,000 leaders. They include the following:

1. Lacking energy and enthusiasm
2. Accepting mediocre self-performance
3. Lacking clear vision and direction
4. Poor judgment
5. Not collaborating
6. Not following standards
7. Resistance to new ideas
8. Not learning from mistakes
9. Lacking interpersonal skills
10. Failing to develop others*

* From Zenger and Folkman, *The Daily Stat: The 10 Most Common Failures of Business Leaders*, Harvard Business Publishing, June 4, 2009.

1.1 INTRODUCTION

This chapter aims to focus on a number of different psychological issues considered critical for any form of medical practice or health-care organization. For that matter, it also deals with the differences between management and leadership; medical ethics; and risk-management classifications, types, and principles.

1.2 EMOTIONAL INTELLIGENCE

Many of us have encountered a person who may intellectually be at upper levels, but whose ability to interact with others appears to be that of one who is highly immature. This is the individual who is prone to becoming angry easily, verbally attacks coworkers, is perceived as lacking in compassion and empathy, and cannot understand why it is difficult to get others to cooperate with them and their agendas. (Think Sheldon Cooper, PhD, DSc, MA, BA, of the TV show *The Big Bang Theory*.)

The concept of emotional intelligence (EQ) was brought into the public domain when Daniel Goleman authored a book entitled *Emotional Intelligence*. According to Goleman, EQ consists of four basic noncognitive competencies: self-awareness, social awareness, self-management, and social skills. These are skills that influence the manner in which people handle themselves and their relationships with others. Goleman's position was that these competencies play a bigger role than cognitive intelligence in determining success in life and in the workplace. He and others contend that EQ involves abilities that may be categorized into five domains:

1. *Self-awareness*: observing and recognizing a feeling as it happens
2. *Managing emotions*: handling feelings so that they are appropriate; realizing what is behind a feeling; finding ways to handle fears and anxieties, anger, and sadness
3. *Motivating oneself*: channeling emotions in the service of a goal; emotional self-control; delaying gratification and stifling impulses
4. *Empathy*: sensitivity to others' feelings and concerns and taking their perspective, appreciating the differences in how people feel about things
5. *Handling relationships*: managing emotions in others; social competence and social skills

In 1995, Goleman then expanded on the works of Howard Gardner, Peter Salovey, and John Mayer. He further defined EQ as a set of competencies demonstrating the ability one has to recognize his/her behaviors, moods, and impulses and to manage them best, according to the situation. Mike Poskey, in "The Importance of Emotional Intelligence in the Workplace," continued this definition by stating that EQ is considered to involve emotional empathy; attention to and discrimination of one's emotions; accurate recognition of one's own and others' moods; mood management or control over emotions; response with appropriate emotions and behaviors in various life situations (especially to stress and difficult situations); and balancing of honest expression of emotions against courtesy, consideration, and respect (Cherniss 2000).

EQ differs from what has generally been considered intelligence, which is described in terms of one's IQ. Traditional views of intelligence focused on cognition, memory, and problem solving. Even today, individuals are evaluated on the basis of cognitive skills.

Entrance tests for medical, law, business, undergraduate, and graduate schools base admissions in large part on the scores on the SAT, GMAT, LSAT, MCAT, etc. Without question, cognitive ability is critical, but it has been demonstrated that it is not a very good predictor of future direct job performance and indirect liability management. In fact, in 1940, Wechsler (1940), the developer of a widely used intelligence test, made reference to "non-intellective" elements. By this, Wechsler meant affective, personal, and social factors.

Goleman became aware of the work of Salovey and Mayer, having trained under David McClelland, and was influenced by McClelland's concern with how little traditional tests of cognitive intelligence predicted success in life. In fact, a study of 80 PhDs in science underwent a battery of personality tests, IQ tests, and interviews in the 1950s while they were graduate students at Berkeley. Forty years later, they were reevaluated, and it turned out that social and emotional abilities were four times more important than IQ in determining professional success and prestige (Feist and Barron 1996).

Undoubtedly, we want to have individuals work with us who have persistence, which enables to them have the energy, drive, and thick skin to develop and close new business, or to work with patients and other members of the staff. It is important to note that coworkers with a "good" personality may be fun, energetic, and outgoing.

However, a good personality does not necessarily equate to success. An individual with a high EQ can manage his/her own impulses, communicate effectively, manage change well, solve problems, and use humor to build rapport in tense situations. This clarity in thinking and composure in stressful and chaotic situations is what separates top performers from weak performers.

Poskey outlined a set of five EQ competencies that have proven to contribute more to workplace achievement than technical skills, cognitive ability, and standard personality traits combined.

1.2.1 Social Competencies

These are competencies that determine how we handle relationships. Intuition and empathy refers to our awareness of others' feelings, needs, and concerns. He suggested that this competency is important in the workplace for the following reasons:

1. *Understanding others*: an intuitive sense of others' feelings and perspectives, and showing an active interest in their concerns and interests
2. *Patient service orientation*: the ability to anticipate, recognize, and meet customers' (patients') needs
3. *People development*: ability to sense what others need in order to grow, develop, and master their strengths
4. *Leveraging diversity*: cultivating opportunities through diverse people

1.2.2 Political Acumen and Social Skills

These refer to our adeptness at inducing desirable responses in others. This competency is important for the following reasons:

1. *Influencing*: using effective tactics and techniques for persuasion and desired results

2. *Communication*: sending clear and convincing messages that are understood by others
3. *Leadership*: inspiring and guiding groups of people
4. *Change catalyst*: initiating and/or managing change in the workplace
5. *Conflict resolution*: negotiating and resolving disagreements with people
6. *Collaboration and cooperation*: working with coworkers and business partners toward shared goals
7. *Team capabilities*: creating group synergy in pursuing collective goals

1.2.3 Personal Competencies

These refer to competencies that determine how we manage ourselves.

1.2.4 Self-Awareness

This refers to knowing our internal states, preferences, resources, and intuitions. This competency is important in the workplace for the following reasons:

1. *Emotional awareness*: recognizing one's emotions and their effects and impact on those around us
2. *Accurate self-assessment*: knowing one's strengths and limits
3. *Self-confidence*: certainty about one's self-worth and capabilities
4. *Self-regulation*: managing one's internal states, impulses, and resources, which is important in the workplace
5. *Self-control*: managing disruptive emotions and impulses
6. *Trustworthiness*: maintaining standards of honesty and integrity
7. *Conscientiousness*: taking responsibility and being accountable for personal performance
8. *Adaptability*: flexibility in handling change
9. *Innovation*: being comfortable with an openness to novel ideas, approaches, and new information

1.2.5 Self-Expectations and Motivation

These refer to emotional tendencies that guide or facilitate reaching goals. This competency is important in the workplace for the following reasons:

1. *Achievement drive*: striving to improve or meet a standard of excellence we impose on ourselves
2. *Commitment*: aligning with the goals of the group or the organization
3. *Initiative*: readiness to act on opportunities without having to be told
4. *Optimism*: persistence in pursuing goals despite obstacles and setbacks

A note of caution is necessary. Goleman and Salovey both stated that EQ on its own is not a strong predictor of job performance. Instead, they contend that it provides the bedrock for competencies that are predictors.

Obviously, EQ is an important attribute, and it behooves each of us to promote EQ in the workplace. A number of guidelines have been developed for the Consortium for Research on Emotional Intelligence in Organizations by Goleman and Cherniss. The guidelines cover 21 phases, which include preparation, training, transfer and evaluation.

1. *Assess the organization's needs*: Determine the competencies that are most critical for effective job performance in a particular type of job. In doing so, use a valid method, such as the comparison of the behavioral interviews of superior and average performers. Also make sure the competencies to be developed are congruent with the organization's culture and overall strategy.
2. *Assess the individual*: This assessment should be based on the key competencies needed for a particular job, and the data should come from multiple sources using multiple methods to maximize credibility and validity.
3. *Deliver assessments with care*: Give the individual information on his/her strengths and weaknesses. In doing so, try to be accurate and clear. Also, allow plenty of time for the person to digest and integrate the information. Provide feedback in a safe and supportive environment in order to minimize resistance and defensiveness. Avoid making excuses or downplaying the seriousness of deficiencies.
4. *Maximize choice*: People are motivated to change when they freely choose to do so. As much as possible, allow people to decide whether or not they will participate in the development process, and have them change goals themselves.
5. *Encourage people to participate*: People will be more likely to participate in development efforts if they perceive them to be worthwhile and effective. Organizational policies and procedures should encourage people to participate in development activity, and supervisors should provide encouragement and the necessary support. Motivation will be enhanced if people trust the credibility of those who encourage them to undertake the training.
6. *Link learning goals to personal values*: People are most motivated to pursue change that fits with their values and hopes. If a change matters little to people, they won't pursue it. Help people understand whether a given change fits with what matters most to them.
7. *Adjust expectations*: This builds positive expectations by showing learners that social and emotional competence can be improved and that such improvement will lead to valued outcomes. Also, make sure that the learner has a realistic expectation of what the training process will involve.
8. *Gauge readiness*: Assess whether the individual is ready for training. If the person is not ready, because of insufficient motivation or other reasons, make readiness the focus of intervention efforts.
9. *Foster a positive relationship between the trainers and learners*: Trainers who are warm, genuine, and empathic are best able to engage the learners in the change process. Select trainers who have these qualities, and make sure that they use them when working with the learners.
10. *Make change self-directed*: Learning is more effective when people direct their own learning program, tailoring it to their unique needs and circumstances. In addition to allowing people to set their own learning goals, let them continue to be in charge of their learning throughout the program, and tailor the training approach to the individual's learning style.

11. *Set clear goals*: People need to be clear about what the competence is, how to acquire it, and how to show it on the job. Spell out the specific behaviors and skills that make up the target competence. Make sure that the goals are clear, specific, and optimally challenging.
12. *Break goals into manageable steps*: Change is more likely to occur if the change process is divided into manageable steps. Encourage both trainers and trainees to avoid being overly ambitious.
13. *Provide opportunities to practice*: Lasting change requires sustained practice on the job and elsewhere in life. An automatic habit is being unlearned, and different responses are replacing it. Use naturally occurring opportunities for practice at work, and in life. Encourage the trainees to try the new behaviors repeatedly and consistently over a period of months.
14. *Give performance feedback*: Ongoing feedback encourages people and directs change. Provide focused and sustained feedback as the learners practice new behaviors. Make sure that supervisors, peers, friends, and family members—or some combination of these—give periodic feedback on progress.
15. *Rely on experiential methods*: Active, concrete, experiential methods tend to work best for learning social and emotional competencies. Development activities that engage all the senses and are dramatic and powerful can be especially effective.
16. *Build in support*: Change is facilitated through ongoing support of others who are going through similar changes. Programs should encourage the formation of groups where people give each other support, throughout the change effort. Coaches and mentors also can be valuable in helping support the desired change.
17. *Use models*: Use modern webinars, patient portals, and live or videotaped models that clearly show how the competency can be used in realistic situations. Encourage learners to study, analyze, and emulate the models.
18. *Enhance insight*: Self-awareness is the cornerstone of emotional and social competence. Help learners acquire greater understanding about how their thoughts, feelings, and behavior affect themselves and others.
19. *Prevent relapse*: Use relapse prevention, which helps people use lapses and mistakes as lessons to prepare themselves for further efforts.
20. *Encourage use of skills on the job*: Supervisors, peers, and subordinates should reinforce and reward learners for using their new skills on the job. Coaches and mentors also can serve this function. Also, provide prompts and cues, such as through periodic follow-ups. Change also is more likely to endure when high-status persons, such as supervisors and upper-level management, model it.
21. *Develop an organizational culture that supports learning*: Change will be more enduring if the organization's culture and tone support the change and offer a safe atmosphere for experimentation.

Finally, see if the development effort has lasting effects through evaluation. When possible, find a true set of measures of the competence or skill, as shown on the job, before and after training, and also at least 2 months later. One-year follow-ups also are highly desirable. In addition to charting progress on the acquisition of competencies, also assess the impact on important job-related outcomes, such as performance measures, and indicators of adjustments, such as absenteeism, grievances, health status, etc.

CLASSIFICATION OF RISKS

As we review the concept of emotional intelligence, it is possible to set up five risk classes, based on the economic consequences of the occurrence of specific individual risks:

1. *Prevented risks*: Risks whose cost of occurrence is higher than their cost of management and whose occurrence may invoke additional legal sanctions. This class would include intentional torts and injuries caused by gross negligence.
2. *Normally prevented risks*: Risks whose cost of occurrence is greater than the cost of their management but whose occurrence will be considered only as negligent. This class includes most negligent injuries and most types of product liability actions.
3. *Managed risks*: Risks whose cost of occurrence is only slightly greater than their cost of management. The plaintiff usually has the burden of showing that the defendant owed the plaintiff a special duty to recover for one of these risks.
4. *Unprevented risks*: Risks whose cost of occurrence is less than their cost of management. The classic example of this class is the cost of railroad crossing barriers compared to the cost of people being hit by trains.
5. *Unpreventable risks*: Risks whose occurrence is unmanageable.

The assignment of a risk to one of these classes is a major problem in medical and health-care quality control, because the class of a risk determines how much effort must be expended to prevent the risk. The misclassification of a prevented or normally prevented risk as a managed or unprevented risk can result in large financial losses.

For example, a medical clinic that does not update obsolete equipment, such as inaccurate oxygen monitors, would be liable for any injuries attributable to the obsolete equipment. The classifications of risk must be reviewed periodically to determine if the cost of the risk-taking behavior has changed, thereby altering the classification. Or, a small hospital in a rural area would not be expected to have the same sophisticated equipment as a major hospital in a city. If an accident victim is brought into the rural facility, the hospital's duty may be to transfer the patient to a better-equipped facility. The patient will face the risk of dying because of the delay in treatment, but the risk of insufficient treatments outweighs the risk of transfer. If the same victim were brought into a hospital in a major metropolitan center, the duty would be to treat the patient without a transfer. The risk of transfer has not changed, but the risk of insufficient treatment has disappeared.

The classification of risks is also complicated by the dependence upon the historical treatment of the risk by similar providers and any EQ limitations of the doctor making the classification decision.

These abilities are important for one to be successful as a manager and even more so as a leader, or physician executive. But, before we begin an examination of strategic leadership, it is necessary to make a deeper distinction between a manager and a leader. There are many different definitions as well as descriptions regarding leadership and management. Many people talk as though leadership and management are the same thing. Fundamentally, they are quite different. Management focuses on work. We manage work activities such as money, time, paperwork, materials, equipment, and personnel, among other things. As can be found in any basic book on management, management focuses on planning, organizing, controlling, coordinating, budgeting, finance, and money management, as well as decision making. In effect, managers are generally those individuals who have been given their authority by virtue of their role. It is the function of a manager to ensure that the work gets done as well as to oversee the activities of others. In many health-care organizations, we find that the elevation of individuals to a managerial position occurs as a result of being a high performer on their previous assignment. A manager receives authority on the basis of role, while a leader' authority is more innate in nature.

1.3 LEADERSHIP VERSUS MANAGEMENT

Leaders are more strategically focused, and rather than directing employees through tasks, they inspire and motivate employees to drive themselves. Leaders are schooled and adept in the use of EQ.

The latter function is somewhat limited for a manager and generally refers to day-to-day functions. To differentiate between a leader and a manager, the focus of leadership is on more abstract concepts, such as vision, inspiration, persuasion, motivation, teamwork, and listening. Additionally, leaders are also involved in coaching and mentoring. Edgar Shein focuses on the differences between management and leadership by stating, "Leaders work on the culture of the organization, creating it or changing it. Managers work within the culture of the organization." One difference that has been widely quoted was presented by Warren Bennis, who states, "Managers are people who do things right and leaders are those who do the right thing." Additionally, Bennis states that "underperforming organizations are usually over managed and under led" (University of Maryland symposium, January 21, 1988). A follow-up to this is that "leadership maintains a focus on: creating a vision and developing strategies; engaging, motivating and inspiring people; building trust and having courage; and creating action" (Jacobson 2002).

In the 1940s, the Ohio State Leadership suggested that "consideration" is an important aspect of effective leadership. The researcher at Ohio State suggested that those leaders who are able to establish "mutual trust, respect, and a certain warmth and rapport" with members of their group will be more effective (Fleishman and Harris 1962).

Often, this includes the principles of shared Boyer education model decision making and Miller Heiman lifelong learning initiatives, combined with the following three proven leadership and organizational skills.

1. *Sensitivity does matter*: A leader treats each employee with respect and dignity, regardless of race, gender, cultural background, or the particular role they actually perform in the practice. Consider how many legal suits are filed against any type

of organization, whether it is a medical practice or a large manufacturing facility, due to perceived disparate treatment toward the employee based on race, religion, gender, sexual preference, or other non-work-related issues.

2. *Real respect is earned*: Having initials after one's name and the wearing of a lab coat do not automatically entitle an individual to respect. Formal authority has been found to be one of the least effective forms of influence. Only by earning the respect of your staff as well as your patients can you be sure that your intent will be carried out when you are not present. Setting the example in performance and conduct, rather than a "do as I say, not as I do" level of activity, enables one to exert influence far greater than titles.
3. *Trust and challenge your employees*: How many times have practices sought to hire the best and brightest only to second-guess the employee. Eric Schmidt, the CEO of Google, describes his management philosophy as having "…an employee base in which everybody is doing exactly what they want every day." Obviously, there are certain policies and procedures, but at the same time, the leader enables decision making to the lowest possible level. This also enables employees to question why certain policies and procedures are still being followed when more effective and efficient methods are available ("How the Army Prepared Me to Work at Google," Doug Raymond, *Harvard Business Review*).

The phrase "physician, heal thyself" (Luke 4:23, King James version) means that we have to attend to our own faults, in preference to pointing out the faults of others. The phrase alludes to the readiness of physicians to heal sickness in others while sometimes not being able or willing to heal themselves. By the same token, it now is necessary for medical professionals to learn how to manage themselves. It suggests that physicians, while often being able to help the sick, cannot always do so and, when sick themselves, are no better placed than anyone else (Martin 2010).

1.3.1 Developing New Leadership Skills for Health 2.0

Medicine today is vastly different than a generation ago, and all health-care professionals need new skills to be successful and reduce the emerging risks outlined in this textbook, as well as the "unknown unknowns" elsewhere. Traditionally, the physician was viewed as the "captain of the ship." Today, the physician's role may be more akin to a ship's navigator, using clinical and teaching skills and knowledge to chart a patient's course through a confusing morass of insurance requirements, fees, choices, rules, and regulations to achieve the best attainable clinical outcomes.

This new leadership paradigm includes many classic business school principles, now modified to fit the Patient Protection and Affordable Care Act (PPACA), the era of health reform, and modern technical connectivity. Thus, the physician must be a *subtle guide on the side, not a bombastic sage on the stage*. These health 2.0 leadership philosophies might include the following:

- *Negotiation*: Working to optimize appropriate treatment plans, i.e., quality of life versus quantity of life.
- *Team play*: Working in concert with other allied health-care professionals to coordinate care delivery within a clinically appropriate and cost-effective framework.
- *Working within the limits of competence*: Avoiding the pitfalls of the medical generalist versus the specialist that may restrict access to treatment, medications, physicians, and facilities by clearly acknowledging when a higher degree of service is needed on behalf of the patient—all while embracing holistic primary care.
- *Respecting different cultures and values*: Inherent in the support of the medical *principle of autonomy* is the acceptance of values that may differ from one's own. As the U.S. becomes more culturally heterogeneous, medical providers are called upon to work within, and respect, the sociocultural and/or spiritual framework of patients, students, and their families.
- *Seeking clarity on what constitutes marginal care*: Within a system of finite resources, providers are called upon to openly communicate with patients regarding access to marginal medical information and/or treatments.
- *Supporting evidence-based practice*: Health-care providers should utilize outcome data to reduce variation in treatments to achieve higher efficiencies and improved care delivery through evidence-based medicine (EBM).
- *Fostering transparency and openness in communications*: Health-care professionals should be willing, and prepared, to discuss all aspects of care, especially when discussing end-of-life issues or when problems arise.
- *Exercising decision-making flexibility*: Treatment algorithms, templates, and clinical pathways are useful tools when used within their scope, but providers must have the authority to adjust the plan if circumstances warrant.
- *Becoming skilled in the art of listening and interpreting*: In her groundbreaking book, *Narrative Ethics: Honoring the Stories of Illness*, Rita Charon, MD, PhD, a professor at Columbia University, writes of the extraordinary value of using the patient's personal story in the treatment plan. She notes that *"medicine practiced with narrative competence will more ably recognize patients and diseases; convey knowledge and regard, join humbly with colleagues, and accompany patients and*

TYPES OF PURE RISKS

Fundamental Risk versus Particular Risk

Fundamental risk affects a large number of people in the economy. Earthquakes and war are good examples. If originated from the nature of society, namely, acts of war and unemployment, then they are not insurable. Meanwhile, fundamental risk as a result of physical or natural causes may be insurable. On the other hand, particular risk affects only individuals, especially managers and leaders, for instance, fire, robberies, and thefts. These risks, like professional liability and medical malpractice, are all insurable.

Dynamic Risk

Dynamic risk occurs due to changes in economy that cause financial loss to certain people. It exists as a result of adjustment to the misallocation of resources in the economy. In modernity, one of the clearer examples is the rapid change in health information technology. Many companies are victims, while others emerge with new successes.

Static Risk

Static risk, on the other hand, happens even though there are no changes taking place. During a stock market boom or collapse, there are people experiencing losses. These types of losses are due to natural perils like earthquakes and typhoons, or moral hazards like cheats. Static risk brings no benefits to society, only pure losses.

Pure versus Speculative Risks

In pure risk, there is either a possible loss or no loss. In contrast, there are possibilities of gain or loss in speculative risk. Pure risk can be insured against, while speculative risk cannot. However, the pure risk consequences of speculative risk are insurable. For instance, the decision to manufacture a new medical product involves speculative risk, either gaining from the product or experiencing losses. So, it is not insurable. But, if the factory burns down by fire, and as a result, cannot supply what is needed by the dealers of durable medical equipment, then the losses are considered a pure risk and therefore insurable.

1. **Personal risks**

Now, there are basically three types of pure risks that concern individual physicians. These incur losses like loss of income, additional expenses, and devaluation of property. There are four risk factors affecting them:

- *Premature death*: This is the death of a breadwinner who leaves behind financial responsibilities.
- *Old age/retirement*: This is the risk of being retired without sufficient savings to support retirement years.
- *Health crisis*: An individual with a health problem may face a potential loss of income and increase in medical expenditures.
- *Unemployment*: A jobless individual may have to live on his/her savings. If savings are depleted, a bigger crisis is awaiting.

2. **Property risks**
   This means the possibility of damage or loss to the property owned due to some cause. There are two types of losses involved.
   - Direct loss, which means financial loss as a result of property damage
   - Consequential loss, which means financial loss due to the happenings of direct loss of the property

   For instance, a medical practice that burned down may incur repair costs as a direct loss. The consequential loss is being unable to run the practice business to generate income.
3. **Liability risks**
   A doctor is legally liable for his/her wrongful act that causes damage to a third party, physically, by reputation, or in property. She/he can be legally sued with no maximum for the compensation amount if found guilty.

   Knowing how risks are classified, and the types of pure risks an individual is exposed to, will provide a fundamental overview on these risk topics and prepare you to further acquire the knowledge of how to deal with and manage them as a physician executive, leader, or manager.

their families through ordeals of illness." In many ways, attention to the narrative returns medicine full circle to the compassionate and caring foundations of the patient–physician relationship.

These thoughts represent only a handful of examples to illustrate the myriad of new skills that tomorrow's health-care professionals must master in order to meet their timeless professional obligations of compassionate care and contemporary treatment effectiveness, all within the context of modern risk-management principles.

1.4 MEDICAL ETHICS

In today's health-care environment, physicians face a myriad of ethical dilemmas in their daily practice. Time constraints, diminished professional autonomy, declining incomes, explosive growth in technology, increasing institutional and payer pressures to lower length of stay and costs, and deteriorating public trust *combined with* increasing public demands for access to services are only some of the most obvious problems plaguing practitioners. Some have been adversely impacted by these changes and were quick to blame managed care organizations (MCOs) of the last decade and, more recently, the PPACA; this anger may be, to some extent, misdirected.

While there were ample concerns with managed care as it was implemented, its theory and principles remained ethically sound. Health care should be *managed*—for continuity, quality, effectiveness, value, and optimal outcomes—regardless of the mechanisms by which the caregivers are paid. Practicing medicine within managed care entailed obligations to care for patients and to respect their autonomy, but providers were also placed in a disquieting role as resource managers. This role required new approaches to finding better, more cost-effective ways to meet these obligations, while being held accountable to a larger community to which the individual belonged (e.g., a health plan or employee group) for the costs incurred in delivering care.

The physician's apparently conflicting role seemed to impinge on the fundamental tenets of patient advocacy articulated in the Hippocratic oath. By the terms of many insurance plans, physicians' incomes are directly related to savings generated in the delivery of care, a tactic criticized by Marcia Angell, MD, former executive editor of the *New England Journal of Medicine*, who noted in a Public Broadcasting Service (PBS) interview that "our health care system creates ethical dilemmas that no health care system should create, doctors are paid for doing less" (capitation environment). As if in reaction to the principles of population health, there is a growing call for a return to the more traditional, market-based model for health care referred to as *consumer-driven* care. Proponents argue that medical decisions should be made by patients, in consultation with their physicians, based on the individual's self-interest and resources. Components of such a system might include individually directed health savings accounts (HSAs) for routine treatments, combined with insurance for catastrophic medical expenses. Economist John Goodman, PhD, argues that in this model, "consumers occupy the primary decision-making role regarding the health care they receive." Others argue that many consumers will not have resources to adequately fund HSAs and, as a result, will defer or delay needed treatments due to high out-of-pocket costs. University of North Carolina political scientist Jonathan Oberlander noted that this model simply shifts "the cost of health care on the backs of patients." Especially hard hit would be consumers with chronic illnesses who may never save enough in their HSAs to meet the costs of care.

Whether it is managed care's emphasis on the care of populations or the PPACA's subsidized care's focus on individual decisions, the issue of cost will continue to drive debate in this troubled environment. In this context, let us examine some specific dilemmas confronting physicians in their daily practice.

And how they fit into your specific medical risk-management equation is to be explored throughout the remainder of this book.

1.4.1 Patient Advocacy

Few areas of life are as personal as an individual's health, and people have long relied on a caring and competent physician to be their champion in securing the medical resources needed to retain or restore health and function. For many physicians, the care of patients was the foundation of their professional calling. However, in the contemporary delivery organization, there may be little opportunity for generalist physician "gatekeepers" or "specialty hospitalists or intensivists" to form a lasting relationship with patients. These institution-based physicians may be called upon to deliver treatments determined by programmatic protocols or algorithm-based practice guidelines that leave little discretion for their professional judgment. In addition, the physician's personal values may be impeded by seemingly perverse financial incentives that may directly conflict with their advocacy role, especially if a patient may be in need of expensive services that may not be covered in their insurance plan or are beyond the resources of a patient's HSA or savings. Marcia Angell, MD, noted during her previously mentioned PBS interview that the "financial incentives directly affecting doctors...put them at odds with the best interests of their patients...and it puts ethical doctors in a terrific quandary."

1.4.2 Conflicts of Interest

Conflicts of interest are not a new phenomenon in medicine. In the fee-for-service system, physicians controlled access to medical facilities and technology, and they benefited financially from nearly every order or prescription they wrote. Consequently, there was an inherent temptation to overtreat patients. Even marginal diagnostic or therapeutic procedures were justified on the grounds of both clinical necessity and legal protection against threats of negligence.

While it could be construed that this represented a direct conflict of interest, it could also be argued that most patients were well served in this system because the emphasis was on thorough, comprehensive treatment—where cost was rarely a consideration. It was a well-known adage that physicians "could do well, by doing good." In managed care, the potential conflicts between patients and physicians took on a completely different dimension. By design, in health plans where medical care was financed through prepayment arrangements, the physician's income was enhanced not by doing more for his/her patients but by doing less. Patients, confronted with the realization that their doctor would be rewarded for the use of fewer resources, could no longer rely with certainty on the motives underlying a physician's treatment plans. One inevitable outcome was the continuing decline in patients' trust in their physicians. This has been exacerbated to some degree by revelations of significant financial remuneration to physicians by pharmaceutical and medical product firms for their services as researchers or active participants on corporate-funded advisory panels, calling into question the physicians' objectivity in promoting the use of company products to their peers or patients.

1.4.3 Communications

In contemporary medicine, ethical dilemmas in communications are increasingly common and may come in many different forms:

- Physician's failing to communicate necessary clinical information to patients in terms and language the patients truly understand
- Physicians' offering only limited treatment choices to patients because alternatives may not be covered by the patient's insurance plan
- Failure to disclose financial incentives and other payment arrangements that may influence the physician's treatment plans and recommendations
- Time constraints that limit opportunities for in-depth discussions between patients and their doctors
- Lack of an ongoing relationship between the patient and physician that would foster open communications
- Physician's failure to present treatment alternatives to a patient due to conflicts with his/her personal moral or spiritual beliefs

Another area where communication is critically important is in the disclosure of medical error or cause of adverse occurrences. In the years since the 1999 publication of the Institute of Medicine's report "To Err is Human: Building a Safer Health System," there has been increasing awareness that the growing complexity of the nation's health-care system, combined with the tightening financial restrictions on treatment, sometimes results in a perfect storm of actions that may lead to patient harm. According to the report, more than half of the adverse events affecting hospitalized patients are the result of medical errors, and between 44,000 and 98,000 persons die each year as a consequence of such errors.

Especially challenging for physicians is the disclosure of errors that may have caused a patient harm. According to Emory University bioethicist John Banja, PhD, author of *Medical Errors and Medical Narcissism*, the "realization that an error has seriously harmed a patient is one of the most psychologically painful experiences a health professional can have." Unfortunately, given malpractice concerns, disclosing such errors to patients may often be as painful as the error itself. Nonetheless, such disclosure is vital to maintain the trust required for supporting the patient through such an experience.

Recent federal regulations have heightened awareness of errors and adverse occurrences through changes in Medicare that now prohibit reimbursements to health-care facilities for extended stays and additional treatments directly related to serious, preventable incidents or occurrences, dubbed "never events." Among more than two dozen identified events are wrong-site surgery, blood incompatibility, medication errors, decubitus ulcers, air emboli, and many more. The economic consequences of these restrictions could prove to be significant.

1.4.4 Confidentiality

Whether it is an employer interested in the results of an employee's health screening, an insurer attempting to learn more about an enrollee's prior health history, the media in search of a story, or health planners examining the potential value of national health databases, the confidential nature of the traditional doctor–patient relationship may be compromised through demands for clinical information by parties other than the patient and treating caregivers.

In addition, without clear safeguards, the growth in use of electronic medical records may put personal health information at risk of tampering or unauthorized access. Clearly, employers and insurers are interested in the status of an individual's health and ability to work, but does this desire to know, combined with their role as payers for health care, constitute a right to know? The patient's right to privacy remains a volatile and unresolved issue.

Counter to this concern is the recognition that electronic records may one day dramatically improve communications by offering greater accessibility of information to clinicians in the hospital or office, potentially reducing medical errors through elimination of handwritten notes, increased use of built-in prompts and clinically derived triggers for orders and treatments, and development of pathways for optimal treatments based on clinically valid and tested best practices.

1.4.5 Cultural Sensitivity

While America has often been called a "nation of immigrants," it has never been more true than today. Consequently, the challenge for physicians and other health-care providers, in both large cities and small communities, is meeting the health-care needs of increasingly diverse and multicultural populations who speak different languages and have social norms, traditions, and values that may substantially differ from their own. Problems arise when clinicians expect, even demand, that patients and their families discard their cultural

Former U.S. Surgeon General David Satcher, MD, PhD, now director of the Satcher Health Leadership Institute at Morehouse College of Medicine in Atlanta, Georgia, helped develop a special curriculum designed to foster greater cultural competence among physicians and health-care providers. Called the "CRASH Course," the program emphasizes the following:

- *Cultural awareness*: acknowledging the diversity and legitimacy of the many cultures that make up the fabric of American Society
- *Respect*: valuing other cultural norms, even if they differ or conflict with your own
- *Assess and affirm*: understanding the points of both congruence and difference among cultural approaches to decision making; learning how to achieve the best outcomes within the cultural framework of the patient and family unit
- *Sensitivity and self-awareness*: being secure in your own values, while willing to be flexible in working through cultural differences with others
- *Humility*: recognizing that every culture has legitimacy and that no one is an expert in what is best for others; being willing to subordinate your values for those of another to achieve the goals of treatment

foundations and adhere to the health-care provider's view of the care and decision-making process.

Instead, the health-care team should be more aware of and sensitive to the values and beliefs of patients who come from other cultures, working within them to ensure that the patient's individual rights are supported and wishes honored to the fullest extent possible. In her award-winning book, *The Spirit Catches You and You Fall Down*, Ann Fadiman chronicled this tragic clash of two cultures in medical care for a child of the traditional Hmong people of Laos, transplanted to California after the Vietnam War. In the book, Fadiman recounts a conversation with Professor Arthur Kleinman of Harvard University, a highly regarded expert in multicultural relations and conflict, who noted, "If you cannot see that your own culture has its own set of interests, emotions, and biases, how can you expect to deal successfully with someone else's culture?"

There is little doubt that multicultural sensitivity will continue to grow as an increasingly integral component of medical education and risk-management in health-care practice.

1.4.6 Being a Patient Educator, Facilitator, and Mentor

It is no longer enough for physicians to be healers, intervening when a patient appears at their door with an acute or chronic illness. They must be proactive educators, providing patients with the information needed to change poor health habits like smoking, drinking, and obesity, and encouraging the adoption of healthier lifestyles. Unfortunately, this task is more difficult than it appears.

Historically, Americans have refused to accept the consequences of their poor health habits, preferring to seek medicine's help in repairing the damage after it has been done. Results from the Gallup-Healthways Well-Being Index (WBI) poll released in February 2009 showed only marginal improvements in the overall health of Americans, with the most gain among those 65 years of age or older, and those with higher incomes. Nonetheless, the report showed that only 46% of Americans consistently follow good health habits. The report's summary concluded that "it is clear that millions of Americans are in need of continued education and encouragement around critical healthy behaviors."

One aspect of this educational process that has both advocates and opponents is direct-to-consumer (D2C) advertising, notably by pharmaceutical firms. In the past, information on medications was provided to physicians, who then made a decision regarding appropriateness for their patients. Today, consumers are bombarded by almost never-ending radio, television, and print advertisements for products to treat almost everything from high blood pressure and intestinal discomfort to erectile dysfunction. These ads, combined with nearly inexhaustible sources of information—some good, some bad—on the Internet, have changed the dynamics of the patient–physician discussions of treatment choices and preferences. On balance, the greater access to information may be of great value to patients and their physicians, but only if it leads to more informed and coherent medical decision making.

Even when confronted with the time constraints and discontinuity inherent in frequently changing health insurance plans, it is clear that physicians must be diligent in assessing their patients' health habits and helping them articulate their health goals; ensuring that patients understand the terms, limitations, and costs associated with their health plan; and serving as mentors and partners to provide them with the knowledge and self-motivation to change for better long-term health.

Instead of being *gatekeepers* charged with limiting access to the system, physicians should view their roles as that of *facilitators*—guiding patients through an increasingly confusing maze of treatment alternatives and leading them in the direction of informed choices and optimal outcomes. In today's health-care environment, the principle of beneficence is inextricably woven into the premise that physicians must do more to help patients help themselves.

1.4.7 Becoming Quality Driven

Whether care should be managed is no longer a legitimate question. The fundamental question now is for what purpose is medical care to be managed, and by whom? The moral vulnerability of managed care rested with its apparent overriding concern with cost reduction through limitations on access and service, possibly at the expense of clinical appropriateness, quality, and the health needs of the individual patient.

If physicians are to be credible advocates for their patients, they must unwaveringly stand for quality and against arbitrary and unjustifiable restrictions on access to clinically justified and appropriate care. This does not imply a return to unregulated, fee-for-service medicine but, rather, a demand that providers and payers be held accountable for *both* cost-effectiveness *and* quality. To date, unfortunately, this has not taken place in a coordinated fashion with any clear goal of establishing a cohesive, seamless health-care system. Consequently, we have a fragmented, patchwork system, described by Marcia Angell, MD, as a "hodgepodge of temporary alignments, existing independently, often working at cross purposes..." that leaves many patients and providers with inadequate tools and information to make truly informed health-care choices. Physicians, other care providers, payers, and regulators should work in concert to develop a system of care that is integrated and coordinated, dependent on epidemiologic data, consumer focused, sensitive to privacy and confidentiality concerns, and clearly responsive to the legitimate health-care needs of individuals and the general population.

As a nation, we can have a health-care system that embraces compassionate, clinically appropriate, cost-effective care, with universal access to basic services, if we are willing to make difficult, but publicly informed and debated, choices regarding our health-care priorities. Physicians must be proactive and central to this process.

1.4.8 Demanding High Moral Standards of Self and Economics Organizations

It has been argued that physicians have abdicated the "moral high ground" in health care by their interest in seeking protection for their high incomes, their highly publicized self-referral arrangements, and their historical opposition toward reform efforts that jeopardized their clinical autonomy.

In his book *Medicine at the Crossroads*, Emory University professor Melvin Konnor, MD, noted that "throughout its history, organized medicine has represented, first and foremost, the pecuniary interests of doctors." He lays significant blame for the present problems in health care at the doorstep of both insurers and doctors, stating that "the system's ills are pervasive and all its participants are responsible." In order to reclaim their once-esteemed moral position, physicians must actively reaffirm their commitment to the highest standards of the medical profession and call on other participants in the health-care delivery system also to elevate their values and standards to the highest level.

In the evolutionary shifts in models for care, physicians have been asked to embrace the business values of efficiency and cost-effectiveness, sometimes at the expense of their professional judgment and personal values. While some of these changes have been inevitable as our society sought to rein in out-of-control costs, it is not unreasonable for physicians to call on payers, regulators, and other parties to the health-care delivery system to raise their ethical bar. Harvard University physician-ethicist Linda Emmanuel noted that "health professionals are now accountable to business values (such as efficiency and cost-effectiveness), so business persons should be accountable to professional values including kindness and compassion." Within the framework of ethical principles, John La Puma, MD, wrote in *Managed Care Ethics* that "business's ethical obligations are integrity and honesty. Medicine's are those plus altruism, beneficence, non-maleficence, respect, and fairness."

Incumbent in these activities is the expectation that the forces that control our health-care delivery system, the payers, the regulators, and the providers, will reach out to the larger community, working to eliminate the inequities that have left so many Americans with limited access to even basic health care. Charles Dougherty clarified this obligation in *Back to Reform*, when he noted that "behind the daunting social reality stands a simple moral value that motivates the entire enterprise. Health care is grounded in caring. And, managing risk is a component of caring. It arises from a sympathetic response to the suffering of others."

1.5 DEVELOPING NEW HEALTH CARE 2.0 MEDICAL PRACTICE SKILLS

Medical practice today is vastly different from a generation ago, and physicians need new skills to be successful and reduce liability risks while improving care delivery at lower

RISK-MANAGEMENT PRINCIPLES

As we have seen, to manage risk properly in an ethical environment, there first must be an awareness of it. The risk can be in the form of loss of income due to death or disability, loss of possession or property, property damage, professional liability, and the like. Second, the measurement of the potential losses associated with the risk must be assessed, as in medical malpractice litigation. And finally, an appropriate method for managing medical practice risk needs to be analyzed to mitigate, reduce, or eliminate it. In general, there are four methods of dealing with risks.

1. *Risk avoidance*: Some risks can be avoided. The risk of airplane accidents can pretty much be avoided by not flying. The risk of a sport-related injury can be avoided by not playing sports. For the majority of us, however, risk avoidance is not a practical solution for the multitude of risks involved in our daily routines.
2. *Risk assumption*: Risk assumption occurs voluntarily or involuntarily due to failure to properly identify risk exposure. The assumption (or retention) of risk can occur from denial or ignorance of the risk, or after careful consideration as a form of self-insurance. If you raise the deductible on your homeowner's policy to lower the annual premium, you are practicing risk assumption. Knowingly driving without a spare tire is another example of assuming a risk.
3. *Risk reduction*: Taking specific precautionary steps may lessen some risks. Within this category, we could include certain aspects of daily living, such as thoroughly cooking meat, the scheduling of periodic maintenance on our vehicles, and the installation of smoke or radon detectors within our living environment. The overall risk remains, but in a somewhat modified, and possibly diminished, capacity.
4. *Risk transfer*: Some of the most important risks faced by individuals and businesses cannot be intelligently avoided or assumed, and reduction doesn't provide adequate peace of mind. A method must then be identified to shift the risk to others willing to accept it. Purchasing an extended warranty on an automobile is one method of risk transfer. Another method could be to form a corporation with which to conduct business. Here, the stockholders would limit their risk to their investment, while any creditors would assume much of the remaining risk. Another "noninsurance" method would be subcontracting. In this case, the general contractor shifts a portion of the risk to the subcontractors.

costs. In order to balance their obligations to both individual patients and larger groups, physicians now must become more than competent clinicians.

Traditionally, the physician was viewed as the captain of the ship, in charge of nearly all the medical decisions, but this changed with the dynamics of managed care and the health reform of the PPACA. Today, the physician's role may be more akin to the ship's navigator, utilizing his/her clinical skills and knowledge of the health-care environment to chart the patient's course through a confusing morass of insurance requirements, care choices, and regulations to achieve the best attainable outcome. Some of these new skills include the following:

- *Negotiation*: Working to optimize the patient's access to appropriate services and facilities.
- *Being a team player*: Working in concert with other care givers, from generalist and specialist physicians to nurses and therapists, to coordinate care delivery within a clinically appropriate and cost-effective framework.
- *Working within the limits of professional competence*: Avoiding the pitfalls of payer arrangements that may restrict access to specialty physicians and facilities, by clearly acknowledging when the symptoms or manifestations of a patient's illness require this higher degree of service, and then working on behalf of the patient to seek access to them.
- *Respecting different cultures and values*: Inherent in the support of the principle of autonomy is acceptance of values that may differ from one's own. As the United States becomes a more culturally heterogeneous nation, health-care providers are called upon to work within and respect the sociocultural and/or spiritual framework of patients and their families.
- *Seeking clarity on what constitutes marginal care*: Within a system of finite resources, physicians will be called upon to carefully and openly communicate with patients regarding access to marginal and/or futile treatments. Addressing the many needs of patients and families at the end of life will be an increasingly important challenge in both communications and delivery of appropriate yet compassionate care.
- *Supporting evidence-based practice*: Physicians should utilize outcome data to reduce variation in treatments and achieve higher efficiencies and effectiveness of care delivery.
- *Fostering transparency and openness in communications*: Physicians should be willing and prepared to discuss all aspects of care and treatment, especially when disclosing problems or issues that may arise.
- *Exercising decision-making flexibility*: Treatment algorithms and clinical pathways are extremely useful tools when used within their scope, but physicians must follow the case-managed patient closely and have the authority to adjust the plan if clinical circumstances warrant.
- *Fostering patient- and family-centered care*: Whenever possible, medical treatments should be undertaken in a way that respects the patient's values and preferences, and recognizes the important role to be played by family in supporting the patient's care and well-being. For details on engaging families in this process, visit the website for the Institute for Family-Centered Care (2015) at http://www.familycenteredcare.org.
- *Becoming skilled in the art of listening and interpreting*: In her groundbreaking book, *Narrative Ethics: Honoring the Stories of Illness*, Rita Charon, MD, PhD, a professor of clinical medicine at Columbia University's College of Physicians and Surgeons, writes of the extraordinary value of utilizing the patient's narrative, or personal story, in the care and treatment process. She notes that "medicine practiced with narrative competence will more ably recognize patients and diseases, convey knowledge and regard, join humbly with colleagues, and accompany patients and their families through ordeals of illness." In many ways, attention to the narrative returns medicine full circle to the compassionate and caring foundations of the patient–physician relationship.

These represent only a handful of examples to illustrate the myriad of new skills that today's savvy physicians must master in order to meet their timeless professional obligation of compassionate patient care, coupled with risk avoidance, assumption, transference, and reduction mechanisms.

Note: Health 2.0 is information exchange plus technology. It employs user-generated content, social networks, and decision support tools to address the problems of inaccessible, fragmentary, or unusable health-care information. Health care 2.0 connects users to new kinds of information, fundamentally changing the consumer experience (e.g., buying insurance or deciding on/managing treatment); clinical decision making (e.g., risk identification or use of best practices); and business processes (e.g., supply-chain management or business analytics.

1.6 ASSESSMENT

The erosion of trust expressed by the public toward the health-care industry may only be reversed if those charged with working within or managing the system place patient and community interests ahead of their own. We must foster an ethical and governing culture within health care that rewards leaders with integrity and vision, those who encourage and expect ethical excellence from themselves and others, and leaders who recognize that ethics establishes the moral framework for all organizational decision-making and risk-reduction methodologies.

And, when it comes to profession liability and medical malpractice, compassion and empathy may be the best risk-management strategy when combined with the tools, techniques, and strategies outlined in this textbook.

1.7 CONCLUSION

Keep in mind these risk classifications, risk types, and risk-management principles in relation to EQ, managerial and leadership, and medical ethics as you read the upcoming chapters on insurance planning, as well as the entire textbook. We trust that you and your patients—and clients—will benefit from it.

1.8 COLLABORATE

Discuss this chapter online with others at http://www.medicalexecutivepost.com.

ACKNOWLEDGMENT

To Rebekah Prather, The Doctors Company, Napa, California.

BIBLIOGRAPHY

American College of Obstetrics and Gynecology: "The Limits of Conscientious Refusal in Reproductive Medicine," Report of the Committee on Bioethics, Washington, DC, November 2007.

Baker, K and Ricciardi, V: *Investor Behavior: The Psychology of Financial Planning and Investing*, pp. 3–24. John Wiley & Sons, Inc., Hoboken, NJ, 2014.

Banja, JD: *Medical Errors and Medical Narcissism.* Jones and Bartlett Publishers, Sudbury, MA, 2005.
Bauer, JC: *Mastering Relentless Progress in Medical Science and Technology Realities of Health Reform: New Strategies for Survival and Growth.* The Governance Institute (Leadership Conference), Naples, FL, 2009.
Beauchamp, TL and Childress, JF: *Principles of Biomedical Ethics*, 6th edition. Oxford University Press, New York, 1989, 2008.
Brescia, F, MD, professor, Medical University of South Carolina, Charleston, SC, interview.
"Bush Plans Last-Minute 'Physician's Conscience' Rule Despite Controversy," December 3, 2008. http://www.findingdulcinea.com.
Center for Ethics in Healthcare: *Integrated Healthcare Ethics.* Department of Veterans Affairs. http://www.ethics.va.gov.
Charon, R: *Narrative Medicine: Honoring the Stories of Illness.* Oxford University Press, New York, 2006.
Cherniss, C: Emotional Intelligence: What It Is and Why It Matters, presented at the Annual Conference of the Society of Industrial and Organizational Psychology, April 2000.
Davis, R: *Medical Ethics for Challenging Times. The Business of Medical Practice*, 3rd edition. Springer Publishing, New York, 2010.
DeGross, J, MD, professor, Mercer University School of Medicine, Macon, GA, interview.
DeRuyter, D, MD, pulmonologist and medical director, Kindred Hospital, Atlanta, GA, interview.
Dougherty, CJ: *Back to Reform: Values, Markets, and the Healthcare System.* Oxford University Press, New York, 1989.
Doyle, JS: *The Business Coach.* Wiley, New York, 1999.
Eastern, JS: "Ingenix Settlements: Don't Drop Your Guard." *Skin and Allergy News*, March 2009.
Emanual, EJ and Dubler, NN: "Preserving the Physician–Patient Relationship in the Era of Managed Care." *JAMA*, Vol. 273, No. 4, pp. 323–329, 1995.
Fadiman, A: *The Spirit Catches You and You Fall Down: A Hmong Child, Her American Doctors, and the Collision of Two Cultures.* Farrar, Strauss and Giroux, New York, 1997.
Feist, GJ and Barron, F: Emotional Intelligence and Academic Intelligence in Career and Life Success, paper presented at the Annual Convention of the American Psychological Society, San Francisco, CA, 1996.
Fleishman, EA and Harris, EF: "Patterns of Leadership Behavior Related to Employee Grievances and Turnover." *Personnel Psychology*, Vol. 15, pp. 43–56, 1962.
Friedman, E: *The Right Thing: Ten Years of Ethics Columns From the Healthcare Forum Journal.* Jossey-Bass Publishers, San Francisco, CA, 1996.
Gallup-Healthways Well-Being Index (WBI) Report, February 2009. http://www.gallup.com.
Gardner, K: *Better CEO Board Relations.* AHA Press, Washington, DC, 2008.
Gardner, K: *The Excellent Board II: Practical Solutions for Healthcare Trustees and CEOs.* AHA Press, Washington, DC, 2009.
Goldsmith, J: *Digital Medicine: Implications for Healthcare Leaders.* Second River Healthcare Press, Bozeman, MT, 2003.
Goleman, D: *Primal Leadership: Learning to Lead with Emotional Intelligence.* Harvard Business School, Boston, MA, 2004.
Healthcare in Crisis, Public Broadcasting, 2000. http://www.pbs.org/healthcarecrisis. Interviews with M. Angell, MD and U. Reinhardt, PhD.
Huff, C: "Attitude and other Adjustments [Helping Physician Fit-In]." *H&HN*, April 2010.
Institute for Family-Centered Care. 2015. http://www.familycenteredcare.org.
The Institute of Medicine: *America's Uninsured Crisis: Consequences for Health and Health Care.* Report from the Committee on Health Insurance Status and Its Consequences. The National Academies Press, February 2009. http://www.iom.edu.
Irelan, C and Irelan, J: *It's Not Rocket Surgery: How to be a Star Leader at Every Level.* Second River Healthcare Press, Bozeman, MT, 2008.
Jacobson, T: "What it Takes to Be an Effective Leader," *Canadian Manager*, Winter 2002.

Kenagy, J: *Designed to Adapt: Leading Healthcare in Challenging Times*. Health Administration Press, Tampa, FL, 2010.

Klontz, B, Klontz, T, Schmuckler, E, Shubin-Stein, K, and Marcinko, DE: *Unifying the Physiologic and Psychologic Financial Planning Divide. Comprehensive Financial Planning Strategies for Doctors and Advisors*. Productivity Press, Boca Raton, FL, 2015.

Konnor, M: *Medicine at the Crossroads*. Vintage Books, New York, 1994.

La Puma, J: "Understand Guiding Principles When Mixing Business, Medicine." *Managed Care Magazine*, July 1998.

Lauer, CS: *Decency*. Second River Healthcare Press, Bozeman, MT, 2009.

Leebov, W: *Essentials for Great Personal Leadership*. AHA Press, Washington, DC, 2008.

Leebov, W: *Great Personal Leadership*. AHA Press, Chicago, IL, 2009.

Loop, FD: *Leadership and Medicine*. Studer Group and Fire Starter Publishing, Breeze Beach, FL, 2010.

Martin, G: *The Praise Finder "Physician Heal Thyself."* 2010. http://phrases.org.uk/meanings/281850.html.

Pellegrino, ED, Veatch, RM, and Langan, JP: *Ethics, Trust, and the Professions: Philosophical and Cultural Aspects*. Georgetown University Press, Washington, DC, 1991.

Phillips, W: "The Complete Continuum of Care." *H&HN*, April 2010.

Pitts, S, Niska, RW, Xu, J, and Burt, CW: "National Hospital Ambulatory Medical Care Survey: 2006 Emergency Department Summary." http://www.cdc.gov.

Pointer, DD: *Getting to Great: Principles of Health Care Organization Governance*. Jossey-Bass, New York, 2002.

Povar, GJ, Blumen, H, Daniel, J, Daub, S et al.: "Ethics in Practice: Managed Care and the Changing Health Care Environment," Managed Care Ethics Working Group Report, American College of Physicians and Harvard Pilgrim Health Care Ethics Program. *Annals of Internal Medicine*, Vol. 141, No. 2, July 20, 2004.

Russler, D, MD, vice president of medical informatics, Oracle, Atlanta, GA, interview.

Schipman, C and Kay, K: *Womenomics: Write Your Own Rules for Success*. Harper Business, New York, 2009.

Schmuckler, E: "Relinquishing the Leadership Role of Physicians," in Marcinko, D.E. (editor): *The Business of Medical Practice*. Springer, New York, 2000.

Schmuckler, E and Marcinko, DE: *Medical Career Leadership and Development. Hospitals and Healthcare Organizations*. Productivity Press, Boca Raton, FL, 2013.

Scott, M, Kaiser, L, and Baltus, R: *Courage to Be First*. Second River Healthcare Press, Bozeman, MT, 2009.

Svorny, S: "Medical Licensing: An Obstacle to Affordable Medical Care." Policy Analysis No. 621, CATO Institute, September 2008. http://CATO.org.

Thorpe, K: "Health Reform Must Include Real Reforms." *Roll Call*, July 7, 2009.

Tuglan, B: *It's Okay to be the Boss*. Collins Business, New York, 2007.

Tuglan, B: *Not Everyone Gets a Trophy*. Jossey-Bass, Hoboken, NJ, 2009.

Wechsler, D: "Non-intellective Factors in General Intelligence." *Psychological Bulletin*, Vol. 37, pp. 444–445, 1995.

2 Life Insurance Planning
Protecting the Doctor

Thomas A. Muldowney, David Edward Marcinko, and Gary A. Cook

CONTENTS

As a doctor or medical professional, your degree and/or state license is likely your most valuable asset next to your life (spouse and/or family notwithstanding). Yet, the irony is that unless you are a financial advisor, Certified Medical Planner™, or insurance agent advising physicians yourself, there will be a strong tendency to skip this chapter. The word *insurance* seems to have that effect on many doctors. The physician or medical professional reader is assured, however, that each topic, while important, will not be covered in laborious detail.

Let's start by recalling that the basis for much of today's insurance evolved from the seventeenth century study of probabilities and what is called the *law of large numbers*. Actually, it's the language of science—mathematics—and more precisely, statistics. Statistically, whenever a potentially random event is to be predicted, the more events recorded or tested, the more likely the final outcome will match the predictions—the first concept of the law of large numbers. Actuaries believe this instinctively. It seems that the rest of us are always trying to beat the odds.

For example, looking at all the readers of this chapter as a sample set, and assuming that they are all licensed drivers, we could predict that the reader has been involved in a minor automobile accident at sometime in his or her lifetime. If only one person ever reads this section, the likelihood of this prediction being wrong is fairly high. The more people that read it, however, the more likely this prediction will be right on target. Depending on the reader's age and sex, the number of miles driven in a year, his or her particular area of the country, and some other factors, the actuary can actually predict how often this will occur and, to an uncanny degree, even the extent of the damage. Accuracy of the predictions, then, leads to profits.

Expanding on this second concept within the law of large numbers, the insurance company's marketing department is tasked with enticing enough drivers (readers) into the company's risk pool to ensure the frequency distribution (experience accuracy) of the actuarial predictions. Insurance coverage can generally be obtained for car-related accidents, tornado damage, cancer expenses, theft losses, cost of repairing tooth decay, being killed by a falling space lab, or any other statistically predictable event. The potential of finding an insurance underwriter willing to predict the event and develop rates usually depends equally on finding enough willing buyers to make the predictions accurate. It's not personal; it's just business. The business of any insurance type coverage is basically that simple.

2.1 GENERAL TYPES OF INSURANCE POLICIES COVERING DOCTORS

2.1.1 Life Insurance Overview

Life insurance transfers the financial loss resulting from death. A myriad of different families of life insurance policies exists, but they basically have two main branches: term insurance and permanent insurance.

2.1.2 Term Insurance

Term insurance is the simplest form of life insurance and is a sensible place to begin any discussion of life insurance. Term insurance is exactly what the name implies: it provides life insurance coverage for a specified period of time, i.e., the term. At the end of the term, the policy is either canceled or continued, typically by paying higher premiums.

2.1.2.1 Annual Renewable Term

The oldest form of term insurance is that of annual renewable term (ART). These policies have premiums that typically begin very low, but increase steadily each year. At the end of each year, the policy owner has the option to renew coverage at the higher premium or cancel the coverage. By the time an insured reaches the age 60, and the probability of dying becomes more pronounced, the premiums start to rise drastically. The increased premium is simply a reflection of the increased chance of dying combined with the obvious fact that there are fewer lives at that age to spread the risk over. ART insurance has lost much of its popularity recently since level-premium term products have captured more market share.

2.1.2.2 Level Term Insurance

Level term policies offer a premium that remains level for a specified period of time, usually 5, 10, 15, 20, 25, or 30 years. The most popular products have premiums that are guaranteed to remain level for the prescribed period. Beware however; policies do exist where the insurance company has the right to change the premiums during this period. Following the selected level-premium period, the term policy is typically canceled, although the owner may keep the policy in force by paying higher premiums. The premiums, however, may increase drastically, sometimes even to the absurd.

The affordability (during the selected term period) and simplicity of these products have made them very popular. It is easy to see why a 40-year-old physician would be attracted to a term policy that guarantees its premium for 20 years. It is entirely reasonable for many to obtain affordable coverage that would end exactly when it is anticipated that it will no longer be needed—at retirement, a seemingly very nice fit, unless justification can be made for longer coverage, like the potential for poor health and the need to renew the policy when needed most (noncancellable feature).

2.1.2.3 Decreasing Term Insurance

Decreasing (or reducing) term is another common style of term insurance that not only lasts for a specified period of time but also reduces in death benefit each year. These are often recommended by lenders to cover mortgages as the mortgage balance decreases each year. These policies have become very rare because level term insurance is so affordable that it makes little sense to buy decreasing coverage.

As currently marketed, term products generally have excellent premiums that allow a policy owner to purchase substantial coverage for a very affordable price. But it is important to keep in mind why the premium is so affordable—because the vast majority of term policies never pay a death benefit. The simple reason for this unexpected fact is that most people outlive the term period or their policies are not in force when they die.

2.1.2.4 Triple X

Regulation XXX, also referred to as Triple X, is a model regulation from the National Association of Insurance Commissioners (NAIC) that was implemented on January 1, 2000. This regulation has substantially changed the manner in which an insurance company must set aside reserves for any term policy with a premium guarantee longer than 15 years, or a universal life policy with a secondary guarantee of more than 5 years (this will be covered soon). It basically requires higher reserves for policies with longer guarantee periods. Higher reserves generally resulted in the insurance companies increasing their premiums. As a direct result, if the physician has a current policy with a premium or death benefit guarantee longer than 5 years, the policy should probably not be replaced or lapsed without some serious thought.

2.1.3 Permanent Insurance

Permanent insurance differs from term insurance in two major ways. First, it is usually designed to last to age 95 or 100 (commonly referred to as the maturity date) without any future requirement to requalify for the coverage by providing proof of good health. Some newer contracts, in fact, have no maturity date at all and are being illustrated as lasting until age 115. Second, permanent policies have built-in reserves, as mentioned above. It is the reserves that end up as a form of cash value accumulation.

One permanent insurance policy can cover a single life, two lives, or an entire family. Policies covering two lives can provide a death benefit either on the first death or the last death.

Generally, permanent insurance has a predefined level-premium payable until a stated maturity, but the premium-paying period can potentially be shortened in a number of ways. Regardless, the predefined premium is substantially higher in a permanent policy than for a comparable face-amount term insurance policy. This higher premium results in the aforementioned aspect of an internal accumulation of cash value.

This accumulation was originally designed by actuaries to help level the premium over longer periods of time. It has since, however, been seen by many as a convenient method of accumulating funds in a tax-deferred manner.

2.1.3.1 Common Types of Permanent Insurance

Permanent insurance comes in four standard variations: whole life, variable life, universal life, and variable universal life. Do not be fooled by the title *permanent*, however. Today's life insurance products are very complex, and few policies are truly permanent. Events can occur, which result in policies lapsing or paying reduced benefits, even when specified premiums have been submitted in a timely manner. The word *permanent* simply reflects the fact that these policies are expected to last until the insured's death no matter when that may be.

2.1.3.2 Whole Life

Whole life, also called straight life or ordinary life, is the oldest and the most classic type of permanent insurance. It typically has the highest required premium of the four standard variations, but it is also the least risky for the policy owner. Whole life remains in force until maturity and is guaranteed to pay the full death benefit if the required premiums are paid in a timely manner. The whole life family of policies also includes those referred to as Life Paid up at 65, 83, 85, 95, etc. The Life Paid up at age "X" refers to the insured's age at which the larger premiums (larger than the premium for whole life) may be stopped, even though the policy death benefits will be guaranteed to remain in force until the insured person dies.

Whole life premiums are fixed, i.e., they cannot be arbitrarily changed from year to year, and they must be paid in a timely manner if the entire death benefit is to be kept intact. Whole life is more rigid than universal life, but it counters by offering the highest level of guarantees. Whole life, like all permanent policies, offers growing cash values that can be borrowed by the policy owner if needed.

Because whole life is considered expensive (high insurance agent sales commission payouts), companies have created ways, such as term riders, to temporarily increase the death benefit but to hold the premium to more affordable levels. However, the drawback of these term riders is that more risk falls upon the policy owner. When term riders are added to a whole life policy, the premium becomes cheaper, but the entire policy is no longer guaranteed to last to maturity and/or may pay reduced death benefits under some situations.

When purchasing a whole life contract, the death benefit is fully guaranteed, as long as the premium is paid on time every year. At the maturity date, the internal cash values (to be discussed later) will equal the amount of guaranteed death benefit: this is called *endowment*.

If the insurance company offers a *participating policy* and has good experiences with its business over the years, i.e., fewer people die than expected, the company may illustrate that the policy *participates* and receives a refund of premiums. These refunds are called *dividends*.

Because dividends are paid to participating policies and are considered a return of the policy owner's premium, they are therefore not taxable income. A policy owner can generally take them in cash, use them to buy paid-up additions, use them to buy one-year term additions, or have them accumulate at interest, like an additional savings account. Using the dividend to buy paid-up additions or allowing them to accumulate at interest will provide the policy owner an additional source of future premiums or increased death benefit.

At some point in the policy's life, these funds may be sufficient to allow the policy owner to cease paying premiums and direct the insurance company to take its annual premium from these excess values. This is sometimes called a *vanishing premium* or a *short pay* premium or a *premium offset*. The premiums are still due and still paid each year, but instead come from the excess external policy values rather than the owner's pocket.

A life insurance agent, or Certified Financial Planner®, may illustrate this discontinued premium flow as a benefit of their policy. Beware! This is only a *projection*. This means the company is not guaranteeing the ability to stop paying premiums. This may possibly occur if the company keeps doing well. It is not guaranteed!

Many whole life policies were sold this way in the past, and while some policies actually did allow the owner to stop paying premiums, many policies did not. This surprised many policy owners who were expecting to cease their premiums. The medical professional or health-care practitioner must make sure they understand what policy aspects are guaranteed and what are merely projections!

A well-informed physician, when purchasing a whole life policy, will ask his/her insurance agent to check both the Standard and Poor's (or Moody's) company rating and the AM Best's Annual Historical Dividend Report (THINK: AIG). The first rates the financial stability of the company, whereas the second reports how a company's actual dividends compared to their projections for each year. It is wise to be leery of illustrations from companies that consistently fail to meet their projections.

Before a whole life product is purchased, ask to see what happens to the death benefit and premiums if the company experiences a lower dividend scale (worse business conditions). This will allow the purchaser to see how sensitive the policy is to different business conditions. Beware of whole life policies that are very sensitive to reduced dividend scales.

2.1.3.3 Universal Life Insurance

Universal life was developed in the late 1970s and has become a very popular product in a very short time. Generally, in terms of price and risk to the policy owner, it falls between term and whole life.

Universal life is similar to a bank savings account but has automatic monthly withdrawals from the account to pay for the death benefit. Each universal life premium goes into the policy and becomes part of the cash value just as a bank savings deposit becomes part of a savings account. Some policies have a premium expense charge that generally is designed to pay the individual state premium tax. The cash value also has monthly debits to pay for the death benefit and/or any riders, and most also charge a monthly administrative fee. The resulting cash value of the policy earns a competitive money market-like interest rate. Finally, policy owners receive an annual report that itemizes all relevant costs to the penny. Universal life has often been called *whole life unbundled* because of this feature.

Clearly, the cash value of the universal life policy will depend on which is greater: the amount going into the policy (premiums and interest) or the amounts leaving the policy (the cost of the death benefit and the monthly administrative fees). Additionally, the charges for the death benefit will rise over time, as the insured doctor gets older (just like the ART rates mentioned at the beginning of this topic).

Typically, in the early policy years, the amounts flowing into the policy are greater than the internal charges, and the subsequent cash value increases. If, at some point, the outflows exceed the inflows, the cash value will cease growing and may even decline. If the cash value falls to zero, the policy generally lapses unless more premiums are paid.

The policy owner can periodically adjust the amount and timing of the universal life premiums and even skip premiums (without incurring a loan, which is the result with whole life). Any change in premium amount or mode of payment will also change the cash value projections on a policy illustration. Skipping premiums will cause a drop in cash values and possibly cause a policy to lapse. If ample cash value has accumulated in the contract, the ability to skip premium without adverse consequences becomes more probable. This flexibility is one of the reasons for the popularity of universal life policies.

Because universal life policies are very interest rate sensitive, a policy owner needs to keep track of the policy values each year to make sure the policy is performing as expected. When a policy owner receives their *annual report*, it is a good idea to use this as a reminder to request (from the agent or the company) a reprojection of future amounts based on the then current assumptions. This is commonly called an in-force projection or midstream proposal.

Just as with *vanishing premium* whole life projections, there have also been problems with universal life. In the 1980s, interest rates were very high, and this made universal life policies appear very inexpensive compared to whole life. Unfortunately, interests rates have declined dramatically, and by now, those policies have been credited far less interest than originally illustrated. As a result, the cash values were lower than expected, and policy owners had to either increase their premiums or risk the policies lapsing.

If purchasing a universal life policy, the doctor should definitely ask to see illustrations reflecting declining interest rates. Typically this does not need to be to the guaranteed rate. Ask the agent, Certified Financial Planner, or insurance broker for a history of the company's rates and gauge your request accordingly. If policy performance is drastically affected, commit to a higher premium so that coverage is not jeopardized in the event of falling interest rates.

Besides being interest rate sensitive, the insurance company can also change the internal cost of the death benefit on a universal life policy. Obviously, increasing these charges could cause the cash values to drop and the policy to lapse. Companies try to avoid doing this, but it can and does happen. A potential buyer should also inquire as to the company's history of *mortality cost* increases before purchasing any universal life policy. Avoid companies that have a history of raising their insurance costs or that fail to provide this vital information.

2.1.3.4 Variable Life Insurance

Variable life is a type of permanent insurance that comes in the same two forms discussed above: universal life and whole life.

The same general designs of whole life and universal life, as just described, also apply to variable whole life and variable universal life. The only real difference is the availability of investment choices for the cash value of the policy. With whole life and universal life, the insurance companies generally invest the money in fixed income investments like bonds and mortgages. The insurance company then declares the interest rate that gets credited to the company's policies (except term, which has no cash value).

With variable policies, the company offers the policy owner a choice of investment options. These investment options are called *separate accounts* and resemble traditional mutual funds. Good variable life policies should offer a wide array of investment choices to include money market funds, bond funds, balanced funds, stock funds, and international funds. It is not unusual to find policies offering in excess of 30 such separate accounts.

The policy owner then chooses the account or accounts that match his/her investment risk. Most policy owners put a majority of their premium dollars into equity accounts because they have historically provided better returns than most other investments. Of course, the higher the actual returns of the separate accounts, the more the cash value grows.

This results because the internal policy expense costs of a variable policy are typically higher than the internal costs of a fixed interest rate policy. It therefore takes a higher return inside of a variable life to offset the effect of these higher internal costs. Generally, one should not purchase a variable policy unless he/she expects the separate accounts to earn an average of at least 8.5% per year.

Variable life policies give the policy owners more control over how their premium dollars are invested. These policies allow greater potential returns, but at greater risk, because the policy owner assumes the investment risk. Variable policies became very popular during the bull market of the 1990s. To their surprise, if they bought the policy during those periods, setting premiums based on those high equity returns, by now they must provide large amounts of additional premium or replace the policy with one that is currently more affordable. These products are most appropriate for policy owners with a moderate- to high-risk tolerance, who believe in the long-term superiority of equities as investments, and who have a long-term time horizon and the ability to pay additional premiums if necessary.

The same principles that apply to investing in general also apply to variable policies. A wise variable policy owner will invest his/her premiums in several separate accounts in order to achieve diversification. Most variable policies will also allow dollar cost averaging and asset rebalancing.

2.1.3.5 Other Varieties of Life Policies

2.1.3.5.1 Survivorship Life Insurance

Survivorship life is commonly referred to as second-to-die life insurance. Unlike the typical life insurance policy that has one primary insured and pays a death benefit when that person dies, a survivorship life policy generally has two insureds and only pays a death benefit when both of the insureds are deceased.

Survivorship products have existed for about 30 years, but became very popular after passage of the unlimited marital deduction in the Economic Recovery Tax Act (ERTA) of 1981. These policies are used almost exclusively in the estate planning realm where the husband and wife have a combined net worth of more than two times the current unified credit, i.e., $5.25 million in year 2016. The amount of the unified credit will increase with inflation. Wealthy couples, with estates in excess of $10.5 million, typically between the ages of 50 and 70, purchase survivorship insurance to assist in providing adequate liquidity for estate transfer and settlement costs routinely due at the second death.

In 1996, a new feature was seen in universal life and, in particular, survivorship universal life policies, that of a secondary guarantee. The primary guarantees in these policies were that of a guaranteed minimum credited interest rate and a maximum amount of monthly charges, and specifically, a maximum charge for mortality. The earlier versions of these policies illustrated poorly with regard to guaranteed cash values, unless a whole life-type premium was paid.

Secondary guarantees have also been called no-lapse guarantees. Basically, these policies are guaranteed to stay in force for a specified number of years as long as the policy owner pays a required cumulative premium as of a particular date, even if the underlying primary guarantees would allow the policy to otherwise lapse. Most importantly, the new no-lapse premiums were still considerably lower than that of a whole life policy. Unfortunately, Triple X regulations have forced most insurance companies to remove these products from sale or substantially increase their premium requirements for this benefit.

2.1.3.5.2 Joint First-to-Die Life Insurance

Just as with survivorship life insurance, a joint First-to-Die policy generally insures two people. Unlike survivorship insurance, however, a joint First-to-Die policy pays upon the death of the first insured.

Joint First-to-Die policies typically make sense in family insurance planning for households who have dependent children and where both parents work, and occasionally they are used for mortgage (loan) protection. The vast majority of joint First-to-Die plans, however, are used in the business world. These policies are particularly well suited for multiple keyperson or for stock redemption (entity) buy–sell plans.

It is important to remember that when the first insured dies under a joint First-to-Die policy, the death benefit is paid, and the policy is terminated: coverage no longer exists on the remaining insured(s). This problem can be solved by buying a guaranteed insurability option on the policy that allows the remaining insured to purchase a new joint policy with no underwriting immediately after the first death.

Another rider that should be considered when joint policies are purchased for business planning reasons is a substitute insured rider. This allows the policy owner to exchange an insured with a new insured. This rider comes in very handy if one of the insureds leaves the business and is replaced by someone else. Many insurance companies, unfortunately, have withdrawn this rider because of the difficulty in administering it.

2.1.3.5.3 Interest Sensitive Whole Life

Interest sensitive whole life, also referred to as current assumption whole life, is a hybrid of whole life and universal life. Like whole life, the premiums are fixed. Some companies fix the premium for the life of the policy, but most fix the premium only for a specified period of time. Like universal life, the current internal mortality charges are lower than for a whole life policy, but the insurance company retains the right to raise them. Also like universal life, a competitive interest rate is credited to the policy cash values each month. These policies are currently not very common.

2.1.3.5.4 Group Life

Group life insurance coverage is very common, and the vast majority of people have this form of coverage at work and/or have the opportunity to purchase more group life insurance coverage through their employer or other associations to which they belong. Most group life insurance policies are group term because term is affordable and easy to understand, but group universal life and group variable universal life policies exist as well.

Many employers, especially larger ones, typically offer a minimum of group life insurance as an automatic employee benefit. Since current tax code provisions allow up to $50,000 of group coverage as a totally tax-free benefit, this is often the initial amount of coverage. Many employers also offer the employee the ability to purchase additional group life insurance with the premium being deducted from each paycheck. The main advantage of group life insurance is its convenience.

The major disadvantages concern the lack of flexibility. It may not be easy to change your coverage under a group life policy, and if you leave your company, it may not be possible to take the coverage with you. For this reason, most doctors prefer to purchase their own individual life insurance policy for the bulk of their life insurance protection.

2.1.3.5.5 Single Premium Life

Single premium life is exactly as the name implies: the owner pays one premium for lifetime coverage. Clearly, the premium will be much larger than any other type of insurance for an equivalent death benefit.

These policies have become quite rare since the modified endowment contract (MEC) rules were established to discourage large premiums early in the life of a policy (see Section 2.3). Nonetheless, these policies still have a limited number of uses. These policies may be appropriate if tax-deferred growth is desired and the money is not needed during the insured's lifetime.

2.1.3.6 The 5–100 Rule

With any universal life insurance policy (and certainly all variable life policies), fluctuating rates of return, the actual timing of the premium payments, and potential internal policy changes by the insurance company, all contribute to results that will probably differ substantially from the original illustration. The 5–100 rule states that as a result of accounting for these elements, all initial projections of cash value beyond 5 years will necessarily be 100% incorrect when compared to actuality. A prudent policy owner should therefore keep on top of any changes and react accordingly. If a policy owner ignores his/her policy for even 5 years, any adverse changes could be so drastic as to make rectifying them very costly.

2.1.4 Death Benefit Settlement Options

Settlement options refer to the different ways a beneficiary can receive the death benefit payable upon the death of the insured. A beneficiary commonly receives the entire death benefit in a lump sum, but that is certainly not the only choice. Another possibility is the interest-only option where the beneficiary leaves the death benefit with the insurer and receives the monthly interest. Another common option is the lifetime annuity option where the death benefit is paid out as a guaranteed lifetime income.

Settlement options can be left to the discretion of the beneficiary. In this way, the beneficiary, with capable advice, can hopefully make an informed choice based on their particular situation at the time. Alternatively, the policy owner can specify a particular settlement option. During the life of the insured, the policy owner can instruct the insurance company to pay the beneficiary according to a design that the policy owner feels appropriate. It is the opinion of the authors, however, that a better alternative would be to establish a trust for any beneficiary unable to manage their funds, rather than use a restrictive settlement option.

2.2 NEEDS ANALYSIS APPROACH TOWARD LIFE INSURANCE

Needs analysis is a generic term used to help quantify the financial need for life insurance. And, whereas a broker or agent may use a simple needs analysis designed to pinpoint a certain life insurance amount, a Certified Medical Planner's™ model should include a more thorough review of insurance needs and a long- and short-term financial analysis. The CMP or trusted insurance agent, broker, or insurance counselor assisting the physician should request

- An in-depth discussion of your goals, both financial and personal
- A review of your current insurance (life, health, disability, property, casualty, etc.) and financial holdings, investment assets, and their projected growth potential
- A review of your current estate plan, including any current wills and trusts
- Any personally owned business information

2.3 TAXATION OF LIFE INSURANCE

Life insurance has a number of tax advantages that can be potentially rewarding. However, there are also some pitfalls that should be avoided.

2.3.1 Income Tax–Free Death Benefit

The simplest tax advantage of life insurance is that the death benefit is received free of any income tax by the beneficiary. When the insured dies, the named beneficiary generally receives all death proceeds free of any income taxes. The word *generally* is used because there are situations that can cause the entire death benefit, or a large part of it, to become subject to income tax.

2.3.2 Transfer for Value Problem

This is a situation that can cause the death benefit of a life insurance policy to be income taxable. This can be a complicated topic, and the situation may arise unexpectedly, especially when life insurance is used for business purposes.

Generally, if an existing life insurance policy is transferred to a new owner for some type of consideration (money, exchange of property, or a *quid pro quo* arrangement), then the death benefit becomes taxable to the beneficiary to the extent that the proceeds exceed the tax cost basis in the policy. Basis becomes the amount of consideration paid at the time of transfer and all future premiums following the transfer paid by the new owner. There are five exceptions to this rule:

1. Transfers by any person or company of their ownership to the person insured by the policy.
2. Transfers by a business partner (in the strictest sense, i.e., not a co-shareholder) to another partner in the same business.
3. Transfers to a partnership by any of the partners.
4. Transfers to a corporation in which the insured is a stockholder or officer.
5. Transfers between corporations (under certain conditions) in a tax-free reorganization.

If a transfer for value falls under one of these exceptions, then the policy retains its tax-free death benefit status.

2.3.3 Tax-Deferred Growth

Another tax advantage of life insurance is its income tax–deferred cash value growth. As mentioned earlier in this section, life insurance products, other than term, have cash accumulation potential. The cash values will depend on the policy style, the amount of the premiums, and also the general economic environment. If there is growth in the cash value, the growth will be tax-deferred under current tax laws.

2.3.4 Withdrawals and Loans

Income taxes are not generally an issue unless cash values are removed from the policy while the insured is still alive. There are three methods of accessing a policy's cash value while the insured is living. The first choice is to surrender the policy. If the policy is surrendered and the cash value is greater than the total premiums paid, the difference is subject to ordinary income tax. A policy owner must ask his/her agent and give careful consideration before surrendering because if done improperly, a portion of the surrendered values may be taxable, plus, once surrendered, the policy no longer exists.

What if you want to access a portion of the cash value but not lose the coverage? There are two methods to accomplish this: withdrawals and loans. A withdrawal, also called a partial surrender, does not cause the policy to terminate, but it does lower the death benefit of the policy by the amount of the withdrawal. If a withdrawal is requested, then under the current first-in first-out (FIFO) accounting rules, the total amount of premiums paid into the policy is removed first, and more importantly, without any income tax liability. Any withdrawals removed in excess of the gross premium paid would be income taxable.

Because withdrawals beyond a policy's basis are taxable, loans are often used at this point, because in most cases, policy loans are not taxable. If the insured dies while a loan is outstanding, the insurance company repays the loan from the death proceeds, and the remaining death benefit goes to the named beneficiary. In other words, the death proceeds will decrease by an amount equal to each loan. Also, unless the interest charged on the loan balance is paid annually, the size of the loan will increase as the interest accrues to the loan. So when withdrawals and loans are combined, a significant portion of a policy's cash value can be accessed while the policy is still in force.

2.3.5 Violating the 2 out of 3 Rule

Another common mistake involves an issue of gift taxation. Violating the 2 out of 3 rule can result in a policy owner unwittingly making a sizable gift of the entire death benefit and wasting a major portion of his/her unified credit as a consequence. The *three* refers to the parties to the policy: the insured, the policy owner, and the beneficiary. *Two* of these *three* parties should almost always be the same.

2.3.6 Policy Replacement—Section 1035 Exchanges

If a policy owner intends to replace an existing policy with a new policy, he/she has two choices regarding the existing policy. Once the new policy is issued, the policy owner can simply surrender the first policy and receive the cash value, if any. Income taxes will be due if there is a gain in the policy.

However, most policy owners would rather transfer the cash value from the old policy into the new policy rather than actually receive it. If this is the case, the policy owner can take advantage of an Internal Revenue Code Section 1035 exchange. This section of the tax code allows a policy owner to transfer cash value from one life insurance policy *directly* to a new policy. The main advantage of a Section 1035 exchange, unlike a regular surrender, is that the transfer is tax free, even if the first policy had a large gain.

Section 1035 exchanges have a definite procedure that requires the insurance companies to conduct the exchange of money, much as in the trustee-to-trustee transfer of qualified funds. Additionally, this procedure only permits the transfer of a life insurance policy to (1) another life insurance policy or (2) an annuity policy. Annuities can *only* be transferred to annuities.

Unfortunately, policy replacement is probably recommended more often than it is really necessary. If replacement and a Section 1035 exchange is recommended, the medical professional or health-care practitioner should carefully review the proposal. Ensure that the assumptions made for projecting the old policy into the future are consistent with those assumptions for the new policy. Also, if replacement is warranted, a policy owner should never cancel an existing policy until the new policy is in force.

2.3.7 Modified Endowment Contracts

MECs are the last tax issue to be addressed with regard to life insurance policies. Because the cash values inside of a life insurance policy grow tax-deferred, many policy owners recognized this advantage and deposited large, single premiums into their policies. Unfortunately, it was perceived as abusive by Congress. It was clear that these people were buying life insurance primarily as a means of escaping income taxation and not actually for the life insurance death benefit.

As a result, the laws were changed in 1984 to discourage putting very large amounts of money into life insurance contracts in the early years. Based on the age, sex, and size of the death benefit, an MEC premium (also referred to as the TAMRA 7-pay guideline) is established for each policy. For the first 7 years of the policy, the policy owner cannot have paid cumulative premiums greater than the cumulative MEC premium.

If a policy is classified as a MEC, then it is treated as an annuity contract, and not a life insurance policy, for any and all lifetime withdrawals or loans. Taxable interest earnings are removed before basis is recovered, i.e., all funds removed from the policy in excess of basis will be immediately taxable. If the insured is under 59 ½, there will also be a 10% tax penalty. Thus, one of the basic tax benefits of life insurance is destroyed. Remember from our previous example that withdrawals of non-MEC policies are not taxable until the withdrawals exceed the cumulative premiums. Finally, once a MEC, always a MEC!

2.4 TAX WARNING!

According to fee-only life insurance expert Peter C. Katt of Kalamazoo, Michigan, doctors should be on guard against believing in the existence of perfect retirement vehicles funded through springing cash value life insurance plans. These plans reportedly feature payments of very large premiums while the policy is subject to favorable tax treatment, and then transferring the policy to the insured doctor when it appears to have no taxable value, after which the cash value *springs* to life.

Unfortunately, in the real world, tax deductible contributions and tax-free benefits do not exist without resorting to fraud or deception. Particularly notorious are the so-called continuous group insurance and Voluntary Employee Benefit Association prepaid retiree plans, despite the fact that the latter has been mistakenly endorsed by state medical societies in certain cases.

So, always remember that no matter how professional and sincere insurance agents and marketers appear, there are no life insurance policies that can legitimately provide tax-deductible insurance with tax-free retirement benefits. Therefore, you should always consult a qualified professional for further information regarding your specific needs.

Overheard in the Advisor's Lounge

Debunking Conventional Whole Life Insurance Selling Points

> You need to protect yourself and your family with life insurance that you won't outlive.

This is one of the common selling points for whole life or universal life rather than term life insurance. At first glance, it seems to make a lot of sense. Of course you don't want to outlive your life insurance. Having it pay benefits upon your death is the reason you buy it. This statement, however, misses one essential fact. Many people don't need to worry about outliving their life insurance, because they outlive their need for life insurance.

OUTLIVING THE NEED

We don't all need life insurance throughout our entire lives any more than we do auto or homeowners' insurance. If you no longer drive a car, you don't need auto insurance. If you no longer own a home, you don't need homeowners' insurance. For example, in circumstances like the following, you may no longer need life insurance:

1. When you and your spouse have accumulated enough assets and income streams to independently care for yourselves
2. When your children are self-sufficient adults
3. When your estate is too small to owe estate taxes or liquid enough to pay the estate taxes

PRIMARY PURPOSE

The primary purpose of life insurance is to replace the future income of a primary breadwinner. Two groups most likely to need it are middle-aged couples saving for retirement and parents of minor children. Ideally, most young families should have over $1 million in life insurance to provide for the children if either parent should die prematurely. Yet many of them are unable to afford the higher premiums for this much "permanent" insurance. Their choices are to underfund their needs with a smaller permanent policy or purchase an affordable 30-year term policy. As we age, the probability of dying becomes greater. Therefore, a $1 million life policy costs much less for a 25-year-old than a 75-year-old. It doesn't matter if the policy is cash value, whole life, universal life, or level term; the cost of providing the life insurance component increases every year.

PSYCHOLOGICAL AVERSIONS

Yet most human brains have a psychological aversion to price increases. In order to please their customers with life insurance premiums that didn't increase every year, insurance companies came out with level term policies. Essentially, the premiums are averaged out by overcharging in the early years of the policy and undercharging in the later years.

HIGHER PREMIUMS

Whole life and universal life insurance policies don't have that same averaging. To be *permanent*, the premiums must be much higher in order to fund a savings account that grows over time and is often used to offset a significant portion of the death benefit in the later years of the insured's life. Usually, if the insured cancels the policy, a portion of the premiums will be refunded.

CASH VALUE

A cash value policy may occasionally be a good estate planning tool, generally for those with substantial wealth. It might be used to fund an irrevocable life insurance trust upon the second spouse's death, perhaps to pay taxes on an illiquid estate like a family farm or other property. It also can be used for those wanting to leave the bulk of an estate to charity and still provide income to their children. These strategies rarely apply to those whose primary goal is basic income replacement for their families. One of the ironies of insurance in general is that we all know it's essential and we all hope never to need it. For most people, life insurance is not really an exception to this. Its primary purpose is not to provide us with investment income, but to provide our families with income if we aren't there.

Rick Kahler, MSFS, CFP®, CLU, ChFC, CCIM
KahlerFinancial.com
Rapid City, South Dakota

2.5 ANNUITY OVERVIEW

Annuity contracts transfer the financial risk of living too long, i.e., outliving one's savings. Annuities are deferred or immediate, fixed or variable, and tax-qualified or non–tax-qualified.

2.5.1 Deferred Annuities

The deferred annuity contract, like a permanent life insurance policy, has been found by some to be a convenient method of accumulating wealth. Funds can be placed in deferred annuities in a lump sum, called single premium deferred annuities, or periodically over time, called flexible premium deferred annuities. Either way, the funds placed in a deferred annuity grow without current taxation (tax-deferred).

2.5.1.1 Fixed Deferred Annuity

Fixed deferred annuities provide a guaranteed minimum rate of return (usually around 3% per year) and typically credit a higher, competitive rate based on the current economic conditions. Fixed annuities are usually considered conservative investments.

2.5.1.2 Variable Deferred Annuity

Recently, variable deferred annuities have become very popular. Like fixed annuities, variable deferred annuities offer tax-deferred growth, but this is where the similarities end. Variable deferred annuities offer separate accounts (similar to mutual funds) that provide different investment opportunities. Most of the separate accounts have stock market exposure, and therefore, variable annuities do not offer a guaranteed rate of return. But the upside potential is typically much greater than that of a fixed annuity.

The value of a variable deferred annuity will fluctuate with the values of the investments within the chosen separate accounts. Although similar to mutual funds, there are some key differences. These include the following:

- A variable annuity provides tax deferral, whereas a regular mutual fund does not.
- If a variable annuity loses money because of poor separate account performance, and the owner dies, many annuities guarantee at least a return of principal to the heirs. It is important to note that this guarantee of principal only applies if the annuity owner dies. If the annuity value decreases below the amount paid in, and the annuity is surrendered while the owner is alive, the actual cash value is all that is available.
- When money is eventually withdrawn from a deferred annuity, the amount withdrawn that is investment gain is taxable at ordinary income tax rates. With taxable mutual funds, funds can be liquidated, and the gains, if held longer than 12 months, are taxed at lower, capital gain rates.
- There is also a 10% penalty if the annuity owner is under 59 ½ when money is withdrawn. There is no such charge for withdrawals from a mutual fund.
- The fees charged inside of a variable annuity (called mortality and expense charges) are typically more than the fees charged by a regular mutual fund.

Variable deferred annuities are sensible for people who want stock market exposure while minimizing taxes during the accumulation phase of their lives. Most financial planners recommend regular mutual funds when the investment time horizon is under 10 years. But if the time horizon is more than 10 years, variable annuities may become more attractive because of the additional earnings from tax deferral.

Both types of deferred annuities may be subject to surrender charges. Surrender charges are applied if the annuity owner surrenders the policy during the surrender period, which typically run for 5–10 years from the purchase date. The charge usually decreases each year until it reaches zero. The purpose of the charge is to discourage early surrender of the annuity. Surrender charges may be eliminated if the annuity purchased is a *no-load* annuity.

2.5.2 Immediate Annuities

Immediate annuities provide a guaranteed income stream that starts at the date of purchase. An immediate annuity can be purchased with a single deposit of funds, possibly from savings or a pension distribution, or it can be the end result of the deferred annuity, commonly referred to as annuitization. Just like deferred annuities, immediate annuities can also be fixed or variable.

Immediate annuities can be set up to provide periodic payments to the policy owner annually, semiannually, quarterly, or monthly. The annuity payments can be paid over life or for a finite number of years. They can also be paid over the life of a single individual or over two lives.

2.5.2.1 Immediate Fixed Annuity

Immediate fixed annuities typically pay a specified amount of money for as long as the annuitant lives. They may also be arranged to only pay for a specified period of time, i.e., 20 years. Either way, they often contain a guaranteed payout period, such that, if the annuitant lives less than the guaranteed number of years, the heirs will receive the remainder of the guaranteed payments.

2.5.2.2 Immediate Variable Annuity

Immediate variable annuities provide income payments to the annuitant that fluctuate with the returns of the separate accounts chosen. The theory is that since the stock market has historically risen over time, the annuity payments will rise over time and keep pace with inflation. If this is indeed what happens, it is a good purchase, but it cannot be guaranteed. Some companies will, at a minimum, provide a guarantee of a low minimum monthly payment no matter how poorly the separate accounts perform.

2.5.3 Qualified Annuities

The term *qualified* refers to those annuities that permit tax-deductible contributions under one of the Internal Revenue Code (IRC) sections, i.e., § 408 Individual Retirement Accounts (IRA), § 403(b) Tax Sheltered Annuities, § 401(k) Voluntary Profit Savings Plans. Qualified annuities can also result from a rollover from such a plan.

Nonqualified annuities, then, do not permit deductible contributions.

There is much debate as to whether an annuity, which is tax-deferred by nature, should also be used as a funding vehicle within a tax-qualified plan, i.e., a tax shelter within a tax shelter. Since the investment options within the annuity are also generally available to the plan participant without the additional management expenses of the annuity policy, it is felt that this could be a breach of fiduciary responsibility, and both the National Association of Securities Dealers (NASDs)/Financial Industry Regulatory Authority (FINRA), and the Securities and Exchange Commission (SEC) have gone on record as criticizing these sales.

2.6 ANNUITY TAXATION

The tax treatment of annuities is extremely dependent on whether it is a qualified or non-qualified annuity. Although both permit the tax-deferred growth of the investment and both have penalties for early distributions, they are governed under different sections of the IRC. Since qualified annuities were just discussed, we will start with them.

2.6.1 Qualified Annuity Taxation

Qualified annuities are treated no different than any other tax-qualified retirement investment. Growth of the investment, whether fixed interest or variable, escapes current taxation under one of the 400-series IRC sections. Additionally, if the funds are withdrawn prior to age 59 ½, there is a 10% penalty. As the money is withdrawn, every dollar is taxed as ordinary income. Finally, fund distributions must begin no later than April 1 of the calendar year following the year in which the owner turns age 70 ½. In addition, withdrawals from the annuity may be subject to the surrender fee charged by the annuity company.

2.6.2 Nonqualified Annuity Taxation

The taxation of nonqualified annuities is generally contained within IRC § 72. Again, the annuity is provided tax-deferred growth and the 10% penalty for early withdrawal. The manner in which distributions are taken, however, will determine the nature of their taxation.

Since the tax act TEFRA of 1982, if non-annuitized funds are withdrawn, they are taxed under last-in first-out (LIFO) accounting rules. Under these rules, the first funds withdrawn are considered the investment earnings, i.e., the last funds credited to the annuity. Ordinary income tax will be paid until all earnings are removed, at which time only the original principal remains. This principal, having already been taxed, can then be withdrawn without any further income taxation.

On the other hand, if in annuitization, the choice for a guaranteed monthly payment option is chosen, an exclusion ratio is developed by the insurance company using governmental tables. This technique causes a portion of each payment to be considered a return of principal, and thus only a portion of each payment is taxable. Generally, the option to annuitize is permanent. This exclusion ratio remains in effect until the insurance company has returned all of the original principals to the owner. After that, each payment received will be considered 100% earnings and totally subject to ordinary income taxation.

2.6.3 Wealth Transfer Issues

Regardless of whether the physician has a qualified or nonqualified annuity, extreme care must be given when specifying beneficiaries. Although these investments have great potential for appreciating sizable amounts of wealth during a lifetime, they are, unfortunately, very poor vehicles for the transfer of this wealth to successor generations after death.

Upon the death of an annuity owner, an annuity can be subject to both federal estate and federal income taxes. This double taxation may result in a 40–70% loss of annuity value before the heirs can receive it. The retired doctor should seek wealth transfer advice if he/she holds a large portion of their wealth in annuities or other qualified plans such as IRAs. One good strategy to consider is the stretch IRA, which spreads the income and the tax liability over a period as long as the life expectancy of the beneficiary.

2.7 HEALTH INSURANCE OVERVIEW

Health insurance transfers the potential financial hardship caused by severe or chronic health conditions resulting from accidents or illnesses (morbidity), whereas life insurance is concerned with death (mortality). Health insurance, like life insurance, also has families of policies. There are medical expense/hospital policies, disability income policies, and long-term care policies. Although the medical professional or financial advisor should be familiar with the medical expense/hospital family of insurance policies, as well as changes brought about by the Patient Protection and Affordable Care Act (PPACA) recently passed into law, they are rapidly changing and will be briefly reviewed here.

2.7.1 What Types of Traditional Health Coverage Are Still Available?

Rising health-care costs have driven the demand for, and the price of, medical insurance sky-high. The availability of group coverage through employment has helped many Americans face such costs. However, people who are not currently covered by their employers have few affordable sources for group coverage currently. Generally, those seeking personal medical coverage can explore purchasing an individual private health insurance policy. And those aged 65 and older may qualify for Medicare coverage.

There are three general classifications of medical insurance plans: fee-for-service (indemnity), managed care (e.g., health maintenance organizations [HMOs] and preferred provider organizations [PPOs]), and high-deductible health-care plans (HD-HCP).

2.7.1.1 Fee-for-Service

With a basic fee-for-service (indemnity) insurance plan, health-care providers (such as physicians, nurse practitioners, surgery centers, and hospitals) are paid a fee for each service on a per-unit basis (Current Procedural Terminology [CPT®] and/or Diagnostic Related Group [DRG®]) provided to insured patients. However, this leads to the quantity-of-care versus quality-of-care conundrum that exists today. In other words, more DRG and CPT coded procedures lead to additional physician/facility reimbursement. This is, rightly or wrongly, recapitulated by the *malpractice phobia* crisis of increased medical testing leading to physician/facility reduced liability, but forcing the cost-curve upward!

Indemnity plans normally cover hospitalization, outpatient care, and physician services in or out of the hospital. You select the health-care provider for consultation or treatment. You are then billed for the service and reimbursed by the insurance company, or you can *assign* direct payment to the provider from the insurance company. Indemnity plans typically require the payment of premiums, deductibles, and coinsurance. Limits on certain coverage or exclusions may apply. Lifetime limits on benefits are prohibited, and limits on annual benefits were prohibited beginning in 2014–2015.

2.7.1.2 Managed Care

Managed care plans became popular in the 1990s as a way to help rein in rising medical costs. In managed care plans, insurance companies contract with a network of health-care providers to provide cost-effective health care. Managed care plans include HMOs, PPOs, and point-of-service (POS) plans.

2.7.1.2.1 Health Maintenance Organizations

An HMO operates as a prepaid health-care plan. You normally pay a monthly premium in addition to a small copayment for a visit to a physician, who may be on staff or contracted by the HMO. Copayments for visits to specialists may be higher. The insurance company typically covers the amount over the patient copayment amount.

Each covered member chooses or is assigned a primary-care physician from doctors in the plan. This person acts as a gatekeeper for his or her patients and, if deemed necessary, can refer patients to specialists who are in the HMO's list of providers. Because HMOs contract with health-care providers, costs are typically lower than in indemnity plans.

2.7.1.2.2 Preferred Provider Organizations

A PPO is a managed care organization of physicians, hospitals, clinics, and other health-care providers who contract with an insurance company to provide health care at reduced rates to individuals insured in the plan. The insurance company uses actuarial tables to determine *reasonable and customary* fees for each type of service, and health-care providers accept the PPO's fee schedule and guidelines.

The insured can see any health-care provider within a preferred network of providers and pays a copayment for each visit. Insured individuals have to meet an annual deductible before the insurance company will start covering health-care services. Typically, the insurance company will pay a high percentage (often 80%) of the costs to the plan's health-care providers after the deductible has been met, and patients pay the balance.

Although insured individuals can choose providers outside the plan without permission, patient out-of-pocket costs will be higher; for example, the initial deductible for each visit is higher, and the percentage of covered costs by the insurance company will be lower. Because PPOs provide more patient flexibility than HMOs, they may cost a little more.

2.7.1.2.3 Point-of-Service Plan

A POS health-care plan mixes aspects of a PPO and HMO to allow greater patient autonomy. POS plans also use a network of preferred providers whom patients must turn to first and from whom patients receive referrals to other providers if deemed necessary. POS plans recommend that patients choose a personal physician from inside the network. The personal physician can refer patients to other physicians and specialists who are inside or outside the network. Insurance companies have a national network of approved providers, so insured individuals can receive services throughout the United States. Copayments tend to be lower for a POS plan than for a PPO plan.

2.7.1.3 High-Deductible Health-Care Plans

HD-HCPs provide comprehensive coverage for high-cost medical bills and are usually combined with a health-reimbursement arrangement that enables participants to build savings to pay for future medical expenses. HD-HCPs generally cover preventive care in full with a small (or no) deductible or copayment. However, these plans have higher annual deductibles and out-of-pocket limits than other insurance plans.

Participants enrolled in an HD-HCP can open a health savings account (HSA) to save money that can be used for current and future medical expenses. There are annual limits on how much can be invested in an HSA. The funds can be invested as you choose, and any interest and earnings accumulate tax deferred. HSA funds can be withdrawn free of income tax and penalties provided the money is spent on qualified health-care expenses for the participant and his or her spouse and dependent children.

Remember that the cost and availability of an individual health insurance policy can depend on factors such as age, health (preexisting conditions), and the type of insurance purchased. In addition, a physical examination may be required.

2.7.2 U.S. Medicare

Medicare is the U.S. government's health-care insurance program for the elderly. It is available to eligible people aged 65 and older as well as certain disabled persons.

Part A provides basic coverage for hospital care as well as limited skilled nursing care, home health care, and hospice care. Part B covers physicians' services, inpatient and outpatient medical services, and diagnostic tests. Part D prescription drug coverage is also available.

Medicare Advantage is a type of privately run insurance that includes Medicare-approved HMOs, PPOs, fee-for-service plans, and special needs plans. Some plans offer prescription drug coverage. To join a Medicare Advantage plan, you must have Medicare Part A and Part B and you have to pay the monthly Medicare Part B premium to Medicare, as well as the Medicare Advantage premium.

Medicare Supplement Insurance (MSI), or Medigap, is sold by private insurance companies and is designed to cover the deductibles and copayments that Medicare doesn't cover. At one point, there were more than 200 different policies available. Then the NAIC stepped in and created 10 standard packages of coverage, designated by the letters A through J. Since June 2010, plans E, H, I, and J have not been sold, although you are able to keep your plan if you already had one of these plans before June 2010. There are also two new policies (plans M and N) that offer different benefits and premiums. Plans D and G bought on or after June 1, 2010, have different benefits than D and G plans bought before June 1, 2010 (although the benefits won't change for those who participated in these plans prior to June 1). Only Medigap insurers are able to offer these plans. Although each standardized plan is identical from insurer to insurer, prices may differ and all these plans may not be available in every state.

2.7.2.1 Medicare Premiums and Deductibles for 2015

A premium is the monthly amount paid for Medicare coverage. It changes each year. The Centers for Medicare & Medicaid Services (CMS) publishes Part A and Medicare Part B rate changes for the following calendar year in the middle of October or November. New premium rates for Medicare Part D and Medicare Advantage Plans become available October 1st, when sponsors are allowed to start marketing their plans.

2.7.2.1.1 Medicare Part A Premiums

Most beneficiaries do not pay a monthly premium for Medicare Part A coverage if they or their spouse paid Medicare taxes while working. In fact, according to CMS, approximately 99% of Medicare beneficiaries do not have to pay Medicare premiums on Part A because they have more than 10 years (or 40 quarters) of Medicare-covered employment. The small percentage of people who do have to pay Medicare premiums will pay up to $426 each month. The monthly amount depends on the number of quarters of Medicare-covered employment the person (or his/her spouse) has

- Those with 30–39 quarters of covered employment paid a monthly rate of $234 in 2014.
- Those with less than 30 quarters of employment and who are not eligible for free or reduced benefits.
- Medicare recipients paid a monthly premium of $426 in 2015.
- Premium amounts may change for 2016 with a 52% increase.

2.7.2.1.2 Medicare Part B Premiums

The Medicare Part B premium is set each year at a level calculated to pay for 25% of the average cost of coverage. The standard premium—the premium for most enrollees—applies to those with annual household incomes that do not exceed a set threshold amount. For 2014, the standard Part B premium was $104.90, and the threshold was $85,000 for single filers or married couples who file separately and $170,000 for couples who file jointly, based on 2012 tax returns.

Although most beneficiaries pay the standard rate, there are three provisions that alter the premium rate for certain Part B enrollees:

1. There is a premium surcharge for those who enroll after the initial enrollment period.
2. A *hold-harmless* provision can lower the premium rate for those who have their premiums deducted from their social security check. This provision limits the dollar increase in the Part B premium to the dollar increase in social security benefits.
3. There are higher *income-related* premiums for those whose annual income exceeds the threshold amount.

2.7.2.1.2.1 2015 Part B Income-Related Premium Amounts If your annual income is percent of cost-covered actual premium and estimated 2015 premium

Individual Tax Return		**Joint Tax Return**
$85,000 or less		$104.90
$170,000 or less	25%	$123.10
$85,001–$107,000	35%	$146.90
$170,001–$214,000		$156.90
$107,001–$160,000	50%	$209.80
$214,001–$320,000		$224.20
$160,001–$213,000	65%	$272.70
$320,001–$426,000		$291.50
More than $213,000	80%	$335.70
More than $426,000		$358.70

2.7.2.1.3 Medicare Part D Premiums

The monthly Medicare Part D base premium is set to pay 25.5% of the cost of standard coverage, established by bids submitted annually by Part D plans. CMS releases the Medicare Part D base premium in early August each year. Actual premiums are based on this set premium but can vary greatly. The premium for 2014 was $32.42.

As of 2011, beneficiaries with higher incomes must pay a premium adjustment based on their income. This premium adjustment is called the income-related monthly adjustment amount (IRMAA) and is paid directly to the federal government (deducted from Social Security, Railroad Retirement Board, or Office of Personnel Management benefits).

2.7.2.1.4 Medicare Part A Deductible

Medicare Part A pays all covered hospital, skilled nursing facility, and home health-care services for each benefit period except for the deductible. For 2014, this deductible was $1216, and the overall cost for coinsurance ranges based on the length of hospital stay:

- 1–60 days: $0
- 61–90 days: $304 per day
- 91 days and beyond: $608 per day

For those on Medicare who receive care in a skilled nursing facility, Medicare will cover days 1 through 20 in full. In 2013, there was a copayment of $148 per day for days 21 through 100, and no coverage after day 100 in a benefit period.

2.7.2.1.5 Medicare Part B Deductible

Medicare Part B included a yearly deductible of $147 in 2014. This deductible was applied to health-care costs that involve physician services, outpatient hospital services, certain home health services, and durable medical equipment. Once the deductible is met, you are required to pay 20% of the Medicare-approved amount charged by providers for health-care services. Because of the new health-care law, many preventive services are provided at no cost. These free benefits are not subject to a deductible.

2.7.2.1.6 Medicare Part D Deductible

The annual deductible for the standard Medicare Part D benefit was $310 in 2014, which is a decrease of $10 from the 2013 deductible. No Medicare drug plan may have a deductible more than $310 in 2014, although some plans may have a lower deductible or no deductible at all.

2.7.2.1.6.1 CMS Part D 2015 Standard Benefit Model Plan Details Here are the highlights for the CMS defined Standard Benefit Plan changes from 2014 to 2015. The list below shows the Standard Benefit design changes for plan years 2011, 2012, 2013, 2014, and 2015. This *Standard Benefit Plan* is the minimum allowable plan to be offered.

- *Initial deductible*: will be increased by $10 to $320 in 2015.
- *Initial coverage limit*: will increase from $2850 in 2014 to $2960 in 2015.
- *Out-of-pocket threshold*: will increase from $4550 in 2014 to $4700 in 2015.
- *Coverage gap (donut hole)*: begins once you reach your Medicare Part D plan's initial coverage limit ($2960 in 2015) and ends when you spend a total of $4700 in 2015. *In 2015*, Part D enrollees will receive a 55% discount on the total cost of their *brand-name* drugs purchased while in the donut hole. The 50% discount paid by the brand-name drug manufacturer will still apply to getting out of the donut hole; however, the additional 5% paid by your Medicare Part D plan will not count toward your true out-of-pocket expenses (TrOOP). Enrollees will pay a maximum of 65% copay on *generic* drugs purchased while in the coverage gap.
- *Minimum cost-sharing in the catastrophic coverage portion of the benefit*: will increase to greater of 5% or $2.65 for generic or preferred drug that is a multisource drug and the greater of 5% or $6.60 for all other drugs in 2015.
- *Maximum copayments below the out-of-pocket threshold for certain low-income full subsidy eligible enrollees*: will increase to $2.65 for generic or preferred drug that is a multisource drug and $6.60 for all other drugs in 2015.

2.7.2.2 The Patient Protection and Affordable Care Act

The opening date was October 1, 2013. And now, the competition is lined up and ready to go after bronze, silver, gold, and even platinum plans. These competitors aren't athletes, but insurance providers. The field they are entering is the new health insurance exchanges

(HIEs) as mandated by Obamacare (PPACA). Beginning January 1, 2014, nearly everyone in the United States was required to have health insurance or pay a tax penalty. Those not insured through their employers can apply for coverage through these HIEs, also called *marketplaces*. Enrollment began on October 1, 2013, for coverage that started in January, 2014. The exchanges were intended to make it easier to find insurance providers and compare coverage and costs. Each state's exchange website lists all the policies available in that state, with prices and policy provisions. So far, over half of the states have opted to use exchanges managed by the federal government instead of setting up their own. But state and national changes, modifications, and exceptions abound by political fiat with this ever changing law.

2.7.2.2.1 The Five Basic (Colors) Health Plan Categories

Bronze, silver, gold, and platinum describe the four basic categories of policies that will be available through the exchanges at different costs. Here is a very brief summary of each category.

2.7.2.2.1.1 Bronze The least expensive option is a bronze plan, which might be the best choice for younger people with lower incomes and good health. The plan will pay 60% of health-care costs, and the insured will be responsible for 40%.

2.7.2.2.1.2 Silver The second level, silver, will pay 70% of health-care costs.

2.7.2.2.1.3 Gold and Platinum Gold covers 80%, and a platinum plan covers 90%. Obviously, the categories with higher benefits also will have higher premiums.

2.7.2.2.1.4 Copper Plans? To add to the above, a recent fifth copper plan legislative proposal covers 50% of medical costs, compared to the 60% actuarial value for bronze plans, 70% for silver plans, 80% for gold plans, and 90% for platinum. This offers the potential for low-deductible, but inexpensive plans, with very high cost sharing.

2.7.2.2.2 The Essential Benefits

All these plans are required to cover ten *essential health benefits*. These include preventive and wellness care like cancer screening, chronic disease management, pediatric care, many prescription drugs, injury rehabilitation, mental health and addiction treatment, maternity and newborn care, hospitalization, and emergency services. Companies are not allowed to deny coverage or charge more for those with preexisting conditions. There are no lifetime benefit limits.

2.7.2.2.3 The Carrot and Stick Approach

The PPACA requirement to have health insurance coverage, the *stick* of Obamacare, is accompanied by a *carrot* in the form of federal subsidies to help pay insurance premiums. It's estimated that two-thirds of Americans are eligible for subsidies, which are figured on a sliding scale. The upper limit for qualifying is four times (400%) the federal poverty level (FPL), which amounts to about $88,000 a year for a family of four.

To find out more about how the PPACA is evolving, it's a good idea to spend some time online, especially at two sites that offer more helpful information.

1. *The first site* is the federal government website at http://www.HealthCare.gov. It provides links to the state exchanges plus detailed information that for the most part is explained in straightforward, plain English (beware—the site is not totally secure, and the integrity of website *navigators* may be suspect).
2. *The second site* is the Henry J. Kaiser Family Foundation at http://kff.org. An especially useful tool is available here (http://kff.org/interactive/subsidy-calculator/). It has a calculator to determine the federal subsidy for specific income levels.

2.7.2.3 Who Gets Government Aid through the HIEs?

According to Lon Jefferies, MBA, CFP, of the financial advisory firm Net-Worth-Advice in Salt Lake City, Utah, the premium assistance tax credit (PATC) was designed to help *lower* income individuals and families pay for health insurance plans purchased through the new health-care exchange program. However, more people may qualify for government assistance when purchasing health care through the HIEs than they may realize (personal communication).

2.7.2.3.1 Understanding the PATC

The program defines *lower* income as households that earn less than 400% of the FPL, which is based on the number of individuals in the home. In 2013, the FPL for a single individual was $11,490. Similarly, the FPL for a household of two people was $15,510, and the FPL for a home of four individuals was $23,550.

Consequently, at least some premium assistance credit is available for individuals earning less than $45,960, couples earning less than $62,040, and a household of four earning less than $94,200. It's important to note that for the purposes of the assistance program, income is defined as modified adjusted gross income (MAGI). This means that a taxpayer's adjusted gross income will include all social security benefits received (whether it was taxable or not) and all bond interest (tax-exempt or not). This factor will reduce a person's eligibility for aid if he or she begins receiving social security before the age of 65 (at which point he or she qualifies for Medicare and can no longer participate in the health-care exchange).

The amount of aid that the government will provide is essentially calculated in reverse—the maximum amount that an individual or family can owe is calculated, and the government will pay the remaining premium. Single persons who don't purchase health insurance will have to pay a tax equal to 1% of their income or $95—whichever amount is greater.

The table below shows the *PATC* thresholds based on income relative to the FPL:

Income Relative to FPL	Premiums Limited to
Up to 133% of FPL	2% of household income
133–150% of FPL	3–4% of income
150–200% of FPL	4–6.3% of income
200–250% of FPL	6.3–8.05% of income
250–300% of FPL	8.05–9.5% of income
300–400% of FPL	9.5% of income

Example: Assume that John LPN is a single 62-year-old man living in Utah and making $30,000 per year. (Again, remember that when calculating the PATC, it really doesn't matter whether John's $30,000 of income is from employment, a social security benefit, or a combination of the two.) John's income is 261% of the FPL amount for singles

[($30,000/$11,490)*100], so this puts his threshold between 8.05% and 9.5% of his income. His exact threshold is 11/50 of the way between 250% and 300% of the FPL, so his maximum premium is 11/50 of the way between 8.05% and 9.5%, which means his maximum premium is 8.37% of his $30,000 income, or $2511 per year ($210 per month). This is the most John will need to pay for an adequate health insurance plan.

What is deemed an adequate health insurance plan? The next relevant figure in the calculation involves determining the cost of the *second least expensive silver plan in the state.* This can be determined by obtaining a quote at http://www.HealthCare.gov. Assuming John lives in Salt Lake County, the second least expensive silver plan available to him costs $5100 per year ($425 per month). Whether or not John decides to purchase this exact policy, the $5100 annual cost of the plan is significant.

Since the second least expensive silver plan available to John costs $5100, but the most John will be required to pay is $2511 per year (8.37% of his income), the PATC program will cover the cost difference of $2589. This amount will be the tax credit available to John for purchasing any health insurance policy through the exchange.

However, this does not mean that John is required to actually purchase and utilize the second least expensive silver plan available to him. If John is so inclined, he can purchase a less expensive policy and he will still receive the $2589 tax credit determined to be available to him. Nevertheless, since the policy is less expensive, John would need to cover less of the cost of the inferior policy out of his own pocket. Similarly, John could also purchase a more expensive policy, but his tax credit would still be $2589, and he would need to cover the additional cost of the superior policy with his own money.

The bottom line is that the PPACA may well mark the beginning of the end of tying health insurance decisions to employment status, which ultimately will reshape important career, retirement, and other financial planning decisions that clients make. Some may find a new freedom in the job decisions that they make—whether changing jobs, starting a new business, or retiring altogether—but will also need help to contend with affordability of health insurance and how to pay for it, including maximizing the PATC. In addition, many clients—and small business owners—will need help in the coming years handling the transition from employer-based to individual-based health insurance, as the system slowly shifts. In the long run, arguably a system where people can make employment and job decisions without being constrained to access to health care may be a huge plus, but there will be much planning to be done, including helping clients to change their mindset, during the coming transition years!

2.7.3 Health Savings Account

The HD-HCPs mentioned above are becoming more common. With a qualifying high-deductible plan comes the chance to contribute pretax dollars to an HSA. Compared with health flexible spending accounts, HSAs have higher contribution limits—$6550 for a family compared with $2500 for a health FSA—and there's no limit to how much can be rolled over year to year. So, sheltering $6550 with a tax rate of 25% could result in annual savings of $1500 on a tax bill.

2.7.3.1 Disability Income Insurance

Disability income insurance is designed to transfer the financial risk of lost wages due to an accident or illness to an insurance company. The actual benefits may be received for as short a period as 6 months in some short-term group policies, to age 65 in both group long-term and many individual policies, and possibly even to lifetime for some individual *professional* policies. The length of the benefit period is one of the main factors in determining the premium to be charged by the insurance company.

2.7.3.1.1 Disability Defined

Arguably, the most important issue when purchasing disability insurance is the definition of disability found within the policy. Disability insurance pays a monthly benefit to the insured if he/she satisfies this definition of disability. Unlike a life insurance policy death claim, a disability income claim can be a far more difficult issue. Different policies from the same insurance company can define disability differently, and a medical professional or health-care practitioner must be sure they are comfortable with the definition found in the policies that they are considering for purchase.

The more liberal the definition of disability in any given policy, the easier it will be to meet that definition, and the more likely the insurance company will pay benefits. Consequently, these are also the most expensive policies. Many agents and financial planners recommend paying the extra premium so that you have a higher chance of receiving benefits. The last thing an insured wants to do after becoming seriously injured is fighting an insurance carrier over benefits.

There are two common definitions of disability:

- The ability to perform the substantial and material duties of your occupation
- The ability to perform any gainful occupation for which you are reasonably trained

Some aggressive insurance companies have even gone so far as to define the disability in terms of occupational and/or medical specialties. Regardless, the definition will almost always end with the words "and under a physician's care."

Some policies will pay benefits under the first definition for a couple of years, and then use a second definition thereafter. This design permits the insured full monthly benefits immediately after a disability and then time to rehabilitate and establish a new career.

2.7.3.1.2 Partial Disability

Some policies also allow fractional benefits for a partial, or residual, disability. Partial benefits can be available under two circumstances:

1. During a disability where the insured cannot perform some of the duties of his/her occupation
2. When the insured can still perform all the duties of his/her occupation, but for a limited period of time during recuperation

The doctor should pay particular attention to the partial disability benefit language in their policy. Some companies require total disability prior to any partial claims payment. Other companies may have no such provision and, in fact, even pay a full benefit for the first 3 months of partial disability. This gives the insurance company the opportunity to give an incentive for the claimant doctor to recover and go back to full-time work.

2.7.3.1.3 Elimination Period

Another aspect used in the development of a disability income insurance premium is the waiting period, i.e., that period of time that elapses, at the beginning of a disability, prior to the payment of any benefits during which the insured must generally be continuously disabled. This is also referred to as the elimination period and in individual contracts is usually specified as 30, 60, 90, 180, or 365 days.

The shorter the elimination period, the higher the potential premium. In short-term group policies, the standard elimination period is the first day for accidents and the seventh day for sickness. Long-term group policies traditionally begin after 6 months. Medical professionals and health-care practitioners with ample savings should consider a longer elimination period in order to save premium dollars, but those with less savings should obviously choose a shorter elimination period. A personal emergency fund can provide the cash flow needed during the elimination period. This emergency fund makes it feasible for a doctor to select a longer elimination period, thus reducing the premiums.

2.7.3.1.4 Coordination of Benefits

Coordination between short-term group and both long-term group and individual contracts is often possible to complete an overall portfolio of coverage. Since most long-term group policies have a provision for coordination of benefits (insurance speak for "reduction of benefit payments") with individual coverage purchased subsequent to the group policy effective date, many financial service professionals will look for the opportunity to place substantial amounts of individual coverage prior to writing the group coverage.

2.7.3.1.5 Monthly Benefit Amount

Yet, another aspect to be taken into consideration for developing the premium to be charged is the monthly benefit amount. The amount of coverage that can be initially purchased is dependent on the current level of pre-disability earnings. Insurance companies have usually been willing to insure up to 50% of current income (for the highest wage earners) to up to 70% of current income (for moderate- to lower-income workers).

2.7.3.1.6 Occupation

The hazard category of the insured's occupation is also important to develop an adequate premium. Obviously bus drivers, fire fighters, cardiovascular surgeons, and financial service professionals face different risks during their typical day. These occupation classifications also take into account the claims experience related to that occupation. For example, dentists at one time were in the same top classification as physicians. However, because of poor claims experience, many companies have since lowered their classification, i.e., raised their premiums.

2.7.3.1.7 Inflation Protection

When purchasing a disability income policy, it is strongly recommended that it includes an inflation rider. In the event of disability, this rider will increase the benefit each year in an attempt to keep pace with inflation. Without this rider, if a young insured becomes totally disabled, their monthly benefit will certainly lose its purchasing power over the years. If the insured is young enough, a level benefit may become almost meaningless 20–30 years in the future. An inflation rider will cost extra, but it is money well spent.

2.7.3.1.8 Renewability

The last major issue to be considered when purchasing a disability policy is the renewal feature of the policy. The typical renewal features are

- Conditionally renewable
- Guaranteed renewable
- Noncancellable

Conditionally renewable policies allow the insurance company a limited ability to refuse to renew the policy at the end of a premium payment period. The insurance company may also increase the premium. Most policies sold to doctors will not contain this limitation.

Guaranteed renewable means the insurance company cannot cancel the policy, except for nonpayment of premium, but it can change the premium rates for an entire class of policies.

Noncancellable means the insurer cannot cancel the policy nor can it change the rates. This added level of security means noncancellable policies are more expensive than guaranteed renewable policies.

Although redundant, many disability income policies specify that they are both *noncancelable and guaranteed renewable.*

2.7.3.2 Disability Income Taxation

The general rule for taxation of disability benefits is that if the policy owner pays the premiums from his/her own funds, then any benefits received as a result of the disability are income tax–free. If the policy owner's employer pays the premiums as an employee benefit, then any benefits are taxable. Therefore, when choosing a monthly benefit amount, the physician should always factor his/her individual tax status of the benefits into the calculations.

2.7.3.3 Disability Income Statistics*

Risk of disability:

- At age 30, long-term disability is 4.1 times more likely than death.
- At age 40, long-term disability is 2.9 times more likely than death.
- At age 50, long-term disability is 2.2 times more likely than death.

Risk of disability within groups of people:

- At age 30, there is a 46.7% chance of any one person having a 90-day disability before age 65.
- At age 40, there is a 43% chance of any one person having a 90-day disability before age 65.
- At age 50, there is a 36% chance of any one person having a 90-day disability before age 65.
- At age 30, there is a 71.6% chance of any one person out of any two people having a 90-day disability before age 65.
- At age 40, there is a 67.5% chance of any one person out of any two people having a 90-day disability before age 65.
- At age 50, there is a 59% chance of any one person out of any two people having a 90-day disability before age 65.

* 2014–2015 National Underwriter Field Guide.

Overheard in the Doctor's Lounge*

Split Benefit Health Insurance?

Traditional cost sharing for health care is stymied by limited patient wealth. The *split benefit* is may be a new way to reduce consumption of high-cost, low-value treatments for which the risk/benefit ratio is uncertain. When a physician prescribes a costly unproven procedure, the insurer could pay a portion of the benefit directly to the patient, creating a decision opportunity for the patient. The insurer saves the remainder, unless the patient consumes.

The reform is promising for further testing since it has the potential to decrease spending on low-value interventions, and thereby increase the value of the health-care dollar.

Christopher T. Robertson
University of Arizona
James E. Rogers
College of Law, Harvard University
Edmond J. Safra
Center for Ethics, Harvard University
Petrie-Flom Center for Health Law Policy, Biotechnology, and Bioethics
Harvard Law School

2.8 LONG-TERM CARE INSURANCE

Long-term care insurance (LTCI) was considered one of the newer forms of personal coverage insurance. LTCI is designed to transfer the financial risk associated with the inability to care for oneself because of a prolonged illness, disability, or the effects of old age. In

* A Randomized Experiment of the Split Benefit Health Insurance Reform to Reduce High-Cost, Low-Value Consumption. Social Science Research Network; January 4, 2015.

particular, it is designed to insure against the financial cost of an extended stay in a nursing home, assisted living facility, adult day care center, hospice, or home health care. It has been estimated that two out of every five Americans now over the age of 65 will spend time in a nursing home. As life expectancy increases, so does the apparent need for LTCI.

2.8.1 Medicare

Currently, the only nursing home care that Medicare covers is skilled nursing care, and it must be provided in a Medicare-certified skilled nursing facility. Custodial care is not covered. Most LTCI policies have been designed with these types of coverage, or the lack thereof, in mind. To qualify for Medicare Skilled Nursing Care, an individual must meet the following conditions:

1. Be hospitalized for at least 3 days within the 30 days preceding the nursing home admission.
2. Be admitted for the same medical condition that required the hospitalization.
3. The skilled nursing home care must be deemed rehabilitative.

Once these requirements are met, Medicare will pay 100% of the costs for the first 20 days. Days 21–100 are covered by Medicare along with a daily copayment, which is indexed annually. After the initial 100 days, there is no additional Medicare coverage.

Medicare Home Health Services cover part-time or intermittent skilled nursing care, physical therapy, medical supplies, and some rehabilitative equipment. These are generally paid for in full and do not require a hospital stay prior to home health service coverage.

2.8.2 Critical LTCI Policy Features and Markets

According to the U.S. Department of Health and Human Services and the Health Insurance Association of America, there are seven features that should always be included in a good long LTCI policy:

1. Guaranteed renewable.
2. Covers all levels of nursing care (skilled, intermediate, and custodial care).
3. Premiums remain level (individual premiums cannot be raised due to health or age, but can be raised only if all other LTCI policies as a group are increased).
4. Benefits never reduced.
5. Offers inflation protection.
6. Full coverage for Alzheimer's disease.
7. Waiver of premium (during a claim period, further premium payments will not be required).

In addition, there are another seven features considered to be worthwhile and are included in the better LTCI policies:

1. Home health-care benefits
2. Adult day care and hospice care
3. Assisted living facility care

4. No prior hospital stay required
5. Optional elimination periods
6. Premium discounts when both spouses are covered
7. Medicare approval not a prerequisite for coverage

Top 25 Most Expensive Markets for LTCI Coverage

Market	Nursing Home Private Room Annual Rate
Bridgeport–Stamford–Norwalk, CT	$159,359
Anchorage, AK	$156,950
New York–Northern New Jersey–Long Island, NY–NJ	$155,180
Poughkeepsie–Newburgh–Middletown, NY	$155,180
Hartford, CT	$154,118
Boston–Worcester–Lawrence, MA	$146,372
Rochester, NY	$141,244
San Diego, CA	$135,554
Seattle–Tacoma–Bremerton, WA	$131,750
San Francisco–Oakland–San Jose, CA	$130,283
Philadelphia–Wilmington–Atlantic City, PA–NJ–DE	$129,239
San Jose–Sunnyvale–Santa Clara, CA	$127,130
Albany–Schenectady–Troy, NY	$126,932
Portland, ME	$121,910
Honolulu, HI	$121,154
Washington–Baltimore, DC-MD	$120,709
Sacramento–Yolo, CA	$120,322
Boise, ID	$118,475
Milwaukee–Racine, WI	$118,005
Manchester–Nashua, NH	$117,264
Miami–Fort Lauderdale, FL	$116,931
Buffalo–Niagara Falls, NY	$116,577
Los Angeles–Riverside–Orange County, CA	$115,165
Detroit–Ann Arbor–Flint, MI	$114,716
Portland–Salem, OR	$111,909

Source: New York Life Insurance Company (NYLIC) 2014.

2.8.3 Activities of Daily Living

Most LTC policies provide benefits for covered insureds with a cognitive impairment or the inability to perform a specified number of activities of daily living (ADLs). These ADLs generally include the inability to perform two of six of the following, in order to file a claim: bathing, dressing, toileting, transferring, eating, and continence.

Another issue is whether the covered insured requires *hands-on* assistance or merely needs someone to *stand by* in the event of difficulty. Obviously, policies that read the latter are more liberal and costly.

2.8.4 LTCI Taxation

Some LTCI policies have been designed to meet the required provisions of the Kassenbaum–Kennedy health reform bill, passed in 1996, and subsequently are *Tax Qualified Policies.* Insureds who own policies meeting the requirements are permitted to tax-deduct some of the policy's premium, based on age, income, and the amount of total itemized medical expenses. The major benefit of the tax-qualified LTC policy is that the benefit, when received, is not considered taxable income.

2.8.5 Selecting Nursing Homes

The following will allow the FA to assist appropriate clients in choosing a nursing home.

2.8.5.1 The Checklist

1. Review the client's requirements. An assisted living facility may suffice instead of a true nursing home, which is required by the frail and elderly needing daily medical care.
2. Pick a location close to home and relatives. Frequent visits are crucial not only to combat loneliness but also to ensure that the resident receives proper attention.
3. Read inspection report (state survey). If the financial advisor encounters difficulties in obtaining a current report, he or she should assume that the home has something to hide. Don't expect perfection. Nursing homes provide a difficult service for difficult residents. If a home is unresponsive to inquiry regarding items in a report, assume a similar response to concerns about the quality of care being provided in the future.
4. Tour the facility on an unannounced basis at different times on different days. Stroll through corridors and look and listen. Trust senses and instincts. Items to consider should include
   - *Appearance of residents' rooms.* Outward decor of facility can be misleading, so the FA should inspect the residents' rooms. To what extent can the rooms be personalized? If rooms are shared, how are good roommate matches made?
   - *Smells.* High-quality homes have no lingering stench of urine or air freshener to cover up bad care and unusually high incidences of incontinence due to lack of attention by staff.
   - *Safety hazards.* Be especially aware of items in corridors that can be obstacles to those with unsteady gait and poor eyesight.
   - *Sufficient staff members who are pleasant and respectful to residents.* Are staff members responsive to residents' needs? Are staff members warm in their interactions with all residents, even those requiring the heaviest supervision? Are aides helping residents with walking or exercise of their arms and legs?
   - *Residents' attitudes toward facility's service.* Talk with residents and staff to determine attitudes toward the facility's service. Does the facility have a family counsel to provide it with input?
   - *Grooming.* A clear sign of neglect is failure to keep residents clean, well dressed, and well groomed.

- *Physical restraints.* Nursing homes that have eliminated restraints also have improved quality of life and more social contact among residents. Ties, belts, vests, and high bed rails are an easy but unsatisfactory solution to managing residents. Count number of residents that are restrained; ask what percentage are restrained and why.
- *Food.* Visit at meal time and sample the food to make sure it is palatable. The setting for meals should be attractive and pleasant, and food should be served at the proper temperature. Staff should be available to help residents who are not able to feed themselves. Review menus and determine the amount of concern for nutrition.
- *Activities.* A wide variety of activities should be provided, and the participation level should be high. Bored residents in front of a television may be a sign of a home's failure to stimulate its residents.
- *Dignity.* Residents should be handled in ways that respect their dignity. For example, are residents properly clothed in public?
- *Bed sores.* Bed sores are a sign of poor care. Review inspection reports and see if they are mentioned, or talk to residents or their families about this topic.
- *Special care units.* Such units are often used as an expensive marketing device. The special care units may not be designed well and may indicate a lack of outdoor facilities.

5. Review the facility's policy on medical care. Will residents be seen by their personal doctors or by staff physicians? Does the home have good infection control and immunization plans? What sort of access to dentists and eye doctors is there?
6. Perform financial analysis. The planner should gain a complete understanding of what the client's and/or his or her family's financial commitments are and how they will be met:
   - Determine the financial strength of the nursing home, particularly if client funds are to be advanced.
   - Consider a single lifetime payment in lieu of monthly rental payments.
   - Consider exclusions in contract. For example, nursing home insurance coverage should include loss of personal property and personal injury.
   - Determine what services the client will require, what is covered under the facility's general fee, and what services are provided for an extra fee. Determine what the extra fee will be for each additional service that will be required. Family members should not agree to pay these charges because this could delay Medicaid funding.
   - Analyze pricing structure in general and what the pattern of increases in fees has been.
   - Determine residents' rights in eviction proceedings for nonpayment of rent, in returning to nursing home after hospital stay, and in having Medicaid make payments on behalf of the resident.
   - Determine residents' rights to appeal decisions and what the appeal procedures are.
7. Obtain and check references, including families of current residents, local hospitals, doctors, and government agencies, particularly the ombudsman at state departments for aging.

2.8.6 New Thoughts on LTCI

To be sure, physicians and FAs are aware that there is a sometime need to recommend an LTCI policy to clients. Of course, in such cases, it is a good idea to work with a low load provider (or the physician or client's agent). Yet, most LTCI policies are sold, not bought, and that most statistics used to sell LTCI policies are fear-based and half-truths. Even the Department of Health and Human Services gets into the fear mongering on their website quoting that "about 70 percent of people over age 65 require some type of long-term care services during their lifetime" (from http://www.longtermcare.gov/LTC/Main_Site/Planning/Index.aspx).

This may be a deceptive statistic as it omits the length of long-term care needed in these 70% of cases. And it is not 3+ years in all these cases (our estimate is closer to 2.5). With the recent stamp of approval by the Supreme Court of the United States on the PPACA, we may be looking at social LTCI in the United States like other social medicine countries and give up on private LTCI altogether. Germany introduced mandatory LTCI in 1995. Japan and France also have an LTCI tax-funded insurance plan. And the poor utilization and growing risks associated with LTCI are leading a growing number of insurance agents, financial advisors, and Certified Medical Planners to recommend alternatives to their clients.

To be a thought leader ahead of the curve, the newest aging trend is away from LTCI and toward *sheltering at home*—living at home and dying at home. Perhaps, this is the way it should be. Dying should not be a for-profit industry.

Overheard in the Doctor's Lounge*

Long-Term Care Insurance Research and Development

The *Center for Retirement Research at Boston College* found that fewer people will need long-term care—some 44% of men and 58% of women will need long-term care versus estimates of 70%—and that those expenses may be less than previously thought.

Yet, "Few individuals would choose to buy insurance even if they were rational, far-sighted, and well-informed," the Center concluded.

Physician Geriatrician
Atlanta, Georgia

2.9 PREPAID FUNERAL EXPENSES

If you're inclined to choose this route for funeral expenses, make sure you're being guaranteed the services you specify at the contracted price (pre-need), because this sort of arrangement is all about contract law. Here is one place that you might not want to make any assumptions. So, realize that some funeral home or mortuary contracts call for additional payments for *final expense funding*. This means that if the funeral home's charges

* Available at http://crr.bc.edu/briefs/long-term-care-how-big-a-risk/.

increase between the time you sign up and the time you sign off, somebody will have to pay the difference. Also consider these questions:

- What if you change your mind? Can you get all or part of your money back?
- Will your money earn interest? If so, how much? Who gets it?
- If there is an insurance policy involved, is there a waiting period before it takes effect? How long?
- What happens when prices increase? Are increases covered by the plan or will your family have to pay extra?
- Does your health affect the terms of the plan?
- What happens if the funeral home goes out of business? Is your plan taken over by another funeral home? If so, which one?
- What happens if you move? Can the plan be transferred to another funeral home in a different state?
- If there's money left over after your funeral, will your heirs get it, or does the home keep it?
- Is the funeral home a stand-alone or family entity, or a local, regional, or national chain?

2.9.1 A Better Way to Pay Ahead?*

According to Kiplinger's, you could simply buy a life insurance policy with the proceeds earmarked for funeral expenses, although the relatively low level of coverage it would take to pay for a funeral doesn't translate to the most economical level of insurance premiums. Or you could even set up your own burial *trust fund*, which isn't as complicated as it sounds! You do it at a bank or credit union through what's often called a Totten trust. Now, a Totten isn't actually a trust. It's a regular bank account with a designated *pay on death* inheritor. When you open the account, you name a relative or friend (or even the funeral home) as beneficiary. You put in the money and collect the interest. You can close the account any time you want, transfer the balance to a different bank, or change the beneficiary. When you die, the beneficiary collects the account balance and pays for the funeral.

2.10 CONCLUSION

Physicians should always consult a trusted fee-only Certified Financial Planner, Certified Medical Planner, trusted insurance agent, insurance broker, or Certified Insurance Counselor to get a second opinion before the purchase of any insurance policy product.

2.11 COLLABORATE

Discuss this chapter online with others at http://www.medicalexecutivepost.com.

---

* *Kiplinger's Personal Finance*, February 2015.

ACKNOWLEDGMENTS

To Cathy D. Belteau, CFP, CLU, ChFC, FLMI; Philip E. Taylor, CLU, ChFC, FLMI; Matthew Lawrence DeSantos, JD; Matthew D. Rogers, CFP, CLU, ChFC; Hope Rachel Hetico, RN, MHA, CMP™; and Lon Jefferies, MBA, CFP, of http://networthadvice.com.

FURTHER READINGS

Dogra, A: Four things everyone should know about end of life planning. http://www.KevinMD, March 9, 2014.

Marcinko, DE and Hetico, HR: *Dictionary of Health Insurance and Managed Care*. Springer Publishing, New York, 2008.

Muldowney, TA, Marcinko, DE and Hetico, HR: Financial Planning for the Elderly. In: Margolis, HS, Esq. [editor]: *Elder Law Portfolio Series*. Wolters-Kluwer and Aspen Publishers, New York, 2007.

Muldowney, TA, Marcinko, DE and Hetico, HR: Postmortem Estate Planning. In: Margolis, HS, Esq. [editor]: *Elder Law Portfolio Series*. Wolters-Kluwer and Aspen Publishers, New York, 2007.

Muldowney, TA, Cook, GA and Marcinko, DE: Establishing a Solid Foundation of Insurance Planning: The Bedrock of Life and Medical Practice. In Marcinko, DE [editor]: *Comprehensive Financial Planning Strategies for Doctors and Advisors: Best Practices from Leading Consultants and Certified Medical Planners™*. Productivity Press, Boca Raton, FL, 2015.

Thompson, J: *Money. Wealth. Life Insurance: How the Wealthy Use Life Insurance as a Tax-Free Personal Bank to Supercharge Their Savings*. CreateSpace Publishing, North Charleston, SC, 2014.

3 Property Insurance Planning
Protecting Possessions

Thomas A. Muldowney, David Edward Marcinko, and Gary A. Cook

CONTENTS

3.1 GENERAL TYPES OF INSURANCE POLICIES COVERING POSSESSIONS

Unlike those insurance policies covering people, where it is mostly a matter of personal choice, most property insurance coverages discussed in this chapter are virtually required by law.

3.1.1 Homeowner's (and Renter's) Insurance Overview

The basic model of the homeowner's contract began in 1958 and contains three areas of coverage: property, theft, and liability. There are seven standard forms of homeowner contracts, and their coverages are contained in two sections.

Section I is for property and theft coverage and typically includes coverage for the

- Structure itself (commonly called the dwelling)
- Appurtenant structures (unattached buildings, fences, swimming pools, etc.)
- Unscheduled personal property (commonly just called contents within the structures and only those not itemized by endorsement)
- Additional living expenses (the increased cost of living during the period after damage occurs while the structure is uninhabitable)

"Contents coverage" is typically 50% of the dwelling coverage for on-premises losses. Off-premises coverage is typically worldwide but limited to 10% of the limit for contents coverage. Typically, there are other restrictions, with some types of personal property being totally excluded and others having a dollar limitation applied against them.

A common mistake is to not have a basic inventory of your property in an off-site location, possibly a safe deposit box. This is often conveniently accomplished by periodically taking photographs of each of the rooms in the house. Should there be a fire that damages that section, the picture may assist in bringing to mind property that was destroyed and for which a claim needs to be filed.

Section II is the liability protection section and covers personal liability for bodily injury to others, or for damage to their property, and includes reasonable medical payments for their injuries. Section II is identical in all seven forms. Liability protection often begins at $100,000, with medical payments at $1000 per person.

Briefly, the seven forms are as follows:

1. *HO-1*: *The basic form* insures against fire, lightning, removal, vandalism or malicious mischief, glass breakage, and theft. It also provides what is called extended coverage for damage from wind, civil commotion, smoke, hail, aircraft, vehicles, explosion, and riot. The dwelling protection is specified as a dollar amount, while the contents are covered at 50% of this amount and the additional living expenses are covered at 10%.
2. *HO-2*: *The broad form* gets its name from broadening the extended-coverage perils of the HO-1. Coverage is now extended to include damage from falling objects; weight of ice, snow, or sleet; accidental damage to steam or hot-water heating systems; accidental discharge of water or steam from those systems or

domestic appliances; freezing of those systems or appliances; and electrical surge damage. Again, the dwelling protection is specified, and the contents are covered at 50%. Additional living expenses are increased to 20% of the dwelling coverage amount.

3. *HO-3*: *The special form*, also called the *all-risk form*, expands on the HO-2 by providing coverage for the dwelling, appurtenant structures, and additional living expenses on an all-risk basis. Rather than naming each peril to be covered, this form covers all perils not specifically named as an exception, such as flood, earthquake, war, and nuclear accidents. Coverage for the dwelling, contents, and additional living expenses is identical to the HO-2.
4. *HO-4*: *The tenant's form* is basically the same as the HO-2 and provides a named-perils basis for the contents of renters. Additional living expenses are provided at 20% of the amount of coverage purchased for the contents.
5. *HO-5*: *The comprehensive form* is seldom seen anymore. It is identical to the HO-3 except contents are covered at 50% of the dwelling amount, and this level is provided for both on and off premises.
6. *HO-6*: *The unit owner's form* is also referred to as the *condominium form*. It is very similar to the tenant's form except additional living expenses are provided at 40% of the amount of coverage purchased for the contents. There are other unique differences with regard to insuring additions and alterations by the unit owner and the availability of optional coverage to protect against the exposure to losses from assessment by the condominium association for uninsured property damage or liability claims.
7. *HO-7*: *The modified coverage form* is designed specifically to provide coverage for older dwellings. Many older homes contain elaborate carvings and specialty features that would cause the replacement value to substantially exceed current market value. This form of coverage has no replacement cost provision but substitutes a "functional replacement" concept for any losses.

3.1.2 Replacement Cost versus Actual Cash Value

Actual cash value settlements provide payments for claims that generally start with the cost today to replace a lost, stolen, damaged, or destroyed item. However, it then takes into account the length of time the item was owned or in service, to develop a deduction for depreciation. Often, this depreciation amount is substantial and severe.

Under replacement cost coverage, insureds are able to collect for their losses without the deduction for appreciation, up to the limits of the policy. This is an automatic but optional provision of all homeowner forms. To take advantage of this provision, the amount of insurance on the dwelling must be at least 80% of its replacement cost at the time of claim.

3.1.3 Inflation Protection

The easiest way for a homeowner to ensure replacement cost coverage is with the addition of a rider that automatically adjusts the value of the dwelling coverage by the inflation rate for his/her community as calculated by the insurance company. This coverage adjusts policy limits periodically to maintain appropriate levels of coverage.

3.1.4 Other Homeowner Policy Endorsements

The homeowner is well advised to also consider a multitude of endorsements and/or potential increases in policy limits. Examples include the following:

- Scheduling personal property, such as jewelry, furs, art, golf equipment, and computers, which has been exempted from coverage or whose coverage has a severe dollar limitation
- Increasing liability coverage to take advantage of the minimums needed for *umbrella liability*, covered in Section 3.3
- Theft extension endorsement to remove the exclusion for loss of unattended property from a motor vehicle, trailer, or watercraft
- Earthquake and/or sinkhole collapse coverage
- Increasing the deductible from the standard $250 to a convenient self-insurance amount

3.1.5 Title Insurance (Lender and Policy Owner)

As a routine part of any home purchase, a history of the title to the property, as well as any liens or conveyances, is completed. This is referred to as title insurance and typically protects the mortgage *lender* from any title defects. If a title defect causes loss, the title insurance company will indemnify the lender, not the homeowner-buyer, to the extent of the loan. These are single-premium policies of indefinite duration but can terminate when the loan is retired.

The physician should also inquire about the cost of a *personally* owned title insurance policy. This second policy would protect him/her (owner) rather than the mortgage lender. Although it adds to the expense of closing, there is no harm in requesting that the seller be responsible for providing this protection to the purchaser as well. In general, items that are covered by title insurance can be determined solely from a review of the property records and court records:

- Judgments
- Liens (except to the extent that they have superiority, i.e., once recorded, they gain priority ahead of things recorded prior to the lien, for example, mechanic's liens)
- Deeds of trust, mortgages, and real-estate contracts
- Easements
- Restrictive covenants
- Rights granted in real property by divorce (half of proceeds of sale of property)
- Mineral rights reserved by prior owner or granted to a third party
- Recorded leases
- Latecomer's agreements
- Recorded no-contest agreements (agreement not to contest future imposition of taxes or assessments, usually for things like traffic, water, and sewer mitigation)
- Deeds transferring ownership of any interests in the property
- Whether the property has access to a public road
- Taxes and recorded assessments
- Condemnation actions filed with the court or property records

3.1.5.1 Items Not Covered

Generally, items that are not covered by title insurance cannot be determined by reviewing the property records and court records:

- Zoning laws, restrictions on the use of property
- Building codes, setbacks, lot coverage, construction standards
- Wetland regulations
- Storm water drainage permits
- Floodplain, location of property in relation to floodplain
- Unrecorded leases
- Use permits
- Hazardous materials, environmental contaminants
- Subdivision regulations
- Shoreline Management Act
- State Environmental Policy Act (SEPA)
- Persons claiming an interest in the property, through adverse possession (both ownership of the property and easement rights)
- Compliance of the property with recorded restrictive covenants

3.1.5.2 Additional Extended-Coverage Policy Items

Coverage extends beyond basic coverage. This covers items that show up during an inspection of the property:

- Additional matters including those that the title company can determine from either an inspection of the property or a review of a survey showing all improvements to the property and the location of all easements.
- Mechanic's liens filed after the date of the policy but that take priority prior to the date of the policy.
- Encroachments (the buildings on the property that overlap the property lines or buildings on adjacent property that overlap onto the client's property).
- Persons claiming an interest in the property through adverse possession (both ownership of the property and easement rights).

3.1.5.3 Additional Matters Covered by Endorsement

- Compliance with subdivision laws (guarantees that the property constitutes one or more legal lots)
- Zoning laws

3.1.6 Renter's Insurance

Renter's insurance can protect you from damage caused by weather events like wind, rain, snow, or lightning, as well as fire, vandalism, or theft. Some policies also include liability protection. This would be valuable if someone got injured in your home and sued you. Renter's insurance tends to be cheap. For a low payment, usually annually, you can often get replacement coverage for your belongings and living expenses if you are displaced. This means that you can get money to replace a damaged or stolen item as well as pay for a hotel or alternative rent if you are forced to leave your home because of damage.

3.1.7 Boat Insurance Overview

Watercraft and small pleasure boats are usually covered within a homeowner policy but generally only for $1000. More expensive boats are often insured either under a separate inland marine policy or as a personal articles floater (attachment) to the homeowner's policy. The decision between these two alternatives usually involves the liability risk element. There is no provision in the personal articles floater for liability, and although it could be increased on the homeowner's policy, it is usually preferable to use a separate policy. Other items to consider are the size of the craft, maximum speed, engine horsepower, waters navigated, and special uses, such as water skiing or racing.

3.2 AUTOMOBILE PURCHASE AND INSURANCE OVERVIEW

With the possible exception of the handgun, the automobile represents the greatest single item of ownership that is capable of inflicting death, injury, and damage. America's fascination with the automobile has resulted in a marked increase in the power and potential speed of our vehicles. The latest trend in sports utility vehicles (SUVs) has also witnessed a substantial increase in damage due to their higher ground clearance and heavier frames. The owners and operators of any vehicle must be financially able to respond to any resulting claims, or they need to transfer the risk through insurance. All states require some minimal coverage for personal vehicles.

3.2.1 Purchasing the Vehicle

Typically, car buyers who wait until the end of the year can score a deal. Buying at the end of the month can also increase negotiating power as dealerships look to move volume, and shoppers in the late summer and early fall may be able to get a deal when the new-model-year vehicles enter inventories. Also, cold or rainy weather can work to a doctor's advantage, since bad weather can discourage people from walking around a lot to look at vehicles, potentially giving those who do show up a bit more negotiating power. Even a serious buyer who goes to a dealership near the end of the day may receive a better price as the dealer makes concessions to speed things up so everyone can go home. So, if you time your car purchase right, and you aren't buying one of the more popular models or colors, you might save $500 to $2000 just by waiting until the end of the month or day to make your purchase.

3.2.2 Insuring the Vehicle

The most frequently used policy to insure individual private passenger vehicle risks is the family automobile policy (FAP). It provides two major types of coverage: liability and physical damage. Liability coverage includes both bodily injury and property damage. Physical damage, on the other hand, includes comprehensive and collision coverage.

3.2.2.1 Liability Coverage

The liability section of the FAP is contained within most policies as Part A—Liability and Part B—Personal Injury Protection.

3.2.2.1.1 Bodily Injury

Bodily injury liability coverage generally includes sickness, disease, and death, and is expressed in dual limits—per person and per occurrence. Nearly half of the states require minimums of $25,000 per person and $50,000 per occurrence. Higher limits of $100,000 per person and $300,000 per occurrence are often a prerequisite for consideration of umbrella coverage.

3.2.2.1.2 Property Damage

Property damage liability is coverage for damage or destruction to the property of others and includes loss of use. Liability coverage limits usually include property damage limits as the third number, i.e., $100/300/25. The coverage here would be for $25,000 of property damage. As automobiles become more expensive, however, coverage to $50,000 is not considered excessive.

3.2.2.1.3 Personal Injury

Personal injury coverage is provided for medical expenses, funeral expenses, and loss of earnings for anyone sustaining an injury while occupying your vehicle, or from being struck by your vehicle while a pedestrian.

Liability insurance follows the vehicle, not the driver. Coverage is extended to the vehicle owner and any resident in the same household. It also covers anyone using the insured vehicle with the permission of the owner *and* within the scope of that permission.

Newly acquired vehicles are usually covered automatically for liability for 30 days after acquisition, but physical damage must have been on all currently covered vehicles to be included. Coverage is also typically extended to a temporary substitute automobile, but only if this vehicle is used in place of the covered automobile, because of its breakdown, repair, servicing, loss, or destruction.

3.2.2.2 Physical Damage Coverage

3.2.2.2.1 Comprehensive

Comprehensive physical damage coverage includes coverage for theft, vandalism, broken windshields, falling objects, riot or civil commotion, and even damage from foreign substances, such as paint. Comprehensive coverage is often described as coverage for all hazards other than collision.

3.2.2.2.2 Collision

Collision coverage involves the upset of the covered vehicle and collision with an object, usually another vehicle, that is not enumerated in the discussion of comprehensive coverage. Colliding with a bird or animal is considered under comprehensive coverage.

The distinction between comprehensive coverage and collision coverage is more than technical. The deductible provisions of the FAP often show a considerable difference in these areas, with the collision deductible typically being much greater.

Damage to tires can be covered by provisions in either comprehensive or collision coverage. Exclusions typically include normal wear and tear, rough roads, hard driving, or hitting or scraping curbs.

3.2.2.3 Repairs after the Accident

Following a collision, the insurance company will assign a claims adjuster to determine the extent of damage and the cost of repairs. If these repairs exceed the estimated value of the vehicle, it may be totaled. Experience tells us that the value of the vehicle to the owner nearly always exceeds that estimated by the insurance company.

The physician is therefore strongly urged to consider purchasing replacement cost coverage rather than accepting actual cash value, which is the depreciated value of the vehicle. The cost may be higher for this coverage, but accepting a larger deductible will often make up the difference. Paying a little more toward the deductible could easily be worth it, if the damage is extensive.

3.2.2.4 Uninsured/Underinsured Motorist's Coverage

Uninsured motorist coverage provides protection from the other driver who is operating his/her vehicle without any insurance coverage. It covers expenses resulting from injury or death as well as property damage. There are currently a dozen states where it is estimated that over 20% of the vehicles on the highway are being operated without any insurance. This is not coverage that should be rejected when buying automobile insurance.

Underinsured motorist coverage provides protection from the other driver who purchased only the state-mandated minimum liability insurance coverage. Again, this is not coverage that the medical professional or health-care practitioner should thoughtlessly reject when buying automobile insurance.

Tip: By failing to check once a year, you might be overpaying for some insurance needs. For example, get quotes online and approach your current insurer about lowering their rate when coverage and quality of insurers are comparable. Also mention life changes, such as an adult child no longer needing auto insurance or a new home security system. Other discounts can typically be had for school-age drivers with good grades or for those who take a defensive-driving class. And, those with older vehicles worth under $1000–$3000 should consider dropping comprehensive and collision coverage. For example, school-age drivers with good grades can save up to 25% on average, depending on the company and the state. Defensive-driving classes can yield about 10% savings depending on the state. Using the national average annual auto insurance payment of $797, these discounts could yield annual savings of about $199.25 and $79.70, respectively. And, dropping some coverage on an old car could bring savings of 15–40%, although you should not drop liability insurance on your car. Of course, there's always the option of switching to a higher deductible—increasing a homeowner's deductible to $1000 from $500, for instance, can save 25% on annual premiums. This strategy amounts to annual savings of $244.50 based on the national average premium of $978 in 2011, the latest year the statistic is available from the Insurance Institute.

3.2.2.5 Most Expensive Cars to Insure in 2015

1. Nissan GT-R Track Edition	$3169
2. BMW M6	$3065
3. Mercedes-Benz CL550 4MATIC AWD	$3019
4. Mercedes-Benz SLS AMG GT	$2986
5. Porsche Panamera Turbo S	$2970
6. Audi R8 5.2 Spyder Quattro	$2917
7. Mercedes-Benz G63 AMG	$2887
8. Audi A8 L 6.3 Quattro	$2869
9. Jaguar XKR Supercharged	$2854
10. Jaguar XK	$2610

Source: Edmunds.com.

3.2.2.6 Automobile Leasing*

The decision of whether to lease or purchase a new vehicle is one of the most important choices for car-shopping physicians to make. There are many important differences between the two, which can help you make your choice:

Monthly payments: Monthly lease payments are always lower than they would be if you purchased the vehicle. That's because you only have to pay for the vehicle's depreciation and additional rent charges. The depreciation estimate is based on the assumption of a certain amount of miles per year and proper maintenance of the vehicle itself.

Sales tax: Typically, drivers who lease a vehicle will only pay sales or use tax on their monthly payments and any capitalized cost reduction. This means less sales tax paid over a longer period. When purchasing a vehicle, sales tax is paid on the full purchase price (although the value of your trade-in is often excluded from this amount).

Who owns the vehicle: During a lease, the leasing company maintains ownership of the vehicle. At the end of a lease, you can choose to renew your lease, purchase the vehicle, or return it to the dealership and pay any associated costs. Purchasing a vehicle means that you are the owner whenever you make your final payment.

Warranty coverage: All vehicle warranties cover terms of 36 months or less, which means it's likely that your full lease term will be covered. This helps ensure fixed costs of driving over that period. If you finance a vehicle, your warranty will expire after a certain period, and your costs of driving will be variable.

* From Leasing vs. Buying a Car (comparing the two major finance choices in car buying), ConsumerReports.org.

Trading vehicles: Drivers who lease have the option to change cars whenever their lease term is up by simply entering into a new lease. Purchasing a vehicle makes it more difficult to change vehicles frequently, since you will be paying for the full cost of the vehicle and the depreciation, including any unexpected depreciation (in a lease, the risk of unexpected depreciation is carried by the lessor).

In a recent study, *Consumer Reports* noted that over the first 5 years of ownership, the median car costs more than $9100 a year to own. However, if you keep the vehicle for 8 years, this cost can be significantly decreased to an average of $7800 per year. So, keep the clunker as long as you can—until the repair bills outweigh the cost of a new car.

Overheard in the Advisor's Lounge

How Much Will a Ticket Raise My Car Insurance Rates?

Be careful out there! A GMAC survey revealed that one in five drivers would not pass the written driver's test if they took it today. And, getting a ticket will raise your car insurance rate, but by how much? The survey found that reckless driving triggers the highest hike—an average increase of 22%—yet many drivers aren't even sure what constitutes reckless driving. Depending on state laws, reckless driving can be defined as driving over 80 mph, driving too fast for weather conditions, or knowingly driving in a way that endangers others.

Jay Smith
Insurance.com
Foster City, California

3.3 UMBRELLA LIABILITY INSURANCE OVERVIEW

Umbrella policies should be considered any time a doctor has substantial current income or has accumulated a sizable estate, and is concerned about asset protection from potential litigation. Umbrella policies vary greatly in structure, so care should be taken to examine all of the various aspects of the policy carefully. Not only do umbrella policies vary in

THE PROPERTY AND CASUALTY INSURANCE AGENT

A good property and casualty (P&C) insurance agent is needed to protect your home, medical practice, and business. The P&C agent should have an array of carriers with which the policy can be placed. One should not hesitate to place different types of coverage with different insurers. Most insurance companies will offer a discount if you place multiple coverages with them. However, this may not be as beneficial as insuring each need with a specialist. But, P&C agents are not fiduciaries; they do not work for you. Rather, they work for their company on a sales commission basis.

structure, but they can also be arranged with many different endorsements to meet the specific needs of the doctor. A few examples would be the following:

- The addition of personal injury coverage (to include libel, slander, and defamation of character)
- Incidental business pursuits (to include coverage to personal automobiles where the business activity was incidental and not the primary purpose of the use of the car)
- The broadening of personal automobile coverage (to the insured regardless of whose vehicle he/she was driving and the coverage afforded that vehicle)

3.4 LIFETIME (VIATICAL AND SENIOR) SETTLEMENTS

A lifetime settlement occurs when a life insurance policy owner sells his/her life insurance policy to a company that specializes (and speculates) in purchasing life policies as an investment. Lifetime settlements began as viatical settlements and were originally created in the late 1980s as a way to provide HIV-infected individuals with much-needed additional income to pay for their increasing medical expenses or for experimental drug treatment. Viatical settlements expanded quickly to include any terminally ill policy owner. Later, they evolved into acceptance of any elderly policy owner.

In the past, when a policy owner determined that a particular policy no longer served a purpose, it could be surrendered for any existing cash value, or merely lapsed without value. Now, the policy owner can sell it to a lifetime settlement company as another alternative. From the perspective of the investor, purchasing a viatical is similar to buying a zero-coupon bond with an uncertain maturity date. However, an annual maintenance fee is payable, i.e., the policy premium. The return depends on the seller's life expectancy and when he/she dies.

3.4.1 HISTORY

A U.S. Supreme Court decision from 1911 provides the legal basis for viatical settlements. In *Grigsby v. Russell*, 222 U.S. 149 (1911), Dr. A.H. Grigsby treated a patient named John C. Burchard. Mr. Burchard, being in need of a particular surgical operation, offered to sell Dr. Grigsby his life insurance policy in return for $100 and for agreeing to pay the remaining premiums. Dr. Grigsby agreed, and as a result, the first viatical settlement transaction was created. When Mr. Burchard died, Dr. Grigsby attempted to collect the benefits. An executor of Burchard's estate challenged Dr. Grigsby in appeals court and won. The case eventually reached the U.S. Supreme Court, where Justice Oliver Wendell Holmes Jr., delivered the opinion of the court. He stated in a relevant part, "So far as reasonable safety permits, it is desirable to give to life policies the ordinary characteristics of property. To deny the right to sell except to persons having such an interest is to diminish appreciably the value of the contract in the owner's hands." It is this *property* characteristic that precludes inclusion of this insurance product in the preceding life insurance chapter.

The Supreme Court's decision set forth the fundamental principle upon which the viatical settlement and, later, the life settlement industry were based: a life insurance policy is private property, which can be assigned at the will of the owner. Viatical settlements were rare for almost eight decades until the onset of the AIDS epidemic.

Unfortunately, early improper activities among a few bad actors produced a fear among consumers regarding viatical settlements. Life insurers became concerned about individuals purchasing policies purely for speculative purposes. Today, many states regulate viatical and life settlements, and many more are developing legislation and regulations. As of June 2011, the states that do not regulate viatical settlements are Wyoming, South Dakota, Missouri, Alabama, and South Carolina. All other states regulate viatical settlements. As lifetime settlements become more popular, as both an investment and a settlement option, more attention and scrutiny from a number of regulators can be expected.

Overheard in the Advisor's Lounge

A New Software Program

The new *Life Settlement NumberCruncher* program by Professor Stephen Leimberg, JD, and Mike Weinberg, JD, AEP, is a tool that helps evaluate whether to keep or settle a policy. It helps address the numerical component of the decision to retain or sell the policy. The program also helps fulfill professional and, perhaps, fiduciary responsibilities to give well-reasoned responses regarding an offer to purchase a policy or if one is asked later why a policy wasn't recommended.

Donald Kelley
WealthManagement.com

3.4.2 Mechanism of Action

A lifetime settlement company may purchase a policy for a percentage of its death benefit value. If the policy owner would not receive more money through this sale than he/she would through simply surrendering the policy, then the lifetime settlement concept should be dropped. The price set by the lifetime settlement company will depend on the insured's age and medical condition. The lower the projected life expectancy, the higher the price paid by the company. To receive 40–80% of a life insurance policy's death benefit while still alive could be very helpful to a family struggling with medical bills and other debts. Once a policy is purchased by a lifetime settlement company, the company becomes the owner of the policy and continues to pay the premiums until the insured dies. The settlement company then receives the full death benefit. The company's profit is the death proceeds minus the amount they paid to the original owner.

As a result of the Health Insurance Portability and Accountability Act (HIPAA) of 1996, the money received by the insured in a viatical settlement may not be subject to income taxes. If the insured is terminally or chronically ill, the money is generally considered an early payment of the death benefit and is not income taxable. If the insured, however, is healthy and just doesn't need the policy any longer, any payment received over the insured's original cost basis will be taxed as ordinary income.

Beware! Lifetime settlements are not always as attractive as they might seem. When such a company purchases a life contract, it is wagering on the death of the insured. The faster the insured dies, the more profit for that company. The various state insurance departments have been slow to respond to this growing trend, and regulation of this activity is sporadic.

So, what should the medical professional or health-care practitioner do if approached about a lifetime settlement? The best thing to do is to keep a number of guidelines in mind.

- Call your state insurance department to find out if the settlement company is licensed or regulated in your state.
- Consult your attorney or financial advisor. Review the current tax ramifications of the recommendation. If you are terminally ill, the viatical settlement will probably be exempt from federal income tax as a result of HIPAA.
- Make sure you contact a number of different settlement companies. Settlements can vary greatly between different companies, and the Viatical Association of America encourages potential "viators" to get at least three different offers before selling.
- Request that the settlement company set up an escrow account for you when you accept the settlement, so the funds will be assured. Any reputable firm should not have a problem with this request.
- Talk with your current beneficiaries. Your decision may affect their lives as well, and if they will be saddled with large, unpaid medical bills upon your death, a viatical or senior settlement may not be the best decision.
- A viatical settlement will likely affect any financial need-based public assistance you may otherwise be eligible for.
- Such settlements are normally fair game for creditors.
- Check into alternatives. Find out how much cash is available in your life insurance policy without selling it, and check if your policy has an accelerated death benefit. An accelerated death benefit will typically allow terminally ill insureds to access a portion of the total death benefit (usually 50%) while still alive.

Remember, unlike a viatical settlement, the insurance policy is still owned by the original policy owner. Thus, when the insured passes away, the named beneficiary will receive the remaining death benefit. This results in all of the death benefit going to the original parties of the contract rather than a viatical company getting a piece of the pie.

CASE MODEL

Dr. Dread has recently learned that he has an inoperable brain tumor. His doctor has given him 6 months to 1 year to live.

He knows that his health insurance will cover most of the bills but realizes his wife would have to pay for the difference from his estate. Although they have not saved excessively, he does own multiple life insurance policies, totaling over $2 million in death benefits. His wife has an excellent job, and they do not depend on his income to survive financially.

After talking it over with his wife, Dr. Dread decides to opt for a viatical settlement on $1 million worth of insurance. He shops his policies through a number of different viatical firms and receives an offer of 70% of the death benefit from Viaticals-R-Us. Dr. Dread can then use the $700,000 to take himself and his wife on the vacation they always dreamed of, knowing his wife will still have $1 million in death benefits to cover any outstanding medical bills, if needed, or supplement her income.

So, despite the bad experience of some investors, viatical settlements remain a valuable tool for the personal financial management of many ill people.

3.5 CONCLUSION

Keep in mind there is a difference between using an agent or broker for these insurance needs and services, and using a Certified Medical Planner. An agent or broker will not normally charge a fee for service. Embedded commissions are usually included in the product sale. A Certified Medical Planner is a fiduciary and will generally charge a set amount, depending on the complexity of the situation being analyzed. Fees of Certified Financial Planners are variable depending on individual certificant transparency (fees or commissions, or a hybrid method) as fiduciary standards are generally *aspirational*.

Lastly, an insurance policy is merely a contract or legal machination; it is not personal. It is just business. So, as your life and practice evolve, an in-depth reanalysis should periodically be performed. This will ensure an accurate, up-to-date plan for the future.

3.6 COLLABORATE

Discuss this chapter online with others at http://www.medicalexecutivepost.com.

ACKNOWLEDGMENTS

To Cathy D. Belteau, CFP, CLU, ChFC, FLMI; Philip E. Taylor, CLU, ChFC, FLMI; Matthew Lawrence DeSantos, JD; Matthew D. Rogers, CFP, CLU, ChFC; Hope Rachel Hetico, RN, MHA, CMP; and Lon Jefferies, MBA, CFP, of http://networthadvice.com.

FURTHER READINGS

Abraham, KS: *Insurance Law and Regulation*. Foundation Press, New York, 2010.

Dogra, A: "Four Things Everyone Should Know about End of Life Planning," http://www.KevinMD, March 9, 2014.

Jensen, JA and Leimberg, SR: "Stranger-Owned Life Insurance," *ACTEC Journal*, Fall 2007, p. 110

Kinder, J and Kinder, G: *Secrets of Successful Insurance Sales*. Napolean Hill Foundation, Hammond, IN, 2012.

Kunreuther, HC and Pauly, MV: *Insurance and Behavioral Economics*. Cambridge University Press, Cambridge, Cambridgeshire CB2-8RV, 2013.

Magner, JC and Leimberg, SR: "Life Settlement Transactions: Important Tax and Legal Issues to Consider," *Estate Planning*, April 2007.

Marcinko, DE and Hetico, HR: *Dictionary of Health Insurance and Managed Care*. Springer Publishing, New York, 2008.

Muldowney, TA, Cook, GA, and Marcinko, DE: Establishing a Solid Foundation of Insurance Planning: The Bedrock of Life and Medical Practice. In Marcinko, DE (editor): *Comprehensive Financial Planning Strategies for Doctors and Advisors: Best Practices from Leading Consultants and Certified Medical Planners*™. Productivity Press, Boca Raton, FL, 2015.

Trivium: *Property & Casualty Insurance License Exam Study Guide: Test Prep and Practice for the Property and Casualty Exam*. Test Prep, Inc., Houston, TX, 2015.

4 Rethinking Risk Management for Physicians

Beyond Professional Liability Insurance

Ike Devji

CONTENTS

Most of us implement some form of asset protection every day without thinking of it. We create limited liability corporations (LLCs) for various enterprises; buy life, health, disability, and car insurance; lock our home doors, use our burglar alarms, and change our Internet and computer account passwords; to name just a few common examples.

4.1 WHAT EXACTLY IS ASSET PROTECTION?

Asset protection can understandably be a confusing term for medical professionals as well as consumers, especially given that it is currently a fashionable marketing phrase used by everyone from insurance agents and annuity salesmen to risk managers and loss prevention specialists, and a wide variety of both lawyer and nonlawyer "promoters" advancing various legal and financial schemes of subjective and dubious value.

> For our purposes, the term "asset protection" refers to the holistic legal practice of proactively managing assets, risk, and liabilities, both personal and professional.

It cannot be stressed strongly enough that prevention always beats treatment with legal and financial exposures. The best asset protection is always preventative and proactive. Timing is crucial and of the essence; you may be legally unable to act (fraudulent conveyance, voidable transaction, etc.) or, at best, end up with results that are more expensive and less predictable if you wait and try to manage *crisis* instead of *risk*. Even the best asset protection strategies *will fail* against a known and preexisting exposure, and create additional financial and legal risk up to the level of being *criminal*.

There are many books and theories on asset protection, with an even wider range of actual skill and legal experience behind them. Just as there may be more than one way to effectively treat a medical condition, there may be more than one specific way to address a particular asset or exposure. Regardless of differences in informed professional opinion on how to achieve a particular result, the best advice, continuing medical education (CME) presentations, and books and articles on asset protection and risk management typically come from attorneys that have actually done the planning for a large number of medical clients for a long period of time with consistent results.

4.2 WHY ISN'T THIS CHAPTER ABOUT SPECIFIC LEGAL STRUCTURES?

Frankly, because it's more important to talk about doctors than attorneys! Don't misunderstand; having the right legal tools in place, including estate planning and business and personal legal structures, is vital for physicians and the substance of what asset protection attorneys do for a living. That said, the majority of asset protection books and articles written by attorneys tend to focus on either specific legal structures they'd like to extol or on defamation of the virtues of works written by traditional estate planners. In particular, they are often very trust heavy and attempt to combine sophisticated multigenerational tax and estate planning with creditor protection. Others extol the virtues of complex (and very fact-specific) structures, like captive insurance companies and private placement insurance, or failingly simple ones, like those advanced by LLC promoters who weave fairytales of secrecy, tax avoidance, and other magic powers with little effect or professional liability, as most promoters are not lawyers.

Furthermore, let's assume that a particular strategy being advanced is objectively sound. Speaking to a wide and diverse group of people about a very fact-specific tool (for instance, some specific form of trust) is a lot like asking a doctor, "What do you think about surgery?" The best answer is "it depends…" for whom and for what comorbidities… The list is long and specific. A deep discussion of most legal tools outside the context of a specific individual's fact pattern can be misleading, if not simply wrong, for those hearing the message.

Nevertheless, a few of the basic factors that should be considered by doctors and their advisors in determining the fit of a specific legal tool are as follows:

- The specific result desired
- The client's need for liquidity
- The client's age and family structure
- The complexity and expense of the structures, both at setup and ongoing
- The tax implications and reporting requirements of the structure
- The long-term history and effectiveness of the structure
- All the legitimate business purposes of the structure
- A thorough understanding of when such structures have failed and why
- The planner's own experience level with a specific set of tools

Even if these risk-management strategies do achieve some result with a specific set of assets, the planners almost universally fail to counsel clients on the minutia and proactive risk avoidance machinations that could keep the client out of harm's way in the first place. As an advisor that helps manage this specific continuum for several thousand physicians, the best work that lawyers practicing in this area do is not *just* making you a hard target if the unthinkable happens; it's first and foremost about helping to keep you from ever having to use those tools in the first place. As such, this chapter will focus on a limited number of specific and actionable risk-management issues that you can address today as a key step in protecting your medical practice, clinic, and/or tangible and financial assets.

Overheard in the Doctor's Lounge

How Much Insurance Is Enough?

I currently have no fewer than 10 separate insurance policies associated with my plastic surgery practice. I understand very little about the policies other than that somebody at some point told me I needed each and every one of them, and each made sense when I bought it. But, I often wonder:

- Am I overinsured and thus wasting money?
- Am I underinsured and thus at risk for a liability disaster?

I never really had the means of answering these questions.

Lloyd M. Krieger, MD, MBA
Beverly Hills, California

4.2.1 Core Universal Concepts about Wealth Preservation and Asset Protection

Think of asset protection the way you teach patients about wellness; it's a system and lifestyle that requires some discipline and good habits in four core areas.

1. A culture of good habits, procedures, accountability, and compliance
   Avoiding or eliminating higher-risk behavior often starts with having good, professionally drafted, legally compliant policies and procedures on a variety of risk-management issues and consistently *implementing and enforcing* them uniformly. There is no more dangerous and ineffective manager than one who is conflict averse or who wants to be everyone's friend. Leadership requires that you help everyone be and do their best by managing them actively and creating expectations and boundaries.
2. Proactively managing all your predictable risks, not just those related to medical malpractice
   We won't dwell on this issue beyond noting that medical malpractice lawsuits are still a real threat, and no matter what various experts tell you about statistics, how many actually go on trial, future reductions due to the Patient Protection and Affordable Care Act (PPACA), etc., we all have seen the devastating first-hand effects of these claims. And, no matter how remote a risk may be, what if it *is* you? Are you emotionally, legally, and financially prepared[1] for an adverse claim or judgment that could potentially stop your income, cost you your hospital privileges or practice, trigger a payer audit, and/or take seven figures off your life's work and net worth? Most physicians are not.
   That said, malpractice liability is not the only, or even the most predictable and recurring, exposure you face. You are a physician, but you are also potentially an executive, a parent, a business owner, a compliance officer, a breadwinner, the driver of vehicle, the owner of a home, and you wear a variety of other hats you may not even think about. Having experienced help in properly identifying as many of these other, nonprofession liability risks as possible, and addressing them proactively both *personally* and *professionally*, is a key part of any defensive strategy.
3. Insurance, all the right kinds and in the right amounts
   Insurance needs to be thought of as an *insurance program*, not a line item, and works as a system of overlapping coverage. Most physicians have an overly simplified vision of what they should have in place, mainly, some form of professional liability insurance, typically a "1–3" policy, meaning $1 million per occurrence with a $3 million aggregate. Many attorneys advise physicians to buy, "every dollar you can afford, then have a back-up plan." This goes far beyond your professional liability or malpractice insurance and includes half a dozen or more varieties of specialty insurance that can be well covered with the help of a top-notch property and casualty (P&C) insurance agent. A word of caution: having an asset protection plan consisting of putting defensive legal tools in place without the complementary insurance, commonly known as "going bare," is never the best idea and, if nothing else, subjects you to the exposure of massive legal fees for defense costs, which are easily six figures.

4. Defensive legal structures

   There will inevitably be gaps in the number of things that can be covered or the dollar limit to which you can insure yourself. Do not ever rely on your umbrella policy alone as effective universal coverage. This is where all the trusts, LLCs, partnerships, corporate structures, and estate-planning techniques that attorneys are fond of come into play. You must have good policies and procedures with insurance against different instances in case those fail, and have a backup plan if the first two layers fail.

Remember that asset protection is fact specific, and use your facts. Every doctor seeking asset protection must have a thorough review of his/her own assets, have his/her personal and professional risks identified, and have tools and solutions implemented by a qualified and experienced professional: in other words, the familiar pattern of examination, diagnosis, and *then* personalized treatment. There may be a reasonable and proven course of treatment for any particular problem, but your advisors should always know what the problems are before they start proposing specific solutions.

4.2.2 What Are the Most Common Mistakes Doctors (and Their Advisors) Make with Asset Protection?

1. *Doing nothing.* Asset protection can be described as "net-worth insurance," and like insurance, you have the best, most effective and legally supportable options available to you when you implement the planning *before* a crisis exists. You cannot insure a car after an accident occurs, and similarly, you must act proactively on the issues covered below. Attorneys regularly get calls from doctors after something

COMMON RISK FACTORS FOR PHYSICIANS

- Do you and or any family members drive a vehicle?
- Do you have employees?
- Do you have a professional malpractice exposure?
- Do you have a legal responsibility to protect medical and/or financial data?
- Are you married, and do you have assets not protected by a prenuptial agreement?
- Do you have a current tax obligation?
- Do you have children?
- Do you own a business?
- Are you a board member, officer, or director of a corporation, foundation, or religious or educational organization?
- Do you engage in activities like hunting, flying, boating, etc.?
- Do you have business or domestic partners whose actions create joint and several liabilities for you?
- Do you have personal guarantees on real estate or for business loans?
- Do you have tail liability for professional services performed in the past?
- Have you made specific legal or financial representations that others have relied upon in a business context?
- What kind and what dollar amount of insurance and legal planning have you implemented against these exposures?

bad has happened and hear the same story about how they always meant to take care of this but just didn't have the time and worked too many hours to get it done. So, if you work hard and are not acting to protect the results of that labor for yourself and your family, you need to put a greater value on your own efforts and act now, especially given the changes in physician compensation and profitability over the last 10 years. Most doctors say that the money they made the last decade was harder earned and of a lower profit margin than what they made the decade before. Imagine having to replace that effort with *the next* 10 years of earnings.

2. *Not thinking that your wealth deserves protection.* This is a common mistake made by both doctors and, more surprisingly, by other professionals like lawyers, certified public accountants (CPAs), and financial advisors. These advisors often tell clients that they are "not rich enough" to worry about asset protection planning and that that only those with a net worth north of $5 million or even $10 million need to worry about it. This advice is dangerous, especially for those in the autumn of their careers. What you have earned is important to you, and there are basic defensive risk-management moves that can be made at nearly any net-worth level. For example, how would you answer these questions?
   a. Are you financially and legally prepared for a lawsuit that either is uncovered by liability insurance or may produce a verdict above the limits you carry?
   b. Do you have assets that would be difficult or impossible to replace given your age, health, current compensation rates, and economic conditions?
   c. If you lost some significant portion of everything you have worked for today, are you at an age, earning level, and financial condition that will allow you to maintain your family's goals and expenses and replace that wealth?
3. *Relying on traditional estate planning, also known as (aka) the emperor's new trust.* "I've already taken care of this. My home, cars and investments are all titled in my trust." This is something asset protection planners hear often. A transfer of these assets to a vehicle like an estate-planning trust, or more specifically, a revocable living trust, is not effective asset protection and leaves assets exposed to your creditors during your lifetime. We distinguish estate planning, as important as it is, as *death planning*. What has been done about your *life planning* and the exposures you face every day as a practicing physician, employer, executive, car driver, parent (with kids driving your car), or property owner?
4. *Using any particular tool as a catchall.* Correctly implementing a tool like an LLC as a barrier between yourself and your investments but failing to adequately segregate and subdivide assets so that they are protected from both the owner and each other is self-defeating. A common example is the case of the physician property owner who has a single LLC that is legally and financially responsible for multiple properties that have different levels of liability, equity, and use. As an example, if you have $10,000 down on three properties in a single LLC, it's probably OK, because total exposure is theoretically limited to $30,000, the value of the LLC's assets. On the other hand, if you have five pieces of real estate with a total equity position of six or seven figures, some paid for, some all debt, including an office condo, a rental home, a triplex, a lot, and a commercial strip mall, grouping them that way could be fatal. Any exposure at a new, zero-equity property could wipe out your entire portfolio of paid-for or partially paid-for properties. Assets should always be divided based on risk, use, and equity, among many other factors.

5. *Not using the right tool for the job.* Certain protection vehicles have great use for specific business functions supported by statute, tax law, and case history. You and your advisor must have a good handle on these issues and know what pros and cons each entity presents, how it will affect access to your liquidity and future options, and what it will take to maintain and support that stated business purpose, as a start, to the detail required. One specific example is the common misuse of what is commonly referred to as a family limited partnership (FLP) to own the client's personal residence. What is the *legitimate business purpose* of using a vehicle that is most often created (and that can be very effectively used) for "investment management and wealth transfer" to own your personally occupied residence? If you're not paying commercially reasonable rent and maintaining some legitimate business purpose, *you don't have one.* In litigation, expect the adverse party (or worse, the Internal Revenue Service [IRS]) to successfully argue that you are using the FLP as a personal piggy bank in way that is not legally distinct and immune from your personal assets and liabilities.
6. *Infecting your plan and assets with unnecessary and unrelated liability.* Attorneys routinely see doctors and their advisors move liability-generating property and activities (like buying or leasing personal vehicles) into structures like an LLC or S corporation that is their primary business or into an entity like an FLP that is holding safe and attractive assets like cash, stocks, bonds, and other assets. If you lease or own your vehicle through your business, your CPA has likely told you that it's a good tax deduction and is probably right. From a liability perspective, however, it's penny-wise and pound-foolish. You have linked the liability of the most dangerous thing you likely do on a repeated daily basis, driving a car, to either the source of your wealth (your practice) or, in the example of your FLP, the place where you stored your liquid wealth.
7. *Relying on "gifting" to spouse and relatives.* In another common example of too little too late, transferring significant assets to your spouse and/or children, especially *after* something has happened, will not protect your assets from a lawsuit and simply opens up another level of liability. As popular as this method is with doctors due to its relatively low cost and DIY ethos, it simply exchanges one person's liability for another's and, when done right, makes a real, binding, and permanent legal transfer of the title to your property to someone else. We've seen disastrous results from this strategy upon divorce, when the person who gifted the assets is estranged, has a substance abuse issue, and/or dies or has their own significant liability.

Example 1

Let's suppose that you transfer all of your assets to your 18-year-old daughter, who causes an auto accident. Several other cars are involved in the accident, and multiple injuries, a fatality, and significant property damage are incurred. Chances are high that the other parties will come looking for the driver with the deepest pockets. If your daughter "owns" your house and business, a sympathetic jury will undoubtedly take the possession away from her in order to teach her a lesson about reckless driving. The same holds true for spouses, parents, and even friends. Also, gifting is limited to about $14,500 annually, per spouse, per donee. Gifts over that amount must be documented with a gift tax return. Failing to do so will result in you having to answer the following question: "Are you lying about the date and validity of this transfer, or did you commit tax fraud by making the transfer and not filing the return?" This is clearly a bad place to be in a time of need, and often, it happens under oath in litigation discovery proceedings.

8. *Using amateur tools like "friendly liens."* Another common play that targets doctors is when promoters of LLC mills set up LLCs that you or a friendly party own and those entities record a "lien" against some valuable asset, most typically real estate. While validly recorded and executed liens can provide a great deterrent against creditors, they have to be backed by a legitimate exchange of value. Your brother's Nevada LLC that holds a lien on your home for most of its value should have included some exchange or "consideration" roughly equal to the amount of the lien. "Your brother has a $400,000 lien against the $500,000 home you live in? OK...then where is the record of the $400,000 (or some other equivalent value) he gave you, as a bank would have in a real secured loan? He didn't actually give you anything in return? He doesn't actually have $400,000 in the bank to give you for that *alleged secured line of credit*? Great, we'll take the house."

4.3 EMPLOYMENT RISK MANAGEMENT

The recurring risk of employment-related lawsuits can be substantially mitigated by following some simple steps. As previously mentioned, a good asset protection plan has multiple layers, including the management of predictable and recurring risks.

4.3.1 Employee Handbooks

According to a recent Equal Employment Opportunity Commission (EEOC) press release,[2] the agency levied nearly $400 million in fines against employers in 2013 alone. This number is the largest collection year in the history of the EEOC, which receives close to 100,000 complaints a year.

4.3.2 What Are All These Lawsuits Actually About?

The EEOC lists the causes of these complaints, in order, as follows:

1. *Retaliation* claims under all the statutes (roughly 40%)
2. *Racial discrimination* (roughly 33%)
3. Sex discrimination, including sexual harassment and pregnancy discrimination (roughly 27%)
4. Disability-based discrimination (about 25%)

Both race and disability discrimination claims have *increased* as a percentage of all charges filed.

There are two layers of distinct financial exposure for physician executives to be aware of with employment-related lawsuits. First, the awards themselves can be financially devastating, with sexual harassment *verdicts*, as one common example, regularly reaching hundreds of thousands of dollars; the national average sexual harassment award is estimated to be as high as $530,000. Second, the *costs of legal defense* alone could put many medical practices out of business. The costs for competent legal defense regularly reach six figures without including the potential dollar value of any award that may be obtained against the physician.

4.3.3 The First Layer of Defense: A Professionally Drafted Employment Manual

Despite this well-known exposure, you may be surprised to find that many, if not most, medical practices fall into one of three basic categories.

1. They have *no* formal manuals.
2. They have generic-form manuals of questionable legality and fit that are not specific to the practice and how it operates, often obtained free from the Internet or from a doctor friend in another state.
3. They have a custom manual but have not implemented it, distributed it to the staff in a formal way, or consistently enforced it. Just *having* it is not enough.

4.3.4 What Does Having an Employment Manual and Policy Guide Do for MDs?

Your employment manual is a vital first line of defense and a compliance guidebook for both management and employees, and prescribes the policies and procedures for the vast majority of employment-related issues at your practice. According to Paul Edwards, CEO of CEDR Solutions, an employment law resource that specializes in medical practices (personal communication),

> An employee handbook is also your first defensive tool in deterring and fighting employment lawsuits. Policies that are well written and in compliance with all state and federal laws can prevent 90% of legal exposures because an employee or manager was not aware of or did not understand a rule or regulation. A strong handbook will also often deter aggressive contingency-fee attorneys who know it is much more difficult to fight and win when a medical practice has implemented written, legally compliant policies.

4.3.5 Why Your Manual Needs to Be Custom Drafted

Four key legal areas require custom drafting in an employment manual:

1. It should comply with and cite the laws of your state. Employment laws vary from state to state. New York and California, as just two specific examples, are more onerous for employers than others. Citing the wrong laws can make your practice noncompliant or subject you to rules that are more onerous than they would have been under the correct choice of law. Remember, if it's in your manual, you are required to follow it, even if the manual is harsher than the actual law.
2. It should be specific to the number of employees you have. Your compliance burdens and legal obligations change with the number of employees you have, so the difference between 49 versus 50 employees (think PPACA), or even 14 versus 15 employees, is very significant from a legal standpoint.

3. It should be specific to the needs and realties of a *medical practice*. In addition to all the general business law issues, you have many additional, unique compliance burdens as a *medical employer* and significantly extended liability for the actions of your employees on issues like Health Insurance Portability and Accountability Act (HIPAA) compliance, credentialing, and many others, which should be specifically and carefully addressed.
4. Your manual should reflect the actual and desired culture of your practice. Every practice and its needs and expectations are different; your manual and polices should match how your practice actually runs and help conform behavior to your ideals.

4.4 EMPLOYMENT PRACTICES LIABILITY INSURANCE

The second layer of employment risk liability management you must have in place is commonly referred to as employment practices liability insurance (EPLI).

4.4.1 What Is EPLI?

EPLI insurance is specialty P&C coverage that can help protect you against both the risks of employee lawsuits against your practice and liability you may bear for the vicarious liability of your employees under the legal theory of *respondeat superior*, or *let the master answer*. One unique feature of the better polices (they are not all the same) is that some of them even cover certain "intentional acts," an important gap in most insurance coverage that you must understand and manage.

It's easy to think of employment liability with tunnel vision and to assume that we are only talking about an employee suing you. As great as that risk is, you are also liable for a variety of acts and omissions, or failures to act, committed by your employees, including the following:

1. How they interact with patients and other third parties, including in the delivery of care
2. How they interact with each other (again, the employment manual is a key control on this issue that can set polices on language, dress codes, harassment, and many other issues)
3. Actions they take while on the job, including while driving and treating patients, and creating risky physical conditions on the property through acts or omissions (e.g., the wet, slippery floor they ignored or created)
4. Anything else that a plaintiff's lawyer can think of to link the claim to your deep pocket instead of what is likely your employee's substantially smaller one

4.4.1.1 Some Unfortunate and Very Real Examples

1. Midwest doctor sued when long-time trusted employee and licensed massage therapist molests 17-year-old girl while performing physician-ordered massage therapy.
2. Florida doctor sued for employee's auto accident involving fatality when employee is sent to pick up lunch for office birthday party.

3. And perhaps the most shocking example, doctor sued for discriminatory conduct of office manager faces $500,000 demand from EEOC. The claim was not by the actually aggrieved employees who were discriminated against. Rather, it was filed by the *discriminating employee, that's right, the bad guy*, when the physician–practice owner learned of his actions and fired him. That employee then went to the EEOC and made a large number of false claims with the help of another disgruntled employee who had also been properly and legally terminated for cause.

4.4.1.2 Aren't These Issues Covered by My Other Existing Insurance Policies?

In most cases, no, and if they are covered as riders under another policy, the coverage usually isn't enough. In fact, most don't provide any coverage at all. Those that do offer EPLI through special riders or bundled programs don't have high enough limits to cover the costs typically involved. Your EPLI coverage should be $1 million as a minimum, ideally more, not the $50,000 or $100,000 we might find in a base policy, if at all. Six figures in legal defense expenses and six-figure awards are now both routine, and that assumes you face only a single plaintiff. The exposure on a class-action suit or one with multiple plaintiffs is a multiple of those figures.

EPLI insurance addresses specific risks and financial and legal gaps that are not adequately covered by the three basic polices we assume you've had counsel in properly implementing already:

1. A medical malpractice insurance policy of *at least* $1 million per occurrence
2. A worker's comp policy (aka employee hurt on the job coverage)
3. A general liability policy (covers slip and fall and other injuries or nonmedical liability related to general function of your business)

4.4.1.3 What Kinds of Employment Claims Are Covered and, Perhaps More Importantly, Are Excluded?

This is a policy-specific question, so the insurance agent you work with must be knowledgeable about the all options available in this area and should give you a very specific list of what is covered and what is not, in writing. Always keep in mind that even the best EPLI is not a license to sin and break labor laws and that you should follow the law and the policies in your manual. Violations that are repeated, *implemented by* and *known to* the organization itself, are often explicitly excluded from your EPLI carrier's liability.

There is an important distinction if the harm complained of is by an employee or manager who is outside the scope of the organization's policies (like the ones found in the manual) and was *unknown* to the employer. In other words, if this is a result of an individual employee or manager generating liability for your practice by not following the rules, it probably will help. Issues commonly covered include various types of harassment and discrimination (sex, age, race, disability, etc.), as well as some general civil torts, like defamation and intentional infliction of emotional distress, which are often related to other claims.

On the other hand—if you have *institutionalized* illegal or actionable employment practices, whether overtly or by failing to correct known problems, EPLI insurance is unlikely to cover it! What is excluded in many cases falls under some sort of institutionalized pattern of an illegal employment practice that is known, open, and part of your practice's policies.

Retaliatory claims and actions seem to be one issue that insurance companies increasingly exclude, and there are a number of other strict liability–type statutory liabilities that may or may not be covered as well for violations of federal or state law. Again, this points out why having a good manual that helps ensure that your practice is compliant on issues like fair wage and labor laws, Consolidated Omnibus Budget Reconciliation Act (COBRA) insurance requirements, the Family Medical Leave Act (FMLA), harassment, and other human resources–related (HR-related) details is so important.

Attorneys often remind doctors that *just* insuring is typically not enough protection against the wide variety of risk this chapter addresses. As vital a line of defense as EPLI insurance is, both *consent-to-settle clauses* (where the insurance company can unilaterally decide to settle out of a claim rather than fight) and *defense-inside-the-limits clauses* (if you have a $1 million policy and $500,000 is spent on legal costs, that leaves only $500,000 for any adverse award) in your policy can significantly reduce your protection. Employee risk requires several layers of risk management and ideally includes personal asset protection planning for medical practice owners and executives.

4.5 EMPLOYEE CLASSIFICATION RISK—THE LIABILITY OF INCORRECTLY CALLING SOMEONE A CONTRACTOR

Medical practices nationally have faced substantial legal and financial jeopardy due to the increasing number and aggressiveness of *employee classification audits* by the Department of Labor (DOL). If you have independent contractors at your practice, you must carefully review the law to make sure that they have been correctly classified as such to avoid substantial fines and both civil and even criminal legal jeopardy.

When lawyers ask how many employees a client has as part of a risk-management analysis, we often hear one of the following frightening responses from practice owners:

1. "None, we don't have to worry about that; they are all contractors."
2. Or even better, "We lease our employees, so we don't really have any employee risk."

Both of these answers are false on many issues and leave your practice substantially exposed to a variety of labor law and tax law claims, including misclassifying someone who is legally an *employee* as a *contractor*. Both are very specific legal terms of art with well-defined definitions that go far beyond "picking their own hours."

Many medical practice managers and owners also don't realize that once a violation is established in a Fair Labor Standards Act lawsuit, the burden is on the employer to prove why double damages should *not* be awarded, in which case the employer is liable for the employee's legal fees in addition to their own legal fees, costs, and penalties. Moreover, the owner of the practice and/or the executive responsible for the decisions that led to the violation can be held *personally* liable along with the company itself, regardless of laws that limit personal liability in many other contexts. Cases brought under Title VII for discrimination, as one example, require a substantial administrative process before employees can go to court. As such, a medical practice's owners, executives, and board members face significant personal jeopardy that will typically not be covered by medical malpractice, general liability, or personal umbrella insurance policies, so adequate directors' and officers' liability insurance is another vital layer in such a plan.

4.5.1 The Tax Consequences of Employee Classification Are Serious

The DOL isn't the only federal agency that has a stake in this issue; the IRS is substantially involved as well. Employment withholding taxes are a major source of both federal revenue and social security payments and are significantly harder to collect directly from contractors than they are from employers. An excellent *Forbes* magazine article[3] recently pointed out the growing scale of this exposure for employers. The DOL and the IRS are now working together under joint agreements, citing one recent government press release: "In the last two years, the Wage Hour Division has secured over $18.2 million in back wages for more than 19,000 workers where the primary reason for minimum wage or overtime violations under the Fair Labor Standards Act was that workers were not treated or classified as employees." This represents a 97% increase in collections and claims.

4.5.2 Heading Off IRS Audit Exposure by Using the Voluntary Classification Settlement Program

If you think you have an audit exposure, it is best to address it up front, i.e., call them before they call you. The Voluntary Classification Settlement Program (VCSP) is a voluntary program that provides an opportunity for taxpayers to reclassify their workers as employees[4] for employment tax purposes for future tax periods, with partial relief from previously misclassified and delinquent federal employment taxes. To participate, you must meet certain eligibility requirements and apply to participate in the VCSP by filing *Form 8952, Application for Voluntary Classification Settlement Program*, and enter into a closing agreement with the IRS.

Managing this risk requires that you have your own contracts, processes, and qualifications reviewed by an employment law specialist to determine if you have tax or labor compliance issues, and to prevent them from happening again.

4.5.3 How Is an Independent Contractor Defined?

Professionals like physicians and podiatrists, dentists and veterinarians, lawyers, accountants, contractors, and subcontractors *who are in an independent trade, business, or profession in which they offer their services to the general public* are generally qualified to act as independent contractors. Whether these people actually are independent contractors or employees depends on the specific context of an employment relationship.

One very general rule of thumb (get the advice of an accounting professional) is that an individual can be classified as an independent contractor if the employer has a right to control or direct the *result* of the work but not *what* will be done and *how* it will be done. The earnings of a person working as an independent contractor are subject to self-employment tax. An employee is generally not an independent contractor if he/she performs services that can be controlled by an employer (what will be done and how it will be done). This applies even if the employee is given freedom of action.

If an employer–employee relationship exists (regardless of what you call the relationship), the employee is not an independent contractor, and his/her earnings are generally not subject to self-employment tax. However, his/her earnings as an employee may be subject to

Federal Insurance Contribution Act (FICA) (social security tax and Medicare) and income tax withholding, for which you, as the employer, are responsible.

The IRS provides specific guidance on determining whether an individual is an independent contractor or an employee.[5] This guidance comes directly from the IRS but is not a substitute for specific tax or legal advice. Use it as a starting point on your personal list of issues to consider and a caveat on the complexity of these issues that must be professionally addressed to protect your practice and comply with tax and labor laws.

4.5.4 Determining Whether Those Providing Services Are Employees or Independent Contractors

Before you can determine how to treat payments you make for services, you must first know the business relationship that exists between you and the person performing the services. The person performing the services may be

- An independent contractor
- An employee (common-law employee)
- A statutory employee
- A statutory nonemployee

In determining whether the person providing service is an employee or an independent contractor, all information that provides evidence of the degree of control and independence must be considered.

4.5.4.1 Common-Law Rules

Facts that provide evidence of the degree of control and independence fall into three categories:

1. *Behavioral*: Does the company control or have the right to control what the worker does and how the worker does his/her job?
2. *Financial*: Are the business aspects of the worker's job controlled by the payer? (These include things like how the worker is paid, whether expenses are reimbursed, who provides tools/supplies, etc.)
3. *Type of relationship*: Are there written contracts or employee-type benefits (i.e., pension plan, insurance, vacation pay, etc.)? Will the relationship continue, and is the work performed a key aspect of the business?

Medical practices and health-care businesses must weigh all these factors when determining whether a worker is an employee or an independent contractor. Some factors may indicate that the worker is an employee, while other factors indicate that the worker is an independent contractor. There is no magic or set number of factors that makes the worker an employee or an independent contractor, and no one factor stands alone in making this determination. Also, factors that are relevant in one situation may not be relevant in another.

The key is to look at the entire relationship, consider the degree or extent of the right to direct and control, and finally, document each of the factors used in coming up with the determination.

Overheard in the Advisor's Lounge

On Asset Protection

From my perspective, asset protection is a team sport, and lawyers rely on financial advisers all the time to spot issues for clients. We do not all share the opinion that non-lawyers are incapable of giving good advice.

J. Chris Miller, JD
Alpharetta, Georgia

4.6 EMPLOYEE CREDENTIALING: LIABILITY FOR MEDICAL EMPLOYERS

Many medical practice employees, including doctors, nurses, and various clinical assistants, must be very specifically credentialed based on both the specifics of your practice and third-party payer contracts. This additional condition of employment requires a variety of credentialing compliance best practices.

4.6.1 Why Is This Such a Big Deal; What's the Worst That Could Happen?

1. Once an error is identified in any one area of your billing practices, you should expect other areas, even nonrelated ones with lower compliance burdens, to be examined.
2. You face potential civil and criminal liability for billing third-party payers that contractually require specific credentialed care providers.
3. Your practice may face a loss of revenue due to failure to comply and substantial disruption of practice cash flow if an audit or questions arise.
4. You are subject to reputational damage, stress, and substantial legal fees easily in the six-figure or seven-figure range.
5. Increased medical malpractice risk for potentially not providing the required *reasonable standard of care* if a noncredentialed employee is in the chain of treatment for an affected patient.
6. It may also potentially induce your liability insurance carriers to either completely exclude an event or reduce applicable coverage.

Although this process can be managed internally with the right training and by a variety of existing administrative staff, there is professional help available at nearly every scale, from small practices to hospitals. Many practices, especially smaller ones that don't have full-time HR managers, find that outsourcing this issue is a time-efficient and cost-efficient form of risk management of this important issue. Outside professional resources are generally known as credentialing organizations (COs), which operate under the wider banner of HR and employee background-check services. Many of these services have accredited certified provider credentialing specialists that can work with your office and staff as outsourced compliance experts.

The biggest benefit a CO can offer is that the best of them go beyond providing just a snapshot of your current credentialing; they also offer a long-range plan to help you implement and maintain it.

4.6.2 Some Advantages of Outsourcing This Issue to a Credentialing Organization

1. They manage credentialing proactively instead of reactively and can help avoid loss of time, efficiency, and revenue when, for instance, doctors or staff are taken out of the office to complete massive amounts of CME all at once on a short deadline.
2. COs are typically better equipped to respond quickly to staff changes, including the onboarding of new staff or doctors, and can help identify and verify what is required to bring any new staff into compliance.
3. They typically have software systems that are more consistent and reliable than the self-created systems implemented by most practices internally, typically Excel spreadsheets that need to be manually updated and checked.
4. Using CO software systems is often time efficient and cost-efficient in related areas, like insurance credentialing, and can help manage a variety of functions including background-check compliance, immunizations, and hospital privilege policy compliance, as just a few examples.

Risk management in this area again requires that your practice is proactive and discovers and corrects any credentialing gaps in your office before they are an unwelcome surprise discovered by a third party. The liability and financial jeopardy is ultimately that of the practice owners and managers regardless of whether you outsource to a CO or not.

4.6.3 Proactively Addressing This Serious Issue Starts with a Few Simple Steps

1. Have a specific written plan to determine and verify all the required credentialing compliance of each employee and to maintain their compliance status. This applies to both statutory compliance required by law and any other credentialing required as a provider that bills third parties under specific and enforceable contractual requirements.
2. Make a specific person accountable for managing this process, and check on that management at least quarterly.
3. Implement appropriate specialty insurance coverage where possible to help protect against any gaps or errors including recovery audit contractor (RAC) audit insurance.

4.7 HIPAA AND DATA BREACHES: MANAGING CYBER LIABILITY RISK

Patient HIPAA and financial data present a daily exposure for physicians and medical practices.

For example, the Anthem breach in 2015 exposed the personal identifying information (PII) records of up to 80 million patients but, at least according to Anthem, not the actual credit card or health-care data. What is less widely known is that nearly 20 million additional patients who thought this had nothing to do with them may also have been exposed as Anthem has systems and records linked to over 30 other smaller providers for national database purposes.

PII typically includes names, dates of birth, member ID/social security numbers, addresses, phone numbers, e-mail addresses, and even employment information: in other words, most of what you'd need to fill out a credit application.

As serious as that exposure is, the recent, much smaller data breach affecting "only" 11 million Premera Blue Cross patients may be even more serious and destructive to both doctors and patients. According to a *New York Times* news report,[6] criminal hackers likely gained access to claims data, including specific clinical information, bank account numbers, social security numbers, dates of birth, and other PII data, in an attack that they believe began in May 2014. The report stated that medical records themselves are highly valuable items sold on underground criminal exchanges, where stolen data are used to engage in insurance fraud and may also be used directly against patients in some blackmail-type scenario; imagine being a public figure on that list with medical data you'd like to keep private.

These are high-profile examples that illustrate the extent of the damage that can be done, but readers should not be lulled into thinking that this risk only applies to hospitals, insurance companies, and other massive providers; quite the opposite is true. Your practice is substantially more vulnerable to any such breach, and we can guarantee that these behemoths have information technology (IT) security resources and compliance programs that are far ahead of your own, not to mention their ability to survive the many costs of such a claim.

Example 2

In Arizona, one privately held and well respected medical practice recently had up to 40,000 patients' financial data exposed when a secretly drug-addicted employee in their billing department used patients' credit cards for shopping online, fast food, rims and tires, and a variety of other charges. This created a massive financial exposure for the practice and a huge reputational hit, the true costs of which are hard to determine. Let's walk through the tangible part of the math:

1. The practice had to notify all of the patients in writing (40,000 letters at an estimated $1.50 each).
2. These notification letters typically offer an apology, inform the recipient of the breach, and offer credit monitoring for a year at cost of $100 per recipient. That's $460,000 in potential exposure plus the incalculable reputational damage, which is actually a low estimate, as you'll see below.

According to a research report on the costs of data breach conducted by the Ponemon Institute and sponsored by IBM,[7] the numbers for 2014 are disheartening. It's unsurprising and recommended reading if you have organizational responsibility for or input on these issues, including having a position on the board of directors. Here's a look at just a fraction of what they report:

1. Breaches have a higher overall cost than in the past.
2. More customers leave a business after a breach than before.
3. The costs of redress are higher than before, including remedial action.
4. The average cost per record exposed by malicious activity is substantially greater than in our example above; they put it at $246 per record.

4.7.1 Perfect Hindsight: Three Essential Layers of Data Risk Management

4.7.1.1 Layer One: Professional IT Security

A professionally implemented IT security system not only provides hardware, software, training, and best practices; it also helps illustrate that you made an effort and have an actual plan in place. Even if you get breached, one of the issues that are evaluated in determining your fines and legal culpability is what you did and how reasonable and effective those measures were.

4.7.1.2 Layer Two: Having Cyber Liability, aka Data Breach Insurance

Cyber liability insurance (CLI) policies cover a variety of exposures in our increasingly computerized world, including not only outside theft of PII and medical records but also the intentional theft and misuse of patient data by employees and even what can happen if you or a connected employee loses a laptop, tablet, or smartphone with protected information. In the Arizona case, both the medical practice and the billing company, which is likely a "business associate" of a medical practice (if not a wholly owned tax shelter set up by the owner's CPA, as we see with many doctors), will face substantial liability. Interestingly, the EPLI, previously covered, may also provide some protection in such cases. While our coverage of this vital issue focused on its value in protecting your office from an employee lawsuit, good policies often include riders that can help protect you from the liability of the intentional, but unpermitted, actions of an employee as well.

4.7.1.3 Layer Three: Background Checks and Proper Employee Credentialing

This specific example involves the billing and subsequent breach that occurred at what is ostensibly a third-party company that we can only hope was properly credentialed and in compliance with the requirements of the dermatology practice's third-party payer contracts. Your HIPAA security procedures should include a review of the entire chain of custody of the confidential data your practice handles and discloses to third parties, and that review should include inquiry into any third party's own background-screening practices. Ask if they indemnify you for loss or misuse of the information you share with them due to their own negligence or breach—and always get a copy of the "in-force" liability policy they carry that covers you in the event of such a breach. Unfortunately, relying on their assurances of being properly credentialed and insured is not a defense for you.

4.7.2 A Word about Equipment Disposal Liability

Medical practices replacing obsolete computer and electronic equipment must safely and securely dispose of a variety of devices, including the following:

- Networked printers, faxes, scanners, etc.
- Computer servers and arrays
- Devices that combine hardware and software for a specific medical or administrative use
- Networking equipment
- Electronic data storage devices and backups
- Desktop and laptop computers, tablets, and smartphones that have been used to access or relay protected data

Computers themselves were listed last and pose only the most obvious threat to the financial and HIPAA-protected information that every medical office in the United States stores and is legally responsible for. The partial list of other devices that store and transfer these data illustrates the true size of the exposure that practices must deal with. Just one example of how onerous the liability the *equipment itself* can be is that a printer can have thousands of patients' PPI and treatment data stored in its memory.

4.7.3 You Can't Just Throw Them Away or Donate Them

You may donate and perhaps take a tax deduction for certain peripherals after determining if they pose a storage risk or not (things like mice, keyboards, and monitors are the most basic examples), but the computers themselves and most other devices that transfer, copy, or store data present a serious exposure to your business. Your responsibility does not end when they go out the door. Regardless of whether the devices are going to be destroyed, donated, or recycled, it's vital that all data on them are permanently wiped out as a basic first step.

Drive cleaner–type software programs or those available at most office stores may already be part of your operating system or part of antivirus programs. Remember that data on personal computers is not actually erased unless the hard drive itself is destroyed. In many cases, a professional ID thief (or an average 12-year-old) will be able to retrieve the data from a computer that you think you wiped clean.

4.7.4 Five Simple Equipment Security Tips

These steps will help mitigate your practice's legal and financial exposures for data, potentially encourage the use of the equipment by a worthy charity or individual, and help your practice be greener.

1. Be proactive about equipment security. Far too often, medical practices put old equipment into a storage closet that no one takes inventory on or responsibility for until there's problem.
2. Disconnect old machines, sign all users out of them, and disconnect them from your network where they are often not maintained or updated and where they may actually create a security risk.
3. Make someone specific responsible for a specific written plan. Create a written chain of custody and inventory, and educate the responsible party about the risks and gravity of the task at hand.
4. Have specific records of how many devices you have and are destroying or donating (make a copy for the CPA, including depreciated value and replacement cost) and where they went or how they were disposed of.

4.8 RECOVERY AUDIT CONTRACTOR RISKS

RACs, or the government's Recovery Audit Program, as many physicians have unfortunately discovered, are part of the government effort to reduce fraud, errors, and waste in insurance billing practices and Medicare and Medicaid in particular. Audits run during the test program between 2005 and 2008 resulted in almost $1 billion in compensation being returned to the Medicare Trust Fund by a wide range of medical service providers. (That $1 billion was the *yearly* dollar number refunded to the government by providers by 2012.)

Government-approved auditors work different regions of the country and conduct audits on providers named in whistle-blower tips and complaints and as a result of irregularities and red flags in their billing and coding practices by "...providers that have a high propensity for error based on the Comprehensive Error Rate Testing (CERT) program and other CMS analysis," according to information available at the government's Center for Medicare Services (CMS) website. The site lists the following key reasons for a finding of provider overpayment:

- Incorrect payment amounts
- Noncovered services (including services that are not reasonable and necessary under section 1862(a)(1)(A) of the Social Security Act)
- Incorrectly coded services (including DRG miscoding)
- Duplicate services

4.8.1 Who RAC Audits Affect; Significant Burdens for a Wide Range of Providers

Almost any health-care provider, including hospitals, doctor's offices, home health-care providers, nursing homes, and medical equipment providers, and all businesses and individuals that submit bills to government programs such as Medicaid or Medicare should expect to be audited at some point.

Many auditors work on a contingency-fee basis, and the five regional auditing firms contracted by the government are paid up to 12.5% of payments they successfully identify as invalid and collect. This places a significant record-keeping manpower and financial burden on health-care providers from a resource, financial liability, and record-keeping standpoint; they can go back as far as 3 years, and the maximum number of requests per 45 days is 400. The maximum request amount is per "campus."

The CMS defines a campus as one or more facilities under the same tax identification number (TIN) located in the same area (using the first three positions of the ZIP code). This means that two of your locations in the same city could theoretically be required to produce and defend up to 800 files in a 45-day period. The average payment denied to hospitals, as one example, on an automatic denial basis is nearly $600, and those defined as "complex" denials on larger cases average a loss or denial to the provider of nearly $6000, yet more than half of hospitals have had no formal training on payment error compliance from CMS or its contracted RACs; the number among smaller private providers is even lower.

4.8.2 Protecting Your Practice against RAC Audits

First, it's vital that you insure yourself against the costs with RAC audit liability insurance. This specialized coverage will often help address the massive research cost and financial burden an audit usually creates. A RAC audit policy may also cover expensive related exposures like the following:

- Medicare and Medicaid audit (RAC audit)
- Commercial payer audits
- STARK violations and HIPAA compliance
- EMTALA violations, etc.

Coverage is typically affordable for practices that don't have a significant claims history and can include the costs of defending a health-care provider, such as legal fees, specialized consultants, secure document reproduction costs, and independent audit work, in addition to the audit fines and penalties themselves.

Once again, being proactive is the key. You are better off identifying any billing issues and correcting them before a RAC auditor does it for you. There are many compliance auditors and software systems that can help identify and correct these issues. Due diligence on your resource is required as well; some are law or accounting firms with extensive training and experience, some are software companies, and some are independent consultants with credentials that may or may not be of value to your purpose.

You must get professional counsel in place if your practice is subject to a RAC audit. A large number of claims get appealed, and some of those denials are actually even overturned in the provider's favor, but hospitals typically fare better than other providers because they were more compliant in the first place.

4.9 MANAGING YOUR MEDICAL EXECUTIVE RISK: YOU ARE NOT JUST A DOCTOR; YOU ARE ALSO AN EXECUTIVE

Another vital area of risk management in physicians' business and asset protection planning in their expanding roles as business leaders, owners, and executives is the need for directors' and officers' coverage, commonly referred to as D&O insurance. This coverage is often confused with a variety of other forms of coverage with similar-sounding names and is overlooked by doctors and insurance agents alike. It is common that doctors who think they have a full suite of liability products by their local P&C insurance agent are not aware that D&O coverage is even available and distinct from their core general liability, malpractice, and Errors & Omissions (E&O) coverage.

Getting the right policy for your role as a physician entrepreneur and executive involves having an expert agent that can explain the different types of coverage available under an E&O policy and what each one does. Policies are different and have different features and pricing.

Three *primary types of coverage* include the following:

- *Side A*—for the officers and directors themselves
- *Side B*—for the corporation if it is required to indemnify
- *Side C*—for security claims

The scope of the liability for doctors is wide; you have all of the conventional medical practice–related issues like HIPAA compliance, Medicare and Medicaid billing regulations, and employee certification, plus the liability for care delivery itself. Add to that responsibility for issues ranging from waste disposal and employment law to accounting and tax reporting, and the scope of the liability grows. This exposure applies not just to medical practices and logically related businesses, including labs and medical supplies, research, and medical device and technology companies, but also to a variety of other businesses that want doctors on their boards and executive management teams for their knowledge, prestige, and connections. This liability extends into service on private foundations, charitable boards, and even boards of religious institutions. If you serve on any of these boards, you should always require that they insure you with their own D&O coverage and that you have a copy of the current policy; again, relying on being told you were covered will not protect you if they are wrong.

The cost of this insurance, like all others, is underwriting specific and is based on your organization's current record. It's exceptionally cost-effective. The principals in one recent intracompany lawsuit between partners at a business without D&O insurance in place paid over $250,000 in legal fees out of pocket; the insurance would cost only a small fraction of that amount.

4.10 MANAGING DRUG-BASED TREATMENT LIABILITY RISK

Medical specialties that use drug-based treatments administered by the physician's office as a routine part of their treatment regimes face additional risks as well. This usage presents several expanding liability issues that require serious proactive risk management.

Using specialty-compounded drugs is increasingly common; one recent report says they account for a full 6% of medical-error claims and so are the associated risks for medical practices. A recent case that made national headlines involved the unknowing use of infected epidural steroid compounds by pain management practices across the country. Over 200 patients across more than 12 states suffered meningitis infection and a variety of other serious ailments, with nearly 50 casualties.

Drug-injury lawsuit websites make it clear that the administering doctor is part of the lawsuit chain in such circumstances. One website reads, in part,

> The doctors who prescribed (or administered) the drug that injured you may also be liable for your injuries because they are part of the chain of distribution of the drug.

Having and enforcing a drug-quality policy regardless of whether you work in pain management, cardiology, or any other specialty is vital. Regardless of actual fault or causation, lawsuits always seek deep, easy pockets like yours for redress.

4.10.1 Steps to Protect Your Patients and Practice

1. *Have a written plan.* Just as with HIPAA liability, a key issue in attributing blame to a medical practice and its owners is whether or not they took any reasonable efforts to ensure quality and prevent harm.

2. *Delegate plan responsibility.* Have accountability for enforcing the plan in place and implement at least one secondary check and failsafe.
3. *Keep records.* Maintain documentation of the quality assurance program and note each time you check the responsible party's work for compliance. Also maintain notes and examples of the correspondence with and marketing of your vendors. Common red flags for suspect drugs include billing from outside the United States, drugs that have been relabeled or those labeled in foreign languages instead of or in addition to English, and prices that are substantially below the market rate.
4. *Perform due diligence on vendors.* Check their licensing, look for lawsuits and complaints, and get specific representations in writing about the quality and source of any pharmaceuticals you personally administer in your office.
5. *Review informed-consent procedures.* Review the procedures in place in connection with such treatments. This area has been the key in establishing liability for the doctors themselves.

Remember that many insurance programs you bill for treatment, including the use of drugs, require that all pharmaceuticals be sourced from licensed U.S. providers. If you use and bill for tainted drugs that do not meet these conditions, you have both the risk of injury to the patient and the potential to face a Medicare fraud claim, another exceptionally onerous issue that will have to be litigated and defended separately if you think you can prove you were an "innocent purchaser."

4.11 MANAGING PREMISES LIABILITY RISKS

One common issue that surprises medical professionals is the liability they face as the owners or operators of a physical facility that is open to the public. This issue extends beyond your office to your home and other investment real estate as well and is more common than you think.

4.11.1 How Great Is the Risk?

Slip-and-fall accidents requiring medical treatment, as just one example of a premises liability, happen half a million times a year and account for some 1500 emergency visits a day. Such accidents are the leading cause of work-related injuries and even deaths, causing an estimated 25,000 deaths a year, and follow only auto accidents as the leading accidental cause of death in the United States. Judgments for such injuries can be financially devastating and range from relatively small amounts to millions of dollars for death and permanent or disfiguring injuries.

4.11.2 Whose Injuries Are You Responsible For?

Pretty much everyone's, but to differing degrees and standards of care! Loosely paraphrased, if you created, knew of, or should have known of dangerous conditions and allowed them to continue or failed to provide warnings, you may be on the hook. The law breaks down the "duty of care" for property owners and operators as follows, from highest to lowest liability:

- *Invitees* are generally defined as those on the property by express or implied invitation for a business purpose.

- *Licensees* or *guests* are persons on the property at express or implied invitation for a social purpose. A higher degree of care is typically due a child guest.
- *Trespassers* are defined as persons on the property without actual or implied permission. A higher degree of care may be owed to trespassing children under the attractive nuisance doctrine.

4.12 OFFICE MAINTENANCE AND SAFETY ISSUES

Being proactive about maintenance and safety issues is vital, especially during months where water and ice pose additional and often unseen risks that arise over the course of a single day or less or cause even durable property like stairs, railings, sidewalks, and parking lots to deteriorate. A good maintenance program including a record of what was done and when it was inspected is a good start and will help prove the fact that you make serious efforts to inspect and maintain the property for any safety-related conditions. Both owners and tenants share this risk, so don't assume that you are off the hook if you lease a property, especially if the condition is in an area you limit access to or control completely. Likewise if you are a property owner that leases to others, don't assume that dangers the tenant creates will not flow up to you.

The first level of defense is as always a good liability insurance policy with limits that are adequate to cover the true scope of the liability, as outlined above; $1 million is the *bare minimum* in bodily injury a commercial insurance policy should cover, and it should ideally be higher and backed up by a higher limit umbrella policy.

4.12.1 Some Specific Examples: Are There Dangerous Conditions in Your Office, or Have You Allowed Patients or Employees to Create Them?

- In a scene right out of *Portlandia*, an elderly medical office patient is injured by the expensive bicycles of two patients, who asked the front desk for permission to bring them inside because of fears that they'd be stolen. The senior citizen tripped over the bikes upon entering and injured his knee and had his cheek pierced by a section of the bike's brake cable that barely missed his eye.
- An inattentive mother leaving the doctor's office lets her child run out from between parked cars, and the child is injured by a vehicle driven by another patient. The doctor is sued for contributory negligence by not having enough warnings and speed bumps in his very small parking lot.
- A tree branch falls on an expensive, collector car in the doctor's parking lot on a windy day. The doctor is sued for diminution in value of the auto due to the improper maintenance of landscaping on her property.
- An employee of a medical practice moves warning signs and a bucket covering a hole in the floor that a contractor was working on and then, the same day, steps in the hole, injures her foot, and sues her employer.
- We've seen a variety of lawsuits where very heavy people have also been injured by falling when a chair, bench, or toilet broke under their weight. These lawsuits sometimes even include an emotional distress claim.
- A large flat screen TV installed in the waiting area of a high-end dentist office is accidentally pulled over by a toddler, falling on top of him and injuring him severely.

As you can see from these examples, wherever possible, liability is going to be attributed to the practice, which is often seen as a more exciting or deep-pocket corporation than just another patient! It makes more financial sense to the lawyers (as one real example) to sue a doctor's office for not having enough signs and speed bumps in their parking lot than it does to sue the retired widow on a fixed income who hit a child in the parking lot.

Someone in the practice should be responsible for a variety of issues like cleaning-crew schedules, waiting-room construction and furniture selection, public access to electricity or electronics with electrocution risks (including medical devices that can cause harm), access to dangerous materials (including biohazards, drugs, and chemicals like cleaning products that may be stored in a bathroom cabinet—restaurants are famous for this unsafe practice), or other publicly accessible space, as just a few specific examples. Considering outsourcing this, at least for an initial review of issues to correct or watch for. Professional safety inspectors can be hired to walk through your facility from the parking lot to the exam room and look for potential issues. Many experts also suggest that clients walk through the entire facility as if they are childproofing it (another common issue) while making sure they wouldn't limit access by a handicapped person. Issues we think of as simple can get complicated relatively quickly!

4.12.2 Americans with Disabilities Act Compliance Liability—Is Your Facility Accessible?

Properly addressing this issue covers basics like having the legally required handicapped-accessible parking and restrooms all the way through specific legal requirements for the construction of public spaces like entrances, thresholds, pathways, elevators, counters, and even your practice signage. Lawsuits on this issue have hit businesses across the United States and can be generated by people who are not even your patients, for instance, when a scout spots a condition that is not Americans with Disabilities Act (ADA) compliant as the basis for a lawsuit. Specialists in ADA compliance are available in nearly every jurisdiction to inspect your facility and provide a list of violations and the required corrective actions. What fully abled people take for granted surprises even physicians, and there's a significant return on investment from a risk-management perspective as the relatively small costs of a compliance review are always less than the cost of responding to an ADA complaint or lawsuit. This is especially true given the fact that some states provide ADA plaintiffs punitive damages, attorney's fees, and fines, and on top of that, your practice will *still* have to make the changes legally required.

4.13 PERSONAL RISK-MANAGEMENT ISSUES FOR PHYSICIANS—YOU ARE NOT "JUST" A DOCTOR

Doctors have strong opinions about liability insurance that are often not realistic. They are not an all-or-nothing tool, and no, having higher limits of liability insurance is not a bad idea "because it makes you a bigger lawsuit target"; it merely makes the target you present harder to penetrate by adding additional layers. Despite their limits, these policies remain a vital tool in your asset protection plan and an important and affordable first line of defense.

4.13.1 Why Personal Liability Insurance Is Vital (and Why Insurance Alone Is Not Enough)

Doctors have wrongly relied on their umbrella polices to provide greater protection on a wider variety of issues than they reasonably can. A few simple issues to consider are gaps in either the *depth* of insurance, meaning the dollar limits of the coverage, as well as the *width* of the coverage, meaning how many specific types of exposure the policy itself actually says it covers. Surprisingly, this cost-effective defensive tool is consistently overlooked by both doctors and insurance agents.

This gap has been fatal for a variety of successful people within the last few years, including several health-care families that were informed by their insurance carriers that they should expect claims over and above the insurance they had in place following serious accidents involving significant property damage, injuries, and fatalities. There are 11 million auto accidents in the United States per year (according to U.S. Census Bureau statistics), resulting in 40,000 fatalities.

Umbrella policies *are not* a complete defense against anything that might happen, no matter how much it costs. They are simply extensions of your basic insurance policy that cover some logically related claims to specific increased limits with a *very* specific list of exclusions. Many doctors don't fully understand that their *personal liability umbrella* on their home and auto coverage, for instance, won't provide any protection from business-related exposures we've discussed, like EPLI, data breach, etc. For example, a dog bite that occurs at your home may be covered, but a lawsuit by an employee almost certainly will not.

Insured persons and their insurers often have frighteningly different ideas about what *umbrella* means. To many insured consumers, umbrella is thought to mean *everything*. On the other hand, your carrier probably thinks it covers only specific events in the scope of the base policy, covered to specific increased limits and governed by a specific set of exclusions detailed in the fine print of your policy, clearly two very different definitions.

There is no form of insurance that will cover you against an infinite universe of possible personal and professional exposures to an unlimited dollar amount, nor is this reasonable to expect of the insurance carrier for what you pay. For example, in Arizona, the top 10 civil verdicts in 2007 ranged from a $6 million judgment against a pharmacy that dispensed prescriptions that, when combined, caused a patient's death to $360 million on a dispute over a real-estate deal. One doubts that every defendant's various liability and E&O coverage, even fully applied, is adequate to cover the claim.

4.13.2 Why Liability Insurance *Alone* Is Inadequate Risk Management

As important as this coverage is, attorneys and insurance agents continue to see both clients and advisors trying to insure their way to safety without solid plan-B defensive structures in place. In the worst cases, uninformed advisors, including lawyers who should be better educated, tell their clients that *the only* asset protection required is a good umbrella policy. This is simply wrong for successful medical professionals and may be professional malpractice on the part of the person giving the advice.

Many lawsuits involve financial gain to plaintiffs and their attorneys, and all are seeking the greatest possible recovery. If we simply examine the gap between the average national medical malpractice verdict of around $3.9 million and the average national liability policy in the area of $1 million, we find that an average physician defendant is *personally* exposed for $2.9 million. Proper defensive legal planning that legally segregates your personal assets from this distinct liability will make it clear that you have a policy in place that specifically covers this event and that there is very little beyond policy limits that they can take from you by force. This securitized financial condition actually often encourages settlement within your policy limits and discourages lawsuits and expenses being generated above that amount that the players are unlikely to collect. If liability or the risk of a misinformed jury prompts your counsel to advise that you offer some additional settlement amount above the policy, you should certainly consider it carefully. In these cases, however, it is important to consider that when properly protected, *you* ultimately control the terms you are willing to offer as opposed to having those terms forced upon you by an unsympathetic jury verdict.

Finally, don't go on past performance and ego (e.g., "I've never been in an accident or faced an employee lawsuit") or your personal assessment of what you think your risks are ("We only have adult drivers in our home"). They are called "accidents" for a reason and happen with supposedly safe adult driving and experienced professional conduct as they do with teens and young adults, in addition to a variety of claims that lack a strong factual basis and are simply made up, regardless of the facts and your actual culpable conduct.

4.14 MANAGING DOMESTIC EMPLOYEE RISKS

Employment-based lawsuits by various domestic help are a serious and growing threat. Claims by domestic staff including maids, nannies, housekeepers, cooks, gardeners, personal trainers, etc. are on the rise and include wage and labor issues, sexual harassment, personal injury, wrongful termination, and discrimination. These claims closely mirror the wide range of employment-related liabilities we've previously discussed but that are often treated much too casually in the home environment despite the level of liability being the same.

These claims also have far-reaching and unintended consequences, including reputational damage and media attention that come from these claims, which can be damaging in many ways beyond just the direct liability of a lawsuit judgment itself. This is especially true for high-profile physicians and individuals with sensitive public personas, even if that public persona is limited to a high profile locally. Negative publicity can affect promotions, board memberships, and speaking engagements and often affects contracts, endorsement deals, and even stock prices.

4.14.1 The Four-Layer Risk-Management Plan: Household Staff

1. Get a high-limit personal liability policy on the home with an umbrella of at least $2 million or, based on your net worth, maybe higher.
2. Have a written employment agreement with staff that includes a confidentiality agreement and mediation and arbitration provisions as conditions of employment. This confidentiality agreement is especially important if you share domestic employees with others in your community or professional and social circles. Due to sheer physical proximity and the casual, if not intimate, professional relationship many of us develop with such trusted employees, they are often privy to the personal details of your life, relationships, finances, and a number of other private details that you probably don't want colored with their interpretation or shared with others.

3. Strongly consider EPLI insurance and worker's comp coverage that is specific to your home; your business policies do not apply.
4. Stop committing tax fraud, and pay them *legally*. The IRS[8] says that household employees include housekeepers, maids, babysitters, gardeners, and others who work in or around your private residence as your employee. And, we continually find that people that pay their domestic employees in cash are "helping them out" and that "it's just casual and does not really need to be reported." You're wrong on both counts and are technically guilty of tax fraud and subject to a variety of the penalties here that we discussed in the employee classification risk section. Reporting and labor law compliance burdens begin at an exceptionally low threshold; less than $200 per month of repeated payments or a total of only $1900 on an annual basis requires that you legally withhold for both social security and Medicare taxes and pay your share of those taxes as an employer. Consult your CPA and local counsel for details specific to your home and employees.

Again, many doctors should consider outsourcing some of this compliance, including how staff is paid. There are a variety of services out there like NannyChex and MyHomePay that offer assistance with domestic HR issues including screening, training, and payroll. When conflicts arise, bear in mind that most juries don't feel sorry for people with household help. In fact, some of them may *be* household help like the allegedly aggrieved party you face. The final, unspoken layer is always the same; examine proactive asset protection strategies with the help of a qualified and experienced professional; this means not just getting the opinion of your brother-in-law the real-estate lawyer.

4.15 MANAGING YOUR RISKS AS A PARENT

The number of ways that children are creating substantial risks for their parents is at an all-time high, as many parents are unfortunately aware. Increased defensive planning or education by most parents despite increasingly common litigation for this vicarious liability has not increased commensurately with this risk.

Some of you believe that your kids are better behaved, smarter, and more sensible than those we hear about in the news. Such exposures are unpredictable and often arise from mundane activities you never imagined could be so serious. Part of the discussion we encourage parents to have with their children includes a detailed explanation of the fact that you as parents are personally, financially, and legally responsible (up to the level of criminal liability) for any harm, damage, or loss caused by your minor children.

In one example; a successful physician left town for the weekend with his wife, and his 17-year-old daughter threw a party at their home, in a pattern repeated in nearly every city in the country every weekend. Tragically, a teenager whom she had never met before crashed the party and died after he overdosed on drugs he brought with him, resulting in a lawsuit against the young lady's parents that sought damages in excess of $3 million. Neither the young lady nor her parents, nor anyone else in the tony private-school community of gated homes imagined, that something like that could happen in their nice neighborhood, and the resulting claim was in excess of the limits of the homeowner's liability policy the family had in place. Dozens of other parental liability exposures seen over the years have come from much more mundane issues.

4.15.1 Negligent Supervision and Negligent Entrustment

Two ways liability is linked back to parents include negligent entrustment (providing the means or access to things or situations where some reasonably anticipatable harm occurs) and negligent supervision (basically infers that the harm would not have occurred if the minor had been properly supervised). This liability extends to others that have custody or are entrusted with supervision, so any guardian is at risk if the harm would have been prevented absent the access to the thing that created the harm and/or inadequate supervision. This also creates potential liability for you for the children of others you have custody of, even overnight for a slumber party.

4.15.2 Some Specific Recurring High-Risk Issues

1. *Automobiles*: Minor children must be specifically named and insured on any vehicle they drive. Parents are generally liable for what minors do behind the wheel, permitted or not. If they are irresponsible drivers or if they take the car without permission, you must take control of the car and treat it like a loaded weapon that's pointed at everything you own and possibly their very own survival. Your high school senior cutting class with his/her friends and piling them into *your car* to go to Starbucks for "ditch day" is remarkably less charming when, for instance, she loses control of the vehicle on the way back to school and two of her passengers are critically injured, as happened in one recent case. Thanks to commonly available and inexpensive software and tracking devices, not to mention the tracking software on your kid's iPhones, you can know where they and your vehicle are at all times.
2. *Access to firearms and other dangerous items*: If you have guns in your home (or bows and arrows, ATVs, jet skis, a swimming pool, prescription drugs, or anything else that can be misused), you are legally and financially responsible for not only personal injury and property damage but, in some states and fact patterns, even criminal liability for the actions of your child and his/her friends. The cost of defense counsel alone could be financially fatal considering the possibility of someone getting injured or killed and the resulting liability and consequences.

4.16 ASSESSMENT

Like all risks, this chapter can only be a starting point for your risk-management endeavors, and even those described in preceding chapters. You must be adequately insured and then take steps beyond insurance to manage these risks and secure your assets before the harm occurs.

4.17 CONCLUSION

Get experienced help[9] from an informed attorney and a knowledgeable insurance agent, who can not only describe their own legal tools and insurance products, but also help you manage the real world, street-level risks outside their office, and formal documents, proactively. This means they need physician and health-care-specific experience and should understand the realities of running a medical practice, office, clinic, or health-care business.

4.18 COLLABORATE

Discuss this chapter online with others at http://www.medicalexecutivepost.com.

REFERENCES

1. The Physician's (and Business Owner's) Asset Protection Self Exam: http://www.proasset protection.com/2012/05/the-physicians-simple-asset-protection-self-exam/.
2. EEOC Press Release: http://www.eeoc.gov/eeoc/newsroom/release/2-5-14.cfm.
3. Feds and New York State Jointly Target 'Independent Contractor' Misclassification: http://www .forbes.com/sites/robertwood/2013/11/19/feds-and-new-york-state-jointly-target-independent -contractor-misclassification/.
4. VCSP Program Details, IRS: http://www.irs.gov/Businesses/Small-Businesses-&-Self-Employed /Voluntary-Classification-Settlement-Program.
5. Independent Contractor (Self Employed) or Employee?: http://www.irs.gov/Businesses/Small -Businesses-&-Self-Employed/Independent-Contractor-Self-Employed-or-Employee.
6. Premera Blue Cross Says Data Breach Exposed Medical Records: http://www.nytimes.com /2015/03/18/business/premera-blue-cross-says-data-breach-exposed-medical-data.html?_r=0.
7. 2014 Cost of Data Breach Study, United States: http://www.accudatasystems.com/assets/2014 -cost-of-a-data-breach-study.pdf.
8. Topic 756—Employment Taxes for Household Employees: http://www.irs.gov/taxtopics/tc756 .html.
9. How to Pick an Asset Protection Attorney—Due Diligence for Physicians: http://www .proassetprotection.com/2011/06/how-to-pick-an-asset-protection-lawyer-—-key-due-diligence -questions-and-caveats/.

FURTHER READINGS

Bennett, J: *The Ultimate Guide to Asset Preservation.* BG Publishing International, New York, 2011.

Gassman, A: *Creditor Protection: A Comprehensive Handbook for Physicians.* Haddon Hall Publishing, New York, 2012.

Marcinko, DE and Hetico, HR: *Insurance and Risk Management Strategies for Physicians and Advisors.* Jones and Bartlett Publishers Inc., Sudbury, MA, 2005.

Marcinko, DE and Hetico, HR: *The Business of Medical Practice*, 3rd ed. Springer Publishing, New York, 2010.

Marcinko, DE and Hetico, HR: *Comprehensive Financial Planning Strategies for Doctors and Advisors: Best Practices from Leading Consultants and Certified Medical Planners™*. CRC and Productivity Press, Boca Raton, FL, 2015.

Minttz, R: *Asset Protection for Physicians and Business Owners.* Francis O'Brien & Sons Publishing, N. Las Vegas, NV, 2011.

4.13* COLLABORATE

Discuss this chapter online with others at http://www.medicalexecutivepost.com

REFERENCES

FURTHER READING

5 The Medical Records Revolution

Modern Concerns and Pitfalls

David Edward Marcinko, Hope Rachel Hetico, and Frederick William LaCava

CONTENTS

Yes, paper medical records are still used in the health-care industry and are, in fact, more numerous, famous, and infamous than their younger electronic siblings. Yet, physicians of all persuasions are still having trouble adjusting to the radically new use of medical records (paper or electronic) in the present era of health-care reform, the Patient Protection and Affordable Care Act (PPACA), managed care, Recovery Audit Contractors (RACs), and various billing practice reviews. An inadequately documented medical chart can mean civil and criminal liability to the sloppy and/or unwary practitioner. So, a brief look at the history of keeping medical records puts this evolving risk in some perspective.

Medical records were previously used to aid in the quality of medical care. Now they are also *the* basis for payment for services, not as a record or reflection of the care that was actually provided but as a separate justification for billing. The lack of appropriate documentation now no longer just threatens nonpayment for services but also risks civil money penalties and criminal charges.

5.1 HISTORIC PURPOSE OF MEDICAL RECORDS

As little as a hundred years ago, detailed medical records were likely to have been compiled by medical researchers such as Charcot and Hughlings-Jackson. The medical record was an *aide memoire* for detecting changes in patients' conditions over time, solely for the benefit of the physician in treating the patient. As health care became more institutionalized, medical records became a communications device among health-care providers. Doctors made progress notes and gave orders. Nurses carried them out and kept a record of patient responses. A centralized record, theoretically, allowed all to know what each was doing. The ideal was that if the doctor were unable to care for the patient, another physician could stand in his/her shoes and assume the patient's care.

Then pressures from third-party payers occurred. As insurance and then government programs became larger players in the compensation game, they wanted to know if the care they were paying for was being delivered efficiently. Why were these tests ordered? Why weren't these studies done? Why had the patient remained hospitalized after his temperature had returned to normal for so many hours and no pain medications had been required? Why couldn't this preoperative work be done on an outpatient basis? Though the real push behind these questions was the desire to save money, utilization review also directly contributed to better patient care. A patient who was being given inefficient care was getting substandard care as well. Utilization review was mainly retrospective; denial of compensation was rarely imposed, and suasion by peers was the main effector of change. Though "economic credentialing" was shouted about, it rarely showed itself in public.

Even health reform, which openly admitted economic incentives as one of its motivators, preferred to find some other reason for deciding not to reimburse or admit Dr. Jones to its narrow panel of PPACA, or other "skinny" network providers, or not renewing Dr. Smith's contract with an HMO. The medical record remained essentially a record of patient care, whether it was good or not, efficient or not. If the record wasn't complete, the doctor could always supplement it with an affidavit, use information from somewhere else, or provide explanations.

Today, the concept known as socioeconomic status (SES) is conceptualized as the social standing, or class, of an individual or group. It is often measured as a combination of education, income, and occupation. Examinations of SES often reveal inequities in access to medical resources, plus issues related to privilege, power, and control. SES is increasingly being considered as another payment component (CPT codes) to medical providers, as reflected in the paper medical record, electronic medical record (EMR), and elsewhere.

5.2 MEDICAL RECORD CONFIDENTIALITY

As a patient—Are my medical records secret? The physician is ethically bound to preserve your confidence and not let anyone find out what is in your medical record. The employees of a physician, clinic, or hospital may review your records, but they are likewise bound to preserve the confidentiality of your records. Only in certain limited situations can your physician be legally required to divulge the contents of your record without your permission. You may, however, request that your records be inspected or copied by anyone of your choice.

When may my physician disclose the contents of my record without my permission?

- Some contagious diseases, including venereal disease, must be reported to the public health department.
- Certain violent injuries (such as gunshot wounds) must be reported to the police.
- If you are involved in a lawsuit where your health or physical condition is an issue, your physician may be called as a witness.
- If you make a worker's compensation claim, the insurance carrier can obtain access to your records, even if you do not consent to their release.

Who else can get my medical records? If you have health or life insurance, you have probably signed a release as part of your policy or as part of a claim form. This allows the insurance company to check your medical records before they insure you or pay a claim. Without such a release, however, such information must not be disclosed.

Is the insurance company required to keep my records confidential? No. Once you give the insurance company your records, they may give the information to other persons without your permission. What about records concerning treatment for mental illness, drug abuse, or alcoholism? There is a new law in Texas that gives records concerning treatment for such conditions additional protection from disclosure. This law prevents your records from being disclosed to other people or used in court, except in a proceeding that involves your mental condition, the care received, payment of your bill, or certain other narrowly defined cases. This law does not protect your records if you release them to anyone. (This will vary from state to state.)

5.3 PHILOSOPHIC MEDICAL RECORDS REVOLUTION

To understand the revolution that has since occurred, place yourself for a moment in the position of a third-party payer. You want to know if Dr. Brown actually gave the care for which he is submitting a bill. You want to know if that care was needed. You want to know that the care was given to benefit the patient, rather than to provide financial benefit to the provider beyond the value of the services rendered. Can you send one of your employees to follow Dr. Brown around on his/her office hours and hospital visits? Of course not! You cannot see what actually happened in Dr. Brown's office that day or why Dr. Black ordered a computerized axial tomography (CAT) scan on the patient at the imaging center. What you can do is review the medical record that underlies the bill for services rendered from Dr. Blue. Most of all, you can require the doctor to certify that the care was actually rendered and was indicated. You can punish Dr. White severely if an element of a referral of a patient to another health-care provider was to obtain a benefit in cash or in kind from the health-care provider to whom the referral had been made (Stark law). You can destroy Dr. Rose financially and put him in jail if his medical records do not document the bases for the bills he submitted for payment.

This nearly complete change in function of the medical record has precious little to do with the quality of patient care. To illustrate that point, consider only an office visit in which the care was exactly correct, properly indicated, and flawlessly delivered, but not recorded in the office chart. As far as the patient was concerned, everything was correct and beneficial to the patient. As far as the third-party payer is concerned, the bill for those services is completely unsupported by required documentation and could be the basis for a False Claims Act (FCA) charge, a Medicare audit, or a criminal indictment. We have left the realm of quality of patient care far behind. Shall we change it back to the way it was? That is not going to happen.

Instead, practitioners must adjust their attitudes to the present function of patient records. They must document as required under pain of punishment for failure to do so. That reality is infuriating to many since they still cling to the ideal of providing good-quality care to their patients and disdain such requirements as hindrances to reaching that goal. They are also aware of the fact that full documentation can be provided without a reality underlying it. "Fine, you want documentation? I'll give you documentation!"

Some have given in to the temptation of "cookbook" entries in their charts, canned computer software programs, or EMR (electronic health record [EHR]) templates, listing all the examinations they should have done and all the findings that should be there to justify further treatment, embedded "billing engines" not withstanding. We have personally seen records of physical examinations that record a patient's ankle pulses as "equal and bounding bilaterally" when the patient had only one leg; hospital chart notes that describe extensive discussion with the patient of risks, alternatives, and benefits in obtaining informed consent when the remainder of the record demonstrates the patient's complaint that the surgeon has never told him/her what he/she planned to do; and operative reports of procedures done and findings made in detail that, unfortunately, bear no correlation with the surgery that was actually performed.

Whether EMRs will really be helpful, in the future, is still not known. In fact, according to Ed Pullen, MD, a board-certified family physician practicing in Puyallup, Washington, EHRs are defined primarily as repositories of patient data (much like paper records). But, in the era of meaningful use (MU), patient-centered medical homes, and accountable care organizations (ACOs), mere patient data repositories are not sufficient to meet the complex care support needs of clinical professionals. These complaints arise because EHR systems are being used as clinical care support systems, which means they *should* enhance the productivity of clinical professionals and support their information needs, not hinder them (personal communication; DrPullen.com).

5.4 ALTERED RECORDS

The health-care provider should not alter the medical record under any circumstances. The office, clinic, or hospital must zealously guard its medical records from alterations by physicians or members of the nursing staff. Even an inconsequential alteration will throw the validity of the entire record into question. If an entry must be changed, a single line should be drawn through the entry, taking particular care to make sure that the original entry is clearly legible. The new entry should be written above or next to the old entry, and the date of the new entry, as well as the name of the person making the entry, should be recorded. The entry must also be signed by that person. Juries are very intolerant of altered medical records; even innocent mistakes, such as the loss of a few pages of a record, will be construed as an intentional cover-up. Under no circumstances should materials such as Liquid Paper or other opaque liquids be applied to the record in order to correct any entry.

Overheard in the Doctor's Lounge

Medical Records as Malpractice Defense

The best defense against any medical malpractice liability claim is a complete and accurate written or electronic record of the facts. In particular, medical malpractice claims will frequently be stalled or thwarted by a consistent written description of the symptoms you observe and the treatments you prescribe.

Extensive record keeping will not only help formulate a defense against a claim but also (and perhaps more importantly) create the appearance that you are careful and highly competent in all of your affairs. Members of a jury may not be able to discern whether the medical judgments you made in a particular case were good or bad, as they do not have the years of education and training that you do.

Jurors can, however, sense whether your practice is organized and professional. If your records are thorough and consistent, jurors will assume that you dedicate as much attention to the substantive aspects of your work as you do to the tedium of record keeping. If you are active in the management of your office, you should keep track of its operations and establish logs for your employees to complete as they perform their daily tasks.

Not all information, however, ought to be written down. Keep your written records to the facts you have observed and leave your speculations for department meetings.

J. Christopher Miller, JD
Alpharetta, Georgia

5.5 MODERN DOCUMENTATION GUIDELINES FOR E&M CODING

The most important document with which every medical practitioner should be intimately familiar is *Documentation Guidelines for Evaluation and Management Services*, published jointly by the American Medical Association (AMA) and the Centers for Medicare and Medicaid Services (CMSs) in 1997. Those guidelines were revised in December 2000 and 2010, and are updated and available on the CMS website. The changes being proposed are almost all in the direction of requirement of more detail in documentation. One of the really nasty, unfair requirements that the guidelines impose is that the records be legible: if the entries cannot be read, then there is no documentation at all. You do not want to join the list of practitioners who, at deposition, under oath, have to admit that they cannot read their own handwriting. By the way, whether you can read the entries is irrelevant—it is the reviewer who must be able to read them.

5.5.1 Evolution of the SOAP Format

The guidelines rank all patient–practitioner encounters by level of intensity of services rendered and require levels of documentation consistent with those intensity levels. The documentation at every level must include "history, examination and medical decision making."*

If you look at the suggested guidelines, you will find our old friend SOAP lurking beneath. *Subjective* and *objective* are combined in the first entry, and then come *assessment* and *plan*. Added to the standard list is a requirement for the date of service and the identity of the doctor providing it. The guidelines suggest beginning with chief complaint. Please note that few patients complain that they have "paroxysmal nocturnal dyspnea." They are more likely to say, "I wake up in the night choking for air." So, we personally advocate keeping subjective reports separate from objective examination to handle those cases when the two do not match up, e.g., the patient who says, "My back is killing me," but has no trouble hopping up onto the examining table.

The detail required for recording the patient's history of the present illness, past medical history, and family history and/or social history varies according to the level of intensity of the encounter. However, the only exception in the proposed changes in the guidelines for the required, detailed history is for emergency conditions that take up so much time and skill of the practitioner that he/she cannot take the time to obtain those facts. The review of systems (ROSs) may be included in the history, and all positive findings must be recorded. The proposed changes, however, no longer allow silence to indicate that there were no significant negative findings. Significant negative findings are proposed to be required as well.

What is new in the guidelines is the requirement that the process the practitioner goes through in determining how to handle a patient's problem be apparent from the documentation. There must be an indication in the records of *why* a test was ordered, for example. This requirement aids a reviewer in judging whether the expense of the test was justified. Another requirement is that if an addendum is made to the record, it must be dated on the day that it was added to the record, not the date of service. This requirement can be troublesome for practitioners who dictate all or a portion of their records and have the typed dictation inserted into the record when the dictation is transcribed. Additionally, Dr. Ed Pullen, MD, states,

> Consultants have known for years that their referring physicians do not want to look through the entire history and physical exam documentation to get to the assessment and plan. Most consultants make notes to their referring physicians with the Impression and Plan/Recommendations at the top.

Now, the entire legal world knows that referring physicians do not want to look through the entire history and physical examination documentation to get to the medical assessment and treatment plan. WOWSA! As the patient, how would you feel about this statement? Furthermore, he stated,

---

* Guidelines, p. 2.

When a physician reviews a prior progress note, the information they usually want to see is the assessment and plan. Much less often they need to know the details of the patient's history, examination, review of systems, etc. In a paper chart it is just a movement of the eyes to find the desired part of the note, and it makes little difference whether the needed information is on the first few lines, or at the end of the note.

The traditional progress note format is the SOAP note: *subjective* history first; *objective* information like vital signs, physical exam, and test results next; *assessment*, including the diagnosis and documentation of the thought process and decision making, third; and the *plan* of treatment last. This reads in a logical fashion and has become the standard format in most paper patient charts. In an EMR note reviewed on a computer monitor, however, the traditional SOAP note simply does not work. The history of present illness, past medical history, family and social history, and ROS and physical exam more than take up the available space on a monitor.

5.5.2 Enter SOAP(IER) Formats

The traditional SOAP format of medical charting was developed by Dr. Lawrence Weed in 1968. More formally, it is known as the problem-oriented medical record (POMR). However, the concept was updated about 25 years ago by adding the extension SOAP(IER), which may work a bit better:

I = intervention
E = evaluation
R = revision

Of course, nurses know this, but some doctors may not. And, some MDs do not read paper nursing notes, and some EMR systems do not integrate MD and RN electronic notes, as seen in the Ebola EHR clinical integration fiasco in October 2014. Or, doctors know but do not execute—a much graver offense.

5.5.3 And Now—The APSO Format

Furthermore, Dr. Pullen says,

> Simply making an APSO note instead of a SOAP note, i.e., putting the Assessment and Plan first, and the Subjective history and Objective information later can make reviewing notes much more efficient. This simple change can be done easily in most EMRs, and just requires thinking about the different work process using a computer monitor to look at information.

Note: APSO = assessment, plan, subjective, and objective.

5.5.4 So, Let's Change the Medical Record—But Not Bad Physician Behavior?

Well maybe; maybe not! The thought process here seems to be that if the physician behavior is wrong (not reading the entirely legible e-note), let's change the paper or electronic algorithm instead. To which we say, let's change bad physician behavior; or, doctor—PLEASE READ THE DAMN NOTES.

5.5.5 From Paper Records to Electrons—A Malpractice Litigator's Dream

It is at best naive, and more frequently closer to a death wish, to think that an unscrupulous practitioner can beat the system with handwritten notes, computer-generated records, or fabricated EMR documentation. And, we do politely disagree when Dr. Pullen opines,

> EMRs also can easily make a document that does a good job of producing a document that can stand up to legal scrutiny. Although there is little data to prove it, some experts believe use of an EMR can reduce liability.

Regardless of the above, whether EMRs will be more helpful, or even read and reviewed in the future, is still not known. And, malpractice insurance authorities, like David B. Troxel, MD, even feel that they may enhance—not reduce—professional liability.

In fact, after serving as a malpractice trial litigator (defense and prosecution) and expert medical witnesses (defense and prosecution) through three decades, beginning during the early digital medical records revolution, we believe that EMRs will actually increase medical liability as astute plaintiff attorneys and skilled litigators portray them as canned, automated, and robotic notes—not at all relative to the real patient. We've seen it before, and it will successfully happen again, as sympathetic jurors buy the argument—*en masse.*

For example, we can just imagine a sly attorney admonishing the lay jury—

> My client, Mrs. Smith, is a human being—a patient; she is not an electronic template. Like you, she exits in the real world, not the virtual world of manipulated bits and fabricated electronic bytes. And, by the way, doctor, did you even read the notes? After all, consultants have known for years that referring physicians do not want to look through the entire history and physical exam documentation to get to the assessment and plan.

Of course, like some other experts, we also believe that EMRs may actually hinder the patient–physician relationship and communication channel.

5.6 LEGAL STATUTES REGARDING MEDICAL BILLING

After the guidelines in importance (but not far behind) are the statutes that punish providers for submitting false claims for services. There is a special FCA for Medicare* and a general FCA.† The original FCA was passed during the Civil War period when unscrupulous traders were bilking the government for war material. The special act provides for coordination of state, federal, and insurance company efforts to monitor and investigate false claims for medical services. The general act provides severe penalties for any person who bills the U.S. government for items or services not actually provided and/or falsely billed. What every practitioner needs to know is that A BILL FOR A SERVICE WHICH IS INADEQUATELY DOCUMENTED (paper or electronic) IS A FALSE CLAIM. Read this sentence over a few times and believe it.

It does not matter if the care was actually given, if it was given properly, or if the patient benefited.‡ A bill for those services is not to be submitted unless the documentation is there before the bill is submitted. If the bill is sent (claim made) without the level of documentation required, then the claim is false. Submitting a false claim is a civil wrong done to the government and may constitute a crime as well. The consequences are so horrendous that they are hard to imagine.

The FCA allows the government not only to get its money back for improperly billed claims, but also to get double or triple that amount. Next come fines called civil money penalties beginning at $5000 up to $10,000 for *each bill submitted.* Finally, criminal punishment can be imposed for knowing violation of the act. In the case of the FCA, there is a special definition of *knowing* and *knowingly*, which mean that a person, with respect to information, (1) has actual knowledge of the information; (2) acts in deliberate ignorance of the truth or falsity of the information; or (3) acts in reckless disregard of the truth or falsity of the information, and no proof of specific intent to defraud is required.

The case of *United States v. Krizek* provides one of the first shocking examples of a physician falling afoul of the FCA. A psychiatrist had his wife bill the government for alleged health-care services and did not check her bills in any way. The bills amounted to more than 24 hours of service in a 24-hour period, so that the government did not have to review the individual documentation to show that the claims were false. Both the doctor and his wife were held liable, and the impossibility of the care having actually been provided was held to be sufficient to amount to knowledge of the falsity of the claims. A chilling detail of this case is that the government wanted to charge a civil money penalty not just for each bill submitted but for each diagnostic code listed on each bill.

Billing for medical services at a higher reimbursement level than was justified by the services actually provided constitutes a false claim. In *United States v. Lorenzo*, a dentist billed for a separate oral examination for cancer that was actually only a part of his regular dental check-up examination. So-called *upcoding* is a basis for an FCA charge, and it can take a number of forms.

---

* 42 U.S.C. 1320a–7c.

† 31 U.S.C. 3729.

‡ U.S. ex rel. Pogue v. American Healthcorp, Inc., 914 F. Supp. 1507 (M.D. Tenn. 1996).

Overheard in the Doctor's Lounge

Inviting Patients to Read Their Doctors' Notes

In an *OpenNotes* study, researchers examined the impact on patients and doctors when patients were allowed access to their doctors' notes via a secure Internet portal. Through the use of surveys, patients' benefits, concerns, and behaviors, as well as physicians' workload, were measured.

Beth Israel Deaconess Medical Center (BIDMC) in Boston, Geisinger Health System (GHS) in Pennsylvania, and Harborview Medical Center (HMC) in Seattle were selected for this quasi-experimental year-long study. The study included 105 physicians and 13,564 of their patients. Patients were notified when their notes were available, but whether or not to open the note was at their own discretion. The authors analyzed both preintervention and postintervention surveys from the physicians who completed the study; 99 physicians submitted both preintervention and postintervention surveys. Of the patients who viewed at least one note, 41% completed postintervention surveys.

Almost 99% of patients at BIDMC, GHS, and HMC wanted to have continued access to their visit notes at the completion of the study; no physician elected to end this practice. Although a limited geographic area was represented, the positive feedback and clinically relevant benefits demonstrate the potential for widespread adoption of *OpenNotes*. Moreover, it may be a powerful tool in helping improve the lives of patients.

Ann Miller, RN, MHA, CMP (candidate)
*Atlanta, Georgia**

OpenNotes, a grantee of the Robert Wood Johnson Foundation, was developed to demonstrate and evaluate the impact on both patients and clinicians of fully sharing (through an electronic patient portal) all encounter notes between patients and their primary care providers.

For example, if a patient comes into the office for a diagnostic test or a session of some therapy that is not personally delivered by a practitioner, and the practitioner tacks on an office visit to the bill, the claim is obviously false. A more troublesome area of potential liability, however, arises when the code and the actual intensity of care match up but the documentation does not. The practitioner may have given all the care needed to justify the billing code, but if the documentation is lacking, the claim may be false. Upcoding levels of intensity of care causes false claims to be submitted.

Potential liability for damages is not linked directly to the amount of money that was lost by the government in the false billing. While the amount of damages starts with triple the government's losses, the civil money penalties can soon overwhelm that amount. In the case of *United States v. Greenberg*, the court awarded the government $78,000 against Dr. Greenberg despite the fact that he only gained $549.09 from the false claims he submitted for his medical services.

* From Delbanco, T. et al., *Ann. Intern. Med.*, 157(7): 523–524, 2012 (October, 2).

The FCAs contain *whistle-blower* provisions for immunity. A person acting in good faith who reports possible false claims to governmental authorities is immune from prosecution for doing so.

Many defendants in such actions have attempted to bring complaints of theft or conversion of trade secrets against those who bring records to the offices of prosecuting attorneys. They have not had much success except when records have actually been stolen rather than copied.

A *qui tam* action may also be brought by civilians on behalf of the government under 31 U.S.C. § 3730. The civilian, known as a relator, brings the claim on behalf of the government to recover the amount of the false claim. (All of those cases that begin "U.S. ex rel." are *qui tam* actions.) If the relator has insider knowledge that allows the claim to succeed, then the relater is entitled to a percentage of the damages ultimately recovered for the government.

5.7 MEDICAL RECORD RETENTION

According to Richard Cahill, JD, vice president and associate general counsel of The Doctors Company, a number of variables affect the length of time a physician should keep a medical record. Factors include state and federal laws, medical board and association policies, and the type of record (for example, that of an adult patient versus that of a pediatric patient). The following information can help guide you in developing a medical record retention policy (http://www.thedoctors.com).

5.7.1 Basis for Keeping Medical Records

The most important reason for keeping a medical record is to provide information on a patient's care to other health-care professionals. Another major rationale is that a well-documented medical record provides support for the physician's defense in the event of a medical malpractice action.

Entries made in the medical record at or near the time of the event are regarded as highly reliable evidence in subsequent judicial procedures. Without the medical record, the physician might not be able to show that the care he/she provided was appropriate and, thereby, met the standard of care. Relying on the practitioner's general habit and practice to show that the standard of care was met—without supporting documentation to establish what treatment was actually rendered—often fails to convince the finder of fact that the treatment the patient received was consistent with community standards.

5.7.2 State and Federal Laws

For the most part, state and federal laws regarding mandatory record retention requirements apply to hospitals or similar facilities rather than to physician practices. The Medicare Conditions of Participation (COP) require hospitals to retain records for 5 years (6 years for critical access hospitals), whereas Occupational Safety and Health Administration (OSHA) requires an employer to retain medical records for 30 years for employees who have been exposed to toxic substances and harmful agents. Health Insurance Portability and Accountability Act (HIPAA) privacy regulations require records to be retained for 6 years from when the record was created, which follows the federal statute of limitations for civil penalties.

5.7.3 Medical Board and Medical Association Policies

When state or federal laws are silent on medical record retention, medical boards may be able to provide policies or recommendations on how long a physician should keep records.

For example, the Colorado State Board of Medical Examiners Policy 40-07 recommends retaining medical records for a minimum of 7 years after the last date of treatment for an adult and for 7 years after a minor has reached the age of majority, or age 25. The California Medical Association has concluded that, while a retention period of at least 10 years may be sufficient, all medical records should be retained indefinitely or, in the alternative, for 25 years.

5.7.4 Case Law

A decision by the California Court of Appeal (Fourth District) discussed the protection traditionally afforded to physicians by the statute of limitations. The court ultimately held (consistent with state law) that when an injury or abnormality does not manifest itself within the statute of limitations or if the patient could not have discovered that the injuries were caused by wrongdoing within the required time frame, the limitation period is not triggered. As such, the required time for the patient to bring a malpractice action may be extended for an additional period after the care was provided.

5.7.5 Considerations

Medical record retention laws and regulations differ from state to state. It should be emphasized that once a record is destroyed, it is difficult—if not impossible—to defend the case. Physicians should contact their attorneys for guidance.

For example, in California, where there is no statutory requirement, the California Medical Association recommends that medical records be retained indefinitely or for at least 25 years after the patient's last visit.

Some states allow records to be retained in an electronic format. For example, a paper record may be scanned to a computer or kept in another electronic format. Paper records should be stored with a reputable document storage company.

Many companies offer alternative methods for document management, such as electronic scanning and storage. Storing closed or archived records at your residence puts the records at risk of damage from fire or flood, loss due to theft, or other unauthorized access. You should also check state statutes and professional licensing agencies for state-specific requirements or recommendations.

5.7.6 What Records Should You Retain?

Retain all records that reflect the clinical care provided to a patient, including provider notes, nurses' notes, diagnostic testing, and medication lists. Retain records obtained from another provider for the same length of time as your own. This is especially true if you have relied on any of the previous records or information when making your clinical decisions.

Review patient bills for any reference to care provided. For example, review a bill to determine if it shows a limited examination or an annual physical with diagnostic tests obtained or requested. If the billing document shows that care was provided, it may be in your best interest to keep the bill for as long as you retain the medical record. Otherwise, you need to retain the bill for the same length of time as other business records and in accordance with federal and state income tax requirements.

We understand that storing medical records for the recommended time can have a financial effect on the physician or practice. Given the importance of the medical record in defending a malpractice action, however, it is vital to ensure that the record is available to defend proper care.

5.8 MEDICAL RECORD REQUESTS AND COPYING COSTS

According to colleague Nicholas Bagley, of the *Incidental Economist*, medical records are technically the property of the physicians and hospitals that compile them. But, the law has long recognized that patients also have rights to those records (personal communication).

Most significantly, under HIPAA's Privacy Rule, a provider must, upon request, give a patient a copy of his/her medical records. But, to cover the costs of copying and postage, the Privacy Rule allows providers to charge those patients "a reasonable and cost based" fee. Many providers don't bother imposing fees at all. But, some claim extraordinary fees—often several hundreds of dollars—for copying and releasing patient records. Responding to the potential for abuse, more than two-thirds of the states have imposed caps on fees. The caps vary, but they typically range from $40 to $70 for a 100-page record.

Excessive charges for patient records are obviously burdensome, especially for the poor. But, the charges might be problematic for other reasons as well. Imagine, for example, that a patient would like to switch doctors. He/she would also like to bring their medical records with them. If it's going to cost hundreds of dollars to get those records, might the patient just sit tight? In other words, could fees for copying medical records impede competition, or enhance liability risk?

Pending research by Laurence C. Baker, Kate Bundorf, and Daniel Kessler brings some data to answer the question. To their surprise, they "find that patients from states adopting caps on copy fees were significantly more likely to switch doctors." In any given year, they find, patients are 11% more likely to switch primary care doctors and 13% more likely to switch specialists.

They also wondered whether providers were more likely to adopt EMRs in states with caps on copy fees. Allowing providers to charge whatever it costs to copy and send medical records dulls their incentives to improve their record-keeping systems. Might caps encourage them to adopt EMRs? Again, the data suggest that the answer is yes. "Hospitals from states that imposed a cap," they opined, "were approximately 8 percentage points more likely to adopt an EMR" (personal communication).

5.9 PHOTOREDUCTION OF MEDICAL RECORDS

Except for the OSHA provisions regarding x-rays, there are no laws limiting the microfilming or storing of medical records in a reduced format. However, it is very important that photographically reduced records and any copies subsequently made from the reductions are completely legible. Ensuring the legibility of photographically reduced records is not a trivial process. It demands that the photoreduction process be carefully controlled and that the reduced records be constantly monitored to make sure that each one is legible. The most difficult problem in ensuring legible photoreduction is in controlling the color of ink used to make entries in the medical record. Photoreduction materials are able to record only certain colors of ink accurately. If the medical record is in several different colors of ink, it may be impossible to record all entries legibly. It is very important to keep exotically colored ink from the medical record. Ideally, all entries in the medical record should be made in black ink. This would make it simple to produce a photoreproduction and ensure that the subsequent copies would be legible. While it may not be possible to require that all entries be in black ink, it should be possible to require that all entries be in either black or neither blue ink, thus excluding such colors as peacock blue. Under no circumstances should entries be made in pencil. While a penciled entry may reproduce satisfactorily, it is easily altered and produces a legally questionable record.

Once photoreductions have been made of the medical record, it is permissible to destroy the original record by shredding or burning. Special precautions are needed when storing the photoreductions. The original paper records can stand quite a bit of abuse and still maintain their legibility. This is not true of photoreductions. Humid conditions of storage can lead to the destruction of the emulsion by mildew, and even a minor scratch can eliminate major portions of a medical record. Access to the photoreductions thus should be limited to members of the medical records department. This will prevent unskilled persons from damaging the reduced records in the process of trying to read them. The facility may even want to make duplicate reduced records and store them separately. Once the record has been reduced, copying the reduction is simple and inexpensive.

Original paper records should be retained for as long as is economically feasible after photoreductions are made. The original paper record is still the most effective documentation of the health care that was rendered to the patient. It is imperative that the paper record not be destroyed if litigation is in progress. If the record is microfilmed and the original destroyed, the plaintiff's counsel may be able to throw the entire record into question over the issue of whether the copying was done to cover up alterations in the original record. Conversely, a properly reduced and stored medical record is the best guarantee against both future alterations in the record and the complete disappearance of the record.

5.10 DISAPPEARANCE OF MEDICAL RECORDS

The disappearance of the entire medical record is extremely damaging in medical malpractice litigation. The disappearance of the records calls into question the care rendered the patient and the integrity of the hospital. The office, clinic, or hospital must carefully guard its medical records to prevent them from being inadvertently misplaced or stolen by an unscrupulous person. Under no circumstances should the medical record be allowed outside the medical records department. If a patient is readmitted to the hospital, the relevant parts of the record (admissions and discharge notes, reports of laboratory tests, and other requested information) should be duplicated, and copies should be sent to the floor to be incorporated in the patient's new medical record. The record of the earlier hospitalization should not be sent to the floor and made the basis of the patient's new records.

Physicians should not be allowed to check out medical records and take them away from the medical records department. The medical records department should provide a comfortable, quiet area for physicians to work on medical records and review charts. Only by enforcing an absolute prohibition on removing records from the medical records area can the medical records administrator prevent the inadvertent loss of a record. If records routinely leave the medical records department, it will be very difficult to guarantee that all the records removed are actually returned to the department. Even if an effective mechanism for checking out the records could be devised, if the physician who checks out the record accidentally loses it, the medical records personnel are in the same position as if the record has been stolen.

Overheard in the Doctor's Lounge

Is there a Migration of Patients to Paper-Based Records?

Starting long ago, I warned that as more dental patients are notified of data breaches—some more than once—we are likely to witness an event mandate stakeholders said would never happen: a migration of patients to paper-based dentists. Now, because of the rapidly escalating costs and liabilities, not only can defiant, slow adopters of electronic dental records (EDRs) expect to provide dental care at a lower cost than "paperless practices," but also, patients are on course to learn that some dentists put their patients at risk of medical identity theft by putting identities on computers. For example, in February 2015, the *Ponemon Institute* published their "Fifth Annual Study on Medical Identity Theft."

> Consumers expect healthcare providers to be proactive in preventing and detecting medical identity theft. Although many respondents are not confident in the security practices of their healthcare provider, 79 percent of respondents say it is important for healthcare providers to ensure the privacy of their health records. Forty-eight percent say they would consider changing healthcare providers if their medical records were lost or stolen. If such a breach occurred, 40 percent say prompt notification by the organization responsible for safeguarding this information is important.

So if your patients start asking you not to put their identities—including medical records—on your computers, what will you do, Doc?

Since encryption is a nonstarter in dentistry for solid, business reasons, and will make paperless practices even less competitive with paper-based ones, would you consider employing staff who know how to use pegboard, ledger cards, and lots of carbon paper (the gold standard of security)? OR would you prefer not to give up computerization, yet keep your patients safe? Deidentification of primary electronic dental and medical records is sounding better all the time. Am I right? If patients' identities are not available, they cannot be hacked.

From: Paper Medical Records Become Popular Again?*

D. Kellus Pruitt, DDS
Fort Worth, Texas

---

* http://medidfraud.org/2014-fifth-annual-study-on-medical-identity-theft/.

5.11 MISFILING RECORDS

Another problem arises in the misfiling of a record. In facilities that have hundreds of thousands of records, the misfiling of a record may lead to its permanent loss. This is not a problem peculiar to medical records storage. Large libraries face the same problem: when books are misplaced, they are effectively lost. In order to combat this problem, such facilities hire persons whose only job is to do what is called "reading" the shelves. They systematically begin at one end of the collection and scan the titles and the access numbers of every book in the collection to flag misfiled books. In the case of books, this is a cost-effective procedure. A person need only recover one or two valuable books a day to offset the salary being paid. When it is realized that thousands of titles may be scanned in a day's time, the probability that several misfiled books will be located is very high.

It is harder to assess the cost-effectiveness of this type of surveillance in a medical records department. First, medical records are not in open stacks, so they are usually filed by skilled personnel. The probability of misfiling a record will be considerably lower than it is in a research library, where the patrons often refile books themselves. Second, unless a malpractice suit has already been filed in a given case, there is no clear economic benefit to finding a misplaced file. The risk manager must be very forceful in arguing that, even though there is no direct economic gain in finding a misplaced file, the potential loss from litigation is great enough to justify the periodic scanning of the files to recover misplaced medical records.

5.12 RETENTION OF RECORDS

There are few legal requirements on how long medical records must be retained after the patient has been discharged from the hospital. From a risk management point of view, it would be desirable for all records to be retained indefinitely. Unfortunately, this would be economically difficult to justify, so reasonable criteria for the retention of records must be adopted. These criteria should balance the risk management benefit of retaining records against the economic problems associated with storing a large quantity of records that will seldom, if ever, be needed.

Overheard in the Doctor's Lounge

Socioeconomic Status

Today, the concept known as socioeconomic status (SES) is conceptualized as the social standing, or class, of an individual or group. It is often measured as a combination of education, income, and occupation. Examinations of SES often reveal inequities in access to medical resources, plus issues related to privilege, power, and control. SES is increasingly being considered as another payment component (CPT codes) to medical providers, as reflected in the paper medical record, EMR, ICD-10, and elsewhere.

Ann Miller, RN, MHA, CMP (candidate)
Atlanta, Georgia

5.13 RISKS OF A SECOND MEDICAL OPINION

What if I want another opinion before undergoing treatment? An opinion from another physician is very important before underlying major therapy, and it is your right to seek one. You may ask your physician to send you to another physician, but it is better if you find the second physician on your own. A second opinion from an independent physician is an especially good idea for nonemergency or *elective* surgery, so that you can fully consider all the possible risks and benefits.

What is the second physician entitled to obtain from my original physician? The physician giving a second opinion should obtain a summary of your medical history from the original physician. This summary should include the results of any tests you were given so that they need not be repeated. If the original physician refuses to provide x-rays, that physician must at least make them available for the second physician to view.

What if the original physician refused to make the records or x-rays available? You should call the physician and explain the situation, and then send a written request for the information. If this does not work, you might consider contacting your local medical society, or an attorney.

5.14 STATUTE OF LIMITATIONS

The statute of limitations for medical malpractice in the state where the facility is located will provide a guide to the absolute minimum period that records should be maintained. Depending on the local state laws, adults have from 1 to 4 years after the occurrence of an injury to file a claim for medical malpractice.

The main problem here is that states tend to define the term *occurrence* differently. In some states, it is the date on which the specific act of malpractice occurred, whether the patient knew about the malpractice or not. Other states date the running of the period from the last date on which medical care was rendered to the patient by the defendant healthcare provider. In states where the running of the statute period of limitations starts from the discovery of the malpractice, it is conceivable that a malpractice suit could be filed 10, 15, 20, or more years after the patient was discharged from the facility. The safest legal course in these states is to retain the medical records until the statute of limitations period has run out after the patient's death. In states where the statute of limitations period runs from the last date that care was rendered to the patient, all records should be kept to the end of the statute period after the patient was last treated at the facility. In states where the statute of limitations period runs from the actual occurrence of the malpractice, it is still best to hold the records through the period of the statute of limitations after the patient was last treated at the facility, because it is impossible to know which treatments will become the subject of litigation.

Records on minors must be maintained for longer periods than the records on adults. The laws vary from state to state, but in many states, the statute of limitations period for medical malpractice on a minor does not begin to run until the patient's 18th birthday. In these states, it is clear that the records must be kept at least until the patient's 18th birthday, plus the period of the statute of limitations. In other states, the statute period begins to run at earlier birth dates, from the age of 14, or even the age of 6 or 8. In facilities located in these states, it is necessary that the records be kept for the statute of limitations period beyond the appropriate birthday. Under no circumstances should the records be kept for a period less than the statute of limitations period after the last discharge from the facility.

5.15 MEDICAL RECORDS WHEN CLOSING A MEDICAL PRACTICE

When a practice closes, the physician or group is responsible for making appropriate arrangements for the disposition of all medical records—regardless of whether the records are in paper or electronic format. The possibility of a lawsuit after a physician has left or a practice has closed always exists. To help defend against any future claims, the retention of records is paramount.

In California, where there is no statutory requirement, the California Medical Association recommends that medical records be retained indefinitely or for at least 25 years after the patient's last visit. Due to the impracticality of this recommendation, the following criteria are suggested as minimum standards in California:

- Adult patients, 10 years from the date the patient was last seen
- Minor patients, 28 years from the date of birth
- Deceased patients, 5 years from the date of death

Physicians who turn their practices over to replacement physicians should have agreements in place that stipulate the recommended retention time and access capability. If a physician chooses to destroy clinical records after a set period of time, confidentiality must not be compromised. There exist record destruction services that guarantee records are properly destroyed without releasing any information.

When a practice closes and medical records are transferred, patients should be notified that they may designate a physician or another provider who can receive a copy of the records. If a patient does not designate a physician, records may be transferred to a custodian (a physician or a commercial storage firm).

Custodians who agree to retain records can be physicians, nonphysicians, or commercial storage facilities. Custodial arrangements for retaining records are usually entered into for a fee and should be in writing. A written custodial agreement should guarantee future access to the records for both the physician and patients and should include the following points:

- The custodian will keep and maintain the medical records for the retention times specified above.
- No one can access the information contained in the medical records without a signed release from the patient or a properly executed subpoena or court order.
- The original physician or physician's personal representative will be notified of any change of the custodian's address or phone number.
- Terms apply to all persons in the custodian's employment and facility.
- Copies of medical records will be released to a person designated by the patient only with the patient's written request.
- The custodian will comply with state and federal laws governing medical record confidentiality, access, disclosure, and charges for copies of the records.

- There are agreed-upon fees for maintaining the records.
- The agreement contains language that addresses any personal practice decisions made by a custodian (retirement, selling, or moving) to ensure the safety of and continued access to the records by the original physician or physician's personal representative.

5.16 ASSESSMENT

In almost an ironic return to the original reason for medical records, FCA suits have been maintained on the basis of claims that the care actually provided to patients was not adequate in quality to justify the claims being submitted. In other words, if the care provided fell below the standard of care provided, not only did the practitioner commit medical malpractice, but he/she also submitted a false claim!

MEDICAL RECORD SCRIBES

Medical scribes, like medical transcriptionists, are important to the health information management (HIM) industry. A scribe is a physician collaborator who fulfills the primary clerical and nonmedical functions of the busy physician or medical practitioner. By focusing on data collection and its documentation in order to establish a rapid and smooth work flow, the physician is relieved from having to make time-consuming phone calls, and can prepare to see the next patient, answer a nurse's concern, or perform the next patient procedure. The scribe will also actively track down delayed lab results, CT scan readings, and any other pertinent information in order to increase the accuracy and velocity of the completed medical record and, ultimately, decrease emergency room (ER) waiting room times and discharge patients faster. This will allow the physician to prioritize tasks he/she must accomplish in a given time period. Medical scribes earn between $10 and $16 per hour and can earn significantly more with increased experience and responsibility as a manager of a hospital's scribe program, either working directly for the hospital or working for a medical scribe company. Of course, the average annual salary varies based on geographic location.

5.17 CONCLUSION

Traditional medical records are undergoing a philosophical, legal, reimbursement, and electronic sea change fraught with many new risks and perils. Therefore, always remember that medical records are no longer a reflection of reality; they are the reality.

5.18 COLLABORATE

Discuss this chapter online with others at http://www.medicalexecutivepost.com.

ACKNOWLEDGMENTS

To Dr. Charles F. Fenton III, JD, Atlanta, Georgia, and to Professor Edward P. Richards, JD, MPH, Program in Law, Science and Public Health, LSU Law Center, LSU.

FURTHER READINGS

29 CFR § 1910.1020(d)(1).

31 U.S.C. §3729(b).

31 U.S.C. 3729.

42 CFR § 482.24(b)(1) and 42 CFR § 485.638(c).

42 CFR Part 1003.132.

42 U.S.C. § 1320a–7c (B)(iii); Mann v. Olsten Certified Healthcare Corp., 49 F. Supp. 2d 1307 (M.D. Ala. 1999).

42 U.S.C. 1320a–7c.

45 CFR § 164.530(j)(2).

111 F.3d 934 (D.C. App. 1997).

237 F. Supp. 439 (S.D.N.Y. 1965).

Fenton, CF: Medical Risk Management Issues. In Marcinko, DE [editor]: *Insurance Planning and Risk Management for Physicians.* Jones and Bartlett Publishing, Sudbury, MA, 2006.

Gallegos, A: EHRs' advantages may carry malpractice risks as well. *ACP Internist*, American College of Physicians Press, Philadelphia, PA, 2014.

Hristidis, V: *Information Discovery on Electronic Health Records.* Taylor & Francis Group, Productivity Press, Florence, KY, 2009.

Kitzig v. Nordquist, 81 Cal. App 4th 1384, 97 Cal Rptr 2d 762 (2000).

Lacava, W: *Medical Records Risks [A Reflection of the New Reality]: Insurance Planning and Risk Management for Physicians.* Jones and Bartlett Publishing, Sudbury, MA, 2006.

Marcinko, DE and Fenton, CF: Medical Risk Management Issues. In Marcinko, DE and Hetico, HR [editors]: *Comprehensive Financial Planning Strategies for Doctors and Advisors: Best Practices from Leading Consultants and Certified Medical Planners™.* Taylor & Francis Group, Productivity Press, Florence, KY, 2015.

Retention of Medical Records, Document #4005, CMA On-Call, http://www.cmanet.org.

Richards, EP: *Medical Risk Management: Preventive Legal Strategies for Health Care Providers.* The Law, Science & Public Health Law Site. Paul M. Hebert Law Center, Louisiana State University, Baton Rouge, LA, 2015.

Trites, P: Medical Records, Insurance Billing and Coding Guidelines. In Marcinko, DE [editor]: *Business of Medical Practice* [3rd edition]. Springer Publishing, New York, 2010.

Troxel, DB: *An EMR-Related Claim.* The Doctor's Advocate. The Doctor's Company, Napa, CA, 2014.

Troxel, DB: SAFER Guides for Electronic Health Record Implementation and Use. The Doctor's Advocate. The Doctor's Company, Napa, CA, 2014.

U.S. ex rel. Mikes v. Straus, 931 F. Supp. 248, motion to certify appeal denied, 939 F. Supp. 301 (S.D.N.Y. 1996).

U.S. ex rel. Pogue v. American Healthcorp, Inc., 914 F. Supp. 1507 (M.D. Tenn. 1996).

U.S. ex rel. Trim v. McKean, 31 F. Supp. 2d 1308 (W.D. Okla. 1998).

U.S. v. Lorenzo, 768 F. Supp. 1127 (E.D. Pa. 1991).

APPENDIX: DISENROLLMENT APPEAL LETTER TEMPLATE

Dear Medical Director,

As a current disenrolled member or nonmember of your managed care/HMO/insurance plan, I would like to take this opportunity to inform you of the activities we have pursued during this past year in order to gain acceptance into your plan.

For example, I have received X hours of clinical continuing education, which is X more than the state requires. Topics included recently developed techniques for pain control, non-hospital-based and non-surgical-based therapy, more effective drug utilization, and a host of other methods of practice to reduce costs and increase patient welfare and mobility. Moreover:

- I have received X hours of medical business management training aimed at reducing office overhead expenses, increasing office efficiency and capacity, and improving patient flow and communications. For example, our computerized callback system is designed to ensure the continuity of patient care.
- We have completed a patient survey that demonstrates that the average patient can receive a regular appointment within X days and urgent appointment within X days. Of course, we are fully staffed for immediate care of emergent patients. Our patient satisfaction rating is high. Most patients spend less than X minutes in the waiting room and are discharged in a timely fashion, with appropriate instructions in order to return them to work efficiently and comfortably.
- We have expanded our office hours to improve access and enhanced the barrier-free design of our office infrastructure. We are OSHA, CLIA, MSDS, PA, Sarbox, and HIPAA compliant, etc.
- Since we believe in preventative care, our diabetic patients are continually screened and evaluated to reduce the potential for infections and other complications. This includes the liberal use of random Accu-Chek blood sugar readings, with neurologic and circulatory assessment, with prompt reporting of aberrant values and findings to their primary care physicians or endocrinologists.
- I will be taking my specialty board certification examination in 2017. Of course, my results will be forwarded to you immediately.
- I will become American Board of Quality Assurance and Utilization Review (ABQAUR) certified and/or a certified physician in health-care quality (CPHQ) this year, after successful completion of all educational requirements and examinations.

Although I realize that this is a challenging time for all concerned, we strive to make every patient's visit to our office a medically and socially positive one. More specific suggestions regarding our practice would be appreciated. Therefore, we hope you will consider the probationary inclusion of our practice into your managed care plan, for the coming enrollment period.

Fraternally,
Joseph A. Smith, MD/DO/DPM

6 Romantic Patient Advances

Medical Office Sexual Harassment Issues

Vicki L. Buba and David Edward Marcinko

CONTENTS

The lesson for fledgling doctors comes early in medical school: getting romantically involved with a patient is forbidden. The problem is that not every patient plays by the rules, and a patient prone to flirtation can create a dicey ethical dilemma for a doctor—or at least make office visits uncomfortable for physicians and staff. Later, in his/her medical career, of greater interest to the physician executive or medical practice owner is under what circumstances doctor employers can be held liable if an employee claims he/she has been sexually harassed.

So, let us start at the beginning.

6.1 INTRODUCTION

Within the medical practice, clinic, hospital, or university setting, faculty and supervisors exercise significant power and authority over others. Therefore, primary responsibility for maintaining high standards of conduct resides especially with those in faculty and supervisor positions. Members of the medical faculty and staff, including graduate assistants, are prohibited from having "amorous relationships" with students over whom they have "supervisory responsibilities." *Supervisory responsibilities* are defined as teaching, evaluating, tutoring, advocating, counseling, and/or advising duties performed currently and directly, whether within or outside the office, clinic, or hospital setting, by a faculty member, staff member, or graduate assistant, with respect to a medical, nursing, or healthcare professional student. Such responsibilities include the administration, provision, or supervision of all academic, cocurricular, or extracurricular services and activities, opportunities, awards, or benefits offered by or through the health entity or its personnel in their official capacity. Employees are prohibited from having amorous relationships with employees whom they supervise, evaluate, or in any other way directly affect the terms and conditions of the others' employment, even in cases where there is, or appears to be, mutual consent.

6.2 CONSENSUAL AMOROUS RELATIONSHIPS DEFINED

An *amorous relationship* is defined as a consensual romantic, sexual, or dating relationship. This definition excludes marital unions. The term also encompasses those relationships in which amorous or romantic feelings exist without physical intimacy and which, when acted upon by the faculty or staff member, exceed the reasonable boundaries of what a person of ordinary sensibilities would believe to be a collegial or professional relationship. The faculty/student and supervisor/employee relationship should not be jeopardized by questions of favoritism or fairness in professional judgment. Furthermore, whether the consent by a student or employee in such a relationship is indeed voluntary is suspect due to the imbalance of power and authority between the parties. All members of the healthcare entity should be aware that initial consent to a romantic relationship does not preclude the potential for charges of conflict of interest, or for charges of sexual harassment arising from the conflict of interest, particularly when students and employees not involved in the relationship claim they have been disadvantaged by the relationship. A faculty member, staff member, or graduate assistant who enters into an amorous relationship with a student under his/her supervision, or a supervisor who enters into an amorous relationship with an employee under his/her supervision, must realize that if a charge of sexual harassment is subsequently lodged, it will be exceedingly difficult to prove blamelessness on grounds of mutual consent. This policy is superseded by the laws governing inability to consent based on age.

6.3 HANDLING ROMANTIC PATIENT ADVANCES

While physicians vary in their approaches to managing flirtatious patients, many agree that nipping the behavior in the bud is critical to maintaining professionalism and upholding ethical standards. "It's flattering to have a flirtatious patient," said Dr. William P. Scherer, MS, professor of radiology at the Barry University School of Medicine, Miami, Florida. "But, we have an obligation to protect the integrity of our medical profession, and to our marital contracts and spousal relationships and family, and to act professionally at all times" (personal communication).

Dr. Scherer finds it helpful to put some professional distance between himself and a flirtatious patient. "I have no problem saying to a patient: I appreciate what interests you may have, but I have to draw the line to take proper professional care of you, instead."

And a good way to derail flirtatious behavior from patients is by deflecting their unwelcome comments. "And, you can't act sheepish about it." When a patient's remark crosses the line from complimentary to something uncomfortable, the doctor may either curtly laugh it off or ignore it. "I don't acknowledge the statement and immediately move the conversation into something clinical in order to put the rest of the visit in a serious tone."

On the other hand, Dr. Barbara S. Schlefman, MS, a fitness trainer and retired podiatrist, instructed her nurses to have another staffer accompany them into an examination room when a patient known for being flirtatious was waiting to be seen, and to leave the door open (personal communication).

Likewise, other physicians use a "more is merrier" approach for themselves and their staff as a defense against flirtatious behavior. Flirtatious behavior is a problem that can be avoided by having physicians never see patients alone. So, as Dr. Schlefman advised, be sure to always have a nurse or medical assistant in the room with the physician, even if you have to see somebody in the office on call after hours. And, be sure to have a call schedule for the nursing and medical assistant staff that includes patients of both genders, regard less of physician gender, since flirtatious behavior can be same-sex flirtatious behavior. Fortunately, adjunct or visiting clinical professors, or doctors on a medical school clinical teaching staff, rarely have patient encounters without a medical student, intern, resident fellow, or nurse in the room during examinations.

6.3.1 Recognize the Signs

While it's important that physicians don't act on a flirtatious patient's advances, it's equally critical to recognize subtle flirtatious signs from a patient, according to Donna Petrozzello, MD, an otolaryngologist at the California Sinus Centers.

A patient that maintains unusually long eye contact with their doctor, engages in talk not related to their visit, or makes a habit of touching the physician when not medically necessary, may be flirting. Additionally, doctors can protect themselves when performing some common procedures that put them in close proximity to a patient's face, breasts, genitals, legs, and even feet. That closeness could turn a clinical exam into a flirtatious event. Wearing a mask to perform each of these local or regional examinations is not only for the purposes of infection control but also gives the added benefit of establishing some personal space and protection, to avoid any potential misunderstanding. For example, auscultating lungs through a shirt, not underneath, is a good idea with this type of exam on a young woman patient.

6.3.2 Potential Outcomes of Flirtatious Behavior

Although flirting may seem innocent in most situations, it can have serious consequences if it persists and escalates between a physician and a patient, particularly if the physician becomes sexually involved with that patient.

For starters, physicians who become romantically involved with patients may lose sight of their professional obligation to be objective in treating them. "When you're biased in your decision making, or so emotionally attached to a patient that you can no longer be objective, then you're no longer on your game, and you're no longer able to provide the best quality of response that the patient deserves," according to Render Davis, MHA, CHE, a medical ethicist formerly from Crawford Long Hospital and Emory Healthcare, in Atlanta, Georgia (personal communication).

Additionally, a physician may be the target of a civil lawsuit by a patient when the relationship comes to an end. Using the defense that the relationship was consensual is typically not a strong one, given societal views that physicians are in the power position when it comes to initiating, or ending, a physician–patient relationship.

If a physician is found to have engaged in sexual misconduct with a patient, he/she may be sanctioned by a state medical board, which can dole out any number of punishments, not limited to censuring the physician privately or publicly revoking his/her license to practice medicine, said Dr. Charles F. Fenton III, JD, PC, a doctor and health-care attorney, in Atlanta.

Fenton advises physicians to tell patients, in no uncertain terms, that flirtatious behavior isn't welcome. "It's very clear that a physician cannot engage in flirtatious activity with a patient. If the activity continues on, the physician has no option but to terminate the relationship," he said. "I would follow up a termination letter in writing and tell the patient: You may seek a physician of your choice, or, if you need a recommendation, we are happy to provide three names."

6.3.3 How to Discourage Flirtatious Patients

- Bring a medical assistant into the exam room. A third person can squash a patient's urge to flirt and also serve as a witness to the appropriateness of the physician–patient encounter.
- Don't let a reassuring pat on the back, warm handshake, or comforting hug become misconstrued. Doctors must be careful that patients don't perceive their compassionate care to mean they are interested in pursuing a deeper relationship.

- Preserve the personal space between yourself and your patient. Wear a protective mask when performing sensitive clinical procedures and exams that require you to be close to a patient's head.
- Keep the conversation polite but focused on a clinical topic. Don't engage in flirtatious banter with patients or entertain their suggestive comments.
- Be sensitive to the fact that flirting can occur. Learn to recognize the subtle signs of flirting and quickly put an end to the behavior.

Now, let us progress from flirtation to harassment.

6.4 SEXUAL HARASSMENT DEFINED

According to the Equal Employment Opportunity Commission (EEOC), sexual harassment is a form of sex discrimination that violates Title VII of the Civil Rights Act of 1964. Title VII applies to employers with 15 or more employees, including state and local governments. It also applies to employment agencies and to labor organizations, as well as to the federal government. Unwelcome sexual advances, requests for sexual favors, and other verbal or physical conduct of a sexual nature constitute sexual harassment when this conduct explicitly or implicitly affects an individual's employment; unreasonably interferes with an individual's work performance; or creates an intimidating, hostile, or offensive work environment.

6.4.1 Facts about Sexual Harassment

Sexual harassment can occur in a variety of circumstances, including but not limited to the following:

- The victim as well as the harasser may be a woman or a man. The victim does not have to be of the opposite sex.
- The harasser can be the victim's supervisor, an agent of the employer, a supervisor in another area, a coworker, or a nonemployee.
- The victim does not have to be the person harassed but could be anyone affected by the offensive conduct.
- Unlawful sexual harassment may occur without economic injury to or discharge of the victim.
- The harasser's conduct must be unwelcome.

It is helpful for the victim to inform the harasser directly that the conduct is unwelcome and must stop. The victim should use any employer complaint mechanism or grievance system available. When investigating allegations of sexual harassment, EEOC looks at the whole record: the circumstances, such as the nature of the sexual advances, and the context in which the alleged incidents occurred. A determination on the allegations is made from the facts on a case-by-case basis.

Prevention is the best tool to eliminate sexual harassment in the workplace. Employers are encouraged to take steps necessary to prevent sexual harassment from occurring. They should clearly communicate to employees that sexual harassment will not be tolerated.

They can do so by providing sexual harassment training to their employees, establishing an effective complaint or grievance process, and taking immediate and appropriate action when an employee complains.

It is also unlawful to retaliate against an individual for opposing employment practices that discriminate based on sex or for filing a discrimination charge, testifying, or participating in any way in an investigation, proceeding, or litigation under Title VII.

6.4.2 The Courts

The courts have extended EEOC definitions and defined sexual harassment as unwelcome sexual advances, requests for sexual favors, and other verbal or physical conduct of a sexual nature under any of the following conditions:

1. Submission to such conduct is an explicit or implicit term or condition of employment
2. Submission to such conduct is used as the basis for a favorable employment decision or the employee's rejection of such conduct is used as the basis for an adverse employment decision
3. Such conduct unreasonably interferes with an employee's work or creates an intimidating, hostile, or offensive working environment*

This definition, although accurate from a legal perspective, offers little or no guidance to a physician or other employer who is trying to articulate to professional or nonprofessional employees what behavior is prohibited and what is acceptable. Unfortunately, there is no clear-cut line to provide an answer to the relevant question: What specific acts are classified as sexual harassment?

Of greater interest to many small employers, such as physicians and health-care professionals, is under what circumstance the doctor employer can become liable if an employee claims he/she has been sexually harassed.†

6.5 PREFERENTIAL TREATMENT

The most easily recognized sexual harassment occurs when a doctor, medical officer, or other supervisor offers an employee a raise or promotion in exchange for sexual favors or when a supervisor demotes or fires an employee who refuses a request for sexual favors. This type of harassment has been referred to as *quid pro quo.*

Over the past decade, a great deal of publicity has been given to this type of behavior. As a result, most employers fully understand the perils of the office romance, and little commentary is necessary. Suffice it to say that it is never acceptable for any doctor or supervisor to offer an employee job-related rewards in exchange for sexual favors. If a supervisor engages in such behavior and the employee complains, it is highly likely that the employer will be liable for sexual harassment.

---

* *See* Meritor Savings Bank, F.S.B. v. Vinson, 477 U.S. 57 (1986).

† Laws prohibiting discrimination and sexual harassment apply equally to behavior of men and women. Throughout this chapter, references to "she" can be read as "he or she."

6.6 HOSTILE MEDICAL OFFICE WORK ENVIRONMENT

Less obvious, and the basis for the majority of the sexual harassment suits brought today, is the area of sexual harassment referred to as "hostile work environment." A hostile work environment claim results from any conduct, verbal or physical, that embarrasses, degrades, offends, or shows hostility toward an individual or a group of individuals, based on gender. Harassing conduct may include gender-related slurs, sexual remarks, negative stereotyping, unwanted touching, or any other type of gender-related behavior that would be offensive to a reasonable person.

It is important to recognize that a hostile work environment is merely a subcategory of sexual harassment. It is unnecessary for a physician employer to become caught up in terminology. Rather, it is important to understand the general characteristics of sexual harassment so that the harassing behavior can be eliminated from the work environment.

Any claim of sexual harassment necessarily involves behavior based on gender, but does not necessarily involve sexual comments or sexual activity. The behavior may be directed toward a particular individual or a group of individuals. It may involve written or graphic material. It may be actions or comments that create a sexually charged atmosphere. It may be conduct by a supervisor or a coworker. Finally, it can be any type of gender-related behavior that creates an intimidating, hostile, or offensive work environment. The key question in deciding whether behavior is sexually harassing is whether the conduct is offensive and unwelcome and whether it has the purpose or effect of unreasonably interfering with an individual's work performance.

6.7 UNREASONABLE INTERFERENCE WITH WORK PERFORMANCE

The most frequently asked question is where the threshold lies for behavior that reaches the level of unreasonable interference with work performance. In other words, what is offensive to the level of interfering, and what is merely annoying? The measure is twofold: how severe is the behavior, and how pervasive is it?

The United States Supreme Court has stated that the behavior must be "sufficiently severe or pervasive" so as to interfere with work performance, but what does *sufficiently* mean? It is actually a test of weight and can be viewed as a continuum of behavior. At one end of the continuum, a single episode may be sufficient if that single act is extremely severe. For example, if a doctor or supervisor forces sexual contact with a subordinate, e.g., genital fondling or sexual intercourse, that single event will likely be sufficient to constitute sexual harassment.

At the other end of the continuum is behavior that, taken in isolation, appears innocent or innocuous, such as a casual remark. Doctor Arni says to Employee Betty, "Nice dress—sexy." Obviously, the comment is inappropriate in the workplace, and potentially, Employee Betty might be offended or embarrassed by the comment. But if that single comment is the only event that occurs, it would not be sufficient to create a hostile work environment, because it is unlikely that this single remark will interfere with Employee Betty's work performance.

Such is the analysis a court will employ in deciding whether behavior is sexually harassing. In the context of the continuum described above, the court will ask how severe the behavior was and how often it occurs. Behavior that is less severe but occurs on a repetitive or frequent basis is likely to create a hostile work environment. Similarly, behavior that occurs on an infrequent basis but is exceptionally crude and offensive is likely to be sufficient to interfere with an employee's work performance and thus form the basis for a claim.

6.8 TWO-PRONG TEST FOR OFFENSIVE BEHAVIOR

One question that often arises is how anyone can ever know for sure what behavior is offensive and what is not. After all, some language may highly offend a person of extreme sensibilities but be everyday language to someone else.

To resolve this issue, courts have established a two-prong test for offensive behavior. That test asks first whether the conduct was severe and pervasive enough to create a hostile and abusive work environment and then whether this victim subjectively perceived the environment to be hostile or abusive.* In other words, would a "reasonable" person be offended, and was this particular person offended? Both questions must be answered *yes* before the behavior is classified as sexual harassment.

6.9 EXAMPLES OF SEXUAL HARASSMENT

Using the continuum approach and the two-prong test, let's examine several examples of behavior and see which might be considered sexual harassment.

6.9.1 Compliments

Simple compliments are part of everyday social interaction, but under certain circumstances, they may create a hostile work environment. Consider the following examples:

Example 1

"You look nice today. That dress really accents your dark hair."

This comment is simply a pleasant remark. Even if the employee to whom it was directed was offended or felt it was too personal, it would not rise to the level of sexual harassment since a reasonable person would not find it offensive.

Example 2

"You look really nice today. With your dark hair, that color really makes you look sexy. You ought to be a model."

Obviously, this comment is more personal than the first. The overtone is that the employee to whom the remark was directed is sexually attractive. Thus, in deciding whether the comment is sexually harassing, a little more analysis is necessary.

The first question is whether a reasonable person would be uncomfortable or embarrassed by such remarks. The personal nature of this comment makes it

* *See* Harris v. Forklift Systems, Inc., 510 U.S. 17 (1993).

more likely that a reasonable person would be offended, particularly if such comments were made on a repeated basis. This example illustrates the fluid nature of the continuum described above. The comment is not extremely severe but certainly is inappropriate for a medical or other office environment. Consequently, if there were several occurrences of this or similar comments, the behavior will likely be determined to be sexually harassing.*

Example 3

"Nice boobs! Are they real? Come on over here so I can really check out your tits."

This comment certainly falls further down the continuum as to the degree of severity. Such a comment is not only inappropriate but also highly offensive and would warrant disciplinary action. One occasion may not reach the level of interfering with work performance, but very few repetitions such as this would be necessary to reach the threshold for sexual harassment.

6.9.2 Sexist Words

Often, certain words are associated with one gender or another and, if used repeatedly, may form the basis for a sexual harassment claim.

Example 1

"You are such a bitch."

There is no question that the term *bitch* refers to a female. However, in today's society, this term has become so commonplace that it is often accepted in conversation. Consequently, use of this term, if there were no other events, would likely not be sufficient to constitute sexual harassment.

Example 2

"All women are c__s and don't deserve to be treated with respect."

Again, the referenced word refers to females only. However, the crudeness of the language places this event further along the continuum in terms of severity. This particular comment becomes even more offensive since it is combined with a stereotyping remark about women. For all of these reasons, it is likely that a few repetitions such as this would be sufficient to constitute sexual harassment and to create a hostile work environment. Accordingly, such language should be prohibited in the workplace.

* Of course, this assumes that the second prong of the test has been satisfied and that this particular victim is offended or embarrassed.

Example 3

"Men are such idiots. I guess that's because they let their little head do all their thinking."

There are several problems with this remark. First, there is a not-so-subtle reference to the male anatomy. There is also the blanket assumption that not only are all men less intelligent than women but also, the reason for this anomaly is that men are more interested in sex than in intelligent pursuit.

Again, one comment such as this is probably not sufficient to form a claim. However, in combination with other behavior or similar behavior on a repeated basis, a claim might be asserted.

6.9.3 Office Jokes

For decades, joke telling has been part of our social interaction, both on and off the job. Over the last several years, thanks in part to Bill Clinton, political jokes have taken a turn to include sexual overtones. What happens when these jokes are introduced into the working environment? The criterion remains the same: would a reasonable person be offended by the jokes, and was the complaining individual offended?

When an employee complains that office jokes are too off-color, such that they are embarrassing and interfere with work performance, the defense is nearly always the same—"It was just a joke; I didn't mean anything." However, such a defense will not be effective.

Remember, the basic definition of sexual harassment is any conduct that has the purpose *or effect* of interfering with work performance. Motive, or lack thereof, is irrelevant. Jokes of a sexual nature that are offensive and embarrassing can create a hostile work environment, *even if the jokester harbored no intent to do so.*

Does this mean an employee cannot tell jokes at work? Of course not! It does mean that if any employee tells jokes that might offend, the employee had better be sure of his/her audience. Two friends kidding around does not mean that one of the friends can suddenly decide to complain of sexual harassment and prevail. However, if one of the parties does decide to complain, an employer may have problems defending the action if the jokes are of a sexual nature and do not belong in the workplace.

It is important to understand a few other aspects of office joke telling. The first is that offensive language and embarrassing jokes may create a hostile work environment, even if two people voluntarily engage in the conduct. The hostile work environment occurs when the off-color jokes are inadvertently overheard by others who find the jokes embarrassing or offensive. Of course, the solution to this potential problem is to keep all such joking out of the office, hospital, or work environment.

Another pitfall of sex jokes may be seen when an individual brings a cartoon to the office and gives it to a friend who finds it highly amusing. That person makes a copy and passes it on to a third person that again finds it amusing, not offensive. This chain continues until eventually, the cartoon comes into the hands of people who are not so amused. Depending on the crudeness (or severity) and the frequency with which such conduct occurs, a hostile work environment could evolve, even though it started as two friends engaging in what they perceived to be harmless fun.

6.9.4 Touching

Touching is an area subject to various interpretations by different individuals. Some people simply do not like touching of any type. Others have difficulty talking to another without some touching. Like compliments, touching can be analyzed along a continuum to see if it is sexually harassing.

Example 1

A dentist walks over and says "good job" and simultaneously pats the employee on the shoulder. Such touching cannot rise to the level of sexual harassment, because no reasonable person would consider such conduct offensive.

Example 2

A female internist says, "Nice tie, you always wear such professional-looking clothes." The comment is combined with the woman fondling the tie followed by rubbing the male employee's arm.

The comment sounds harmless, but combined with the touching described above, it takes on a personal feeling and becomes more intrusive. Although not extremely severe, if such conduct occurs on a regular basis, it is likely to make the male employee uncomfortable and create a hostile work environment.

Example 3

A chiropractor employer walks over and says, "You look tired; let me give you a massage." This conduct definitely has a personal overtone and is inappropriate in the workplace. The problem is that even if the employee is uncomfortable with such touching, she may not feel comfortable telling her doctor employer to stop. Consequently, the conduct can recur, resulting in the employee feeling very oppressed or uncomfortable about what goes on in the workplace, and eventually she may complain of sexual harassment.

Example 4

A male podiatrist says "good job" and pats a female employee on the rear. Again, she may not feel comfortable telling the supervisor to stop. However, the personal nature of the conduct can create a hostile work environment if the behavior is repetitive.

6.9.5 Invitations

Employees often ask if the state of current sexual harassment law means there can no longer be any romance or dating between persons who work together. Of course not! Employees and even health-care supervisors and subordinates are still free to engage in consensual relationships. However, this area warrants a few pertinent comments.

6.9.5.1 When "Yes" Becomes "No"

Two individuals may engage in a romantic relationship without any legal consequences. However, if one of the individuals becomes disenchanted, the rules change. Any further pursuit, which may be unwanted, can create a hostile work environment, regardless of what the previous relationship was like.

6.9.5.2 A Sense of Obligation

Often, when an employee asserts a claim of sexual harassment against a doctor supervisor, the defense will be, "But it was mutual. She participated voluntarily." The employee will respond by saying, "I didn't feel like I had any choice; he was my boss." This issue has come before the courts on many occasions, and the U.S. Supreme Court has resolved the issue by affirming that a plaintiff who voluntarily participates may still have a claim. The test is whether the conduct was unwelcome, not whether participation was voluntary.*

Obviously, a doctor who engages in an office romance had better be sure the other party's participation is voluntary and not something that stems from a sense of fear or obligation. Under any circumstances, a supervisor who engages in such relationships in the workplace runs the risk of having a sexual harassment complaint filed against him/her.

6.9.5.3 Listening for Clues

Another word of advice, particularly to physicians, is to be perceptive in listening to the response to an invitation. An employee may feel nervous about refusing an invitation from a medical supervisor but may still give hints as to her feelings.

For example, the doctor supervisor asks, "How about dinner Friday?" and the employee responds, "No thanks, I already have plans."

The following week, the doctor supervisor again asks, "How about dinner Friday?" and the employee responds, "I'd love to, but I'm visiting a sick friend."

The following week, the doctor supervisor again asks, "How about dinner Friday?" and the employee responds, "Sorry, I have to stay home and sort my sock drawer."

Consider what is going on. The employee has not said, "Please don't ask me out; I don't want to go out with you." However, the message should be just as clear as if she had.

6.9.6 Demands or Threats

Demands for sexual favors, sometimes combined with threats if sexual favors are not forthcoming, often form the basis for sexual harassment complaints. If the demands or threats are made by supervisors, there is no question that such conduct is sexually harassing. However, similar behavior occurring between coworkers may also form the basis for a claim.

An employee who repeatedly invites another employee on dates sets up a hostile work environment if the second employee refuses. In some cases, the invitations may be combined with following the employee home or the giving of gifts to persuade the employee to change her mind. In extreme cases, it may be combined with threats against the invitee if she does not agree to some relationship.

As an employer physician, if you learn of such a situation, it is imperative that it be stopped. If knowledge of the threats or persistent unwanted demands are ignored, you will be held liable if a claim is raised.

---

* *See* Meritor, 477 U.S. 57 (1986).

6.10 GENDER-BASED ANIMOSITY

A sexually hostile work environment often results from comments or actions that contain some sort of sexual connotation. However, this cause of action stems from actions that are based on gender. Consequently, sexual content is not required. Acts that fall into this category are easily recognized because they are generally based on negative stereotyping.

Example 1

"Women are not as intelligent as men, so men make better physical therapy department managers."

Obviously untrue, this comment demonstrates a bias against women and, if often repeated, certainly is likely to interfere with a female's work performance. Notice that the characteristics of gender-based animosity are much like ordinary gender discrimination. Consequently, it would not be uncommon for a woman to bring both a hostile work environment claim and a discrimination claim. Since they both arise out of the same body of law, either claim could be viable.

Example 2

"I don't understand why she works in this office. Women belong at home, taking care of the house and raising kids. They don't belong in the workplace."

Again, there is no reference to any sexual terms, but there definitely is an overtone of gender bias. These two examples are obvious ones. Consider the following example of gender bias that might not be so obvious.

Example 3

"We have an opening for a computer medical technician. Since men tend to be better at wiring and configuring a computer, let's hire a man."

Obviously, gender has nothing to do with technical ability. Does this mean that if an employer hires a man, the decision will be challenged? Certainly, if the hiring is accompanied by statements like those outlined above. However, the best way to avoid lawsuits in this area is to refrain from making remarks and to utilize neutral testing procedures to screen candidates.

6.11 SAME-SEX HARASSMENT

Before 1998, courts around the country were split on the issue of whether sexual harassment claims could be asserted only if the behavior occurred between a male and a female. Some courts held that sexual harassment can occur only if the harasser and the victim are of different sexes. Other courts held that sexual harassment is illegal, even if both parties are of the same sex. Still other courts held that sexual harassment between two persons of the same sex can occur only if one of the parties is a homosexual.

In 1998, the U.S. Supreme Court settled the issue in its ruling in *Oncale v. Sundowner Offshore Services, Inc.*, when it ruled that sexual harassment is behavior based on gender and it applies whether the parties are different sexes or the same sex.* The court also said that the relevant question was whether there was a hostile work environment because of gender, and therefore, the sexual orientation of the parties was not to be considered.

With this ruling, the court expanded the body of law previously delineated as sexual harassment. The ruling affirmed that the test was whether the behavior was offensive and whether it was sufficiently severe or pervasive to be actionable. The court emphasized that male-on-male horseplay is not prohibited. However, when it rises to the level of more serious acts, such as genital grabbing, threatened sexual acts, or severe language that offends or frightens the victim to the extent it interferes with the victim's work performance, it is prohibited under the law governing sexual harassment.

6.12 DOCTOR-EMPLOYER LIABILITY

A key question is under what circumstances the physician or other employer will be liable for sexual harassment in the workplace? The rules vary, according to whether the harassing party is a supervisor or a nonsupervisor.

6.12.1 Liability for Supervisor's Harassment

For many years, the courts held that where the harasser is also a supervisor, the employer will be absolutely liable. This liability is based on the premise that a doctor, or other employer, must have notice of the harassment in order to be liable and that since supervisors are agents of the employer, there is notice. In 1998, the U.S. Supreme Court clarified

* *See* Oncale v. Sundowner Offshore Services, Inc., 523 U.S. 75 (1998).

the employer's liability, and although the court said that employers are not absolutely liable, the course prescribed for avoiding liability placed a high burden on the employer.

The court outlined an affirmative defense that would permit the employer to avoid or limit liability. An affirmative defense exists where the employer exercised reasonable care to prevent and promptly correct harassing behavior and where the victim unreasonably failed to take advantage of any preventive or corrective opportunities to avoid harm.*

What does this mean in everyday language? It means the physician employer must have a strong policy defining and prohibiting sexual harassment. It must be adequately disseminated to all employees, and it must include a reporting procedure. It is important that the policy specifically identify the individuals to whom an employee may address a complaint and also include alternate reporting procedures in cases where the harasser is the supervisor of the complaining individual.

It is not sufficient to merely have a policy in place and to disseminate it to employees. In addition to developing the policy, the physician employer must be prepared to uniformly enforce the policy once it has been established.

6.12.2 Reporting Procedure

It is also essential that the doctor employer have some procedure in place for investigating sexual harassment complaints. As noted above, the efficiency with which an employer investigates a complaint will play into the court's decision as to whether the employer is able to take advantage of the affirmative defense. This means that you should take all claims seriously. The result of an investigation may be a report back to the complaining individual that there is no evidence to substantiate the complaint but that all individuals involved, including the alleged harasser, have been warned that such behavior will not be tolerated and will be the subject of disciplinary action.

6.13 DISCIPLINARY ACTIONS

Many events may contribute to a sexual harassment claim, even though each of them standing alone may be insufficient to prevail in a court of law. However, because the threshold for a sexual harassment claim falls in a gray area, employers have the right to protect themselves by establishing rules that may be more stringent than those imposed by a court. Many doctors and employers adopt a zero-tolerance policy. Such a policy means that when any employee engages in behavior described above, that employee will be disciplined, even for a single incident.

The important point to remember is that the discipline must be uniformly imposed. In other words, an employer cannot discipline one employee for telling off-color jokes and then ignore the same behavior by another employee because "he was only joking around." Disciplinary action may be something as simple as a verbal conversation explaining to the alleged harasser that these things do offend some people and that the harasser should avoid such behavior in the future. Obviously, more serious violations may warrant more serious disciplinary action, up to and including termination of employment.

The bottom line is that doctor employers must be able to show they have done everything within their power to prevent sexual harassment and when complaints are made, they have

---

* Faragher v. City of Boca Raton, 524 U.S. 775 (1998).

immediately investigated and, when necessary, taken corrective action. Such is the only way in which a doctor employer may avoid liability for sexual harassment complaints.

6.14 TANGIBLE EMPLOYMENT ACTION

If harassment results in a tangible employment action (e.g., discharge, demotion, or undesirable reassignment), and the harasser is a supervisor, the affirmative defense is not available.* A tangible employment action does not necessarily mean the employee has lost some economic benefit. It could also mean a loss of status, loss of promotion opportunities, or loss of anything perceived to be a benefit of the job.

Further, threats of loss of tangible benefits may form the basis for a hostile work environment claim, even if there is no follow-through with the threatened action.† An example of this would be when a doctor or supervisor continuously threatens to fire or demote a female employee because "as a woman, she's not smart enough to do the job." The threat itself is sufficient; no action is required.

6.15 PUNITIVE DAMAGES

Punitive damages are sums of money that are awarded to a plaintiff to punish the defendant. The sum of money awarded relates to the assets of the defendant and the need to punish that defendant, rather than to the economic loss of the plaintiff.

Until recently, many courts felt that although an employer could be held vicariously liable for damages resulting from a sexual harassment complaint, punitive damages would not be appropriate. However, the U.S. Supreme Court addressed the issue in 1999 and stated that punitive damages may be imposed if the conduct is "that of a managerial agent."‡ Punitive damages do not require a showing of egregious or outrageous discrimination. However, punitive damages will not be imposed when the decisions of the managerial agent are contrary to the employer's good-faith efforts to comply with the laws governing sexual harassment.

The question becomes "who is a managerial agent?" A court will look at all of the circumstances to determine if the individual is a managerial agent. Questions a court will ask may include what the supervisory responsibility of the individual is, how much power the individual has to enforce company policies, how much authority the individual has to hire and fire employees, and other similar questions. In a small medical office, an office manager who has merely a title and no real managerial duties will likely not be deemed to be a managerial agent. Conversely, a doctor in an office, even if he/she does not ordinarily hire and fire staff members, may likely have sufficient authority and power to be deemed a managerial agent of the group.

6.16 FINANCIAL AND ECONOMIC COSTS

There are positive reasons to consider your medical practice climate. Preventing discrimination and harassment boosts worker morale and productivity. But, there are also costly negatives you want to avoid: discrimination and harassment lawsuits cost companies more

---

* Id.

† Burlington Industries, Inc. v. Ellerth, 524 U.S. 742 (1998).

‡ Kolstead v. American Dental Association, 527 U.S. 526 (1999).

and more each year. A study released in January 2002 by Jury Verdict Research, Inc., found the following:

- The national median jury award for employment-practice liability cases, which include discrimination and retaliation claims, rose 44%—from $151,000 to $218,000—between 1999 and 2000. The median award had stayed level at about $150,000 between 1997 and 1999.
- Of all discrimination types, age discrimination plaintiffs won the most money from 1994 to 2000.
- The overall median jury award in discrimination cases was $150,000 for the 7-year span.
- The study also showed an increase in public awareness and jury sympathy for the plaintiffs in discrimination cases:
  - In 2000, 62% of plaintiffs in sex discrimination cases (including sexual harassment) won their cases, compared with only 43% in 1994.
  - 67% of race discrimination plaintiffs won their cases in 2000, compared with 50% in 1994.
- A 1999 survey of 496 companies published by the Society for Human Resource Management found that
  - Sexual harassment complaints increased at those companies by almost 140% between 1995 and 1998.
  - Small businesses averaged nearly one claim per 100 employees in 1998—five times higher than the rate of one claim per 500 among large businesses.
  - Only 51% of small businesses said that they offered sexual harassment prevention training, while 76% of large companies did.

These statistics suggest that whether your medical practice is large or small, you need to take harassment and discrimination prevention training seriously.

Overheard in the Doctor's Lounge*

Do We Need More Medical Chaperones?

First of all, it's clear that both men and women are capable of illicit sexual behavior. And, that's just in the traditional straight sense. However, with ever-evolving definitions of sexuality, how is our view of chaperones altered?

From what I have read online, one of the fundamental beliefs of lesbian, gay, bisexual, and transgender (LGBT) physicians is that nobody feels they should be compelled to reveal their sexuality. Fair enough. But, what does that mean in terms of chaperones?

If a gay physician examines a straight man's genitals, or performs a rectal exam on him, should that physician bring a male or a female chaperone? What about the sexuality of the chaperone? If the gay physician has a male chaperone, shouldn't we ensure that the chaperone is straight? And, if the female chaperone is a lesbian, I suppose it would be better than having a straight female chaperone, as she might also find the exposed man sexually interesting. Or, if a lesbian physician performs a pelvic on a

* From http://www.kevinmd.com/blog/2015/04/were-going-to-need-more-medical-chaperones-heres-why.html.

woman, it makes sense that she have a straight female chaperone. But, would a gay male be just as good? A straight man certainly wouldn't do.

Wait, what if the patient is gay? Would a lesbian physician need a chaperone? Or, would a lesbian patient need for her gay physician to have a chaperone? What about a patient or provider who is bisexual? Does that require two chaperones? Should chaperones be chaperoned? What a vast cauldron of lust might ensue if we kept adding chaperones to the mix! And, would we explain the sexual melting pot to the poor patient, who reclines in stirrups or bends over the table, potentially unaware that he/she is the object of so much potential controversy, lust, and litigation?

Sexuality aside, what happens when a patient, or physician, has alternate genders? And what if those genders have alternate sexualities? I mean, I'm a baby boomer and a little behind, I admit. But, it stands to modern reason that a man who self-identifies as a woman could be a lesbian who is thus attracted to women and comes sort of, you know, full circle. Can a female physician, who is a self-identified male, be trusted to examine, alone, a lesbian patient? Or, indeed, a gay patient?

Dare we inquire, in medicine, about both gender and sexuality as it pertains to being alone with a patient? And, should we update the charts of our patients regarding gender, which appears to be endlessly mutable, unlike what our culture believes sexuality to be, which is carved in stone? And is it the duty of the provider to discuss his/her own personal sexuality before performing such exams on patients?

And, what happens when the accusations fly in any of these scenarios? Who will be liable when someone alleges that he/she was assaulted or touched by someone who was sexually attracted to him/her, but whom the patient never realized was of an alternate gender or sexuality? Who will be liable when the provider is the one faced with unwanted, and unforeseen, advances? And, will we be concerned that chaperones can, themselves, be compromised by attraction or group allegiance? After all, that's one reason we had females chaperone males: for fear, in part, that "the boys" would cover up misbehavior.

Finally, is this an open field for litigation? Or simply an open field for more and more regulations in health care?

Of course, this is not to suggest that any of the above groups are particularly prone to sexual predation. This is not some "everyone but straight people are dangerous" assault on those who are different. However, neither is it safe to assume that those of alternate sexualities and genders are not prone to such behaviors. Most of us, even the whitest, most male, and straight, are not sexual predators. But, for the good of our patients, it is always assumed that we might be.

Edwin Leap, MD
Emergency room physician

6.17 CONCLUSION

This chapter does not begin to cover all of the examples of behavior that may constitute sexual harassment or a hostile work environment. It is, however, intended to illustrate that a physician employer who wishes to avoid sexual harassment claims will be more successful if he/she exercises common sense in this area. A workplace, even a small doctor's office, should always be viewed as a professional environment. Employees should be viewed as just that. When an individual walks through the office door in the morning, that individual is not a female, not a Jew, not black, but is simply an employee there to do a job. An employer who makes attempts to enforce such an attitude will go far in eliminating sexual harassment in the workplace.

6.18 COLLABORATE

Discuss this chapter online with others at http://www.medicalexecutivepost.com.

FURTHER READINGS

Buba, VL: Sexual Harassment Risks in Medical Practice: He Said, She Said … There is No Quid Pro Quo. In Marcinko, DE [Editor]: *Risk Management and Insurance Planning for Physicians and Advisors—A Strategic Approach*. Springer Publishing, New York, 2004.

Davis, R: Medical Ethics for Challenging Times. In Marcinko, DE [Editor]: *The Business of Medical Practice*. Springer Publishing, New York, 2010.

Emanual, EJ and Dubler, NN: "Preserving the Physician–Patient Relationship in the Era of Managed Care." *JAMA: The Journal of the American Medical Association*, Vol. 273, No. 4, pp. 323–329, 1995.

Friedman, E: *The Right Thing: Ten Years of Ethics Columns from the Healthcare Forum Journal*. Jossey-Bass Publishers, San Francisco, CA, 1996.

Jessani, A and Marcinko, DE: Special Situations Financial Planning. In Marcinko, DE [Editor]: *Comprehensive Financial Planning Strategies for Doctors and Advisors*. Productivity Press, Boca Raton, FL, 2015.

Konnor, M: *Medicine at the Crossroads*. Vintage Books, New York, 1994.

La Puma, J: "Mixing Business, Medicine." *Managed Care Magazine*, July 1998.

Miller, C: Asset Planning and Protection Principles. In Marcinko, DE [Editor]: *Comprehensive Financial Planning Strategies for Doctors and Advisors*. Productivity Press, Boca Raton, FL, 2015.

Pellegrino, ED, Veatch, RM, and Langan, JP: *Ethics, Trust, and the Professions: Philosophical and Cultural Aspects*. Georgetown University Press, Washington, DC, 1991.

Povar, GJ, Blumen, H, Daniel, J, Daub S, Evans, L, Holm, RP, Levkovich, N, McCarter, AO, Sabin, J, Snyder, L, Sulmasy, D, Vaughan, P, Wellikson, LD and Campbell, A, the Medicine as a Profession Managed Care Ethics Working Group: "Ethics in Practice: Managed Care and the Changing Health Care Environment: Medicine as a Profession Managed Care Ethics Working Group Statement." *Ann Intern Med*, Vol. 141, No. 2, pp. 131–136, 2004.

SAMPLE

Sexual Harassment Policy For Health-Care Facility Employees

To: All Hospital/Medical Office and Clinic Employees
From: CEO
Subject: Sexual Harassment Policy
Date: ______________________________

This health-care facility believes that each employee has the right to be free from harassment because of age, color, creed, national origin, or sex. Because of the current rise in sexual harassment charges across the country, we wish to clarify our procedure for dealing with this problem.

It cannot be stressed enough that this hospital will not tolerate any form of sexual harassment. Should you feel you are being harassed, please follow these guidelines to help remedy the problem.

Harassment by other employees or by patients at the individual units should be brought to the attention of the head nurse, who will then investigate the matter. If the allegation is sustained, the responsible employee or parties will be disciplined. If harassment continues, the responsible individual will be terminated immediately. Responsible patients who do not change their behavior after a polite request from the head nurse will be provided legal counseling.

Should you feel the head nurse has not investigated the matter to your satisfaction, contact ______________________________ at ______________________________ immediately!

Should the harassment originate from management or the head nurse, the regional medical or administrative supervisor for that unit is to be contacted. If, for any reason, that supervisor cannot be reached, any supervisor will respond to your complaint.

Should the harasser be the regional supervisor, or medical or health-care administrator, please contact me directly.

Sexual harassment is defined as any of the following:

- Unwelcome physical contact
- Sexually explicit language or gestures
- Uninvited or unwanted sexual advances
- An offensive overall environment, including the use of vulgar language, the presence of sexually explicit photographs or other materials, and the telling of sexual stories

It can come from superiors, fellow employees, doctors, nurses, medical technicians, or patients. Men as well as women can be victims of sexual harassment.

Please sign and date the attached, acknowledging that you have read this notice.

Signed ____ Date ____________

7 Divorce and the Mediation Process

Pre-, Intra-, and Postnuptial Considerations

Anju D. Jessani

CONTENTS

The federal and state governments, as well as corporate America, confer many benefits, protections, and obligations to married couples. This is colloquially known as the ABCs of Marriage Benefits:

- Assumption of spouse pension
- Automatic housing lease transfer
- Automatic inheritance
- Bereavement leave
- Burial determination
- Child custody
- Confidentiality of conversations
- Crime victim's recovery benefits
- Divorce protections
- Domestic violence protection
- Exemption on property tax upon partner's death
- Family leave to care for sick partner
- Immunity from testimony against spouse
- Insurance benefits and breaks
- Joint adoption, foster care, and custody
- Joint bankruptcy
- Joint parenting to care for partner
- Medical decisions on behalf of partner
- Property rights
- Reduced rate membership
- Social security benefits
- Tax advantages
- Visitation of partner's children
- Visitation of partner in hospital or prison
- Wrongful death benefits

7.1 INTRODUCTION

The divorce statistics are high and, for the medical profession, exceed those of the general population. While few people intend to divorce when they marry, it is certainly wise to understand steps that can either reduce the risk of divorce or lessen the financial impact should divorce occur. When divorce does occur, it is unfortunate that the professional often neglects to discuss the details of their proposed settlement with a trusted advisor or financial planner. Perhaps this is because the topic may be viewed as too delicate. Nevertheless, the truth is that much financial damage is done by this lack of disclosure. In this chapter, we will provide an outline of divorce issues that will provide an overview of divorce issues that may remove some of the mystique surrounding this topic.

Overheard in the Advisor's Lounge

The Financial Case against Marriage

When it comes to death, divorce, and taxes, two people are probably better off financially if they don't marry. Intentionally or not, many federal and state laws reward couples who choose to live together without marriage. For example, laws relating to Worker's Compensation insurance are one example of this. Someone whose spouse has died in a work-related accident may be eligible to receive a monthly benefit, paid for the rest of his or her life. However, most state laws provide that the benefits end if the recipient remarries. This puts a real cost to remarrying.

WORKER'S COMPENSATION

Example: Consider as an example a woman who at age 50 loses her husband to a work-related accident and receives a settlement of $2000 a month for life. Assuming she will live another 35 years and could invest the proceeds in a 3% bond, the present value of that income stream is $520,000. That means a person would need $520,000, invested at 3%, to give a monthly income of $2000 for 35 years. Therefore, if this woman fell in love and wanted to remarry 2 years into receiving the payments, the remaining 33 years of monthly payments she would forfeit has a value of $502,000. This puts a rather quantifiable cost on one's social, emotional, and religious values.

TAX CODE

Example: Take a couple who both earn high incomes. Suppose each has taxable income of around $400,000, which is the breakpoint where the 39.6% tax bracket begins. As two singles, as long as their taxable income is $400,000 or less, they both remain in the 35% tax bracket. However, if they marry, their joint income goes to $800,000 while the 35% tax bracket only expands to $450,000 for couples. That means they now pay an additional 4.6% in federal income taxes on the excess of $350,000, or $12,600. Some may be quick to dismiss that amount as trivial, given their income level, but the point is still that marriage for them brings a tangible cost in higher taxes.

PRIOR MARRIAGES

Those with previous marriages may find another disincentive to marriage in the challenge of passing on assets to children upon your death or if the new marriage should end in divorce. If leaving assets to children is a priority, you will probably need to negotiate a prenuptial agreement with your fiancé. This is especially important for couples with unequal assets.

A prenuptial agreement is a real romance killer. It highlights the reality that every marriage is a business deal, with the added emotional weight of negotiating the divorce settlement before there is a wedding. Some couples find it easier to live together without marriage and keep their assets largely separate.

THE UNMARRIEDS

For couples that decide not to marry, the potential tax planning is ripe with opportunity. Such couples can do anything that the tax code or state statutes prohibit married or related parties from doing. This provides some great tax savings and asset protection opportunities. For example, spouses cannot be the trustees of each other's irrevocable or asset protection trusts, but unmarried partners absolutely can. Choosing not to marry is becoming especially popular with older couples. This is because many older people with previous marriages have accumulated two things: assets and children. They find marriage less compelling when they and their new partner won't have children together. Younger couples who do plan to have children still recognize that marriage is important.

For many reasons, marriage isn't going out of style any time soon. Few of those reasons, however, are financial ones.

Rick Kahler, MS, CFP, ChFC, CCIM
Rapid City, South Dakota

7.2 IMPLICATIONS OF DIVORCE STATISTICS

Married couples strive to stay together for richer or poorer, and in sickness and health. But, the reality is that more than 2 million people get divorced each year in the United States. Divorce is a $50 billion annual industry. Divorce rates for first marriages are between 52% and 60% (75–90% if there's a special needs child). So, it pays for all medical professionals to be aware of this reality.

As Barbara Dafoe Whitehead writes in her book *The Divorce Culture*,* "Divorce is now part of everyday American Life. It is embodied in our laws and institutions, our manners and mores, our movies and television shows, our novels and children's storybooks, and our closest and most important relationships."

Divorce can be devastating in many ways. It has created both economic and emotional disadvantages for many children. Nationally, over 1 million children are affected each year by the divorce of their parents. As Whitehead illustrates, divorce figures prominently in the altered fortunes of middle-class families. It has reduced both the levels of parental time and money invested in children. The various studies suggest that divorce carries multiple risks and losses for children including loss of income, loss of ties to father, loss of residential stability, and loss of social resources. For families where money is tight during the marriage,

* Random House, 1999.

separation and divorce is even more financially difficult. Adding an additional residence with its prerequisite overhead to an already tight budget is obviously a daunting task. The income that used to support one home and lifestyle is now split between two homes and two lifestyles.

There has been a great deal of controversy in trying to quantify how much the standard of living declines following divorce for women. Adding to the complexity of the issue was the proclamation of Lenore Weitzman in her book *The Divorce Revolution*,* published in 1985, that after a divorce, women and children suffer on average a 73% decline in standard of living, whereas divorced men's standard increases by 42%. Seven years later, it was revealed that her conclusions were based on faulty computer calculations, and her numbers actually yielded a milder 27% drop for women and children and a 10% increase for men. More recently, Sanford Braver, PhD, of the University of Arizona has shown that when these numbers are adjusted for taxes and expenses fathers usually have during parenting time, mothers and fathers fare about equally about 1 year after divorce.

7.3 DIVORCE WITHIN THE MEDICAL PROFESSION

A Johns Hopkins University study, by Michael J. Klag, MD, in 1997, found that physicians in some specialties—chiefly psychiatry and surgery—are at higher risk for divorce than their medical brethren in other fields. But the results did not support the common view that job-related anxiety and depression are linked to marital breakup. Alerting medical students to the risks of divorce in some specialties may influence their career choices and strengthen their marriages whatever field they choose. The study, supported by the National Institutes of Health, was published in the March 13 issue of *The New England Journal of Medicine*. Results also strongly suggested that the high divorce risk in some specialties may result from the inherent demands of the job as well as the emotional experiences of physicians who enter those fields.

7.3.1 Divorce-Prone Medical Specialties†

For example, the Hopkins team assessed the specialty choices, marriage histories, psychological characteristics, and other career and personal factors of 1118 physicians who graduated from The Johns Hopkins University School of Medicine from 1948 through 1964. For over 30 years of follow-up, the divorce rate was 51% for psychiatrists, 33% for surgeons, 24% for internists, 22% for pediatricians and pathologists, and 31% for other specialties. The overall divorce rate was 29% after three decades of follow-up and 32% after nearly four decades of follow-up.

Physicians who married before medical school graduation had a higher divorce rate than those who waited until after graduation (33% versus 23%). The year of first marriage was linked with divorce rates: 11% for marriages before 1953, 17% for those from 1953 to 1957,

---

* Free Press/MacMillan 1985.

† Coauthors of the study, which was part of the Johns Hopkins Precursors Study, an ongoing, prospective study of physicians from the Hopkins Medical School graduating classes of 1948 through 1964, were lead author Bruce L. Rollman, MD, Lucy A. Mead, ScM, and Nae-Yuh Wang, MS.

24% for those from 1958 to 1962, and 21% for those after 1962. Those who had a parent die before medical school graduation had a lower divorce rate.

Female physicians had a higher divorce rate (37%) than their male colleagues (28%). Physicians who were members of an academic honor society in medical school had a lower divorce rate, although there was no difference in divorce rates according to class rank. Religious affiliation, being an only child, having a parent who was a physician, and having a divorced parent were not associated with divorce rates. Physicians who reported themselves to be less emotionally close to their parents and who expressed more anger under stress also had a significantly higher divorce rate, but anxiety and depression levels were not associated with divorce rate.

7.3.2 The Painful Truth

In their article "The Painful Truth: Physicians Are Not Invincible" (Miller and McGowen 2000), Miller and McGowen state that divorce rates among physicians have been reported to be 10–20% higher than those in the general population. They explain that for many years in premed college, medical school, and residency, physicians focus on getting through the next hurdle. They may postpone the pleasures of life that others enjoy. Compulsive traits that allow them to postpone enjoyment may have the unwanted consequence of leading to more distant relationships, thus placing strain on intimate relationships.

A 2002 study looking at dual physician marriages found that they have a relatively low divorce rate of 11%. "They're a happily married cohort," says Dr. Wayne Sotile of the Sotile Center for Resilience (http://www.sotile.com). "They're more compassionate about the passion for the career—they understand the calling because they share it."

7.4 GENDER DIFFERENCES IN MARRIAGE AND DIVORCE REGARDING FINANCIAL ISSUES

Whatever the statistics regarding standard of living, the reality is that within most marriages, the husband more frequently takes responsibility for understanding and managing the finances. Additionally, women are more likely to remain in the marital home following a separation, thus inheriting a large fixed expense that may prove to be an excessive, albeit short-term burden to them. At the time the decision is made to separate or divorce, many women do not have an understanding of how to manage their household budget or how to manage their assets and liabilities.

An issue many divorcing physicians face is that the other spouse (in the past, the wife) may have concentrated their energies on managing the home, while the physician concentrated on earning and managing the finances. The problems of the spouse of a physician are often compounded in divorce; not only do they not understand their personal finances, but also their absence from the workforce has made them financially dependent on the other. At what is probably the most emotionally taxing time in their lives, they are forced to play catch-up.

Taking a more active role in their own financial planning during the marriage may help the spouse of a physician avoid some of the financial pitfalls of separation and divorce. There any many resources available for this; http://www.womenswire.com/money is a good starting point for more information for both women and men. Barbara Stanny provides an excellent overview and reading bibliography on how people can get smart about money in her book *Prince Charming Isn't Coming*.*

7.5 SAME-SEX MARRIAGE AND DIVORCE

James Obergefell had sued to put his name on his husband's Ohio death certificate as the surviving spouse. On June 26, 2015, the U.S. Supreme Court ruled on the case of *Obergefell v. Hodges* that it is legal for same-sex couples to marry in every state. Prior to the Supreme Court ruling, only 37 states recognized gay marriage, and gay and lesbian couples could only divorce in states that recognized gay marriage.

With the expansion of marriage to same-sex couples in all states, we now have the expansion of divorce, with the same laws applying to same-sex couples. While with marriage equality comes divorce equality, in practice, there might be some differences in how settlements look, especially in the short term.

In divorce, custody and parenting time can be problematic unless both parties are the legal parents of the children. Parentage presumptions and adoption laws differ from state-to-state. On the money side, in divorce, the length of the marriage is a factor in determining the length and/or amount of alimony, and how marital assets and liabilities are divided. How do the state guidelines address the couple that has cohabited for 30 years, but married when their state law was changed 5 years ago? How do they establish when the couple went from cohabiting to being in a marriage-like relationship?

The subject of same-sex marriage and divorce is evolving; at some point, it may look no different than heterosexual marriage and divorce. Same-sex couples should consider utilizing the services of knowledgeable and gay-friendly mediation and legal professionals for marriage- and divorce-related services.

7.6 PRENUPTIAL AND RELATED AGREEMENTS

Although one can hardly plan for such an event such as divorce, there are certain steps to take that may lessen the financial impact of separation and divorce. One of the tools is the *prenuptial agreement (PNA)*.

A *PNA* is a contract between prospective spouses. Most PNAs contain provisions limiting the distribution of marital property and alimony in the event of divorce and limiting the distribution of property to a spouse in the event of death. It is important to note that most states specifically prohibit provisions regarding child support.

With more people getting married later for the first time, often with substantial assets, and people getting married for the second or more times with children from previous marriages, the prevalence of PNAs is increasing. It is particularly important in the case of a female physician, especially if she has been married before, has substantial assets, owns a closely held business, marries a spouse with substantial debt, has agreed to pay for the medical or professional education of a soon-to-be spouse, or who has children from a previous marriage.

Some couples feel that discussing what happens if the marriage fails hinders the romance and shows a lack of commitment toward the marriage. However, at the end of the marriage, few couples agree on how to split their assets or on what a fair amount of support would be.

---

* Penguin USA (paper), 1999.

Whether parties choose to have a PNA, communicating about financial issues strengthens the trust and starts the marriage off on the right foot. The signing of a PNA, or not, finally comes down to a decision that the couple will have to make together. Parties don't need to have the PNA to have the discussion and information sharing that is part of the PNA process.

Wills, insurance policies, pension plans, individual retirement accounts (IRAs), and other assets from prior marriages should also be addressed, updated, and changed if needed, along with beneficiary designations as part of the process of PNA planning.

Because of past uncertainty whether courts could enforce PNAs, a uniform treatment of PNAs was sought through the Uniform Premarital Agreement Act (UPAA). The UPAA was approved by the National Conference on Uniform State Laws in 1983 and has been adopted in whole or in part by approximately half the states. While the standards for enforcing PNAs vary from state to state, in almost all states, four conditions are imposed:

- Each party must make complete disclosure to the other of his or her assets, liabilities, sources of income, and any other facts likely to affect his or her financial position.
- Each party must be represented by separate and independent legal counsel (or must make a voluntary and well-considered decision to waive such independent legal counsel).
- The terms of the agreement must be *fair* at the time the agreement is entered into, a standard with respect to which even reasonable people may differ.
- Finally, the agreement may be set aside by the courts if enforcement of the agreement would impoverish either party and thereby create a risk that either party (or any minor children of either party) would require public assistance.

The value of a PNA is much like other legal contracts, and it can be challenged for a myriad of reasons. In looking at the validity of PNAs, the courts have sometimes overturned agreements signed under duress such as the night before the wedding, even when both parties have had legal counsel. So it makes sense to take the time to put together the PNA in an orderly fashion.

Since divorce may affect an existing medical practice in many ways, including a forced sale, a PNA may well complement a properly drawn-up buy/sell agreement and practice equity sharing agreement.

Often, the couple may go through prenuptial planning to discuss financial issues that are emotionally difficult to bring up on their own, but may choose not to have a formal document drawn up. In some cases, this decision is based on the understanding that in most states, premarital assets—if kept separate from marital property—remain separate property and are not subject to distribution at the time of divorce. In other cases, a trust or a will may serve the same function as the intent of a PNA.

An additional point to note for men or women marrying a party who is divorced and has child and/or spousal support payments is that the earnings from income-producing assets may be included in the paying party's income for the purposes of calculating support. Therefore, it would make sense to keep your income-producing assets such as bonds in your own name, so that that income is not perceived as belonging to the paying party, thus increasing his/her support payments.

"The Commitment Conversation" brochure is a resource that can be downloaded from http://www.equalityinmarriage.org/cc.pdf. It is an excellent tool that allows couples to sit together and review some important issues they need to discuss prior to taking their vows, regardless of state residence. The book *Prenups for Lovers: A Romantic Guide to Prenuptial Agreements** by Arlene Dubin, a New York City matrimonial lawyer, may also be helpful in this regard, whether or not you ultimately decide to execute a PNA.

7.6.1 Intramarital, Intranuptial, Antenuptial, and Mid-Marriage Agreements†

The intramarital agreement, also known as a mid-marriage, intra-, or antenuptial agreement, is a relatively new concept that has been addressed by the Appellate Division in New Jersey only once, in the case of *Pacelli v. Pacelli*. In that case, the Appellate Division determined that intramarital agreements are enforceable *only if* the agreement is fair and equitable at the time of its entry and remains fair and equitable at the time of its sought enforcement.

A simple interpretation was that in a PNA, while pressure exists on both parties due to an impending marriage, each party remains free to make their own decisions and look out for what is best for them. They are also free to walk away from a marriage that hasn't occurred yet, with little or no financial penalty. This presumes of course that both parties have sufficient time and advice prior to entering into a PNA. If they don't, the agreement is sure to be challenged if the parties divorce. When a marriage is over, save the entry of a judgment by the court, the parties can enter into a property settlement agreement. As with the PNA, the parties are free to make their own decisions based on what is in their best interest. They will also have a lawyer in their corner providing advice.

In a mid-marriage agreement, however, the potential for abuse and the leveraging of power by one individual over another is high. So, while some mid-marriage agreements are entered into with the best of intentions, it is still strongly advised that both parties have their own counsel.

7.7 THE DECISION TO DIVORCE

Sanford Braver, PhD (Braver and O'Connell 1998), has conducted research on who leaves whom; the wife was identified as the initiator in approximately two-thirds of his samples. In Braver's research on divorcing parents, the top two ranked factors for both men and women in initiating a divorce were gradually growing apart and losing a sense of closeness, and serious differences in lifestyle and/or values. For men, the third ranked factor was severe and intense fighting/frequent conflict, while the third ranked factor for women was not feeling loved or appreciated by their spouse. Contrary to popular wisdom, extramarital affairs and abuse rank much lower in factors for divorce.

The level of commitment both in training and in practice that is required of a physician can weigh heavily on a marriage for the very reasons Braver illustrates. It is understandable how both the physician and his/her spouse may have a hard time maintaining a sense of closeness with the excessive time demands of a busy practice and being constantly on-call. That spouse may feel that he/she is less important to their physician spouse than his/her job.

---

* Villard (paper), 2001.

† From James P. Yudes PC; Springfield Township, NJ.

Additionally, if the physician sees his or her role as a breadwinner, more important than a spouse's role, the power imbalance that the situation creates can lead to marital discord.

As difficult as marriage is, it remains the condition or goal of the vast majority of Americans. Married couples that seek a stable marriage may want to take a careful look at the research conducted by University of Washington psychologist John M. Gottman, PhD. He researched 140 newlyweds over a 6-year period. To his surprise, he found that the marriages that did work all had one thing in common—the husband was willing to give in to the wife! Unfortunately, despite Gottman's research, couples continue to divorce. We don't appear to be able to live with people very well, but we are not very good at living alone either.

Despite the rhetoric about people rushing into divorce, research shows that people who initiate the breakup have usually contemplated the possibility of divorce for more than a year before they take a strong stand. Especially for the abandoned spouse, the emotional upheaval of divorce can be overwhelming and disorienting because he or she is not even aware of the impending doom. Then, at one of the most emotionally vulnerable points in their life, parties are forced to make important financial decisions and parenting decisions that could impact the rest of their lives. It is a good idea to seek emotional support from a professional during this time of crisis to help deal with the anger, grief, hurt, and guilt that are normal to experience at this period of loss. Many people find that joining a support group and hearing other people's stories helps. You have the names of support groups in your area through local newspapers, church, and synagogues, and you can also find them on the web at http://www.divorcesource.com and other sites.

7.7.1 Divorce-Prone Cities

The divorce laws in all 50 states were evaluated relative to the waiting period required before a divorce is finalized, residency requirements, whether mandatory counseling exists, or whether a separation period is required for a no-fault divorce.

The 10 Worst Cities for Marriage*:

- Toledo, Ohio
- Boise Idaho
- Las Vegas, Nevada
- Tulsa, Oklahoma
- Jacksonville, Florida
- Little Rock, Arkansas
- Cheyenne, Wyoming
- Norfolk, Virginia
- Albuquerque, New Mexico
- Charleston, West Virginia

"The Commitment Conversation" Brochure is a resource that can be downloaded from http://www.equalityinmarriage.org/cc.pdf. It is an excellent tool that allows couples to sit together and review some important issues they need to discuss prior to taking their vows, regardless of state residence.

* From Covert, J., MensHealth.com, March 31, 2014.

7.8 DIVORCE MEDIATION

Divorce usually requires a division of all assets and liabilities including investments, pensions and business holdings, custody and parenting time decisions, establishment of child and sometimes spousal support, planning for educational funding, and tax, insurance, and estate planning. Many of the decisions divorcing parties make are best made in a collaborative manner. Therefore, you and your spouse may want to consider mediation. A step-by-step approach to the divorce mediation process follows later in this chapter.

Mediation is a court-approved process in which a trained neutral person, called a mediator, encourages and facilitates the resolution of a dispute between two or more parties. The mediator does not replace the services of attorneys, but supplements their role to first an advisory position and later as someone who assist you in processing your divorce complaint through the court system. Mediators include attorneys, mental health practitioners, accountants, and other professionals with special training and experience in the practice of family and divorce mediation.

On average, even with attorney costs for each party, the cost of a mediated divorce is about one-third the cost of a litigated divorce. Additionally, as Jessica Pearson and Nancy Thoennes found in their Denver study of 120 mediated and 120 litigated cases, the parents in the mediated cases were more pleased with and more likely to follow their agreements than the parents who went to court. Other benefits of mediation include the following:

- *Mediation is not adversarial.* The nature of the legal system requires the participants to be adversarial. Many people in disputes are not adversaries. Rather, they may want to problem-solve because they understand the importance of maintaining their ongoing relationship.
- *Mediation is private.* In many states, divorce records and divorce proceedings are open to outsiders. Resolving the conflict in the confines of the mediator's office limits the information available to the public to what the parties agree will be included in their divorce judgment.
- *Mediation is faster.* Since all discussions are held face-to-face, resolving the dispute takes less time in mediation than resolving it through intermediaries.

The mediator usually meets with a client anywhere from three to eight sessions. At the end of the process, the mediator will draft a memorandum of understanding (MOU), which summarizes in plain English what the clients agreed to and, where appropriate, why they made the agreement. The spouses take the MOU to their respective separate attorney for review, advice, and incorporation into their formal legal agreement that is ultimately filed with the court as part of the divorce decree.

Successful mediators come from many different backgrounds. As http://www.mediate.com indicates, competence depends partly on the context of the dispute and the parties' expectations. It also depends on whether the mediator has the right mix of acquired skills, training, education, experience, and natural abilities to help resolve the specific dispute. Important skills and abilities include neutrality, the ability to communicate, the ability to listen and understand, and the ability to define and clarify issues.

To learn more about the mediation process and/or acquire a list of advanced practitioner level mediators (those with the highest level of training and experience), you can contact the Academy of Professional Family Mediators (http://www.apfmnet.org) and the Association for Conflict Resolution (http://www.acrnet.org). These sites also provide a list of state mediation organizations, some of which may have their own accreditation procedures. A mediator's accreditation will help assure you that your mediator has the education, experience, skills, and ethical standards necessary to help address your conflict, and that your mediator has a commitment to the process and the practice of mediation.

Recommended reading for parties contemplating mediation is John Haynes textbook for mediators, *The Fundamentals of Family Mediation*,* as well as Sam Marguelies' book, *Getting Divorced without Ruining Your Life*.†

7.9 COLLABORATIVE LAW

Another alternative dispute to litigation is collaborative law (see https://www.collaborativepractice.com). This is a voluntary dispute resolution process in which parties settle without resort to litigation. In this process

- The parties sign a collaborative participation agreement describing the nature and scope of the matter.
- The parties voluntarily disclose all information that is relevant and material to the matter that must be decided.
- The parties agree to use good faith efforts in their negotiations to reach a mutually acceptable settlement.
- Each party must be represented by a lawyer whose representation terminates upon the undertaking of any contested court proceeding.
- The parties may engage mental health and financial professionals whose engagement terminates upon the undertaking of any contested court proceeding, and may jointly engage other experts as needed.

7.10 DIVORCE ARBITRATION

Another alternate dispute resolution process is arbitration where a neutral third party called the *arbitrator* makes decisions for the couple. The couple decides in advance whether the arbitration is binding or nonbinding. Although not used as frequently as mediation, where the mediator facilitates a nonbinding agreement, arbitration can be a less expensive process than going to trial and is a helpful tool if parties to a divorce seem hopelessly deadlocked on an issue in mediation or litigation. Many of the arbitrators in divorce mediation are retired judges where the decisions provided reflect how they might have ruled if they were still *on the bench*.

7.11 CHOOSING A DIVORCE ATTORNEY

Whatever dispute resolution process you choose, you will still require the services of an attorney. As a medical professional or the spouse of a medical professional, you will probably have more at stake in your divorce than the average person getting divorced. Selecting

* State University of New York Press, 1994.

† Fireside, 1992.

the wrong lawyer can cost you untold aggravation and expense. You are paying the bills and you will have to live with the results.

If you choose collaborative law, you will have to choose from a list of collaborative lawyers. If you are litigating or mediating, you may also use the collaborative lawyer list as a resource. Most family law practitioners would suggest that you ask relatives and friends for referrals as the best source for professional service providers comes from satisfied clients. You can call your local bar association and chamber of commerce for additional names and do a search on the Internet for practitioners. It is recommended that you interview at least three law firms before choosing an attorney. Many attorneys provide free initial consultations or will ask for only a nominal fee, and explain when you are setting up the initial consultation that you wish to obtain a sound evaluation of your legal situation, and to see if you are comfortable about working together. Bring all pertinent written information with you such as last year's tax return, bank account and brokerage statements, mortgage statements, and recent credit card bills.

The following tips on how to choose a divorce lawyer are from the late Elaine Majewski, an advocate for divorce reform:

1. *Qualifications.* Ask the attorney to describe their legal training, how long they have practiced family law, how many family law cases they have handled, and what proportion of their time is spent on family and divorce matters. If the answer is less than 30%, this attorney may not spend sufficient time in this practice area to stay abreast of new developments and current case law.
2. *Attorney's philosophy.* Ask the attorney about his/her view on child custody, visitation/parenting time, support, etc. What are his/her feelings about shared custody? Inquire about his/her outside activities and professional associations, as they will tell you a lot about his/her views. Will the lawyer first seek to resolve the matter amicably in lieu of the traditional adversarial approach? Seek to work with any attorney who is receptive to your ideas and desires. It's always for telling to meet the attorney at his/her office as you can learn much about their outlook from the awards they have received, the photographs they display, the books they read, etc.
3. *Fees.* Inquire how much do they charge, in what increment of billable time, who will actually do the work, and whether a flat or mixed fee arrangement be worked out. Be aware that novices often charge less for an hour but may require more time to handle a problem. What are the specifics of the retainer arrangement as well as costs for travel, meals, administrative assistance, etc.? Is this attorney willing to submit an itemized bill each month?
4. *Point of view.* Once you have presented the facts, the attorney should be able to point out the strengths and weaknesses of your case, assess your probability of achieving your goals, and be able to give you an estimate of how long your matter will take to resolve and make an estimate of the approximate legal fees they would anticipate. Some lawyers neglect to give honest appraisals, and clients are then misled and spend large sums of money on losing causes. Ask the lawyer to also estimate what the minimum and maximum of the fee might be.
5. *Work style.* Will the attorney return phone calls within 24 hours? In his/her absence, how will your inquiries be answered? How are you charged for these inquiries? Does the attorney utilize e-mail? Will the attorney agree to keep you apprised of

all developments in your case and make no offers or agreements without first consulting you? Make sure that the attorney will be available to you, and that you are comfortable with his/her work style and manner.

6. *Handling your case.* Be sure that the lawyer of your choice will be working on your matter. People often go to prestigious firms expecting their problem to be handled by the lawyer they contacted initially, only to be surprised that the case had been turned over to a junior associate. To avoid this situation, state in the retainer agreement that the matter is to be handled by the lawyer of your choice.
7. *Referrals to others.* Does your attorney work with or refer clients to mediators, mental health professionals, tax professionals, appraisers, etc. when appropriate? Does he get a fee or any type of remuneration for these referrals (he/she should not be in a position to gain financially from these referrals)?

It is important to leave the interview feeling that the lawyer is open and responsible to your needs, and that the case would be prepared and handled properly. Majewski offers the following clues to look for at the initial interview:

- Were you received at the appointed hour or kept waiting?
- Did the attorney present an outward appearance of neatness and good grooming?
- Did the attorney discuss the fee arrangement with you up front?
- Was the lawyer a clock watcher?
- Did the attorney leave the room frequently during the interview or permit phone calls?

Majewski also suggests that you may want to observe the attorney in a courtroom setting to see how he/she handles himself/herself. Find out when the attorney will be in court and sit in and observe. You can look up the attorney's rating at Martindale-Hubbell. Inquire if you can speak to previous clients; references will help you learn more about an attorney. If you do not feel comfortable with a lawyer you interviewed, shop around.

7.12 SOME DOS AND DON'TS AND PITFALLS AS YOU PREPARE TO SEPARATE

Marriage involves a legal contract; therefore, the legal system must be involved when changing the status of the contract. Use the legal system for division of property, custody and parenting time arrangements, and child and spousal support. Do not use the legal system to

- Punish an ex-spouse
- Get even for years of problems
- Resolve who was bad or good, right or wrong, etc.
- Show the children "who really loves them"
- Maintain control over an ex-spouse
- Get something from an ex-spouse that you didn't get in marriage

Carol Ann Wilson, CFP, President of the Institute of Certified Divorce Planners, suggests that the first financial agenda for the medical professional when contemplating divorce is to continue paying bills and the mortgage payment, and maintain joint accounts even if no longer living in the same house. Insurance policies should not be canceled, credit card debt should not be increased, and no money should be transferred. Moreover, couples should register accounts in both names with bilateral signatures required to make withdrawals or investments. Duplicate copies should be forwarded to each party.

According to Esther M. Berger, CFP, be prepared to deal with the following *dirty trick* financial tactics, regardless of which spouse you may be

- Your wife asks her physician hospital organization to delay paying part of her salary, bonus or yearly withhold, until after the divorce, making her income appear low, in order to pay you less than entitled.
- Your spouse funnels savings into his/her own account weeks before filing for divorce.
- Your wife's medical convention trips to the Caribbean are visits to an offshore bank that you knew nothing about.
- You discover that your husband has generously gifted joint assets to friends, family members, and medical colleagues so the assets can't be split during a property settlement.
- To your wife's amazement, her almost worthless stock options in a limited partnership suddenly become worth a bundle, 6 months after the divorce.

7.13 EASIEST AND DIFFICULT STATES TO DIVORCE

As many states have residence requirements, it's not easy to venue-shop your divorce. However, a few states have very short or no residency requirements, and a handful have no residency requirements such as Alaska. If the parties are separated and living in different states, they may be able to choose between the two states. An article from Huffington Post online entitled the "Five Best and Worst States for Getting a Divorce" by Brittany Wong dated April 15, 2014, rated states on ease of filing, processing fees, and minimum processing time. The states that came out on top were Alaska, South Dakota, Wyoming, Iowa, and Washington.

In an article on ABC News online dated August 6, 2014, divorce attorney Bruce Provda said that these seven states have among the most expensive filing fees and extensive waiting periods. He also has found that these states' length of residency requirements and minimum separation periods are particularly stringent: Nebraska, New York, California, Arkansas, South Carolina, Rhode Island, and the worst of the worst—Vermont, where Provda states, "A year's residency is required before the divorce will be granted and then there's a three-month 'decree nisi' period to go through before the judge's approval is absolute."

Overheard in the Advisor's Lounge

January Is Divorce Month

January is nicknamed the *divorce month* because of an uptick in activity for divorce lawyers after the New Year. Yet, January to April 15th is also a very low period in terms of people inquiring about divorce mediation. The reason is that couples generally want to know where they stand financially before pursuing divorce. And, with the economy improving, people may be less inclined to wait. While anecdotal evidence abounds, hard figures are more elusive. An analysis of national divorce filings between 2008 and 2011 by legal information website http://FindLaw.com found a spike in January and a gradual rise until a peak in late March.

Sean G. Todd Esq., CPA, MTax, CFP, CMP (Hon)
Roswell, Georgia

7.14 AN OVERVIEW OF FAMILY AND DIVORCE LAW

Which state you file for divorce will determine grounds for filing, child custody and parenting time options, how property is divided, and guidelines for child and spousal support. As a result, a New York divorce decided by the courts may look very different from a California divorce, even though the circumstances of the parties may be quite similar.

Almost every state now offers some form of uncontested divorce with grounds of *irreconcilable differences*, which either states or implies that the marriage is irretrievably broken with no chance of reconciliation. You should check your state statute for the grounds that apply to your case. In most states, no matter what the grounds, fault usually does not impact how assets are divided, how custody is decided, or how alimony is established.

In the following sections, we will take a look at each of these major components you need to decide as you face a divorce:

- Custody options and parenting time issues
- Child support and other financial issues related to the children
- Distribution of marital assets and liabilities
- Spousal support/alimony and tax issues related to alimony
- Other tax considerations of separation and divorce

7.15 CUSTODY OPTIONS AND PARENTING TIME ISSUES

The standard most courts look for custody in adversarial situations is the *best interests of the child*. However, no matter what the custody arrangement, both parents usually do have rights with the child. Additionally, most states offer some form of joint custody as an option, and joint custody is a presumption in approximately one-third of the states. James

Cooke, President of The Joint Custody Association, Los Angeles, California, offers the following custody definitions.

- *Sole custody*: An award of custody to one parent with parenting/visitation rights to the noncustodial parent. The custodial parent retains exclusive authority and control regarding the education, medical care, religion, discipline, and financial support of the child or children.
- *Joint legal custody*: Both parents retain and share responsibility and authority for the care and control of the child or children. The sharing of that responsibility can traverse an entire spectrum, from casual cooperation to specifically delineated times and functions. In its broadest interpretation, joint legal custody has encompassed nearly all major responsibilities and opportunities that are relegated to custodians (e.g., medical, schooling, religion, etc.), except for day-to-day residence.
- *Joint physical and legal custody*: Joint legal custody plus the allocation of significant periods of time for the child or children with each parent. Variations for sharing physical custody can include freedom of movement between two homes, school year versus summer vacation with exchange weekends and nights, workday versus weekends, with special vacation periods, etc.
- *Split custody*: Awards one or more of the children to one parent and the other child or remaining children to the alternate parent. Parents and courts considering the split custody alternative will wish to weigh carefully the wisdom and necessity of ensuring that the children do or do not have significant time together with their siblings.

Beyond negotiation of the types of custody, divorcing parties need to focus on the parenting time needs of their children. Perhaps the most frequent mistake seen in couples returning to court for postdivorce litigation is no specific parenting schedule. At the time of the divorce, sometimes one or both parents state that they don't need a schedule—they can work the schedule out, and both parents are free to see the children anytime they want. This doesn't give the children much assurance. Most children need the security of knowing where they are going to be and with whom. Holidays can become complete chaos with both parties wanting the children at the same time; right after Thanksgiving and Christmas, family courts are clogged with unhappy parents upset because they assumed they were going to have their children over the holidays and were disappointed. Sometimes, the parenting schedule breaks down completely when the first of the parties starts dating.

Furthermore, divorcing parents should work out a schedule with clear pickup and drop-off times and locations. Getting copies of their children's school schedules is essential so that the couple can account for all the children's holidays including teachers' conventions and winter and spring break. As the children get older, you also have to take into account after-school activities and athletic schedules. Once the parties have a schedule, they can always adjust it to meet each other's needs. However, it is important that clients commit to schedules that are workable; if they know they have to work late most weekdays, scheduling a Wednesday midweek visitation may not make sense.

Divorcing parents should try to determine at what age (if any) they or the children can elect to change the arrangements. Finally it is helpful for parties to establish a venue such as mediation for resolving inevitable conflict that will come up in coparenting their children after their divorce.

When it comes to decisions regarding the children, there are only win/win and lose/lose options; there are no win/lose situations. Should a parent win something that is unfair to the other parent, the parties are likely to wind up back in court at some later date, with the child ultimately being exposed to harmful parental conflict, in addition to the financial and emotional cost to both parents. Half of divorced couples with children go back into litigation after their divorce is final. Working out a comprehensive and fair divorce agreement is a cooperative endeavor and may seem daunting when the parties are in the throes of mourning the loss of the marriage and possibly experiencing a great deal of anger; however, it's worth the upfront time and effort in terms of future returns and savings.

7.16 CHILD SUPPORT AND OTHER FINANCIAL ISSUES RELATED TO THE CHILDREN

Parents have a legal and moral obligation to provide their children with the necessities of life. Child support is mandated by law. Most states have a variation of the following formula—17% of net income for one child, 25% of net income for two children, 29% of net income for three children, 31% of net income for four children, and 35% of net income for five or more children. If physical custody is shared for long or frequent periods of time, depending on the financial circumstances of the parents, the needs of the children, and the time spent with each parent, support payments may or may not be required and may be subject to state guidelines. Always check the formula and guidelines for your state.

In most instances, child support is paid to the custodial parent and not the children. Child support covers food, clothing, and shelter for the child. Additional expenses that are usually not included in the basic child support obligation include medical insurance, child care needs, and private school tuition, if appropriate. Such states provide for these expenses to be shared, whereas other states suggest that the parents pay for these expenses based on their percentage of income. As opposed to alimony, child support is not taxed as income to the recipient and is not deductible to the payer.

A frequent question is when does child support end? With the ratification of the twenty-sixth amendment to the Constitution granting 18-year-olds the right to vote in 1971, many states reduced the age of majority from 21 to 18. According to the law, most college students are now adults. Some states adhering strictly to the law limit parental obligation for support to the age of minority. Other states authorize child support during higher education up to a certain age. A third group of states have ambiguous statutes.

The child support guidelines were enacted because many women with children were falling into poverty because of inadequate levels of support. The federal legislation requires the states to develop a formula for determining child support in the hope that the formula raises the level of support and makes support more uniform. The Child Support Enforcement Amendments of 1984 require state child support enforcement agencies to initiate wage withholding when the parent obligated to pay support falls behind in an amount equal to 30 days of support.

Related to the issue of postmajority child support is the issue of whether parents are required to pay for their children's college education. Some courts refuse to authorize college expenses on the argument that if the marriage had continued, the parents would be under no requirement to pay for college. Some states provide that both (divorced) parents are responsible for providing a college or other postsecondary education for their child dependent on their ability to pay at that time and the child's aptitude, opportunities, and inclinations. Some states will actually specify a dollar limit for educational expenses such as the cost of the state university. It is therefore important to look to your state's statute. Additionally, you should know that even though the state may lack the power to order college expenses, the court may look to your divorce order to establish an enforceable obligation.

7.17 DISTRIBUTION OF MARITAL ASSETS AND DEBTS

In the United States, a few states, influenced by their French or Spanish heritage, have the continental system of community property (50/50), which essentially means that property or assets acquired by either husband or wife during the marriage, except for gifts from third parties, belong equally to the husband or wife. Community property does not mean that each asset is divided 50/50. Rather the net value of the assets received by each spouse must be equal. Thus, it is not uncommon for one spouse to be awarded the family residence, with the other spouse receiving the family business and investment real estate. Community property states include Arizona, California, Idaho, Louisiana, Nevada, New Mexico, Texas, and Washington.

The majority of states base their marital law on British common law and provide for equitable rather than equal distribution. In equitable distribution states, the court determines a fair and reasonable distribution that may be more than or less than 50% of any asset to either party. The equitable distribution laws vary from state to state. Each state has its own factors in determining what an equitable fair and just division of assets are. You should check what the factors are for your state. Factors may include

- The duration of the marriage
- The age and physical and emotional health of the parties
- The income or property brought to the marriage by each party
- The standard of living established during the marriage
- Any written agreement made by the parties before or during the marriage concerning an arrangement of property distribution
- The economic circumstances of each party at the time the division of property becomes effective
- The income and earning capacity of each party including educational background, training, etc.
- The contribution by each party to the education, training, or earning power of the other
- The contribution of each party to the acquisition, dissipation, preservation, depreciation, or appreciation in the amount or value of the marital property, as well as the contribution of a party as a homemaker
- The tax consequences of the proposed distribution to each party
- The present value of the property
- The need of a parent who has physical custody of a child to own or occupy the marital residence and to use or own the household effects
- The debts and liabilities of the parties
- The need for creation, now or in the future, of a trust fund to secure reasonably foreseeable medical or educational costs for a spouse or children
- Loss of inheritance rights upon dissolution as of date of dissolution

- Loss of pension rights upon dissolution as of date of dissolution
- Any award of maintenance
- The amount of each person's separate property
- Any other factors that the court may deem relevant

There are a few states that provide that whoever has title to the property is the owner. While this was the prevalent system throughout the United States in the first half of the twentieth century, most states realized that this system was fraught with problems and changed to the community property or equitable distribution process of division. In both community property and equitable distribution states, it does not matter who holds title to the asset or property acquired during the marriage. The property may have been acquired by either the husband or the wife during the marriage and may be in either party's name.

In both community property and equitable distribution states, marital property usually does not include property provided for in a written agreement such as a PNA. It also does not include *separate property*, which is defined as property acquired before marriage and property acquired by bequest, devise, descent, or gift from a party other than the spouse, and also does not include compensation for personal injuries. However, the increase in value of separate property may or may not be considered marital property in some states, and in other states is only considered marital property to the extent that the appreciation is due in part to the direct or indirect contributions or efforts of the other spouse.

It is important to note that the enhanced earning capacity from an educational degree or license earned during the marriage may be considered a marital asset in some states, giving the other spouse the right to a percentage of the enhanced earnings, while in other states, the other spouse may only be entitled to be reimbursed for the costs of acquiring the degree or license.

Businesses and professional practices, real estate, 401(k) plans and other qualified plans, IRAs, pension plans, bank accounts, brokerage accounts, whole life insurance policies, business interests, stock options, automobiles, profit sharing plans, income tax refunds, and other assets acquired during the marriage are considered marital assets. Some assets may have tax ramifications. The parties must factor in tax consequences of the gain or loss as well as the impact of depreciation in determining the true value of an item.

7.17.1 Businesses and Professional Practices

Certified public accountant and business appraisers are hired to determine the value of a business or professional medical practice. The accountant or appraiser who is hired reviews the books and records of the practice and prepares a written report. Since a practice, unlike a bank account, cannot usually be divided in a divorce, judges will look to provide the non-physician spouse with another asset from the marriage. This is commonly referred to as an offset against the value of the practice that the physician is maintaining. Of course, if the divorcing physician is selling the practice because of retirement or for other reasons, the need for an offset is eliminated as the non-physician can share in the proceeds from the sale.

7.17.2 Pension Plans (Defined Benefit Plans)

Pension plans usually specify the monthly benefit the retiree will receive upon retirement at a specified age. If there are no other assets to offset the present value of a pension plan as determined by an actuary, the other spouse may receive a percentage of each future pension check, or at some other designated time as allowed by the pension plan, based on the number of years the spouses lived together as husband and wife and the total number of years the employed spouse has been participating in the pension plan.

The laws governing pensions are different for private corporate physicians than they are for government and military health-care workers. Private corporate employees are usually covered under the Federal Retirement Equity Act of 1984, which created what is known as the *Qualified Domestic Relations Order* or *QDRO* (pronounced as "quadro"). The QDRO is a court order to designate how a specific retirement plan will be divided, and to whom it will be paid, and whom, and requires the employer to comply with the terms of the order. If you or your spouse is a government or military employee, you and your attorney should seek to understand the nuances of the specific plan.

7.17.3 401(k) Plans and Other Qualified Plans (Defined Contribution Plans) and IRAs

If there are no other assets to offset the net value of a 401(k) plan, other qualified plan, or IRA, the other spouse may receive a percentage of these accounts. This distribution usually occurs concurrent with the divorce. He or she will be able to defer taxes on the distribution by placing the funds in a rollover IRA account. Please note that while there is usually an additional 10% penalty for early liquidation of these accounts, the early distribution tax does not apply for receipts from 401(k) plans and other qualified plans paid to an alternate payee through a QDRO.

7.17.4 Real Estate/Marital Residence

There are some financial pitfalls that must be considered in dealing with the marital residence. For physicians, ignoring these could be a financial disaster since it is not unusual for a doctor to have a significant part of his or her net worth tied up in home ownership.

The Taxpayer Relief Act of 1997 provided new rules for home sales. The Act provides for a couple to exclude $500,000 in capital gains and for an individual to exclude $250,000 in capital gains, every 2 years. Additionally, the Act states that to qualify for this exclusion, this home must have been your primary residence for two of the past 5 years. (As a medical professional, if you have an office at home, any portion that qualified for the home office tax deduction does not qualify for this tax-free profit.)

There are special rules in the Taxpayer Relief Act for divorcing couples regarding home sales. Divorcing couples should be entitled to a partial exclusion of taxes even if they don't meet the 2-year time test. For example, if a divorcing couple had a $375,000 gain during their 18 months of home ownership (i.e., $500,000 × 75%), they could exclude the whole gain. Additionally, a taxpayer is treated as using his/her home as his/her principal residence during any period that the taxpayer's spouse or former spouse is granted use of the residence under a divorce or separation agreement.

Where minor children are involved, it is common for the custodial parent to be allowed to live in the residence with the children for a specified period of time after the Dissolution of Marriage is finalized. During that period of time, the spouse who lives in the home is usually required to make all mortgage, property tax, and homeowner insurance payments when due. The house may be sold when there are no children living at the property, when the youngest child attains the age of majority, or at any date as otherwise agreed by the parties or specified by the court, with the proceeds to be divided based on the agreement in the divorce settlement. In this situation, the parties will still be entitled to take the $500,000 joint exclusion after the divorce.

If there is a large gain on the house at the time of the divorce, a pitfall to avoid is transferring the entire house to one of the parties in the divorce settlement. If that spouse subsequently were to sell the house and has to report the entire gain on his/her separate return, only $250,000 of the gain (from the time of the original purchase of the house) would escape taxation.

7.18 SPOUSAL SUPPORT/ALIMONY AND TAX ISSUES RELATED TO ALIMONY

During the divorce process, no one word seems to incite riot as easily as *alimony* (also known as spousal support or maintenance). Issues such as closure, dependency, and deservedness come into play. However, once you separate the emotions and stereotypes from the actual mechanics, alimony can offer some couples financial advantages. As attorney Steve Abel states in *The Friendly Divorcebook*,* "allowing your feelings to take over on the matter may prevent you from saving a great deal of money. Maintenance might save money by means of smart tax planning, just at a time you both need it."

Publication 504 issued by the Department of the Treasury provides information for divorced or separated individuals, including the federal rules regarding alimony. "Alimony is a payment to or for a spouse or former spouse under a divorce or separation instrument... Alimony is deductible by the payer and must be included in the spouse's or former spouse's income."

The crux of the benefits of alimony relates to taxes. We have a progressive tax system in the United States. People who earn more are taxed at a higher percentage than those who earn less. By shifting earnings to the lower taxpayer, both parties can benefit. An illustration may help.

Let's say that a doctor husband has $200,000 in taxable income and the wife has $30,000 in taxable income. Based on the 2014 tax tables, assuming each party is filing as head of household, the husband will owe about $46,586 in federal taxes and the wife will owe $3856 in federal taxes. Together, they will owe $50,442 when filing separate returns as head of household. Now let's shift $50,000 of the husband's income to the wife based on an arbitrary theoretical taxable alimony obligation. The doctor/husband's taxable income would now be $150,000, and he would owe $32,586 in taxes, while the wife's taxable income would now be $80,000 and she would owe $14,419 in taxes. Together they would owe $47,005—a savings of $3437 in taxes. As the differences in income become larger, the savings also become larger.

* Bradford Publishing Co., 1996.

If you have children, most courts are looking for child support by that state's child support guidelines in your divorce agreement. It is therefore wise to calculate the child support guidelines and not to muddy the waters by calling child support alimony. However, there will still be situations where the higher paying spouse intends to provide support beyond the child support guidelines or plans to make periodic payments to the other spouse. It may benefit the parties to structure these payments as alimony.

To be alimony, a payment must meet certain requirements:

- The payment is made pursuant to a divorce or separation instrument—it cannot be a verbal agreement.
- The instrument does not designate the payment as not alimony.
- Alimony does not include child support or payments pursuant to equitable distribution.
- The parties should live in separate households (there are some exceptions).
- The parties must file separate tax returns and also live in separate households.
- The payment must be in cash (or check, etc.); transfer of services or property is not permitted.
- There is no liability to make payment after the death of the recipient spouse.
- Alimony cannot terminate or drop by more than $15,000 from the prior year in the first three calendar years of payment. There is the potential to have to recapture if this does occur, unless the drop is due to death or the remarriage of the person receiving payments.
- There must be no contingency related to payment of alimony based on an event impacting your child or children such as leaving school or the children becoming employed.

There is always some risk involved with actually getting payments over a period of time versus getting a lump sum payment upfront. The factors that often lead to these risks include additional expenses from a new marriage or new family, cohabitation (although some agreements specifically have clauses addressing this issue), inability to pay as a result of incapacitation through illness, payment withheld as punishment, and refusal to pay.

To avoid some of these risks, another way to receive alimony is through a so-called *alimony substitution trust*. In this vehicle, liquid investments such as stocks and bonds are placed in trust with a custodian with generated interest and dividends sufficient to pay each month's agreed alimony stipend. Stipulations are made in the trust provisions to sell portions of the portfolio if sufficient cash is not generated by the portfolio's investments. Some professionals feel that this arrangement is a better vehicle for periodic alimony payments than the goodwill of the payer spouse, as the *check is in the mail* syndrome is avoided.

While many people believe alimony is assumed, it is not as common as you may think it to be. Nearly one out of six divorce cases even considers it as an option. Temporary spousal support is more common and occurs at time of separation, mostly to help the receiving spouse get on his or her feet again. It is either agreed upon or an order is issued. However, if your marriage is a long-term marriage in the eyes of the court (this usually means over 20 years), and your spouse has had income that is less than one-third of your income, you may be expected to pay alimony. While few states have alimony guidelines as they do for child support, most have statutory criteria for an award of alimony.

Some of the factors that may be part of your state's criteria may include

- Parental responsibility
- Income available to either party through investments or any assets held by that party
- The tax treatment and consequences to both parties of any alimony award including the designation of all or a portion of the awarded alimony
- The actual need and ability of the parties to pay
- The duration of the marriage
- The age and physical and emotional health of the parties
- The standard of living established in the marriage and the likelihood that each party can maintain a reasonably comparable standard of living
- The earning capacities, educational levels, vocational skills, and employability of the parties
- The length of absence from the job market and custodial responsibilities for children of the party seeking maintenance
- The time and expense necessary to acquire sufficient education or training to enable the party seeking maintenance to find appropriate employment, the availability of the training and employment, and the opportunity for future acquisitions of capital assets and income
- The history of the financial or nonfinancial contributions to the marriage by each party including contributions to the care and education of the children and interruption of personal careers or educational opportunities
- The equitable distribution of property ordered and any payout on equitable distribution directly or indirectly, out of current income, to the extent this consideration is reasonable, just, and fair
- Any other factors that the court may deem relevant

Most alimony falls under the category of term alimony where alimony is paid for a specific period of time, usually based on the length of the marriage. For a spouse that has been away from the work force, there may also be *rehabilitative alimony* in that it is paid until the spouse has acquired job skills or experience. Often, term and rehabilitative alimony may both be awarded. In cases where the spouse has not worked during a long-term marriage, that spouse may be awarded *lifetime alimony* or alimony for an indefinite period of time, which ceases upon the death of either party or the remarriage of the person receiving the support, and would be subject to a review at the time the payor retires, usually after the age they can collect full social security.

Some states also provide for *reimbursement alimony*, which is intended to reimburse one party who supported the other party usually through an advanced education. It is assumed that the supporting party anticipated participation in the fruits of the earning capacity generated by the education. Basically, there is an attempt by some states to reimburse the person who did not go to school for an advanced degree because they will not benefit from the increased salary or earnings of the person who received the degree. (Other states may value the advanced degree or licenses, and look to reimburse the other spouse for the value of that education or degree.)

Invariably, when there is alimony, a court will also order the payor to carry life insurance to secure payments to the payee spouse in the event of the payor's death. Usually, the amount of insurance required will match the outstanding payment owed.

In the past, the wife was almost always the recipient of alimony, but the courts no longer view gender as a consideration. In most states, marital conduct is also not a consideration. It is purely a decision made due to the economic consequences of each spouse. If an agreement between spouses is reached out of court regarding any aspect of your divorce, the court will give it significant consideration, and the court usually encourages litigants to mediate or otherwise resolve their cases themselves.

Overheard in the Doctor's Lounge

The Likely to Be Married List

Bloomberg *Businessweek* has a fun breakdown of which occupations have had the highest shares of people who are married from 1950 to 2010, based on data from the Census Bureau. While engineers, mathematicians, and scientists today are (unfairly) stereotyped as awkward nerds who don't know how to interact with the opposite sex, in 1950, they were among the occupations most likely to be married.

Today, the most commonly conjugated occupations are instead more often medical professionals with doctorates, starting with dentists (81% of whom are hitched): occupations in which people are most likely to be married, 2010: (1) dentist, (2) chief executive, (3) sales engineer, (4) physician, (5) podiatrist, (6) optometrist, (7) farm product buyer, (8) precision grinder, (9) religious worker, and (10) tool and die maker.

Catherine Rampell
Washington Post, January 8, 2015

7.19 OTHER TAX CONSIDERATIONS OF SEPARATION AND DIVORCE

To stay up-to-date on tax issues and for the most recent tax tables and forms, please visit the IRS site at http://www.irs.ustreas.gov.

7.19.1 Filing Status

As previously mentioned, child support is not taxed as income to the recipient and is not deductible to the payer, while alimony is usually taxed as income to the recipient and is deductible to the payer. The tax laws impose other rules for separated or divorced individuals. If you are in the process of going through a divorce, it would be wise to read through the IRS publications related to separation and divorce, as well as to consult with your tax advisor, so that you are in the best position to negotiate these monetary aspects of your divorce.

Your filing status for your tax return is your status on the last day of the year for the year you are filing. If you and your spouse are living apart but are not legally separated, or if your divorce decree is not final, you may file a joint tax return. You should know that married filing separately currently results in the highest tax rate; it pays if both parties can cooperate—better to share the savings than pay more to the IRS out of spite. You are considered single if you are unmarried or separated from your spouse either by a divorce or a court-approved separate maintenance decree and that you don't qualify as a head of household.

Because the head of household tax rate is lower than the single tax rate, you may want to see if you can qualify for this status—you can qualify as a head of household only if you were unmarried on the last day of the year or separated for over 6 months, and have at least one dependent child and pay more than half the cost of keeping a home for yourself and this dependent, which was the dependent's main home for more than half the year. In a family with two or more children, with proper tax planning, both parents could qualify as head of household if the parents structure their parenting time so that each parent has physical custody of at least one child more than 50% of the time. If your taxable income is $150,000, you would save over $2588 in taxes by filing as head of household rather than single, and nearly $4867 as head of household rather than married filing separately.

7.19.2 Exemptions for Dependents

Only one parent can claim a child on their tax return. The parent who had custody of the child for the greater part of the year is generally treated as the parent who provided more than half the child's support and is usually allowed to claim the exemption for a child. Noncustodial parents can still claim the child exemption if the custodial parent signs a statement (using Form 8332), agreeing not to claim the child's exemption, and the noncustodial parent attaches this statement to his or her return or attaches a copy of certain pages of his/her divorce decree or separation agreement addressing exemptions. There are separate rules for divorce agreements made prior to 1985.

Generally, you can deduct $4000 (as of 2015) for each exemption for a dependent you can claim on your tax return. If you are at a 33% tax bracket, each deduction results in a net saving of $1320 on your federal tax return. High-income earners should be aware that the exemption is subject to a phaseout that begins with adjusted gross income of $258,250 for singles and $309,900 for married couples filing jointly. For these classes, it phases out completely at $380,750 and $432,400, respectively.

7.19.3 Child Tax Credit

Additionally, the IRS provides a child tax credit for each qualifying dependent under age 17 (see Exemptions for Dependents). The parent who claims the exemption for the child is also entitled to claim the child tax credit. A tax credit is a dollar-for-dollar reduction in your tax liability. Each dollar in tax credit results in a dollar offset against your income tax. As of 2015, the maximum tax credit is $1000 per child, with the credit subject to phase out for adjusted gross income (AGI) over $100,000 for married filing jointly, $75,000 for head of household or single, and $55,000 for married filing separately. Usually, if your credit exceeds your income tax, you won't get a check for the difference. However, if your income is below a threshold, you may qualify for the "Additional Child Tax Credit," which allows you to receive the difference.

7.19.4 Child Care Tax Credit

If you paid someone to care for your child under age 13, or other qualifying person, in order to work or look for work and you have physical custody of a child, you may also be able to take the credit for child and dependent care. If you are divorced or separated and you have physical custody of the child, you can treat your child as a qualifying person, even if you cannot claim the child's exemption. If you are the noncustodial parent, you cannot treat your child as a qualifying person even if you can claim the child's exemption.

While the White House is proposing increasing the child care tax credit to $3000 per child, the maximum child care expense allowed is currently 35% of $3000 for one dependent and $6000 for two or more dependents. The credit percentage is reduced in steps to 20% as gross adjusted income increases.

7.19.5 Education Credits

The American Opportunity Tax Credit (AOTC, formerly the Hope Credit) provides a credit of up to $2500 for the first 4 years of college. The Lifetime Learning Credit (LLC) provides up to $2000 per return for all years of postsecondary education. Both follow the same rule as the Under Age 16 Child Tax Credit. For a student, you cannot take both credits in the same year. The parent who claims the exemption may also claim these education credits. The Education Credits have income tests associated with them of a maximum of $80,000 for a single or head of household return and $160,000 adjusted gross income for a joint return for the AOTC, and $55,000 and $110,000 AGI for the LLC.

7.19.6 Earned Income Tax Credit

The earned income credit is a tax credit for certain people who work and have earned income under a specified threshold; for 2015, the maximum AGI before phaseout is $18,110 for single taxpayers with one or more children. It is likely that most medical professionals will not qualify for this credit. There are different thresholds for people without children, people with one child, and people with two or more children.

7.19.7 Child's Investment Income

If your dependent children have unearned income (income-producing property or investment property) of more than $1050 as of 2015, they will have a tax liability on this earning. The custodial parent or parents may choose to include this income on their return rather than file a return for the child. The IRS specifically states not to use the return of the noncustodial parent. Note that if your child's interests, dividends, and other investment income total more than $2100, unearned income above that threshold will be taxed at the parent's highest tax rate instead of the child's tax rate.

7.20 OLDER DIVORCING MEDICAL PROFESSIONALS (GREY DIVORCE)

While marriages are more apt to break up at around the 7-year mark than at the silver anniversary, divorce among people 50+, has also become more common, sometimes attributed to the empty next syndrome. When divorce does occur in later years, it can present more complicated financial issues when compared with earlier breakups, says Gregg Parish of the College for Financial Planning.

If for example a party dies or becomes incapacitated during the divorce, the surviving spouse will completely retain control of the finances. A common situation, Parish says, is when a couple owns a home in joint tenancy with rights of survival. Thus, if one spouse dies, the other automatically inherits the house. Parish recommends that older couples in the throes of separation situation change the ownership to tenants in common, in which each party is considered to own half the property.

Another area older physicians going through a divorce should be especially cautious about is inheritances or gifts from their own parents. They may want to stop or delay distribution of their estate to you to reduce the chance that the property would become mixed into marital property. Or the recipient might put any gifts or inheritances into a separate account or trust.

Alimony is more prevalent among this age group of divorced couples. It is not uncommon to find a woman who may not have employable skills and who must rely on her former spouse for support. As is the case for child support payments in younger parties, steps should be taken to ensure continuation of funds to the recipient if the obligated party dies before the recipient through instruments such as life insurance.

For most older divorcing couples, after their house and their pension, their next most valuable asset is their social security rights. Each party vests in the other's social security account after 10 years of marriage. That means that even a nonworking spouse can usually collect 50% of benefits of the earning spouse; alternatively, the spouse with lower earnings can either collect benefits based on their own earnings or collect 50% of the benefits their spouse is entitled to. This collection does not impact how much the higher earning spouse can collect. You can learn more about social security benefits and rules by contacting http://www.ssa.gov.

What is often missed in the analysis of divorce is the inequity in social security benefits for the nonworking spouse or lower-earning spouse after separation or divorce. The issue of social security benefits can easily be addressed in the divorce agreement by stipulating that the parties will equalize social security benefits with the higher-earning spouse providing to the lower-earning spouse one-half the difference between the payments provided by the Social Security Administration to each of them. As social security benefits are taxable, it is further recommended that these payments be regarded as alimony, and therefore will be taxable to the recipient.

Another divorce area often overlooked, given today's older physician population, is eldercare obligations. For example, if a doctor is involved in the care and financial assistance of an older family member, this must be placed on the table at the divorce resolution planning discussions. America is aging and 25% of its population is 60 or older. Every 7 seconds someone turns 50. It is not unusual to live many miles from aging parents.

Imagine the impact if an in-law is in a long-term care facility that is dependent upon the financial help of the children who now get divorced. What happens to the elder persons' ability to meet their financial obligations and to stay in the current facility? How can quality care be coordinated? Who will monitor the ongoing health, mental, and physical issues? When does the aging parent need in-home care? Assisted living arrangements or a skilled nursing facility? Yet, the generation of medical professionals between the ages of 40 and 60 is dealing with aging parents at the same time their children are entering college. This double financial squeeze has created a new set of eldercare issues.

Most cities and local government agencies are addressing this issue, and many nonprofit organizations are attempting to fill the gap in this growing societal issue. The following information resources are helpful in this regard: http://www.eldercaredirectory.org; http://www.medicare.gov; http://www.medicaid.gov; http://www.careguide.com; http://www.seniorhousing.net; http://www.caregiver911.com; and http://www.n4a.org.

7.21 ASSESSMENT

Although one can hardly plan for an event like divorce, this information and the steps outlined in the mediation process may lessen the financial impact of divorce.

7.22 CONCLUSION

The information in this chapter does not take the place of legal, accounting, and/or financial planning advice from competent professionals. As providers of expert services to others, the medical professional should seek sound personal advice when contemplating a change in marital status.

7.23 COLLABORATE

Discuss this chapter online with others at http://www.MedicalExecutivePost.com.

ACKNOWLEDGMENTS

To John R. Connell, MBA, JD, CPA, PFS, Denver, Colorado, and Dr. David Edward Marcinko, MBA, CMP.

BIBLIOGRAHPY

Braver, S and O'Connell, D: *Divorced Dads—Shattering the Myths*. Penguin Putnam, New York, 1998.

Eddy, B and Kreger, R: *Splitting: Protecting Yourself While Divorcing Someone with Borderline or Narcissistic Personality Disorder*. New Harbinger Publications, New York, 2011.

Elliott, SJ: *Getting Past Your Breakup: How to Turn a Devastating Loss into the Best Thing That Ever Happened to You*. Da Capo Lifelong Books, Boston, 2009.

Green, J: *Divorce After 50: Your Guide to the Unique Legal & Financial Challenges*. Berkeley, CA, 2013.

Haynes, JM: *The Fundamentals of Family Mediation*. State University of New York Press, 1994, p. 31.

Koenig, F: *Divorce: No-Nonsense Practical Advice for Men (Divorce: No-Nonsense Practical Advice Book 1)*. New York, 2013.

Lander, JA: *DIVORCE: Think Financially, Not Emotionally® Volume I: What Women Need To Know About Securing Their Financial Future Before, During, and After Divorce*. San Clemente, CA, 2015.

Marcinko, DE: *Special Situations Financial Planning. Comprehensive Financial Planning Strategies for Doctors and Advisors*. Productivity Press, Boca Raton, FL, 2015.

Miller, MN and McGowen, R: The painful truth: Physicians are not invincible. *Southern Medical Journal* 2000;93:966–973.

Poindexter, V: *Divorce: Complete Guide to Fast Recovery, Emotionally and Financially with Proven Strategies For Success*. Amazon Digital Services, 2014.

Rollman, BL, Mead, LA, Wan, NY, and Klag, MJ: Medical specialty and the incidence of divorce. *The New England Journal of Medicine* 1997;336:800–803.

APPENDIX

A.1 A STEP-BY-STEP APPROACH TO THE DIVORCE MEDIATION PROCESS

As opposed to psychological therapy, which is often open-ended, mediation should be approached in a structured manner so as to minimize mediation fees, maximize the productivity of sessions by keeping clients focused, and expedite a fair resolution before the conflict escalates. The reality of divorce is that most clients have similar issues they need to address such as the house, the pension, and college education for the children. Nevertheless, the process should also be flexible to properly address the uniqueness of each client situation such as different religious requirements or the needs of a gifted child.

Described herein is an approach to the divorce mediation process with the caveat that each mediator has his/her own style, that there are many right approaches to this process, and that the process can take more or less sessions and time than described depending on the complexity of the issues, the availability of documentation and third-party appraisals, and preparedness of the parties, and the parties' readiness to proceed. On average, there are three to eight 90-minute client meeting sessions over a 2- to 3-month time frame. However, there are some clients who literally take years to work through the issues, and others clients who have completed the mediation process over two weekends.

The objective is to provide information that demystifies what happens behind closed doors during the divorce mediation process. Although outlined as an approach that assumes the couple has children, the same approach can be used in a more contracted fashion for couples without children.

The mediator helps the separating couple address the custody and parenting time issues, distribution of assets and liabilities, child and spousal support amounts, insurance, income tax, and other decisions needed to restructure their family into two units.

The mediator's role is to help the couple explore options and their consequences, and bring knowledge and experience that provide a context for decision making. Mediation is guided by the concept of self-determination—decision-making authority in the mediation process rests with the parties. When necessary, the mediator will refer the couple to experts for services such as appraisals.

At the end of the mediation process, the mediator prepares a *memorandum of understanding* (MOU) that summarizes the agreements reached. Although attorneys generally do not participate in the mediation sessions, the two spouses are advised to have their attorneys review the memorandum. They may also use the services of an attorney or attorneys to prepare their separation or divorce agreement based on the decisions in the memorandum.

The success rate for divorce mediation, which may be defined as the parties coming to agreement, is higher than in other civil mediation cases. Additionally, the success rate for couples voluntarily seeking divorce mediation is significantly higher than for court-mandated mediation. From usual experience, 90% of separating clients who voluntarily come to mediation complete the process.

A.2 SCHEDULING THE FIRST MEDIATION SESSION

A client may phone or e-mail to either learn more about mediation or to make an appointment. In his book *The Fundamentals of Family Mediation*, John Haynes, the Founding President of the Academy of Family Mediators, states that "the mediator is presented with a classic dilemma: how to provide sufficient information so she can make an intelligent decision about the suitability of mediation while at the same time not developing a relationship with the client" (Haynes 1994).

During this initial inquiry, the mediator will try and ascertain the following:

- How the prospect received their name
- The names of the parties and their attorneys
- Where the parties are in the divorce process with their attorneys
- Whether there is domestic violence that precludes the couple from mediating
- The length of the marriage and the ages of the children, if any

The mediator will provide the following information during the conversation:

- Description of the mediation process and the role of the mediator
- The role of the mediator versus the role of the attorney in the divorce process
- Typical number of sessions, fee structure, and available times for sessions
- Information on background, training, and experience

A.2.1 Mediation Session #1

The first session serves as an introduction and overview of the mediation process. The agenda for the first session will usually encompass the following:

- Description of process, the mediator's role, the number of sessions/fees
- Parties' objectives for today and for the mediation process
- Review of the mediation agreement (not to be signed that day)
- Grounds for filing for divorce/separation with summary of legal process
- Issues that must be addressed today
- Description of issues to be addressed in the mediation process
- Development of list of documents for clients to bring in for the next session

This session is usually highly emotionally charged. There may be great anxiety about the session, anger between the parties, and apprehension about the mediator and the mediation process. A number of things help to put the clients at ease during this session. Mediators may remind clients that the purpose of the first session is to provide them with information, and that they are under no pressure to make any decision until they are comfortable.

The most helpful information obtained during this session is each of the party's objectives for the mediation. What mediators hear most frequently is that the parties don't want to spend unnecessary money, don't have the intestinal fortitude for a court battle, want to keep their conflict private, and want to remain friendly with each other for the sake of any children.

The mediation agreement includes the following:

- The parties have entered mediation voluntarily, and it is understood that they may discontinue the mediation process at any time.
- They have not waived the right to consult with and/or retain their own attorney.
- The mediation process is confidential with the exception of information regarding abuse, neglect, abandonment, or exploitation of a child.
- Neither the mediator nor his/her records shall be subject to subpoena.

- Good faith disclosure requires full disclosure of information and production of documents; if documents requested are not provided, the mediator reserves the right to terminate the mediation.
- If the services of other experts are required such as appraisers, the parties will retain neutral experts and will pay their fees directly to them.
- The hourly fee for the mediation and the payment schedule (usually pay-as-you go).
- The MOU is not a legal document; their attorney(s) will include information from the MOU in the Property Settlement Agreement/Divorce Agreement.
- The parties are urged to consult with attorneys prior to signing the Property Settlement Agreement/Divorce Agreement.

The mediator may provide legal information but should not provide legal advice. They may cover the grounds for filing for divorce for their state, who may file for divorce, any residence requirements, as well as a timeline of the legal process.

Toward the end of the first session, the mediator will provide a list of documents needed for the next session. If either party has a defined benefit pension plan, the mediator will provide forms so that they can request a valuation of the pensions. If there is a business like a professional medical practice, the mediator will suggest that the parties need a business valuation by a neutral business appraiser, and may provide a list of professionals they recommend. Other documents that are usually requested include

- The children's school schedules with holidays
- Pay stubs
- Last year's W-2 Forms for each party (summarizing annual earnings)
- Most recent federal tax return
- Copies of all bank, brokerage, and 401(k)/403(b) statements
- Most recent mortgage statement showing outstanding loan balances
- A summary of all insurance policies and coverage
- A market assessment of real estate if property values are in dispute
- A list of household items if the parties cannot agree how to divide them
- A credit report for each party

With the exception of medical practice business appraisals, which can be very time consuming, it usually takes 2 or 3 weeks for clients to collect the other requested documentation and deal with getting a market assessment on the house. Therefore, scheduling the second session for 3 weeks later makes sense. The time lapse is also helpful in allowing the client to process what happened in mediation and their emotional issues regarding their impending separation and divorce.

A.2.2 Mediation Session #2

The focus of this session is on developing the parenting plan and on data collection. The agenda for the second session will usually encompass the following:

- Sign the mediation agreement
- Develop the parenting plan and address related issues
- Meet with each party alone (caucus)

- Collect requested documentation
- Provide budget worksheets for completion by the next session

Many states require parents in divorce proceeding to file parenting plans, with the hope that the parties will be encouraged to fulfill their parenting responsibilities through their agreements rather than rely on judiciary intervention. The parenting plan typically encompasses nonfinancial parenting issues, including

- The type of custody chosen and reasons for selecting it (usually either sole custody to one parent with parenting time to the other, joint legal custody with one parent having primary residential care, or joint physical custody)
- A specific schedule for parenting time for each party including weeknights, weekends, vacations, religious holidays, school vacations, birthdays, and special occasions, and including procedures for transferring the child
- Access to various records including educational and medical records
- Provisions or restrictions on domestic or international travel
- The impact if there is a contemplated change of residence by a parent
- Participation in making decisions regarding the child including decisions about religious upbringing, health care, and education

In some other states, child support is based on a number of factors including the number of overnights each parent has with the child/children. By first developing the parenting plan, the mediator has an essential building block to assist the clients in structuring their financial settlement.

During this session, the mediator may meet with each party alone (caucus) for approximately 10 minutes with the idea of providing equal time to each participant. Different mediators have different views on whether the caucus is confidential; they should share this information, so you can proceed accordingly. Most clients appreciate the time in caucus, as it allows them to share the emotional details of their personal situation without worrying about their spouse's reactions.

If the case appears appropriate for spousal support because of a large difference in party incomes, or if one party is a supported spouse, budgeting is a necessity. However, even for clients who have similar incomes, preparing a budget can help reduce the level of anxiety about separating. The mediator may provide budget work sheets for clients to complete outlining current and projected expenses. As time is needed to go through the documents provided by clients, for them to collect budget information, and for the return of the business appraisal, it is good to schedule the next session at least 2 weeks out.

A.2.3 Mediation Session #3

The focus of this session is on data analysis for child support and distribution of assets and liabilities. The agenda for the third session will usually encompass the following:

- Review child support based on child support guidelines
- Discuss other financial issues related to the children
- Review inventory of assets and liabilities
- Decide how to divide assets and liabilities
- Collect budgeting information

By the third session, most clients feel comfortable with the mediation process and the routine of going through the agenda. This session will be pivotal and requires that clients be ready to make key financial decisions. However, because the clients have provided the necessary documentation that has allowed the mediator to conduct data analysis, they will now be in a position to make decisions based on information.

Each state has its own child support guidelines and formulas, and many of the courts will require proof that parties have been provided with information regarding what child support would be by the state's child support guidelines. Therefore, the mediator should be able to perform these calculations. Clients may choose to adjust the child support—that is also something the mediator should work through with clients. Additionally, if spousal support is also warranted, child support may be revised upward or downward depending on the amount of spousal support agreed to in Session 4.

There are frequent and recurring child expenses that must be also addressed during this session including

- Work-related childcare
- Child's share of health insurance premiums
- Out-of-pocket health-care expenses of the child such as for orthodontia
- Other extraordinary but forecastable expenses such as SAT preparation classes

Some child-related costs cannot be anticipated at the time of the divorce such as fees for summer camps or karate lessons. Parents often choose to share these costs or pay them in percentage to their incomes. The mediator may also bring up the following issues:

- Frequency and/or events that should trigger a child support modification
- Age of emancipation for the children as related to the child support obligation
- Any religious rights-of-passage and how funded such as bar mitzvahs
- The parties' desires regarding the child's college education and costs

The first area discussed with respect to assets and liabilities is personal property. If the parties can decide how to divide their personal property on their own such as furniture, stereo equipment, television, computer equipment, antiques, and photographs, the mediator will usually stay out of that process. If they cannot, the mediator may suggest that they make an inventory of household items, place a fire sale price next to each item, and then take turns picking which items they desire. If one person ends up with significantly less, they can ask for reimbursement from the other party.

The parties have provided documentation including copies of bank statements, business valuations, brokerage statements, and pension statements. Once all the information has been collected, one method for dividing assets and liabilities is to prepare a three-column spreadsheet program such as MS Excel. The total estate would be in column 1. Column 2 would be reserved for assets and liabilities the wife is receiving, and column 3 would be reserved for assets and liabilities the husband is receiving.

As an example, if the parties have a car worth $10,000 with a $5000 loan, a house worth $250,000 with a $125,000 mortgage, and a bank account with $130,000, the total value of their entire estate as indicated in column 1 would be $260,000. If the parties decide that the wife is keeping the car, the car loan, the house, and the mortgage, those values go in column 1; it is clear that she is getting 50% of the total assets. Please note that this is a simple illustration and does not adjust for potential taxes, sales commissions, and closing costs that may or may not be considered in the mediation process.

During the mediation session, the mediator may go through numerous alternatives on how he/she could divide up the marital assets and liabilities, and may look for ways to balance the division through vehicles such as qualified domestic relations orders (QDRO) that allow the transfer of part of a pension of deferred savings plan to the other party.

As time is needed to analyze budget information provided by the clients, it is wise to schedule the next session for 2 weeks later.

A.2.4 Mediation Session #4

The focus of this session is on budgets, spousal support, and other outstanding. The agenda for the fourth session will usually encompass the following:

- Review parties' current and forecasted budgets
- Discuss what is needed if there are shortfalls like spousal support
- Review outstanding issues like taxes, religious issues, divorce cost, etc.
- Provide agenda for next session

As with the balance sheet, the mediator will take data provided by the clients and create a spreadsheet with the parties' marital budget, and the projected budgets for each of the parties after the separation and divorce. There are many issues that influence the ease or difficulty of this task. It is usually easier if the parties are already living in separate residences and if both parties are employed and working at their full earning capacity. It is harder if the parties are self-employed, and also if they have a lot of cash expenditures that are hard to track. The parties' capacity for record keeping will influence the accuracy of the budget. For most clients, the goal is to capture the 20% of expenses that account for 80% of their budget.

During the session, the mediator will review the current and forecasted budgets with the clients and try and help them jog their memories for expenditures as well as income sources that they may have missed. The budgets either provide reassurance that both parties will be self-sustaining and relatively comfortable, or help identify shortfalls. The budgeting exercise provides for a more rational discussion regarding spousal support, be it some type of interim support, support for a number of years, or in longer-term marriages, permanent alimony. Because establishing both the amount and the term of spousal support is highly subjective, it is advisable that that clients seek advice from counsel, and even get a second opinion, if they are not comfortable.

Outstanding issues usually addressed in this session include

- Income taxes including exemptions for children and filing status during separation
- Religious issues like annulments for Catholics and Gets for Jewish clients
- Whether the wife plans to change her name following the divorce
- Social security issues for equalizing benefits for long-term marriages
- How the parties plan to pay the legal costs and fees for the divorce

Once the mediator has gathered the remaining information, he/she will be in a position to write a draft version of the MOU. The next session will be scheduled for at least 2 weeks later.

A.2.5 Mediation Session #5

The focus of the fifth and usually the last session is on reviewing the draft MOU and amending/correcting it.

The draft MOU summarizes everything the parties have agreed to in the mediation process. The MOU is not intended as a legal document and will remain unsigned by the parties. It serves the purpose of putting in writing the goals, intentions, and attitudes of the couple. The mediator will give each client a draft copy of the MOU and then should go through it in as great detail as is needed to ensure that the document reflects the intentions of the clients. The final MOU will be mailed to clients shortly after the session.

Generally, the text of the MOU does not come as a surprise to the client. But seeing the document itself can be upsetting to some clients, as it reminds them that they are moving along in the process. If any of the issues appear to be creating conflict, the mediator may caucus with the parties to try and bring it to closure. If it appears that the clients could benefit from another mediation session, the mediator will suggest it. However, this is the exception rather than the rule.

If clients have not secured legal counsel, most mediators will supply a list of mediation-friendly attorneys and will encourage their clients to make contact with a few attorneys so that they can inquire about fees, availability, and approach.

Frequently, mediators will suggest that clients also review the MOU with their accountant, tax accountant, and financial planner. This review often helps identify or confirm strategies that may be mutually advantageous. As an example, there may be a tax benefit to waiting until the next year for the divorce to be finalized. In that situation, the parties can instruct their attorneys accordingly.

The last part of this session will be spent answering questions and addressing concerns. Most clients are comfortable with the MOU but apprehensive about moving forward. They should be assured that the hardest part of the process is done—the decision making. Their attorneys will review the MOU and help them implement the agreement. For some clients, there is sadness in moving on. The mediator will assure them that if any conflicts arise during the filing process, during the divorce, or after the divorce, they are free to come back to mediation to address those issues.

8 Asset Protection Fundamentals

How Doctors Protect What Is at Risk

J. Christopher Miller

CONTENTS

This chapter will illustrate how avoiding risk and handling your assets can minimize the chance of losing your assets to creditors. Asset protection receives attention from medical professionals in all spheres who have accumulated wealth. Some have conservatively built their nest eggs with careful savings over decades of work, some are health-care entrepreneurs, and others have seen their fortunes rise and fall with the economy, and even the Patient Protection and Affordable Care Act (PPACA). The real-estate bubble and the Great Recession of the past decade have also taught many doctors and nurses a difficult lesson that highlights the vulnerability we all face in safeguarding the earnings for which we have worked so hard.

8.1 INTRODUCTION

The first step in constructing a solid asset protection plan (APP) is to assemble an experienced attorney and professional advisory team that can be trusted to stay current on the swift changes in this area. Together, you will be able to plan and execute a course of action customized to your needs and objectives.

8.2 BEGINNING THE JOURNEY

Strong asset protection depends substantially on timing. The sooner you act to protect your assets, the greater the odds of your success. Many asset protection strategies construct barriers between assets and creditors, and if those barriers are built when creditors are closing in, courts will not respect them. If, on the other hand, you use the asset protection tools described in this chapter when your financial outlook is healthy, the tools can be an effective barrier between your wealth and the reach of future creditors.

8.3 UNDERSTANDING THE RISKS

Physicians and medical professionals share a unique disadvantage when it comes to asset protection. They are constantly haunted by the prospect of being sued for malpractice. Most have solid malpractice insurance coverage in force, but if that pool runs dry, the courts may look to the professional individually to compensate patients for injuries suffered while under the professional's care. Malpractice insurance itself may not be sufficient to completely protect a physician against professional liability claims. As verdicts increase in size, policy limits may become inadequate. Likewise, insurance companies have a strong incentive to deny coverage by arguing that a claim falls outside the scope of coverage. Preparing for these possibilities will leave you much more financially sound than if you had not planned ahead.

Aside from the professional risks you take merely by agreeing to examine and treat a patient, dangers to your assets surround you. As discomforting as it may sound, your practice partners, your family, and even your neighbors are in fact potential adversaries. Unfortunately, your position as a medical professional in today's society subjects you to elevated risks of a nasty lawsuit if you are negligent in your personal conduct.

An accident while driving to the hospital in response to a call, or a simple slip-and-fall incident on your home's sidewalk, will more likely find its way into a courtroom because plaintiffs (and their lawyers) perceive you as a deep pocket.

On a more personal level, there may come a time when your marriage fails, and you are faced with equitably dividing property between you and your spouse. Asset protection strategies act differently in the context of a divorce, and family-oriented claims need to be treated differently in the scope of creating a plan. In the event that a claim arises from outside your professional activities, or if you find yourself swallowed by consumer debts, several asset protection methods will help you to prevent your assets from slipping away.

Overheard in the Doctor's Lounge

On Asset Protection for Physicians

The first step in the asset protection process for all physicians is to acknowledge the reality of risk and then devise ways to mitigate it. Unfortunately, denial is a common tactic that substitutes deliberate ignorance for thoughtful risk management planning.

Dr. Charles F. Fenton III, JD, PA
Atlanta, Georgia

8.4 TOOLS OF ASSET PROTECTION

8.4.1 Good Medical Record Keeping

The best defense against any claim is a complete and accurate record of the facts. In particular, medical malpractice claims will frequently be stalled or thwarted by a consistent written or electronic (e-healthy records [eHRs]) description of the symptoms you observe and the treatments you prescribe. Extensive record keeping will not only help formulate a defense against a claim, but it will also (and perhaps more importantly) create the appearance that you are careful and highly competent in all of your affairs. Members of a jury may not be able to discern whether the medical judgments you made in a particular case were good or bad, as they do not have the years of education and training that you do. Jurors can, however, sense whether your practice is organized and professional. If your records are thorough and consistent, jurors will assume that you dedicate as much attention to the substantive aspects of your work as you do to the tedium of record keeping. If you are active in the management of your office, you should keep track of its operations and establish logs for your employees to complete as they perform their daily tasks. Not all information, however, ought to be written down. Keep your written records to the facts you have observed and leave your speculations for department meetings.

8.4.2 Insurance Protection

The next line of defense against creditors having an adverse effect on your net worth is insurance. Insurance is the easiest way to avoid risk because you are paying someone else to pool your risk with the risks of hundreds or thousands of others. Insurance carriers derive their profit from estimating and managing that risk and then paying only a few claims from among their many policyholders. As frustrating as they can sometimes be, they do provide a valuable service to society.

The best piece of advice anyone can share with someone about to purchase an insurance policy is to compare insurance policies before signing up. Just as you should comparison shop for a new car, you should ask your agent to present you with the offerings of multiple carriers and take the time to discuss with him/her the gaps and exclusions that might be addressed with riders or additional policies. Rates for comparable policies vary widely, and policies may differ significantly in the size and scope of coverage they offer. Research the attributes of a policy, such as its deductible and the extent of its exclusions. Find out whether the insurance carrier is financially secure and whether its investments are liquid. Deciding which combination is right for you requires careful consideration and a trusted advisor, insurance agent, or councilor.

8.4.2.1 Professional Liability (Malpractice) Insurance

With respect to the scope of malpractice coverage, many liability insurance policies will deny coverage if an intentional tort is alleged. A *tort* is an injury inflicted by one person on another, and an *intentional tort* is when the person intends to do an act that the law decides is wrong, even if the person does not intend to injure the victim. One example of an intentional tort is intentional infliction of emotional distress, which doctors may need to defend against if they misdiagnose a patient while having a financial interest in the treatment of the diagnosis. Battery is another intentional tort with which doctors are often charged. *Battery* can be defined as any injurious contact without consent.

The necessity of obtaining informed consent from each patient is becoming increasingly important as a defense against such claims. Intentional torts are different from torts of negligence, which are usually covered under most liability insurance policies. Negligence claims arise out of mistakes usually attributable to carelessness. Make sure your insurance policy extends to intentional torts to prevent these kinds of cases from being denied coverage by your insurance company.

8.4.2.2 Life and Disability Insurance

The most valuable asset of most physicians is not their homes or their stock portfolios; rather, it is their future income potential. You can protect against its loss by ensuring that its full value is replaced if you are unable to continue working into the future. Life and disability insurance are the tools used to protect this value. An easily overlooked factor to consider when buying life insurance is the amount of debt you have outstanding. Be sure that the proceeds will satisfy any obligations you have assumed, such as the mortgage on your home or continued payments on automobiles or boats, as well as provide enough money to satisfy known future expenses like a child's college education or wedding and to support your spouse and children until they can find other sources of income. In some cases, you may need to plan for a spouse's retirement. If you are an insurable candidate, think twice before turning down additional coverage, because sometime later, you might lose that status and be unable to add to your insurance posture.

8.4.2.3 General Liability Insurance

When consulting with an insurance agent, inquire about umbrella general liability policies. These policies protect you from a plaintiff adopting a shotgun approach to litigation, because the general liability insurer bears a burden to defend covered claims as well as to indemnify against losses. That is, the insurance carrier pays the legal fees and expenses that build up while the claim is being litigated. Because of this duty, consider the stress and money you would save in finding good representation in addition to the possible damage awards when considering the purchase of an umbrella policy.

8.4.2.4 Natural Disaster Insurance

Finally, protect against the loss of accumulated assets by insuring them against the wrath of Mother Nature. Most homeowner's policies do not cover damages arising from floods or earthquakes. If a home, or any other real property like a vacation home or beach condo, is in an area subject to floods or earthquakes, consider the value of purchasing insurance that covers such catastrophes. Take the time to review your homeowner's policy, making sure that it will repair or replace your roof if damaged by hail and will apply in the event of high winds, rather than only in tornadoes. The key to the maintenance of any type of insurance is to anticipate all of the possible calamities and then to decide whether you can afford to lose the assets exposed to those calamities.

8.4.3 Layered Organizations

8.4.3.1 Practice Format

The format and corporate structure of your medical practice is another way to limit personal liability and protect your assets. The most successful means of reducing the risk from your professional conduct is the creation of a layered organization. Your practice should operate through an entity (or set of entities) that limits the liability of its owners. A series of subsidiary organizations operating under a parent entity may limit your personal liability after a colleague suffers liability in a claim or if the practice is found liable for a breach of contract.

Traditionally, layering of a physician's business structure involved the use of a professional corporation governing an office whose stockholders were either the physicians themselves or other professional corporations embodying each practicing physician. Nowadays, new and different forms of business entities do not require the time-consuming formalities associated with a corporation, but they still benefit from statutory limits on the liability of their owners. Such entities include limited liability companies (LLCs) and limited liability partnerships (LLPs). Layering these types of organizations on top of one another can provide the same protection from claims by creditors without incurring the double income taxation of more traditional corporations. Many entity types are designed to make asset protection easier, although sorting through the alphabet soup created by these new entity types and deciding which one to use can be difficult.

8.4.3.2 Comparing Business Entity Types

8.4.3.2.1 Corporations

Generally speaking, a corporation consists of one or more shareholders that appoint one or more directors, who in turn manage the corporation and its actions. Shareholders suffer a loss for the liabilities of the corporation only to the extent they have value in their shares. More specifically, the shareholders' personal risks are limited by the interest they have in the corporation, which equals the investment they made when buying or subscribing for the shares, plus any corporate earnings that have not yet been distributed as dividends. Except for special circumstances discussed later in this section, personal assets of each shareholder are not at risk when a corporation suffers losses or is presented with a liability. For this reason, many professional corporations make annual or more frequent distributions to their owners of most of the earnings gained by the corporation, leaving only enough assets in the corporation to cover its outstanding known debts and enough capital to weather cash flow fluctuations.

8.4.3.2.2 Limited Liability Companies

A limited liability company (commonly known as an LLC) is very similar to a corporation in its role as a barrier between the personal assets of its owners and its liabilities. An LLC can also be owned entirely by one person, by a parent entity, or by more than one person, which makes it a convenient format for a medical practice. LLCs also offer increased flexibility for tax planning and management purposes. Certain single-member LLCs can be entities that are disregarded for tax purposes but, in many states, still provide a layer of insulation between the owner's assets and the LLC's operational debts. Florida is a notable exception to this rule because it allows creditors to treat assets of a wholly owned LLC as if there is no liability shield.

You can think of an LLC as a hybrid or crossover entity using the best parts of both corporation law and partnership law to build a separate type of business. Instead of shareholders, an LLC is owned by members who can all have the same rights and responsibilities, or if you choose, the members can be split into managers and nonmanagers. The managing members of an LLC have the right to make decisions on behalf of the business and have a say in its operations, but they have no additional liability like they would in a general partnership or in a limited partnership (LP).

8.4.3.2.3 Limited Liability Partnerships

An LLP is much like an LLC, except that as a form of partnership, there must be more than one partner. You would likely use an LLP instead of an LLC in a situation where you want cohesiveness among several people or bodies but want to minimize subjecting each partner to the risks carried by other partners. An LLP has several advantages over a general partnership because, as its name suggests, the liability of each of the partners is limited to the value of the partners' interests in the partnership. That is, a partner in an LLP would not risk personal assets to the same degree as a partner in a general partnership. In a general partnership, any liabilities that the partnership incurs flow back to the partners, and each partner is jointly and severally liable for those general partnership debts.

The difference between an LLP and an LP is rather subtle. Both types of entities are improvements over a general partnership from an asset protection standpoint in that not every partner puts the partner's assets on the line when partnership liabilities arise. The difference between the two is that in an LP, there must be at least one general partner who risks paying for liabilities of the LP beyond the general partner's interest in the partnership. In other words, the general partner exposes personal assets to creditors of the partnership. In an LLP, every partner can absorb the benefit of limited liability, but every partner must be given management authority.

8.4.3.2.4 Limited Liability Limited Partnerships

The last type of entity is a limited liability limited partnership (LLLP), sometimes called a "triple LP." These entities are harder to form and less common. Their rarity makes them hard to deal with as banks may refuse to lend to them, and both judges and jurors may view the entity as a type used only by someone trying too hard to avoid liability rather than

BUSINESS ENTITY TYPES AND THEIR IDENTIFIERS

- General partnership
- Limited partnership (LP)
- Corporation (Inc. or Corp.)
- Limited liability company (LLC)
- Limited liability partnership (LLP)
- Professional corporation (PC)
- Professional limited liability company (PLLC)
- Limited liability limited partnership (LLLP)

conducting an operating business. The mere sound of the name makes it suspect in the eyes of too many people, and for that reason, the author discourages their use when it is also possible to build a two-layer organization with an LP and an LLC. The LLC can serve as the general partner of the LP, and this accomplishes the same level of protection and additional flexibility without sounding quite so defensive as an LLLP.

8.4.3.3 An Ideal Approach

A modern structure of a practice might be an LLP in which several LLCs are general partners. The LLP would be the umbrella organization in which all of the pratice's operations take place. Each of the general partner LLCs might be wholly owned and managed by an individual practicing medical professional, and each general partner LLC would have a voice in the management of the LLP. Each of the LLCs and the physicians owning them would also be insulated from liability arising from the acts or omissions of the other physicians in the practice, whether such harms were intentional or not.

In this hypothetical organization, the LLP would be the practice's umbrella and would be at the forefront of litigation proceedings. It would also be the primary operational entity to which patients remit payments and would pay staff members. The LLP would then distribute its profits and the physicians' negotiated compensation to the various LLCs. The LLCs would employ the physicians that were part of the practice and then pass along the earnings received from the LLP to the doctors individually. To be effective in insulating the LLCs, the LLP would need to make distributions of its profits promptly and regularly, so those profits are not exposed to the claims of plaintiffs. Also, the operational entity would not own the building in which the office is housed. Instead, a holding company of some form would be created, and a lease signed between the holding company and the LLP would help prevent the building from exposure to seizure by creditors. The operating LLP cannot be merely a phantom. It must have some working capital of its own to be respected as a litigable party. It must also have its own incidents of business, such as a checking account and letterhead, and the functional differences between the LLP, the facilities holding company, and the LLCs should be respected in practice to ensure the success of the shields created by layering the organization.

The benefit of layering an organization derives from the fact that courts treat corporations, LLPs, and LLCs as individual legal entities. Certain claims against the entity must first exhaust the assets of the entity before attaching the assets of the entity's owners. In summation, it is a good idea to minimize the value of assets held by the businesses conducting the operations of your practice but not allow those quantities to be so small as to make reasonable the argument that the LLP is merely a shell that carries no weight.

As stated above, the owners of LLPs and LLCs, as opposed to partners in a general partnership, will not be liable for more than their investment and their share of the profits unless a claimant can pierce the veil of the entity. Although this rule, like any summary of the law, has several exceptions in cases where there are egregious facts, courts now allow plaintiffs and creditors to pierce the veil only when the alternative would sanction fraud or promote injustice, or when the entity and its owners have commingled their assets, which leads to the conclusion that they have perfectly aligned interests. This lumping of an entity and its owners into the same category is called an "alter-ego" theory. In other words, treating each part of the layered organization as a separately functioning entity gives them separate personalities and makes it more difficult for plaintiffs to reach the assets of the owners. Because the owners of the LLP in the sample model are LLCs, plaintiffs would need to pierce two veils and show two alignments of interest before getting to the assets of the physicians themselves.

Layering an organization, however, does not protect an individual from direct *tort liability* if the individual is negligent or has committed fraud. In cases of potential professional tort liability, such as a malpractice claim, the professional is personally liable for any claims arising from his/her negligent conduct. Layering a business organization will not protect you against medical malpractice claims or other tortuous wrongdoing. The layering of a business organization is instead meant to prevent claims based in contract and vicarious claims against colleagues' negligent or intentional acts (i.e., harassment, violence, or discrimination claims) from reaching the personal assets of a physician. For these sources of liability, treating each layer as serving a different function in the business, and dealing with each entity as a separate business, has proven to be effective at protecting the assets of the owners of the business.

8.4.4 Qualified Retirement Plans

Current tax laws encourage both employers and employees to create and regularly contribute to retirement plans for use at a later stage in life. Qualified retirement plans (QRPs) may be set up by individuals in the form of an individual retirement account (IRA) or in employer-sponsored plans meeting the requirements of Internal Revenue Code (I.R.C.) sections 401(k) and 403(b), from which 401(k) plans get their name.

In general, employer-sponsored QRP assets are protected from the claims of creditors under the provisions of the Employee Retirement Income and Security Act (ERISA). Thus, it makes for good long-term planning to contribute as much as possible to retirement plans created by your employer during your career. Under ERISA, contributions made to a QRP are treated as being withheld from the employee, or not paid to them, so they cannot be subject to any claims against the employee. Although the employee holds the promise of future payments from the plan assets, he/she may not make use of those funds or have any of the other benefits of present ownership of those funds. Because of the restricted nature of the employees' access to plan assets, the creditors of the employees are likewise prevented from seizing those assets while they are in the plan.

The general rule for IRAs is not the same as the rule applied to employer-sponsored plans. Contrary to popular belief and to the surprise of many, IRAs are *not* protected under ERISA and thus may be exposed to creditors' claims unless state law provides creditor protection. The good news is that the laws of many states protect IRAs from creditors' claims in a manner similar to the way ERISA shields employer plans from creditors. For example, in the state of Georgia, IRAs are exempted from the claims of creditors by statute, and in the event of bankruptcy, IRAs are not considered available assets for liquidation.

Claims for alimony and child support, however, are given an exception to this rule, proving once again that no single tool of asset protection should be relied upon exclusively. Additionally, several states consider the value of an employee's retirement plan contributions when deciding how to split the assets of a couple during a divorce. Because of the variety of rules applied by different states, and the speed with which those rules change in this field, you should consult with an expert in the area of deferred compensation before relying heavily on retirement plans for protection of your assets.

Another factor in making the most out of a retirement plan is having a robust succession of designated beneficiaries. If a spouse or child is named as a beneficiary, then that non-probate transfer at an employee's death entitles the beneficiary to the funds built up in the plan without exposure to the creditors of the employee or his/her estate. Without a designated beneficiary, however, IRA assets do flow into and through a decedent's estate, which is a pool of resources used by an Executor or personal representative to pay any debts left behind before distribution to the beneficiaries. Consult with the plan administrator to establish a structured retirement plan providing the most protection for you retirement assets but not negatively impacting the ability to enjoy those assets when they become available.

The theory supporting the protective value of retirement assets is that the nominal owner does not actually own the assets. In most cases, a brokerage or investment company will serve as a custodian of the IRA for the investor, holding the account for the benefit of that investor and agreeing to comply with the complex rules governing the administration of retirement accounts. The benefits are not permanent, however, in that once a person has reached retirement age (currently 59.5), the custodial relationship does not give the custodian sufficient power to withhold assets from the investor if the investor wishes to dissolve or cash out the IRA. This right of immediate access to the funds may give creditors the right to demand the same access, again depending upon relevant state law. It not only allows creditors to seize the assets held in a custodial IRA, but it also imposes adverse tax consequences on the investor because of the early termination of the IRA.

A relatively new development in this area is the enactment of the Roth IRA. A Roth IRA is an IRA in which the participant receives no income tax deduction for a contribution to the Roth IRA. That sounds bad, but the trade-offs can easily make it worthwhile. In addition to its principal and income growing tax-exempt, the distributions to a participant from a Roth IRA are tax-free. In many states, the ability of the Roth IRA to escape the claims of creditors is similar to that of a traditional IRA, especially when a flurry of legislative activity overruled a renegade court ruling that a Roth IRA was accessible to a judgment creditor because Roth IRAs were not specifically mentioned in the statute providing protection from seizure.

8.4.5 Separate versus Joint Ownership of Assets

Do you remember when Andy DuFresne confronts the chief guard of his prison in *The Shawshank Redemption* and tells him to divert an inherited sum of money into his wife's name? Even 65 years after the 1949 setting of that conversation, a common means of protecting assets from the reach of creditors is to transfer property into a spouse's name.

Assuming that the spouse is not also at substantial risk of being the target of lawsuits because of the spouse's profession or lifestyle, it is an effective means of accomplishing that goal. Creditors with valid judgments against an individual may only attach and seize those assets owned by that individual. Anything worth doing is worth doing right, however, and there are several pointers to structuring asset ownership in a way that maximizes its protective value.

A small number of states, such as Hawaii, Pennsylvania, and Florida, have statutes that automatically protect property jointly owned by spouses from creditors of either spouse but often not from creditors of both spouses together. Property that benefits from this characterization is held in as a *tenancy by the entirety* and prevents only one spouse from transferring away property that the married couple obtained together. Again, variation in state law determines just how beneficial the formation of a tenancy by the entirety can be from an asset protection standpoint. This protection comes from a public interest in the preservation of marital assets, such that one spouse's indiscretion may not harm the position of the other spouse. The most significant limits to the advantage provided by the tenancies of the entirety are, first, that the creditors with claims against both spouses may seize such jointly held property and, second, that upon the first death between the spouses, the property flows directly to the surviving spouse alone, who then no longer has the benefit of the creditor protection. Moreover, in April of 2002, the U.S. Supreme Court sharply curtailed the benefit provided by tenancies by the entirety by ruling that it does not shield an asset from the federal authorities, even if the tax liability was incurred only by one spouse.*

Some states in the South and West are community property states; community property is similar to, but not the same as, tenancy by the entirety. Under the community property theory, all property acquired by either spouse during the residency in that state (or in some states, prior to or during the residency) will be considered jointly owned property even if titled to an individual spouse. Merely by moving to one of these community property states, a person can automatically shift assets, thus reducing the quantity of assets subject to the creditors of the wealthier spouse.

Community property and land owned as tenants by the entirety is different from a third type of ownership called joint tenancy with rights of survivorship, sometimes abbreviated as *JTWROS*. Joint tenancy with rights of survivorship may ease some burdens associated with probating a decedent's estate, but this form of ownership is not ideal when viewed through the asset protection prism. An alternative is to hold assets in the name of one spouse or the other, or as *tenants in common*. Tenancy in common is best described as a situation in which each spouse owns a one-half undivided share in the property but does not have the automatic right to full ownership at the death of the other spouse. Three advantages flow from this form of ownership:

- Neither spouse owns the property exclusively.

  A creditor seizing the interest of one spouse would not have a valuable asset because it could not evict the remaining spouse, so creditors will attack these assets only as a last resort to satisfy their claims. However, a lien recorded against either fractional interest would have to be satisfied upon its sale, so that the net proceeds would be reduced by the amount of the lien. For this reason, tenancy in common is only a temporary means of protecting an asset from an adverse judgment and

---

* *See* United States v. Craft, 535 U.S. 274 (April 17, 2002).

not quite the same as fully separate ownership. This flaw is one reason why many estate planners recommend the funding of property into the name of a spouse or family member less vulnerable to adverse judgments.

- If either spouse were to die, only half of the property would be subject to estate tax.

  Ownership of property as tenants in common helps in the estate planning arena by facilitating the process of equalizing the assets held by each spouse. Changes made during 2010 and 2013 to the estate tax laws have pushed the federal estate tax exemption above $5 million, so fewer individuals (less than half of 1% of the general public by some estimates) will realize an actual tax savings from such planning. Even more appealing is that surviving spouses can now claim the unused exemption left behind by a deceased spouse. Estate tax concerns are now playing a much smaller role in recommending how spouses own their property.
- A dying spouse has the ability to control how his/her interest is distributed.

  In many simple wills, all property of a spouse is given by bequest to the surviving spouse. Such a bequest could include partial ownership interests in real estate. If the surviving spouse is concerned about asset protection, this additional property would not be beneficial, because it would easily be sacrificed to the survivor's creditors. One way of avoiding this result is to build an estate plan in which each spouse bequests the partial interest owned by that spouse to a trust. At the first death between two spouses, the trust will hold the partial ownership interest for the benefit of the surviving spouse. The trust holding the partial residence interest preserves the deterrent faced by creditors of the surviving spouse because seizure of the surviving spouse's interest would not terminate the spouse's right to use the land provided for in the trust.

A different set of rules applies to property held jointly by medical professionals who are not married to each other. If property is owned jointly among siblings or business associates instead of a business entity, the owners should make sure that the deed names them as tenants in common. Otherwise, each successive death among the owners will shift the ownership to the survivors and leave the family of the deceased owner with no lasting value from the owner's investment into the property and its improvements.

Assets should be held in a way that protects them from creditors for the long term. The form of asset holdings should thus be a significant part of the discussions held with professional advisors, so that the protection lasts beyond your death or that of your spouse. Structure the protected assets so that they do not flow back to you if your spouse should pass away. In this manner, integrated asset protection, estate planning, and financial planning unite to protect the family's interests by extending the benefits of creditor protection for the long term.

8.4.6 Gifting

One easy asset protection tool you can use to ensure that your children inherit your legacy is to begin giving assets to them early, before your future creditors claim them. Gifting should be used much more frequently than it is, but the obvious disadvantage of gifting property to children is that the donor no longer has the use of or control over the property. More emphatically, you must commit to the permanent loss of the property, so you must be

FORMS OF JOINT OWNERSHIP

- Tenancy by the entirety
- Tenancy in common
- Community property
- Joint tenancy with rights of survivorship (JTWROS)

absolutely sure that you will not ever need the gifted assets. This risk is especially significant when planning for future possibilities of creditor invasion.

Gifting is an effective protection against creditors, and a number of different methods are available to effect this intent, without always subjecting the assets to the whims of descendants not ready to handle money. First, small outright gifts to multiple beneficiaries may be made annually. This has the effect of reducing the quantity of assets subject to creditors' claims, but it also entrusts the donee receiving those gifts with control over those assets. Some recipients of gifts given to them are not appreciative of the work that went into earning the gifted property, so while gifting is an effective asset protection strategy when timed properly, it sometimes has an unwanted impact on the family dynamics.

Gifts made to any individual other than a donor's spouse are subject to gift taxation if they exceed $14,000 in a calendar year. Amounts less than $14,000 are exempted from gift tax under I.R.C. § 2503(b), also known as the annual exclusion. Spouses may combine their exclusions to provide up to $28,000 in benefits to their children or other beneficiaries, but it is important to consult with a tax professional before making sizable gifts.

One alternative to outright gifting is to gift property in trust. This option involves giving your property to a trustee, who holds the property for the benefit of a beneficiary other than the donor. The trustee bears a fiduciary duty to obey the instructions set forth in the document establishing the trust, otherwise known as the trust instrument or trust agreement. The transfer of property into a nongrantor, or third party, trust is still considered a gift for tax and property ownership purposes, but the trust instrument may include spendthrift provisions, which prohibit the trustee from distributing assets to certain beneficiaries except for specific uses and at particular times. The vital point here is that the trust separates creditors of both the donor and the beneficiary from the assets.

8.4.7 Spendthrift Trusts

Despite a handful of exceptions discussed near the end of this chapter, retaining control or the benefit of assets held in a trust you create and fund means that state and tax law treat the gift as illusory and will ignore the creation of the trust, allowing your creditors to reach the property. Control of a trust is determined by several factors, including the power to exchange trust assets and the ability to withdraw money.

If the reality of the situation is that the trust was created merely as a smokescreen, and the assets are still within your reach, courts in most jurisdictions will reach through the formalities and treat the property as held solely in the donor's hands.

If that is the case, then how can a trust be considered an asset protection tool? The protection found in a spendthrift trust lies in your sacrifice of such rights in favor of third

SAMPLE SPENDTHRIFT LANGUAGE

No interest in this Trust shall be subject to the beneficiary's liabilities or creditor claims, assignment, or anticipation. If the Trustee shall determine that a beneficiary would not benefit as greatly from any outright distribution of trust income or principal because of the availability of the distribution to the beneficiary's creditors, the Trustee shall instead expend those amounts for the benefit of the beneficiary. This direction is intended to enable the Trustee to give the beneficiary the maximum possible benefit and enjoyment of all of the trust income and principal to which the beneficiary is entitled.

parties, such as your spouse and children. Suppose that after your death, a trust you create instructs the trustee to hold assets for the benefit of your spouse and or children and to distribute assets to them only at the trustee's discretion to meet the actual needs of your children. If the trust has good language preventing the beneficiaries from ordering the trustee to withdraw those assets from the trust, those assets will, for the most part, be inaccessible to the claims of any creditors of your children. Once a child has the right to request those assets from the trustee, however, that spendthrift protection falls away, and the trust assets become part of the child's assets in a debtor–creditor dispute.

A gift in trust can be made without saddling the beneficiary with the responsibility of managing the money wisely, and the beneficiary may still gain the benefits of the appreciation and income derived from the gift. The gift in trust is most useful when beneficiaries are too young to effectively manage the assets, or perhaps too immature to invest the money wisely. To educate the beneficiaries in money management, trust provisions often allow the income and principal of the trust to be distributed to the beneficiaries in stages. These stages often are delayed until the beneficiaries have reached adulthood and are intended to ease the transition from beneficiary to owner. While you would like your children or grandchildren to turn a gift into something more valuable, trial and error plays a significant role in money management. Giving incremental gifts to the beneficiaries over time creates the opportunity for beneficiaries to learn the lessons of finance with smaller quantities of money, preserving the remainder of the trust property for a later distribution. Long-term asset protection means more than just protection from creditors. It means protecting the beneficiaries from themselves as well.

In addition to the stages of distribution, many trusts give the trustee the power to distribute assets to beneficiaries or on behalf of beneficiaries for specific purposes. In this way, a trust that delays distribution of money until after a child reaches the age of 25 may still pay for the beneficiary's college and postgraduate education. The trustee may also be allowed to pay for such specific events as weddings and home purchases. This power must be discretionary, however, to preserve the asset protection features of the trust, and the beneficiary may refuse the distributed proceeds, though such an occurrence is extremely rare.

If a creditor can point to gifts made just prior to the effective date of the creditor's judgment, the creditor may be able to persuade a court to forcibly return the gifted property to the ownership of the donor and subject it to the claims of the creditors.

Overheard in the Doctor's Lounge

Don't Leave Yourself Unprotected

The best asset protection plan (APP) for a physician or high-net-worth client may be to remove all assets from the doctor's name. The worst plan has all the assets in the doctor's name. You will need to work with a specialized attorney to find the ideal plan for you. In many cases, your largest assets are the funds in your retirement plan or IRA. The good news is that creditors cannot reach ERISA-qualified plan assets. Common ERISA plans include the following:

1. 401(k) or 403(b) plan
2. Profit purchase plan
3. Money purchase plan
4. New comparability plans
5. Defined-benefit plan

Keep in mind that IRAs are not considered ERISA-qualified plans and have no federal protection from creditors. Many individual states have protected IRAs in part or in full. In my state, New York, IRAs are fully protected. If you live in a state where they are not, you should seriously consider moving the money into an ERISA-qualified plan. This can be accomplished even if you are retired.

Most effective APPs involve the use of a corporate structure, limited liability company (LLC), or family limited partnership (FLP). Keep in mind that the entity you choose will have its own unique asset protection and tax consequences.

- Sole proprietorships and partnerships are the worst way to own a business. If a sole proprietor is found negligent in his/her duties for the business that injures a third person, the sole proprietor is personally liable. If a product or employee harms a third person or someone is harmed on the premises, the sole proprietor is personally liable. With a partnership, you have all of the above risks coupled with a partner who can cause you even more liability.
- LLCs, family limited liability companies (FLLCs), and FLPs are the most commonly used tools by asset protection specialists today. A creditor attempting to obtain assets of a debtor when the assets are in an LLC will likely have very limited success. In fact, a charging order is the only remedy a court can give a creditor. A charging order does not allow creditors to sell assets of the LLC or force distributions of income. It also cannot transfer interest in the LLC to the creditor. A creditor who obtains a charging order against an LLC may in fact receive a K-1 for income they never did and never may receive.

Also, it is never a good idea, from an asset protection standpoint, to own property in just your name. If you get sued, the property is almost entirely at risk. Owning the marital home jointly with your spouse can be effective. You will protect the home from each other's individual creditors (though not joint creditors). You should not title many assets as tenants by the entirety for several reasons. Physicians suffer a higher divorce rate than the already high national average of 50%. Should a divorce occur, you will have ensured that the spouse will receive half of that asset. You do nothing to protect the asset against joint creditors.

I advise my physician clients to consider holding rental real estate, after tax investment accounts, planes, boats, and any personal assets of value, in an LLC. Unless you are single and your home is titled in your name alone, the marital home may not be a good candidate for transfer to an LLC. By doing so, you forgo the capital gains exemption of $250,000 per spouse. Brokerage accounts can be owned by an LLC, and when constructed correctly, you will have full ability to invest as you desire. The investments within the account would then be protected. Assets such as planes and boats may be best held in their own LLCs to protect the rest of your estate from their unique risk profiles. For example,

- Personal residence, $750,000: tenants by the entireties
- Vacation property, $300,000: LLC #1
- Investment account, $900,000: LLC #1
- 401(k), $2,400,000: ERISA plans are federally protected
- Boat, $55,000: LLC #2

Remember, advanced thought and action is the best way to succeed with any APP. So, be proactive—to be protected.

Nicholas Efthemis, CFP
Snyder, New York

8.5 SOPHISTICATED ASSET PROTECTION TOOLS

The following methods of asset protection are significantly more sophisticated than those described above and will often require a substantial investment of time and money. They are also much more effective at sheltering large quantities of assets from creditors. A working knowledge of their availability will help you know to what degree you might wish to carry out your asset protection efforts.

Complex or more sophisticated asset protection tools are aimed at deterrence rather than bulletproof shelter. They make the seizure of assets more difficult than it would otherwise be and make those assets less attractive to creditors. Although asset protection specialists now practice each method with regular frequency, there are exceptions to almost every rule. Your likelihood of success depends in large part on the factual circumstances surrounding the inception of your APP. The primary object should be to steer clear of transfers that could be characterized as fraudulent conveyances. You should discuss the following ideas at length with your advisory team before making any moves with respect to these tools.

8.5.1 Avoiding Fraudulent Conveyances

As a general rule, courts respect the efforts of people to preserve and foster the growth of their assets. Courts balk, however, if such efforts seem fraudulent or are made when there is potential liability to creditors or plaintiffs. The courts then label such efforts unethical, void, or even criminal. If you skipped to this part of the chapter because you see trouble on the horizon or are already involved in litigation, it is too late to act. A rescue attempt using the suggestions in this chapter will not patch existing problems. Despite your best intentions, you could be committing fraud.

Fraudulent conveyances are transfers made by a debtor with the intent to hinder, delay, or defraud creditors. In the absence of concrete evidence of intent, such as a "smoking gun" memorandum, or the availability of testimony, courts look to a number of factors in deciding whether a debtor has the requisite intent. Among these factors are familial relationships between the debtor and the person receiving the conveyance, the timing of the transfer in relation to a creditor's threats of collection or litigation, and a whether the debtor received fair value in exchange for the transfer.

There is no bright-line rule to help determine whether a conveyance will be deemed fraudulent, because courts use such factors and arbitrarily weight them to decide the existence of intent. This makes predicting the outcome of any particular fraudulent conveyance case almost impossible. There does, however, seem to be a spectrum along which some landmarks may be plotted. For instance, a physician with a thriving practice, a happy marriage, and a healthy financial balance sheet will not likely be charged with fraudulent conveyance, even if he/she does not receive full value in exchange for a transfer. On the other hand, a defendant in the midst of litigation making a transfer that leaves him/her without sufficient assets to pay a reasonable estimate of the damages will probably be accused of making a fraudulent conveyance.

One of the key factors in determining the fraudulent nature of a conveyance is whether the transfer leaves the transferor either unable to pay his/her debts or with fewer assets than potential liabilities. In other words, if a transfer makes a person insolvent, or if the person is already insolvent, the transfer will likely be ruled a fraudulent conveyance. Thus, a doctor with an $8 million net worth who has recently become liable for a claim worth $3 million ought not to convey any amount close to $5 million at the risk of being punished for conveying the property fraudulently.

The punishment for a debtor found to have made a fraudulent conveyance is harsh. Creditors' remedies vary from state to state, but creditors are often given the option of voiding the transfer and taking back any property that was given. The debtor, however, may not undo the transfer in the same way. Additionally, the debtor will likely be forced to pay all of the creditor's expenses incurred in revoking the fraudulent conveyance. This rule of law leaves more power in the hands of creditors and makes it wiser to avoid making fraudulent conveyances at all costs rather than risk the potential for punishment.

8.5.2 Relocation

Relocation to another state that has passed debtor-friendly laws is a drastic step but nevertheless a popular one. Some of the friendlier states include Florida, Arizona, and Nevada. These states have enacted laws that create special rights of ownership for debtors when creditors attempt to collect on judgments. Several states make joint ownership of property between spouses into an effective asset protection device.

Another debtor-friendly rule of law pertains to a debtor's ownership of the cash value of life insurance. Some life insurance policies accrue a cash surrender value, against which the policyholder may withdraw an advance on the death benefit payable, or for which the policyholder may exchange the policy. The cash surrender value turns the insurance policy into a liquid asset, which creditors could seize and then exchange for money. Florida and some other states offer their residents protection against creditors for the cash value of life insurance policies by declaring the surrender value exempt from garnishment upon an adverse judgment. This convenient legal feature makes the purchase of selected life insurance policies an even more attractive asset protection tool because creditors will choose not to seize the policy in an effort to recover the debt.

8.5.3 Homestead Exemption

Florida also offers a generous homestead exemption. A homestead exemption is an asset protection shelter created by statute that prevents one parcel of real estate and its improvements from being attached and levied upon by creditors. By investing money in luxurious homes on large tracts of land in rural areas of Florida, many wealthy individuals are prudently protecting their estates from the reach of creditors.

Example: Dr. Josh Clemm, a Florida resident and domiciliary, invests $4 million of his earned cash into a home with acreage in Florida. The home fully qualifies for the homestead exemption. If Dr. Clemm later declares bankruptcy, his home will be exempt from the liquidation of his assets. After the liquidation, all of his debts will be discharged by the bankruptcy court. Although Dr. Clemm may have lost his nonexempt assets, he will still own a $4 million asset free and clear of outstanding creditors, with which he may rebuild his accustomed lifestyle.

Another effective use of the homestead exemption is to backstop an incorrect form of jointly owned property. Although tenancies by the entirety and joint tenancies with rights of survivorship automatically leave the surviving spouse with the full ownership of property, the surviving spouse often may use the homestead exemption to preserve a primary residence against creditors' claims.

8.5.4 Irrevocable Life Insurance Trusts

An irrevocable life insurance trust (ILIT) is a specialized trust instrument designed primarily to reduce estate taxes or to enable a client with significant nonliquid assets an opportunity to generate liquidity to pay estate taxes or other obligations without increasing the total estate tax liability. The client creating an ILIT transfers to the ILIT a preexisting life insurance policy on his/her life, or enough money to pay the premiums on a new life insurance policy. If the client survives 3 years beyond the contribution of an existing policy to the trust, or if the policy is a purchased by a trust, the proceeds of the insurance policy payable on the client's death will not constitute part of his/her taxable estate. An ILIT is also helpful in protecting the cash value of policies from creditors in states where the cash value of life insurance is not protected from creditors' claims.

The primary drawback of the ILIT is that you cannot change the terms of the trust after it is signed, such as the lineup of the trustees or the list of beneficiaries. The second drawback is that money spent on the premiums is not returnable to the creator of the trust, and the proceeds of the insurance policy owned by the trust must flow into the trust at the death of the person on whose life the policy was purchased. Even though the ILIT is not revocable, it may nevertheless be drafted with great flexibility.

For example, terms such as "grantor's spouse" may be defined broadly as "the person to whom Grantor is married at the time of Grantor's death." As with any irrevocable document, care must go into its structure and textual references so that the document will have relevance and utility long after its creation.

ILITs also provide creditor protection to beneficiaries because the trust assets are not necessarily immediately available to them. If the ILIT is properly drafted, creditors will not be able to capitalize on an influx of money to the beneficiaries, as they would if the insurance proceeds were paid directly to the beneficiaries. Rather, as with spendthrift trusts created by a third party, the ILIT will serve as a barrier between creditors and beneficiaries, ensuring that the proceeds are spent for the benefit of the beneficiaries, rather than being ceded to their creditors. In favorable comparison to retirement assets, the ILIT can even protect a beneficiary from prioritized claimants, such as a beneficiary's former spouse.

Moreover, an irrevocable trust may prove to be a much more palatable alternative than a prenuptial agreement from the beneficiary's standpoint, particularly in a first-marriage situation. In this regard, ILITs and other irrevocable trusts provide creditor protection in a number of ways to both the creator and the beneficiaries.

8.5.5 Family Limited Partnerships

FLPs are business entities specializing in the management and prudent investment of family assets. They are used for the same reasons that professional business offices use layered organizations. As with other complex asset protection tools, FLPs do not necessarily make it impossible for a creditor to access an asset, but they instead place obstacles between some claims of creditors and the valuable assets of the family. An FLP will often keep potential claims against individuals from endangering the assets held by the partnership by deterring creditors from pursuing the assets. An FLP is a business and must be treated as a separate functioning entity, or the partnership will not be respected by the courts, and the protections it offers will be unavailable. The creation and proper funding of an FLP are highly technical maneuvers with serious income tax and estate tax implications, and the timing of your transfers of property is critical to the success of this planning technique.

FLLCs

A modern alternative to the FLP, allowed in a growing number of jurisdictions, is a family limited liability company (FLLC). With respect to the FLLC's asset protection capabilities, the structure of an LLC is similar enough to that of a partnership to indicate that creditors will not wish to seize interests in the LLC.

FLPs are different from general partnerships in that some, but not all, of the partners are insulated from liability for losses of the partnership. In a general partnership, all of the partners share liability for losses of the partnership. In an LP, at least one partner is appointed as general partner, and that general partner is fully liable for losses of the partnership. In exchange for this disadvantageous position, the general partner has the power to manage the assets of the partnership.

Limited partners are passive owners and have very limited powers under the laws of most states. Additionally, LPs are almost always governed by an agreement among the partners containing provisions that further limit the rights of the limited partners. One caveat must be raised, however, about the characterization of general partners as opposed to limited partners. If limited partners are proven to be making decisions about the operations of the partnership, limited partners may be treated as general partners and may be forced to share the liability for losses with the general partner.

In a typical LP agreement, a limited partner may have the power to assign, or transfer, all or part of the economic value of his/her partnership interest to another person with the prior consent of the general partner. The person receiving that assigned interest, called an *assignee*, often receives the right to receive the distributions that would otherwise have been delivered to the transferor, but the assignee does not become a limited partner. As a result, the assignee is unable to exert much power within the partnership or redeem his/her interest in exchange for partnership assets. Even worse for the assignee, the tax attributes of an FLP often require that the assignee pay income tax on a share of the LP's income. Unless distributions are issued to the assignee by the general partner, the assignee will actual experience a negative cash flow upon gaining possession of the LP interest.

Forming an FLP requires a significant amount of advanced planning and legal advice. FLPs are not appropriate for all situations, and the Internal Revenue Service (IRS) has, in recent years, devoted increased attention to the practice. If successful, however, an FLP can be used to discount the value of assets, and thus reduce estate tax liabilities, as well as provide a formidable barrier to the reach of creditors.

Example: Dr. Mom and Dr. Pop each contribute assets to form an FLP, and in exchange, each receives an LP interest. Mom and Pop also form an LLC to serve as a third partner, which will act as the general partner and thus the lightning rod for any partnership liability. Mom and Pop then assign portions of their LP interests to their three lovely children, Faith, Hope, and Charity, who each become limited partners in the FLP.

Creditors of the limited partners are not able to force their way into the partnership in the capacity of a limited partner. Instead, courts will allow creditors to step into the shoes of a limited partner, or assignee, by means of a charging order. A charging order gives the creditor an assignment interest similar to that of any other assignee. However, it is only an economic interest in the distributions of the partnership. The creditor (or, for that matter, any other assignee) does not have any right to immediate payment, because distributions are determined by the general partner according to the terms of the partnership agreement, or by statute.

FLPs are particularly effective in some states, such as Georgia, because a creditor levying on the partnership interest does not have the power to force dissolution of the partnership. In some other states, a limited partner (as opposed to an assignee) may have the ability to force the partnership to exchange its interest in the partnership for a *pro rata* share of the partnership assets by requesting redemption. Thus, choosing the appropriate jurisdiction in which to form the FLP is very important.

Another disadvantage faced by the creditor seeking to take over a partnership interest from a limited partner (or an assignee) is that the general partner has the ability to make or withhold distributions of cash to the creditor. Since partners are taxed on income realized by the partnership, regardless of whether that income is actually distributed to partners, the general partner's control over distributions places the creditor in peril of realizing income without receiving any cash with which to pay the tax generated by his/her share of the FLP's income.

Finally, the partnership agreement may provide that the existing partners have a right to purchase the assigned partnership interest from the creditor (or assignee) at the fair market value of the partnership interest. Since the fair market value of an assigned partnership interest is usually less than the value of that partner's percentage share of the partnership's assets, the creditor may be forced to settle for less than the value it had expected to realize from the assigned partnership interest. These significant drawbacks to the remedy of a charging order usually deter creditors from attempts to become an assignee of a partnership interest. Instead, creditors will often negotiate a reduced payment schedule or turn to other nonexempt assets of the debtor.

FLPs are also very useful in segregating separate property from marital property in the context of a divorce. If a spouse enters the marriage with a partnership interest, that partnership interest will usually not be blended into the marital estate for purposes of dividing property in a divorce. This attribute enables newlyweds to shelter family assets without the awkwardness of negotiating a prenuptial agreement.

When properly constructed and implemented, FLPs have the potential to significantly reduce the taxable estate of the partners contributing assets. It is vital that only an experienced practitioner well versed in the statutes and case law surrounding FLPs implement the FLP.

8.5.6 Asset Protection Trusts

The transfer of assets to a specifically designed asset protection trust is a technique designed to deter creditors from seeking assets, by putting those assets in a trust governed by laws that both protect the trust from certain claims of creditors and still permit the creator of the trust to receive discretionary distributions of principal and income from the trust. Laws that permit this type of trust exist in selected foreign countries and a growing number of states, starting with Alaska and Delaware. Before then, all states followed the common-law rule against creditor protection through self-settled trusts. In other words, until very recently, trusts in which the trust creator was a controller of the assets or a beneficiary of its resources could be accessed by creditors of the trust creator. These states passed such laws with the intent to attract investment capital and, as a result, imposed certain restrictions on the trustee and the investments made with the trust assets.

The difference between the asset protection trusts discussed in this section and the spendthrift trusts introduced above is that specialized asset protection trusts may provide creditor protection benefits to the person who contributed the assets to the trust without forbidding the trustee from distributing trust assets back to the creator of the trust. Generally speaking, asset protection trusts have at least four common elements:

- The trustee is independent, meaning someone other than a relative, partner, or employee.
- A high level of discretion is given to the trustee so that distributions are made only when the trustee decides it is appropriate.

- A spendthrift provision preventing the beneficiary of the trust from assigning or conveying the beneficiary's interest in the trust for his/her own benefit.
- An irrevocability clause that keeps the trust creator from making changes to the trust or unwinding it under pressure from a court or creditors.

An asset protection trust generally provides that a trustee has exclusive control over the trust management, and also that the trustee be permitted to distribute or withhold the trust income and principal, at the trustee's sole discretion, provided that the trustee follows the instructions contained in the trust instrument. Often, the trustee is advised, but not directed, through the language in the trust not to distribute assets when the grantor or beneficiary is insolvent or involved in collection proceedings. This type of provision, called an *antiduress clause*, shelters the trust proceeds from exposure to the creditors during the time when creditor protection is needed most.

The most important requirement of the asset protection trust is that it be established in a jurisdiction with laws that provide that judgments against the trust's grantor will not be enforced against the trust assets. In 1997, Delaware and Alaska each established laws providing some protection for certain trusts established in those states, and states like Nevada, Missouri, Ohio, South Dakota, Tennessee, Rhode Island, Virginia, and Wyoming have jumped on the bandwagon since then.

In addition to the states that now permit self-settled trusts to offer some sort of creditor protection, offshore jurisdictions such as the Cook Islands, the Cayman Islands, and the Bahamas offer exotic asset protection alternatives. Such offshore alternatives have advantages and disadvantages when compared with domestic trusts and are addressed separately.

8.5.6.1 Domestic Asset Protection Trusts

Domestic asset protection trusts (DAPTs) are created by transferring property to a trustee under a trust instrument that includes very narrow instructions for returning property to the trust creator and will be interpreted under the laws of a state that allows such trusts. The states enacting DAPT laws have shrewdly drafted those statutes to maximize the in-state benefit realizable from the trusts. In Alaska, for example, the trust merits protection only if it is closely connected to Alaska, in that both a trustee and some trust assets are located there, as well as several other requirements contained in the statute. If all of these requirements are met, the Alaska courts will assert jurisdiction over lawsuits attempting to seize the property, and the courts will apply Alaska law.

Alaska law validates and will enforce trusts that give a trustee the power to distribute assets, at the trustee's exclusive discretion, to a person who transferred property into the trust. The Alaska statute furthermore refuses to permit judgments of any creditor to impact property that was placed in a qualifying trust, unless one of several exceptions applies. Among the exceptions are fraudulent conveyances and trusts requiring the trustee to distribute assets to the grantor. Additionally, the law forbids most suits alleging that a transfer into the trust was fraudulent unless those suits are brought within 4 years of the transfer into the trust. This means that a qualifying trust properly funded at least 4 years before the grantor faces potential liability stands a good chance of being protected under the Alaska statute because a creditor may not raise the argument that the transfer into the trust was a fraudulent conveyance.

Delaware's statute regarding asset protection trusts is very similar to the law in Alaska. Delaware also requires that a trust be closely connected with the state of Delaware before extending its influence to the assets held by that trust, but once qualified, the trust may provide both optional distributions to the grantor creating the trust and trustee discretion in making those distributions. The 4-year rule against lawsuits alleging fraudulent conveyance is carried over as well, but the statutes are not identical in their requirements. Delaware, for example, provides a more extensive list of rights that trust creators may retain without allowing creditor access. All jurisdictions permitting a DAPT, however, allow the trust creator to be a potential distributee of income and principal of the trust at the discretion of the trustee. The two pioneer states in this field, Delaware and Alaska, also differ in the way they treat claims among family members, such as judgments for child support and alimony. Lastly, each transfer into an Alaska DAPT must be accompanied by an affidavit of the transferor establishing his/her solvency after the transfer. On the contrary, Delaware does not require such an affidavit before honoring the trust. The choice among selecting Delaware law, Alaska law, or another more recently enacting jurisdiction for the establishment of DAPT is one that must be made with great care.

Nevada and South Dakota are currently viewed as the states with the most debtor-friendly DAPT laws. This is because the statute of limitations barring claims against the transfer of property into the trust is only 2 years, or one-half of the 4-year window set forth in Alaska and Delaware. Furthermore, the Nevada statute provides no exception for divorcing spouses to attach DAPT property or for claims of unpaid alimony and child support to breach the trust protection. Nevada and South Dakota are also jurisdictions following Delaware's lead in not requiring a transferor's affidavit of solvency when transfers are made to the trust.

If an attorney successfully drafts a trust that may be interpreted only under the laws of a jurisdiction with an asset protection trust statute in effect, several advantages fall to the grantor. For example, the laws regarding trusts in several DAPT-friendly states allow trusts to last indefinitely, whereas in most other jurisdictions, a trust's lifetime is limited. In addition, few of those states apply an income tax to income realized by trusts. Thus, it may be possible to escape state income tax on trust income by creating a trust to which only the law of the trust *situs* applies.

Despite these elements, the creator of a DAPT runs the risk that a court will object to the constitutionality of the statutes that make them possible, leaving the grantor with a trust vulnerable to the claims of its creditors. Several academic arguments have been raised that the statutes allowing self-settled asset protection trusts violate the Full Faith and Credit Clause of the U.S. Constitution, which requires states to enforce judgments of sister states. To date, the Supreme Court has yet to rule on these issues, so that the validity of these statutes is neither certain nor implausible.

Another source of concern is that the Supremacy Clause enables federal bankruptcy courts to overrule the statutory language of the states and reach into asset protection trusts to satisfy creditors in a bankruptcy proceeding. The bankruptcy laws were substantially rewritten in 2005 so that fraudulent transfers may be unwound by a bankruptcy trustee up to 10 years after the transfer.*

One recent example of when a DAPT was ruled ineffective using the new rules is in the case of *In re: Huber*.† In that case, a set of unpleasant facts was used by the bankruptcy trustee to persuade a bankruptcy judge that Alaska law did not apply to a trust that

* 11 U.S.C. 548(e) (2005).

† Waldron v. Huber (In re: Huber), Bankr. W.D. Wa. Adv. No. 12-04171, May 17, 2013 (opinion available at http://goo.gl/1TPMn).

purportedly claimed to take advantage of the Alaska creditor protection statutes. Relying on the state of Washington's public policy against self-settled spendthrift trusts, the opinion treated all of the assets of the trust as part of the bankruptcy estate available for the trustee to distribute to creditors. In *Huber*, the bankruptcy trustee was able to show that the transfers into the DAPT occurred at the same time that creditors were closing in, and used correspondence of the trust creator and his attorneys to demonstrate that the trusts were set up with the intent of hindering the access of creditors to the trust assets. This *fraudulent conveyance* treatment underscores why the timing of asset protection planning is so critical to its success.

An earlier example of an Alaska DAPT failing to accomplish the goal of shielding trust property from inclusion in the bankruptcy estate is found in *In re: Mortensen*.* In that estate, the trust creator tried drafting the trust on his own and funded the trust with property after he had burned through most of his liquid assets in dealing with a divorce and several years of low income. Even though Mr. Mortensen claimed that he was solvent at the time of the trust creation and transfer, the bankruptcy court found evidence to the contrary and ruled that the transfer was fraudulent and fell within the 10-year window of his bankruptcy filing. The court then allowed the trustee to liquidate the trust property for the benefit of the estate's creditors.

Despite these warning tales, it is generally believed among lawyers practicing in the area that when DAPTs are set up well ahead of creditor threats and when a person is solvent, they present the opportunity for individuals to transfer property to a trustee subject to the laws of the United States. This provides a level of comfort for people that would not be available to creators of offshore trusts. DAPTs, furthermore, are generally less expensive to create and maintain than foreign asset protection trusts. A medical professional interested in creating one of these trusts should adopt a cautious approach and be ready to initiate a backup plan in the event that the trusts are invalidated or disrespected.

8.5.6.2 Foreign Asset Protection Trusts

Offshore trusts are trusts established under the laws of a foreign jurisdiction, with foreign trustees, and using assets transferred outside the United States. The laws of the United States thus do not apply to the administration of those trusts, and the assets within offshore trusts are not subject to the jurisdiction of any United States court. Although the foreign venue may make it more difficult to pursue claims against trustees who mismanage money, the difficulty in pursuing claims is also faced by creditors, who must fight a legal battle in a foreign land to reach the assets of the trust. That can be very expensive, not just because the creditor will need to hire lawyers who can practice there but also because the procedural laws of these jurisdictions make it very difficult to sue. Some jurisdictions require that a sizable bond be posted before a suit may be filed. Once in court, the rules of law in the foreign nation also apply to the trust, and several popular nations follow a rule of law allowing much more protection from creditors than would be available in the United States. Trusts created that provide the grantor with benefits at the discretion of the trustee are often insulated from creditors' attempts to seize them. Many jurisdictions do not enforce the fraudulent conveyance doctrine. A few nations even bestow upon the grantor some control over the size and timing of distributions by enforcing antiduress provisions. These provisions in

---

* Battley v. Mortensen (In re: Mortensen), Bankr. D. Alaska, Adv. No. 09-90036, May 26, 2011 (opinion available at http://goo.gl/7gWjA).

an offshore trust advise the trustee to follow the directions of the grantor when the grantor is giving directions using his/her independent free will. If a court or a creditor is forcing the grantor to ask the trustee for money, however, the trustee has the power to refuse to comply with the request.

Tactics such as the use of antiduress provisions inspire disfavor by the U.S. courts no longer having jurisdiction over the assets. In a ruling by the Ninth Circuit Court of Appeals in California, Denyse and Michael Anderson were held in contempt of court and sentenced to time in jail because they did not prove that their assets held in an offshore trust were impossible to reach.* That court stopped short of declaring the trust invalid, but its hostility to the trust's creation may be reflective of how other courts might view offshore trusts. Although the Andersons served a sentence for angering the court, the United States courts' inability to assert jurisdiction made it impossible for the creditor to access the assets. Ultimately, the asset protection device succeeded. Now that the contempt sentence has been served, and the Andersons are back to their usual shenanigans, it is arguable that the benefits were worth the price paid. On the other hand, however, any assets that may later be repatriated to the United States be will be subject to creditors' claims immediately upon arrival. The outcome in *Anderson* is therefore a mixed blessing.

Several asset protection specialists point to the extreme facts of the *Anderson* case and dismiss the notion that offshore trusts are a dangerous strategy. The Andersons were found guilty of managing a Ponzi-type pyramid scheme, and the court was attempting to recover the proceeds for the investors. Such facts would not arise in a case of medical malpractice, for example, because the patient would not have been the traceable source of the full amount of the damages.

Another demonstration of disfavor given offshore trusts was decided by a bankruptcy court in the case of *In re: Stephan Jay Lawrence*.† Mr. Lawrence was an options trader who had moved several million dollars into an offshore trust just before a $20 million award was granted against him. When he later attempted to have the debt discharged in a bankruptcy proceeding, the bankruptcy court refused to grant the discharge because it viewed Mr. Lawrence as undeserving. In Mr. Lawrence's case, the asset protection trust effectively protected his assets, but the court ruled that he could not protect his assets under foreign law and protect himself under U.S. law as well, because that was not consistent with the spirit of the Bankruptcy Code. The court then ordered Mr. Lawrence to repatriate the assets in the offshore trust. In rehearing the case a year later, the same bankruptcy court held Mr. Lawrence in civil contempt of court and sentenced him with heavy daily fines and incarceration.‡ The court refused to believe Mr. Lawrence's testimony that he did not have the power to comply with the order. It specifically denied Mr. Lawrence the argument that compliance was impossible because, said the court, Mr. Lawrence himself had created the impossibility. On appeal, both the district court and the Eleventh Circuit Court of Appeals affirmed the decision of the bankruptcy court, reasoned that the actions of Mr. Lawrence were entirely voluntary, and denied him the benefits of a true discharge available to most debtors in bankruptcy.§ Refusing to give up, Mr. Lawrence filed a lawsuit

* *See* Federal Trade Commission v. Affordable Media, L.L.C., 179 F.3d 1228 (9th Cir. 1999).

† 227 B.R. 907 (Bankr. S.D. Fla. 1998).

‡ *See* In re: Stephan Jay Lawrence, 238 B.R. 498 (Bankr. S.D. Fla. 1999).

§ *See* Lawrence v. Goldberg, 279 F.3d 1294 (11th Cir. 2002).

against the bankruptcy trustee from his prison cell, but the district court and the court of appeals have dismissed those claims.*

The common thread in cases like *Anderson* and *Lawrence* is the courts' hostility to transfers they determine to be fraudulent conveyances. Without the taint of fraud, the creation of an offshore trust would stand a greater chance of being supported.

Offshore trusts were once used to hide assets from the IRS, such that the income they generated would avoid tax, although all foreign income of U.S. citizens is, and always has been, part of their taxable income. In response to this fraud, the IRS now requires that each offshore trust created by a U.S. citizen be registered and that continuous reporting be provided to the U.S. government. This requirement substantially increases the cost of creating and maintaining an offshore trust.

Both domestic and foreign jurisdictions giving shelter to trust assets against creditors' claims provide an opportunity to place sizable quantities of assets into a trust, while still having the potential to receive the funds at the discretion of the trustee. The asset protection trust is a very effective tool against creditors, notwithstanding the court rulings that have frowned on them so.

8.5.6.3 Asset Protection Trusts and Divorce

One area in which asset protection trusts are not typically successful is in the context of a divorce. In an equitable division of marital property, courts will frequently rule that assets placed into an asset protection trust are marital assets and subject to the jurisdiction of the court. The court will then shortchange the spouse contributing to the asset protection trust, or order that spouse to terminate the trust and split the income and principal with the divorcing spouse. Two recent examples of the latter type of ruling, in New York, have created the precedent that asset protection trusts are ineffective against spouses in a divorce. In most other contexts, however, the asset protection trust remains a viable solution to the challenges of creating an asset protection strategy.

Overheard in the Advisor's Lounge

Asset Protection and Records

A basic strategy for asset protection is to hold various assets in different entities. Putting real estate, small businesses, and other assets into trusts, corporations, or limited liability companies (LLCs) is effective protection that is relatively easy to put into practice. Not only do I recommend this strategy to clients; I use it myself. Recently, however, I discovered a potential downside.

About 25 years ago, I invested in some rare coins in a corporation I owned and put them into a safe deposit box owned by the corporation. When my business relocated 12 years ago, the safe deposit box billing was not forwarded to the new address and was never paid again. Last year, I went to retrieve the coins from the safe deposit box, which I had not visited in 25 years. I discovered that the box had been drilled open 3 years earlier and my collection turned over to the unclaimed property division of the state treasurer's office.

I was told that getting the coins back would be simple enough. I just needed to verify that I owned the company that owned them by providing the corporation's tax ID

* *See* Lawrence v. Goldberg, 573 F.3d 1265 (11th Cir. 2009).

number. However, the corporation no longer existed. I didn't have a record of its tax ID number. The IRS wouldn't verify the number without my giving them the address the company had used. That address was a post office box number that I no longer used and couldn't remember. The state's position was "no tax ID, no coins." The only verification of my identity as owner of the corporation was my signature on the bank's safe deposit box application. Eventually, with the support of bank officers who were willing to swear that I was who I claimed to be, I got my coin collection back. The hassle involved in this process was a reminder of an important component of asset protection. Maintain accurate records so you don't end up hiding assets from yourself.

A good start is to create a master file of all the entities that hold your assets. This can be any system that's easy for you to use: a computer spreadsheet, a set of file folders, or a single paper list. Share it as appropriate with your certified public accountant (CPA), attorney, or financial planner. The master list should include the name of each company, its date of incorporation, tax ID number, address, and other relevant information like phone or bank account numbers. Also keep an inventory of the assets each company owns.

Once you've created a master list, it's essential to keep it up to date as you buy or sell assets, close companies, or transfer ownership. Set up a system, as well, to remind yourself of tasks like filing tax returns, completing minutes of annual meetings, and paying the annual safe deposit box rent. Make your record keeping easier by eliminating unnecessary complications. For example, you probably don't need a separate address for each trust, corporation, or LLC. Instead of creating a separate company for each asset, you might consider grouping smaller assets within one entity. I'd suggest first discussing the pros and cons with an attorney or financial planner. For larger assets like real estate, I do recommend holding each one separately.

When I talk to clients about asset protection, I mention that part of the price we pay for it is an increase in paperwork. It's easy to accept that idea with casual good intentions. The case of my reclaimed coin investment is a good reminder of the importance of keeping up with that paperwork. If we don't, we might protect ourselves right out of access to our own assets.

Rick Kahler, MS, CFP
Rapid City, South Dakota

8.6 TIMING IS EVERYTHING

It merits repeating: timing is everything! Each method of asset protection introduced in this chapter works best if completed before danger of creditors appears on the horizon. Advanced planning is key to the success of an asset protection strategy, and the ideas were intended to inspire present action, rather than provide an escape route for medical professionals already nearing financial difficulty. Much like the diversification of assets in an investment portfolio, the methods are frequently used in concert with one another as redundant strategies to ensure effectiveness. Sanguine asset protection planners will employ several of them collectively because they each provide a unique approach to the challenge of asset protection. The tools in this chapter are also qualified with the intent that they be used with the consultation and advisement of professionals, since there are loopholes and pitfalls that make asset protection into a legal and financial planning subspecialty itself.

The complex forms of asset protection are primarily used because they require creditors to expend additional time, effort, and money, and in this way are often more effective than the simple ones and used frequently by physicians and couples of high net worth. Implemented properly and at the proper time, complex asset protection tools have proven highly effective at sheltering millions of dollars from the hands of creditors and plaintiffs, to the betterment of the people who use them wisely.

8.7 CONCLUSION

This chapter demonstrated how to reduce and avoid risk, and handle assets to minimize the chances of losing them to creditors, regardless of how acquired. If used early when your financial outlook is healthy, these strategies can be an effective barrier between your wealth and the reach of future creditors.

8.8 COLLABORATE

Discuss this chapter online with others at http://www.medicalexecutivepost.com.

ACKNOWLEDGMENTS

This chapter is modified from Miller, J.C., Asset Protection and Planning Principles: What is at Risk and How to Protect It, in Marcinko, D.E., and Hetico, H.R., *Comprehensive Financial Planning Strategies for Doctors and Advisors: Best Practices from Leading Consultants and Certified Medical Planners*™, CRC and Productivity Press, Boca Raton, FL, 2015.

FURTHER READINGS

Adkisson, J and Riser, C: *Asset Protection*. McGraw-Hill, New York, 2006.

Gassman, AS: *Creditor Protection for Florida Physicians: A Comprehensive Handbook for Physicians and Advisors*. Haddon Hall Publishing, New York, 2012.

Gassman, AS and Markham, MC: *Gassman & Markham on Florida and Federal Asset Protection Law*. Haddon Hall Publishing, New York, 2013.

Korn, DJ: Are your HNW clients covered? *Financial Planning*, March 12, 2014.

Marcinko, DE and Hetico, HR: *Comprehensive Financial Planning Strategies for Doctors and Advisors: Best Practices from Leading Consultants and Certified Medical Planners*™. CRC and Productivity Press, Boca Raton, FL, 2015.

Miller, C: Asset Protection for Physicians. In Marcinko, DE [editor]: *Financial Planning for Physicians*. Jones and Bartlett, Sudbury, MA, 2007.

Presser, H: *Asset Protection Secrets*. Brookline Press, LLC, Boston, 2013.

Taylor, CC: *Asset Protection Made Easy: How to Become Invincible to Lawsuits, Save Thousands in Taxes, and Set Up a Successful Estate Plan*. Mount Lanai Publishing, Vista, CA, 2011.

9 Functioning as a Physician in a Regulatory Environment

Controlled by Board Governance and the Medical–Industrial Complex

Eric A. Dover

CONTENTS

> Unless we put medical freedom into the Constitution, the time will come when medicine will organize into an undercover dictatorship. To restrict the art of healing to one class of men and deny equal privileges to others will constitute the Bastille of medical science. All such laws are un-American and despotic and have no place in a republic... The Constitution of this republic should make special privilege for medical freedom as well as religious freedom.
>
> **Dr. Benjamin Rush**
> *George Washington's personal physician*

How true Dr. Rush's words ring today. They are no doubt prophetic. Then again, it seems medicine, in the general sense, has been fighting this battle for centuries. Innovative and questioning "healers" have always fought uphill against the establishment and its restrictive "idea" of medicine. The medical establishment, for various reasons including greed, pride, power, and the demise of their closely held medical beliefs and treatments, has typically punished medical pioneers. These pioneers suffer greatly at the hands of those who control the medical system and wield immense power over them. Many have lost careers, families, and some, even their lives, as a result.

9.1 INTRODUCTION

During the past few decades, physicians have faced ever-increasing challenges to the practice of medicine that I'm not sure even Dr. Rush could have fully envisioned. There have always been mental, physical, and financial challenges. But now, physicians deal with a system that is so overreaching in its effect and so wholly protected legislatively that it can, without hesitation, destroy them and their careers. The labyrinth that physicians must maneuver, especially those in small groups or solo practice, is vast. The very essence of this system is to make all of medicine an allopathic algorithm and healthcare providers just a cog in it. The system is destroying the art of medicine and its advancement, patient lives, and our country. The system doesn't allow alternatives unless "blessed" by those in power, and still only as a substandard alternative to their allopathic treatments.

Little is written on the subject of medical boards, physician health programs (PHP), or the medical–industrial complex and their adverse affects on physicians and other healthcare providers' lives. There is rare media coverage of medical boards' despicable behaviors directed toward physicians; yet, like police violence, it's occurring on a daily basis. An occasional article or editorial is seen in a medical journal or blog regarding the subject. So, physicians suffer silently, typically alone and without support, as their lives and financial stability crumble around them. No one has researched the professional, social, and psychological outcomes of physicians who have been "disciplined," nor is there research regarding patient outcomes post physician discipline by a medical board or other entity.

9.1.1 Impact of the Challenge

Most physicians lack a basic understanding or knowledge of their state's medical practice laws, medical board process, state administrative law, federal law, the National Practitioner Data Bank (NPDB or just Data Bank), hospital peer review, or any other oversight entity until they become entangled in its webs. Even then, most physicians lean heavily on their lawyer's understanding of this overwhelming event, and that knowledge can be quite variable. One thing lawyers overwhelming understand is that medical boards and other similar entities are politically and legally protected. Physicians are naive to this, believing in the justice of the system to protect them.

The social and psychological upheaval the physician will experience dealing with medical board or other oversight entity investigation is sudden and dramatic. The physician will be caught completely off guard lacking any education, or time to educate themselves, on how to deal with such a catastrophic event. There will be a *loss of income* related to their practice of medicine for months or years, or forever. The physician may become *financially destitute* as a result of legal costs, absence from work, and mandated program costs. Physicians will probably suffer *marital and social discord*, no matter how strong their relationships, as a result of institutional intrusion, right or wrong. Many times, there is associated *psychological damage* such as anger, alienation, social withdrawal, posttraumatic stress disorder (PTSD), depression, and even suicide [1]. There will be *difficulty reintegrating into the work force* for those who lose their ability to practice medicine, especially older physicians, who typically have no skills other than medicine. There will be *loss of faith in the system*, and the protections it should provide, as physicians find they are helpless to these entities that are protected by the courts, administrative law, past legislative decisions, the media, and politicians.

9.2 MEDICAL BOARDS

9.2.1 Brief History

The first medical board was established in Connecticut in 1792 by the state legislature. It consisted of a group of physicians who evaluated the competency of physicians wishing to practice in the state. Medical boards eventually evolved and became very powerful with the addition of medical practice acts containing a plethora of administrative rules. The medical boards' stated mission was, and still is, the protection, health, and safety of the public. State boards formed a national group, the Federation of State Medical Boards (FSMB), in 1912. The FSMB was the first institution to publically list names of disciplined physicians in a monthly bulletin [2,3].

In the 1980s and 1990s, there were a number of high-profile cases involving physicians and public safety. One such case, international in scope, concerned surgeon Dr. Jayant Patel. Significant news coverage regarding his surgical outcomes and knowledge resulted in the heightened questioning of medical boards and whether they were actually fulfilling their mission of protecting public health and safety. The Oregon Medical Board (OMB) was scrutinized for allegedly "ignoring" 79 complaints and at least three deaths, attributed to Dr. Patel's surgical care from 1989 to 1998. The OMB abdicated all responsibility for the situation with a myriad of excuses for why they had no control over this physician or the HMO he worked for.

The OMB then came to the state legislature with a "fix" to supposedly prevent any further such incidents. The OMB advocated for greater authority over physicians and greater independence from government oversight. With the din of the press and public, the Oregon legislature gladly granted the OMB their wish. Other states followed Oregon's example [4–6]. Not a single individual associated with the OMB, whether administrative or board member, was investigated in any meaningful way for their horrendous dereliction of duty. Not one of them had their license restricted, suspended, or revoked for such serious offenses. None of them were ordered to pay out of pocket to go to programs for competency evaluations, psychological examinations, or courses to help them become better board members. No one resigned, nor was anyone dismissed, from his/her position of power. The OMB's inaction led to a number of deaths and numerous patients with chronic postsurgical medical disorders, yet all individuals involved with the OMB were protected from malpractice lawsuits.

With cases such as Dr. Patel's featured prominently in the mainstream media, medical boards nationwide came under intense public pressure and scrutiny as it became clear they were not fulfilling their mission of protecting the public's health and safety. The public saw physicians as a privileged class, protected by their colleagues and medical boards. They were correct to a degree. Public safety groups like Public Citizen, who had been taking medical boards, hospitals, and large clinics to task for years regarding what they felt was a lack of physician oversight and discipline, began ranking state medical boards based on how many disciplinary actions they handed out each year. In their 2011 report, "Public Citizen's Health Research Group Ranking of the Rate of State Medical Boards' Serious Disciplinary Actions, 2009–2011," the authors made the *erroneous assumption* that the greater the number of physician "disciplines" (actions) per 1000 physicians, the better the job that state's medical board was doing. Therefore, at 6.79 actions per 1000 physicians, Wyoming was doing the "best" job, and at 1.33 actions per 1000 physicians, South Carolina was doing the "worst" job [7–9].

Medical boards vary remarkably from state to state. There are only two constants among them. First, each state has a medical board. Second, the board makes all final decisions concerning licensees. Otherwise, there's no consistency when it comes to what's sandwiched in between. The medical board's authority is grounded in the state's medical practice act, which gives them the authority to enforce laws for licensing, monitoring, and disciplining physicians in the state. Every state has its own unique laws and processes, but every medical practice act covers the basics regarding oversight of physicians practicing medicine in the state. The U.S. FSMB periodically issues guidelines on the essential elements of a medical practice act [10].

9.2.2 Medical Board Structures—"The Tale of Two Boards"

The great majority of states have, in reality, two medical boards. All states have a *board proper*, and all but a handful have an *administrative board*.

The board proper is, depending on the state, made up of 7 to 16 individuals. There will be a president (chairperson) and president elect. The board members are "volunteers," typically appointed by the state's governor. The individuals who constitute the board vary greatly and are somewhat determined by the medical disciplines overseen by the medical board. Oklahoma presently separates the boards overseeing medical doctors (MDs) and doctors of osteopathy (DOs) [11]. Other medical boards may oversee physician assistants (PAs), midwives, respiratory therapists, podiatrists, athletic trainers, etc., who may, but typically don't, have direct board representation. All states have MDs on the board. Some boards are made up of all MDs. Others members of the board may include DOs, PAs, podiatrists, midwives, respiratory therapists, a representative from the secretary of state's office, the commissioner of state boards, or an educational director. Many, but not all, medical boards will have anywhere from one to three public members. Some states require that public members come from a specific profession, such as a lawyer or hospital administrator. Other states have no such qualifications; therefore, the public members can come from any profession.

The administrative board is the other medical board. They run and supervise the operations throughout the year. Their personnel, structure, and operation vary widely from state to state.

Most states have an executive director who supervises the board. Some states, such as New Mexico [12] or Indiana [13], use a state board director who operates as the executive director for all state boards. Pennsylvania uses a state administrator in lieu of an executive director [14]. Individuals who fill these positions are typically legally or administratively trained and *without any medical or scientific background.*

Many states have a medical director who is a physician. His/her tasks include working with investigators, lending medical expertise, and working on board committees. Some state medical boards, such as Delaware, don't have a medical director [15].

Medical boards are divided regarding legal staff. Oregon has an executive director who is a JD along with additional in-house legal staff. They also rely heavily upon a single assistant attorney general from the state department of justice [16]. In Pennsylvania, all boards use the Office of General Counsel for legally related issues [14].

Each state handles their medical board investigations differently. Some boards have in-house investigators. They frequently are ex–police detectives *with no medical background.* California's investigators are called *peace officers*, and they aren't typically ex-police [17]. In North Dakota, the board members act as the investigative staff and will hire outside investigators if necessary [18]. In Delaware, investigations are handled for all boards in the state by the Division of Professional Regulation [15].

9.2.3 Anatomy of a Complaint

A complaint to a state medical board regarding a physician can arise from anyone. It could be a patient or his/her family, physician colleague or competitor, pharmacist, hospital personnel, insurance company, Medicare, Medicaid, the legal system, Internal Revenue Service (IRS), medical board member or staff, wife, partner, family member, or neighbor. Again, anyone.

There are two types of complaints, legitimate and illegitimate. *Legitimate complaints* would be for offenses such as medical errors, drug abuse, sexual improprieties, prescribing concerns, abusive behavior, or inability to practice safely. Examples of *illegitimate complaints* would be a medical insurance company unhappy with a physician because of disagreements over prescriptions or procedures; an unhappy spouse or family member, especially if there's conflict such as divorce or child custody; board members on a crusade against physicians utilizing evaluations or treatments not embraced by the board and their allopathic algorithms (in Oregon, this has occurred regarding assisted suicide and alternative medical care such as chelation or medical cannabis); physicians looking to remove competitors from their community; individuals with a personal vendetta against certain types of health-care providers such as PAs, DOs, family physicians, and chiropractors; or retaliation by anyone who so chooses to cause harm.

Complaints are always anonymous. The complainant is never directly named, although it may be obvious from medical board correspondence, questions, or chart requests. Anonymous complaints from nowhere, not linked to a specific patient interaction, are the most ominous because the physician is unaware of who made the complaint and what specifically it is based upon.

The potential for abuse is obviously very high. Two examples of this come from Texas. One is described in *AAPS v. Texas Medical Board*. The complaint of the Association of American Physicians and Surgeons (AAPS) alleged abuses perpetrated on physicians by means of anonymous complaints, harassment of doctors who complained about the board, conflicts of interest by decision makers, and violation of AAPS members' constitutional rights. This case ultimately forced the resignation of the medical board's executive director [19]. The other example is the Texas Medical Board's (TMB's) and Food and Drug Administration's (FDA's) unending attacks on Dr. Stanislaw Burzynski and other alternative health-care providers [20,21].

Another example is unfolding in Oklahoma, where the medical board is seemingly being used to remove competition. This has prompted an investigation of the medical board and has one state representative asking the governor for the resignation of the board's executive director [22,23].

Every medical board has an algorithm for processing a complaint from start through finish. Most don't have any diagrammatic depiction of their algorithm available on their website. Many board websites have a brief written description of the process, and others, nothing at all.

When medical boards violate their own processes and procedures, they almost never suffer any repercussions. These violations are easily kept from public view. Many times, physicians and their lawyers aren't even aware of these violations, but even if they are, they usually won't complain. Any complaints about, or demands for, due process by a physician are termed "arrogant" by the board. Most physicians' lawyers understand that you do whatever the medical board says, right or wrong, or else their client will lose their license.

9.2.4 Investigative Process

The investigative process is the most critical step of the complaint progression. It determines whether the case moves forward with further scrutiny or is closed. Again, the individuals and system used varies from state to state. Medical board members have become extremely reliant on investigators and administrative staff to feed them what they assume is reliable and well-investigated case material.

A state audit of the OMB in 1996 found the following [24]:

- Investigators were overwhelmed with work.
- Investigators had limited time available per case.
- A significant number of cases were taking a very long period of time to close.
- Investigators were doing a very poor job of documentation.

It has been almost 20 years since this audit was performed, and these and other issues have not been revisited since.

9.2.5 When an Investigation Is Not Closed

If an investigation is not closed, then the case moves forward with further exploration of charts, witnesses, medical experts, etc. The process varies remarkably from state to state. In Delaware, the Division of Professional Regulation does the investigation up through the hearing, if needed [25]. In Minnesota, the medical coordinators on the Complaint Review Committee act as a mini investigative committee (IC) [26]. In Oregon, the complaint and investigation are moved to the IC, which consists of board physicians, physician "expert(s)," an assistant attorney general who works directly with the board on a routine basis, investigator(s), the medical director, and the executive director. These individuals conduct an "interview" (interrogation) of the physician in a Star Chamber setting where your lawyer, if you decide to bring one, is not allowed to intercede on your behalf [16].

9.2.6 Due Process

Due process is guaranteed to American citizens by the Fifth and Fourteenth Amendments. The *Fifth Amendment's* Due Process Clause applies to the *federal government* ("No person… shall…be deprived of life, liberty, or property, without due process of law"). The *Fourteenth Amendment's* Due Process Clause applies to *state and local governments* ("nor shall any State deprive any person of life, liberty, or property, without due process of law") [27].

Procedural due process is "a course of formal proceedings [legal proceedings] carried out regularly and in accordance with established rules and principles" (Webster's Online Dictionary). It focuses on fair and timely procedures.

Substantive due process is "a judicial requirement that enacted laws may not contain provisions that result in the unfair, arbitrary, or unreasonable treatment of an individual" (Webster's Online Dictionary). It focuses on government regulation.

9.2.7 Consent Agreements/Stipulated Orders

Once the entirety of the investigation is finished, the board can choose to close the case, send a letter of concern, or pursue discipline of the physician. Discipline can come in many forms, such as a restricted, suspended, or revoked license; evaluations of all types; refresher courses; proctors; and, always, a fine. Physicians are given the choice of *signing a forced confession* called a consent agreement or stipulated order, or requesting a hearing. By signing these consent agreements/stipulated orders, physicians admit their guilt to medical board charges made against them. These legal documents also preclude future litigation by the physician against the board. With the threat of license revocation, physicians, under duress, will sign almost any document in the hope of placating the medical board and keeping their license. There are few, if any, compromises available to the physician, yet the entire deception gives those outside the process the illusion of compromise between the medical board and physician and an aura of integrity and fairness. If physicians are resolute in their innocence or demand due process, they are labeled "arrogant" or "disruptive." The medical board will then become dogged in their pursuit to exile the physician from medicine forever. Therefore, physicians are apt to sign legal documents that may not have a modicum of truth to them and many times aren't in their best interest.

9.2.8 Hearings

Hearings are offered to physicians by the medical board, or other governmental agency in charge at that juncture of the process, as a means to redress and contest the board's charges and decisions. Physicians decide if they desire a hearing to challenge the medical board. Each state has a format for hearings. Hearings are held in an administrative law setting with an administrative law judge (ALJ) presiding. Medical boards are not bound by the ALJ's decision and can ignore any or all parts of it. Many physicians see hearings as nothing more than a facade of due process with the actual intent being revocation of the physician's license. A physician is very *unlikely* to win a hearing with his/her license fully intact. It's very likely to be revoked.

Administrative law has a separate set of rules/laws/procedures than trial court. There is *no jury*, and very *low evidentiary standards* are allowed to determine the outcome of cases. "Administrative law uses the lowest evidentiary standard termed a *preponderance of the evidence*. The evidence is not sufficient to free the mind wholly from all reasonable doubt, but is sufficient to incline a fair and impartial mind to one side of the issue rather than the other. *Clear and convincing evidence* involves evidence indicating that the [charge] to be proved is highly probable or probably certain. This is a greater burden than preponderance of the evidence, and is the standard applied in most civil trials, but is less than *evidence beyond a reasonable doubt*, the [norm] in criminal trials [emphasis added]" [28].

9.2.9 Posthearing

A physician, if unhappy with the hearing outcome and the medical board's final order, may appeal the board's decision. *Appeals* look at nothing but the process of the physician hearing. They do not retry the case.

All states have an appeal process. In most states, you appeal directly to an appellate court and then onto the state supreme court if indicated. In a handful of states, such as Nevada or New Hampshire, you appeal to the state supreme court. Some supreme courts decide whether the case should be referred to the appellate court or closed. Other supreme courts actually hear the appeal if they don't close the case [29].

It is uncommon to win an appeal of a medical board decision. Physicians in Oregon have never won a state appeal of a medical board decision (at least in recent decades), except one, where only the fine was overturned, not the medical board's decision. The OMB is quite proud of this as they boast in their self-generated 2013 performance document [30].

9.2.10 The Entirety of the Process—Complaint to Discipline

Unfortunately, even with state and federal laws and rights in place to supposedly protect physicians, there are, in most cases, no protections. The process is typically opaque, secretive, and extremely psychologically and financially taxing to physicians and their families. Going through a hearing or appeal at this point in time should be avoided if possible. The cards are stacked in the board's favor, and no matter how wrong they may be or how right the physician is, it is a monumental battle in any court to overturn a medical board decision. *No physician should expect that there is, or will be, a "day in court" that exonerates them or provides them with justice* [31].

Medical boards are given broad latitude and treated as if they are infallible by the government, courts, media, and public. Most medical boards have *little, if any, effective oversight.* Most states have *no system, let alone functional ones, for public or physician complaints* regarding their medical board. In addition, legislation and courts have granted *these boards immunities unimaginable to the general public.* This creates a recipe for disaster that has played out and is playing out in many states, some mentioned previously. Medical boards control all information regarding physician cases, and only their opinions are published for public consumption. Medical boards have every opportunity to do damage control regarding their poor judgment, sloppy work, and criminal actions. Physician's licenses are routinely restricted, suspended, or revoked for much less, but medical boards almost never suffer any repercussions for their extraordinary malfeasance.

State legislatures throw softball questions and criticisms at medical boards but seem reticent to question their decisions. These legislatures are politically paralyzed, unable or unwilling to implement effective oversight or reforms of their medical boards. Federal courts, in particular the district courts, have been unwilling to question the constitutionality of state medical practice acts or address physician charges of medical boards acting unconstitutionally [32].

There have been a limited number of cases that have gone to federal appeals courts and, rarely, to the Supreme Court.

Medical board members and associated governmental figures are, in general, granted absolute immunity for any wrongdoing or errors, no matter how serious they may be or how adversely their actions effect physicians, their families, and patients. Immunity is not constitutionally warranted. The courts state that the Eleventh Amendment gives these boards immunity. *First*, the *Fourteenth Amendment* supersedes the Eleventh Amendment, as was the intent of Congress. Section 1 of the Fourteenth Amendment reads, "All persons born or naturalized in the United States, and subject to the jurisdiction thereof, are citizens of the United States and of the state wherein they reside. *No state shall make or enforce any law which shall abridge the privileges or immunities of citizens of the United States; nor shall any state deprive any person of life, liberty, or property, without due process of law; nor deny to any person within its jurisdiction the equal protection of the laws* (emphasis added) (Fourteenth Amendment U.S. Constitution).

Second, the Eleventh Amendment reads, "The Judicial power of the United States shall not be construed to extend to any suit in law or equity, commenced or prosecuted against one of the United States *by Citizens of another State, or by Citizens or Subjects of any Foreign State* (emphasis added)" (Eleventh Amendment U.S. Constitution). Nowhere in this amendment does it state that a citizen can't sue their state for constitutional violations against them; nor does it claim immunity for government or even use the word immunity. The Eleventh Amendment is the result of the Supreme Court case Chisholm *v.* Georgia (1793), which permitted a suit to be brought by a citizen of South Carolina against the state of Georgia. Fearing that other states would follow suit, the amendment was proposed on March 4, 1794. It was ratified by 12 of the then 15 states on February 7, 1795. South Carolina ratified the amendment in 1797; New Jersey and Pennsylvania did not ratify the amendment [33]. The federal courts subsequently perverted the Eleventh Amendment and extended undeserved immunity to state actors.

One recent case appealed to the Fifth Circuit Court of Appeals was a victory for physicians. The Fifth Circuit, on December 2, 2010, in the case *AAPS v. Texas Medical Board* (2010), ruled against the TMB, allowing landmark litigation by the AAPS to proceed to prove wrongdoing by the board [34]. Unfortunately, in 2013, this all came to an end when the district court judge made a bench decision and dismissed the case. AAPS was not financially able to appeal the decision a second time.

9.2.11 Medical Boards' Targeting of "Outliers"

On January 9, 2015, Alex M. Siegel, JD, PhD, who is director of professional affairs for the Association of State and Provincial Psychology Boards, spoke to the Oregon Psychology Board. He stated that "outlier" psychologists, who don't fit in with the mainstream herd mentality and organizations, are going to be the target of board investigations and discipline. As repugnant as his words were, they were truthful and insightful. This same doctrine holds true for medical boards who target what they consider to be outlier health professionals.

Their primary targets have been the following [20,35–39]:

- Solo practitioners
- Alternative medicine adherents who utilize such treatments as chelation, medical cannabis, and other nonallopathic medications and procedures
- Those who question vaccines
- Those working outside the mainstream insurance model
- "Loners"
- Those not involved in mainstream medical associations
- Assisted suicide advocates
- Mavericks and nonconformists
- Physicians working with malpractice lawyers
- Whistle-blowers
- Possibly particular races, as accused in California

9.2.12 Medical Board Overreach

Medical boards have morphed into a disciplinary arm of the state and federal government for non-medically-related issues. Medical boards control the means of a physician's livelihood via their license. This holds true for any licensed profession. Medical license suspensions and revocations are occurring for non-medically-related issues such as nonpayment of child support [40]; default on student loans [41–43]; IRS problems; or not participating in a state medical insurance program, as has been threatened in Massachusetts [44].

9.2.13 Medical Board Oversight

Let's be bluntly honest. There is *none*. Yes, there's plenty of rhetoric about government oversight and supposed legal protections for physicians, but in practice, they are nonexistent. Most states have no system to file a complaint against a medical board, and if they do, it's dysfunctional and ineffective. Many physicians have contacted all levels of state and federal government, but to no avail. Usually, the government just doesn't respond. It is a rare, almost extinct, government servant who will stand up against state medical boards and administrative law [45]. Without oversight, there is no accountability. No accountability means absolute power, and as we all know, "absolute power corrupts absolutely."

9.3 MEDICAL–INDUSTRIAL COMPLEX

9.3.1 Brief History

The term *medical–industrial complex* was first coined in 1980 by Arnold S. Relman, MD, who was, at the time, editor in chief of *The New England Journal of Medicine*. He adopted the concept from President Dwight Eisenhower's farewell address, which warned of the dangers of the military–industrial complex [46]. With government meddling in medicine and the extreme amounts of money at stake, so was born the medical–industrial complex. It is now a behemoth in size and reach, both politically and financially. It becomes more powerful each year as it further insulates itself politically and legally.

"The driving principle of medicine is revenue generation," says Diane Meier, MD, who directs the Center to Advance Palliative Care at Mount Sinai Health System [47]. Health-care spending in the United States for 2014 was somewhere between *$3 and $4 trillion*, depending on whose numbers you use [48]. That's an unfathomable sum of money flushing through the system. Each year, it grows, especially with an aging population. For comparison, the U.S. defense budget averages about $700 billion a year, about a fifth of health-care expenditures [49].

Doctors in the classical sense don't exist anymore. They have been reduced to technicians who follow only the allopathic medical regimens allowed by the medical–industrial complex and its political servants that dominate the profession. Doctors have lost control of their profession. According to Alexandra Meyer Tien, MD, "Everyone but the doctors is involved in big policy issues related to medicine—politicians, hospital administrators, bureaucrats, insurance companies and the pharmaceutical industry. Doctors' incomes have decreased while nonclinical medical bureaucrats' incomes have skyrocketed. We are refashioning primary care into a field that will be dominated by so-called physician extenders, who have far less training than physicians. What does this say about what we value as a society in our health care?" [50].

Who is responsible for the current state of medicine? I would propose that everyone is to some extent: the government, hospitals, HMOs, pharmaceutical industry, insurance companies, Wall Street, physicians, and even the public. Shareholders aren't concerned about medical care; they want profits, even at the expense of the well-being of their family, friends, neighbors, and fellow citizens.

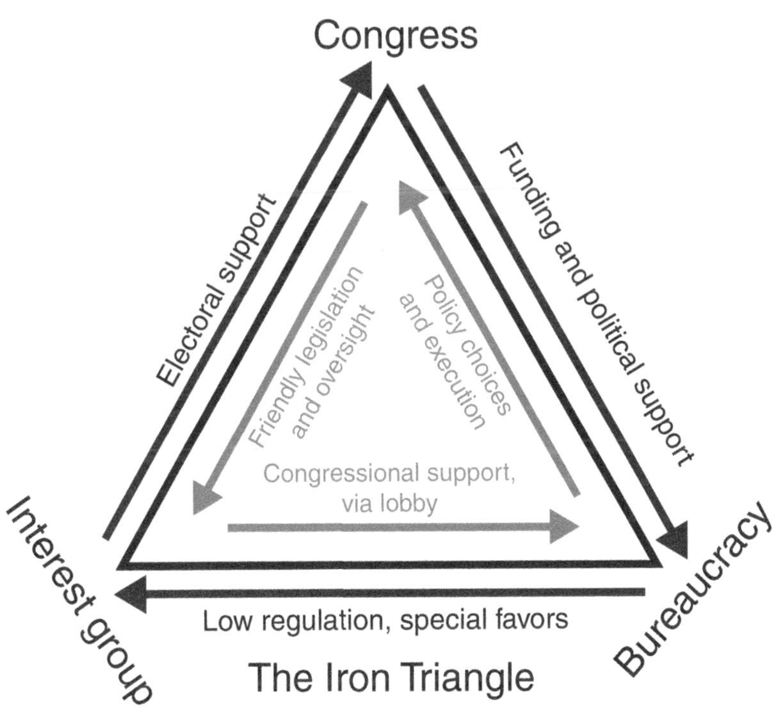

For "interest group," insert any health-care-related entity such as insurance companies, the American Medical Association (AMA), pharmaceutical corporations, Medicare, etc. [51]. (From Fisher, W., The Health Care Industrial Complex Is Stronger than Ever, May 30,

2014, available at http://www.kevinmd.com/blog/2014/05/health-care-industrial-complex-stronger-ever.html.)

9.3.2 Pharmaceutical and Insurance Industries

These two powerful components of the medical–industrial complex are well known. Medical dollars flow through and are controlled by insurance companies. Medicare and Medicaid dollars now flow to and through private insurance companies via government privatization projects. Insurance companies decide which treatments, surgeries, medications, services, or providers they will or won't pay for.

Pharmaceutical companies, along with the FDA, determine which allopathic medications are available to the public. The pharmaceutical company's tentacles reach deeply into medical schools, research facilities, physician offices, families' homes, hospitals, medication formularies, the FDA, and other government institutions and leaders. These companies pay for advertising in multiple venues, including health-care journals, mainstream magazines and newspapers, television, radio, and the Internet. They sponsor public events for diseases that their medications treat. They subsidize continuing medical education (CME) conferences for physicians while they lobby them from their sales booths. The pharmaceutical corporations pay medically related institutions and physicians to research their drugs and thereby contractually control all information that comes from that research. Therefore, they completely control all information that's outputted to physicians and the public regarding the benefits and side effects of any particular treatment.

"Now we have the private sector providing funding for our instruments of health care. We see companies that supply medical devices, drugs, insurance, electronic medical records and companies that support lobbying efforts and data mining and richly-paid oversight entities. Today, however, the budget is much, much larger for medicine than the military. Our health care industrial complex has grown into the monster it is today with a supporting flotilla of corporate, special interest, regulators and oversight entities, with doctors and patients swept up by its wake," according to cardiologist Wes Fisher, MD [51].

9.3.3 Antiphysician Acronyms

There are numerous agencies, entities, and authorities who earn their living regulating, auditing, monitoring, disciplining, prosecuting, and punishing physicians. Any action by them against a physician will be costly to defend, may be career ending, and may even place the physician's liberty at stake.

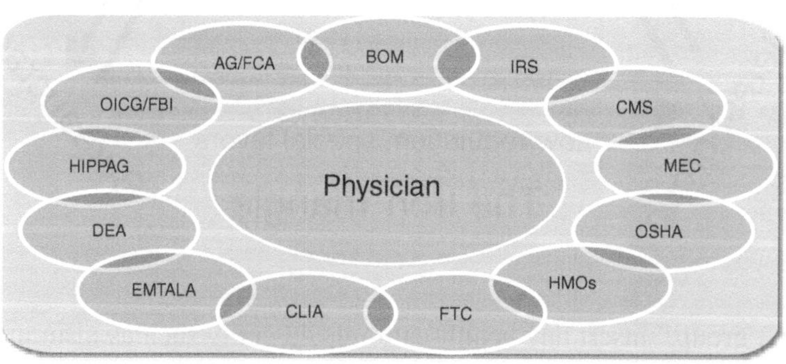

Note: Attorney General (AG), Board of Medicine (BOM), Federal Bureau of Investigation (FBI), Federal Trade Commission (FTC).

Medical records are reviewed, audited, analyzed, and scrutinized at an ever-increasing rate by these entities and many others. Most complaints, and the resulting investigation and actions, are initiated by and predicated upon the negative conclusions derived from review of medical records. This is done without any direct discussion with the physician [31].

9.3.4 Physician Health Programs

Once a need is in place, there is financial incentive to fill it. Nature abhors a vacuum, especially if money is involved. In this case, we had a "need" to fix "broken" physicians. PHPs were developed to fill that void. The need and the programs have grown congruently. PHPs are now an "industry" ingrained in the system. This has made it difficult, if not impossible, to extricate or even prune back these programs. The industry now requires a steady diet of broken physicians; otherwise, it financially collapses.

In 2013, the North Carolina State Auditor's Office (NCOSA) audited the PHP to which North Carolina's medical board "refers" their broken physicians. What they found was lack of oversight of the PHP and plenty of room for exploitation [52].

PHPs are now solidly established in the medical–industrial complex web. They see physicians as "food" that they drain of financial resources. It's only once the physician is drained of all assets and is no longer able to find work in medicine that his/her carcass is disposed of.

9.3.5 Healthcare Quality Improvement Act of 1986

The Healthcare Quality Improvement Act of 1986 (HCQIA) was the destructive handiwork of Congressman (now Senator) Ron Wyden of Oregon (Title 42 of the United States Code, sections 11101–11152). Representative Wyden introduced HCQIA legislation in response to a *federal* antitrust *suit* brought by Surgeon Timothy A. Patrick, MD, who practiced in Astoria, Oregon, against the city's only hospital and members of the Astoria Clinic. Dr. Patrick, the plaintiff, claimed that antitrust actions were affected through the mechanism of peer review in the hospital. Dr. Patrick's suit claimed that the Astoria Clinic initiated the action due to an ongoing dispute between himself and the clinic. Dr. Patrick had worked for the Astoria Clinic for 1 year. When offered a partnership in the clinic, he declined and opened an independent practice. That is when the attacks by the Astoria Clinic and Columbia Memorial Hospital (CMH) began. In 1979, Dr. Gary Boelling, a partner of the Astoria Clinic, complained to CMH's executive committee about Dr. Patrick. This complaint was forwarded to the OMB, where Dr. Franklin Russell, another partner at the Astoria Clinic, chaired the IC of the OMB. The IC criticized Dr. Patrick's medical practices to the full OMB, which then issued a letter of reprimand that had been drafted by Dr. Russell. The OMB retracted their letter in its entirety after Dr. Patrick sought judicial review of the OMB proceedings [53].

In 1981, at the request of Astoria Clinic surgeon Dr. Richard Harris, the executive committee of the CMH's medical staff initiated a review of Dr. Patrick's hospital privileges. The committee voted to recommend the termination of Dr. Patrick's hospital privileges on the grounds that the care of his patients was below the standards of the hospital. Dr. Patrick demanded a hearing, as provided by hospital bylaws. A five-member *ad hoc* committee, chaired by Dr. Boelling, heard the charges and defense. Dr. Patrick requested that the members of the committee testify as to their personal bias against him, but they refused. Before the committee rendered its decision, Dr. Patrick resigned from the hospital staff rather than risk termination [53]. Dr. Patrick, during the course of these proceedings, filed an antitrust lawsuit in the Oregon Federal District Court, where he eventually prevailed in a jury trial and was awarded $650,000. This decision was later overturned by the Ninth Circuit Court of Appeals on the grounds that existing Oregon statutes already protected the peer-review committee members from prosecution and that these protections should extend to federal antitrust suits brought by individuals for monetary, but not injunctive, relief [54]. Congressman Wyden then imprudently introduced HCQIA to extend state peer-review immunities on a federal level. "However, the consequences of the Act have instead helped promote an environment that protects those physicians on a peer review committee when they distort the review process for their own gain, by maliciously disciplining those physicians that may be in political or economic competition" [55].

Dr. Patrick took his case to the Supreme Court. The Supreme Court justices ruled in favor of Dr. Patrick, but by then, Congress had passed Wyden's damaging legislation that would negatively impact all future physicians' legal attempts. The system had learned well from Dr. Patrick's lawsuit and immediately adjusted. Wyden's legislation is responsible for the ultimate tyrannical, totalitarian power that all medical boards, and other peer-review health-care-related entities, now wield. HCQIA is what gives the governmental entities of the medical–industrial complex their ultimate power—*unconstitutional legal immunity.*

"HCQIA has provided a shield of nearly absolute immunity for bad faith, malicious peer reviewers," according to Lawrence R. Huntoon, MD, PhD, FAAN, chairman of the AAPS Committee to Combat Sham Peer Review [56].

9.3.6 National Practitioner Data Bank

The NPDB, also known as the Data Bank, was written into HCQIA. It is the national database for all adverse physician reports. Entities that are required to report physicians to this government program are the following [57]:

- Medical malpractice payers
- State health-care practitioner licensing and certification authorities
- Hospitals
- Health entities with peer review (HMOs, group practices, managed care organizations)
- Professional societies with formal peer review
- Federal and state government agencies
- Health insurance companies

The information collected by the NPDB includes the following [57]:

- Medical malpractice actions against a health-care provider
- Any adverse licensure actions by medical boards or peer-review entities, including revocation, reprimand, censure, suspension, probation, or dismissal or closure of any proceedings by reason of the practitioner surrendering the license or leaving the state or jurisdiction
- Adverse clinical privileging actions
- Adverse professional society membership actions

- Private accreditation organization negative actions or findings against health-care practitioners
- Criminal convictions that are health-care-related
- Exclusions from federal or state health-care programs

Entities that can query the NPDB include the following [57]:

- Hospitals, health-care entities, and professional societies with formal peer review
- State health-care practitioner licensing and certification authorities
- Agencies or contractors administering federal health-care programs
- State agencies administering state health-care programs
- State Medicaid fraud units
- U.S. comptroller general, U.S. attorney general, and other law enforcement
- Self-query by health-care practitioner
- Plaintiff's attorney/*pro se* plaintiffs, but under limited circumstances
- "Quality improvement organizations"
- Researchers (statistical data only)
- Federal and state government agencies
- Health plans

Once physicians are reported to the NPDB, their careers, if they still have one, are dramatically changed forever. There is no expunging process to remove defamatory physician reports, whether true or not. The stain is there forever. You have the opportunity to write a rebuttal for what it's worth—unfortunately, not much—but it should still be done. Actions reported to the NPDB by one entity will most likely trigger cross-investigations and actions by other entities [31]. It is easy to comprehend the simplicity of destroying a physician's career, psyche, and family with the untenable protections afforded by HCQIA to those responsible for the destruction.

9.3.7 Hospitals and Sham Peer Review

An excellent reference and starting point for a physician regarding peer review is *The Basics: What Every Physician Needs to Know About Medical Staff and Other Types of Disciplinary Proceedings*, by Thomas R. Bradford [58].

From the AAPS:

> Traditionally, physicians have reviewed the medical care provided by other physicians with the goal of improving the quality of care. That is known as *peer review done in good faith* [emphasis added].
>
> *Sham peer review* is peer review *done in bad faith* for some purpose other than the furtherance of quality care [emphasis added]. It is an insidious and spreading evil which threatens to destroy not only the integrity of the medical profession but quality care for all patients. It is eliminating some of the most competent, ethical and caring physicians from our hospitals. Sham peer review is being used by unethical physicians to attack other physicians so as to eliminate competition. It is a process which is being driven by money. As reimbursements to hospitals and physicians decline, sham peer review increases. Increasingly, hospitals are retaliating against

physician whistle-blowers to silence them and to end their careers. Sham peer review has become the weapon of choice used by hospitals to eliminate these good, conscientious physicians from the hospital.

Although thousands of patients die every year from preventable errors which occur in hospitals, many physicians today are afraid to come forward to report problems in hospitals out of fear that their careers will be ended by a retaliatory sham peer review. Fewer and fewer physicians are willing to risk their career and livelihood to protect patients in hospitals. It is easier and far safer for physicians to simply look the other way and remain silent. [56]

From Medscape:

In *Austin v. McNamara* (9th Cir. 1992), the Court of Appeals for the Ninth Circuit interpreted HCQIA to bestow immunity on a hospital *regardless of its animosity, hostility or bad faith* in revoking a physician's privileges at the hospital [emphasis added]. The Court held that "the test [for immunity under § 11112(a)] is an objective one." This precedent has been widely followed to exclude evidence of bad faith from lawsuits against hospitals for sham peer review. This precedent was distinguished by *Clark v. Columbia/HCA Info. Servs* (2001), as follows.

The presumption of immunity has been interpreted by the federal courts almost exclusively in favor of finding immunity for peer review board members [citing Austin as an example]. ...in only two cases have federal courts reversed an order of summary judgment based on immunity because the physician demonstrated by a preponderance of the evidence that the board failed to give appropriate fair notice and procedures in accordance with § 11112(a)(3)—*Islami v. Covenant Medical Center, Inc.* and *LeMasters v. Christ Hospital.* In addition, in *Brown v. Presbyterian Healthcare Services*, the Tenth Circuit upheld a district court's finding that the peer review board lacked immunity because the board only investigated two patient charts before deciding to revoke the physician's privileges, which was not a reasonable effort to obtain facts under § 11112(a)(4). Moreover, in *Brown* the board reported false findings to the National Practitioner Data Bank pursuant to § 11137(c).

Not only is the peer-review process corrupt, it's ineffective, says Ralph M. Bard, a physician turned attorney in Tullahoma, Tennessee. *To Err Is Human*, the Institute of Medicine's report on patient safety, was released after HCQIA and the NPDB had been in place for many years. Yet the report shows a high rate of medical errors—and that error rate remains high. Rather than being used to weed out bad doctors, peer review as it exists today is used primarily as a weapon against young, vulnerable practitioners. "Peer review wasn't intended as a means to oust qualified physicians to the benefit of their more economically successful competitors," says James Lewis Griffith Sr., a malpractice attorney in Philadelphia.

When coupled with mandated reports to the state medical licensing board and the National Practitioner Data Bank, hospital discipline—even if it is a sham—can ruin a physician's career and make it virtually impossible for the doctor to relocate and start again.

Compounding the problem of sham peer review is sham due process, in which hospital lawyers—who usually control sham peer-review proceedings—afford the targeted physicians little or no meaningful rights to exonerate themselves. Sham peer review and sham due process are made possible by medical staff bylaws which for the most part are written by lawyers selected and paid for by the hospital. Not surprisingly, these hospital lawyers create bylaws that protect the hospital's interests, not the interests of the medical staff or individual physicians. In voting on medical staff bylaws, most physicians are either naive or apathetic, thinking, "Peer review only happens to bad doctors; it'll never happen to me." Experience shows, however, that it is often good, strong doctors who are targeted by sham peer review. No physician is immune from attack [59].

9.3.8 Medical Boards

> …I am persuaded that licensure has reduced both the quantity and quality of medical practice…It has reduced the opportunities for people to become physicians, it has forced the public to pay more for less satisfactory service, and it has retarded technological development…I conclude that licensure should be eliminated as a requirement for the practice of medicine. [60,61]
>
> **Milton Friedman**
> *Nobel Prize–winning economist*

> As a rule, regulation is acquired by the industry and is designed and operated primarily for its benefit. [61,62]
>
> **George J. Stigler**
> *Nobel Prize–winning economist*

> Licensing has served to channel the development of health care services by granting an exclusive privilege and high status to practitioners relying on a particular approach to health care, a disease-oriented intrusive approach rather than a preventive approach… By granting a monopoly to a particular approach to health care, the licensing laws may serve to assure an ineffective health care system. [61,63]
>
> **Lori B. Andrews**
> *Professor of law at Chicago-Kent College*

> Let us allow physicians, hospitals and schools to spring up where they're needed, abolish the restrictive licensure laws, and simply invoke the laws against fraud to insure honesty among all providers of health care…That will make health care affordable for everyone…. [61,64]
>
> **Ron Paul, MD**
> *Former Texas congressman*

America for the first 140 years was fundamentally a free market in health-care services. Few licensing laws or other barriers to entry into the healing arts existed [65]. America's founders opposed licensing, a common practice in England. They believed in (1) a right to work, (2) a right to freedom of choice for practitioners and consumers, and (3) the government as a neutral party to protect those rights. Many types of healing schools and clinics operated without government interference. Competition kept prices down. The government protected the consumer against fraud and negligence. No healing modality or group of healers had a legal advantage over the others. Whoever helped people the most prospered [61].

In 2012, the American Medical Association (AMA) wrote:

> With State and Federal legal immunity protections and no oversight, Medical Boards nationally have increased their staffs and expanded their abilities to investigate and discipline doctors. The result has been more disciplinary actions against doctors. Board actions against physicians increased 6.8%, from 5652 in 2010 to 6034 in 2011; prejudicial actions—such as license suspensions, revocations, probations and other restrictions—rose 4.1%, from 4798 in 2010 to 4996 in 2011; and non-prejudicial actions, for less serious offenses, jumped 21.5%, from 854 to 1038 during the same period according to the Federation of State Medical Boards (FSMB). Disciplinary actions nationwide rose 13.4% from 2007 to 2012.

Legislation passed in Washington in 2008 created a 5-year pilot project to grant the Washington State Medical Quality Assurance Commission *greater control over its staff and budget*. Subsequently, there was a 42.1% *rise* in the commission's actions since 2007.

The number of disciplinary actions by the Florida Board of Medicine jumped from 215 in 2010 to 332 in 2011. "While the state medical association supports prosecution of physicians who are prescribing illegally, the new laws go too far," Jeff Scott, general counsel with the Florida Medical Association, said in 2012. He added, *It's going to make it difficult for a legitimate pain patient to see a doctor.* He said, "It's going to limit access, and it's going to compound the problem" [66].

Most medical boards are composed of physicians that practice and believe in allopathic medicine exclusively. Typically, PAs or other health-care providers aren't allowed to participate on medical boards, even though they typically practice allopathic-based medicine and are licensed by the same board. Medical boards definitely don't include alternative medicine practitioners, but do routinely investigate, harass, and revoke them.

According to Dr. Sydney Wolfe of Public Citizen (see also Medical Boards—Brief History [Section 9.2.1]). "There is considerable evidence that most boards are inadequately disciplining physicians. Action must be taken, legislatively and through public pressure on medical boards themselves, to increase the amount of discipline and thus the amount of patient protection." How Dr. Wolfe makes such a correlation regarding physician discipline and patient protection is unknown. There are no data to support his statement. There are data that show no change in patient protection with an increase in physician discipline. Dr. Wolfe's unsubstantiated statements are causing significant harm to physicians, their families, and patients.

States vary in how a medical board's budgets are financed and determined. Some boards have, or are seeking, semiautonomous status, which gives little, if any, legislative control over their budget and, therefore, less control over the medical board. These boards are supposedly financing themselves with licensing fees and fines. This presents an obvious *conflict of interest*, especially related to physician fines. An environment is created that gives these medical boards a *financial incentive to discipline physicians*. Boards end up cannibalizing their licensees to survive financially.

9.3.9 Sticks and Stones Break My Bones, and Yes, Words Hurt Me

> So, Peer Review has changed the basic nature of medical practice. It has selected for a certain kind of personality, the kind that gets along, and is not threatening. It has led to a rejection of other kinds of personalities. Clinic medicine looks more like IBM than rugged pioneer types. [59]
>
> **Tony Francis, MD**

Medical boards, hospitals, and other entities have developed *derogatory, demeaning, dehumanizing* terms to describe and psychologically attack physicians. These prejudicial expressions are also concocted for public consumption so as to destroy a physician's practice and name. The primary terms used are *arrogant, disruptive, impaired, and outlier.* They are no different than labels used to denigrate race, religion, country of origin, sex, sexuality, style of dress, politics, socioeconomic status, intelligence, etc. The labels given to physicians are frequently used very subjectively and are broadly applied to attack them for various nefarious reasons.

Physicians are typically labeled arrogant if they stand up for themselves; demand due process; question the entity; or expect legal protections, accountability, and integrity from those in control of their livelihood. All physicians are "arrogant" to at least a mild degree. If they aren't "confident" (a preferred term), patients will notice and retreat from them. Patients like confident physicians. Physicians are expected to be in control. They make life-or-death decisions while carrying an enormous weight of responsibility. Therefore, a physician's underlying personality trait must be one of "healthy" confidence. This invariably makes it much easier for entities such as a medical board to label a physician arrogant.

Michael J. Schoppmann, Esq., sums it up:

> Physicians, as their medical license is a privilege and not a right under the law, hold a set of dramatically compromised rights under the law and are routinely, and increasingly, wrongfully labeled as "Disruptive," "Impaired" and/or an "Outlier." Any one of these "Scarlet Letter" labels is a virtually permanent and potentially career ending accusation.
>
> In the new investigatory, regulatory and competitive climate of healthcare, it is critical for physicians to avoid even the inference of being "disruptive." In order to do so, every physician must acquire an understanding of the new healthcare risk landscape and know how to maintain a risk-prevention state.
>
> Disgruntled patients can complain to health plans/managed care companies, leading to investigations that can result in the termination of the physician's contract and dramatic losses of income. Action can be taken against a physician's hospital privileges for intimidating, uncooperative or insensitive behavior.
>
> Moreover, these types of behaviors are reportable to the NPDB and thereby may trigger cross-investigations and/or actions as the physician seeks credentialing or re-credentialing.
>
> The critical first step in avoiding the label of "disruptive" is to immediately obtain any and all rules, regulations, policies or protocols (most commonly referred to as a code of conduct) under which the physician currently practices. [31]

9.3.10 Medical Schools, Residencies, and Primary Care

Medical schools and residencies are indoctrination centers for the medical–industrial complex. They teach one discipline of medicine, the allopathic branch. They gloatingly teach young physicians to be prejudiced against nonallopathic medical modalities. This is where young physicians are introduced to the pharmaceutical industry, the sole keeper of medications.

College has become quite expensive. Total student debt presently exceeds $1 trillion in the United States. When students finish medical school, they have typically studied for at least 8 years. Many of them will have an enormous amount of debt to repay. These costs are pushing medical students toward specialty residencies and fellowships that typically result in higher pay. Primary care is seen as a poor option to repay loans over the typical 10-year repayment plan, yet primary care physicians, the backbone of medicine, are what this country needs more of.

According to Marsha Mercer, writing for the *AARP Bulletin*, March 2013,

> Today [2012], the United States is short about 16,000 primary care doctors—the very doctors (family practitioners, internists and pediatricians) who offer the treatments and preventive screenings that save lives and head off expensive emergency room visits and hospitalizations.
>
> Why the shortage? It starts with huge medical school debts and ends with a doctor who is often overworked and underpaid. While students may enter medical school wanting to practice primary care medicine, they graduate saddled with heavy debt—$250,000 is not unusual—which prompts them to switch to a more lucrative specialty. Only one in five graduating internal medicine residents plans to go into primary care medicine, the *Journal of the American Medical Association* reports.
>
> "The doctor shortage is worse than most people think," says Steven Berk, M.D., dean of the School of Medicine at Texas Tech University. "The population is getting older, so there's a greater need for primary care physicians. At the same time, physicians are getting older too, and they're retiring earlier," Berk says. And graying doctors—nearly half the nation's 830,000 physicians are over age 50—are seeing fewer patients than they did four years ago. [67]

Stephen C. Schimpff, MD, professor of medicine and public policy, author, and former CEO of the University of Maryland Medical Center, wrote: "Less prestige, high debt loads and a knowledge that PCPs work in a non-sustainable business model forcing them to see an excessive number of patients per day in order to meet overhead and still garner an income about one half that of the specialist is, combined, enough to discourage medical school graduates from selecting primary care as a career" [68].

Doctors Insurance Company did a survey of their clients in 2012 and wrote an article titled "Nine out of 10 Physicians Unwilling to Recommend Health Care As a Profession, Exacerbating Anticipated Physician Shortage" [69].

Lynnette Khalfani-Cox wrote in Daily Finance in 2010:

> …with enormous student loans, [and you] can't wipe out college debt in bankruptcy court. Under the law, professionals with any kind of state license—doctors, lawyers, accountants and so on—can all have their professional licenses revoked if they default on federal student loans.

> Such defaults are particularly troublesome for health-care workers because borrowers in default also get excluded from the Medicare and Medicaid programs by the U.S. Department of Health and Human Services. For existing doctors and health-care providers, they'd be unable to accept Medicare payments, which is critical for hospitals, clinics, physicians and others.
>
> Moreover, for medical professionals, a federal student loan default "effectively eliminates 98% of your employment opportunities," says Michael Smith, an attorney with *The Health Law Firm*, an Altamonte Springs, Fla.–based company that provides legal services to the health-care industry. [42]

Many state medical boards determine whether their state's medical school(s) and residency programs meet their "standards." They also determine whether out-of-state or internationally trained physicians who apply for licensure meet their standards. In many states, especially smaller ones, there is a very closely linked relationship between medical boards, medical schools, and the state medical association. It's cronyism. They feed off of and into each other, with a small pool of physicians who lead these entities. The physicians chosen have a specific personality type and the same belief in how medicine should be practiced in their state. These physicians are then used interchangeably in the hierarchal positions of these organizations. These incestuous relationships result in not just an allopathic approach to patients but a *singular* allopathic approach. For students and physicians who choose not to follow this specific allopathic approach, there will be definite negative sequelae.

9.3.11 Medical Societies

There are a number of medical societies. They may be local, state, national, or international in scope. They may focus on a singular or diverse group of medical issues. The biggest such society in the United States is the AMA, which was organized in 1847. The AMA's supposed mission was to protect the public from quacks; however, their actual objective was to increase the income of its members, allopathic physicians. A report submitted at the AMA convention in 1847 was unusually candid in stating, "...The very large number of physicians in the United States has frequently been the subject of remark.... No wonder that the merest pittance in the way of remuneration is scantily doled out even to the most industrious in our ranks..." [70].

An excellent article written by Lawrence Wilson, MD, states, "The method adopted by the AMA to increase their members' incomes was to eliminate the competition by passing licensing laws. Virtually every law restricting the practice of medicine in America has been enacted not on the crest of public demand, but due to intense pressure from the political representatives of physicians" [61].

State medical society hierarchy is a common source of state medical board members but varies with each state. In Oregon, only 54% of physicians belong to the Oregon Medical Association (OMA), yet the Oregon Medical Practice Act commands that every MD or DO that's considered for the OMB *must only* come from a list of potential candidates provided by the OMA to the governor's office [71]. Mississippi, with a participation rate of 70%, has the same system for placing physician medical board members as Oregon. This should immediately trigger conflict-of-interest concerns, especially for those who aren't members of the state's medical society.

Physician participation rates in state medical societies differ significantly. In Colorado and Nebraska, participation is as low as 25%, whereas in Kansas and Vermont, it is 70–75%, and in South Dakota, it is upward of 90%. Most states don't require that physician recommendations for medical board positions come directly from state medical societies. Frequently, though, physicians on medical boards are also state medical society members. There are exceptions, such as Washington, where 40% of physicians are members of the state medical society, and presently, none of them are on the state's medical board.

The same physicians on medical boards have also typically been on hospital, medical society, and medical school boards and peer-review committees. A specific personality seems drawn to, and then retained within, these administrative physician positions. This level of collusion between organizations such as medical boards, medical societies, hospitals, medical schools, and residency programs certainly raises concerns of abuse and retaliation against physicians and health-care providers. Unfortunately, that's exactly what we are seeing across the United States; therefore, it's of no surprise that state medical societies are silent on medical board and PHP abuses and on legislation that affects physician due-process rights.

9.3.12 Physician Burnout

American medicine is undergoing vast changes, placing the status of physicians in the medical–industrial complex at great risk. Most physicians feel overwhelmed by increasing bureaucratic mandates from insurers, hospitals, and government. At the same time, physicians are the frontline employees of health care and assume the majority of the risk for patient care. This has left many in the profession with increasing disillusionment [72].

Samantha Meltzer-Brody, a psychiatrist and director of Taking Care of Our Own, University of North Carolina, Chapel Hill, North Carolina, states it best:

> Daily, I am contacted by good doctors who are struggling with symptoms of burnout syndrome and who have become overwhelmed by the challenges of attempting to practice medicine in today's health care environment. As a psychiatrist who runs a program to address and treat these distressed doctors, I am troubled by the ever-growing number of calls I receive.
>
> The burned-out physician is exhausted—mentally and physically—and often no longer able to find empathy or connection with patients. The question of how to escape from what has become a highly unpleasant situation becomes a frequent one. Given the high demands of the profession and serious consequences of mistakes, the burned-out doctor is a potentially impaired one. And the impaired physician is not able to maintain the unflappable, perpetually cool under fire, always objective, professional and yet compassionate demeanor that is expected by society. Worst of all, the impaired physician is at great risk for developing depression, suicidal ideation, or a serious addiction.
>
> The doctors who contact me report feeling beaten down by an increasingly hostile work environment. They say that they don't have time to take care of patients the way they envisioned when they decided to apply to medical school. Many describe feeling

> betrayed by a system that they say seems focused on achieving the bottom line with little regard for the impact on both doctors and patients.
>
> Most of these doctors report spending a significant amount of their time dealing with the electronic medical record and documentation. The ratio of time spent on doctor–patient interactions compared to physician–computer ones appears so horribly skewed that it has reached the point of complete dysmorphia. These good physicians call me when they feel like they can't continue any longer in the profession. They want to quit medicine. They report a loss of joy and meaning in their work. They describe the toll that the profession has had on their mental health, physical health, and personal lives. And most wrenchingly, they don't see an end.
>
> What can we do? There are no easy answers to the complex issues that threaten our profession. *The Taking Care of Our Own Program...has had an over 200% rate of growth in the first year, reflecting the enormous need...* [emphasis added]. [73]

Burned-out physicians will eventually be labeled as disruptive, impaired, an outlier, or arrogant. There's a reason it's difficult and extremely expensive for physicians to find disability insurance: psychiatric claims. Burnout leads to depression, anxiety, PTSD, suicide, divorce, drug abuse, surly behaviors and interactions, etc. It's nothing new; it's been occurring for a long time. Go without routine sleep, eat erratically, work long hours, operate under constantly stressful situations, and have no time for your family or self, and most individuals will decompensate physically and psychologically within weeks. Physicians operate within these parameters year after year. How are they to remain healthy, functional humans? They can't. Even a superhero couldn't, yet physicians are expected to endure and thrive under such conditions. If a physician makes a single mistake, or snaps just one day, his/her entire career is on the line.

9.4 ASSESSMENT

Physicians should protect themselves from all professional risks and perils, legally and financially, now. Prior to practicing in any state, physicians should thoroughly educate themselves regarding the following:

- State medical practice laws
- State medical board discipline rates
- State medical board process for complaints, investigation, and discipline
- How medical board hearings are held
- How are appeals handled
- What percentage of appeals result in a reversal of medical board decisions
- Hospital bylaws, procedures, and other associated legal materials
- Clinic bylaws, procedures, and other associated legal materials
- All financial contracts
- Legal documents associated with contracting entities like Medicare, private insurance, etc.

9.5 CONCLUSION

Being a physician has never been easy, but the task has become so onerous and dangerous that physicians are either leaving the profession or thinking about it daily. Medical schools may be full, but those idealistic and naive students cannot imagine the system they are about to encounter. They are only aware of a romanticized notion of practicing medicine and caring for patients. This is reinforced in medical school, internship, and residency. These physicians in training focus only on studying allopathic medicine and caring for patients. Nothing of merit is taught about the business of medicine or what residents will encounter once in the real world. Many physicians remain ignorant of the financial, legal, and political ramifications of their chosen profession.

It is time for physicians to move away from just a steady diet of medical training. We must become better educated financially, legally, and from a risk management perspective regarding all aspects of the medical milieu in which we operate.

9.6 COLLABORATE

Discuss this chapter online with others at http://www.medicalexecutivepost.com.

ACKNOWLEDGMENTS

To Kernan T. Manion, MD, Work/Life Design, Wrightsville Beach, North Carolina, and Michael Lawrence Langan, MD, Boston, Massachusetts.

REFERENCES

1. Wible, P, December 12, 2012—TED speaker. http://www.idealmedicalcare.org/blog/why-physicians-commit-suicide/.
2. https://s1.fsmb.org/Docinfo/History.aspx.

3. http://en.wikipedia.org/wiki/Federation_of_State_Medical_Boards.
4. http://medtech1.com/new_tech/newtechnologyfeature.cfm/212/61.
5. http://blog.oregonlive.com/oregonianextra/2009/02/_australia_ready_to_charge.html#2.
6. https://www.themedicalbag.com/despicabledoctor/this-surgeon-spent-his-entire-career-as-a-defendant-in-court.
7. http://www.citizen.org/hrg1937.
8. http://www.citizen.org/Page.aspx?pid=1248.
9. http://www.citizen.org/documents/2034.pdf.
10. http://www.fsmb.org/policy/what-is-a-smb-faq.
11. http://www.okmedicalboard.org/.
12. http://www.nmmb.state.nm.us/.
13. http://www.in.gov/pla/3638.htm.
14. http://www.dos.pa.gov/ProfessionalLicensing/BoardsCommissions/Medicine/Pages/default.aspx#.VOO-ZfZ0zIU.
15. http://dpr.delaware.gov/boards/medicalpractice/members.shtml.
16. http://www.oregon.gov/OMB/Pages/index.aspx.
17. http://www.mbc.ca.gov/.
18. https://www.ndbomex.org/.
19. http://www.aapsonline.org/index.php/site/article/high_noon_in_aaps_vs._tmb_-_be_there_feb._19/.
20. http://healthimpactnews.com/2014/texas-medical-board-tries-to-eliminate-alternative-health/.
21. http://articles.mercola.com/sites/articles/archive/2013/01/19/cancer-doctor-burzynski.aspx.
22. http://www.reddirtreport.com/red-dirt-news/state-medical-board-spent-more-700000-investigate-spine-surgeon.
23. http://www.reddirtreport.com/red-dirt-news/supreme-court-justices-admonish-state-medical-board-due-process-concerns.
24. State of Oregon Auditors Division, *Board of Medical Examiners, Special Review*, November 19, 1996.
25. http://dpr.delaware.gov/index.shtml.
26. http://mn.gov/health-licensing-boards/medical-practice/.
27. http://nahmodlaw.com/?s=substantive+due+process.
28. Garner, B.A. (editor), *Black's Law Dictionary* (10th ed.). MA, Thompson, 2014.
29. http://en.wikipedia.org/wiki/State_court_(United_States).
30. http://www.oregon.gov/omb/board/Documents/performance-measures/2013-annual-report.pdf.
31. http://www.drlaw.com/Articles/White-Paper—The-Targeting-of-Physicians—Insigh.aspx.
32. http://law.justia.com/cases/federal/appellate-courts/ca9/12-35705/12-35705-2014-05-29.html.
33. http://www.britannica.com/EBchecked/topic/184510/Eleventh-Amendment.
34. http://www.aapsonline.org/index.php/article/another_victory_againstbr_texas_medical_board.
35. https://www.facebook.com/video.php?v=678202715563198.
36. http://www.anh-usa.org/milestone-victory-texas-state-medical-board-attack-on-leading-integrative-doctor-beaten-back/.
37. http://www.salem-news.com/articles/december092013/david-allen-es.php.
38. http://www.cnn.com/2015/02/05/health/anti-vaccine-doctor-jack-wolfson/.
39. http://www.forbes.com/sites/peterlipson/2015/01/30/anti-vaccine-doctors-should-lose-their-licenses/.
40. http://www.ncsl.org/research/human-services/license-restrictions-for-failure-to-pay-child-support.aspx.
41. http://forums.studentdoctor.net/threads/doctor-doesnt-pay-student-loans-medical-license-suspended.734666/.
42. http://www.dailyfinance.com/2010/08/20/student-loan-horror-stories-whats-the-worst-than-can-happen/.

43. http://www.uvm.edu/~vlrs/Education/studentloansprofessionallicenses.pdf.
44. http://scholarship.law.wm.edu/cgi/viewcontent.cgi?article=1692&context=wmborj.
45. http://www.reddirtreport.com/red-dirt-news/lawmaker-demands-resignation-medical-board-executive.
46. http://www.michaeleglasscockiii.com/28/The_Medical_Industrial_Complex_And_Health_Care_Reform.htm.
47. http://lowninstitute.org/news/barriers-to-de-innovation-diane-meier-on-the-medical-industrial-complex-how-regional-variation-affects-patients/.
48. http://www.forbes.com/sites/danmunro/2014/02/02/annual-u-s-healthcare-spending-hits-3-8-trillion/.
49. http://www.usgovernmentspending.com/defense_budget_2012_3.html.
50. http://www.providencejournal.com/article/20140905/Opinion/309059914.
51. http://www.kevinmd.com/blog/2014/05/health-care-industrial-complex-stronger-ever.html.
52. http://www.ncauditor.net/EPSWeb/Reports/Performance/PER-2013-8141.pdf.
53. http://www.peerreview.org/patrick.htm.
54. http://en.wikipedia.org/wiki/Healthcare_Quality_Improvement_Act.
55. http://www.hcqia.net/.
56. http://www.aapsonline.org/index.php/article/sham_peer_review_resources_physicians/.
57. http://www.npdb.hrsa.gov/.
58. http://www.peerreview.org/hospital/what_every_physician_should_know.htm.
59. http://boards.medscape.com/forums/?128@@.2a349bb6!comment=1.
60. Friedman, M, "Medical Licensure," in *Dangers of Socialized Medicine*, eds. Hornberger, JG and Ebeling, RM. Future Freedom Foundation, Fairfax, VA, 1994, p. 68.
61. Andrews, LB, *Deregulating Doctoring: Do Medical Licensing Laws Meet Today's Health Care Needs?* People's Medical Society, 1983, 1986.
62. Andrews, L, "The Shadow Health Care System: Regulation of Alternative Health Care Providers," *Houston Law Review*, Vol. 332, No. 5, 1996.
63. Paul, R, "Health Care," *Health Freedom News*, Monrovia, CA, February 1989, pp. 18–19.
64. http://drlwilson.com/Articles/licensing.htm.
65. Goodman, J and Musgrave, G, *Patient Power*. Cato Institute, 1992, Washington, DC, p. 140.
66. http://www.amednews.com/article/20120604/profession/306049944/1/.
67. http://www.aarp.org/health/medicare-insurance/info-03-2013/how-to-beat-doctor-shortage.html.
68. http://www.kevinmd.com/blog/2014/02/shortage-primary-care-physicians.html.
69. http://www.thedoctors.com/TDC/PressRoom/PressContent/CON_ID_004671.
70. Wilson, L. "Proceeding of the National Medical Convention," *NY J Med*, 9 (July 1847):115.
71. http://www.theoma.org/.
72. Jauhar, S, "Why Doctors are Sick of Their Profession," *The Wall Street Journal*, August 29, 2014.
73. http://www.kevinmd.com/blog/2014/08/epidemic-physician-burnout-heartbreaking.html.

FURTHER READINGS

Biggs, E, *Healthcare Governance: A Guide for Effective Boards (American College of Healthcare Executives Management)*. Healthcare Administration Press, Boca Raton, FL, 2011.

Johnson, D and Chaudhry, H, *Medical Licensing and Discipline in America: A History of the Federation of State Medical Boards*. Lexington Books, Lanham, MD, 2012.

10 Understanding Medical Practice Cybersecurity Risks

Mitigations for the Digital Health Era

Shahid N. Shah

CONTENTS

There has been a tremendous explosion of information technology (IT) in health care caused by billions of dollars of government incentives for usage of digital health-care tools. But, IT systems face threats with significant adverse impacts on institutional assets, patients, and partners if sensitive data are ever compromised. Every health enterprise is required to ensure confidentiality, integrity, and availability of its information assets (this is called *information assurance* [IA]). Confidentiality means that private or confidential information must not be disclosed to unauthorized persons. Integrity means that the information can be changed only in an authorized manner so as to maintain the correctness of the information. Availability defines the characteristic that information systems work as intended and all services are available to their users whenever necessary.

It is well known that health-care organizations face and have been mitigating many risks, such as investment risk, budgetary risk, program management risk, safety risk, and inventory risk for many years. What's new in the last decade or so is that organizations must now manage risks related to their information systems because operating systems (OSs) are also at risk. IT is now just as critical an asset as most other infrastructure managed by health systems. It is important that information security risks are given the same or more importance and priority as given to other organizational risks.

As health records move from paper native to digital native, it's vital that organizations have information risk-management programs and security procedures woven into their culture. For this to happen, basic requirements of information security must be defined and implemented as part of both the operational and management processes. A framework that provides guidance on how to perform these activities, and the coordination required between these activities, is needed.

10.1 INTRODUCTION

The Risk Management Framework (RMF) is supported and provided by the National Institute of Standards and Technology (NIST). The NIST 800 series of publications provides a structured approach to achieve risk management. It provides broad guidance and not necessarily all the prescriptions, which means it can be tailored to meet the organization's specific needs and provide the flexibility needed for the different organizations. Using the NIST RMF helps organizations with risk management not only in a repeatable manner, but also with greater efficiency and effectiveness. Health-care information assurance is complex, and without a framework that takes into account a broad risk-management approach, it is difficult to consider all the intricacies involved.

As shown in the diagram, the NIST RMF consists of a six-step process designed to guide organizations in managing the risks in their information systems.

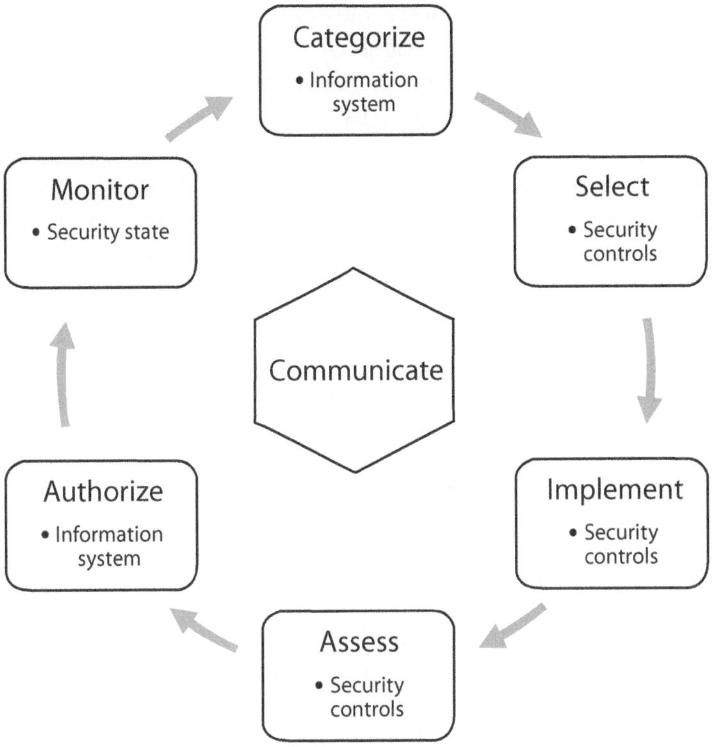

The various steps as defined in the NIST specifications are the following:

- *Categorize* the information system and the information processed, stored, and transmitted by that system based on an impact analysis.
- *Select* an initial set of baseline security controls for the information system based on the security categorization, tailoring and supplementing the security control baseline as needed based on an organizational assessment of risk and local conditions.
- *Implement* the security controls and describe how the controls are employed within the information system and its environment of operation.
- *Assess* the security controls using appropriate assessment procedures to determine the extent to which the controls are implemented correctly, operating as intended, and producing the desired outcome with respect to meeting the security requirements for the system.
- *Authorize* information system operation based on a determination of the risk to organizational operations and assets, individuals, other organizations, and the nation resulting from the operation of the information system and the decision that this risk is acceptable.
- *Monitor* the security controls in the information system on an ongoing basis, including assessing control effectiveness, documenting changes to the system or its environment of operation, conducting security impact analyses of the associated changes, and reporting the security state of the system to designated organizational officials.

All information systems process, store, and transmit information. What is the possible impact if a worst-case scenario occurs that endangers this information? A structured way to find out the potential impact on the confidentiality, integrity, and availability of information can be done through the first step of NIST Risk Management Profile (RMP), the *categorization of information systems*. The NIST SP 800-60[1–4] provides such guidance. The potential impact is assigned qualitative values—low, moderate, or high. Based on these impact levels for each of the information types contained in the system, the high-water-mark level is calculated, which helps in selecting the appropriate controls in the subsequent steps.

Organizations need to mitigate risks adequately by selecting an appropriate set of controls that would work effectively. In the *selection of security controls* step, the set of controls are chosen based on the categorization of the information system, the high-water mark, and the goals of the organizations. These baseline controls are selected from the NIST SP 800-53[5] specification, one of three sets of baseline controls, corresponding to a low, moderate, and high impact rating of the information system. These baseline controls can be modified to meet specific business needs and organization goals. These tailored controls can be supplemented with additional controls, if needed, to meet unique organizational policies and environment factors and their security requirements and its risk appetite. The minimum assurance requirements need to be specified here.

All the activities necessary for having the selected controls in place are done in the *implementation of security controls* step. The implementation of the selected security controls will have an impact on the organization risks and its effects. NIST SP 800-70[6,7] can be used as guidance for the implementation. An implementation strategy has to be planned, the actions have to be defined, and the implementation plan needs to be reviewed and approved before the implementation is done.

Once the controls are implemented, the *assessment of security controls* is done to find out whether the controls have been correctly implemented, work as intended, and give the desired output with respect to the security requirements. In short, whether the applied security controls are indeed the right ones, done in the right way, and give the right outcome. NIST SP 800-53,[5] NIST 800-53A,[6] and NIST 800-115[8–11] can provide the necessary guidance here.

The *authorization of information systems* is an official management decision, authorizing that the information system can be made operational, with the identified risks mitigated and the residual risks accepted, and is accountable for any adverse impacts on the confidentiality, integrity, and availability of information systems. If the authorizing personnel find that the risks are not mitigated and hence can compromise the sensitive information, they can deny authorizing the information system. NIST SP 800-37[2] provides guidance on authorization. The authorizing personnel are to be involved actively throughout the risk-management process.

Risk management is not a one-time process, which, once done, is forgotten. It is a continuous process, to be integrated with day-to-day activities. One of the key aspects of any risk management is the *monitoring of security controls* to check whether they are performing as intended. The main focus of monitoring security controls is to know whether the controls are still effective over a period of time, given the changes that occur in the information systems—the changes in hardware, software, and firmware; environment factors; operating conditions, etc. NIST SP 800-37[2] provides guidance about this. And if the security controls are found to be ineffective, the cycle starts again, with recategorization or selection of another set of baseline controls, or assessment of the effectiveness of the controls once more, etc.

And, in all the steps in the RMF, one of the important aspects is communication. Appropriate documents need to be generated in all the steps, reviewed, and kept up-to-date.

Organizational risk management provides great benefits to the organization because it helps to prioritize resources, increase interoperability, and reduce costs incurred due to adverse effects. It helps to prevent unauthorized access to personally identifiable information, which will lead to security breaches.

10.2 EXPLANATION OF THE MOST COMMON TYPES OF INFORMATION ASSURANCE RISKS

10.2.1 Administrative Risks

10.2.1.1 Example 1

Risk: Lack of documentation to mitigate threats and vulnerabilities.
Explanation: Not having a formal, documented program, which is always secondary to thorough risk analysis, might be the reason why you're not able to implement effective safeguards to protect your electronic Private Health Information (ePHI) against possible vulnerabilities and security threats. This may compromise your ePHI security in several ways:

- You may face medical identity theft due to unauthorized access, theft, or disclosure of ePHI.
- Unauthorized access to your practice's ePHI may leave it inaccessible, compromised, and exposed.
- The ability of health-care professionals to correctly diagnose and treat patients may be severely compromised due to the corruption of your practice's ePHI.

Mitigation: Conduct an annual risk analysis and document all possible threats and vulnerabilities to your practice's ePHI. Based on the documented risks and vulnerabilities, implement appropriate security measures specifically targeted to mitigate the vulnerabilities to an appropriate level!
Success criteria: Documentation of possible risks and implementation of safeguards leading to reduction in security breaches.

10.2.1.2 Example 2

Risk: Lack of security awareness and training.
Explanation: The security of your practice's ePHI might be at risk if your workforce members don't comply with the standard security protocols, either due to the lack of awareness or due to the lack of training. Several factors that may contribute to such behavior may include the following:

- Workforce members not really knowing what security is and why it is so important when it comes to ePHI
- Lack of sanction policies and procedures that make crystal clear to the workplace members their respective duties to uphold the integrity of ePHI, or lack of compliance on the part of workers to the sanctioned policies and procedures
- Security awareness and training programs being noninteractive and inappropriate

- A person not having the right skills, qualities, and knowledge in running the process of security awareness and training
- Not having enough metrics on whether all your arrangements are actually improving security awareness among your workplace members
- Unrealistic expectations
- Conducting a once-a-year training exercise only

Mitigation: You can strengthen security awareness and training among your workplace members and thereby improve the security of your practice's ePHI by taking the following steps:

- Make the sanction policies and procedures as explanatory as possible.
- Apply appropriate sanctions against members who fail to comply with the security protocols and policies.
- Make security awareness and training programs more interactive and periodic.
- Appoint the right person with the perfect skill set to head this process.
- Collect metrics on a periodic basis to see the progress of your training activities.
- While it is important that you collect metrics to know if your efforts are actually producing enough results, in the meantime, you have to be realistic. Promoting awareness is not a one-day process; it takes time and patience.

Success criteria: Improved awareness and better compliance on the part of the workplace members, leading to strengthened security.

10.2.1.3 Example 3

Risk: Lack of role delegation.
Explanation: Your business associates or workforce members can, knowingly or unknowingly, access the confidential ePHI if your practice doesn't clearly define, along logical lines, the roles and responsibilities allocated to each member. This is important as this will ensure that no member has too much authority and makes decisions on his/her own that can compromise access to critical and confidential systems and information.

Let's explain this by a simple example. Say one of your workplace members is responsible for reviewing the access logs. Due to your practice's poor role delegation, the same person is also responsible for updating patient records. In this scenario, that member is essentially left to monitor his/her own access to ePHI, facilities, and systems. This can result in unauthorized access attempts by the same member to your practice's ePHI.
Mitigation: Some important safeguards that may help solve this issue include the following:

- Implementing procedures and policies ensuring that all the workforce members have appropriate access to ePHI and no member gets too much authority.
- Assigning a senior-level manager who authorizes operations before commencing.
- Assigning different duties to the workforce members.
- Developing and distributing among your workplace members a work control policy that explains to the members things like their roles, degree of coordination between members, their responsibilities, compliance requirements, and so on.

Success criteria: Decrease in the incidence of security breaches from within the organization.

10.2.1.4 Example 4

Risk: Lack of business associate agreements when a business has a contractor creating, transmitting, or storing ePHI.
Explanation: The safeguard of your ePHI is incomplete until enough security safeguards are provided by the service providers, as per agreement. If your service provider fails to provide enough safeguards, it may result in the following:

- Unauthorized access or disclosure of your ePHI
- Compromising the ability of your workplace members to efficiently serve patients
- Medical identity theft

Mitigation: Before getting into a contract with your service provider, make sure that they give satisfactory assurances regarding the creation, transmission, storage, and handling of ePHI. Such assurances may include the following:

- Limiting the use/access to ePHI as required by law
- Employing enough safeguards to prevent unauthorized use or disclosure of ePHI
- Following the same or substantially similar good practices followed by your own institution

Success criteria: Highest level of security services further strengthened by the service providers, leading to improved experience and better security.

10.2.1.5 Example 5

Risk: Not having a process for periodically reviewing risk analysis policies and procedures and making updates as necessary.
Explanation: In something as dynamic as health-care security, the nature of risks and threats changes with time. That's why the efficacy of the safeguards you put to mitigate those risks declines with time. The security of your ePHI might be at risk if you fail to periodically assess the nature of risks and the validity of your policies and procedures, and undermine the importance of making regular updates for improving the safeguards.
Primary mitigation: Do a periodic risk analysis to determine the nature and severity of emerging risks to your ePHI. Keeping in mind the result of the analysis, make upgrades in your policies and procedures. Once you're done with the paperwork, translate what you've learned from the risk analysis and the changes you've made in your policies into actually strengthening the safeguards of your ePHI.
Secondary mitigation: Risk analysis and making changes in your policies and procedures is not a one-time job. Make sure to repeat the same routine periodically—have daily, weekly, monthly, quarterly, and annual checklists to review different types of risks.
Success criteria: Successive risk analysis reports will show that the changes made in the policies and, subsequently, in ePHI safeguards lead to a significant decrease in security breaches.

10.2.1.6 Example 6

Risk: Not having a senior-level person whose job it is to develop and implement security policies and procedures or act as a security point of contact.

Explanation: Not having a senior-level person who manages your security team can be jeopardizing the safety of your operations. Although security implementation and maintenance is a team effort, having a capable person who leads that team is equally important. Moreover, the head of your security will act as a liaison between the security department and the policy makers. If that link is missing, you might not be able to influence the decisions of your higher-ups when it comes to defining policies and procedures.

Primary mitigation: Identify the security official who is responsible for heading the security team. Define his/her role as being an individual who actively takes part in policy making. Finally, he/she should be responsible for the implementation of the policies for strengthening ePHI security.

Success criteria: Having a senior security officer who actually influences policy making, reviews documentation, runs scans, establishes a secure infrastructure, and strengthens ePHI security as a result.

10.2.1.7 Example 7

Risk: Not having an emergency-mode operation plan to ensure the continuation of critical business processes that must occur to protect the availability and security of ePHI immediately after a crisis situation.

Explanation: The functioning of health-care processes, including ePHI, is always a tug-of-war between the security safeguards and security threats. The security can be compromised anytime, by both extrinsic and intrinsic threats, which might compromise the functioning of your entire business operation.

Having an emergency mode helps you carry out critical operations and assists you in practicing operations and securing the integrity of your ePHI in the event of an emergency. Emergency operation allows you to access controls, back up the data, and access logging, and it allows encryption while other things occur. If your practice does not have an effective emergency mode, you might not be able to provide services to end users in the event of an emergency. In addition, you not being able to carry out important business processes may compromise the security of your process and ePHI even further.

Primary mitigation: Primary mitigation of this risk may include the following:

- Establish and implement the set of procedures that enable you to carry out important business processes, like the functioning and security of ePHI, when operating in emergency mode.
- Employ audited and automated override of the access control mechanism and implement role-based access control (RBAC) for an emergency.
- Establish a plan that determines the activities and related requirements, for instance, process, roles, and responsibilities for full system restoration.

Secondary mitigation: Test the continuity of operations during emergency mode, at regular intervals, so that the system can be promptly shifted to the emergency mode in case of need.

Success criteria: Your ability to readily shift to the emergency mode in cases of system collapse, run critical operations, and maintain ePHI security all mark the success of emergency mode establishment and implementation.

10.2.1.8 Example 8

Risk: The practice of not having policies and procedures for the creation and secure storage of an electronic copy of ePHI that would be used in the case of system breakdown or disaster.
Explanation: Like any other form of data, ePHI may be lost in case of system breakdown or disaster, if a proper backup in not kept and maintained. Backup of an ePHI is important as it allows you to create and maintain retrievable copies of ePHI in case of emergency. The exact retrievable copies of ePHI can be established and maintained in media like physical, removable media (e.g., CDs, USBs) or virtual media (e.g., cloud storage).
Primary mitigation: Establish and implement policies and procedures for making copies of ePHI on either physical or virtual media that can be retrieved when there is a breakdown of the system.
Secondary mitigation: Make sure that the retrievable copies of ePHI are safe and protected against unauthorized use and disclosure.
Success criteria: Being able to retrieve ePHI from the backup sources when the main source breaks or faces a disaster.

10.2.1.9 Example 9

Risk: Not having policies and procedures for the review of information system activity.
Explanation: Reviewing the activity of the information system enables one to identify and investigate irregular use of the system, which might be due to some breach in your security protocols or may be a violation of your security policies. Reviewing the activity of the information system includes the following:

- Analyzing the audit reviews
- Analyzing system activities and incident reports
- Analyzing the audit logs
- Reviewing the exception reports

If you don't have defined procedures or policies to analyze these activities, you might not be able to detect and analyze security violations, unauthorized disclosure, or use of ePHI.
Mitigation: Establish a system for reviewing the records of activity of the information security system. This includes reviewing incident tracking reports, audit logs, access reports, and so on.
Success criteria: Being able to detect and analyze any anomalies after reviewing information security system activity records.

10.2.1.10 Example 10

Risk: A practice that doesn't identify members of its incident response team and assures that workforce members are trained and that incident response plans are tested.
Explanation: An incident response consists of defining, clearly, what constitutes a security incident and a step-by-step approach to how to deal with the situation afterward. Without an effective incident response and training of the workforce involved, the security of ePHI will always be a far cry. In the absence of incident response and workforce training, the security of your system will be compromised. Not to mention, it will also increase the cost and time of recovery and will exacerbate the damage done to your critical processes.

Primary mitigation: An effective incident response plan would consist of the following components:

- Identifying the roles that will participate in incident reporting and response
- Providing role-based training to the workforce involved
- Incident response testing
- Making observations and recommendations on how to improve incident response
- Identifying who will speak to law enforcement, business associates, the media, and patients in the event of an incident
- Carefully training the members of the incident response team

Secondary mitigation: Training and increasing awareness regarding incidents in other workforce members too.
Success criteria: Successfully identifying which situations qualify to be labeled as an incident and successfully handling those uneventful events without compromising the security and mitigating the cost and time of recovery.

10.2.1.11 Example 11

Risk: Not implementing the information system's security protection tools to protect against malware.
Explanation: It is important that you complete regular and real-time scans of your servers, workstations (including laptops and other electronic devices), and information systems so that you're able to identify and respond to the known or suspected cases of security incidents. If you're not implementing these protocols, the security of your ePHI and other critical business operations may get compromised.
Mitigation: Mitigation steps may include the following:

- Identifying the known or suspected cases of security incidents
- Decreasing, as much as possible, the harmful effects of these incidents
- Documenting these incidents and their potential outcomes
- Employing automated mechanisms and tools to assist you in keeping track of the incidents and collection and analysis of the information gathered as a result

Success criteria: Improved protection against malware, decrease in the incidence of malware attacks, and mitigation in the compromise of the sensitive business components as the result of malware attacks.

10.2.1.12 Example 12

Risk: Not regularly reviewing information system activity.
Explanation: Reviewing the activity of your business operations and system activity is a periodic process that you have to go through on a day-to-day basis. If you're not doing that, then perhaps you're overlooking some very crucial threats to your system security.
Mitigation: Establish a system for reviewing the records of activity of the information security system on a day-to-day basis. This includes reviewing incident tracking reports, audit logs, access reports, and so on.
Success criteria: Being able to detect and analyze any anomalies after reviewing information security system activity records on daily basis.

10.2.2 Technical Risks

10.2.2.1 Example 1

Risk: Lack of unique user identification for every workforce member prior to obtaining access to ePHI.

Explanation: A user identifier is typically a name or a number or a combination of numbers and characters put together to form a string of characters that uniquely identifies a user. This unique user identifier allows the information system to track the activities of a user in the information system. This is done so that every user of the system can be held accountable for his/her functions performed on the information systems that have ePHI in it.

Major mitigation: Physician practices must determine the user identification strategy that best fits with the organization's policies and processes. Some organizations use employee codes, variations of names, or even identifiers that have been randomly generated using a combination of characters and numbers. The advantage of using randomly generated identifiers is that it is difficult for an unauthorized user to guess it. On the flip side, it may be difficult for the actual user to remember it. Physician practices must consider all these factors while determining a user identifier. Whatever be the format, the important thing is that only the user of the identifier needs to remember the identifier.

Secondary mitigation: User activity in information systems containing Private Health Information (PHI) must be tracked and monitored on a regular basis to watch for unauthorized access.

Success criteria: Periodic audits need to be performed that prove the following:

- Unauthorized access to ePHI has not taken place.
- Regular monitoring of user activity has been carried out religiously.

10.2.2.2 Example 2

Risk: Lack of unique passwords for each member of the workforce. Sharing of passwords. Access to ePHI is not based on the job function of the workforce.

Explanation: Passwords allow the team to gain access to information systems using ePHI. Each password has to be unique and assigned to individual users. A password given to a user, whether it is system generated or assigned, should not be shared with anyone. Users in an organization may require more or less access to ePHI based on their job function, and so all users will not need equal access to ePHI.

Major mitigation: Access to systems containing ePHI should be given to only those individuals who require the access as part of their job function. Additionally, the access given to the workforce should be only the minimum access needed for them to carry out their job function. Users should have the privilege to change the passwords, and the passwords must be changed periodically so that they are not compromised in any way. Each member of the workforce should be trained on the password protection policies and should be held accountable for slippage.

Secondary mitigation: Workforce members' access to ePHI must be periodically reviewed and updates made as their job functions change so as to ensure minimum access to ePHI. Access details must be documented and updated. Periodic audits must be carried out. A sanction policy must be implemented for sharing passwords.

Success criteria: Reports from the periodic audits will show how the defined policies are carried out and how they are periodically updated. User access logs also can be checked to verify users' access to ePHI based on their job functions.

10.2.2.3 Example 3

Risk: Lack of policies and procedures in place to provide appropriate access to ePHI in emergency situations.

Explanation: During an emergency situation, it is vital that doctors still have access to ePHI. There must be documented instructions along with practices and policies that need to be in place so that they are readily available for access in an emergency. The authorized personnel must be aware of how to get to these emergency procedures and operations in the event of an emergency. Physician practices must also determine the various types of emergency situations that would require access to ePHI.

Major mitigation: Emergency procedures, processes, and policies should be easily and readily accessible in the event of an emergency. The severity of emergencies may vary; for example, an emergency may result from an electrical power outage due to a natural or manmade disaster. Workforce members must be trained on the procedures and processes so that they are equipped to handle critical situations. With well-trained workforce members, there is little chance of confusion in these kind of situations. They must also be aware of ways to gain access to ePHI in these conditions.

Success criteria: Emergency situations happen rarely, and hence, proof that the procedures and policies are in fact working can only be obtained for sure when such an emergency occurs. However, every physician practice must be well equipped in all aspects to face such an emergency. Frequent audits and periodic emergency drills need to be carried out to mimic emergencies and test out the policies and procedures in place.

10.2.2.4 Example 4

Risk: Lack of automatic log-off capability for applications or workstations accessing ePHI.

Explanation: Sometimes, users working on workstations running applications that access ePHI may forget to log off or may not have the time to log off when they move away from their workstation. This may pose a threat since the workstation is left unattended, and unauthorized users can easily access ePHI, tamper with it, or even steal the data. An effective way to prevent this kind of unauthorized access is automatic log-off.

Major mitigation: The mitigation can be carried out in 2 ways:

- Configure the applications that access ePHI to automatically log off after a predetermined period of inactivity.
- For systems with limited capabilities, activate a password-protected screen saver after a period of inactivity.

In either of the above two cases, unauthorized users do not have access to the workstation containing ePHI.

Secondary mitigation: There needs to be a shorter log-off period for computers in high-traffic areas.

Success criteria: Applications that log log-off activities along with the time when the log-off took place show if the automatic log-off has taken place after a specific period of inactivity. Random and periodic testing of automatic log-off by the system administrators on all workstations accessing ePHI can verify if this risk has been taken care of.

10.2.2.5 Example 5

Risk: Lack of audit control mechanisms to record and examine activity in information systems that contain or use ePHI.
Explanation: It is necessary that information systems be equipped with audit controls that track and record system activity. This is important especially for detecting security violations. Most audit controls also provide audit reports of the system activity.
Major mitigation:

- Evaluate and understand the current technical infrastructure, hardware, and software security capabilities.
- Perform a risk analysis; determine the risks and possible mitigation/avoidance strategies.
- Decide on the audit controls that work for information systems in the physician's practice containing ePHI.

Secondary mitigation: The organization must have more than one person to conduct the audit process and report the results. It may also be a good idea to have IT vendors explain how audits are conducted and have the process documented.
Success criteria: Data gathered from audit controls and periodic review of data can help verify if the audit control mechanisms are tracking activity in information systems. Auditing the audit control system by outside third-party organizations can verify the proper working of the audit controls in the organization.

10.2.2.6 Example 6

Risk: Lack of proper mechanisms to authenticate ePHI.
Explanation: It is essential that the integrity of ePHI is given high importance. Compromises to the integrity of ePHI occur due to human errors that caused incorrect information to be stored into the database, or due to system crashes, the stored information gets altered/damaged. ePHI integrity can also be compromised if the backups are not ensured to be accurate. Intentional unauthorized access to ePHI through hacking can also destroy the integrity of ePHI.
Major mitigation: Controls to validate human data entries and that check for errors must be employed. Also, controls that ensure the accuracy of backups of data must be in place. Intrusion detection services can be used to detect intrusions or attempts to tamper with data. Vulnerability scanning can also be employed, which will scan the systems on a predetermined basis. Malware-scanning tools must be used and configured to scan the systems in frequent intervals to ensure no malware is present. Patches for applications, operating system (OS), etc. must be tested and ensured to be the latest.
Secondary mitigation: Designing policies and procedures to ensure that the integrity of ePHI is maintained. The policies and procedures must include all the above-mentioned mitigation steps and additionally can include a policy that ensures that data integrity tests are conducted on a regular basis. All log-in attempts can be logged and checked to ensure the access controls are in place as intended.
Success criteria: Audit of the logs from the different tools/services can help in knowing whether the risks have been mitigated. If data integrity tests are run, those logs can also be audited to know the exact status. Also, the reports of the risk analysis/risk assessment can

be used to understand whether the risk is mitigated and the current controls are effective, or more controls are to be added.

10.2.2.7 Example 7

Risk: Lack of proper authentication.
Explanation: The first step to gain access to ePHI must be authentication, which is verifying whether the entity trying to access ePHI is really the one it claims to be. If persons or entities (can be other software programs) are not authenticated, this can lead to the risk of ePHI being compromised. Proper authentication also needs to be done, before ePHI is shared with anyone in any manner. Without doing so, ePHI may end up in the wrong hands.
Major mitigation: In the simplest form, the authentication mechanism includes a username and a password, which has to be used to gain access. This authentication mechanism can be either at the workstation level or at the application level, or both, depending on the level of security that is needed. There must be defined policies and procedures that lay out the authentication mechanisms to be followed. These policies and procedures must include the mechanism to be adopted when sharing ePHI with another person/entity.
Secondary mitigation: A combination of authentication mechanisms can be used for a more advanced level of authentication, a multifactor authentication.
Success criteria: Each and every access to the systems needs to be logged. An audit of these logs can give a clear picture. Also, the risk analysis/assessment reports will give a clear indication whether any risks exist, and whether the controls are effective or not.

10.2.2.8 Example 8

Risk: Lack of encryption of ePHI in transmission and at rest.
Explanation: ePHI is vulnerable to compromise in all the states it is in, whether it is at rest (in databases and files), in motion (being transmitted through networks), in use (being updated or read), or disposed of (discarded paper files or electronic storage media). Using encryption puts an extra layer of security for ePHI because even if someone gains access or reads ePHI, if it is encrypted, then the chances of ePHI getting compromised diminish. It makes the data unreadable and unusable by unauthorized persons. When ePHI is transmitted through networks, it is possible that it will be accessed by unauthorized persons, thus compromising it. These types of unauthorized access hacking may not be immediately known but can cause much damage.
Major mitigation: ePHI should be encrypted, and there must also be reasonable and appropriate mechanisms in place to prevent access to ePHI so that it is not accessed by persons or software programs that have not been granted access rights.

There are many different encryption methods and technologies to encrypt data in motion (Secure Sockets Layer [SSL], Virtual Private Network [VPN]) or at rest. Choose the methods and technologies that best meet the requirements of the physician's office.
Success criteria: The risk analysis/assessment reports will provide a clear indication of whether these types of risks exist or have been mitigated with appropriate controls.

Auditing logs that track access to ePHI can be verified periodically to check if there has been unauthorized access by persons or software programs that have not been granted access rights.

10.2.3 Physical Risks

10.2.3.1 Example 1

Risk: Lack of procedures and contingency plans in the event of an emergency.

Explanation: In the event of an emergency, a well-defined contingency plan helps the team to allow for data restoration in addition to providing physical security. A contingency plan is usually used when there is an emergency, for example, when there is an outage. During the crisis, it is important that the doctors still have access to ePHI so that the quality of care is not compromised.

Major mitigation: Based on the size of the physician's practice, the contingency plans in place may vary. For small doctor's offices, the whole staff may need to be involved in restoration. In the case of large physician practices, authorized personnel may need to be accompanied into the buildings by guards.

A contingency plan should be in place that ensures that the right people have access to where the PHI is physically housed. This would mean that there need to be procedures and processes that are well established so that in the case of an emergency, authorized people who have access can retrieve the PHI or even make a backup copy of the PHI data. For example, this can mean bringing up the application in another data center if the primary data center housing the application becomes inaccessible. This should be done so that the physicians have uninterrupted access to their patients' PHI even in the event of an emergency.

Success criteria: Periodic third-party audits of contingency plans and mock emergency drills can help ensure that this risk has been taken care of.

10.2.3.2 Example 2

Risk: Lack of controls to prevent unauthorized physical access, tampering, and theft.

Explanation: The physician's facility should be secure so that PHI and related equipment cannot be tampered with in any way. Securing PHI would mean that only the staff who are authorized to access PHI must access it. This would mean securing equipment, workstations, and in some cases, entire facilities so that only authorized staff are allowed to enter these facilities.

Major mitigation: Review of risk data on anyone requiring access to ePHI, whether they are staff, patients, visitors, or business partners, needs to be done.

The following are some methods for mitigating this kind of risk as suggested by the Department of Health and Human Services in their HIPAA Security Series[9–11]:

- Locked doors, signs warning of restricted areas, surveillance cameras, alarms
- Property controls such as property control tags, engraving on equipment
- Personnel controls such as identification badges, visitor badges, and/or escorts for large offices
- Private security service or patrol for the facility

Secondary mitigation: All persons accessing PHI must be well aware of their roles in maintaining security in the facility. Procedures and processes would also need to be kept up-to-date when there are changes in the information systems or the environment.

Success criteria: Periodic monitoring of facilities to ensure that policies and procedures are being followed. Third-party audit of physician practices.

10.2.3.3 Example 3

Risk: Lack of procedures defining the use of electronic devices.

Explanation: Different electronic devices are used to access ePHI. These devices include desktops, laptops, mobile devices, and tablets. These electronic devices may be used within the practice building, or in homes and other places. If there is no defined procedure on how to use these devices to access ePHI, including what not to do using these devices, then there is a risk of ePHI being compromised.

Major mitigation: Specific policies and procedures must be defined that spell out how ePHI needs to be accessed, in other words, a clear description of what can be done and what cannot be done in the devices that are used to access ePHI. For example, it can be defined that in the devices that are used to access ePHI, no other software program can be installed and used without prior permission. Or it can be defined that no personal e-mails or social media sites can be accessed through these devices. These policies can be defined to the level of detail deemed appropriate. For example, a policy can just define what can be done or what cannot be done by the device types. Or it can very specific, detailing each electronic device by its ID and describing how it must be used. Also, separate policies must exist for those devices that are used to access ePHI remotely. In addition, scenarios where the staff bring in their own devices to the workplace need to considered, and policies governing their use must be defined.

Secondary mitigation: The environment surrounding the devices used for ePHI is also to be considered. Policies and procedures describing how the environment that houses the devices must be when they are used to access ePHI must be written down. For example, a policy can be defined that privacy filters need to be installed on desktop monitors so that ePHI is not visible to others nearby. Another example is a policy that mentions that all ePHI information access is done only on a particular floor of the building, where unauthorized persons will not have entry.

Success criteria: Regular audits and reports of these audits along with the risk assessment reports can be used to know whether there is risk of ePHI being compromised in this manner.

10.2.3.4 Example 4

Risk: Lack of guidelines governing the physical protection of electronic devices.

Explanation: The electronic devices used to access ePHI need to be protected physically from theft and unauthorized access. If not, these devices could be accessed by unauthorized persons, and ePHI will be compromised. Physical protection of devices is as important as other security mechanisms used to protect ePHI. Physical protection is often not taken into consideration, while other security measures like authorization, authentication, etc. are given more importance. But the loss of a mobile device or a laptop or tablet poses the same degree of risk as any other unauthorized access.

Major mitigation: The policies laying down the measures to be adopted for each of the electronic devices as appropriate need to be defined. For example, if it seems appropriate to keep desktops and other electronic devices in locked rooms to prevent unauthorized access, a policy to that effect should be in place. Policies must also consider the portable electronic devices, and if needed, mechanisms for tracking their use and whether they are returned before the staff leave the workplace can be defined.

Success criteria: Regular audits and physically checking the environment to see the protections in place can give a clear picture as to whether the policy is being followed and whether we need additional measures. So, too, can the risk assessment reports be considered to know whether these risks are present.

10.2.3.5 Example 5

Risk: Lack of mechanisms that keep an inventory of hardware and electronic media.
Explanation: An inventory of all types of hardware and electronic media needs to be tracked and maintained. With the advancement of technology, the use of portable devices is on the rise, and hence, the movement of these devices needs to be tracked and accounted for. Without having this kind of inventory, it is difficult to know when a device is lost and thereby accessed by unauthorized persons, exposing ePHI to unintended persons.
Major mitigation: Policies and procedures defining the mechanisms to be adopted maintaining the inventory of hardware and electronic media. The policy must define that there must be a person who is accountable for this. For example, if a faulty hard disk is taken out to the service center, the necessary bookkeeping along with the person accountable for it must be logged.
Secondary mitigation: The procedures can define the tools that are to be used to track and maintain the status of each of these media. Since there are many tools that are available in the market, they can be used for easily doing this bookkeeping. The level and detail of bookkeeping needed depends on each organization's needs.
Success criteria: Audit of the inventory logs, or if tools are used, the reports from these, can provide the status. Also, the risk assessment report can give a clearer understanding of whether these types of risks are mitigated or not.

10.2.3.6 Example 6

Risk: Lack of guidelines on how hardware or electronic media are to be disposed of.
Explanation: It is not just important to protect and secure the devices in use. It is equally important to consider what will happen to ePHI stored in these devices when they are not in use and are being disposed of. If these media are not properly disposed of, it poses the same level of risk as when they are in use. This is often an overlooked scenario.
Major mitigation: When each electronic medium reaches the stage when it is ready to be disposed of, policies and procedures must be laid down that describe how ePHI can be completely erased before the medium is disposed of. One of the methods used is degaussing (a magnetic field is used to erase the data) to clean up the medium before disposal. Or damaging the medium beyond repair, so that it cannot be accessed any further, can also be done. The policies must also define the need for logs/bookkeeping of the disposed medium and how the data were erased.
Secondary mitigation: Organizations also may defer the disposal of these media until a period of time, maybe years, so that the data contained therein becomes obsolete. Yet, these same policies of erasing these obsolete data before they are disposed of need to be in place. Also, the security of these "going to be disposed of" data must be considered.
Success criteria: Audit of the logs and bookkeeping records will provide information on whether the policies are being followed. And the risk assessment report will give a clearer picture as to whether this risk has been mitigated or not.

10.2.3.7 Example 7

Risk: Lack of guidelines on reuse of hardware or electronic media.
Explanation: It is a common scenario that the hardware and electronic media are reused instead of being simply disposed of. They either can be reused either internally within the organization or can be resold or donated to other organizations/individuals. Whatever may be the nature of reuse, it is important that all ePHI are completely erased using official government-approved wiping methods, before they are given out for reuse. If this is not done, there are fairly high chances of the data being exposed, thereby compromising ePHI.
Major mitigation: Specific policies and procedures need to be defined that clearly provide guidelines on the measures to be adopted when hardware or electronic media are reused. Often, the risks associated with internal reuse of these media are overlooked, and as such, there are no guidelines. Even if it is internal reuse, the same level of risks associated with unauthorized access exists here.
Secondary mitigation: Policies and procedures that advocate the use of logs and bookkeeping for media reuse would help to track these media in a better way.
Success criteria: Audit of the logs and bookkeeping records will provide information on whether the policies are being followed. And the risk assessment report will give a clearer picture on whether this risk has been mitigated or not.

10.2.4 Assessment

It is vital to understand the cybersecurity risks associated with medical practice today.

10.3 CONCLUSION

This chapter illustrates some of the medical practice security risks to any small, medium, or large physician's office, or medical clinic, in order to highlight or even eliminate them by securing the environment, in turn securing ePHI. However, it is not all inclusive, due to the fluid nature of contemporary cybersecurity risks.

10.4 COLLABORATE

Discuss this chapter online with others at http://www.medicalexecutivepost.com.

REFERENCES

1. National Institute of Standards and Technology Special Publication 800-30 Revision 1, *Guide for Conducting Risk Assessments*, http://csrc.nist.gov/publications/nistpubs/800-30-rev1/sp800_30_r1.pdf.
2. National Institute of Standards and Technology Special Publication 800-37 Revision 1, *Guide for Applying the Risk Management Framework to Federal Information Systems*, http://csrc.nist.gov/publications/nistpubs/800-37-rev1/sp800-37-rev1-final.pdf.
3. National Institute of Standards and Technology Special Publication 800-60 Volume I, Revision 1, *Guide for Mapping Types of Information and Information Systems to Security Categories*, http://csrc.nist.gov/publications/nistpubs/800-60-rev1/SP800-60_Vol1-Rev1.pdf.
4. National Institute of Standards and Technology Special Publication 800-60 Volume II, Revision 1, *Appendices to Guide for Mapping Types of Information and Information Systems to Security Categories*, http://csrc.nist.gov/publications/nistpubs/800-60-rev1/SP800-60_Vol2-Rev1.pdf.

5. National Institute of Standards and Technology Special Publication 800-53 Revision 4, *Security and Privacy Controls for Federal Information Systems and Organizations*, http://nvlpubs.nist.gov/nistpubs/SpecialPublications/NIST.SP.800-53r4.pdf.
6. National Institute of Standards and Technology Special Publication 800-53A Revision 4, *Assessing Security and Privacy Controls in Federal Information Systems and Organizations*, http://nvlpubs.nist.gov/nistpubs/SpecialPublications/NIST.SP.800-53Ar4.pdf.
7. National Institute of Standards and Technology Special Publication 800-70 Revision 2, *National Checklist Program—Guidelines for Checklist Users and Developers Recommendations of the National Institute of Standards and Technology for IT Products*, http://csrc.nist.gov/publications/nistpubs/800-70-rev2/SP800-70-rev2.pdf.
8. National Institute of Standards and Technology Special Publication 800-115, *Technical Guide to Information Security Testing and Assessment*, http://csrc.nist.gov/publications/nistpubs/800-115/SP800-115.pdf.
9. National Institute of Standards and Technology Special Publication 800-137, *Information Security*, http://csrc.nist.gov/publications/nistpubs/800-137/SP800-137-Final.pdf.
10. U.S. Department of Health and Human Services, *HIPAA Security Series, Security Standards: Technical Safeguards*, http://www.hhs.gov/ocr/privacy/hipaa/administrative/securityrule/techsafeguards.pdf.
11. U.S. Department of Health and Human Services, *HIPAA Security Series, Security Standards: Physical Safeguards*, http://www.hhs.gov/ocr/privacy/hipaa/administrative/securityrule/physsafeguards.pdf.

11 Medical Malpractice and Tort Reform
Urgent Crisis or Red Herring?

Robert James Cimasi and Todd A. Zigrang

CONTENTS

An analysis of premium trends and a comparison to industry actions within the context of the historical crises and bubbles is presented in this chapter, and touches on the effects of physician regulation, the impact of the *Patient Protection and Affordable Care Act* (PPACA), the increased incidence of reported medical errors, and the costs related to them.

11.1 MALPRACTICE INSURANCE INTRODUCTION

Since the turn of the century, increased media attention has placed the political spotlight on medical malpractice and the issue of tort reform. There have been particular problems within medical malpractice insurance that have been observed for years. Since a 1969 report from a Senate subcommittee presented various "observations,"[1,2] the volume of malpractice litigation has increased, and physicians have been confronted with higher premiums for malpractice insurance. In an effort to put this subject into context, we present a brief consideration of the significant elements of the debate, tracing the roots of the issue from the history of medical education to the development of the medical malpractice insurance industry, as well as the origins of the present-day tort reform movement.

11.1.1 History of Medical Education and Practice

U.S. medical education began in the late eighteenth century as an apprenticeship program in which physicians taught their trade to a few pupils, a pedagogical learning style that relied heavily upon the capacity, skills, and knowledge of the individual physician (see Ref. 3, pp. 22–23). However, as learning newly discovered information and utilizing new technologies became more necessary to the industry's practice, many physicians found the apprenticeship system no longer adequate as a manner of educating the next generation of physicians.[4] As a result, the conventional concept of medical education that originated in the United States in the 1750s was manifested through informal courses and demonstrations by private individuals or for-profit institutions. Those individuals who were not satisfied with a typical U.S. medical education, consisting of two identical 16-week lecture terms, might venture to Europe for a more formalized and detailed manner of learning (see Ref. 5, p. 4).

One of these students who studied in Europe was William Shippen, who began teaching an informal course on midwifery when he returned to the American colonies in 1762 (see Ref. 6, pp. 3–5). He later addressed the limitations of what might be taught in one informal course when he began teaching a lecture series on anatomy to help educate those who wished to be a physician but could not travel abroad. John Morgan, a classmate of Shippen, noticed the potential of his friend's endeavor and proposed the idea to create a professorship for the practice of medicine to the board of trustees of the College of Philadelphia (see Ref. 6, pp. 3–5). Just across town, Thomas Bond, who conceived the idea of, and successfully established, the Pennsylvania Hospital with Benjamin Franklin, recognized the value to allowing medical students to participate in bedside training (see Ref. 6, pp. 3–5). When Bond agreed to a partnership with the College of Philadelphia, the University of Pennsylvania became home to America's first medical school.[4]

In 1893, Johns Hopkins University also made history by housing the first medical school that was able to operate out of a university-owned hospital (see Ref. 5, pp. 18–19). The medical school not only encouraged clinical research to be performed by every member of their faculty, but the program also included a clinical research clerkship for every student during their rotation (see Ref. 5, pp. 18–19). This program quickly became the model to which schools aspired and set the foundation for national medical education by connecting science and medical research with clinical medicine.[7]

With these early examples of medical schools, America's field of medical education and clinical medicine made monumental strides. However, the societal pressures, caused by the U.S.'s population growth and demand for educated physicians (see Ref. 6, pp. 6–7), did not allow many other universities to build on Johns Hopkins' or the University of Pennsylvania's foundation model and led to the development of medical schools that had their own unique set of entrance and graduation requirements. While some focused entirely on medicine, other schools (termed *studia generalia*) also incorporated law, theology, and philosophy in their curricula.[8] In an attempt to both understand and make uniform the field of medical education, the American Medical Association (AMA) founded the Council on Medical Education (CME) in 1904.[8] The CME created minimum national educational standards for training physicians and subsequently found that many schools did not meet these established standards.[8] However, the CME did not share the ratings of any of these medical schools "outside the medical fraternity."[8]

In 1910, the AMA commissioned the Carnegie Foundation for Advancement of Teaching to conduct a study of medical education and schools.[9] Abraham Flexner conducted the inquiry and detailed his findings in what became known as the *Flexner Report* (see Ref. 6, pp. 3–19). In his review of the U.S. medical education system, Flexner found that many of the proprietary medical schools met the AMA's educational goals, but an imbalance existed between the pursuit of science and medical education (see Ref. 6, pp. 3–19). Professors were focused solely on student throughput and did not ensure a high level of medical training that reflected the developments in the medical industry (see Ref. 6, pp. 3–19). As aptly noted by Dr. John Roberts in his book entitled *The Doctor's Duty to the State*, "[m]any of you remember the struggle to wrest from medical teachers the power to create medical practitioners with almost no real knowledge of medicine. The medical schools of that day were, in many instances, conducted merely as money-makers for the professors."[10] As the AMA gained more influence over the provision of health care in the United States, the value and power of medical education also gained recognition. Notably, teaching hospitals had the power to influence the development of their disciplines through their research initiatives, the quality of care they provided, and their ability to operate as an economy of scale, allowing them to dictate the evolution of medical education (see Ref. 5, p. 19).

Since the establishment of the first medical school in the United States, medical education has been the foundation for shaping standards of care in the practice of medicine and defining *medical errors* as *deviations from the norms of clinical care*.[7] When Thomas Bond helped establish the University of Pennsylvania medical school, he envisioned a normal day where the physician

> …meets his pupils at stated times in the Hospital, and when a case presents adapted to his purpose, he asks all those Questions which lead to a certain knowledge of the Disease and parts affected; and if the Disease baffles the power of Art and the Patient falls a Sacrifice to it, he then brings his Knowledge to the Test, and fixes Honour [sic] or

> discredit on his Reputation by exposing all the Morbid parts to View, and Demonstrates by what means it produced Death, and if perchance he finds something unexpected, which Betrays an Error in Judgement [sic], he like a great and good man immediately acknowledges the mistake, and, for the benefit of survivors, points out other methods by which it might have been more happily treated. (see Refs. 6 [p. 4] and 11)

Originally, students were to study and learn from *medical errors* and *adverse events* through medical education as a means of improving the quality of care. However, it is difficult to effectively implement any significant advancement learned through the research and investigation of prior errors in a timely and cost-effective manner. Additionally, physician supply shortages have only increased the amount of patients that a physician must see daily, while simultaneously decreasing the amount of time they can spend with each patient. Although medical education continues to be one of the central underpinnings to the development of the medical industry, outside pressures that shape the clinical practice of physicians continue to limit physician effectiveness in providing quality care to patients (see Ref. 5, p. xxi).

While improving the quality and rigor of medical education has been a constant focus throughout the history of U.S. medical education, the challenges of replicating it on a scale that produces enough qualified physicians to meet the growing demands of the U.S. population, with constantly changing technologies, has consistently been a central issue. Notably, in the 13 years preceding 1980, the ratio of actively practicing physicians to patients increased by 50%.[12] This increased physician-to-patient ratio led to concerns over quality of care and cost-effectiveness, which in turn caused the creation of a government committee to evaluate physician manpower allocation and distribution. The *Graduate Medical Education National Advisory Committee* (GMENAC) was first chartered in April 1976 and later extended through September 1980 (see Ref. 13, pp. 5, 16). Its purpose was to "analyze the distribution among specialties of physicians and medical students and to evaluate alternative approaches to ensure an appropriate balance," as well as to "encourage bodies controlling the number, types, and geographic location of graduate training positions to provide leadership in achieving the recommended balance" (see Ref. 13, p. 73). GMENAC produced seven volumes of recommendations regarding physician manpower supply (see Ref. 13, pp. 5–6), through the development of several models by which to determine the projected number of physicians that would be needed in the future by different subspecialties to achieve "a better balance of physicians."[14] Ignoring critics of the report, U.S. medical schools adjusted their enrollment numbers in response to the GMENAC's recommendations, causing a significant decrease in the supply of new physicians going into the twenty-first century.

11.2 INCIDENCE AND PREVALENCE OF MEDICAL ERRORS

> Knowing is not enough; we must apply. Willing is not enough; we must do.
>
> **Goethe (see Ref. 15, front matter)**

As developments in research and technology have advanced medical practice, the improved ability to diagnose and treat patients has led to an increased volume of medical assessments and procedures performed. However, these increases in the volume of procedures performed by physicians have led to an increase in both the risk of harm to patients and the exposure to liability for physicians.[16] Today, most health-care services are delivered not by individual *Marcus Welby* type of physicians,[17] but through a group practice, health-care organization, or hospital system. While there are numerous advantages to physicians providing care as employees of a health-care enterprise, some of the unintended consequences exhibited under physician employment arrangements (e.g., diminishing physician autonomy, patient quotas, and limited time to spend with patients) have led to an increase in the potential for patient harm and subsequent physician liability (see Ref. 18, p. 507). Additionally, as the overlap between the scope of practice for physicians and nonphysicians continues to increase, the complexities of malpractice liability, which may jeopardize the licenses of both the supervising physician and the nonphysician professional, may similarly increase.[19] The result of these increased risks, medical errors, disgruntled patients, and changing scopes of practice has produced an environment that is ripe for malpractice litigation (see Ref. 18, pp. 506–507).

Numerous studies and examinations of the reality of medical errors demonstrate the varied nature and causes contributing to these errors, and the need for the medical malpractice system. The 2000 Institute of Medicine's (IOM's) landmark report, entitled *To Err is Human: Building a Safer Health System*, conservatively estimated that in 1997, "at least 44,000 and perhaps as many as 98,000 Americans die in hospitals each year as a result of medical errors."* Moreover, the IOM report noted that out of 30,000 discharges at 51 randomly selected New York hospitals in 1984, *adverse events* occurred in 3.7% of all hospitalizations or (1110 hospitalizations), with 58% of adverse events (approximately 644 hospitalizations) caused by *preventable medical errors* and 27.6% (approximately 306 hospitalizations) caused by *negligence* (see Ref. 20, p. 30). In addition to *medical errors*, more than one million serious *medication errors* occur every year in the United States (see Ref. 20, p. 1).[21] As observed in the Leapfrog Group's study, one *adverse drug effect* (ADE) adds, on average, $2000 to the cost of a hospitalization, which totals over $7.5 billion per year nationwide.[22]

Other studies have updated the figures relied upon in the IOM report. In 2010, the Office of the Inspector General (OIG) estimated that approximately 13.5% of hospitalized Medicare beneficiaries experienced adverse events during their hospitalizations, 44% of which were deemed preventable by independent physician reviewers (see Ref. 23, pp. 15, 22). Within this estimate, the OIG subdivided the adverse events into four clinical categories:

1. Events related to medication—31%
2. Events related to ongoing patient care—28%
3. Events related to surgery or other procedures—26%
4. Events related to infection—15% (see Ref. 23, p. 15)

A 2013 study published in *Journal of Patient Safety* combined the OIG's estimate with the estimates of three other studies[24–26] relating to the prevalence of medical errors to conclude that over "210,000 preventable adverse events per year...contribute to the death of

---

* The IOM study extrapolated data from the 1984 New York study, as well as a 1992 study from Colorado and Utah, to the number of hospitalizations in 1997 to estimate the number of deaths due to medical errors in 1997 (see Ref. 20, p. 26). The report authors note that these extrapolations may be low because the studies (see Ref. 20, p. 31)

1. "Considered only those patients whose injuries resulted in a specified level of harm"
2. "Imposed a high threshold to determine whether an adverse event was preventable or negligent"
3. "Included only errors that are documented in patient records."

hospitalized patients," with numerous additional errors shortening patients' life spans and causing other harms (see Ref. 27, p. 125).

The debate surrounding medical errors focuses not only on the *number* of adverse events in hospitals and deaths due to these adverse events, but also the *causes* of these adverse events. Although the 2000 IOM report is widely cited for its estimate of deaths due to medical errors,[28] the report also provided one of the first arguments that many medical errors "could likely have been avoided had better systems of care been in place," framing the medical error debate not solely on "incompetent or impaired providers" but also on the process of care delivery (see Ref. 20, p. 30). These process improvements can center on infrastructure as well as policies and procedures regarding the provision of medical care. The same IOM committee that published the 2000 report released a second report in 2001 entitled "Crossing the Quality Chasm: A New Health System for the 21st Century" which advocated for widespread change in overall structures and processes in the health-care environment as a means to preventing medical errors and improving quality, and listed six "aims" for high-quality care: safety, effectiveness, efficiency, equity, timeliness, and patient-centeredness (see Ref. 15, pp. ix, 25). However, a 2013 IOM report entitled "Best Care at Lower Cost: The Path to Continuously Learning Health Care in America" noted that, 12 years later, these six aims still had not been achieved and attributed the "fragmented, uncoordinated, and diffusely organized" infrastructure of the U.S. health-care delivery system to the lack of systemic processes in place.[29] Specifically addressing outpatient enterprise structures, a 2011 study on ADEs in ambulatory care settings noted the potential for infrastructure improvements to support the reduction of medical errors, stating that "as health information technology becomes more widespread in ambulatory health care delivery… automated surveillance for (adverse drug events) will become more feasible."[30]

The OIG has provided similar guidance to health-care providers regarding the relationship between structure and quality. In its revised guidance to nursing homes, the OIG recommended that nursing facilities can "promote compliance by having in place proper medication management processes," such as utilizing a consultant pharmacist and continually training staff in proper medication management.[31] Nevertheless, criticism still exists regarding the processes utilized by health-care providers to reduce medical errors. In its 2010 report on adverse events suffered by Medicare beneficiaries, the OIG recommended that the Centers for Medicare & Medicaid Services (CMS) "influence hospitals to reduce adverse events through enforcement of the conditions of participation" in Medicare, which includes sanctioning physicians through the peer-review process (see Ref. 23, p. 32). Other studies have advanced the OIG's claim a step further, arguing that "the hospital peer-review system has widespread failures that permit negligent care by physicians" (see Ref. 27, p. 127).

In an attempt "to improve patient safety by encouraging voluntary and confidential reporting of events that adversely affect patients,"[32] the Patient Safety and Quality Improvement Act (PSQIA) of 2005, effective January 19, 2009, established a voluntary reporting system for medical errors (see Refs. 33 and 34 [p. 70732]). Under PSQIA, to address provider fear that "patient safety event reports could be used against them in medical malpractice cases or in disciplinary proceedings,"[32] *confidentiality provisions* regarding the protection of "patient safety work product" were established (see Ref. 34, p. 70734). Patient safety work product includes any information that is collected while reporting and analyzing a *patient safety event* (see Ref. 34, p. 70739), i.e., "a process or act of omission or commissions that resulted in hazardous health care conditions and/or unintended harm to the patient."* Under PSQIA, *patient safety organizations* (PSOs) are charged with collecting and analyzing data under the supervision of the *Agency for Healthcare Research and Quality* (AHRQ).[33]

Despite the numerous attempts and strategies to curtail the prevalence of medical errors, no definitive answer exists as to whether medical errors are properly attributable to process or physician errors on a large scale. If it were determined that most medical errors are mistakes from *breakdowns in processes of care* rather than the *negligence of physicians*, improving and implementing new and effective process controls may best reduce medical errors—and the resulting incidence of medical malpractice cases (see Ref. 20, p. 30). However, to date, the health-care industry and the U.S. tort system are far from reaching this conclusion, leaving the tort system—as well as malpractice insurers and their physician insureds—to continue to grapple with this uncertainty.

11.3 BACKGROUND OF THE MALPRACTICE INSURANCE INDUSTRY

Malpractice, defined as "an instance of negligence or incompetence on the part of a professional,"[35] has always been a risk inherent in the practice of medicine. Specifically, *medical malpractice* is defined as "a doctor's failure to exercise the degree of care and skill that a physician or surgeon of the same medical specialty would use under similar circumstances."[35] Malpractice litigation stems from the U.S. tort system, which allows patients who are injured in some way to sue the wrongdoer, also known as a *tortfeasor* (see Ref. 35, pp. 352, 864, 1335). If found liable, the tortfeasor is held accountable for his/her actions, and the injured party is able to recover for damages incurred as a result of the tort.[36]

The goal of medical malpractice is to function as a *quality control measure*, creating an incentive to prevent medical errors and reduce accident-producing behavior by awarding damages, i.e., "money claimed by or ordered to be paid to a person as compensation for loss or injury,"[35] to plaintiffs who have been found to have been harmed by the physician's error (see Ref. 18, p. 508). The result is that the wrongdoer is held accountable for his/her actions,[36] the injured party is able to recover for damages incurred as a result of the tort, and the public is provided with a means to incentivize physicians and hospitals to improve the quality of their care.

Damages for medical malpractice are monetary and are typically awarded in three categories: (1) *economic damages*, (2) *noneconomic damages*, and/or (3) *punitive damages*. Economic damages compensate victims for actual monetary losses, such as medical expenses, lost wages, and rehabilitation costs, while noneconomic damages compensate victims for losses that are not traditionally measured in monetary terms, including pain and suffering, disfigurement, and loss of companionship.[37] To punish the defendant's conduct and deter future wrongdoers, punitive damages may be awarded in cases where the defendant has acted in a reckless or deceitful manner.[35]

Litigating a medical malpractice case is typically more expensive compared to other types of lawsuits, because these cases usually require one or more expert witnesses to help explain very complex and specific details to juries in order to meet burdens of proof and establish defenses. Figure 11.1 illustrates the cost difference between malpractice litigation and other civil litigation categories, with malpractice litigation costs outpacing other types of civil cases (see Ref. 38, p. 7).

* See Ref. 34, referring to footnote 7 in Ref. 34, p. 8113.

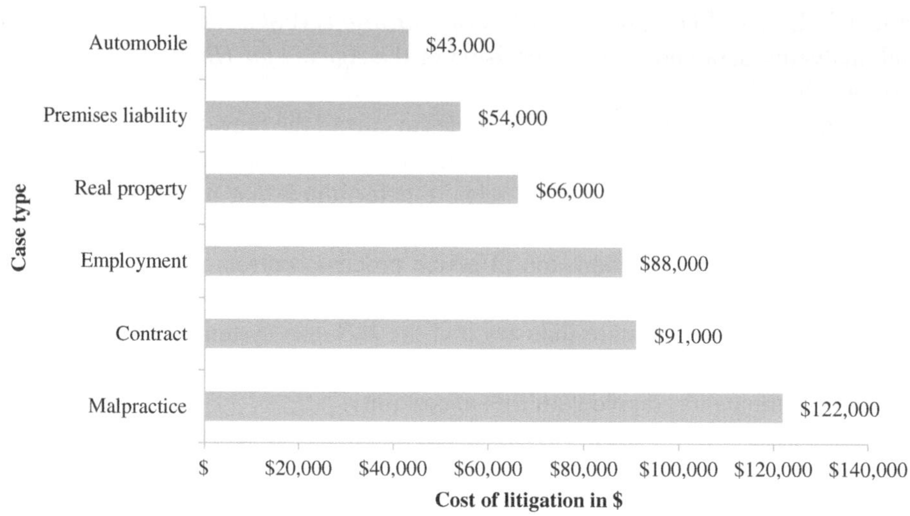

FIGURE 11.1 Average cost of litigation by case type (see Ref. 38, p. 7). (From Hannaford-Agor, P., and Waters, N.L., Estimating the Cost of Civil Litigation, Court Statistics Project, *National Center for State Courts Highlights*, vol. 20, no. 1, p. 7, 2013.)

While the damages awarded in medical malpractice suits tend to be larger compared to other types of lawsuits, evidence has shown that these cases involve higher levels of economic damages and that the damages awarded are not adequately compensating the plaintiff after deducting the cost of litigation and rate of compensation.[38] *Death* was the top reported severity of injury for closed medical malpractice cases, followed by (1) organ failure, (2) brain or head injury, and (3) chronic pain. *Death* constituted 27% of all *closed claims* (i.e., "a claim that has been resolved, either with or without payment to the claimant" [see Ref. 39, p. 4]) from 2004 to 2013,[39] while only comprising 3% of other personal injury cases (see Ref. 40, p. 6). Additionally, for medical malpractice cases where the plaintiff received a favorable verdict and award, and the primary injury was listed as *paralysis* or *amputation*, 100% involved *paralysis* caused by injury to the *spine* or *brain* (see Ref. 40, p. 7). This is compared to only 75% of the injuries in the paralysis or amputation category for an *arm*, *leg*, *hand*, or *foot* in nonmedical malpractice cases in which the plaintiff received a favorable verdict and award (see Ref. 40, p. 7). Further, research has demonstrated that even in cases where liability is or should be clear, compensation for damages ranges from 32% to 89% (see Ref. 41, p. 159). Due to the high costs of medical malpractice litigation, plaintiffs typically will only keep 40–60% of their awards, with the rest allocated to attorneys, expert witnesses, or other administrative costs (see Ref. 41, p. 160).

11.4 INSURANCE ECONOMICS AND POLICIES

The insurance industry is a function of *risk pooling** in a manner that transfers risk from the insured to the insurer. All of the insureds in the insurer's pool pay a premium rate each year to insure themselves from the risk they purchase insurance to cover. By attaining a large enough pool of insureds that represent the actuarially predicted amount of risk, the

* Risk pooling is an insurance industry function that ensures risks related to insuring the insureds are borne by all members of the pool and not by each contributor individually (see Ref. 42).

insurer is able to adequately spread the risk among numerous individuals and manage the associated costs. If the insurer has a pool that is less risky than what was actuarially predicted, the insurer should be able to maintain low expenses and high profit margins. This permits the insurer to remain competitive with their premium rates and attract low-risk insureds. However, if the insurer's risk pool is higher than the actuarial risk assumed, they may not have a large enough pool of money to cover their expenses, forcing the insurer to increase premium rates and harming their ability to competitively attract low-risk insureds (see Ref. 18, pp. 506–513).

11.4.1 Premium and Policy Options

In general, insurance premiums are determined based on what insurers expect to pay for claims filed by their insureds in that calendar year. To set prices, the insurer predicts the amount necessary to cover total costs for that year and subtracts any income received from the interest on the *reserve funds* they have invested. One-third of an insurer's costs are attributed to underwriting, administrative expenses, and legal fees for policyholders who are sued (e.g., physicians sued for medical malpractice claims). The other two-thirds of an insurer's costs are typically related to the payments of claims.[43] Since these types of fees change based on their geographic markets, the process of predicting costs resembles more an art form than a mathematical science. For this reason, short-term factors, such as the cycling patterns of the insurance market, sudden changes in the plans' physician market share, rapid inflation, fluctuation in reserve rate levels, and the varying amounts of profits, have the potential to affect the stability of the medical malpractice industry.

Once costs are evaluated and predicted, the insurer will set its medical malpractice insurance rates based on which of the two different types of policies the insured physician selects. An *occurrence policy* is a type of coverage that insures the physician for any incident that occurred during the time the policy was actively in force. This means that regardless of when the claimant files the claim, the physician will be covered if the incident occurred on a date that falls within the policy range. In contrast, a *claims-made policy* insures the physician for any claims that occur and are reported when the policy is actively in force. Since a claims-made policy only insures for claims made when the policy is actively in force, it tends to be less expensive than an occurrence policy. Additionally, many claims-made policies offer an option for the physician to purchase additional coverage, known as *tail coverage*, to cover any lawsuits that may arise within an extended, specified time period after the initial policy coverage period ends.[44]

11.4.2 Reserves and Loss Ratios

An insurer's ability to survive in the market is centered upon its aptitude for *predicting future income*, *predicting future expenses*, and *properly calculating premium rates*. The insurance industry calculates an insurer's loss ratio to determine the percentage of incurred losses to earned premiums.[45] When an insurer *overestimates* its expected *income*, *underestimates* its *losses*, or does a combination of both, the impact increases the insurer's loss ratio. However, when the insurer *underestimates* its expected *income*, *overestimates* its *losses*, or does a combination of both, the insurer is left with a surplus amount. To protect against the risks associated with future claims, insurers typically move a portion of these excess funds into reserves to protect against future losses.

In order to determine its capacity to take on additional risk, an insurer must assess the value of its assets. *Capacity*, determined by calculating the difference between an insurer's assets and liabilities, establishes whether or not an insurer will be able to continue its current business and take on new risks. Consequently, it has become common insurance industry practice to maintain investment portfolios from the company's reserve funds as a practice to grow assets to increase capacity and to pay for future losses. This typically involves investing in short-term, low-risk investments, including government and corporate bonds.[46]

11.4.3 Economic Factors in the Medical Malpractice Insurance Industry

In an ideal market, the pool of potential insureds is large and comprised of similar risk-based insureds with the propensity to have independent, random adverse events that are *actuarially predictable*. In the medical malpractice market, myriad issues render this economic theory difficult to implement in practice. First, medical progress has increased the ability to diagnose and treat patients, which has similarly increased the liability associated with treating patients. Second, the health-care industry is experiencing an intense period of corporatization/industrialization that has resulted in the system operating through a managed care format that limits physicians' autonomy to set their own prices, meaning they can no longer shift their increased cost of malpractice insurance onto their patients, because prices are set through their integrated delivery system. Additionally, cost containment policies that cause physicians to spend less time with their patients to establish a working relationship are becoming more prevalent throughout the market. This reduced interaction time expands the potential of being sued for medical malpractice by increasing the risk of error and disenfranchising the patient (see Ref. 18, pp. 506–508). Ultimately, these two factors together have resulted in an escalated risk of adverse events and errors, producing a market that is both less stable and less profitable than a typical insurance market (see Ref. 47, p. 33).

The medical malpractice market tends to be exhibited through a cycle that results in what is often characterized as a medical malpractice "crisis." This cycle begins with competitive entry into the market by multiple insurance plans. As more plans enter the market, insurers drop their prices to attract a larger and better risk pool. As a result, the insurer's returns begin to drop, forcing them to rapidly increase their premium rates. Insurers who cannot recover their losses or compete are forced to leave the market, limiting the choices and options of the insureds. As premium rates increase and insurer options decrease, the insureds' need for insurance coverage remains constant. The lack of access to insurers, combined with the high premium costs, frustrates many insureds and results in a period of high market scrutiny and attention to multiple reform initiatives. Inevitably, the need for insurance coverage by insureds drives the market back to a period of competitive entry for insurers, recommencing the cycle (see Ref. 18, pp. 506–513). Historically, this has been the pursuit of "equilibrium" in the medical malpractice system.

11.5 THE MEDICAL MALPRACTICE CRISIS

Beginning in the 1970s, the perception of malpractice claims as a growing problem emerged. Of the total number of medical malpractice suits filed between 1935 and 1975, 80% were filed between 1970 and 1975.[48] Along with the rise in the number of claims during the 1970s, malpractice insurance premiums also increased. As a result of these increases, several states passed tort reform legislation in the mid-1970s, while, during the same period, several physician-owned insurance companies were created in an effort to contain premiums.[48] After a brief respite, the 1980s experienced new premium increases and an increase in large jury verdicts.[48]

Although there were increases in large jury verdicts, the insurers' monetary losses did not amount to what was predicted by their actuaries, resulting in high reserve rates entering the 1990s.* Insurers used these high reserve rates to engage in high investment returns that allowed insurers to increase their income profitability and grow their market share at the expense of their reserve rates. Further, the growth in market share allowed insurers to keep their premium rates growing at a flat rate, sometimes even decreasing, throughout much of the 1990s.* However, these behaviors by insurers kept an increasing amount of losses hidden. By the mid- to late 1990s, much of the excess reserves of insurers were depleted, with income from investments falling below expectations and profitability declining.[47]

A common theory the 1990s was that the influx of *frivolous lawsuits*, and the concept that insurers had to settle them to make them go away, were causing premium rates to increase at a rapid pace. However, to this day, many insurers insist that they do not settle frivolous lawsuits.[50] Additionally, the high cost of litigation has served as an entry barrier to the justice system, since patients may find it difficult to secure legal representation if there is not a reasonable expectation of a large payment. In a 2014 survey published in the *Vanderbilt Law Review*, lawyers stated they cannot accept claims that do not have the potential to earn $250,000 or more, because it is not economically feasible (see Ref. 41, p. 193). The predicted result of this epidemic is that roughly 95% of potential medical malpractice plaintiffs will have a difficult time finding legal representation unless their anticipated damages are substantially more than what is typical for their type of injuries (see Ref. 41, p. 193). Data from the *Physician Insurers Association of America* (PIAA) has reinforced this concept, specifically showing that the number of payments to defendants that were below $250,000 in 2010 was less than half the number of payments that occurred during the 1980s, when there was a peak in the number of litigation payments.† Similar to the decrease in the number of lower payments, the volume of tort cases declined 25% between 1999 and 2008.[51]

Despite the decrease in medical malpractice cases and frivolous lawsuits, insurance premiums have continued to rise and fall at uneven rates. Using data compiled from the Medical Liability Monitor's *Annual Rate Surveys* from 1991 to 2014–2015, Figure 11.2 illustrates the increase in premium rates across all types of plans; however, the overall increase in price is also marked by periods of year-to-year price decreases followed by steep price increases.‡

* See Ref. 49 (data compiled from Annual Rate Survey Issues for years 1991 through 2001).

† See Ref. 41, p. 194 (the study was performed by the author using a data analysis of PIAA data).

‡ The Pearson correlation technique allows one to examine and determine the strength of the relationship between two variables (see Ref. 52, p. 238). Using a correlation matrix with the data compiled from the Medical Liability Monitor Annual Rate Surveys, it was determined that the correlation between the average internal medicine rate and the average general surgery rate is $r = 99.33\%$, the correlation between the average internal medicine rate and the average OB/GYN rate is $r = 98.93\%$, and the correlation between the average general surgery rate and the average OB/GYN rate is $r = 99.70\%$. Since an r above 80% is considered to represent a strong correlation, here we can conclude that the changes in these rates are correlated and the percentage of change from year to year is occurring at approximately the same percentage rate regardless of the type of medical practice being insured (see Ref. 52, p. 239).

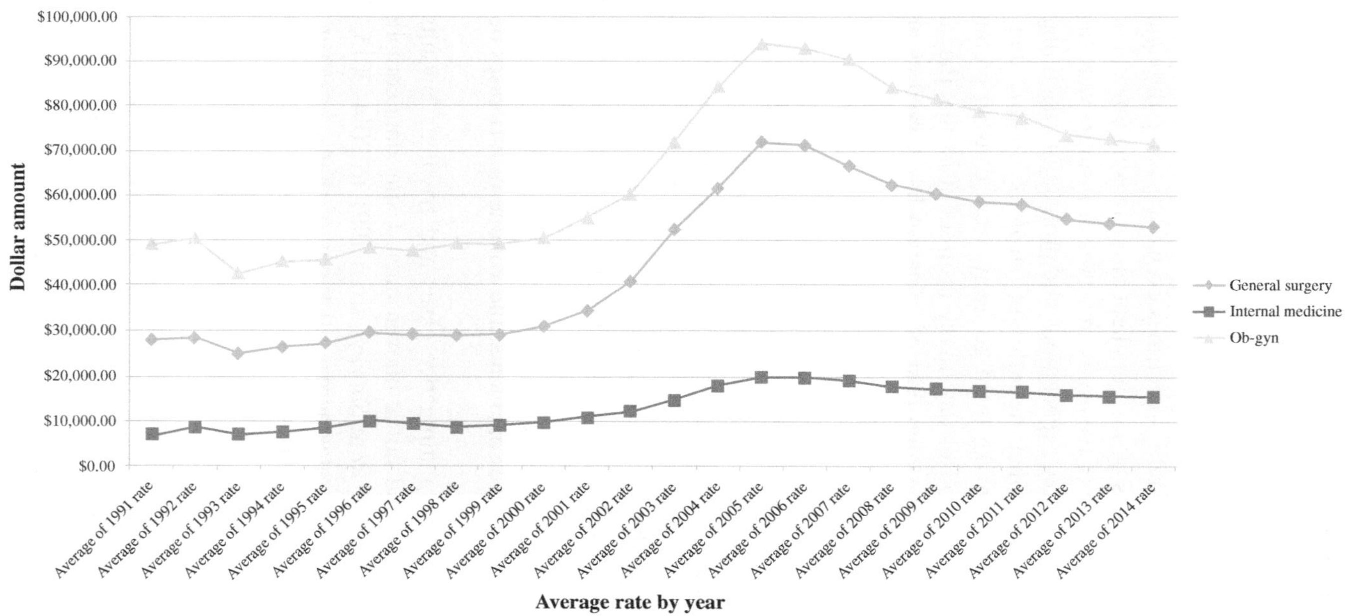

FIGURE 11.2 Average cost of medical malpractice insurance premiums in the United States from 1991 to 2014. (See Ref. 49 [data compiled from Annual Rate Survey issue for 1991 through 2014]. Premium insurance cost amounts were calculating by averaging the reported rates in the Annual Rate Survey issues. These rates were separated by the three reported practice types, states, and years. The chart represents the calculated average amount from all participating states for each of the years for each type of medical practice.) (From *Annual Rate Survey* issues, Medical Liability Monitor, Oak Park, IL, 1991–2014.)

While factors such as large jury verdicts, frivolous lawsuits, and inadequate physician practice typically receive the bulk of media and public attention, other less documented factors—most notably the behavior of medical liability insurers—significantly contribute to the fluctuation in the price of malpractice premiums. The critical stakeholders in this debate (e.g., medical liability insurers, physicians, and consumer advocacy groups) have firmly entrenched positions that give the tort reform debate its current focus; however, this entrenchment may also limit the focus, preventing discovery of the underlying influences on malpractice premiums and how new stimuli can influence prices. Arguably, by turning away from the "headline" causes for tort reform and focusing instead on the complex, multivariable nature of medical malpractice, more sound policy perspectives might be developed and considered in the tort reform debate.

11.5.1 Viewpoints from Competing Perspectives

The United States has the most expensive tort system in the world, with total costs of $264.6 billion in 2010 and costs per citizen of about $857 per year (see Ref. 53, p. 6). Product liability suits against tobacco companies and vehicle manufacturers; toxic torts (including the Deepwater Horizon oil spill, which accounted for $19 billion in total tort costs for 2010); and medical malpractice and negligence generally top the list of the largest jury awards (see Ref. 53, p. 3). Personal automobile torts and medical malpractice often constitute a large portion of aggregate costs in the U.S. tort system, with medical malpractice costs (not including the costs of defensive medicine) estimated at $29.8 billion in 2010 (see Ref. 53, pp. 3–4).

Maintaining a broad, critical perspective on the competing players in the medical malpractice arena is essential to fully understand the U.S. malpractice system. Tort reform stakeholders, including physicians, medical liability insurers, and other corporations, claim that the high cost of the tort system amounts to "tort abuse" by personal injury lawyers and their clients.[54,55] These proponents of tort reform have suggested some possible solutions to the "problem" they have claimed. These solutions, detailed in Section 11.6: Tort Reform Solutions across the United States, include tort reforms at the federal and state levels, such as class-action reform, medical malpractice reform, and a national settlement related to asbestos-related disease claims, as well as controlling the amount of noneconomic and punitive damages (see Refs. 56 [pp. 2–6] and 57). In contrast, consumer advocacy organizations, such as Public Citizen, and attorneys representing plaintiffs assert that the tort system must maintain the ability to provide sufficient legal remedies on a case-by-case basis for those injured by the actions of another, often more domineering, party. Understanding the perspectives and motivations of these players in the tort reform debate can shed light on the inconspicuous conditions contributing to the current medical malpractice environment and the potential for another crisis in the future.

11.5.1.1 Allegations of Greed: Traditional Physician and Insurance Company–Based Arguments

A common argument made by insurance companies and businesses is that greedy juries are awarding larger verdicts because of litigious plaintiffs and ruthless lawyers.[55] In 2012, over 58 medical malpractice cases resulted in a payout of over $5 million, with 15 cases resulting in jury verdicts over $50 million and 5 cases resulting in awards over $100 million; none of these awards included punitive damages.[58] In 2013, 65 malpractice verdicts and settlements exceeded $5 million, with the largest amounting to $140 million.[59] Although a 2003 GAO report observed that jury verdicts that award punitive damages are rare for medical malpractice cases (see Ref. 47, p. 51), the number of indemnity payouts over $5 million in the United States doubled from 2008 to 2013 (see Ref. 59, p. 18). Although large jury verdicts are increasing, this increase in large payouts does not reflect average claim indemnities. The average indemnity paid on a medical malpractice claim (in real 2013 dollars) decreased from $406,689 in 2004 to $342,384 in 2013 (see Ref. 39, p. 8). Proponents of tort reform argue that with the increase in substantial jury verdicts, the volume of malpractice litigation increases as well, due in part to profit-motivated lawyers who typically are paid on a *contingent-fee* basis.[61] The number of paid medical malpractice claims *increased* from 11,989 in 2004–2008 to 12,804 in 2009–2013, although the number of paid claims actually *decreased* between 2012 and 2013, from 2613 paid claims in 2012 to 2093 paid claims in 2013.[39]

11.5.1.2 Patient Legal Protections—Checks and Balances on Abuse: Traditional Market Based and Consumer Advocate–Based Arguments

For years, consumer advocates have argued that sufficient legal remedies must remain in the tort system to protect the legitimate interests of patients who have been damaged, in part, due to the reckless business decisions of medical liability insurers.[62] As discussed in Section 11.5, in the late 1990s, when the economy was strong, premium and reserve rates did not reflect actuarially sound principles; rather, the soft and profitable medical liability insurance market decreased premium rates based on competitive concerns. Specifically, rates of reinsurance, required for risk management for smaller insurance companies, were comparatively low, prompting new insurance companies to enter the market (see Ref. 47, p. 32). New competition encouraged existing insurance companies to compete for market share, and insurers often lowered their premiums beyond actuarially sound levels to maintain their market share (see Ref. 47, p. 31). This led to the increasing practice of underreserving by medical liability insurers, which insurance rater Weiss Ratings noted as one cause of the crisis of the early 2000s.[63] Consumer advocates argue that, in the face of unsound actuarial practices that encourage profitability in the short term, tort reforms intended to reduce jury verdicts are an ineffective means to reform these behaviors, and because tort reform measures will not impact insurer behavior concerning reserving and premium rate setting, these measures serve not to promote the laudable goal of reducing medical errors, but instead hinder a victim's ability to recover from these errors.[62] Their statements are buttressed by Bob White, the former president of First Professionals Insurance Company (which was acquired by The Doctors Company in 2011[64]), who stated, "No responsible insurer can cut its rates after a [medical malpractice tort reform] bill passes."[65]

Concerns about insurer behavior may stem from one aspect unique to the medical liability insurance market—medical malpractice insurance has a long "tail," meaning that there is a typically a significant *time lag* between a malpractice act resulting in a cause of action and the liability exposure for damage awards to plaintiffs. For the over 90,000 closed medical malpractice claims between 2004 and 2013, an average of 1.7 years passed from the time that an incident occurred until the claim was *reported to the insurer*, and another 2.7 years passed before the average claim was *closed* (see Ref. 39, Exhibit 4.2). Because of this delay (an average of 4.4 years), insurance companies that underreserve their risk pools at one point in time may then lack sufficient funds to pay claims when the end of the malpractice tail is reached, forcing them to raise premiums.

11.5.1.3 Other Approaches to Controlling Premiums: The Debate on Physician Self-Regulation

Several other solutions for controlling medical malpractice premiums have been proposed, focusing primarily on the *processes* in which medicine is practiced. Advocates such as Public Citizen recommend reforming the peer-review process so that it effectively reprimands, sanctions, or removes those physicians who account for a significant number of medical malpractice claims.[66] Another proposed "solution" is for physicians and payors who provide reimbursement (based in part on the costs of providing those services) to simply accept that malpractice premium costs are subject to cyclical variation and that the lower premiums of the 1990s and the early portion of the 2010s represent a break from this cycle due to prosperous markets.

11.6 TORT REFORM SOLUTIONS ACROSS THE UNITED STATES

11.6.1 Private Action: Changes in Insurance Practices

As described in Section 11.4.3, the medical malpractice insurance market tends to operate on a cycle varying among stages of competitive entry by insurance plans; insurers lowering prices to increase market share by gaining more insureds; insurers who cannot compete with these tactics dropping out of the market; premium rates increasing; and eventually, a new demand for competitive entry beginning again (see Ref. 18, pp. 506–513). In 1997, insurers indicated a resurgence of the competitive tactics portion of the cycle, noting that many companies were gaining market share at the expense of good underwriting, In the August 1997 issue of the Medical Liability Monitor's *Annual Rate Survey*, an anonymous insurer stated, "Pricing is absurd in some situations and commercial carriers are exhibiting no underwriting discipline."[67] However, the difference between this cycle in theory and the malpractice insurance market between 1996 and 1999* was the insurance industry's diminishing reserves. By 1999, many insurers in the medical liability industry noted that companies were still managing to cut rates even though there were slight indications of an impending market hardening.[68]

The aggressive competitiveness to attract market shares through risky underwriting techniques put many insurance plans in a difficult situation, as it negatively impacted their loss ratios and reserve funds. Many plans began investing their reserve funds in high-risk stock investments, instead of in the normal low-risk bonds market, to increase their returns, improve profits, and stabilize loss ratios. While this decision helped to delay the predicted approach of rate hikes, the timing of the 2001 market recession decreased the value of high-risk investments and resulted in rapid, sweeping price increases across the board, ranging between increases of 10% and 80%.† Physicians who were upset by what they saw as irresponsible and reckless underwriting practices began turning to other means of mitigating their risk and the risks to the market. Many physicians vowed not to do business with those participating in these techniques, and some even began considering self-insuring options. Others began self-regulating‡ or looking to tort reform§ to help limit their risk.

---

* See the first shaded portion of Figure 11.2.

† See Figure 11.2; see Ref. 69.

‡ See Section 11.6.4.2.

§ See Section 11.6.3.

These conflicting approaches that were taken to address the increase in malpractice premiums in the early 2000s resulted in a patchwork of state political and legal actions meant to limit problems such as preventable medical errors and/or large jury verdicts. While actions taken by the public and its political representatives addressed certain issues at the heart of this malpractice crisis, i.e., excessive verdicts and the validation of expert witness testimony, actions taken in response to the crisis of the early 2000s were not uniform and did not effectively decrease or eliminate medical errors nationally. Additionally, these actions did nothing to control the private practices of the insurance companies. As a result, medical liability insurers, doctors, and patients were left to grapple with the effects of patchwork solutions; this patchwork reconciliation continues to date.

11.6.2 Federal Tort Reform Measures

Though medical malpractice law has traditionally been regulated at the state level, the federal government has taken an interest in tort reform. A 2002 U.S. Department of Health and Human Services (HHS) report alleged that the legal system was to blame for rising medical malpractice premiums over the past two decades, citing California's noneconomic damage caps as a model for national tort reform.[70] While there have been efforts to implement federal tort reform, a federal cap on damages has yet to be signed into law. The most recent effort to cap damages at the federal level, the *Help Efficient, Accessible, Low-Cost, Timely Healthcare (HEALTH) Act of 2009*, was introduced before the U.S. House of Representatives in February 2009.[71] This bill was a new attempt to pass a federal cap on noneconomic damages in medical malpractice suits, which has been a continuing congressional goal since the same bill was first introduced in the House in 2002.[71] Similar bills have repeatedly passed in the House; however, no version of the bill has been passed in the Senate.[72]

Proponents of tort reform have historically pushed for caps on punitive damage awards (see Refs. 73 and 74 [p. 2]). However, it has been widely proposed that more viable reform proposals may include shifting tribunals (e.g., from judicial to administrative panels) and/or the creation of federal safe harbors for physicians who practice in accordance with credible comparative-effectiveness research (see Ref. 74, p. 3). Additionally, insurance companies are experimenting with disclosure and offer programs, in which providers offer compensation to patients immediately upon disclosure of a negative outcome, reducing the number of malpractice lawsuits (see Ref. 74, p. 3).

11.6.3 State Tort Reform Measures

States have historically sought to resolve the tort reform crisis by enacting a *cap* on payments for noneconomic damages, including payments for *pain and suffering*, *loss of consortium*, and *emotional distress*. In 1975, California first modeled this approach by passing the *Medical Injury Compensation Reform Act* (MICRA), which enacted a cap of $250,000 for awards based on noneconomic damages.* After the passage of MICRA, other states followed California's lead in enacting similar legislation. By 2002, over 30 states had active legislation that capped noneconomic damages in medical malpractice cases; generally, these caps ranged from $250,000 to $500,000, with some states capping noneconomic damages at $1 million.[76] Additional states enacted caps in 2003 at the height of the crisis, reflecting the continued

* California Civil Code § 3333.2 (West 1975); see also Ref. 75.

belief of tort reform advocates that noneconomic damage caps can limit the increase of medical costs and liability insurance premiums.* As discussed in Section 11.7.1.1, courts have attacked the validity of many of these statutes over the past 15 years. In addition to noneconomic damage caps, by 2002, 20 states had passed limits on the amount of punitive damages an injured party could receive in a medical malpractice case.[76] Similar to the rationale for capping noneconomic damages, states that passed laws creating punitive damage caps and other limitations sought to limit the "prospect of receiving a big 'bonus'" that may prolong cases that would otherwise be settled.[61]

In addition to enacting statutes that cap noneconomic damages, in 2002, 49 states had limited malpractice suits by granting immunity against malpractice to a limited group of physicians and institutional providers who provide emergency aid or care.† These statutes, called *Good Samaritan laws*, work to "protect health care professionals who render emergency aid" and usually apply to medical care given at the scene of the accident.[77] While these statutes generally serve the same purpose of limiting liability when providing medical care in emergencies, each statute differs in the amount of medical training required for a person to gain immunity under these statutes.[79]

As discussed in Section 11.5.1.1, proponents of tort reform in the early 2000s asserted that too many plaintiffs filed frivolous lawsuits in medical malpractice cases. To combat this issue, over 30 states passed statutes regarding the standards of expert witnesses utilized by a party in a medical malpractice case.[76] The various state requirements ranged from mandating a plaintiff's expert witness to practice in the same medical specialty as the accused defendant physician to requiring a physician to certify the validity of a medical malpractice complaint as a prerequisite to filing a complaint in court.[76]

Other methods that have been proposed to limit the financial risk of insurers have included the following:

1. Establishing statutes of limitations on claims made by plaintiffs[80]
2. Enabling or enhancing the ability of defendants to countersue claimants who file frivolous lawsuits[81]
3. Implementing compensation programs outside of the courts to handle malpractice cases[82]
4. Developing solutions in the health-care delivery process, including building rapport with patients, reducing medical errors, and establishing honesty policies for full disclosure of errors[83]

11.6.4 Physician Self-Regulation and Patient Safety

As tort reform advocates sought to impose statutory reforms meant to limit the remedies and damages available to plaintiffs in medical malpractice cases, patient safety advocates worked to address a related problem—flaws in the *process* of providing and regulating medical care to patients. Motivated in part by the 2000 IOM report (discussed in Section 11.2), the "patient safety" movement sought to reduce medical malpractice cases with a forward-thinking approach—eliminate medical errors by

* 2003 Florida Laws 2003-416; 2003 Idaho Session Laws H.B. 92.

† See Ref. 77. Currently, all 50 states and the District of Columbia have some form of a *Good Samaritan Law* (see also Ref. 78).

health-care professionals in the provision of medical care. Although payments for medical malpractice litigation have decreased in recent years, which signifies changes in the adjudication of medical malpractice cases (see Section 11.5.1.1), wholesale changes in health-care delivery processes that reduce medical errors continue to be slow. As discussed below, patient safety advocates point to state licensing boards, the hospital peer-review process, and consumer access to physician discipline data as areas of physician regulation in need of improvement.

11.6.4.1 Process of State Licensing of Physicians

Every state and the District of Columbia require the licensure of all *allopathic* (MD) and *osteopathic* (DO) physicians.[84] Although the specific criteria for licensure vary by state, each state requires candidates to submit proof of completion of the requisite number of years of *graduate medical education* and passage of examinations verifying that "the physician is ready and able to practice competently and safely in an independent setting" (see Refs. 3 [pp. 449–450] and 84).

Additionally, a physician applying for licensure is typically required to have "good moral character," absent his/her involvement in illegal activities.[85] Most physicians satisfy the exam requirement by submitting proof of their successful completion of the *United States Medical Licensing Examination* (USMLE) or the *Comprehensive Osteopathic Medical Licensing Examination* (COMLEX-USA) to the licensure board.[86,87] However, as some practicing physicians may have been licensed under a previously administered exam, certain state licensing boards may consider a combination of other examinations sufficient to meet licensure requirements, so long as those exams were completed prior to 2000 (see Refs. 3 [p. 450] and 86).

The licensure of physicians is governed by a state medical board, the "primary responsibility" of which, according to the Federation of State Medical Boards, is to "protect consumers of health care by ensuring that all physicians…are properly licensed and comply with various laws and regulations pertaining to the practice of medicine."[88] To accomplish this goal, state legislatures have delegated certain powers to the state's medical board, including the power to grant, suspend, and revoke licenses; conduct investigations into complaints against physicians; and release guidelines related to best medical practices.[88] State medical boards have traditionally consisted solely of physicians; however, there has recently been an increase in the number of nonphysician board members on state medical boards (see Refs. 88 and 89 [p. 291]).

Over the last 50 years, state medical boards have faced intense scrutiny regarding their commitment to disciplining physicians based on quality concerns (see Refs. 89 [p. 287, n. 7] and 90). In 1960, the AMA heard "sobering" facts from the Federation of State Medical Boards that "much confusion over the definitions and objectives exists," related to state medical board enforcement of medical standards.[91] From 1963 to 1967, 0.06% of all physicians were subject to discipline, while in 1981, 0.14% of all physicians were subject to discipline, due in large part to the problems identified by the AMA (see Ref. 92, p. 66). Although the rate of physician discipline rose eightfold by the mid-1990s, to date, there are continuing concerns regarding state medical board enforcement of quality standards. A March 2011 report by advocacy group Public Citizen found that over 55% of physicians who faced clinical privilege disciplines by hospitals from 1990 to 2009 did not have a corresponding action from a state medical board.[93] Additionally, in 2011, state medical boards imposed 3.06 "serious disciplinary actions" (e.g., revocations, surrenders, suspensions, and probations of medical licenses) per 1000 physicians, an increase from the 2010 rate of 2.97 per 1000 but a decrease from the 2004 rate of 3.72 per 1000.[94] Numerous reasons have been offered to explain the disparity in quality enforcement by state medical boards, the most prominent being that physicians are loath to report fellow physicians for major disciplinary actions such as licensure revocation.[95] Other reasons include a focus by state medical boards on "character-related misconduct" over clinical quality standards (see Ref. 89, p. 287), as well as a lack of resources to investigate and enforce quality standards, which forces state medical boards to rely on physicians and hospitals to "police" themselves (see Refs. 91 and 92 [p. 90]).

11.6.4.2 Self-Regulation

Although critics have argued that physicians tend not to punish other physicians, physicians and other health-care providers have active mechanisms to monitor the quality of a physician's medical care, most notably the peer-review process in hospitals. For hospitals accredited by the Joint Commission, the hospital credentialing body used by CMS, "it is the hospital medical staff's obligation to bear 'the overall responsibility for the quality of the professional services provided by individuals with clinical privileges'."[96] Hospitals typically meet this responsibility through *peer review*, a term to describe the process by which physicians review and evaluate the performance of another physician on that hospital's medical staff (see Ref. 97, pp. 1189–1190). Each hospital's medical staff bylaws determine the specific process for review, and each physician receiving privileges at a particular hospital is required (as part of its conditions of privileges or employment contract), absent extraordinary circumstances, to follow the medical staff bylaws as an enforceable contract (see Ref. 97, p. 1191). Hospitals can suspend, limit, or revoke a physician's privileges through the peer-review process, among other responses (see Ref. 97, pp. 1190–1191). Because of this ability, hospitals commonly utilize the peer-review process as a risk-management tool to "improve quality and patient safety by learning from past performance, errors, and near misses."[98] As of 2009, over 10,672 of the approximately 970,000 U.S. physicians—approximately 1 in 100 physicians—had "one or more clinical privilege actions" listed in the National Practitioner Data Bank (NPDB).[93] However, many physicians fear that adverse actions in the peer-review process may negatively affect their practices—through licensure restrictions, hospital privileging in the future, or health plan participation—because adverse actions must be submitted to the NPDB, and this information can be accessed by other hospitals and insurance companies.[98] This fear, coupled with the allegation that hospitals do not want to sanction physicians to prevent harm to their own reputations,[99] has, rightly or wrongly, brought the validity of the peer-review process under scrutiny.[98]

In addition to the peer-review process, provider organizations police physicians who provide expert witness testimony in a medical malpractice case. The AMA has endorsed expert witness disciplinary programs, and several professional physician specialty associations, e.g., the American Association of Neurological Surgeons (AANS), instituted programs to discipline their member physicians who do not provide "truthful, scientifically correct and appropriate" expert witness testimony in medical malpractice cases.[100,101] Since the Seventh Circuit Court of Appeals holding that the AANS may continue its expert witness disciplinary program, other professional organizations have moved forward to develop similar programs.* Noting that programs that self-regulate the testimony of expert witnesses

* Austin v. American Association of Neurological Surgeons, 253 F.3d 967 (United States 7th Circuit 2001).

support the efforts of judges to allow only admissible evidence, thereby "rather further[ing] than imped[ing] the cause of justice," the Seventh Circuit upheld a neurosurgeon's 6-month suspension by the AANS for false testimony in a neurosurgery case.* Although the Seventh Circuit issued its opinion in 2001, professional associations and courts are still grappling with issues facing the self-regulation of medical expert witnesses. For example, in 2014, a Maryland court upheld a trial court's decision to bar testimony of a pharmacist in an informed-consent case against a physician.† The court held that a pharmacist is not "per se unqualified to testify in an informed consent action when a physician has been sued" and also held that the pharmacist was unqualified to render an expert opinion on the likelihood that a medication's side effects would occur, a central issue in the case.‡

11.6.4.3 Public Access to Physician Data on Quality

The public has limited access to information regarding the quality of medicine practiced by physicians both inside and outside the hospital setting. Over the last decade, state medical boards have improved public access to its licensure actions against physicians by posting disciplinary actions on state websites, although inconsistencies and fees among various reporting organizations hinder full access to these databases. Currently, the Federation of State Medical Boards provides public access to DocInfo, a searchable database on all actions handed down by state medical boards across the country. Although there is a nominal fee to request a report on DocInfo,[102] a search of the database will provide the following information:

1. Physician disciplinary sanctions
2. Medical school name, year of graduation, and degree earned
3. Licensure history, including state name, date of license issue, and license number
4. Medical specialty, as reported by the *American Board of Medical Specialties* (ABMS)
5. City, state, and zip code of practice[102]

In addition to utilizing DocInfo, members of the public can examine the licensure status of a physician through their state's medical board website, although the level of access, search formats, and time frames of listed actions differ across the states.§

Consumers also lack access to hospital actions regarding a physician's clinical privileges. As part of the *Health Care Quality Improvement Act of 1986*, Congress established the NPDB to improve the availability of information obtained during the peer-review process.¶ The HHS is responsible for overseeing the NPDB system and requires state medical and dental licensing boards to report disciplinary action taken against a licensed professional

* Austin v. American Association of Neurological Surgeons, 253 F.3d 967, 972 (United States 7th Circuit 2001).

† Shannon v. Fusco, 438 Md. 24 (Maryland 2014).

‡ Shannon v. Fusco, 438 Md. 24 (Maryland 2014), p. 54.

§ In Missouri, the State Board of Healing Arts, which licenses physicians to practice in Missouri, publishes an updated list of all disciplinary actions taken by the board against a physician. This list includes the licensee's information, the board action, facts triggering board action, and the effective date of the board's action. Moreover, the board also provides a searchable database of its licensees (see Ref. 103).

¶ See Ref. 99; "Health Care Quality Improvement Act of 1986," 42 U.S.C. Section 11111 et seq. (2006).

in regard to his/her professional competence and professional conduct.* Hospitals are also required to periodically check the database for the status of each member of their medical staff and report adverse actions against a physician's privileges to the NPDB.† The general public does not currently have access to this data bank.‡

11.7 ENVIRONMENT FOR TORT REFORM

11.7.1 Political Responses

Even with the soft market for medical liability insurance and the continued profitability of medical liability insurers, states and physician advocates continue to press for reductions in malpractice litigation volume. While legislative, lobbying, and industry tactics have seemingly evolved since the height of the crisis in the early 2000s, much of the nonuniformity surrounding tort reform nationally remains in effect to date. Further, as malpractice suits moved through state court systems over the last 10 to 15 years, state supreme courts began to more closely scrutinize the constitutionality of the damage caps and, at times, invalidate these caps. What is left today is the continued patchwork of laws that increases the unpredictability of underwriting in malpractice liability policies, as well as the ability of the legal system to provide adequate protection to a growing number of persons with access to health insurance.

11.7.1.1 Legislative Action

The number of states with active caps on noneconomic and/or punitive damages has decreased slightly over the past 15 years. From 2002 to 2013, the number of states with active caps specifically for noneconomic damages decreased slightly from 30 to 27,[104] as a result of state supreme courts invalidating such caps.§ Similarly, within the same time frame, the number of states with active caps specifically targeted at punitive damages decreased from 20 to 19.[105] Because of this decrease, legislators—as pressed by physi-

* "Health Care Quality Improvement Act of 1986," 42 USC Section 11132-33, 11151 (2006).

† "Health Care Quality Improvement Act of 1986," 42 USC Section 11133(a) (2006).

‡ "Health Care Quality Improvement Act of 1986," 42 USC Section 11134-35 (2006).

§ In Alabama, Florida, Georgia, Illinois, Louisiana, New Hampshire, Oregon, and Washington, state supreme courts have invalidated relevant state statutes that imposed caps on noneconomic damages. For example, see McCall v. U.S., No. SC11-1148 (Fla. Mar. 13, 2014).

cian organizations and tort reform advocates—have passed new types of legislation meant to reduce medical malpractice litigation.[56] Prominent among new forms of tort reform legislation include the "apology law," which has been adopted in some form by nearly two-thirds of the states.[106] Generally, an apology law "prohibit[s] the use of a physician's apology as an admission of fault" when a court is adjudicating a medical malpractice case (see Ref. 107, p. 302). To many physicians, apology laws are necessary to promote the full and honest disclosure of medical errors to patients, which would support healing within the trust-based patient–physician relationship.[108] Moreover, physicians argue that apology laws are necessary because they directly counteract a common theme in the law of evidence—statements against one's own interest are able to be used as evidence against the asserting party in a courtroom.* However, consumer advocates argue (and physicians acknowledge) that apology laws have also reduced medical malpractice litigation by "mitigat[ing] the results of an unanticipated or poor medical outcome" (see Ref. 107, p. 302), specifically by diffusing the anger that often motivates medical malpractice lawsuits (see Ref. 107, p. 303), as well as attempting to restore a patient's wounded sense of dignity.[108] This reduction in the number of lawsuits may have positive financial effects on medical liability insurers, potentially leading some insurers and hospitals in the medical liability market to encourage their insured physicians to apologize to patients for their medical errors.[109,110]

11.7.1.2 Ballot Initiatives

In 2014, consumer advocates employed a new tactic in the tort reform arena, ballot measures, and advocates such as Consumer Watchdog have targeted the first noneconomic damage cap passed in the United States—California's MICRA. Unlike some state laws, MICRA, discussed in Section 11.6.2, imposed a $250,000 cap on noneconomic damages *without* an inflation adjustment, which has kept medical malpractice payouts constant since 1975 and may have contributed to lower malpractice premium rates in California than in other high-population states, including New York and Florida (see Refs. 75 and 111 [pp. 8–10, 12–13, 29–30]). Consumer advocates pushed the measure to repeal the law, noting that the nonadjusted cap had an alternative effect of limiting incentives that make physicians conscious of safety concerns.[75] Ultimately, in November 2014, California voters rejected the ballot initiative; this campaign resulted in more than $60 million in contributions to stakeholders for and against the measure.[75]

11.7.2 Relationship between Medical Liability Insurance and Health-Care Industry Consolidation

There has been a noticeable shift in the competitive landscape for physicians since the most recent medical liability insurance "bubble" in the early 2000s, largely due to increased provider consolidation. Originally, many physicians operated as independent competitors, perhaps allied only with the hospital(s) to which they referred patients.[112] The mid-1990s experienced a frenzy of physician practice acquisitions by hospitals, health systems, and large integrated groups as *managed care organizations* and *health maintenance organizations* (HMOs) boomed. With the collapse of the managed care–driven integration efforts of that era, buyers experienced significant financial losses on their practice acquisitions, and many integrated systems divested physician practices.[113,114]

* See Federal Rule of Evidence 804(b)(3).

Although the managed care boom was short-lived, consolidation efforts have rekindled in recent years. Providers are turning to alignment, integration, and cooperation as key strategies to create high-performing, high-quality, and high-efficiency organizations[115] in the face of various legislative initiatives, including the PPACA and its creation of *accountable care organizations* (ACOs); changing reimbursement patterns due to the uncertain future of the *sustainable growth rate* (SGR) formula; changing physician demographics and demands (i.e., a greater number of older physicians and increased importance of work/life balance for physicians); and the implementation of new infrastructure systems such as the 10th revision of the *International Statistical Classification of Diseases and Related Health Problems* (ICD-10) and *electronic health record* (EHR) systems (see Ref. 3, pp. 154–155, 523). These initiatives may be contributing to the decrease in the number of self-employed physicians. A 2004 Medical Group Management Association (MGMA) study found that over half of physicians worked in physician practices in 2003.[116] The 2014 version of the same study found that the share of physicians employed in physician practices had fallen to less than one-third of the physician population by 2013.[117] Conversely, over the same time period, the share of physicians employed by hospitals more than doubled.[116,117] This trend in physician employment is displayed in Figure 11.3.

Consolidation among health-care providers (either through physician employment or mergers and joint ventures between health-care enterprises) has begun to impact the medical liability insurance market. Since the passage of the PPACA in 2010, medical liability insurers have openly stated their concerns regarding "hospitals purchasing [physician] practices and rolling the physicians' exposure [to malpractice liability] into their self-insureds programs" (see Ref. 118, p. 5). Their concerns reflect the long-standing benefits practices of health systems and other health-care providers. In 1996, 97% of health-care organizations (representing over 20,000 physicians) surveyed by the Hay Group provided full coverage of malpractice insurance premiums to their physicians.[119] In 2013, only 81% of health-care organizations responding to a 2013 survey by Sullivan, Cotter, and Associates provided coverage of malpractice insurance premiums, although 90% of these organizations provided full coverage for the premiums.[120] This common benefit practice, coupled with increasing provider consolidation, continues to concern medical liability insurers, who worry that hospitals and health systems, as their former clients, will now become their competition (see Ref. 111, p. 6). These reservations correlate with the additional concern that medical liability insurers, in order to keep clients and other business, are dropping premium rates, even absent a firm actuarial basis for doing so (see Ref. 111, p. 6). Their concerns are supported by declines in the average national premium rates since 2007, as discussed in Section 11.5, further calling into question whether the market is gearing up for the next malpractice bubble and the continuation of the premium pricing cycle in the medical liability industry.

	A	B	C
	Year	**2003**	**2013**
1	Physician practice	65.67%	32.45%
2	Hospital	23.95%	49.40%
3	Other	10.38%	18.15%

FIGURE 11.3 Physician employment by site.

When the next malpractice bubble occurs, health systems may act as larger players than physicians in what could be an energized debate on tort reform. Due to the likely increase in self-insurance by hospitals and the growing number of employee physicians, the success of tort reform legislation in the future may increasingly impact the bottom lines of hospitals and their ability to pay claim awards. Yet unlike medical liability insurers, health systems will likely be on the front lines to address one of the main causes of preventable adverse events that give rise to malpractice errors in the *process* of receiving or providing care (see Ref. 20, p. 30). The continued implementation of EHR systems, including EHR implementation in accordance with the *Health Information Technology for Economic and Clinical Health (HITECH) Act of 2009*, and administrative rules regarding the requirement for the "meaningful use" of EHR systems will likely increase the ability of providers to have accurate and timely information during patient care, a central recommendation of the 2000 IOM report (see Ref. 20, p. 177). However, not all is rosy in a tort reform debate increasingly involving health systems. If and when the renewed tort reform debate occurs, the priorities of health systems—either to reduce the processes and clinical incompetence associated with medical errors or to lobby for lower malpractice suit costs—may significantly contribute to the politics of tort reform. Considering the uncertainty surrounding physician self-regulation, discussed in Section 11.6.3, continued conflict and patchwork solutions are plausible.

11.7.3 PPACA's Impact on Medical Liability Insurance

Aside from differences in insurer behavior, malpractice lawsuit rates, and political responses at the state level, the PPACA may also have an impact on the medical liability insurance market. Following several months of partisan controversy and political debate during President Obama's first term, Congress passed the PPACA in March 2010.* While not achieving a universal coverage insurance program or a single-payor system, the 2010 health-care reform legislation marked the beginning of a new era in health-care reform, resulting in a paradigm change in the way health-care services are delivered and paid for in the United States. Some of the PPACA's initiatives have already had significant impact upon many aspects of the health-care delivery system, including (1) increased regulatory scrutiny aimed at combating fraud and abuse and antitrust violations; (2) health plan regulation; (3) addressing physician shortages; (4) access to and quality of care initiatives; and (5) increased attention to public health and wellness activities, among others.[121]

In contrast, the PPACA's impact on the medical liability insurance market, and the medical malpractice system, is relatively unknown. The Medical Liability Monitor's 2010 *Annual Rate Survey* noted that 41% of medical liability insurers did not believe that the PPACA would impact medical liability insurance markets (see Ref. 118, p. 4); however, by 2011, as stated above, this attitude had changed to reflect increasing concerns about provider consolidation and self-insurance for professional liability by providers.[122] These concerns continue to reflect the thinking of medical liability insurers, in part, because there have been few, if any, answers to alleviate their concerns and measure the PPACA's impact on the incidence and cost of medical malpractice.

* "Patient Protection and Affordable Care Act," Public Law 111-148, 124 Stat. 119 (March 23, 2010); "Health Care and Education Reconciliation Act," Public Law 111-152, 124 Stat. 1029 (March 25, 2010).

Some of the medical liability insurer concerns regarding the PPACA's impact stem from the reality that only one of the two sections of the PPACA directly relating to medical liability insurance and the current medical malpractice system have been implemented. Section 6801 of the PPACA simply provides a policy statement regarding medical malpractice, stating that the U.S. Senate believes that "health care reform presents an opportunity to address issues related to medical malpractice and medical liability insurance," and encourages Congress, as a whole, to develop demonstration programs with the goal of discovering alternatives to the current civil litigation system for medical malpractice.* Additionally, section 10607 of the PPACA authorizes HHS to award grants to states "for the development, implementation, and evaluation of alternatives to current tort litigation" for medical malpractice claims.† This section allows HHS to make $50 million available for these demonstration projects subject to congressional approval.‡ To date, neither Congress nor the president has requested funding for these projects.[123]

Even without these direct impacts, the medical malpractice system may still face changes as a result of the PPACA. First, as providers consolidate with larger health systems, medical liability insurers fear that the medical liability insurance market "will shrink as their former customers become their competitors."[122] From 2011 to 2014, medical liability insurers consistently noted to the Medical Liability Monitor that hospital or ACO acquisitions of physician practices act as "the biggest threat to their market share" because of the entity's ability to better absorb the risk related to malpractice liability.[124,125] In theory, this ability to absorb medical professional liability risk will allow higher rates of self-insurance, which can affect the rates of straight indemnity insurers. Second, the number of malpractice claims is expected to increase as more individuals gain health insurance coverage as a result of PPACA enactments. A 2007 *Journal of the American Medical Association* study concluded that insured persons who suffer a chronic condition receive higher-quality and increased care compared to noninsured persons, reinforcing earlier studies suggesting that insured persons receive more care than uninsured persons.[126] Building on this premise, a RAND report on the PPACA and liability insurance relationships estimated that with the expected influx of newly insured individuals, particularly in states expanding Medicaid, more physician–patient encounters will increase the volume of overall medical errors, leading to an increase in medical malpractice lawsuits (see Ref. 127, p. 30). Consequently, the RAND report estimates that the number of liability payments in medical malpractice actions will increase by 3.4% between pre-PPACA insurance plan enrollment and enrollment post-PPACA implementation (see Ref. 127, p. 30).

Additionally, the RAND report argues that, due to an increase in insurance plan enrollment, medical malpractice payments per claim will actually *decrease* in states adopting limitations to the *collateral source rule*. Under the collateral source rule, the damage awards for injured parties do not take into account payments previously received from other sources; consequently, the damage award includes the value of funds collected by another source (e.g., insurance) while allowing the injured party to keep the benefits of that previous value received (see Ref. 127, p. 18). In the medical malpractice context, plaintiffs in states adopting the collateral source rule can collect from the physician (or his/her medical liability insurer) as well as keep the benefits of health care reimbursed by their own health

* "Patient Protection and Affordable Care Act," Public Law 111-148, 124 Stat. 804 (March 23, 2010).
† "Patient Protection and Affordable Care Act," Public Law 111-148, 124 Stat. 1009 (March 23, 2010).
‡ "Patient Protection and Affordable Care Act," Public Law 111-148, 124 Stat. 1014 (March 23, 2010).

insurer. However, some states limit the application of the collateral source rule in medical malpractice cases where the plaintiff's health insurance already paid for care resulting from the negligent actions of the physician, thereby preventing the plaintiff from receiving this double windfall. As insurance rates rise, RAND estimates that payouts per claim will decrease by 0.6% nationally (see Ref. 127, p. 18). Considering the three effects together, RAND projects that total liability claim costs will increase by 2.8% nationally by 2016 as a result of the PPACA (see Ref. 127, p. 37).

Conversely, other health-care industry commentators argue that the PPACA's expansion of coverage to previously uninsured individuals, as well as quality-of-care initiatives, will actually *decrease* malpractice costs by reducing the number of adverse events suffered by patients (see Ref. 127, pp. 40–41). In a 2010 editorial in the *Journal of Law, Medicine, and Ethics*, Mark A. Rothstein, the director of the Institute for Bioethics, Health Policy, & Law at the University of Louisville, Louis D. Brandeis School of Law, argued that quality and infrastructure initiatives such as increased EHR usage, expansion of outcomes research and use of evidence-based medical standards, and better care coordination will limit the number of adverse events that provide the basis for a medical malpractice claim.[128] Further, Rothstein posited that by simply being insured, "significant numbers of injured patients are likely to forego medical malpractice claims" (see Ref. 127, p. 872).

Although President Obama signed the PPACA in 2010, the effects of this landmark law on the medical malpractice market remain hazy. The current trend toward health-care consolidation, accountable care, and self-insurance mirrors similar consolidation practices in the mid-1990s, which increased competition in the medical liability insurance market and eroded proper underwriting practices. Nevertheless, other critical PPACA effects remain unknown. The impact of the expansion of health insurance coverage will likely remain unclear for the near future because new enrollees began receiving coverage through health insurance exchanges in 2014, limiting the amount of exposure to health-care interactions that could give rise to an adverse event and result in a medical malpractice suit. Additionally, the average length of litigation surrounding preventable adverse events lasts 43.1 months from the date of the incident to the date of resolution,[129] which limits medical liability insurers from realizing the full costs of a claim and the aggregate of claims in its risk pool. Assuming that increased enrollment does not affect the average length of medical malpractice litigation,* the average newly insured person who suffered a preventable adverse event in July 2014 will not resolve his/her claim until March 2018. With this lag time of almost 4 years between adverse events and claims, it is likely that the full impact of the PPACA on the medical malpractice market and medical liability insurance premiums will not be fully known until the next decade.

11.8 CONCLUSION

In 2005, we posited in the book *Insurance and Risk Management Strategies for Physicians and Advisors* that "it is the rise in malpractice premiums that is the gravamen of the crisis" regarding medical malpractice.[130] The statement focused on the impact of the actions by medical liability insurers in setting rates for liability policies. The other chapters in that book noted many complex, if not widely discussed, causes of the crisis of the early 2000s,

* This assumption is faulty, as it is unknown at this point whether or not claims will increase, whether insurers will or will not enter the market, and whether malpractice caseloads will increase due to the PPACA.

including the widespread underreserving practices in the late 1990s, as well as the decrease in premiums to maintain market share in an era of increasing provider consolidation, and observed that "when so many different forces come together at once, it is not enough to remove any one factor and to leave the crisis, or storm, largely intact."[131]

With this in mind today, many of the same seeds that spawned the crisis of the early 2000s are reappearing in the market again, perhaps exacerbated by the dynamic volatility of the post-PPACA health-care arena. Increased competition due to rising numbers of self-insureds may have lowered malpractice premium rates beyond actuarially sound levels, in turn forcing medical liability insurers to release reserves to maintain profitability. Stock indexes are at all-time highs, just as they were in the late 1990s. Medical errors are still prevalent in U.S. medicine at a time when more than 8 million newly insured individuals will begin to utilize their new health insurance policies. Together, it is plausible that these factors will set in motion another malpractice bubble that, without proper action, could repeat the uncertain history of the early 2000s for physicians and their patients.

The U.S. health-care delivery system appears to be at a crossroads. The accusatory discord of the last tort reform debate did not lead to a better understanding of the underlying issues, nor a proactive improvement in the *processes* of providing medical care and adjudicating tort disputes. Given the current dynamic of the volatile U.S. health-care industry environment, there may never be a more propitious time for legislators, health-care industry leaders, physicians and other providers, patient representatives, or the malpractice bar to put in place a process to openly and rationally examine issues related to the medical malpractice system and tort reform issues. Lacking this discourse, we may well deserve the admonition in Henry Kissinger's comment, "It is not often that nations learn from the past, even rarer that they draw the correct conclusions from it."

11.9 COLLABORATE

Discuss this chapter online with others at http://www.medicalexecutivepost.com.

ACKNOWLEDGMENT

REFERENCES

1. U.S. Congress. Senate Committee on Government Operations, Subcommittee on Executive Reorganization, *Medical Malpractice: The Patient Versus The Physician*, 91st Cong., 1st Session, Washington, DC: GPO, 1969, pp. 1–2.
2. B. Webel, *CRS Report for Congress: Medical Malpractice Insurance: An Economic Introduction and Review of Historical Experience*, Congressional Research Service, The Library of Congress, January 19, 2005, pp. CRS-7–CRS-8.
3. R.J. Cimasi, *Healthcare Valuation: The Four Pillars of Healthcare Value*, Volume 1, Hoboken, NJ: John Wiley & Sons, 2014.
4. American Medical Student Association, "Before There Was Flexner," 2014, http://www.amsa.org/AMSA/Homepage/MemberCenter/Premeds/edRx/Before.aspx (accessed 01/07/15).
5. K.M. Ludmerer, *Time to Heal: American Medical Education from the Turn of the Century to the Era of Managed Care*, New York: Oxford University Press, 1999.

6. A. Flexner, *The Flexner Report on Medical Education in the United States and Canada in 1910*, Bethesda, MD: Science and Health Publications, Inc, 1910.
7. S.A. Kirk and W.J. Reid, *Science and Social Work: A Critical Appraisal*, New York: Columbia University Press, 2002, Chapter 1, pp. 2–3.
8. I. Loudon, *Western Medicine: An Illustrated History*, New York: Oxford University Press, 1997, p. 58.
9. K. Hillstrom, *U.S. Health Policy and Politics: A Documentary History*, Thousand Oaks, CA: CQ Press, 2012, p. 141.
10. J.B. Roberts, *The Doctor's Duty to the State: Essays on The Public Relations of Physicians*, Chicago, IL: American Medical Association Press, 1908, p. 23.
11. C. Bridenbaugh, "Dr. Thomas Bond's Essay on the Utility of Clinical Lectures," *Journal of the History of Medicine*, Vol. II, No. 1, (Winter 1947), p. 14.
12. J.E. Harris, "How Many Doctors Are Enough?" *Health Affairs*, Vol. 5, No. 4 (1986), p. 74.
13. Graduate Medical Education National Advisory Committee, *Report of the Graduate Medical Education National Advisory Committee to the Secretary, Department of Health and Human Services—Volume VII*, Washington, DC: U.S. Government Printing Office, 1981.
14. D.R. McNutt, "GMENAC: Its Manpower Forecasting Framework," *American Journal of Public Health*, Vol. 71, No. 10 (1981), p. 1119.
15. Institute of Medicine, *Crossing the Quality Chasm: A New Health System for the 21st Century*, National Academy of Sciences, Washington, DC, 2001.
16. M. Garrouste-Orgeas et al., "Overview of Medical Errors and Adverse Events," *Annals of Intensive Care*, Vol. 2, No. 2 (2012), p. 6.
17. R.J. Cimasi, *Healthcare Valuation: The Financial Appraisal of Enterprises, Assets, and Services*, Volume 1, Hoboken, NJ: John Wiley & Sons, 2014, p. xiii.
18. B.R. Furrow, T.L. Greaney, S.H. Johnson, T.S. Jost, and R.L. Schwartz, *Health Law: Cases, Materials, and Problems*, 7th Edition, St. Paul, MN: West Publishing Company, 2013.
19. S. Becker (ed.), "Licensure of Health Care Professionals," in *Health Care Law: A Practical Guide*, 2nd Edition, New York: Matthew Bender Co., 1998, § 16.02[4], pp. 16–23.
20. Institute of Medicine, *To Err is Human: Building a Safer Health System*, National Academy of Sciences, 2000.
21. The Leapfrog Group, "Fact Sheet: Computerized Physician Order Entry," March 3, 2009.
22. The Leapfrog Group, "Leapfrog Hospital Survey Results," 2008, p. 3.
23. Office of Inspector General, "Adverse Events in Hospitals: National Incidence among Medicare Beneficiaries," November 2010.
24. D.C. Classen et al., "'Global Trigger Tool' Shows That Adverse Events in Hospitals May Be Ten Times Greater than Previously Measured," *Health Affairs*, Vol. 30, No. 4 (2011), pp. 581–589.
25. Office of Inspector General, "Adverse Events in Hospitals: Case Study of Incidence Among Medicare Beneficiaries in Two Selected Counties," December 2008, http://oig.hhs.gov/oei/reports/OEI-06-08-00220.pdf (accessed 02/17/15).
26. C.P. Landrigan et al., "Temporal Trends in Rates of Patient Harm Resulting from Medical Care," *New England Journal of Medicine*, Vol. 363, No. 22 (2010), pp. 2124–2134.
27. J.T. James, "A New, Evidence-Based Estimate of Patient Harms Associated with Hospital Care," *Journal of Patient Safety*, Vol. 9. No. 3 (2013).
28. M. Allen, "How Many Die from Medical Mistakes in U.S. Hospitals?" National Public Radio (September 20, 2013), http://www.npr.org/blogs/health/2013/09/20/224507654/howmanydiefrommedicalmistakesinushospitals (accessed 12/03/14).
29. Institute of Medicine, *Best Care at Lower Cost: The Path to Continuously Learning Health Care in America*, Washington, DC, National Academy of Sciences, 2009, p. 134.
30. U. Sarkar, A. López, J.H. Maselli, and R. Gonzales, "Adverse Drug Events in U.S. Adult Ambulatory Medical Care," *Health Services Research*, Vol. 46, No. 5 (2011), p. 1527.
31. Health Resources and Services Administration, HHS "OIG Supplemental Compliance Program Guidance for Nursing Facilities," *Federal Register*, Vol. 73, No. 190 (2008), p. 56837.

32. Agency for Healthcare Research and Quality, "Patient Safety and Quality Improvement Act of 2005," June 2008, http://archive.ahrq.gov/news/newsroom/press-releases/2008/psoact.html (accessed 03/05/15).
33. U.S. Department of Health and Human Services, "Health Information Privacy: Understanding Patient Safety Confidentiality," http://www.hhs.gov/ocr/privacy/psa/understanding/index.html (accessed 03/05/15).
34. "Patient Safety and Quality Improvement: Final Rule," *Federal Register*, Vol. 73, No. 226 (2008).
35. *Black's Law Dictionary*, 9th Edition, Eagan, MN: West Publishing Company, 2009.
36. "Justice for the Injured: Defending the Civil Justice System from the Corporate 'Tort Deform' Movement," Multinational Monitor, March 2003, pp. 23–26.
37. National Governors Association Center for Best Practices, "Addressing the Medical Malpractice Insurance Crisis," December 5, 2002, p. 5.
38. P. Hannaford-Agor and N.L. Waters, "Estimating the Cost of Civil Litigation," *Court Statistics Project, National Center for State Courts Highlights*, Vol. 20, No. 1 (2013).
39. Physician Insurers Association of America, "Closed Claim Comparative: 2014 Edition," 2014.
40. C.G. Lee and R.C. LaFountain, "Medical Malpractice Litigation in State Courts," *National Center for State Courts*, Vol. 18, No. 1 (2011).
41. J. Shepherd, "Uncovering the Silent Victims of the American Medical Liability System," *Vanderbilt Law Review*, Vol. 67, No. 151 (2014).
42. P.C. Smith and S.N. Witter, *Risk Pooling in Health Care Financing: The Implications for Health System Performance*, World Bank's Human Development Network, Washington, DC, HNP Discussion Paper, September 2004, p. 1.
43. P. Beider, *Limiting Tort Liability for Medical Malpractice*, Washington, DC, Congressional Budget Office, 2004, pp. 3–4.
44. V.B. Hedrick, "The Medical Malpractice Crisis: Bandaging Oregon's Wounded System and Protecting Physicians," *Willamette Law Review*, Vol. 363 (2007), pp. 375–376.
45. NAIC Research and Actuarial Department, National Association of Insurance Commissioners, "Glossary of Insurance Terms," 2015, http://www.naic.org/consumer_glossary.htm (accessed 01/23/15).
46. E. Nordman, D. Cermak, and K. McDaniel, *Medical Malpractice Insurance Report: A Study of Market Conditions and Potential Solutions to the Recent Crisis*, To [The NAIC's Property and Casualty (C) Committee]: National Association of Insurance Commissioners, 2004, pp. 25–26.
47. U.S. General Accounting Office, "Medical Malpractice Insurance: Multiple Factors Have Contributed to Increased Premium Rates," Washington, DC, June 2003, http://www.gao.gov/new.items/d03702.pdf (accessed 01/14/15).
48. B.R. Furrow, T.L. Greaney, S.H. Johnson, T.S. Jost, and R.L. Schwartz, *Health Law: Cases, Materials, and Problems*, 3rd Edition, St. Paul, MN: West Publishing Company, 1997, p. 310.
49. "Annual Rate Survey Issue," *Medical Liability Monitor*, Oak Park, IL: Medical Liability Monitor, 1991–2014.
50. American Trial Lawyers Association, "Fact Sheet: Medical Malpractice Fibs and Facts," http://www.atla.org/ConsumerMediaResources/Tier3/press_room/FACTS/medmal/medmalfibsfacts.aspx (accessed 10/16/03).
51. Court Statistics Project, National Center for State Courts, "Examining the Work of State Courts," National Center for State Courts, 2010, p. 26.
52. J.W. Kuzma and S.E. Bohnenblust, *Basic Statistics for the Health Sciences*, 5th Edition, New York: McGraw-Hill, 2005.
53. Towers Watson, "U.S. Tort Cost Trends: 2011 Update," January 2011, http://www.casact.org/library/studynotes/Towers-Watson-Tort-Cost-Trends.pdf (accessed 01/14/15).
54. D. Dial, Esq. et al., *Tort Excess 2005: The Necessity for Reform from a Policy, Legal and Risk Management Perspective*, Insurance Information Institute, AIG, and U.S. Chamber of Commerce, 2005, p. 7, http://www.iii.org/sites/default/files/tortexcess2005.pdf (accessed 01/14/15).

55. American Tort Reform Association, "Mission," 2011, http://www.atra.org/about/mission (accessed 01/14/15).
56. American College of Physicians, "Medical Liability Reform: Innovative Solutions for a New Health Care System," 2014, https://www.acponline.org/acp_policy/policies/medical_liability_reform_2014.pdf (accessed 01/09/15).
57. A. Ridenour, "Time to End the Asbestos Lottery," National Policy Analysis, August 2003, http://www.nationalcenter.org/NPA478.html (accessed 01/14/15).
58. The Risk Authority & Stanford University Medical Network, "2013 Medical Malpractice Trend Review," 2013, http://theriskauthority.com/wp-content/uploads/2013_Medical_Malpractice_Trend-_Review.pdf (accessed 01/14/15).
59. The Risk Authority & Stanford University Medical Network, "2014 Medical Malpractice Trend Review," 2014, p. 14, http://theriskauthority.com/wp-content/uploads/2014-Medical-Malpractice-Trend-Review.pdf (accessed 01/14/15).
60. L.F. Nadrowsk, "Malpractice Crisis Gravely Threatens Surgical Care," *General Surgery News*, Vol. 32, No. 5 (2005), http://generalsurgerynews.com/ViewArticle.aspx?d_id=66&a_id=3782 (accessed 01/21/15).
61. Insurance Information Institute, "Liability System," September 2014, http://www.iii.org/issue-update/liability-system (accessed 10/31/14).
62. T, Lincoln, "Medical Malpractice Payments Remained at Historic Low in 2013 Despite Slight Uptick," Public Citizen, October 2014, pp. 3–4, http://www.citizen.org/documents/Medical-malpractice-2013.pdf (accessed 01/16/15).
63. Weiss Ratings, Inc., "Medical Malpractice Caps: The Impact of Non-Economic Damage Caps on Physician Premiums, Claims Payout Levels, and Availability of Coverage," June 3, 2003, pp. 9–10, http://www.weissratings.com/pdf/malpractice.pdf (accessed 01/16/15).
64. The Doctors Company, "Subsidiaries of The Doctors Company," 2015, http://www.thedoctors.com/TDC/subsidiaries/index.htm (accessed 01/16/15).
65. P. Galewitz, "Underwriter Gives Doctors Dose of Reality," Palm Beach Post, January 29, 2003, p. 1A.
66. S. Oldmixon, "The Great Medical Malpractice Hoax: NPDB Data Continue to Show Medical Liability System Produces Rational Outcomes," Public Citizen, January 2007, p. 12, http://www.citizen.org/documents/NPDB%20Report_Final.pdf (accessed 01/21/15).
67. "Annual Rate Survey Issue," *Medical Liability Monitor*, Vol. 22, No. 8, Oak Park, IL: Medical Liability Monitor, August 1997, p. 2.
68. "Annual Rate Survey Issue," *Medical Liability Monitor*, Vol. 24, No. 9, Oak Park, IL: Medical Liability Monitor, August 1999, p. 3.
69. "Annual Rate Survey Issue," *Medical Liability Monitor*, Vol. 24, No. 9, Oak Park, IL: Medical Liability Monitor, August 2002, pp. I–IV.
70. Department of Health and Human Services, "Confronting the New Health Care Crisis," July 24, 2002, p. 1.
71. govtrack.us, "H.R. 4600: Help Efficient, Accessible, Low-Cost, Timely Healthcare (HEALTH) Act of 2002: Related Legislation," http://www.govtrack.us/congress/bill.xpd?bill=h107-4600&tab=related (accessed 09/08/09).
72. W.E. Encinosa and F.J. Hellinger, "Have State Caps on Malpractice Awards Increased The Supply of Physicians," *Health Affairs*, Web Exclusive (2005), p. W5-251.
73. American College of Physicians, "Beyond MICRA: New Ideas for Liability Reform," *Annals of Internal Medicine*, Vol. 122, No. 6 (1995), p. 466.
74. M.M. Mello and T.V. Brennan, "The Role of Medical Liability Reform in Federal Health Care Reform," *New England Journal of Medicine*, Vol. 361, No. 1 (2009).
75. CBS San Francisco, "Voters Turn Down Proposition 46 to Lift Medical Malpractice Cap, Require Drug Tests for Doctors," November 4, 2014, http://sanfrancisco.cbslocal.com/2014/11/04/proposition46doctorsdrugtestsresults/ (accessed 12/10/14).

76. National Conference of State Legislatures, "State Medical Liability Laws Table," October 16, 2002, http://www.ncsl.org/programs/insur/medliability.pdf (accessed 10/03/03).
77. B.R. Furrow, T.L. Greaney, S.H. Johnson, T.S. Jost, and R.L. Schwartz, *Health Law: Cases, Materials, and Problems*, 4th Edition, St. Paul, MN: West Group, 2001, p. 231.
78. E. Morris, "Liability under 'Good Samaritan' Laws," *AAOS Now*, American Academy of Orthopedic Surgeons, January 2014, http://www.aaos.org/news/aaosnow/jan14/managing3.asp (accessed 03/09/15).
79. V. Sutton, "Is There a Doctor (and a Lawyer) in the House? Why Our Good Samaritan Laws Are Doing More Harm than Good for a National Public Health Security Strategy: A Fifty-State Survey," *Journal of Health & Biomedical Law*, Vol. 6, No. 2 (2010), p. 272.
80. M.M. Mello, D.M. Studdert, and T.A. Brennan, "The New Medical Malpractice Crisis," *New England Journal of Medicine*, Vol. 348, No. 23 (2003), p. 2283.
81. *Modern Physician*, "Docs Return Fire: Countersuing in Frivolous Malpractice Cases," September 2003, p. 6.
82. P. Eisler, J. Appleby, and M. Kasindorf, "Special Report: Hype Outraces Facts in Malpractice Debate; Degree of Crisis Varies among Specialties and from State to State," *USA Today*, March 5, 2003, p. A.01.
83. M. Crane, "A New 'Malpractice Crisis'? Why Premiums Are Soaring Again," *Medical Economics Magazine*, July 9, 2001, http://medicaleconomics.modernmedicine.com/medical-economics/content/new-malpractice-crisis-why-premiums-are-soaring-again (accessed 03/05/15).
84. J.N. Thompson, "State Medical Boards: Future Challenges for Regulation and Quality Enhancement of Medical Care," *Journal of Legal Medicine*, Vol. 33, No. 9 (2012), pp. 93–114.
85. S.S. Sanbar, J. Daniel, and J.D. Gamino, "Medical Practice: Education and Licensure," in *Legal Medicine*, 6th Edition, Mosby, United States, 2004, p. 81.
86. American Medical Association, "Medical Licensure," 2014, http://www.ama-assn.org/ama/pub/education-careers/becoming-physician/medical-licensure.page (accessed 12/19/14).
87. National Board of Osteopathic Medical Examiners, "COMLEX-USA," 2014, http://www.nbome.org/exams-faq.asp (accessed 12/19/14).
88. Federation of State Medical Boards, "What is a State Medical Board?" 2014, http://www.fsmb.org/policy/what-is-a-smb-faq (accessed 12/19/14).
89. N.N. Sawicki, "Character, Competence, and the Principles of Medical Discipline," *Journal of Health Care Law & Policy*, Vol. 13, No. 1 (2010).
90. L.T. Kohn, J.M. Corrigan, and M.S. Donaldson, Institute of Medicine, *To Err is Human: Building a Safer Health System—Summary*, 2000, National Academy Press, Washington, DC, http://www.iom.edu/~/media/Files/Report%20Files/1999/To-Err-is-Human/To%20Err%20is%20Human%201999%20%20report%20brief.pdf (accessed 12/19/14).
91. "Medical Licensure Statistics for 1960," *Journal of the American Medical Association*, Vol. 176, No. 8 (1961), p. 694.
92. M.T. Law and Z.K. Hansen, "Medical Licensing Board Characteristics and Physician Discipline: An Empirical Analysis," *Journal of Health Politics, Policy and Law*, Vol. 35, No. 1 (2010).
93. A. Levine, R. Oshel, and S. Wolfe, "State Medical Boards Fail to Discipline Doctors with Hospital Actions against Them," Public Citizen, March 2011, http://www.citizen.org/documents/1937.pdf (accessed 12/19/14).
94. S.M. Wolfe, C. Williams, and A. Zaslow, "Public Citizen's Health Research Group Ranking of the Rate of State Medical Boards' Serious Disciplinary Actions, 2009–2011," Public Citizen, May 17, 2012, http://www.citizen.org/documents/2034.pdf (accessed 12/19/14).
95. W.J. Guglielmo, "Medical Boards are Too Lax, Critics Claim," MedScape, October 17, 2014, http://www.medscape.com/viewarticle/833141 (accessed 12/03/14).
96. The Joint Commission, *Comprehensive Accreditation Manual for Hospitals: The Official Handbook*, Oakbrook Terrace, IL, 1996, p. MS-2.

97. K. Van Tassel, "Hospital Peer Review Standards and Due Process: Moving from Tort Doctrine toward Contract Principles Based on Clinical Practice Guidelines," *Seton Hall Law Review*, Vol. 36 (2006).
98. S.J. Jayasankar, "Medical Peer Review and Risk Management," American Academy of Orthopedic Surgeons, October 2008, http://www.aaos.org/news/aaosnow/oct08/managing9.asp (accessed 12/22/14).
99. T.A. Brennan, "Hospital Peer Review and Clinical Privilege Actions: To Report or Not Report," *Journal of the American Medical Association*, Vol. 281, No. 4 (1999), p. 381.
100. American Medical Association, "Case Summaries by Topic—Expert Witnesses," 2014, http://www.amaassn.org/ama/pub/physicianresources/legaltopics/litigationcenter/casesummaries topic/expertwitnesses.page (accessed 12/03/14).
101. American Academy of Orthopedic Surgeons, "Standards of Professionalism—Orthopedic Expert Opinion and Testimony," May 12, 2010, http://www3.aaos.org/member/profcomp/ew testimony_May_2010.pdf (accessed 12/22/14).
102. Federation of State Medical Boards, "Welcome to DocInfo: The Premier Physician Profile and Disciplinary History Report Service," 2014, https://s1.fsmb.org/docinfo/ (accessed 12/03/14).
103. State Board of Registration for the Healing Arts, State of Missouri, "Disciplinary Miscellaneous Actions Taken," http://pr.mo.gov/boards/healingarts/Disciplinary%20Miscellaneous%20Report.pdf (accessed 12/22/14).
104. Thomson Reuters, "Health Care—Medical Malpractice: Tort Reform (Statutes)," September 2013.
105. Thomson Reuters, "Health Care—Medical Malpractice: Punitive Damages in Medical Malpractice Cases (Statutes)," September 2013.
106. H. Morton, "Medical Professional Apologies Statutes," National Conference of State Legislatures, January 21, 2014, http://www.ncsl.org/research/financial-services-and-commerce/medical-professional-apologies-statutes.aspx (accessed 01/09/15).
107. N. Saitta and S.D. Hodge, Jr., "Efficacy of a Physician's Words of Empathy: An Overview of State Apology Laws," *Journal of the American Osteopathic Association*, Vol. 112, No. 5 (2012).
108. A. Lazare, "Apology in Medical Practice: An Emerging Clinical Skill," *Journal of the American Medical Association*, Vol. 296, No. 11 (2006), p. 1402.
109. R.E. Ebert, "Attorneys, Tell Your Clients to Say They're Sorry: Apologies in the Health Care Industry," *Indiana Health Law Review*, Vol. 5, No. 1 (2008), pp. 356–357.
110. N.M. Saitta and S.D. Hodge, Jr., "Is it Unrealistic to Expect a Doctor to Apologize for an Unforeseen Medical Complication?—A Primer on Apologies Laws," *Pennsylvania Bar Association Quarterly*, July 2011, pp. 99–101.
111. C.C. Karls, "The Slinky Effect," *Medical Liability Monitor*, Vol. 39, No. 10: Annual Rate Survey Issue (2014).
112. H.H. Pham and P.B. Ginsburg, "Unhealthy Trends: The Future of Physician Services," *Health Affairs*, Vol. 26, No. 6 (2007), pp. 1587, 1589.
113. R.L. Vance and R.B. Goodspeed, "Back to the Future for Many Hospital-Physician Relationships: Where Do We Go from Here?" *Journal of Ambulatory Care Management*, Vol. 25, No. 4 (2002), p. 59.
114. G. Anders, "Hospitals That Gobbled Up Physician Practices Feel Ill—High Costs and a Decline in Productivity among Doctors Bring Losses," *Wall Street Journal* (June 17, 1997), p. B4.
115. American Hospital Association, "A Guide to Physician Integration Models for Sustainable Success," September 2012, pp. 1–5, http://www.hpoe.org/Reports-HPOE/guide_to_physician_integration_models_for_sustainable_success.pdf (accessed 05/19/2014).
116. Medical Group Management Association, "Physician Compensation and Production: 2004 Report Based on 2003 Data," 2004, p. 23.

117. Medical Group Management Association, "Physician Compensation and Production: 2014 Report Based on 2013 Data," 2014, retrieved via MGMA DataDive at http://data.mgma.com/datadive/rdPage.aspx (accessed 09/03/14).
118. C.C. Karls, "Now Hard & Crunchy on the Outside: Could Strong Financials Be Hiding a Market That's Growing Soft Within?" *Medical Liability Monitor*, Vol. 35, No. 10 (2010).
119. Hay Management Consultants, "Physician Compensation: 1996 Physicians' Total Compensation Survey," May 1996, p. IX-25.
120. Sullivan, Cotter, and Associates, Inc., "2013 Physician Compensation and Productivity Survey Report," January 2013, p. 131.
121. S. Carhart et al., "Restructuring, Consolidation in Health Care Make Reform Top Health Law Issue for 2010," *BNA Health Law Reporter*, Vol. 19, No. 5 (2010).
122. C.C. Karls, "From Crunchy Candy to Simmering Frogs: Waiting and Hoping for a Hardening Market as the Market Trends Slowly, Steadily Softer," *Medical Liability Monitor*, Vol. 36, No. 10 (2011), p. 5.
123. American College of Physicians, "Medical Liability Reform—Demonstration Grants," 2013, http://www.acponline.org/advocacy/where_we_stand/assets/iii12-medical-liability-reform-demo.pdf (accessed 12/23/14).
124. C.C. Karls, "The Slinky Effect: With Medical Professional Liability Insurance Rates Continuing to—Slowly and Steadily—Decline during the Most Recent Soft Market, It Appears It Will Take Several More Years before the Market Hardens and Rates Accelerate Upward," *Medical Liability Monitor*, Vol. 39, No. 10 (2014), p. 6.
125. "Casualty Actuarial Society Session Debates Potential Medical Professional Liability Implications of PPACA," *Medical Liability Monitor*, Vol. 39, No. 7 (2014), p. 4.
126. J. Hadley, "Insurance Coverage, Medical Care Use, and Short-Term Health Changes Following an Unintentional Injury or the Onset of a Chronic Condition," *Journal of the American Medical Association*, Vol. 297, No. 10 (2007), p. 1080.
127. D.I. Auerbach, P. Heaton, and I. Brantley, *How Will the Patient Protection and Affordable Care Act Affect Liability Insurance Costs?* RAND Corporation, 2014.
128. M.A. Rothstein, "Currents in Contemporary Bioethics: Health Care Reform and Medical Malpractice Claims," *Journal of Law, Medicine, and Ethics*, Vol. 38 (Winter 2010), p. 871.
129. S.A. Seabury, A. Chandra, D.N. Lakdawalla, and A.B. Jena, "On Average, Physicians Spend Nearly 11 Percent of Their 40-Year Careers with an Open, Unresolved Malpractice Claim," *Health Affairs*, Vol. 32, No. 1 (2013), p. 114.
130. R.J. Cimasi, "Medical Malpractice and Tort Reform Risks (Crisis…or Red Herring?)," in *Insurance and Risk Management Strategies: For Physicians and Advisors*, David Marcinko (ed.), Jones and Bartlett, Sudbury, MA, 2005, p. 203.
131. R.J. Cimasi, "Medical Malpractice and Tort Reform Risks (Crisis…or Red Herring?)," in *Insurance and Risk Management Strategies: For Physicians and Advisors*, David Marcinko (ed.), Jones and Bartlett, Sudbury, MA, 2004, p. 204.

12 The Malpractice Trial
From First Service to Final Verdict and Emotional Relief

Jay S. Grife and David Edward Marcinko

CONTENTS

Primum non nocere

This Latin phrase is axiomatic in intent and is one of the earliest inoculations students of medicine receive. It dovetails the Hippocratic oath to provide both a moral and ethical foundation for physicians in furtherance of their mission to heal the sick. It asks little in objective terms but demands an immense measure of dedication and knowledge from those who practice their profession. Yet, it is roughly estimated that one of every five practicing health-care professionals will confront the enigmatic process of medical malpractice within a 12-month span. Despite the fact that most health-care practitioners will never see the inside of a courtroom, the sequelae of the event itself can scar the psyche forever after. What can be done when the inevitable happens, and what can you as a practicing doctor do to confront the process?

"Even among the sciences, medicine occupies a special position. Its practitioners come into direct and intimate contact with people in their daily lives; they are present at the critical transitional moments of existence. For many people, they are the only contact with a world that otherwise stands at a forbidding distance. Often in pain, fearful of death, the sick have a special thirst for reassurance and vulnerability to belief."*

When this trust is violated, whether rooted in factual substance or merely a conclusion lacking in reality, American jurisprudence offers several remedies with the core being civil litigation. We have personally witnessed a vast spectrum of reasons that prompts a patient to seek the counsel of an attorney. Whether it be an untoward result of treatment or surgery, an outstanding invoice being mailed to a less-than-happy patient who decides that the doctor's treatment did not measure up to expectations, a physician's wife employed as the office manager charging a patient $85 to complete a medical leave authorization form, or simply a perceived lack of concern on the part of the doctor or his/her personnel, patients can be motivated to seek redress outside the realm of the doctor's office. Compound any of the above scenarios with well-meaning friends and family, and the proverbial prescription for litigation has been certified.

Woven throughout this discourse will be suggestions that might obviate the foregoing. While it is not a panacea, nor a cure-all for medical negligence cases, we believe it to be an effective methodology for resolving those differences that see the growth of a medical malpractice lawsuit: honest communications.

12.1 UNDERSTANDING WHAT IS AT STAKE

At times, medical malpractice can be attributed to simple misdiagnosis on the part of the medical fraternity, but at other times, it may be some serious medical or criminal offense

* Paul Starr, *The Social Transformation of American Medicine*, Basic Books, pp. 4–5, 1982.

done on purpose. In either case, it's difficult to forget and forgive a mistake that can spoil someone's life.

Medical malpractice is a specific legal term that defines an act of negligence on the part of a professional health-care provider, which may result in further complications in the condition of the patient, even resulting in death. It can occur when the health-care providers deviate from the accepted standards either by mistake or on purpose. Cases may range from a misdiagnosis of disease, such as cancer, to botched birthing delivery, which results in physical or mental damage to the child.

Here are some of the most common instances of wrongful activities in the medical field.

- Anesthesia errors
- Birth injury
- Cancer misdiagnosis
- Dental malpractice
- Institutional sexual abuse
- Medical errors
- Nursing home abuse
- Surgery mistakes

Medical malpractice lawsuits are proceedings pertaining to an allegation in the court of law, wherein the plaintiff, most often the patient or the relative of the patient, is expected to prove that the injury or casualty was caused due to negligence on the part of the medical fraternity. The defendant, most often the representative of the health-care facility, is expected to defend the institute against these allegations.

According to Thomas H. Cohen, JD, PhD, of the 1156 medical malpractice trials litigated in the nation's 75 most populous counties during 2001, most were disposed of by jury trial (96%). In an estimated 9 out of 10 medical malpractice trials, the alleged harm involved either a permanent injury (57%) or a death claim (33%).

About half of the sampled medical malpractice trials were brought against surgeons, while a third were against nonsurgeons. Dentists accounted for 5% of medical malpractice defendants. Medical malpractice trials with nonsurgeons had the highest estimated percentage of injuries involving a death claim (43%). Death claims arose in 30% of trials with a surgeon defendant.

The overall win rate for medical malpractice plaintiffs (27%) was about half of that found among plaintiffs in all tort trials (52%). Plaintiffs prevailed in nearly 39% of trials against dentists and in about a quarter of trials against nonsurgeon (23%) and surgeon (27%) defendants. The median award of $425,000 in medical malpractice trials was nearly 16 times greater than the overall median award in all tort trials ($27,000). Median award amounts were higher among plaintiffs who won malpractice trials against medical doctors, both surgeons ($575,000) and nonsurgeons ($511,000), than against dentists ($53,000).

Plaintiff winners were awarded $1 million or more in approximately a third of medical malpractice trials brought against nonsurgeon and surgeon defendants. The type of injury giving rise to a medical malpractice trial also had an impact on damage awards. Median award amounts for medical malpractice trials arising from death claims ($837,000) and permanent injuries ($412,000) were higher than the median awards for medical malpractice trials that stemmed from temporary injuries ($77,000).

The number of medical malpractice jury trials since 1992 has remained stable, as the reported differences were not statistically significant. Since 1992, the percentage of plaintiff winners ranged from 22% to 30%. After remaining stable in 1992 and 1996, the median amount awarded in jury trials to plaintiff winners increased from $287,000 in 1996 to $431,000 in 2001. The percentage of plaintiff winners receiving awards of $1 million or more also rose from an estimated 25% in 1992 and 1996 to 32% in 2001. Punitive damages remained rare in medical malpractice jury trials. From 1992 to 2001, 1–4% of plaintiff winners in medical malpractice jury trials received punitive damages. The median punitive damage awards for medical malpractice jury trials in two of the three study periods (1992 and 2001) were $250,000.

More recently, according to *Becker's Hospital Review*, statistics show that the number of medical malpractice cases being filed in the United States is increasing every year. In 2011, there were over 12,000 payouts made for medical malpractice. The majority of claims were settled outside of court. Statistics showed that 93% of payouts resulted from settlements in 2011. And most recent statistics from Diederich Healthcare's "2013 Medical Malpractice Payout Analysis" are based on data from the National Practitioner Data Bank (medical malpractice payouts and statistics for 2012) and are noted below.

Medical malpractice payouts:

- Dollars in payouts: $3.6 billion (3.4% less than in 2011)
- Total payouts for medical malpractice: 12,142 (one every 43 minutes)
- Payouts resulting from judgments: 5%
- Payouts resulting from settlements: 93%

Payouts by patient type:

- Inpatient: 45%
- Outpatient: 41%
- Both: 9%

Top five states for medical malpractice payouts:

- New York: $763,088,250
- Pennsylvania: $316,167,500
- California: $222,926,200
- New Jersey: $206,668,250
- Florida: $203,671,100

Severity of alleged injury in medical malpractice claims:

- Death: 31%
- Significant permanent injury: 19%
- Major permanent injury: 18%
- Quadriplegic, brain damage, lifelong care: 12%
- Minor permanent injury: 8%
- Major temporary injury: 7%

- Minor temporary injury: 3%
- Emotional injury only: 1%
- Insignificant injury: 0.4%

Types of allegations in medical malpractice claims:

- Related to diagnosis: 33%
- Related to surgery: 24%
- Related to treatment: 18%
- Related to obstetrics: 11%
- Related to medication: 4%
- Related to monitoring: 3%
- Related to anesthesia: 3%
- Other: 4%

More poignantly, in late 2014, the *Dallas/Fort Worth Healthcare Daily* ran a fascinating excerpt from Steve Jacob's book *So Long, Marcus Welby, M.D.* The excerpt contained some very interesting assertions and statistics:

- Consultant PwC, relying on a Congressional Budget Office (CBO) report, estimated that malpractice insurance and defensive medicine accounted for 10% of total health-care costs. A 2010 *Health Affairs* article more conservatively pegged those costs at 2.4% of health-care spending.
- In a 2010 survey, U.S. orthopedic surgeons bluntly admitted that about 30% of tests and referrals were medically unnecessary and done to reduce physician vulnerability to lawsuits.
- A 2011 analysis by the AMA found that the average amount to defend a lawsuit in 2010 was $47,158, compared with $28,981 in 2001. The average cost to pay a medical liability claim—whether it was a settlement, jury award, or some other disposition—was $331,947, compared with $297,682 in 2001.
- Doctors spend significant time fighting lawsuits, regardless of outcome. The average litigated claim lingered for 25 months. Doctors spent 20 months defending cases that were ultimately dismissed, while claims going to trial took 39 months. Physicians who were victorious in court spent an average of 44 months in litigation.
- A study in the *New England Journal of Medicine* estimated that by age 65, about 75% of physicians in low-risk specialties have been the target of at least one lawsuit, compared with about 99% of those in high-risk specialties.
- According to Brian Atchinson, president of the Physician Insurers Association of America (PIAA), 70% of legal claims do not result in payments to patients, and physician defendants prevail 80% of the time in claims resolved by verdict.

12.2 WHAT EVERY DOCTOR MUST REALIZE

Doctors depend on their trusted advisors to be a source of information on a wide variety of complex topics. As we have seen, one of the areas in which physicians are increasingly seeking guidance from their attorney, accountant, consultant, or financial advisor is in the area of risk management, insurance planning, and asset protection.

The best experts and consultants seek to create safe steady growth and avoid losses and exposures to things like malpractice judgments integrated with asset protection. A natural extension of this stewardship is making sure that the growth and balance of assets are safe from exposure to an increasingly predatory and hostile litigation system. Most doctors have obvious daily risks like malpractice exposures. Other sources of exposure are more insidious, such as merely being affluent and visible, owning income property, or something as simple as owning and driving a car every day. The numbers are staggering; we are at a point in our litigation system where we have 70,000 lawsuits filed per day in the United States alone, many without any real merit. Unfortunately, being right is not enough to keep physicians safe.

12.2.1 Why Doctors Are Concerned

As illustrated by the numbers above and below, awards continue to spiral out of control, fueled by litigation attorneys who have become partners in lawsuits and who are economically incentivized to create and magnify adversarial relations between parties who might otherwise reach some reasonable, if not amicable, settlement. So, here are additional facts about our litigation system to consider, for 2016:

- The average medical malpractice award is now $3.9 million, and some authorities put this number substantially higher.
- The average legal cost of settling a frivolous lawsuit is $91,000—plus the actual settlement amount itself.

The average sexual harassment suit against a small medical practice produces a verdict of $530,000. Employees are suing more often, winning more often, and winning proportionally larger judgments. They win 75% of the time. Moreover, only the top 5% of Americans have a net worth of over $1 million. Using this baseline, it's pretty easy to see where even a doctor who is worth only a few million dollars fits on the food chain.

Here is more proof why doctors and allied medical providers are sued:

- MDs are high net worth, high liability, or they will be soon (i.e., new practitioners).
- DOs have assets that would be difficult to replace if lost or reduced.
- DPMs have professional surgical liability.
- DDSs have employees and own their practice.
- CRNs are highly visible, traceable, and/or collectible.
- ODs own liability-generating assets, i.e., rental property.
- NPs and ANPs have a spouse and/or children.

What doctors and all medical professionals must take to heart is that litigation attorneys are in business. Just like any business, including a medical practice, they have weekly meetings in which they examine growth, cash flow, revenue goals, and new leads or opportunities. This economic motivation is a key and explains in part why we see awards rising and why plaintiffs' attorneys regularly seek and obtain awards above the limits of applicable liability insurance policies.

12.3 DEAR DOCTOR, YOU HAVE BEEN SERVED A LAWSUIT...NOW WHAT?

In the United States, a trial is thought to be the most common manner in which disputes are resolved. Contrary to what we see on television, very few cases actually make it to trial, with most either dismissed or resolved through mediation or arbitration. The U.S. Department of Justice recently reported that only about 3% of all civil cases are resolved by a trial. The vast majority of civil lawsuits, and in particular, medical malpractice cases, are settled or dismissed before any of the litigants see a courtroom.

So, when served, don't run to the nearest bridge or fly into an explosive tantrum. Don't throw your hands up in the air and blame the world. It is estimated that one in every two health-care professionals will be the recipient of such news at some time during their professional careers.

12.3.1 First Steps

Take a deep breath and exhale. Devastation isn't knocking at your door, but at the same time, Perry Mason is not your attorney. Finish the day, and when things are subdued, sit down and slowly assess what has happened. If you read and believe the complaint that the plaintiff's lawyer has served upon you, likely you will conclude that as a health-care professional, not only are you negligent, but you border upon the criminal. Our advice: do not read it, but who among us won't?

At this point, take the patient/plaintiff's medical records and make exact copies of every single document contained within. Copy your computer files that reference this patient onto a portable medium of your choosing. Put the originals in an envelope and seal it. *Do not make any changes to the medical records or to the computer data.* Your patient's medical records are your best evidence, and in the world of medical–legal jurisprudence, an inference of truth and fact immediately attach to these, which can be permanently shattered by any changes, well meaning or otherwise.

12.3.2 Call Your Medical Malpractice Insurance Company

At this time, contact your medical malpractice insurance company. Speak to a representative in the claims department, advise them of the current situation, and follow their instructions as to reporting the claim. Your cooperation with your carrier is essential in order to conform to most policies and to insure that you do not do anything to waive the coverage subscribed to. At some time in the immediate future, your insurer will assign your case to a defense attorney, who will become your constant companion for the next several years. It is this person who will undertake the investigation of your case and the study of your patient's allegations. At times, your lawyer will appear to be your therapist, knight in shining armor, and may even seem to be working against your best interests. None of this is factual. Your lawyer is an expert assigned to investigate your case and to provide you with the best defense and advice available, all the time looking through the lens of objectivity. Remember, your view is tinted with emotion and the passion that you have done nothing wrong. But make no mistake about it; it is this person who will tell you when you should hold them and when you should fold them.

12.3.3 Personal Counsel

What is personal counsel? Personal counsel is an attorney with extensive experience in the management of medical negligence cases and one that handles these on a daily basis. Personal counsel should be an attorney who has been researched by you and/or your associates so that you feel comfortable knowing that this person has the understanding and skill necessary to represent your interests. It is a lawyer whom you may retain *independent of* counsel assigned by your insurance carrier. In the vast majority of cases, personal counsel is an attorney whom you will retain to represent your interests at your cost. The essential difference to appreciate is that counsel assigned to you by your insurance company will be retained and reimbursed by your insurer, but personal counsel is an attorney of your choosing whom you agree to retain and compensate.

Is this necessary? If you are a health-care professional who has no insurance coverage, chances are your decision to go bare will necessitate the retaining of personal counsel. Of course, those who have adeptly concealed their personal assets so as to be judgment proof might not deem it necessary, but in that event, the doctor must be ready to accept the possibility of an adverse final money judgment and the necessity of a bankruptcy proceeding if legally applicable. While those doctors going bare might consider the fact that they have no insurance to be the best insurance against a plaintiff's lawyer filing suit, do remember that it takes only one compassionate plaintiff's lawyer to upset that apple cart.

Those doctors who have malpractice insurance have a different type of decision to make in retaining personal counsel. The malpractice insurance company has assigned an attorney to you and will be compensating that attorney for his/her efforts in defending you. That same attorney and/or his/her law firm may have numerous other doctors they are representing who maintain coverage with the same insurance company. Some view this as a conflict of interest. Is the assigned attorney representing your interests or that of the insurance company? Despite the best efforts of the assigned defense counsel, it is not out of the question for that counsel to appreciate the financial realities of the situation. Once your case is over, new business is dependent upon the insurance company and not you. So the dilemma of the personal counsel evolves as to whether you deem it prudent to retain and compensate an attorney to, solely and without question, represent your interests, even at the expense of your assigned counsel and the insurance company. The decision is solely an individual one but, in all fairness, a decision we feel necessary. In those case where we have been retained as personal counsel, our job has been to review the case and decide whether the plaintiff's case has merit and, if we decide it does, whether or not our client, the defendant doctor, is at risk of an adverse judgment greater than the amount of insurance coverage available. If deemed a possibility, it becomes our job to insure that the client does not face that eventuality, and our exclusive duty is to the doctor who has retained us.

12.4 THE TRIAL PLAYERS

In every civil trial, besides there generally being counsel for the respective parties, there is a plaintiff (patient) and a defendant (doctor). While it is not mandatory that the plaintiff be represented by an attorney, an unrepresented plaintiff who is *pro se* most likely will find the course difficult to traverse. The plaintiff is the aggrieved party, or accuser, who files a complaint, and the defendant is the party against whom a complaint is lodged, or the accused. Some cases may involve multiple plaintiffs, multiple defendants, or both. Regardless of the numbers of parties involved, there must be, *de facto*, two opposing sides to a lawsuit. Often, those respective sides make for interesting bedfellows, such as where several of the named defendants each perceives the other as being at fault. In those cases, the finger-pointing often is directed away from the plaintiff and toward the other defendant(s) in the case. At those times, the mentality can often shift toward a Darwinian one of survival, leaving the plaintiff the sole benefactor.

In addition to the parties and their respective counsel, witnesses, both lay and expert, form the main body of testimony that will be elicited and heard by the judge and jury. The respective parties both present their witnesses in a procedural order as determined by the venue of the litigation. Both lay and expert witnesses serve to tell the story of the parties to the court. In a medical malpractice case, a lay witness generally explains the facts of specific events that they have witnessed, or more likely, how the plaintiff has been affected by the alleged negligence. The parties may also call a special kind of witness, called a medical expert, to testify on their behalf. An expert witness is simply a witness with experience in a particular field, whose testimony will aid the lay jury in understanding the medical aspects of the case. Oftentimes, the expert witness can be the trump card necessary for that party to prevail, but all too often, medical experts tend to "cancel each other out," leaving a jury to decide based upon the remaining evidence presented.

In most medical malpractice cases, the plaintiff must present expert testimony from a health-care practitioner that the defendant fell below the standard of care required and caused injury to the patient. These are the two essential prongs, which, when conjoined, equate to negligence in legal terminology, liability being a breach in the standard of care and causation being that the negligence caused the plaintiff damages. It is essential to understand that a plaintiff cannot prevail in litigation if only one of these two prongs has been left unsatisfied. For example, if a physician failed to diagnose cancer in a terminally ill patient, the fact that the diagnosis was not made can be deemed negligent, but the negligence in the failure to diagnose did not damage the patient in that she was terminal when she initially presented. It is this two-pronged test that delineates legal negligence from commonly expressed negligence or a bad result from the care and treatment provided.

In rare instances, and in ever-diminishing jurisdictions, expert testimony is not required in medical negligence matters. In those instances, the legal doctrine of *res ipsa loquitur*, or "the thing speaks for itself," often will attach to obviate the expert's place. Normally, in a medical malpractice case, a plaintiff is required to establish the following: (1) a breach in the standard of care or an act or omission by the defendant that was not in keeping with the degree of skill and learning ordinarily used under the same or similar circumstances by members of defendant's profession and (2) causation or that such negligence or omission caused the plaintiff's injury. However, the doctrine of *res ipsa loquitur* exists to preclude the need for direct proof of negligence through medical testimony and allows cases submitted under the doctrine to proceed to the jury even in the absence of testimony as to negligence because a jury is permitted to draw an inference of negligence from the specific act itself. The classic example of such an incident would be the leaving of a surgical instrument inside a patient's body; or operating upon the wrong eye, kidney, hand, foot, or limb; etc.

The judge and jury are the final participants in a trial. The judge presides over the trial and makes rulings regarding the law and its application to the case. Only the judge is permitted to rule upon issues of law. The jury members are called the triers of fact in that the body listens to the evidence, and determine the facts, based upon their collective wisdom. For example, when two parties tell different versions of an event, the jury must decide which side it believes is true. In cases where there is no jury, the judge decides both the law and the facts.

12.5 BURDEN OF PROOF

In all civil trials, the plaintiff, as the accuser, has the burden of proving his/her case. Much like a criminal defendant, a civil defendant has no burden of proof and is presumed innocent of any claim as alleged by the plaintiff. As a result, if the plaintiff presents insufficient evidence to support his claim, the defendant's counsel will likely seek a directed verdict pursuant to the prevailing law from the judge. Should the judge conclude that the plaintiff has failed to establish those elements of medical negligence as required, the judge will order the directed verdict in favor of the defendant doctor. In other words, the defendant wins without having to present his/her case. The burden the plaintiff carries in a civil arena is that he/she must prove his/her case by what is called a preponderance of the evidence. In other words, the plaintiff must prove that it is more likely than not that the facts as presented prove his/her case. The burden is distinct from that in criminal law, where proof beyond a reasonable doubt is necessary. The best way to visualize this burden is to imagine a set of scales. If the scales are even, or tipped in favor of the defendant, then the plaintiff has not carried his/her burden, and loses. In order to prevail, the plaintiff must tip the scales in his/her favor. And it can be tipped by no more than 50.1–49.9%.

To succeed in a case of alleged medical malpractice, a plaintiff patient must present evidence that the defendant doctor was negligent, and the plaintiff does this by proving that the treatment provided was below the applicable standard of care. This phrase is often misapplied and misunderstood but in essence means that the health-care provider failed to use the degree of care and skill that a reasonably prudent practitioner under similar circumstances would have used in treating a patient. While the standard of care has a fairly universal legal meaning, it has variances throughout the different states. In some jurisdictions, a national standard of care is the accepted norm, while in others, it can be a locality rule. The difference is of vital significance because when expert testimony is sought, that expert must be knowledgeable and able to testify as to the standard of care pursuant to that jurisdiction, regardless of whether it is local or otherwise. In those minority areas where the locality rule remains in effect, often, an expert must be from that specific community or have discussed the standard of care with a local doctor so as to be sufficiently versed in it.* In addition, the standard of care, while established by the medical community at large, is constantly evolving. Care that violates the standard of care today may not necessarily violate the standard of care several years ago. This distinction is an important one, since most cases take several years to reach trial readiness. Of critical importance is to appreciate that while the public at large often will equate a bad result to negligence, legally, it may not be due to a violation of the standard of care.

For the plaintiff to succeed in tipping those scales in his/her favor, expert medical testimony is required to establish a violation of the standard of care in virtually all medical malpractice cases. A plaintiff that fails to present the required expert medical testimony in a medical malpractice case, but for those instances where *res ipsa loquitur* is applicable, will lose. As noted above, the plaintiff must also produce expert medical testimony as to a violation of the standard of care and that the alleged negligence caused the injury.

---

* Idaho is an example of such a jurisdiction.

Finally, it is an unfortunate reality that the jury often does not have the medical knowledge necessary to appreciate the nuances of medicine and the clinical judgment afforded doctors. That is not to say that juries do not do their utmost to reach a reasoned verdict, but medicine can be a difficult proposition for the trained individual, let alone a layman. In a case several years ago in California, a jury listened to the evidence in a medical malpractice case for several weeks. Following a plaintiff's verdict, several of the jurors agreed to discuss their deliberations with the parties' counsels. When asked for a reason that the jury found for the plaintiff against the physician, one specific juror admitted that it was because of the expert medical testimony. When probed further, the juror stated that he believed the plaintiff's medical expert to be the most credible and knowledgeable because while the defendant's expert had charged $500.00 per hour to testify in court, the Plaintiff's expert had charged $650.00 per hour.

12.6 TYPES OF TRIAL

There are two types of trials available to the parties, trial by jury or a bench trial exclusively by the judge. In a trial by jury, the judge determines the law, and the jury determines the facts. In a bench trial, the judge wears both the hats of being the trier of law and the trier of fact. The U.S. Constitution guarantees a trial by jury. If a party does not request a jury trial, that right may be deemed forfeit, and by the same token, both sides must agree to waive a jury trial.

So why would anyone choose to have a case heard by a judge as opposed to a jury, or vice versa? The reasons are mainly based on preconceived notions about judge and juror biases. Generally, most litigants favor a jury over a judge because the decision is put into the hands of many rather than in the hands of one.* Plaintiffs usually like juries because lay individuals are believed to be more sympathetic, and a plaintiff can appeal to the emotions of a jury. Conversely, defendants usually prefer bench trials because a judge is thought to be more objective in deciding a case. Requesting a bench trial can also result in a much quicker trial date. Since court dockets in most large cities are becoming increasingly congested, the time difference between a jury trial date and a bench trial date can be literally years.

None of the perceptions about the benefits of a jury trial or a bench trial apply to all situations—every case is different. There is at least some empirical evidence that some of the commonly held conceptions about bench and jury trials are actually misconceptions. For example, while it is almost universally believed that juries tend to favor plaintiffs and award much higher monetary amounts, a study by the Department of Justice† suggests that *judges* favor plaintiffs and return higher verdicts. Still, jury trials outnumber bench trials by about two to one.

12.7 DISCOVERY PROCESS

In that most medical negligence cases are fact driven, the topic of discovery demands a specific and integral role in the trial process. Discovery simply is the methodology used in American jurisprudence for each side to discover all of the evidence that is available in the

---

* The actual number of jurors can vary from state to state in civil trials.

† See Civil Jury Cases and Verdicts in Large Counties, and Civil Justice Survey of State Courts at http://www.usdoj.gov/bjs/abstract/cjcavilc.htm.

case and to have that documentation analyzed. While specific states have rules that may limit discovery, the purpose is to prevent trial by ambush.*

According to the Federal Rules of Civil Procedure, discovery can include written interrogatories or questions; requests for production; deposition, either oral or through written statements; request for examination; request for inspection of evidence; requests for admission; and finally, independent or, as plaintiffs' lawyers commonly label them, compulsory medical examinations.

The scope of the above discovery methods is generally a book onto itself, so suffice it to say, discovery is the process where each party exchanges information so the merit of their respective cases can be evaluated. Lawyers will use this evidence in developing the theory of their case and the order in which that evidence will be presented to the trier of fact. While discovery is often viewed as a mundane part of the process, in reality, it is the very topic that often proves dispositive in the ultimate outcome of the case, whether it be tried, settled, or rejected.

12.8 DEPOSITIONS

One of the discovery methods listed above does deserve specific discussion because the deposition, or oral statement under oath, is such a vital piece of the puzzle. In general, either party may depose any other person, but usually, a deponent has some relevance to the case, whether it be as a fact witness, an expert witness, or a before-and-after witness (a person who can testify as to the state of affairs of a person before and after the incident in question).

Depositions are taken to gain an insight into what information will be necessary in order to prosecute or defend a case. Even more important is that the oral deposition provides the respective lawyer with a chance to evaluate that person's reactions to stress, to personally see the temperament of the witness, to view the witness' demeanor, and to analyze how that person responds to spontaneous events. The format is typically oral and in-person question-and-answer dialogue, although recent technology has permitted depositions via telephone conference, video conference, and Internet-medium exchanges, like Skype. Depositions can be taken via written-question format, but often, this type has limited value because the deponent will not be asked any follow-up questions and a statement cannot be investigated further.

There are lists of dos and donts that lawyers provide their clients, but the fundamental character of the deposition is for the deponent to tell the truth. While it is rare that a trial sees the Perry Mason moment, this does, in fact, happen, and when it does, the result is often exactly what viewers of that classical television series see. As a rule, in light of the attorney–client privilege, we insist upon knowing whatever skeletons are in a client's closet, past or present. It is of ultimate importance that clients confide the truth to their lawyer so that any adverse issue can be addressed through cognizant decision, rather than surprise. In one case, our client was being deposed and admitted that she was a lesbian. Her sexual preferences did not matter, but the fact that she disclosed a misdemeanor arrest for marijuana did. She was advised to tell the truth about both issues, and it was explained why this was important. During her deposition, when the homophobic defense counsel abrasively

* It is interesting to note that in New York State, the identity and/or deposition of a medical expert is not disclosed until the time of trial, so in this venue, ambush can be a tactical weapon.

probed her sexuality, she readily admitted her own sexual preference. That was fine, but the defense lawyer continued to push her buttons until she finally screamed at him to "shut the f... up." The die was cast because the next line of questioning involved her arrest record as to the marijuana. When the client denied any other arrests but for the drugs, it was simple for the defense counsel to show her documentation of four earlier felony arrests including one for fraud, which ultimately cost her the case. The important fact to remember is that we all have a past and that being truthful as to its content can often dictate a successful outcome of a case.

12.9 MOTIONS *IN LIMINE*

Motions *in limine* are one of the many weapons lawyers use to limit the jurors hearing evidence that is deemed to be irrelevant or too prejudicial to a party. A lawyer must be tactical in this area so that the jury never can appreciate that information is being withheld, thereby creating doubt as to the honesty of that lawyer. A typical example and one that we confront is whether to permit the jury to know that in addition to being a lawyer, the attorney may also be a doctor, for example. In every case, we must gauge the advisability of disclosing this to the jury or simply using a motion *in limine* to prevent that fact from being disclosed. Can you imagine the impact upon the jury if the fact of the trial attorney–doctor was withheld and a witness, expert or lay, through intention or true neglect, testified something to the fact of "come on now, you are a doctor, you know it's true." The jury might interpret this as a conspiracy to have a special hired gun doing that party's bidding rather than a simple advocate of the truth. Or the jury may interpret this as part of a game plan to protect one's own physician colleagues despite the apparent negligence.

12.10 JURY SELECTION

The selection process for a jury begins with what is called the jury pool. A number of citizens are selected as potential jurors, usually several times the number of jurors needed for a trial. From this pool of potential jurors, the jury panel is selected.

The size of the jury panel varies by state and locale. Most juries consist of 6 to 12 individuals on a panel. In addition, one or more alternate jurors may also be selected. Alternate jurors sit with the jury and hear evidence just as all the other jurors. In some states, they also sit in on jury deliberations, though they are not allowed to participate. If for some reason, a member of the selected jury is unable to continue with the trial or deliberations, the alternate juror fills in. The number of alternate jurors varies, and determining that number is usually left to the discretion of the judge. Generally, the longer the trial, the more alternate jurors are sworn in.

Before any potential juror appears at the courthouse for a trial, usually, a questionnaire form is mailed for the individual to complete and return to the court. Such forms generally request demographic information such as name, age, occupation, educational background, participation as a party or witness in previous litigation, previous jury service, etc. Attorneys for the parties are able to obtain and review these questionnaires in advance of the trial date.

On the day of trial, when the potential jurors arrive at the courthouse, the judge typically asks some generic questions about their ability to serve. The judge may ask whether any potential juror has a problem staying for the duration of the trial, or whether the potential jurors know any of the parties or their attorneys. The purpose of these questions is for the judge to determine which, if any, of the potential jurors will be excused immediately from service.

Many juries tend to be comprised of citizens with little or no college education. One of the possible reasons for this result is that many professionals, especially medical professionals, request to be excused from jury service, citing their professional commitments as justification. Ironically, professionals are usually the first to complain when juries who lack any representatives with advanced education hear their own cases. Once the judge is finished with the preliminary screening of the jury pool, *voir dire* begins.

12.10.1 *Voir Dire*: Questioning of the Jurors

Voir dire literally means "to speak the truth." It is the term used to represent the preliminary questioning of potential jurors. The purpose of *voir dire* is to uncover any prejudice or bias in potential jurors. Plaintiffs' attorneys in medical malpractice cases will try to determine if the potential jurors have any strong connection to a health-care provider that might make the juror favor the defendant doctor. Similarly, medical malpractice defense attorneys will try to uncover any bad experiences the potential jurors may have had with a health-care practitioner, which may make the juror biased in favor of the patient. The judge, the attorneys, or both can conduct the questioning. Most jurisdictions allow the attorneys to conduct *voir dire*. The key to successful *voir dire* is not changing an avowed racist into a liberal but discovering that juror's attitudes and position as to issues, and thereafter appropriately responding to that disclosure.

Voir dire is such an important aspect of the trial process that often, studies conclude that the trial is over when *voir dire* ends. Attorneys will spend a great deal of time toward *voir dire* preparation in order to detect juror bias, adverse attitudes and thoughts, as well as prejudice, be it overt or covert. This is simply a human exercise using intuition, gut feelings, and common sense where the input from a plaintiff or defendant often has as much influence as that of counsel. In some cases, jury specialists and consultants such as psychologists are retained to provide expertise in the process. These experts often provide invaluable insight into the process, but as any consultant worth his/her salt will admit, it is an inexact science. The essence of the process is to identify those potential jurors who tend to exhibit a positive identity toward your case facts or those who react adversely, while at the same time not being so blatant as to tip your hand to the opposition.

Beyond trying to eliminate bias against their clients, attorneys often use the *voir dire* process to try to "educate" the jury along with developing a rapport in their favor. They also use *voir dire* to begin placing before the potential jurors the theories of the complaint and defense thereto to try to gauge their reactions. Skillful attorneys will tacitly use the questioning process of *voir dire* to prepare the jury to find in favor of their clients.

12.10.2 Challenges of Jurors

When the attorneys and/or the judge have finished *voir dire* of the potential jurors, challenges may be made to remove potential jurors from serving on the sworn jury panel. Attorneys use the challenge phase of jury selection to remove jurors who may favor the other side's case. To remove potential jurors, two types of challenges may be made to "strike" the individual from the jury.

The first type of challenge is a challenge for cause. A for-cause challenge is one in which the attorneys are required to state and present reasons for removing the potential juror. The rationale given is usually that the challenged juror cannot hear the case fairly for one reason or another. For example, a juror may have stated that he/she will not abide by a judge's instructions as to application of the law, because he/she does not think the instruction is fair. Such a situation is a clear case to have the juror removed for cause. The number of for-cause challenges is unlimited, and the judge decides whether to excuse the challenged potential juror. Other challenges for cause may be based on a claim of juror bias. In practice, however, very few for-cause challenges based on alleged bias are sustained. In the famous Attica prison riot trial in New York, Ernie Goodman, counsel for one of the alleged rioting prisoners, was fortunate enough to have law students use questionnaires, canvass the neighborhoods of potential jurors, and provide insight into what make of automobile was in the driveways and whether any bumper stickers were attached. That information, along with the typical television habits of the potential jurors, and the complexion of the neighborhood environment served the purpose of ferreting out a majority of racial predisposition. Discovering that persons living in a certain neighborhood were more prone to racial bigotry served Goodman well during the *voir dire* process. The process is inexact, and a juror can fool the system.

The second type of challenge is a peremptory challenge (note that the challenge is peremptory, meaning absolute, not preemptory). Each party is given a certain number of peremptory challenges in which to remove any potential juror from the panel. In civil trials, each side generally has two or more peremptory challenges.

No reason is needed to strike a potential juror when using a peremptory challenge, and the individual is automatically excused. The only exception is that the strike must be race and gender neutral. Where a pattern of strikes suggests that peremptory challenges were used to remove potential jurors because of their race or gender, the entire process must be restarted. Volumes of law journal articles have been written about race- and gender-based peremptory challenges, and an extensive discussion is beyond the scope of this chapter. Suffice it to say, objecting to peremptory challenges because they are race or gender based is the exception rather than the rule. In most cases, the number of challenges allowed is too small to show any pattern.

Challenging a juror can often be a tactical decision, which often entertains far-reaching issues. Certainly, it seems simple enough to strike a juror who has voiced concerns that doctors are all quacks, but caution must be exercised so that the opinion of that one potential juryperson will not poison the attitudes of the remaining jury panel. It could be catastrophic for an attorney to continue questioning and to elicit responses from that potential juror so that persons in the courtroom can all listen to it. On those occasions, counsel may request that the court permit the examination of that juror *in camera*, or outside the hearing of the remaining jury panel. In this manner, an attorney can more freely delve into the prospective biases that juror may harbor and, if necessary, establish a for-cause strike rather than a peremptory strike.

12.10.3 Jury Selection Logistics

Ordinarily, the jury box is filled with potential jury panel members by randomly selecting names from the pool of potential jurors. When a potential juror is removed by a challenge, that juror is replaced with another member of the jury pool. Each newly selected potential juror is questioned and then, if appropriate, challenged. When each side has exhausted all of its challenges, the jury selection is complete.

The time to conduct jury selection varies. Supposedly, in the old days, jury questioning would take many days. In our current heavily congested court system, however, most judges limit the *voir dire* process to just a few hours.

12.10.4 Preliminary Instructions to the Jury

Once the jury is selected, the judge will swear in those selected and give them preliminary instructions. These instructions usually involve statements of the law and the case such as the basic allegations in the lawsuit, which side carries the burden of proof, and the presentation of evidence. The judge will also instruct the jury regarding more general issues such as note-taking, limitations on discussing the case, and breaks in the trial. Of course, in a bench trial, no preliminary instructions are necessary. After the judge gives the jury preliminary instructions, the formal presentation of the case begins with opening statements.

12.11 OPENING STATEMENTS

The opening-statement phase of a civil trial is when the case really begins. Some lawyers very firmly believe that cases are won or lost during opening statements and *voir dire*. In this phase, attorneys provide a road map of the trial by telling their client's side of the story, while at the same time trying to convince the jury to find in their client's favor. Lawyers will use this opportunity to build upon the rapport developed during *voir dire* so that the jury will appreciate the theory of the case in factual terms.

Arguments are not allowed during opening statements. Rather, attorneys are only allowed to state what the evidence will show. Most attorneys find this to be a distinction without much of a difference. For example, the statement "Dr. Smith crippled Mrs. Jones by performing unnecessary surgery" could be considered argument and not allowed during opening statements. Stating "the evidence will show that Dr. Smith crippled Mrs. Jones when he performed unnecessary surgery," however, is not considered argument, because the attorney is merely stating what he believes the evidence will show.

Depending on the complexity of the case, attorneys may use exhibits during opening statements. Such exhibits are not considered evidence but are only illustrative of what each side intends to prove. Some attorneys may even use very technical computerized presentations during opening statements. Any such "props" are fair game as long as the information presented can be described fairly as "what the evidence will show."

The time length for opening statements varies from jurisdiction to jurisdiction, and from case to case. Cases that take several weeks to try may involve half-day-long or longer opening statements. Cases that take a few days to try—which is probably most cases—involve an hour or so per side for opening statements.

During the *voir dire* process and again during the opening statement, jurors will take measure of the attorney's credibility and use this later in the decision-making process to see whether that attorney really did establish those points of fact as promised. Gaining the trust of the jury can oftentimes trump the factual evidence elicited during the trial. It is important to remember that the jury has the role of trier of the facts, and it is the attorney who presents these facts to the jury throughout the trial process.

12.12 PRESENTATION OF EVIDENCE (HOW LAWYERS TELL A STORY)

12.12.1 Order of Evidence Presentation

Since the plaintiff has the burden of proof, he/she presents his/her case first. The presentation of the plaintiff's case is called the plaintiff's case-in-chief. The plaintiff's case-in-chief includes what are called the essential elements of the complaint. These elements are what the law requires every plaintiff to prove in order to prevail in his/her case. It is the minimum amount of evidence necessary for the court to permit the case to proceed. For example, and in very general terms, in a medical malpractice or tort case, the plaintiff must prove that there was a duty owed by the defendant to the plaintiff, that the defendant breached that duty or standard of care, that the breach in the standard of care proximally or directly caused damage or injury to the plaintiff, and the extent of damages sustained by the plaintiff. A failure to present evidence on any one essential element produces a failure of the plaintiff to carry his/her burden. When the plaintiff finishes presenting his/her evidence, the defendant has the opportunity to make a motion for what is called a directed verdict.

When a defendant moves for a directed verdict, he/she is asking the judge to enter a judgment in his/her favor because the plaintiff has failed to present evidence essential to the elements of the plaintiff's case. If the plaintiff has in fact failed to present evidence on a crucial aspect of his/her case, the judge will enter a verdict in favor of the defense. The case is over, and the defendant need not present his/her case.

If, however, the plaintiff has presented sufficient evidence, regardless of how weak that evidence may be, then a directed verdict motion will be denied. The judge will not substitute his/her judgment for that of the jury in determining whether evidence is strong enough for the plaintiff to win. In that situation, the defendant will have to present his/her case-in-chief.

Following the defendant's case-in-chief, the formal presentation of evidence is usually concluded, unless the plaintiff wants to present rebuttal evidence. Rebuttal evidence is evidence that may be presented to address any new issues raised by the defense that were not previously addressed by or disclosed to the plaintiff. The decision of whether to allow rebuttal evidence lies in the judge's discretion. In some cases, the defendant's "response" to rebuttal evidence may even be allowed.

12.12.2 Witnesses

After the attorneys finish telling the jurors what the evidence will show in opening statements, the formal presentation of evidence begins. Trial evidence is presented primarily by calling witnesses to testify on the client's behalf. The party calling the witness first asks questions during what is called direct examination, or "direct." The opposing party then gets an opportunity to ask questions of the witness during cross-examination, or "cross."

Questions on cross must be limited in scope to those asked on direct. Issues not raised during the direct examination may not be raised exclusively during cross. Cross-examination is not required but is generally a part of the witness examination. In some instances, an opposing party may have no questions at all for tactical reasons or because the witness testified to unimportant or uncontested issues. During cross-examination, the attorney will try to show how that witness' testimony should not be given the authority for which it was elicited. Television is a wonderful medium for showing how cross-examination is used to discredit, weaken, impeach, and undermine a witness' testimony, but a good attorney will often use this time to simultaneously curry favorable opinions from the witness toward that attorney's client's position. Through the strategic use of leading questions, which are questions that call for a yes or no response, an attorney can often use the opponents' witness to limit issues, if not actually help their own cause. Don't you agree?

Following cross-examination, the party calling the witness has an opportunity to conduct redirect examination, or "redirect," and following any redirect, re-cross-examination may take place. Each subsequent examination, however, is limited in scope by the subject matter of the previous examination. Lawyers use redirect to rehabilitate their own witness, who may have been weakening during cross-examination. The idea is that as each round of questioning is concluded, the focus gets narrower and narrower. Consequently, for example, if no questions were asked on cross, redirect is not allowed. After recross, the process is usually concluded, although on rare occasions, a judge may allow further direct and cross if circumstances so warrant.

12.12.3 Exhibits

Exhibits are tangible pieces of evidence that are relevant to the case. Medical records, photographs, and diagrams are common examples of exhibits that may be used during a civil trial. Basically, any tangible object may be used as an exhibit if it will aid the trier of fact in understanding the issues of the case.

The introduction of exhibits at trial is done primarily through witnesses. In order for an exhibit to be introduced into evidence, a witness must testify that the exhibit to be introduced is authentic, true, and accurate, and it must be relevant to an issue in the case. Such testimony is called foundation testimony. Before any exhibit can be introduced into evidence, a foundation must be laid.

Not all exhibits are introduced into evidence. For example, a skeletal model of the skull may be offered as an exhibit in a neurosurgery injury case because it might aid the jury in understanding the case. The skull model, however, may not be relevant to any issue in the case and therefore cannot be introduced into evidence. Such an exhibit is called a demonstrative exhibit.

In contemporary trial presentations, parties are using computer-generated exhibits to assist in the telling of their stories. Studies have often conflicted but, in general, conclude that juries retain only 10% of the oral evidence that they hear and 20% of the visual evidence, but almost 70% of evidence that combines the two aspects into a common presentation. PowerPoint and Excel* presentations provide a mechanism wherein a party can present visual explanations of what a lawyer is orally describing to a jury so that the picture adds a thousand extra words to that said in court. A day-in-the-life video is a short 10-minute or so presentation that plaintiffs' counsel use to show the tragedy of the plaintiff's daily travails to the jury. Overhead projections and computer-generated graphics can vividly exclaim the importance of the evidence. The impact of this type of demonstrative evidence should not be mistaken, because despite the lofty cost for the preparation of these types of exhibits, the impact can be dispositive.

In a case from Mississippi, a plaintiff claimed that since the defendant's orthopedic ankle surgery, she was essentially disabled from doing those activities that she deemed essential. For 3 years, discovery and depositions tested those claims, and she always maintained them under oath and before God. The weekend or so prior to trial, defense counsel contacted the plaintiff's lawyer and asked that she come over to view video surveillance that would be used at trial. Sure enough, there was the plaintiff parking in a handicapped parking space, walking into the gym in a workout uniform, and thereafter, doing aerobics. When confronted, her explanation was that she could do this only at times when she had taken sufficient doses of pain medication and that was the case in the surveillance videos. It took the jury only 20 minutes to decide otherwise.

12.12.4 Objections

During the course of witness testimony or the attempted introduction of an exhibit into evidence, an attorney may state an objection. The main purpose of an objection is to prevent the presentation of certain information to a jury. Information that is not relevant or otherwise prohibited from being presented to a jury is objectionable. It is important to know that the conduct of a trial is not a wide-open search for the truth. Rather, it is a decision-making process in which the parties present their cases according to rules of evidence and procedure.

For routine objections, the attorneys will make brief statements in open court in support of or in opposition to an objection. The judge will then issue a ruling out loud from the bench. In some situations, however, an attorney may object to potentially damaging testimony that he/she wants to keep from the jury, in which case arguing the objection in open court may reveal the damaging information. In such an instance, the attorneys may ask to approach the bench for a *sidebar*. Each attorney then approaches the judge's bench and will discreetly argue the objection out of the jury's earshot. If the objection involves a major issue that requires extensive argument, the judge will excuse the jury from the courtroom so the attorneys can present their arguments out loud and on the record.

If evidence is excluded and an attorney feels that the judge's ruling was incorrect, the attorney may make what is called an offer of proof. In this instance, the excluded evidence

* Microsoft Incorporated.

is presented on the record but out of the presence of the jury. In this way, the evidence is preserved if the party decides to appeal the decision. An offer of proof is rare but effective if an appeal is contemplated.

12.13 SUMMATION

When each side has concluded its case, closing arguments begin. As with opening statements, the length of time allowed varies from case to case and court to court. Unlike opening statements, summation provides the attorney with a final opportunity to convince those jurors who may be in limbo as to the merits of their case as presented. In addition, skillful counsel will focus upon those jurors whom they perceive to be aligned with their position and provide these jurors with the ammunition or evidence necessary to convince other potentially undecided jurors during deliberations. It is the lawyer's final occasion to argue all of the elements of their case, from proving liability to maximizing damages. Conversely, defense counsel will use this opportunity to debunk the plaintiff's case and argue for a defense verdict.

The court does limit exactly what an attorney can argue in closing, but latitude is generally the name of the game. Counsel may draw inferences from the evidence, and while these inferences may be less than factual, if they are grounded in the truth, they are not improper. Courts often advise the attorneys that the final summation is meant as a time to convince the jury of the truth of their argument.* Lawyers do this through a skilled recitation of the evidence, but there is one golden rule about what is considered a closing taboo. Lawyers for the patient are not permitted to ask the jurors to put themselves in the place of the plaintiff and ask the jurors to decide the matter at hand based upon that perception. Similarly, it is improper for defense counsel to ask the jurors to be the defendant. Lawyers are skilled orators who use their abilities to persuade a jury to accept their version of the facts. Yet, fairness and objectivity are the goals that the court should strive to maintain, and most lawyers work within those parameters.

12.14 FINAL INSTRUCTIONS

Following closing arguments, the judge usually excuses the jury so that the attorneys can argue over final instructions. Final instructions are the instructions on the law the judge gives to the jury to guide them in reaching a decision. Only instructions of law that are supported by evidence in the case are given, and that is what the attorneys argue about. Each side will try to persuade the judge to read an instruction to the jury that is favorable to its case.

As noted above, the jury, as the fact finders, will determine what they believe to be the true version of the facts presented at the trial. The jury will then apply those facts to the law as provided in the final instructions. For example, a final instruction may read as follows:

"In order for the plaintiff to prevail, the plaintiff must prove that A, B, and C occurred. If you find that the plaintiff has proven each of these elements, your verdict must be for the plaintiff. If you find that the plaintiff patient has failed to prove even one of these elements, your verdict must be for the defendant doctor."

As with preliminary instructions, final instructions are omitted in a bench trial.

---

* O'Barr v. United States, 105, p. 938 (Oklahoma 1910).

When the judge has decided which final instructions he/she is going to give, the jury is brought back into the courtroom, and the final instructions are read. The judge also instructs the jury on the logistics of reaching a decision, such as choosing a foreman and taking breaks. The jury then retires to the jury room to deliberate.

12.15 JURY DELIBERATIONS

During jury deliberations, the jury is allowed to discuss the case among themselves. If the jury members have followed the judge's preliminary instructions, this will be the first time they discuss the case. Jury research shows that the process of reaching a decision varies widely from jury to jury, as does the time to reach a decision. Like many aspects of the trial process, a lot of conceptions exist about jury deliberations. If the jury deliberates for a relatively short period of time, it is believed that they will return a verdict in favor of the defense. This conception comes from the belief that even if the jury quickly decided in favor of the plaintiff, it usually takes a long time to calculate damages. This conception, however, has proven to be a misconception in many cases.

While the jury is deliberating, the parties and their attorneys usually leave the courthouse and wait at a more comfortable location (usually a nearby restaurant because, for some reason, most jury trials conclude at the end of the day). When the jury returns with a verdict, the parties are contacted to return to the courtroom.

If the jury is unable to reach a verdict, then the jury is considered to be a hung jury. The remedy in the case of a hung jury is a new trial. Because most judges, parties, and plaintiffs' attorneys would rather crawl across a room full of broken glass than retry a case, judges will pressure the jury to keep deliberating until they are able to reach a decision. Can you see any reason why a defense attorney might not mind a hung jury or retrial? If that fails, the judge declares a mistrial, and a new case is eventually scheduled.

12.16 THE VERDICT

When the jury returns to the courtroom to announce its verdict, the collective hearts of the parties and their attorneys can probably generate a registration on a Richter scale. It is the moment of truth, the climax of the entire trial process. After the verdict is read, either party may poll the jury to verify that each juror supports the decision, though a polling of the jury is always done, if at all, by the losing party.

Once the jury is polled, the losing party can also ask the judge to overturn the jury decision, called a motion for judgment notwithstanding the verdict, or judgment *non obstante veredicto* (JNOV). A motion for JNOV is only granted if the judge, in hindsight, believes that the case should not have been submitted to a jury, because there was no evidence that a reasonable person would have credited on an essential element of the plaintiff's case. The judge has the discretion to enter a JNOV, but such discretion is rarely invoked. In most situations, judges are very hesitant to substitute their own judgment for that of the jurors. Once the judge enters a verdict, the trial is over. In a 2002 case involving a professional football player, the jury returned a $5.2 million verdict in favor of the player, but the trial judge, stating at that late date that the plaintiff had failed to prove his case, awarded the defendant a JNOV. As is often the case in that situation, the parties compromised the jury verdict so that neither side was happy with the result.

A medical malpractice trial is nearly always a roller coaster ride of emotions. When the opposing side is putting on its case, you can feel as though you are being pummeled over the head with a baseball bat, and defeat is inevitable. Moments later, your attorney can perform a stunning cross-examination, and victory seems certain. Such is life in our adversarial system, where two parties present the case in a punch, counterpunch format. When the verdict is finally entered, regardless of the outcome, most parties are relieved that it is over. All have a more thorough understanding as to why 97% of civil cases never make it this far.

12.17 PREVENTING/REDUCING INCIDENTS OF MALPRACTICE

As a practicing medical professional, it is important to realize that while you can accept your position in a malpractice case as a passive victim, alternatively, there are numerous methods at your disposal to protect you, your practice, and your family from potential litigation. Certainly, there is not any one approach currently available that would guarantee that a health-care practitioner will never become involved in malpractice litigation. Despite this lack of assurance, there remain alternatives that might well be the divining wand as to whether a potential case spouts success.

12.17.1 Honesty

At each and every risk-management conference, the universal principle promoted by insurance carriers and the foundation that cements a successful doctor–patient relationship is honesty. The ability to honestly communicate with a patient is of such fundamental importance that it is often taken for granted. It is a simple truism that we as human beings want to be told the truth and be told it in such a way that it is beyond reproach. As Paul Starr wrote, patients are often marginalized when they seek the care and treatment of a physician and look up toward that person for those words of reassurance and certainty. In no way are we suggesting that doctors should simply tell the patient the truth that the patient wants to hear. The communication should be one that displays a sense of reality, credibility, compassion, and earnestness. *It can't be stressed to any degree more than this.*

All too often, clients whom we interview ask why their doctor did not tell them the truth. It might not be presented in such a straightforward manner, but it often is as simple as that. On numerous occasions, clients have told me that "if only my doctor had told me the truth, I would never have sued him," or "why didn't my doctor tell me that there was a problem following surgery," or "why did my doctor not tell me that the nerve in my arm was cut by mistake," or "if only my doctor had fessed up." Patients want to know the truth, and despite any hesitance that you might harbor, tell them the truth. Patients are human beings, as are doctors. Patients make mistakes, as do doctors. Car mechanics often don't fix a problem the first time they try, and plumbers often return to fix a leak in a pipe they just soldered closed. Patients know and understand this, so don't sell them short.

We know that at first blush, you are sitting here saying to yourselves that there is no way I can tell the patient what really happened because, if I tell them, they will think I am admitting I was negligent, run to a lawyer, and sue me. Honesty is not the best policy, you conclude. Sorry to rain on your parade, but you are dead wrong. We only wish that we could statistically recount to you the times when we did exactly as we have advised and told the truth. We will say it again and again. Look the patient in the eyes and simply explain to them what happened, why it happened, and what you plan to do to help them overcome the complications that they perceive are existent. Candor is a must, yet the same must be dosed with a touch of caution. While not admitting liability *per se*, don't sugarcoat it so as to appear condescending. Speak up in a timely manner because avoidance can readily be misconstrued. It is not a contest of wills but a willingness to provide a person with the reality of his/her condition and the assurance that you, as his/her physician, care, will listen, and will work with them to resolve the crisis.

Yes, we will admit that there are those instances where a patient will do the exact opposite of what we suggest will be their reaction. If that is the case, then we would submit to you that the patient would have jumped in their car, run, looked in the yellow pages, consulted a lawyer, and filed a lawsuit regardless of the fact. Tell the truth, and the truth will set you free.

12.17.2 Medical Records

Not only are the patient's medical records (paper or electronic) a legal document, these documents remain the central focus of any competent medical malpractice investigation. The records should honestly and in detail reflect the care and treatment provided to that patient based upon the presenting circumstances. Self-serving statements about what the patient did to cause the current complications not only wave a red flag; they hoist it high. This can't be emphasized beyond underscoring the fact that the medical records create the very nature of one's credibility.

In one case, the defendant doctor's notes stated that postoperative problems were caused by chasing after a cat that escaped, in the house. The records stated that the patient came into the office the following day with tree bark and dirt all over the operative bandages. The doctor wrote that her patient told her that she had to climb a tree in her yard to rescue the cat. The problem faced was that the patient/plaintiff denied that the entire episode ever happened. While admitting that she did have a pet cat run out of the house, she steadfastly denied climbing tress or running to catch the animal. The case in question was settled within a few weeks after the doctor's deposition following the doctor's averment that her notes were truthful and accurate. Why? It was simply because we showed the doctor pictures of the patient's home and yard and, as you might have surmised, there were not any trees to be found.

The proverbial subjective, objective, assessment, and plan (and intervention, evaluation, and revision) (SOAP[IER]) method of charting still reflects a professionalism that is so imperative when case records are reviewed. Medical records should be typewritten or computer generated if at all possible, electronic medical records (EMRs) notwithstanding. Each entry should be dated and endorsed by the treating doctor. Notes that are still handwritten need to be legible. Despite any situation that you may encounter and even under the most careful of conditions, do not, we repeat, do not ever modify or alter your medical chart. Scientific advancements in time dating of paper and ink make alterations the easiest way to ensure a plaintiff's success. Any paper record can be changed to modify an error, but you should simply draw a line through the errant portion, note the correction, and date both entries. Not only does this insure the integrity of your medical chart; it also presents a reviewer with the image of a conscientious and honest practitioner. EMRs are date-stamped.

12.18 ASSESSMENT

As hard as it might be for you as a defendant doctor to accept, every trial lawyer will tell you that despite the jury's most earnest efforts, there are those cases that you should win and those cases that you should lose that turn out exactly opposite. Despite the best efforts of all concerned, sometimes, the decision is not the proper one. We leave you with this thought.

During one jury trial, the defendant was a well-known hospital affiliated with the community's largest church. In fact, the name of the hospital reflected the church's denomination. During *voir dire*, the plaintiff's lawyer was specific in asking the jury panel about their religious affiliations, their membership in church-related groups, and almost every other conceivable situation that might have a root into jury prejudice in support of the hospital. The judge provided unlimited *voir dire*, and there were numerous *in camera* examinations of prospective jurors. The jury was selected, and the case was set to begin that following Monday morning. With a packed courtroom, and with the judge and parties all present, the jury members were escorted into their respective seats. Juror number two, a middle-aged female, took out a pink bible, put it between her hands, and prayed during the entire trial.

We think you can appreciate the significance and the regrettable outcome for the plaintiff whose 7-week-old child died during an anesthesia-related incident at the hospital.

12.19 CONCLUSION

As a medical provider, it is important to realize that while you can accept your position in a medical malpractice case as a passive victim, you can also study the more active trial defense methods in this chapter to help protect your practice, family, and professional reputation from harm during litigation.

12.20 COLLABORATE

Discuss this chapter online with others at http://www.medicalexecutivepost.com.

ANONYMITY

Examples are from actual legal cases, but the venue and details of the parties were modified to enhance confidentiality and protect the privacy of participants.

FURTHER READINGS

Aksu MN. Expert witness or "hired gun?" *J Am Coll Dent.* 1997; 4:25–28.

Allen AM. The nurse and the deposition. *Orthop Nurs.* 1987; 6:50–51.

American Psychiatric Association resource document on peer review of expert testimony. *J Am Acad Psychiatry Law.* 1997; 25:359–373.

Annas GJ. Medicine, death, and the criminal law. *N Engl J Med.* 1995; 333:527–530.

Banja JD. *Medical Errors and Medical Narcissism.* Jones and Bartlett Publishers, Sudbury, MA, 2005.

Beckman HB, Markakis KM, Suchman AL, Frankel RM. The doctor–patient relationship and malpractice: Lessons from plaintiff depositions. *Arch Intern Med.* 1994; 154:1365–1370.

Berlin L. On being an expert witness. *AJR.* 1997; 168:607–610.

Bertin JE, Henifin MS. Science, law, and the search for truth in the courtroom: Lessons from Daubert v. Merrell Dow. *J Law Med Ethics.* 1994; 22:6–20.

Black B. Subpoenas and science—When lawyers force their way into the laboratory. *N Engl J Med.* 1997; 336:725–727.

Black E. What to expect at your deposition: A guide for physicians and health care professionals. *Pa Med.* 1998; 101:24.

Blake BL. Sgt. Friday, Dr. Welby, and the demand for patient information: What to do when the police knock. *Mo Med.* 1998; 95:567–573.

Boyarsky S. Practical measures to reduce medical expert witness bias. *J Forensic Sci.* 1989; 34:1259–1265.

Brennan TA, Leape LL, Laird NM et al. Incidence of adverse events and negligence in hospitalized patients: Results of the Harvard Medical Practice Study I. *N Engl J Med.* 1991; 324:370–376.

Brent RL. Bringing scholarship to the courtroom: The Daubert decision and its impact on the Teratology Society. *Teratology.* 1995; 52:247–251.

Breyer S. The interdependence of science and law. *Science.* 1998; 280:537–538.

Buba DJ. Anatomy of a Civil Trial. In Marcinko DE (Editor): *Financial Planning for Physicians.* Aspen Publishing, New York, 2003.

Buba VL. Sexual Harassment Risks in Medical Practice [He Said, She Said … There is No Quid Pro Quo). In Marcinko DE (Editor): *Risk Management and Insurance Planning for Physicians and Advisors—A Strategic Approach.* Springer Publishing, New York, 2004.

Carter R. The subpoena: Coping with the anxiety and stress. *NY State Dent J.* 1997; 63:16–17.

Clifford R. Deposition abstracts provide insights into personal injury cases. *Natl Med Leg J.* 1997; 8:4.

Cohen TH. Medical Malpractice Trials and Verdicts in Large Counties, 2001. BJS Statistician, April 2004, NCJ 203098.

Craft K, McBride A. Pharmacist–patient privilege, confidentiality, and legally-mandated counseling: A legal review. *J Am Pharm Assoc (Wash).* 1998; 38:374–378.

Francisco CJ. Confidentiality, privilege, and release of medical records under a subpoena duces tecum. *Tex Med.* 1991; 87:34–35.

Gilbert JL, Whitworth RL, Ollanik SA, Hare FH Jr. Evidence destruction—Legal consequences of spoliation of records. *Leg Med.* 1994; 181–200.

Hood RD. Some considerations for the expert witness in cases involving birth defects. *Reprod Toxicol.* 1994; 8:269–273.

Hupert N, Lawthers AG, Brennan TA, Peterson LM. Processing the tort deterrent signal: A qualitative study. *Soc Sci Med.* 1996; 43:1–11.

Jessani A, Marcinko DE. Special Situations Financial Planning. In Marcinko DE (Editor): *Comprehensive Financial Planning Strategies for Doctors and Advisors.* Productivity Press, Boca Raton, FL, 2015.

Karp D. Deposition preparedness is essential to malpractice defense: Experienced defense attorneys offer advice for physicians. *Mich Med.* 1994; 93:27–29.

Kern SI. Responding to subpoenas and other demands for records and testimony. *NJ Med.* 1996; 93:85–88.

LaCava W. Medical Malpractice Trail Primer. In Marcinko DE (Editor): *Insurance and Risk Management Strategies for Doctors and Advisors.* J B Publishing, Sudbury, MA, 2004.

Licata LJ, Allison TH. Subpoenas for medical records served upon physicians. *Ohio Med.* 1989; 85:48–51.

Lindauer C. The video deposition—"You are the witness." *Natl Med Leg J.* 1990; 1:7–8.

Localio AR, Lawthers AG, Brennan TA et al. Relation between malpractice claims and adverse events due to negligence: Results of the Harvard Medical Practice Study III. *N Engl J Med.* 1991; 325:245–251.

Mandell MS. 10 legal safeguards for giving a deposition. *Nurs Life.* 1988; 8:50–51.

Marcinko DE, Hetico HR. *Dictionary of Health Insurance and Managed Care.* Springer Publishing, New York, 2007.

Marcinko DE, Hetico HR. *Dictionary of Health Economics and Finance.* Springer Publishing, New York, 2008.

McAbee GN. Improper expert medical testimony: Existing and proposed mechanisms of oversight. *J Leg Med.* 1998; 19:257–272.

Meadow W, Lantos JD. Expert testimony, legal reasoning, and justice: The case for adopting a data-based standard of care in allegations of medical negligence in the NICU. *Clin Perinatol.* 1996; 23:583–595.

Miller C. Asset Planning and Protection Principles. In Marcinko DE (Editor): *Comprehensive Financial Planning Strategies for Doctors and Advisors.* Productivity Press, Boca Raton, FL, 2015.

Millock PJ. The Harvard Medical Malpractice Study and the malpractice debate in New York State. *Leg Med.* 1991; 111–125.

Neoral L. Forensic medicine, its tasks and duties in medical malpractice and medico–legal litigation. *Med Law.* 1998; 17:283–286.

Perry C. Admissibility and per se exclusion of hypnotically elicited recall in American courts of law. *Int J Clin Exp Hypn.* 1997; 45:266–279.

Peters BM, Rosenbloom AG. The physician's deposition: Preparation and testimony of the medical malpractice defendant. *Pediatr Emerg Care.* 1987; 3:194–201.

Plunkett LR. Anatomy of a dental malpractice case: Subpoenas and confidentiality. *NY State Dent J.* 1997; 63:8–11.

Purnell L. What to do if called upon to testify. *Accid Emerg Nurs.* 1995; 3:19–21.

Rappeport JR. Effective courtroom testimony. *Psychiatr Q.* 1992; 63:303–317.

Reed ME. Daubert and the breast implant litigation: How is the judiciary addressing the science? *Plast Reconstr Surg.* 1997; 100:1322–1326.

Richards EP, Walter C. Science in the Supreme Court: Round two. *IEEE Eng Med Biol Mag.* 1998; 17:124–125.

Rosenbaum JT. Lessons from litigation over silicone breast implants: A call for activism by scientists. *Science.* 1997; 276:1524–1525.

Smith RH, Griffin M Jr. A keep-your-cool guide to giving a deposition. *RN.* 1988; 51:77–79.

Stinson V, Devenport JL, Cutler BL, Kravitz DA. How effective is the motion-to-suppress safeguard? Judges' perceptions of the suggestiveness and fairness of biased lineup procedures. *J Appl Psychol.* 1997; 82:211–220.

Strasburger LH, Gutheil TG, Brodsky A. On wearing two hats: Role conflict in serving as both psychotherapist and expert witness. *Am J Psychiatry.* 1997; 154:448–456.

Tammelleo AD. Nurse asks "Should I get a lawyer?" *Regan Rep Nurs Law.* 1994; 35:1.

Ventura MJ. Are these nurses criminals? *RN.* 1997; 60:26–29.

Walter C, Richards EP. Keeping junk science out of the courtroom. *IEEE Eng Med Biol Mag.* 1998; 17:78–81.

Walter C, Richards EP. The social responsibility of scientists: The scientific impact statement. *IEEE Eng Med Biol Mag.* 1998; 17:94–95.

Weirich AM. The deposition. *Home Health Nurse.* 1996; 14:876–877.

Zonana H. Daubert v. Merrell Dow Pharmaceuticals: A new standard for scientific evidence in the courts? *Bull Am Acad Psychiatry Law.* 1994; 22:309–325.

TIPS FOR LOOKING FOR MEDICAL PROFESSIONAL LIABILITY COVERAGE

The following are buying tips for health-care professionals who are shopping for medical professional liability insurance coverage:

- Shop well in advance of your renewal or expiration date. Your agent should have all of the necessary information to the insurer at least 6 to 8 weeks before your coverage expires. See the attached checklist for the types of information your agent will need.

- If you do not know an agent who can place your coverage, the bureau of insurance has a list of agencies that are licensed and appointed with at least one of the insurers on the bureau's list of "Insurers Writing New Business for Physicians and Surgeons."
- Contact one or two agents and be sure to ask each agent which insurer will be contacted for a quote. Ask the agent if an application will also be submitted to a surplus lines broker. If so, ask for the name of the surplus lines broker and ask which surplus lines insurers will be contacted. Provide this information to the other agent to avoid multiple applications being submitted to one insurer from different agents. If the application is being submitted to a surplus lines broker, be sure to ask the agent for information on the coverage provided and specifically request information on exclusions.
- If the agent recommends coverage through an unlicensed company (such as a surplus lines insurer or a risk-retention group), be aware that, in the case of insolvency, the insured will not have coverage through the (state) property and casualty insurance guaranty association. However, if health-care professionals have had several claims or an open claim, they may only be able to obtain coverage through a company not licensed in their state.
- Ask the agent for information on the financial rating of the company and if the surplus lines insurer has its own guaranty fund. Also, if shopping, the medical professional should feel free to check with the insurance bureau of their respective state to see if the company and agent are licensed or authorized to do business.
- The agent should fully understand the health-care professional's business. If incorporated, ask the agent what coverage is needed to protect the corporation as well as any individual doctors.
- Ask the agent about the availability of "tail coverage" or if the new insurer will provide coverage for "prior acts." If coverage is offered with two insurers, ask the agent what each insurer charges for tail coverage. This information may help in deciding which insurer has the most competitive price.
- Complete the application for coverage in its entirety. Don't omit any information, and be sure to provide as much detail as possible, especially about prior claims. Many insurance companies want 10 years of information. They may also request information about any risk-management practices and procedures.
- Discuss deductible options with your agent. These may help lower your premium.
- Find out if the insurance company offers any risk-management or loss-prevention programs. Such programs may lower the premium and help reduce exposure to losses.

INFORMATION CHECKLIST FOR PHYSICIANS SEEKING INSURANCE

The following are sample questions and information gathered for professional liability coverage.

Background, Education, and Certifications

- Medical specialty information by percentage of practice
- Information on medical education, including information on medical school attended; internship information, residency information, and fellowship information, if any
- Information on medical experience, including information on military discharge (DD214), public health service, moonlighting, "locum tenens," and private practice information

Have dates and locations available (the first four items may be contained in a *curriculum vita*, if you have one):

- Information on completed continuing education hours in the past 2 years
- Publications, speeches, instruction, etc.
- Information on medical licenses, including state, license number, expiration dates, and current status
- Information on board certifications
- On an as-applicable basis, complete details including dates and outcomes of any board certification revocations or suspensions, license revocations or suspensions, alcohol or drug addictions and treatments, criminal or sexual misconduct charges, or Medicare or Medicaid charges
- Previous insurance information: insurance history, including the name, policy number, whether the coverage form was occurrence or claims made, policy period, limits of liability, deductible amount, and prior acts date, for your current carrier, and your first, second, third, and fourth prior carrier, if applicable
- Information on any insurance company cancellations or nonrenewals
- If the current policy is a claims-made policy, whether you are obtainnig tail coverage from your current insurance company
- Copies of prior policies, if available

Current Medical Practice Information

- Information on supervision and employment of residents, physician assistants, nurse practitioners, certified registered nurse anesthetists (CRNAs), nurse midwives, and other physicians
- Information on networks or managed care organizations associated with (IPA, PHO, MSO, etc.), including group name, type of organization, and relationship
- Information on other contractual relationships, other than PPOs, HMOs, IPAs, etc.

- Full information on all hospital privileges, including hospital name, location, and type of privilege
- If any, information on any suspension, denial, revocation, restriction, or other sanctioning of hospital privileges

Classification and Specialty Identification

Full information on procedures performed, including details of surgeries, average number of patients seen weekly, specialty practice areas, etc.

Prior Claims History (If Any)

For each claim, patient's name; date of occurrence; insurance carrier; location of occurrence; date claim was reported; date claim was closed (if applicable); copies of subpoenas, pleadings, or judgments; amount reserved on your behalf; and amount paid on your behalf. Provide as complete a description of the allegations as possible.

Important Note

This is provided as a guide to assist the health-care professional in gathering the information that insurance companies typically request. Discuss this checklist with your insurance agent, attorney, or councilor to identify additional information as needed.

Section II

The Physicians Foundation Issues a List of Concerns for 2016–2017 and Beyond

MEDICAL PRACTITIONER BUSINESS ISSUES

(Corporate Liability Is Just the Tip of the Risk Management Iceberg)

For modern physicians and medical providers, a comprehensive enterprise risk management plan must acknowledge more business and corporate risks than ever before, and in an economically sound manner not counterproductive to individual components of the plan. These business risks include those not considered just a decade ago, in addition to the personal perils reviewed in the first section of this book.

For example, evidence-based medicine (EBM) and health economics outcome research (HEOR) risks necessitate billing company reviews; debt and accounts receivable (AR) protection strategies with internal controls for office embezzlement protection; patient Internet portals, data breaches, cybersecurity, and digital asset protection architectures; and LGBT (lesbian, gay, bisexual, and transgender) discrimination issues with workplace violence risks; all while pay-for-performance (P4P), global reimbursement, and capitation payer risks increase, along with whistleblower, *mystery shopper*, and reputation management concerns for blogging doctors and social media medical aficionados.

Now, add peer-review perils, state medical licensing board overreach, hospital credentialing, and physician hospital organization (PHO) risks to the mix. And, don't forget the psychological stress of change management, career depression, physician self-burnout with premature retirement, and the ultimate—doctor suicide.

Moreover, a plethora of acronymic risks include the Patient Protection and Affordable Care Act (PP-ACA), the Health Insurance Portability and Accountability Act (HIPAA) and the Health Information Technology for Economic and Clinical Health (HITECH) Act, Occupational Safety and Health Administration (OSHA) Act, Clinical Laboratory

Improvement Act (CLIA), Emergency Medical Treatment and Active Labor Act (EMTALA), Comprehensive Error Rate Testing Contractor (CERT), Nation Provider Identification (NPI) number, National Correct Coding Initiative (NCCI), Health Care Fraud and Abuse Control Program (HCFACP), Medicare Drug Integrity Contractor (MEDICP), Environmental Protection Agency (EPA) Act, Limited English Proficiency (LEP) Act, Drug Enforcement Agency (DEA) Act, Recovery Asset Contractors (RACs), Medicare Administrative Contractors (MACs), Medicaid Integrity Contractor (MIC) programs, Zone Program Integrity Contracts (ZPICs), Corporate Integrity Agreements (CIAs), Regional Extension Centers (RECs), Civil Asset Forfeiture (CAF) Act, Federal False Claims Act (FFCA), National Supplier Clearinghouse Contractors (NSCs) and Coordination of Benefits Contractors (COBCs), Preventing and Reducing Improper Medicare and Medicaid Expenditures Act (PRIME), Department of Transportation, Employee Retirement Income Security Act (ERISA), Consolidated Omnibus Budget Reconciliation Act (COBRA), Federal Trade Commission (FTC) antitrust risks, etc.; the list seems endless.

Therefore, much like the personal risks reviewed in Section I, the integration of these enterprise practice issues is no longer an academic luxury for modern health-care business entities, office practices, medical clinics, and/or providers, but a pragmatic survival imperative long recognized by the Institute of Medical Business Advisors Inc. (iMBA Inc.) and presented in Section II of this textbook.

On December 14, 2015, the Physicians Foundation released its *2016 Physicians Watch List*, an insight into the business and management trends physicians are witnessing or predicting will occur in health care.

The *Watch List*, based on the results of a survey of over 20,000 physicians, noted "five critical areas that will have major impact on practicing physicians" during the 2016–2017 calendar period, and beyond: (1) increasing provider consolidation; (2) increased strain on the physician–patient relationship; (3) electronic health records (EHRs) and the implementation of International Classification of Diseases (ICD)-10; (4) liability and the cost of care transparency for both patients and physicians; and (5) telemedicine and access to medical care.

Health-care providers, administrators, risk managers, and compliance personnel can use this information to develop courses of action to mitigate these liability concerns while also promoting high-quality, cost-efficient medical practice.

Therefore Section II, on the business risk of medical practice, summarizes these five known areas of management concern and includes many additional new-wave risks, perils, hazards, menaces, dangers, pitfalls, and future threats. And, it suggests possible courses of action that all physicians, medical providers, health-care administrators, and risk managers may take to potentially mitigate these impending concerns, at least in some small increment.

Remember, forewarned is forearmed.

Professor Hope Rachel Hetico, RN, MHA, CPHQ, CMP™
Distinguished Professor of Health-Care Administration

13 Business Insurance Planning
Protecting the Medical Practice

Thomas A. Muldowney, David Edward Marcinko, and Gary A. Cook

CONTENTS

Insurance is not only an important component of a personal financial plan; it also plays a key role in the financial stability of a medical practice, clinic, or health-care business entity. Life insurance can keep a medical practice or clinic going should the physician-executive owner die, as well as prevent financial hardship for the doctor's family. Without life insurance, the family of a doctor may need to liquidate the practice assets quickly to come up with cash upon the owner's death. A liquidation sale often results in the family receiving far less than market value for the assets. Life insurance can provide the money that eliminates the urgency in liquidating the practice assets.

13.1 BUSINESS USES OF LIFE INSURANCE

13.1.1 Key Person Insurance

Hospitals, a local family practice office, and a pharmaceutical company, all likely have one thing in common. Somewhere within these companies or partnerships, there are key employees or profit makers. Due to their expertise, management skills, knowledge, or "history of why," they have become indispensable to their employers.

If this key employee were to die prematurely, what would potentially happen to the company? In many cases, especially in smaller companies, it would have a devastating effect on the bottom line, or even precipitate a bankruptcy. In these circumstances, a form of business insurance, called key person coverage, is recommended in order to alleviate the potential financial problems resulting from the death of that employee.

The business would purchase and own a life insurance policy on the key person. Upon the death of the employee, the life insurance proceeds could be used to

- Pay off bank loans
- Replace the lost profits of the company
- Establish a reserve for the search, hiring, and training of a replacement

13.1.2 Business Continuation Funding

See the chapters on buy–sell agreements (Chapter 18) and asset protection planning (Chapter 8).

13.1.3 Executive Bonus Plan

An executive bonus plan (or Section 162 plan) is an effective way for a company to provide valued, select employees an additional employment benefit. One of the main advantages to an executive bonus plan, when compared to other benefits, is its simplicity. In a typical executive bonus plan, an agreement is made between the employer and employee, whereby the employer agrees to pay for the cost of a life insurance policy, in the form of a bonus, on the life of the employee.

The major benefits of such a plan to the employee are that he/she is the immediate owner of the cash values and the death benefit provided. The only cost to the employee is the payment of income tax on any bonus received. The employer receives a tax deduction for providing the benefit, improves the morale of its selected employees, and can use the plan as a tool to attract additional talent.

13.1.4 Nonqualified Salary Continuation

Commonly referred to as deferred compensation, this is a legally binding promise by an employer to pay a salary continuation benefit at a specific point in the future, in exchange for the current and continued performance of its employee. These plans are normally used to supplement existing retirement plans.

Although there are different variations of deferred compensation, in a typical deferred compensation agreement, the employer will purchase and own a life insurance policy on the life of the employee. The cash value of the policy grows tax deferred during the employee's working years. After retirement, these cash values can be withdrawn from the policy to reimburse the company for its after-tax retirement payments to the employee.

Upon the death of the employee, any remaining death benefit would likely be received income tax–free by the employer. (Alternative minimum taxes could apply to any benefit received by certain larger C corporations.) The death benefit could then be used to pay any required survivor benefits to the employee's spouse, or provide partial or total cost recovery to the employer.

In a typical plan, the terms of the agreement are negotiated as to the amount of benefit received by the employee, when retirement benefits can begin, how long retirement benefits will be paid, and if benefits will be provided for death or disability. The business has established what is commonly referred to as "golden handcuffs" for the employee. As a result, the benefit will only be received if the employee continues to work for the company until retirement. If the employee is terminated or quits prior to retirement, the plan would end, and no benefits would be paid.

13.1.5 Split-Dollar Plans

Split-dollar arrangements can be a complicated and confusing concept for even the most experienced insurance professional or financial advisor. This concept is, in its simplest terms, a way for a business to share the cost and benefit of a life insurance policy with a valued employee. In a normal split-dollar arrangement, the employee will receive valuable life insurance coverage at little cost to them. The business pays the majority of the premium but is usually able to recover the entire cost of providing this benefit at termination of employment, death, or surrender of the policy.

Following the publication of Internal Revenue Service (IRS) Notices 2002-8 and 2002-59, there are currently two general approaches to the ownership of business split-dollar life insurance: employer-owned or employee-owned.

13.1.5.1 Employer-Owned Method

In the employer-owned method, the employer is the sole owner of the policy. A written split-dollar agreement usually permits the employee to name the beneficiary for most of the death proceeds. The employer owns all the cash value and has the unfettered right to borrow or withdraw it as necessary. At the end of the formal agreement, the business can generally (1) continue the policy as key person insurance, (2) transfer ownership to the insured and report the cash values as additional income to the insured, (3) sell the policy to the insured, or (4) use a combination of these methods. This is commonly referred to as "rollout."

Practitioners should be careful not to include rollout language in the split-dollar agreement. The reason the rollout should not be included is that if the parties formally agree that after a specified number of years—or following a specific event, related only to the circumstances surrounding the policy—the policy will be turned over to the insured, the IRS could declare that the entire transaction was a sham and that its sole purpose was to avoid taxation of the premiums to the employee, generating substantial interest and penalties in addition to the additional taxes due.

The death proceeds available to the insured employee's beneficiary are considered a current and reportable economic benefit (REB), and it is an annually taxable event to the employee. If an individual policy is involved, the REB is calculated by multiplying the face amount by the government's Table 2016 rates or the insurance company's alternative term rates, using the insured's age. If a second-to-die policy is involved, the government's PS38 rates or the company's alternative PS38 rates will be used. Any part of the premium actually paid by the employee is used to offset any REB dollar for dollar.

13.1.5.2 Employee-Owned Method

With the employee-owned method, the insured employee is generally the applicant and owner of the policy. Any premiums paid by the business are deemed to be loans to the employee, and the employee reports as income an imputed interest rate on the cumulative amount of loan based on Code § 7872. A collateral assignment is made for the benefit of the business to cover the cumulative loan amount. In some cases, the assignment may allow the assignee to have access to the cash values of the policy by way of a policy loan. This method is unavailable for officers and executives of publicly held corporations because of the current restrictions on corporate loans (the Sarbanes–Oxley Act of 2002).

The employee-owned method is somewhat similar to the older collateral assignment split-dollar form. The benefits for the employee are both the ability to control large amounts of death proceeds as well as developing equity in the policy. Whether or not this new method catches on will depend greatly on the imputed interest rate published by the IRS every July. If set low enough, this may be an excellent opportunity for the employee to use inexpensive business dollars to pay for life insurance.

13.2 OTHER MEDICAL PRACTICE AND BUSINESS-RELATED INSURANCE

There are other important medical practice, and business-related, insurance products that physicians should be aware of, including the following.

13.2.1 General Commercial Property Insurance

Commercial or business insurance protects against those perils and losses that a healthcare practitioner routinely faces in the practice of medicine. These exposures are both wide and varied and include aspects that may never affect most practitioners, such as the explosion of boilers, aviation mishaps, or a ship's hulls failing. However, many risk exposures should be considered.

13.2.1.1 Covered Property

- Buildings
- Business personal property, which may be the practice/business
- Property and equipment used in the business
- Personal property of others in the care and custody of the policy owner

13.2.1.2 Covered Perils

This topic defies clear summarization because it usually defines the exposures unique to the health-care practice. The risks of loss for a radiology practice are different from those of an obstetrician/gynecology office. Within numerous policy forms, "named perils" are identified in addition to the "all-risks" form that generally cover common perils such as crime or fire. In addition, just like with the individual homeowner's policies, endorsements can be obtained to cover unique and specific risks, such as earthquakes in California and hurricanes in Florida.

13.2.1.3 Loss Settlement

This special provision of commercial policies provides for the settlement of losses on a cash-value basis. Most policies are subject to a deductible amount, although "full loss replacement value" coverage is usually available. Typically, the deductible is 20% of the covered value, with the insurance company only covering the balance. As with personal lines of coverage, the amount of the deductible affects the premium charged.

13.2.2 Commercial General Liability Insurance

Commercial general liability (CGL) provides coverage for a wide variety of risks that a medical/health-care facility may face. In brief, these exposures will include the following (there are others in a general liability policy that may be "endorsed out" for the particular practice):

- Premises liability—injuries on the property owned or occupied by policy owner
- Business operations liability—losses caused by business activities of employees
- Contractual liability—litigation arising from oral or written contracts

Unfortunately, for the medical practitioner, as with many property and liability contracts, liabilities that occur "from the rendering or failure to render professional services" are standard exclusions from this section of liability coverage.

Often, insurance companies offer "packaged" programs, or business owner's policies (BOPs), especially for small to medium practices. These policies include all-risks coverages for the property and limited liability. Most BOP programs include such coverages as the following:

- Debris removal
- Fire department service charges
- Pollutant cleanup and removal
- Water damage

Most importantly, BOP contracts will cover the following:

- *Loss of business income* (it is difficult to run the practice if half of it was destroyed by water damage from the fire in the office upstairs)
- *Extra expense coverage* (the cost of renting substitute property while the covered property is being repaired)
- *Payroll expense* (the need to retain specialists or key employees while the property is being rehabilitated)

Although the latter is limited in amounts and period of coverage, it is valuable coverage, especially for professional practices. Finally, the BOP will cover losses due to crime (such as forgery and alteration). As with commercial liability coverage, professional liability is excluded from BOPs.

13.2.3 Professional Liability (Medical Malpractice) Coverage

For liability protection not covered under the general liability provisions, the health-care professional can obtain *professional liability coverage*. This coverage is generally defined as insurance to protect against failures to use the degree or skill expected of a person in a particular profession. This coverage is also known as *malpractice insurance*.

A discussion of the current issues regarding this particular coverage is unnecessary. The debate continues, even among health-care professionals, as to the causes of the dramatic increases in premiums—and claims—in recent years. Insurance company underwriting losses (generally speaking, claims) increased to 160–170% of the premiums collected in 2012–2013. Combine this with poor investment returns in 2007 and 2008, and the result is substantially increased insurance premiums—which will probably continue into the future. Fortunately, professional liability coverage is universally offered through professional organizations and associations. It would be prudent to investigate coverage through these groups because the policies are often structured and created for the specific requirements of the specialty and are frequently more financially attractive.

Professional liability coverage is specified in a general liability endorsement policy. Doctor policy owners should take care in specifically reviewing this provision of the contract with their insurance professional, especially one with thorough knowledge and experience in this significant area. The terminology used in the policy language may have long-reaching effects on practitioners and their practice.

Since most insurance companies develop unique policies with specialized language for the medical profession, policies are, therefore, quite varied. The general provisions typically include the following:

- *Covered acts*: Although the language will vary widely among insurers, this agreement generally covers acts, errors, or omissions that occur while performing professional services.
- *Coverage—occurrence versus "claims made"*: This area needs particular scrutiny and discussion with your insurance professional. The confusion here concerns what coverage (most particularly, what insurance company) was in force when the event causing the liability *occurred* versus what coverage was in force when the *claim was made*. Review this language to ensure that the contract contains the proper

endorsements. If the coverage is on a "claims made" form, an extended reporting period—also known as a "tail coverage" option—should be included. Some states restrict the premium that can be charged for this feature, and it is often not included. Secondly, new limits on the coverage are often offered, and the period of any tail coverage varies. The new limits and period of coverage are important issues since extended coverage is considered "long tail" and should be reviewed carefully to ensure that the health-care professional policy meets your risk-management tolerance. The policyholder should attempt to get unlimited tail coverage and consider 36 months to be the minimum acceptable period.

- *Definition of "medical services" or "professional liability"*: This definition is the foundation of the policy and must fit the practitioner's level of comfort.
- *Definition of "incident"*: Each policy provides a broad definition of *incident*, thereby providing coverage for claims that arise while health-care professionals are doing their job.
- *Defense coverage*: This provision identifies that the cost of defending against a civil action suit, proceeding, or demand by any person arising out of any actual or alleged act, error, or omission will be covered by the policy. Defense coverage may be provided even if the allegations of the claim are groundless, false, or fraudulent. The contract may also include the costs of depositions and peripheral legal expenses. This would include the loss of income and extraordinary expenses incurred for the practice. The medical practitioner should review these provisions carefully, since some policies include these costs under the "total limits" of the policy, while other companies may cover this provision only by an additional endorsement.
- *Personal injury protection*: This provision may also be included in any individual malpractice policy. This coverage protects the health-care professional from any lawsuit resulting from allegations of personal injuries like breach of a patient's privacy or confidentiality, slander, and libel during the performance of your professional services. This coverage part is usually consistent with the professional liability coverage limits.
- *Broad range of limits of liability*: All insurance programs offer a wide range of limits health-care professionals can select to fit their professional liability exposure. Limits typically range anywhere from a minimum of $250,000/$500,000 (limit per claim/annual aggregate limit) to a more typical $2,500,000/$5,000,000. Some locations, where malpractice coverage has been difficult to maintain, have limits nearing $10,000,000.

The following are buying tips for doctors and health-care professionals who are shopping for medical professional liability (malpractice) insurance coverage:

- Shop well in advance of your renewal or expiration date. Your agent should have all of the necessary information to the insurer at least 6 to 8 weeks before your coverage expires.
- If you do not know an agent who can place your coverage, the bureau of insurance has a list of agencies that are licensed and appointed, with at least one of the insurers on the bureau's list of "Insurers Writing New Business for Physicians and Surgeons."

- Contact one or two agents and be sure to ask each agent which insurer will be contacted for a quote. Ask the agent if an application will also be submitted to a surplus lines broker. If so, ask for the name of the surplus lines broker and ask which surplus lines insurers will be contacted. Provide this information to the other agent to avoid multiple applications being submitted to one insurer from different agents. If the application is being submitted to a surplus lines broker, be sure to ask the agent for information on the coverage provided and specifically request information on exclusions.
- If the agent recommends coverage through an unlicensed company (such as a surplus lines insurer or a risk-retention group), be aware that, in the case of insolvency, the insured will not have coverage through the (state) property and casualty insurance guaranty association. However, if health-care professionals have had several claims or an open claim, they may only be able to obtain coverage through a company not licensed in their state.
- Ask the agent for information on the financial rating of the company and if the surplus lines insurer has its own guaranty fund. Also, if shopping, medical professionals should feel free to check with the insurance bureau of their respective states to see if the company and agent are licensed or authorized to do business.
- The agent should fully understand the health-care professional's business. If incorporated, ask the agent what coverage is needed to protect the corporation as well as any individual doctors.
- Ask the agent about the availability of tail coverage or if the new insurer will provide coverage for "prior acts." If coverage is offered with two insurers, ask the agent what each insurer charges for tail coverage. This information may help in deciding which insurer has the most competitive price.
- Complete the application for coverage in its entirety. Don't omit any information, and be sure to provide as much detail as possible, especially about prior claims. Many insurance companies want 10 years of information. They may also request information about any risk-management practices and procedures.
- Discuss deductible options with your agent. These may help lower your premium.
- Find out if the insurance company offers any risk-management or loss-prevention programs. Such programs may lower the premium and help reduce exposure to losses.

13.2.4 Worker's Compensation

While medical practitioners and facilities can operate without professional liability coverage, one type of business-related insurance that cannot be avoided is worker's compensation. Employers in all but seven states—so-called monopolistic states because they have their own state funds—are under statutory obligation to provide coverage for their employees. Historically, worker's compensation predates social security entitlements and was present well before the emergence of employer-sponsored group benefits.

The coverage under worker's compensation provides for lost income due to on-the-job accidents or work-related disability or death, and the amount of benefits vary by state. In some instances, the coverage will reimburse the employee for medical expenses incurred due to the accident. The four general benefits covered under worker's compensation are as follows:

- *Medical care*—for expenses incurred usually, without limitations on amount or period of care.
- *Disability income*—payable for both total and partial disability and usually based on 66.66% of the employee's wage base.
- *Death benefits*—generally fall into two categories: (1) a flat amount for "burial" insurance and (2) survivor benefits. Though varying by state, these benefits are similar to the disability payment (a percentage of weekly base wages) but may be capped as to total benefit, such as $50,000, or a period, such as 10 years.
- *Rehabilitation benefits*—includes not only medical rehabilitation but also vocational rehabilitation, vocational counseling, retraining or educational benefits, and job placement.

Traditionally, the secondary purpose of worker's compensation was to reduce potential litigation, because employees accepting the benefits from a worker's compensation claim generally waived their right to sue their employer. However, in our litigious society, this "protective shelter" has been severely tested and is crumbling.

Employers may provide their worker's compensation in three ways:

- Private commercial insurance
- State government funds
- Self-insurance

Very few factors drive the premium structure—the occupation of the workers is the single most important determinant of premiums. An office worker may have premiums as low as $0.10 per $100 of wages, and a coal miner may exceed $50.00 per $100 of wages. Generally speaking, however, worker's compensation premiums for the medical profession or health-care worker are among the lowest available.

Therefore, for the medical practice, some physicians may consider self-insurance because the weekly benefits are typically below $500, thus making this decision attractive. Alternatively, because officers and owners can elect not to be covered by worker's compensation, the decision to purchase coverage from a private insurance company may afford inexpensive assurance that the benefits will be conveniently provided, and administered, by a private insurance company for the employees.

13.2.5 Other Forms of Property and Liability Coverage

Obviously, not all forms of coverage can be described in detail; however the medical practitioner should consider other forms of commercial property and liability coverage.

13.2.5.1 Directors and Officers Liability Insurance

The officers and directors of large practices, or health-care facilities, can be held personally accountable, and thus liable, for breaches of their duties by a number of parties.

Overheard in the Advisor's Lounge

Directors and Officers Insurance Policy

One of my clients owns and is the president of a multistate health business entity that produces over $10 million a year in annual revenue. The business faces numerous regulatory requirements and, because it is being closely held and managed by my client, he would certainly face direct personal liability for decisions, acts, and omissions he made in his executive capacity, including data breach and labor-related claims as two specific examples.

When he contacted his insurance agent for quotes on directors and officers liability insurance (DOLI) adequate for his liability level, I was shocked to learn that his agent had informed him that he couldn't get DOLI coverage unless he was on the board of a homeowners' association (HOA) or a big corporation. Not only was the agent just plain wrong; he likely committed some professional malpractice by not doing a little research and making a sale to a client that actually needed help. To confirm, I checked with commercial liability insurance agent Dallas Cowan at Minard-Ames Insurance in Phoenix. The agent was shocked and confirmed that the insurance was in fact available and that it was especially important for medical practice owner/operators who have direct liability for a variety of issues, compared to those in deeper management structures of larger public or private corporations with multiple layers of management and a system of checks and balances under a board of directors.

Honestly, fewer people to blame means more blame for each medical executive or business owner for more issues, including, in some cases, criminal liability, even for acts committed without the health-care executive's direct knowledge or permission.

Ike Devji, JD
Phoenix, Arizona

13.2.5.2 Commercial Automobile/Vehicle Insurance

As the name suggests, this coverage provides protection for any commercial (not personal) vehicles owned and operated by the health-care corporation. If the practice or facility owns automobiles or other vehicles that are used in the "usual and customary" business activities, this coverage is required. The policy owner should be aware of the nine classifications of automobiles insured to ensure that coverage is appropriate.

13.2.5.3 Commercial Umbrella Liability Insurance

This coverage is very similar to the personal umbrella coverage discussed under the personal coverage area. Again, risks above the limits established by the underlying commercial liability coverage trigger the umbrella policy. The word of caution for this coverage is "read the provisions carefully," as there is little standardization among insurance companies. Make sure the umbrella policy covers what you want it to cover, with the right limits of benefits and trigger points, with proper exclusions and proper endorsements (if being used specifically for a medical practice).

EXAMPLE:

- A claimant won a $1,500,000 judgment against the insured.
- The insured's CGL policy and excess liability (umbrella) policy both covered the claim.
- Each policy had an "each occurrence" limit of $1,000,000.

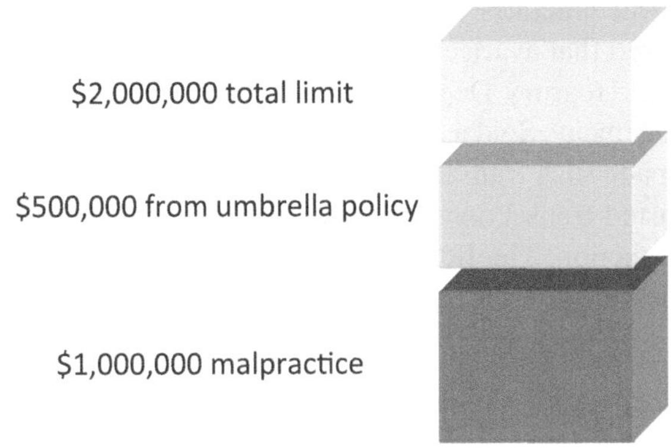

Overheard in the Advisor's Lounge

Welfare Benefit Trust Plans for Physicians

Physicians unfortunately often become unwitting targets of some very egregious investment advice. Usually, it involves an investment product with an imbedded fat commission just waiting to be deposited in a "financial advisor's" bank account.

In the "Hall of Fame" of egregious investment advice is the welfare benefit trust. About 10 years ago, while I was working for a top-five national brokerage firm (this was before my fee-only days when I was still on the "dark side"), our internal insurance products department at the brokerage firm's head office presented an amazing investment product. This "welfare benefit trust," we were told, should be shown to our profitable small-business owners, and doctors, as a cure for their every ill caused by paying too much taxes. A welfare benefit trust essentially works like this:

- The business or medical practice provides a fringe benefit for its employees, such as health insurance and life insurance.
- The benefit is established in the name of a trust and funded with a cash-value life insurance policy.
- Here is the gravy: the entire amount deposited into the trust (insurance policy) is tax deductible to the company.
- The owners of the company can withdraw the cash value from the policy in later years tax-free.

Yes, the holy grail of tax avoidance has been achieved: tax deductible up front and tax-free when you withdraw. By the way, if you are not familiar with such investments, there is a reason. They are not legal by the tax code. Physician practices, as well as other small and midsized businesses, became buyers into these welfare benefit trusts as they were sold as a way for the practice to "protect" a large profit in a certain year from being taxed. We were told it was not uncommon for a single transaction into a welfare benefit trust to be $200,000 to $300,000 or more in a single premium payment, yielding typically a six-figure commission check.

A few years later, the jig was up as it became obvious these could not be tax legal. My understanding is that most medical practices that bought these "unrolled" them when the major brokerage firms realized that avarice got the best of them and stopped selling them. In 2007, the IRS and the Treasury Department issued a formal warning cautioning "about certain Trust Arrangements Sold as Welfare Benefit Funds." The IRS called these "abusive schemes" and made such transactions what the IRS lovingly calls "listed transactions." Essentially, a listed transaction is a transaction that the IRS has determined to be a tax avoidance transaction. The IRS even keeps these listed transactions on their website, listed in chronological order from 1 to 34. Welfare benefit trusts is number 33.

GOOD WELFARE BENEFIT TRUSTS

First of all, it is important to mention that "there are many legitimate welfare benefit funds that provide benefits," according to the IRS. Internal Revenue Code sections 419 and 419(a) spell out the rules allowing employers to make tax-deductible contributions to welfare benefit plans. There is nothing wrong with these plans and no mystery to them. After all, a medical practice or any business, for that matter, is allowed to deduct the costs of doing business as an expense. This includes employee salary and benefits.

Voluntary employee benefits associations (VEBAs) have been around since 1928 and are used by employers to provide health, life, disability, education, and other benefits for their employees and are the original welfare benefit trusts. When properly established and executed, a VEBA can be a legitimate employee benefit structure. In 2007, the United Auto Workers (UAW), in order to relieve the Big Three automakers from carrying the liability for their health plans on their accounting books, formed the world's largest VEBA with over $45 billion in assets.

BAD WELFARE BENEFIT TRUSTS*

However, the IRS does have a problem with welfare benefit plans that are promoted to doctors and small-business owners as a scheme to avoid taxes and provide medical and life insurance benefits to key employees that, in substance, primarily serve the owner(s) of the business. These 419 welfare benefit plan schemes claim that the employer's contributions are deductible under Internal Revenue Code (I.R.C.) section 419 as ordinary and necessary business expenses, allowing business owners to provide a life insurance policy for their favorite employees and themselves, and accumulate cash value in a life insurance policy. Lest there be any confusion or debate, I.R.C. 264(a)(1) states:

> (a) General rule. No deduction shall be allowed for—
> (1) Premiums on any life insurance policy, or endowment or annuity contract, if the taxpayer is directly or indirectly a beneficiary under the policy or contract.

---

* Making Welfare Plans Work, *Advisor Today*, p. 110, September 2000.

While VEBAs have been used properly, as in the UAW example above, unfortunately, they are often a front for an abusive tax shelter. In the 1970s VEBAs were being used by the wealthy as a popular tool for tax reduction and asset protection. In 1984, Congress passed the Deficit Reduction Act, which limited the use of VEBAs. In the 1990s, however, VEBAs were structured to give business owners tax benefits not allowed and got back on the IRS radar. Two state medical societies along with a neonatology group practice became test cases by the IRS that helped close those VEBAs with abusive tax structures and purporting to be employee welfare benefit plans: Southern California Medical Professionals Association VEBA; New Jersey Medical Profession Association VEBA; and Neonatology Associates, Pennsylvania. Although the VEBAs claimed to have favorable determination letters, the actual execution of the plan did not comply with the law, mainly by allowing the employees to hold term policies in the plan that could be converted into universal life policies at the same insurer and use the conversion credit account to spring cash value in the policy. This then allowed policyholders to borrow against the Universal Life (UL) policy as a supposedly nontaxable source of retirement income, with the repayment of the loan paid out of the policy's death benefits. This, of course, is not allowed under the tax code.

There are those that think they may be in the clear with their abusive tax shelter for the following reasons:

1. A large passage of time has occurred since they have owned it.
2. They have a favorable determination letter.
3. Other honorable businesses/medical societies have similar tax shelters.

My insurance agent manager who said it was legal may want to read the 98-page ruling by the United States Tax Court filed on July 31, 2000, in the case of the above-mentioned Neonatology and related cases. The long arm of the IRS reached back 9 years to 1991, 1992, and 1993, disallowing hundreds of thousands of dollars and assessing deficiencies and huge "accuracy-related" tax penalties. Even the doctors who had died since then were not given a break either; their estates and surviving widows were assessed the deficiencies and penalties.

In 2002, the IRS talked Congress into passing new laws basically killing the use of multiple-employer 419 plans. Some third-party administrators (TPAs) that had set up the multiple-employer plans discovered that they could use single-employer 419 welfare benefit trusts and VEBAs because Congress forgot to include them when they passed the negative laws shutting done the multiple-employer plans. This forced the IRS to issue notices 2007-83 and 2007-84 and Rev. Rul. 2007-65, and to place welfare benefit trusts on the listed tax transactions list.*

UGLY WELFARE BENEFIT TRUSTS

I call these "ugly" because these welfare benefit trusts were sold to physicians and small-business owners *after* the 2007 IRS listed-transaction warning and after the multiple IRS notices and revenue rulings. The major brokerage firms, by 2004, had stopped selling welfare benefit trusts to protect their own financial interests, realizing these were compliance and lawsuit time bombs. The 2007 IRS listed-transaction notice along

* Defrancesco, R.M., Negative IRS Notices On 419 and VEBA Plans, Nov. 1, 2007.

with multiple other notices, however, did not seem to stop some smaller broker-dealer firms and life insurance agents from promoting these. I have become aware of the fact that welfare benefit trusts that are in violation of the basics of the tax code (unlimited full deduction of premium, 100% tax-free distribution to owner of cash value) are still being sold even today and are affecting existing clients. These welfare benefit trusts go by many different names, and the insurance agents selling them are using a number of different insurance companies to fund the plan. These plans involve the sale of an insurance policy, usually with a six-digit premium, that often pays the insurance agent a six-digit commission, so perhaps I should not be surprised that individuals (physicians?) are still being victimized.

CONVERSATION WITH AN IRS ATTORNEY ON WELFARE BENEFIT TRUSTS

In 2015, I discussed with Betty Clary, an IRS attorney who helped draft listed transaction number 33 on the IRS website, what exactly the IRS considers an abusive welfare benefit plan. She stated that once you take out the fact that the trust cannot be offering a collective bargaining element that is covered by another IRS code, there are three elements they look for

1. There has to be a trust that claims to be providing welfare benefits.
2. There is either a cash-value policy involved that offers accumulation or a policy in which money is set aside for a future policy in which accumulation occurs, such as a term policy that can then offer a higher accumulated value.
3. The plan cannot deduct in any year more than the benefit provided. For example, if the plan just provides a death benefit, the most that can be deducted in a year is only the term cost of that benefit, not the entire premium. If the plan offers medical benefits, then only the cost (what was paid out to the employee) for that benefit can be deducted in that year.

I found it interesting that the IRS is pursuing this broader definition as an abusive plan. Betty explained that in the case of a discovered abusive welfare benefit plan, the IRS would disallow the deductions, assert income back to the owner as a distribution of profits, and assess penalties. The courts are clear that you cannot get out of penalties by claiming you are relying on the person that sold you the welfare benefit plan.

WHAT IF YOU CURRENTLY HAVE A WELFARE BENEFIT TRUST FOR YOUR PRACTICE?

Realizing that someone you trusted has financially devastated you, carelessly misguided you, and sold you a bogus tax program in order to pay cash for his new 7 Series BMW can be a difficult and rude awakening. After accepting the fact that the welfare benefit plan you have for your practice meets the basic criteria as mentioned in this article for an abusive transaction, I would recommend that you consult an attorney who specializes in pursuing promoters of abusive welfare benefit plans and discuss your options. I have had discussions with Lance Wallach, an accountant and expert witness used in a number of welfare benefit trust cases, which have confirmed to me that you must be proactive. You may be advised to file an IRS Form 8886, which is a disclosure form related to prohibited tax shelter transactions. The penalties for failure to file a Form 8886 can be stiff. Of course, filing this form will open the Pandora's box of your welfare benefit trust to the IRS. Lance has told me that many of these 8886 filings are done incorrectly. An incorrectly filed IRS form is an unfiled IRS form, so please consult a certified public accountant (CPA) who is experienced in this area. Your attorney who has expertise with welfare benefit trusts will be able to guide you with this. Regarding recourse, according to Lance, most all cases are settled out of court, as the insurance company, the agent, and the agency prefer to avoid the publicity.

David K. Luke, MS-PFP, MIM, CMP
New Worth Advice
Sandy, Utah

13.3 MISCELLANEOUS INSURANCE POLICIES

The following insurance policies should be carefully considered before purchase, since they may be unnecessary, be too expensive, provide only minimal benefits, or be duplicated in your other policies.

These include credit life or home mortgage insurance (decreasing term); life insurance for children; accident policies for students; hospital indemnity policies; dread disease insurance; credit card insurance; pet health insurance; life insurance for the elderly; funeral insurance; flight insurance; prepaid legal insurance; and most extended warranties on automobiles, televisions, stereos, home computers, and the like.

On the other hand, the following types of coverage may be important, in selected cases: trip cancellation insurance, termite insurance, and flood and earthquake insurance.

Overheard in the Advisor's Lounge

Critical Illness Insurance Coverage

From 2016 to 2020, medical expenses are expected to outpace inflation at an annual rate of 5.3% versus 2.1% for general inflation, according to the Department of Labor (DOL). As a result, most Americans will be unprepared financially to cope with an illness without significant savings, despite the Patient Protection and Affordable Care Act (PPACA). So now, Prudential Group Insurance is offering critical illness insurance through employers. For about $200 to $250 per year or $8 to $10 a month, employees who fall ill with cancer, kidney failure, stroke, heart attack, coronary artery disease, and other serious illnesses can receive a lump-sum payment upon documented diagnoses.

Although Prudential does not offer the product to individuals, insurers, such as Mutual of Omaha, do (http://www.criticalinsurance.com).

Lon Jefferies, MBA, CFP
New Worth Advice
Sandy, Utah

13.4 ASSESSMENT

Traditionally, physicians protected their families with whole-life, disability, and long-term care insurance, and their practice with malpractice liability and business interruption insurance. For modern physicians however, a comprehensive risk-management and insurance plan must acknowledge more risks than ever before and in an economically sound manner not counterproductive to individual components of the plan.

For example, with the acceleration of private, state, and federal managed care initiatives, and the PPACA, physicians may be facing the ultimate personal contingent liability by selecting the *wrong profession*, as suggested by Yale University economist Robert J. Shiller, PhD. In his book *The New Financial Order: Risk in the 21st Century*, Shiller states that a new risk-sharing paradigm to protect us from "gratuitous random and painful inequality" is required.

The solution? *Livelihood insurance*, framed as a risk-management insurance contract.

13.5 CONCLUSION

Doctors, like most people, tend to experience losses more intensely than gains and evaluate risks in isolation. So it's no surprise that goaded physicians might prefer vehicles like the guaranteed minimum death benefit of variable annuities, or the assurance that comes with disability or long-term care insurance, or traditional cash-value life insurance policies, despite their decidedly higher costs and commissions. Now, after reading the insurance chapters in this book, you will know better.

For insurance professionals, on the other hand, this is an exciting time to work with the medical sector because there is much research and creative enlightenment occurring in academic and practitioner communities. But, one must be willing to abandon ancient thoughts and remain open to new ideas that identify and provide solutions to the contemporaneous problems of physicians.

As an example of this epiphany, the economist Christian Gollier revisits the *raison d'être* of insurance, by asking: *should one even buy insurance since the industry itself is so skilled at exploiting human foibles?* Although this emerging work is descriptive, it is not yet time tested, since some of it aspires to be normative, as developing modern models of savings and consumption hint that insurance may deserve a smaller role in personal risk management than previously believed.

So, physicians should always consult a trusted fee-only Certified Financial Planner, Certified Medical Planner, trusted insurance agent, insurance broker, or Certified Insurance Counselor (CIC) to get a second opinion before the purchase of any insurance policy product.

13.6 COLLABORATE

Discuss this chapter online with others at http://www.medicalexecutivepost.com.

ACKNOWLEDGMENTS

To Cathy D. Belteau, CFP, CLU, ChFC, FLMI; Philip E. Taylor, CLU, ChFC, FLMI; Matthew Lawrence DeSantos, JD; Matthew D. Rogers, CFP, CLU, ChFC; Hope Rachel Hetico, RN, MHA, CMP; and Lon Jefferies, MBA, CFP of http://www.networthadvice.com.

FURTHER READINGS

Muldowney, TA, Cook, GA and Marcinko, DE: Establishing a Solid Foundation of Insurance Planning: The Bedrock of Life and Medical Practice. In Marcinko, DE (editor): *Comprehensive Financial Planning Strategies for Doctors and Advisors: Best Practices from Leading Consultants and Certified Medical Planners™*. Productivity Press, Boca Raton, FL, 2015.
Reavis, MW: *Insurance: Concepts and Coverage*. Friesen Press, Victoria, BC, Canada, 2012.
Rejda, G and McNamara, M: *Principles of Risk Management and Insurance (Pearson Series)*. Prentice-Hall, New York, 2013.

14 Accounts Receivable Management and Safeguarding
Asset Protection Strategies

Gary L. Bode, Perry D'Alessio, and David Edward Marcinko

CONTENTS

All hospitals, clinics, health-care entities, and doctors are aware that accounts receivable (ARs) represent money that is owed to them, usually by a patient, insurance company, health maintenance organization (HMO), Medicare, Medicaid, or other third-party payer. In the reimbursement climate that exists today, it is not unusual for ARs to represent 75% of a hospital's investments in current assets and as much as 85% in medical private practice. As a result, ARs are the major source of cash flow, and cash flow is the lifeblood of any health-care entity. It pays bills, meets office payroll, and satisfies operational obligations. Emphasis on predictability of payments and safeguarding of ARs are vital to day-to-day operations. Poor planning can lead to late payment of medical entities' bills, creating late fees and interest due on credit lines, or worse, credit lines being unavailable can cause the entity to fail.

14.1 INTRODUCTION

A feature of ARs in health-care organizations that differentiates them from ARs in other types of business is that they are often settled for less than the billed amounts. These allowances include four categories that are used to restate ARs to realizable expected values:

- Professional or courtesy allowances
- Charity (*pro bono* care) allowances
- Doubtful account allowances
- HMO and managed care organization (MCO) contractual and prospective payment allowances

14.2 TERMS AND TOOLS TO HELP MANAGE ACCOUNTS RECEIVABLE

Hospitals generate a patient account or an AR at the same time as they send the patient a bill or the insurance company a claim. ARs are treated as current assets (cash equivalents) on the health-care entity balance sheet, usually with a percentage markdown to reflect historic collectability.

According to the *Dictionary of Health Economics and Finance*, an AR aging schedule is a periodic report (30, 60, 90, 180, or 360 days) showing all outstanding ARs identified by patient or payor, and month due. The average duration of an AR is equal to total claims, divided by ARs. Faster is better, of course, but it is not unusual for a hospital to wait 6, 9, or 12 months, or more, for payment.

Predictability and more timely collections are the goals of all ratios and analysis performed. Each of the measures seeks to answer two questions:

1. How many days of revenue are tied up in ARs?
2. How long does it take to collect ARs?

AR ratio = current AR balance/average monthly gross production (Suggested between 1 and 3 for hospitals)

AR turnover rate = AR balance/average monthly receipts

Average days receivable = AR balance/daily average charges (Suggested <90 days for medical practices)

Current ratio = current assets/current liabilities. The current ratio is important since it measures short-term solvency, or the daily bill-paying ability of the hospital or practice. *Current assets* include cash on hand (COH), and cash in checking accounts, money market accounts, money market deposit accounts, U.S. Treasury bills, inventory, prepaid expenses, and the percentage of ARs that can be reasonably expected to be collected. *Current liabilities* are notes payable within 1 year. This ratio should be at least 1, or preferably in the range of about 1.2 to 1.8 for medical practices.

The *quick ratio* is similar to the current ratio. However, unlike the current ratio, the quick ratio does not include money tied up in inventory, since rapid conversion to cash might not be possible in an economic emergency. A reasonable quick ratio would be 1.0–1.3 for a hospital, since this ratio is a more stringent indicator of liquidity than the current ratio.

A point of emphasis in the case of both the current ratio and the quick ratio is that higher is not necessarily better. Higher ratios denote a greater capacity to pay bills as they come due, but they also indicate that the entity has more cash tied up in assets that have a relatively low rate of earnings. Hence, there is an optimum range for both ratios: they should be neither too low nor too high.

The *collection experience table* method plots on Excel the expected collection of receivables by receivable, based not on stated collection terms but on payment experience of the provider. This table is a layered approach that lends itself to more predicable cash flow planning.

Good stewardship requires that one must be concerned with significant economic losses not only due to professional conduct (professional malpractice liability concerns and issues raised by the Equal Employment Opportunity Commission [EEOC], Office of Civil Rights [OCR], Occupational Safety and Health Administration [OSHA], and so on) but also due to physician partner(s) and even the financial failure of contracted private insurers, payors, MCOs, HMOs, etc. ARs are often the biggest asset to protect against creditors or adverse legal judgments. It is not unusual to have ARs in the range of millions of dollars. In working with the collection experience table, pay close attention to any provider that makes up more than 10% of total ARs. Follow up with the provider to be certain they are in good standing and not at risk of default.

14.2.1 Proactive Accounts Receivable Monitoring

The best way to manage AR problems is to avoid them in the first place by implementing a good system of AR control (McLean 2003). Typically, poor control occurs because the doctor and/or hospital is too busy treating patients, or the front office or administrative staff does not have or follow a good system of AR control.

Answering the following questions may help upgrade a system of AR control:

- Is an AR policy in place for the collection of self-pay accounts (*de minimis*/maximum amounts, annual percentage rate [APR], terms, penalties, etc.)?
- Do employees receive proper AR, bad-debt, and follow-up training within legal guidelines?

- Are AR exceptions approved by the doctor, office manager, or accounting department, or do they require individual scrutiny?
- Are AR policies in place for dealing with hardship cases, *pro bono* work, co-pay waivers, discounts, or no-charges?
- Are collection procedures within legal guidelines?
- Are AR policies in place for dealing with past-due notices, telephone calls, dunning messages, collection agencies, small-claims court, and other collection methods?
- Are guidelines in place for handling hospital, clinic, or medical practice consultations; unpaid claims; refilling of claims; and appealing claims?
- Are office AR policies periodically revised and reviewed, with employee input?
- Does the doctor, hospital, or clinic agree with and support the guidelines?

14.2.2 The Need to Protect Accounts Receivable

The quality of medical practice and hospital ARs is high in that the creditors are mostly large insurance companies and federal and state government. As a result, plaintiff law firms are willing to invest in litigation against them because satisfying a judgment secured in a court room is made easy by simply placing a lien on incoming ARs.

Further, a judgment creditor pursuing a doctor for a claim may pursue the assets of the clinic, and ARs and cash are the most vulnerable assets. ARs are as good as cash to a creditor, who usually has to do no more than seize them and wait a few months to collect them. If a creditor seizes ARs, the clinic or entity may be hard pressed to pay its bills as they become due. One must therefore be vigilant to protect AR assets from lawsuit creditors.

With this in mind, every effort should be made to deter litigation and to protect ARs.

14.2.3 Accounts Receivable Protection Strategies

Since ARs are a vital asset for short-term survival, they must be protected from creditors. Several asset protection strategies are reviewed below.

14.2.3.1 Incorporation Strategy

If a clinical practice becomes a corporation, it could be an Inc., Corp., professional association (PA), or professional corporation (PC), depending on the state in which the clinic entity is organized. In addition, almost every state has enacted legislation to create limited liability entities, such as limited liability partnerships (LLPs) and limited liability companies (LLCs), that provide the liability protection afforded a corporation while having the attributes of a partnership. These entities are popular with physicians because they allow much flexibility with regard to buy-ins and buyouts, and in the allocation of clinic income and practice deductions. If ARs are significant in value, one strategy to protect them is to create liens, secured by a loan against the ARs, which will have priority over subsequent creditors.

Doctors in a professional practice can make loans to the corporation for working capital or other needs. The loan proceeds are not taxable income to the practice, and the interest payments on the loan are tax deductible, making the effective cost of the loan considerably lower. In today's low-interest climate, the effective interest rate can be as low as 3–5%. This security interest is called a UCC-1 filing under the provisions of the Uniform Commercial

Code (UCC). The hoped-for result of this UCC-1 filing is that ARs will be protected. A judgment creditor would find that the equity in these assets is subject to the superior claim of the clinic doctors and cannot be used to satisfy the judgment.

14.2.3.2 Multiple-Corporation Strategy

If the clinic of a parent hospital corporation is divided into separate business entities, ARs may be protected using multiple corporations. For example, a single corporation may own and operate several medical clinics in different locations. If something happens at one of the clinics, giving rise to potential liability, the ARs of the other successful clinics must be isolated from these claims.

Example

A physician-hospital organization (PHO) had three offices in different locations run by a physician-executive. All of the offices were held in one corporation. Business at one of the locations slowed down substantially. That clinic became a financial drain on the others, absorbing all of the available cash in the company. Eventually, the corporation had to file for bankruptcy, wiping out all of the equity that had been built up.

A better approach to avoid this eventuality would have been to have each office separately incorporated. Then, if one location were to falter, it would not drag down the others. A judgment creditor of one corporation would not be able to reach the ARs and assets of the other companies.

This strategy is also useful for physicians who provide different high-risk medical services like reconstructive or orthopedic surgery, polytrauma treatment, diabetic wound care, osteomyelitis infection management, ob-gyn services, and the like. Practices like these face enormous potential liability, and whenever a particular service line is deemed too risky, the use of multiple corporations is an effective technique for insulating each separated service from liability caused by another.

Classically, in the medical manufacturing space, recall how pharmaceutical company A.H. Robbins was forced into bankruptcy by liability in connection with its intrauterine devices (IUDs) and how giant Dow Corning had similar classic liability concerns associated with its silicone breast implants.

14.2.3.3 Purchased Accounts Receivable Strategy

AR purchase financing is a potential strategic tool for managing a health-care organization's working capital needs. But before entering into a financing agreement, hospitals need to consider and take steps to avoid serious problems that can arise from participation in an AR financing program.

For example, the purchaser may cease purchasing the receivables, leaving the organization without funding needed for operations. Alternatively, the financing program may be inordinately complex and unnecessarily costly to the organization. Sometimes, the health-care organization itself may fail to comply with the terms of the agreement under which the ARs were sold, thus necessitating that restitution be made to the purchaser or provoking charges of fraud.

These potential problems should be addressed as early as possible—before a health-care organization enters into an AR financing program—in order to minimize time, effort, and expense and to maximize the benefits of the financing agreement.

As another example, a few years ago, some medical practices, clinics, and hospitals were sold to physician (public) practice management companies (PPMCs) or other corporate buyers. However, many of those transactions have soured since the securitized PPMC business model failed and was not able to generate the earnings that Wall Street investors desired. Investors increasingly abandoned the industry as behemoths like MedPartners and PhyCor called off merger plans, and, in 1998, FPA Medical Management filed for chapter 11 bankruptcy protection.

In fact, a more recent review of the Cain Brothers Index of publicly traded PPMCs revealed losses of up to 95%, as many other smaller entities collapsed ignominiously. Also, the publicized financial difficulties of formerly successful PPMCs are becoming transparent as the accounting debacle at behemoth HealthSouth Corporation (HLS) continues to unwind because of allegedly fraudulent behavior. HLS common stock price fell from $60 to $10 this decade.

For example, in a denied February 16, 2007, *ex parte* petition against General Medicine PC, HealthSouth asked for a writ of mandamus* directing the Jefferson Circuit Court to enter a summary judgment on the grounds that General Medicine had no standing to bring the underlying action against it.†

And, on January 12, 2009, the U.S. Supreme Court rejected the appeal of former HealthSouth chief financial officer (CFO) Malcom "Tadd" McVay's attempt to avoid prison. The justices, without comment, let stand an appeals court ruling that threw out McVay's sentence of 5 years' probation as too lenient. The decision sent the case back to a lower court, where McVay had a third sentencing hearing in Birmingham, Alabama, late in 2009.‡

Today, many of these practices, clinics, and their ARs are being bought back by the same doctors that sold out years earlier. If such an entity and its ARs are repurchased, be careful not to pick this item up twice as income. The costs can be immense to the practice or clinic.

Example

A medical practice purchased itself back from a PPMC. Part of the mandatory purchase price, approximately $3 million (the approximate net realizable value of the ARs) was paid to the PPMC to buy back ARs generated by the doctors buying back their practice. The office administrator unknowingly began recording the cash receipts specifically attributable to the purchased ARs as patient fee income. If left uncorrected, this error could have incorrectly added $3 million in income to this practice and cost it (a C corporation) approximately $1,050,000 in additional income tax ($3 million in fees × 35% tax rate).

The error in the above example is that the PPMC must record the portion of the purchase price it received for the ARs as patient fee income. The buyer practice has merely traded one

* *Mandamus* (man-dame-us), n: Latin for "we order," a writ (more modernly called a "writ of mandate") that orders a governmental entity to perform an act required by law when it has neglected or refused to do so.

† Jefferson Circuit Court, CV-05-1483.

‡ Docket and citation number available at http://www.versuslaw.com.

asset—cash—for another asset—the medical ARs. When the practice collects these particular receivables, the credit is applied against the purchased ARs (an asset), rather than to patient fees.

14.2.3.4 Accounts Receivable (Credit) Insurance Strategy

Hospital or health-care business credit insurance, also known as AR insurance, bad-debt insurance, or credit risk insurance, is a custom-tailored financial management tool used to eliminate the risk of a large unexpected credit loss resulting from the insolvency or past-due nonpayment of accounts by patients and/or other creditors. Credit insurance is available from only a limited number of insurance carriers who specialize in this unique type of coverage.

Credit insurance is an asset protection plan for ARs that minimizes exposure to large or unexpected loss. It assures the clinic or health-care entity of getting paid despite intervening economic events, industry competitive factors, changes in business cycles, political fiats, or overambitious managed care expansion. It can protect all ARs, a set of designated accounts, or even one or two large HMO contracts since uncomfortable levels, greater than 15–25%, of health-care entity ARs may occur as health-care insurance mergers, acquisitions, and consolidations continue. Further, disclosure of credit insurance in financial reports can inform bankers and prospective investors that an effective strategy is in place to manage receivable risks. Like most insurance policies, be sure to compare and evaluate premiums, fees, deductibles, coinsurance payment, policy limits, and maximum payment terms, if any.

Premium rates are based on AR aging schedules (terms), spread of intrinsic medical specialty risk versus systemic health-care industry risks, HMO/MCO insurer corporate credit risks, and even previous personal and/or practice credit risks of involved doctors. The cost is low, typically a small fraction of 1%, and payable monthly, quarterly, or annually.

Example

A large West Coast medical clinic felt that credit insurance was important due to a recent rash of HMO insolvencies in the area but found that it was not cost-efficient to insure all its ARs. Upon review of its AR aging schedule and list of managed care contracts, it was determined that only five to six accounts were large enough (>68% of all ARs) for consideration or in danger of economic default. The solution was key account AR coverage for the at-risk ARs, while the clinic remained responsible for the remaining accounts. The key account policy was obtained without a deductible, with the insurer approving all the AR contract limits. Later, the assumption of a policy deductible further reduced costs for the West Coast clinic.

14.2.3.5 Accounts Receivable Financing Strategy

Medical AR financing is a means by which the health-care provider is granted an asset-based credit line that is dependent on the net realized value for his/her billings to third-party payors (i.e., commercial insurance companies, HMOs, Blue Cross-Blue Shield, Medicare, and Medicaid).

AR financing occurs when a loan is received against clinic ARs that are not taxable until given to the doctors. Payment to the doctor is, in turn, a deduction to the clinic (S flow-through corporation, limited partnership, or LLC).

For example, if the clinic received a loan and paid $25,000 to each doctor, each doctor would have to report $25,000 of taxable income to the Internal Revenue Service (IRS). If the clinic were able to report an operating loss on the loan for the distribution, each doctor would get an offsetting $25,000 K-1 deduction or reduction. The "cost" of this transaction is interest on the loan that must be paid back. Today, some insurance companies will finance ARs if the clinic uses the loan to purchase life insurance and pledge the policy as secondary collateral.

Financially, this strategy may allow the proceeds to work in a tax-deferred manner with interest rate arbitrage potential. After a decade or two, each doctor is allowed a tax-free loan from the policy to pay back his/her share of the AR loan. The remaining insurance policy's cash value may be available through tax-free loans to the doctor; if not, a modified endowment contract (MEC) and the death benefit remain. If correctly used, this strategy will protect ARs from creditors and may increase after-tax retirement income by a nominal amount.

However, caution must be exercised when pursing this strategy since this concept is new to the industry. Insurers have not had extensive claims experience, and commissions on this type of insurance product are hefty and not always transparent to the doctor or clinic.

14.2.3.6 Accounts Receivable Factoring Strategy

Invoice factoring, or the sale of ARs, is one of the oldest forms of financing. Factoring began in the garment industry in the nineteenth century and has grown steadily and expanded into other industries, like health care. Invoice factoring provides an advance on slow-paying billings so that accounts payable can be satisfied or discounts taken from vendors or suppliers.

Invoice factoring is not free and is not a substitute to assuming more debt. However, by factoring ARs, funds are quickly received, allowing the health-care entity to concentrate on operations (advertising, inventory, staffing, expansions, equipment purchases, marketing, and so on) while a third party collects the owed money.

AR factoring occurs when a clinic or medical practice sells its ARs to a third party, removing them from the clinic. The proceeds are given to each doctor to hold in a personally owned and asset-protected account. This does result in tax liability to the doctor for receiving the payment from the clinic, and the maneuver must be done continuously to deplete ARs.

14.2.3.6.1 Advantages

Basically, a health-care entity might benefit from invoice factoring, if dealing with patients, clients, customers, and vendors that are credit worthy, stable, and reliable. Invoice factoring can loosen cash flow and be especially helpful with business lines like the following:

- Health-care organizations and hospitals
- Medical and outpatient centers and clinics
- Large and medium-sized medical offices
- Durable medical equipment manufacturers
- Health-care trucking, construction, and transportation vendors
- Health-care recruiters and employment staffing agencies
- Government health agencies
- Health-care professional service providers (such as lawyers, advertisers, accountants, engineers, and consultants)

Indeed, nearly any health-care-related business that is experiencing cash flow problems—or has issues with its own credit—may benefit from prudent invoice factoring.

14.2.3.6.2 Disadvantages

A drawback of this strategy is greatly reduced AR value and more robust collection policies than might otherwise be pursued, especially on at-risk, increasing professional liability concerns. Thus, it is an expensive strategy for protecting ARs. Another drawback is size in that most third parties do not offer factoring with a net realized AR value of $500,000 or less.

Currently, some third-party benefits companies may purchase ARs for almost the same amount as the health-care entity might collect. The entity will then receive the funds from the benefits company and use the proceeds to operate the entity. This protects the ARs since it removes ownership of them from the entity. The entity then invests the after-tax profits into an investment account for each doctor. This money is invested on an after-tax basis, so all proceeds to the doctor in retirement would be tax-free. Usually, this strategy increases the retirement income of the doctor, while reducing current tax liabilities and protecting the ARs from creditors.

14.2.3.7 Accounts Receivable Leveraging Strategy

Leveraging of ARs is a complex method of protecting ARs in a way that makes retirement money available to the doctor. It can provide protection for his/her family in case of death, or serve as a way to buy out older doctors. According to Frank J. Kalenda, CPA, of Houston, Texas, other reasons for consideration include the following:

- Leveraged ARs protect the physician and the medical practice from attachment of all creditors, not just malpractice claims.
- Leveraged ARs convert ARs to funding and capital resources, which can aid the practice and physician with issues common in the day-to-day operation of the medical practice.
- Leveraged ARs offer lump-sum funding of individual retirement planning for the physician.
- Leveraged ARs offer potential discounts on malpractice insurance.

Although attractive, the practice must invest AR loan funds in a way that is asset protected and allows them to grow in a tax-advantaged manner, while not exposed to clinic creditors.

According to David Mandell and Chris Jarvis, leveraging (financing) of ARs works something like this (Jarvis and Mandell 2002):

- A clinic and doctor use AR loan proceeds to invest in an LLC that also uses after-tax dollars. (The LLC must be created with a legitimate business purpose, not just to own life insurance.)
- The LLC buys a life insurance policy on the doctor. If actuarial assumptions are correct and the policy is properly substantiated, there is no taxable transfer of value between the clinic and the physician. Under the LLC agreement, the doctor owns a cash-value position in the life insurance policy, and the clinic owns the death benefit.

- If the doctor retires, the LLC takes a loan from the policy, pays the clinic back the loan principal amount, and pays off the AR lender. The doctor owns the remaining cash balance in the policy through the LLC. He/she can then take tax-free loans from the policy paying throughout retirement.
- The clinic gets the death benefit when the doctor dies, which can be used as a buyout.

Be sure this strategy satisfies all applicable state and federal deferred compensation laws, forfeiture risks, and Internal Revenue Code (I.R.C.) Section 83 constructive receipt requirements. Further, when implemented with the correct primary UCC lien status, all asset protection benefits are usually available.

14.2.3.8 Accounts Receivable Buyout/Buy-In Strategies

Although not proactive in nature like the above strategies, it is important to have some idea of clinic AR buyout/buy-in strategy should the need arise. The obvious question that most doctors wonder about is the inclusion of ARs in a practice buyout situation. The short answer is *yes*, if structured in the form of deductible deferred compensation to the practice. This allows the practice to deduct payments on its federal income tax return, since ARs are really an *income asset.*

On the other hand, as part of a buy-in strategy, the ARs should *not* be included, since they only inflate the value of the practice and make the buy-in more expensive. Rather, they might be declared as a bonus to practice equity owners and paid out over time, as regular overhead cost disbursements (2–4 years). In other words, all the new doctor actually purchases is the practice's net fixed-asset value and goodwill, reduced by any debt liabilities.

14.2.4 Fair and Accurate Credit Transactions Act

The Fair and Accurate Credit Transactions (FACT) Act of 2003 includes provisions designed to curb identity theft in the United States. It requires financial institutions, hospitals, clinics, health systems, and creditors with ARs to submit to the IRS, by November 1, 2008, a written program to identify and manage so-called red-flag accounts.

14.2.4.1 What Are the Core Elements of the Red-Flag Rules?

Pursuant to the FACT Act of 2003, financial institutions and health-care creditors with covered ARs must have identity theft prevention programs to identify, detect, and respond to patterns, practices, or specific activities that could indicate identity theft (i.e., red flags).

The core elements of the red-flag rules are identification; detection; and response to patterns, practices, or specific activities—known as red flags. They include these two key issues:

- *Identification/detection*: Inconsistencies in addresses constitute a red flag to the registrar and organization.
- *Response*: When a red flag is found, predetermined work flows guide the registration process and the financial relationship with patients.

The red-flag rules provide all financial institutions and many health-care creditors with the flexibility and opportunity to design and implement a program that is appropriate to their size and complexity, as well as the nature of their operations.

A white paper* on guidelines issued by the Federal Trade Commission (FTC), the federal banking agencies, and the National Credit Union Administration (NCUA) is helpful in assisting covered entities in designing their programs.

14.2.4.1.1 The 26 Red Flags

Six agencies were involved in drafting the red-flag rules: the Treasury Department's Office of Thrift Supervision, Office of Comptroller of the Currency, Federal Deposit Insurance Corp., FTC, NCUA, and Federal Reserve System. They developed the following examples of red flags, gleaned from the "Identity Theft Red Flags" and "Address Discrepancies" portions of the FACT Act of 2003:

1. A fraud alert is included with a consumer report.
2. Notice of a credit freeze is issued in response to a request for a consumer report.
3. A consumer reporting agency provides a notice of address discrepancy.
4. There is unusual credit activity, such as an increased number of accounts or inquiries.
5. Documents provided for identification appear altered or forged.
6. Photograph on ID is inconsistent with appearance of customer.
7. Information on ID is inconsistent with information provided by person opening account.
8. Information on ID, such as signature, is inconsistent with information on file.
9. Application appears forged or altered, or destroyed and reassembled.
10. Information on ID does not match an address in the consumer report; social security number has not been issued or appears on the Social Security Administration's Death Master File (a file of information associated with social security numbers of those who are deceased).
11. Lack of correlation between social security number range and date of birth.
12. Personal identifying information is associated with known fraud activity.
13. Address is suspicious (like a mail drop or prison), or phone number is associated with pager or mobile phone.
14. Social security number matches that submitted by another opening an account.
15. An address or phone number matches that supplied by a large number of applicants.

* See http://ftc.gov/opa/2007/10/redflag.shtm.

16. Inability to supply identifying information in response to notification of incomplete application.
17. Personal information is inconsistent with information already on file at financial institution or creditor.
18. Person opening account or customer is unable to correctly answer challenge questions.
19. Shortly after change of address, creditor receives request for additional users of account.
20. Most available credit is used for cash advances, jewelry, or electronics; plus customer fails first payment.
21. There is a drastic change in payment patterns, use of available credit, or spending patterns.
22. An account that has been inactive for a long time suddenly exhibits unusual activity.
23. Customer mail is repeatedly returned as undeliverable despite ongoing transactions on active account.
24. Financial institution or creditor is notified that customer is not receiving paper account statements.
25. Financial institution or creditor if notified of unauthorized charges/transactions on customer's account.
26. Financial institution or creditor is notified that it opened a fraudulent account for one engaged in identity theft.*

These red flags can be grouped into the following five categories:

1. Alerts, notifications, or warnings from a consumer reporting agency
2. Suspicious documents
3. Suspicious personally identifying information, such as a suspicious address
4. Unusual use of—or suspicious activity relating to—a covered account
5. Notice from customers, victims of identity theft, law enforcement authorities, or other businesses about possible identity theft in connection with covered accounts.

These categories are intended not as a checklist but as a starting point for identifying possible problems. For more information, please contact redflags@ftc.gov.

14.2.4.2 Who Must Comply with the Red-Flag Rules?

The red-flag rules initially applied to "financial institutions" and those "creditors" with "covered accounts."

Under the rules, a *financial institution* is defined as a state or national bank, a state or federal savings and loan association, a mutual savings bank, a state or federal credit union, or any other entity that holds a "transaction account" belonging to a consumer and/or patient. Most of these institutions are regulated by the federal bank regulatory agencies and the NCUA, an independent federal agency that charters and supervises federal credit unions and insures savings in federal and most state-chartered credit unions. Financial institutions under the FTC's jurisdiction include state-chartered credit unions (medical and nonmedical) and certain other entities that hold consumer transaction accounts.

A *creditor* is any entity that regularly extends, renews, or continues credit; any entity that regularly arranges for the extension, renewal, or continuation of credit; or any assignee of an

* *From* the Federal Trade Commission.

original creditor who is involved in the decision to extend, renew, or continue credit. Accepting credit cards as a form of payment does not, in and of itself, make any entity a creditor.

This definition of a creditor can, of course, include such entities as a medical clinic, hospital, insurance company, or HMO. Other entities that qualify as creditors include medical and nonmedical related finance companies, automobile dealers, mortgage brokers, utility companies, and telecommunications companies. Where nonprofit and government entities defer payment for goods or services, they, too, are considered creditors. Most creditors, except for those regulated by the federal bank regulatory agencies and the NCUA, come under the jurisdiction of the FTC.

A *covered account* is an account used mostly for personal, patient, family, or household purposes that involves multiple payments or transactions. Covered accounts include credit card accounts, mortgage loans, automobile loans, margin accounts, cell phone accounts, utility accounts, checking accounts, and savings accounts. A covered account is also an account for which there is a foreseeable risk of identity theft—for example, health insurance accounts, and small-business or sole-proprietorship accounts.

A *transaction account* is a deposit or other account from which the owner makes payments or transfers. It is considered a covered account within the terms of the act. Transaction accounts include checking accounts, negotiable order of withdrawal (NOW) accounts, and savings deposits subject to automatic transfers. For health-care organizations, transaction accounts may include automatic share draft accounts for medical savings accounts (MSAs), health savings accounts (HSAs), ARs, and time-payments, among others.

14.2.4.3 Impact on Health-Care Organizations

Although the red-flag rules were initially applied to creditors and financial institutions, it was soon obvious that these terms were open to much broader and more detailed interpretation than originally understood. The FTC staff therefore launched outreach efforts to explain the regulations to the many different types of entities covered by the red-flag rules. The agency published a general alert on what the rules require—and in particular, the types of entities covered by the rules.*

For example, health-care organizations, health-care financial institutions, and independent health-care debt-collection agencies (e.g., http://www.searchamerica.com) offer accounts that enable consumers and patients to write checks or to make payments to third parties through other means, such as negotiable instruments or telephone transfers. If these entities therefore qualify as financial institutions, this means that certain hospitals, medical offices, clinics, ambulatory surgery centers (ASCs), outpatient treatment centers (OTCs), and the entire related ecosystem of the health-care industrial complex are not immune from FACT Act compliance.

14.2.4.4 Enforcement

During the course of their efforts, FTC staff realized that some industries and entities within their jurisdiction—notably health-care organizations—were uncertain about coverage under the red-flag rules. These entities indicated that they were not aware that they were engaged in activities that would cause them to fall under the FACT Act's definition of a creditor or financial institution. Many entities also noted that, because they generally are not required to comply with FTC rules in other contexts, they had not followed or even

---

* See http://www.ftc.gov/bcp/edu/pubs/business/alerts/alt050.shtm for details.

been aware of the rule making, and therefore learned of the requirements too late to be able to come into compliance by November 1, 2008.

Therefore, on October 23, 2008, the FTC suspended enforcement of the red-flag rules until May 1, 2009, for certain entities, including patient creditors and health-care institutions, to allow additional time in which to develop and implement written identity theft prevention programs. This announcement, and the release of an enforcement policy statement, does not affect other federal agencies' enforcement of the original November 1, 2008, deadline for institutions subject to their oversight.

14.2.4.5 FTC as Patient Advocate

The FTC works for consumers and patients to prevent fraudulent, deceptive, and unfair business practices and to provide information to help spot, stop, and avoid them. To file a complaint against a health-care organization or other entity or seek rule clarification in English or Spanish, visit the FTC's complaints and assistance line by calling 1-877-FTC-HELP (1-877-382-4357). The FTC enters complaints into Consumer Sentinel, a secure, online database available to more than 1500 civil and criminal law enforcement agencies in the United States and abroad. The FTC's website provides additional information on a variety of related red-flag topics.*

14.3 CONCLUSION

A medical practice, clinic, or hospital is unlike other nonmedical businesses. Rather than extend credit terms to grow in a competitive environment, third-party medical payers are constantly seeking ways to delay, reduce, or cancel payments to health-care entities. ARs balloon, and it often seems that doctors or hospitals suffer AR loss without recourse. Even worse, open-account patients and HMOs may file bankruptcy, run into cash flow problems, face adverse liability judgments, lack sufficient insurance protection themselves, perpetrate balance sheet fraud, or fail to satisfy ARs for a variety of reasons.

Doctors and health-care entities must be willing to abandon ancient thoughts and remain open to new ideas that identify and provide solutions to the contemporaneous problem of protecting their ARs. When a solution is backed by an insurance policy, particular care in evaluating the need and all associated costs is essential since, according to the economist Christian Gollier, PhD, "the insurance industry itself is so skilled at exploiting human foibles" and AR protection is not the *raison d'être* of insurance.

Although this emerging work is descriptive, it is not yet time-tested. Some of it aspires to be normative, as developing modern models of AR protections hint that insurance may deserve a role in AR protection for only the savviest of practitioners, clinics, and hospitals.

14.4 COLLABORATE

Discuss this chapter online with others at http://www.medicalexecutivepost.com.

* See http://www.ftc.gov. For more information, contact FTC Media Contact, Office of Public Affairs, 202-326-2180.

REFERENCES

Jarvis, C. and Mandell, D. *Wealth Protection: Build and Preserve Your Financial Fortress*. John Wiley and Sons, New York, 2002.

McLean, R. *Financial Management in Health Care Organizations*. Thompson, DelMar, Clifton, New York, 2003.

FURTHER READINGS

Comptroller of the Currency Administrator of National Banks. *Accounts Receivable and Inventory Financing*. Create Space Publishing, Amazon Digital Services, New York, 2014.

Dhruy, A. *Accounts Receivable*. Amazon Digital Services, New York, 2014.

Dunn, M. *How to Start a Successful Accounts Receivable Outsourcing Program*. Amazon Digital Services, New York, 2014.

Garrison, R.H. and Noreen, E.W. Financial Statement Analysis. In *Managerial Accounting*. Irwin, Boston, 2000.

Gollier, C. "Intergenerational Discrimination in Insider–Outsider Models with Implicit Contracts." *The Geneva Papers on Risk and Insurance*. 14 (1989): 26–54.

Green, I. *Accounts Receivable Factoring Guide—Definition, Best Companies, Cost Guidance. Expedite Your Business Cash Flows Today*. Amazon Digital Services, New York, 2014.

Hermanson, R.H. and Edwards, J.D. *Financial Accounting*. Irwin, Boston, 1999.

http://www.frankjkalenda.com.

http://www.ftc.gov.

http://www.ftc.gov/bcp/edu/pubs/business/alerts/alt050.shtm.

http://www.ftc.gov/opa/2007/10/redflag.shtm.

http://www.hcla.com.

http://www.managedcaredigest.com.

http://www.managedcaremag.com.

http://www.redflags@ftc.gov.

http://www.sec.gov/litigation/complaints/comphealths.htm.

Marcinko, D.E. and Hetico, H.R. *Dictionary of Health Economics and Finance*. Springer Publishing, New York, 2007.

Marcinko, D.E. and White, K. Understanding Cash Flows and Medical Accounts Receivable. In Marcinko, DE [editor]: *Hospitals and Healthcare Organizations*. Productivity Press, Boca Raton, FL, 2013.

Neumann, B.R. *Management Accounting for Healthcare Organizations*. Precept Press, Chicago, 1998.

CASE MODEL: ST. IGNATIUS MEDICAL PRACTICE, INC.

St. Ignatius Medical Practice is in an urgent cash-crunch situation. Fortunately, it has $500,000 in ARs from a third-party payer that historically pays 96% of the claims in 60 days, denying the remaining 4%. A benefits company has offered the clinic $475,000 for the ARs. If St. Ignatius can earn 6% on excess cash, should it sell these ARs?

KEY ISSUES

Considering the tools and techniques reflected in this section, what factors should the St. Ignatius Medical Practice consider in making its decision?

1. What is the actual cost?
2. What is the benefit?
3. On what grounds could you argue that selling would be a sound financial move?

SOLUTION

The benefit to St. Ignatius is less than the cost.

The cost is $475,312, and the benefit is $475,000, calculated in this manner:

$$\$500,000(0.96)/1 + [1 + (0.04/365) * 60] = \$476,864.$$

SAMPLE FORM

ACCOUNTS RECEIVABLE DOS AND DON'TS

As an accounts receivable (AR) manager in a health-care organization, you should monitor ARs to ensure that ongoing significant events are identified, reported, and appreciated. Readers involved in these activities should continue to review their changing amounts and at-risk percentages.

Determine if the following AR financial benchmarks (absolute numbers and percentages) are appropriate for your health-care organizations:

Am I an AR manager?	o Yes	o No
If not, is there an AR audit committee in place?	o Yes	o No
If so, what is my department's AR size and amount?		
If so, how old are my ARs (days aging schedule)?		
—Are AR collections behind, on track, or ahead of schedule?		
—What are the AR collection write-off or charge-back amounts?		
Do I know my AR ratio?	o Yes	o No
Do I know my average AR turnover rate?	o Yes	o No
Do I know my gross AR collection percentage?	o Yes	o No
Do I know my net AR collection percentage?	o Yes	o No
Do I know my average daily AR collection rate?	o Yes	o No
Are the ARs exposed to creditors?	o Yes	o No
—If so, how much money is exposed to creditors?		
—Is the exposed AR amount too much?		
—Does the exposed AR amount need protection?	o Yes	o No
—Can I collect the ARs faster or more efficiently?	o Yes	o No
Has the health-care organization evaluated all AR collection transactions:		
—In-house?	o Yes	o No
—Complied with legal pursuit limitations?	o Yes	o No
If, not, have the AR collection strategies been outsourced?	o Yes	o No
If not, have I reviewed my department's current ratio, current assets, current liabilities, and quick ratio amounts relative to ARs?	o Yes	o No

If so, are all material statements of financial information made in compliance with generally accepted accounting principles (GAAPs), or presented along with either historical information or industry comparables?	o Yes	o No
If not, is there an auditor or supervisor informed of this information regularly?	o Yes	o No
Is the health-care organization incorporated?	o Yes	o No
Is its corporate entity status correct for AR collection maximization?	o Yes	o No
Am I in control of corporate/departmental cash?	o Yes	o No
How much cash and control do I have?		
How much cash is at risk from creditors?		
Is the corporate cash protected?	o Yes	o No
If not, why not?______________________________		
What is the best AR protection strategy for my department or health-care organization?______________________________		
Have I evaluated my fiduciary responsibilities to the company and its shareholders regarding appropriate AR protection strategies?	o Yes	o No

Checklist 14.1: Accounts Receivable Protection Strategies	Yes	No
Are you familiar with these accounts receivable (AR) protection strategies for your health-care entity?	o	o
Incorporation strategy?	o	o
Multiple-corporation strategy?	o	o
Purchased AR strategy?	o	o
AR credit insurance strategy?	o	o
AR financing strategy	o	o
AR factoring strategy?	o	o
AR leveraging strategy?	o	o
AR buy-in/buyout strategy?	o	o

Checklist 14.2: Accounts Receivable Credit Insurance	Yes	No
Does your health-care entity have accounts receivable (AR) credit insurance?	o	o
If you answer YES:		
Does it cover all the health-care entity's ARs?	o	o
Does it cover a portion of the health-care entity's ARs?	o	o
Does it cover the health-care entity's designated ARs only?	o	o
Have you investigated the cost/benefits of AR credit insurance?	o	o
If you answer YES:		
Is AR credit insurance helpful to the public investors of your health-care entity?	o	o
Is AR credit insurance helpful to the private investors of your health-care entity?	o	o
Is AR credit insurance helpful to your retail lenders or investment bankers?	o	o
Is AR credit insurance dependent on the systemic/nonsystemic risks of your entity?	o	o

Have you identified your systemic health entity risks?	o	o
Have you identified your nonsystemic health entity risks?	o	o
Is AR insurance dependent on entity deductibles and premium?	o	o
Is AR credit insurance dependent on your health entity AR aging schedule?	o	o
Is there a limit or percentage amount of AR credit insurance for your health entity?	o	o
Is AR credit insurance premium cost dependent on your specific health-care entity?	o	o
Is AR credit insurance premium cost dependent on systemic and nonsystemic risks?	o	o
Is AR credit insurance premium cost dependent on AR aging schedules?	o	o
Is AR credit insurance premium cost dependent on insurance amounts, etc.?	o	o

15 Internal Office Control Mechanisms

Detecting Medical Practice Fraud

Perry D'Alessio, Gary L. Bode, and David Edward Marcinko

CONTENTS

Internal controls are simply those systems, processes, procedures, and mechanisms controlled by management that make it possible for a medical practice, clinic, or any health entity to successfully achieve its goals and objectives. Internal controls designed and implemented by the practice physician-owner help prevent bad things from happening. Embezzlement protection is the classic example.

However, internal controls also help to ensure that good things happen, at least most of the time. A procedural manual that teaches employees how to deal effectively with common patient complaints is one example. Operating efficiency, safeguarding assets, quality patient care, compliance with existing laws, and accuracy of financial transactions are common goals of internal controls.

15.1 INTRODUCTION

Congress approved the Health Information Technology for Economic and Clinical Health Act in 2009, which mandated the health-care industry to undertake a massive digitization of patient medical records. Electronic medical records (EMRs) are a digital version of the paper charts in the clinician's office. An EMR contains the medical and treatment history of the patients in one practice.

As a result of the Federal EMR Electronic Medical Records Mandate 2014/2015 Deadline, more than 75% of all physicians now use some type of electronic records system, up from 18% in 2001, according to the Office of the National Coordinator for Health Information Technology at the U.S. Department of Health and Human Services.

Software providers understood that practice managers hoped for a solution that would not only manage medical records but also aid work flow management, accounting, and internal-control auditability, so they quickly worked to provide a solution to manage it all. However, the products proved to be little more than a paperless system for medical records with the ability to capture the patient encounter to aid in the billing process.

The accounting, payroll, and process management portions of the software were not as robust as pre-EMR software, so practices reverted back. Software that does not integrate (migrate data) with the EMR solution software created a weakened internal-control environment. For example, it is common to see billing and accounts receivable functions take place in the EMR software, and deposits are recorded in the accounting software. Without a reconciliation of total collections posted to the EMR system to total deposits in accounting software and bank records, misappropriation can easily occur.

15.2 HEALTH-CARE FRAUD DEFINED

According to Marcinko and Hetico, in the *Dictionary of Health Insurance and Managed Care*, *health-care fraud* may be defined as any illegal health-care activity where someone obtains something of value without paying for, or earning it. In health care, this usually occurs when someone bills for services not provided by a physician or medical provider.

And, health-care *abuse* is the activity where someone overuses or misuses services. According to the Center for Medicare and Medicaid Services (CMS), "although some of the practices may be initially considered to be abusive, rather than fraudulent activities, they may evolve into fraud."

Example

In the case of health-care abuse, this may occur when a physician sees a patient for treatment more times than deemed medically appropriate. If there are reported issues or actions from other sources, such as the National Practitioner Data Bank (NPDB) or a medical board, a health insurance program can take that opportunity to review health-care providers' activities. Most participation agreements allow for this type of scrutiny.

After a workable definition of health-care fraud and abuse has been proposed, and we have some definitional clarity, any preliminary billing, invoice review, or intern control program will usually request a sampling of specific medical records. This may progress to an on-site review of any and all medical records of patients that participate in a CMS program. These activities can be generated by the plan's quality assurance, or quality improvement, program and often are tied to the credentialing process for a provider's participation.*

* From *Medicare Carrier Manual* (14-3-14001) 14001, Part B, Medicare Fraud.

15.3 PREVENTIVE INTERNAL CONTROLS

On the other hand, employee theft in a medical practice is an often underreported business matter. The emotional trauma of such an event often transcends the financial loss. Opportunity is the main causative factor in embezzlement, and a scenario can be constructed under which anyone would feel justified in "borrowing" money. Perceived need, rationalization, and opportunity compose the commonly accepted model used in ethics classes.

Be careful to manage employee perceptions of internal practice-accounting controls. Their implementation and maintenance can be seen as oppressive to some employees. A strong system of internal controls is important to every health-care organization regardless of type and size.

However, it is possible to go too far. An unnecessarily strong system of internal controls may actually cost the practice more than it saves. How much internal control or process is enough? Physician-executive management, of course, should use judgment to determine. The focus should be to care if your office is far to the left with very little attention to process and not benefiting from organizational effectiveness.

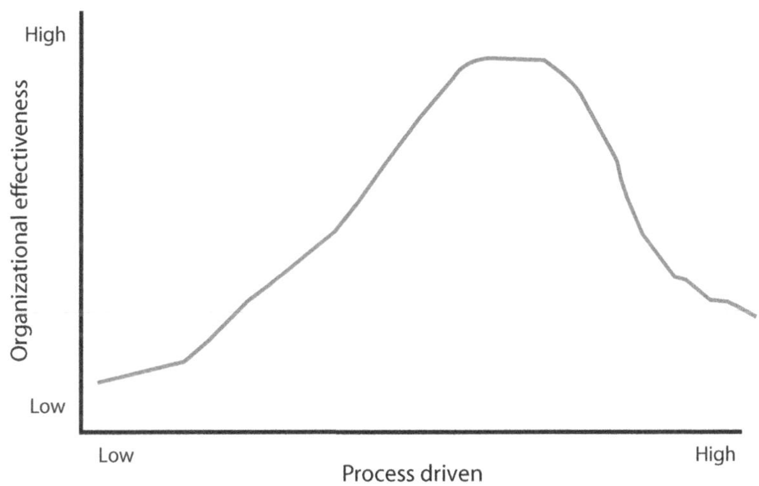

Office staff are responsible for adhering to the established procedures and for reporting to the physician executive or management when controls are not working as designed. Audit is responsible for assessing whether internal controls are present and functioning as designed.

Proactively setting up internal controls can help retain good employees, as it prevents some embezzlement. Controls can make honest employees feel more comfortable in that it is harder to be falsely suspected.

Example

During the holiday season, a medical practice manager suspected misappropriation of gift cards. His suspicion led him to call the gift card issuer to find that the office manager had been spending the cards intended for staff gifts, as witnessed on a retail store camera.

Preventive internal controls include the following:

- Daily inspection of the practice's online checking, savings, and credit card accounts by the owner. This is the vital first line of defense against most embezzlement scenarios.
- Separation of duties in all financial matters. This makes embezzlement only possible with collusion of at least two employees. This can be hard to implement in smaller medical practices with fewer personnel. Only the physician executive or management should have check-signing privileges. A staff member may prepare the checks, and present them, along with all appropriate documentation, for management's perusal and signature. Only preprinted checks should be used: avoid using check creation programs that allow printing of blank checks. Void checks, and subsequent sequential numbering should be retained. The checking statement should be sent to the physician-owner's home, and it, and the checks, should be inspected thoroughly. A different staff member can reconcile the checking statement if you chose not to do it yourself.
- Rotation of duties, as most prolonged embezzlement schemes will be uncovered if a different person periodically performs each duty. The "perfect" office employee who refuses to take a vacation may in fact be hiding such a scheme. Rotation of duties has the side benefit of cross-training employees, an important factor in small and medium-sized practices.
- Bonding of key employees. Bonding companies pursue criminal matters as a matter of policy, once you prove guilt. The fear of certain prosecution is sometimes a deterrent.
- Don't let the staff order anything with a practice credit card. If you do, have the statement sent to your home and check it against documentation.
- Physical safeguards by locking up theft-prone items.
- Enable software audit trails. If your software tracks corrective entries and deletions, use it. In addition to documenting possible fraud, this allows examination of which things go wrong and how to, and how not to, fix them.
- Internal mini-audits with frequent random checks of theft-prone systems can be easily set up and quickly performed.
- Security cameras.
- Computer monitoring programs that allow real-time, key-stroking or logged inspection of the employee's computer screen.

15.3.1 Common Embezzlement Schemes

- The physician-owner pocketing cash off-the-books. To the IRS, this is like embezzlement to intentionally defraud it out of tax money.
- Employees pocketing cash from cash transactions. This is why you see cashiers following protocol that seems to take forever when you're in the grocery checkout line. This is also why you see signs offering a reward if the customer is not offered a receipt. This is partly why security cameras are installed.
- Bookkeepers or your accountant writing checks to themselves. This is easiest to do in flexible software programs like QuickBooks and Peachtree Accounting (http://www.peachtree.com) and financial software. It is one of the hardest schemes to detect. The bookkeeper self-writes and cashes the check to his/her own name, and

then the name on the check is changed in the software program to a vendor's name. So a real check exists that looks legitimate on checking statements unless a picture of it is available.

- Accountants or bookkeepers paying bills of others and posting the disbursements as if they were for a practice obligation. Checks payable to the Internal Revenue Service, for example, can be used to pay tax obligations of another and are described in the bookkeeping as practice taxes due.
- Employees ordering personal items on practice credit cards.
- Bookkeepers receiving insurance company checks or patient checks, demonstrating the receipt of such in the EMR software and not posting in the practice bookkeeping software. Instead, checks are illegally deposited in an unauthorized, pseudo practice checking account, set up in a bank different from yours. They then withdraw funds at will. If this scheme uses only a few patients, who are billed outside of the practice's accounting software, this is hard to detect. Executive management must have a good knowledge of existing patients to catch the ones "missing" from practice records. Monitoring the bookkeeper's lifestyle might raise suspicion, but this scheme is generally low profile, yet protracted. Checking the accounting software audit trail shows the required original invoice deletions or credit memos in a less sophisticated version of this scheme.
- Bookkeepers writing payroll checks to nonexistent employees. This scheme works well in larger practices and medical clinics with high seasonal turnover of employees and in practices with multiple locations the physician-owner doesn't visit often.
- Bookkeepers writing inflated checks to existing employees, vendors, or subcontractors. Physician-owners should beware if there are romantic relationships between the bookkeeper and other practice-related parties.
- Bookkeepers writing checks to false vendors. This is another low-profile, protracted scheme that exploits the physician-owner's indifference to accounts payable.

15.3.2 Positive Internal Controls

- Tone at the top—high ethical standards of physician-management. A bit philosophical, but true. Human standards often follow those of their executive leaders.
- A standard operational procedural (SOP) manual is a must—samples of which are available on the Internet for every aspect of medical practice. Once downloaded, sections can be easily updated and reprinted whenever changes occur. This should include how things should be done, and, why. Give examples of common problems and how to avoid/solve them. This should include the practice's human resource policies, an important legal concern in any business. For example, ensure that the person who posts payments to patient accounts does not open the mail or prepare the deposit slip.
- Regular reporting. Each employee should submit regular reports (i.e., the daily transaction log, which becomes part of the managerial report).
- Install a biometric time clock. They have become very cost-effective and eliminate buddy punching and the hassle of lost time cards or ID badges.
- Use of a segregated payroll account. By reviewing your payroll history and calculating average monthly payroll cost, monthly transfers for the average amount

of payroll are made. The bank will alert when low a balance occurs, giving you awareness of possible payroll errors or fraud.
- Obtain copies of electronic receipts for all tax returns filed. Be certain the tax checks mailed contain only the practice entity's tax identification number on them. Mail them from your office in lieu of trusting your outside accountant to this task.

15.3.3 Spot Audits

Spot audits are an important medical practice control. Here, physician-owners use their expertise with the logistics and dynamics of their practice to devise a series of regular inspections to see if anything is going wrong and ensure that everything is going right. Frequent, small spot audits, perhaps different in nature, are best. These are nondisruptive. Implementation and application of these spot audits can make the difference between them being perceived (by employees, patients, and vendors) as prudent and responsible versus petty and mistrusting. Nothing erodes a practice's efficiency faster than physician indifference. Nothing demoralizes a practice more than a petty, mistrusting doctor. Spot audits, however, are not complex when the framework and forms to comply are in place and it therefore need not be performed by a seasoned auditor; an accounting junior will suffice, which makes this effort cost-effective.

Examples of possible spot audit components include the following:

1. Payroll monitoring (follow the complete payroll process sporadically on random employees):
    - Is the time clock accurate and, can it be manipulated or tampered with?
    - Is this a real employee? Perform random identification and inquiry.
    - Is there the correct number of employee days being paid?
    - Is there the correct number of employee hours being paid?
    - Is the compensation level accurate?
    - Is petty cash reimbursement fully documented?
    - Are withheld funds appropriate? Review W-4 tax withholding information for a match with paycheck withholding.
    - Do the net pay figures in the accounting software agree with the bank records?
    - Are payroll tax and liability correct (i.e., child support checks accurate and timely)?
    - Are payroll reports being properly generated and submitted?
2. Patient audits:
    - Co-pay control report—From the daily patient show report, create a random sample of patients. Start with around 10% of the patients encountered and adjust that percentage up or down based on your findings. Locate the patient file chosen and note the co-pay paid on the encounter along with the method of payment. Trace the patient co-pay amount presented to the deposit amount on your bank statement or to the credit card statement. Note for completeness and discrepancies of any kind.
    - Patient satisfaction surveys, properly done, can reveal surprising patient perceptions—Patient satisfaction occurs when their perceptions exceed their expectations. Perceptions can be influenced.

- Sporadically check the complete accounts receivable cycle for random patients—internal billing data, timeliness of patient invoices, documentation, write-offs, credit memos, payment process, consistent accounts receivable collections, guideline enforcement, accuracy of accounting software to bank records, etc.

3. Quality checks for manufactured products and maintenance inspection of practice equipment.
4. Sporadic physical inventory counts of random stock items.
5. Monitor the list of approved vendors.
6. Monitor the list of patients. Remember to try and reactivate old patients.
7. Sporadically check the accounts payable cycle on random vendors:
   - Follow the purchase order protocol.
   - Cross-reference invoices.
   - Check for late fees and interest.
   - Check the accuracy of payment; match to approved billing.
   - Check timeliness of payment.
   - Ask if payment internal guidelines are being followed.
   - Is accounting software checked for audit trail anomalies?
   - Does the bank reconcile records themselves?
8. Employee monitoring—Workplace monitoring is a practice that involves keeping an eye on activities and conditions in a workplace for health, security, and business reasons. Both employers and employees are concerned with the ethical implications of constant monitoring. While employers use monitoring devices to keep track of their employees' actions and productivity, their employees feel that too much monitoring is an invasion of their privacy. It is clear, however, that the practice will suffer if it is not aware of counterproductive activity. Employees downloading personal e-mails can expose the company computer to a virus, for example.

15.4 CERTIFIED FRAUD EXAMINER

The certified fraud examiner (CFE) credential denotes proven expertise in fraud prevention, detection, and deterrence. CFEs are trained to identify the warning signs and red flags that indicate evidence of fraud and fraud risk (http://www.ACFE.com). CFEs, and forensic accountants and attorneys, focus on detecting fraud and providing litigation support.

15.5 FORENSIC ACCOUNTING VERSUS FRAUD EXAMINATION

Forensic accounting and fraud examination are different, but related, specialties. According to expert Ashrafi Adhau, forensic accounting work is done by accountants in anticipation of litigation and can include fraud, valuation, bankruptcy, and a host of other professional

MEDICAL PRACTICE INTERNAL-CONTROL CHECKLIST

- Check that superbills (patient encounter forms) are prenumbered and accounted for on a daily basis.
- Reconcile the patients listed on the sign-in sheet to the appointment book and either the daily report of charges (computerized system) or the day sheet (pegboard system).
- Review the daily report of payments (computerized system) or the day sheet (pegboard system) to detect any payments by patients that may not have been posted.
- Review the practice's contractual adjustments for the period and year to date. Does the amount appear to be reasonable after taking into account the practice's payer mix?
- Take a sample of patient charges and trace the information on the related explanation of benefits (EOB) to each individual ledger sheet. Trace payment per EOB to the deposit slip. Investigate any discrepancies.
- Review all patients' ledger cards to detect if any balances were written off in their entirety.
- Make sure that the practice has a policy in place so that an account cannot be written off as a bad debt without the authorization of a physician.
- Have end-of-month closing and end-of-year closing performed by an outside bookkeeper or accountant. This approach of independent reconciliation is a great safeguard against collusion or misappropriation.
- Implement a password into the computer system. Supply the password only to authorized practice personnel.
- For a pegboard system, reconcile the accounts receivable balance per the day sheet to the individual ledger cards.
- Are all practice employees bonded?
- Is a physician the only one who is authorized to sign checks?
- Does a physician review and approve vendor invoices before signing checks?
- Review endorsements of canceled checks and investigate any irregularities.
- Reconcile EMR payments received to bank deposits. Match payments posted to the EMR software system to the bookkeeping effort and, ultimately, to the bank deposit. As mentioned, most practices use at least two different software solutions that do not integrate or sync with each other. This check will ensure that no received checks are misappropriated.

services. Fraud examinations can be conducted by either accountants or nonaccountants and pertain only to antifraud matters. The difference between a "normal" accountant and a forensic accountant is that the latter seeks a level of evidentiary detail and analytical precision that will be sustainable with legal scrutiny or review (personal communication).

Forensic accounting focuses on both the evidence of economic transactions and reporting, and the legal framework that allows such evidence to be suitable for establishing accountability and/or valuation. Forensic accounting engagements include transaction reconstruction, bankruptcy, family law issues, asset identification and valuation, fraud examination/detection, and many other issues.

Auditing is performed either by an employee (internal audit) or by an outside accounting firm (external audit). Internal audits examine operational evidence to ensure that the prescribed practice operating procedures have been followed. External audits examine the assets and records of a company, leading to the expression of a professional opinion by the outside certified public accountant (CPA), which gives credibility to the financial reports presented by the company. A key component of an audit is the review of internal-control weaknesses.

15.6 ASSESSMENT

Medical practice success does not just happen. Physician executives and managers do not achieve stated objectives and performance goals without processes and systems in place to mitigate the unexpected (risks). A medical practice needs to ensure that the chances of detrimental financial events occurring are minimized and the chances of positive events occurring are maximized. A prerequisite to optimizing this is a thorough understanding of the financial and nonfinancial aspects of the underlying practice logistics. Internal controls are the systems implemented to make this optimization happen.

15.7 CONCLUSION

In a health-care practice, internal controls can be extended to ensure quality patient care and prevent malpractice suits. Internal controls are long-standing business practices and do not need to be reinvented. But, they do need to be formally addressed for the practice to reach peak economic efficiency.

15.8 COLLABORATE

Discuss this chapter online with others at http://www.MedicalExecutivePost.com.

FURTHER READINGS

Bode, GL and Marcinko, DE: *Internal Audit Control Measures for Medical Practices and Clinics. Financial Management Strategies for Hospitals and Healthcare Organizations*. Productivity Press, Boca Raton, FL, 2014.

Bragg, SM: *Accounting Control Best Practices*. Wiley, New York, 2009.

Brown, E: *Internal Controls—Conversations about Effective Internal Control Procedures*. Amazon Digital Services, New York, 2013.

Graham, L: *Internal Control Audit and Compliance: Documentation and Testing under the New COSO Framework*. Wiley, New York, 2015.

Grant, BJ: Fundamentals of Healthcare Accounting and Finance. In *Practicing Medicine in the 21st Century*, Nash, DB (Editor). American College of Physician Executives, Tampa, FL, 2007.
Joyce, J: *Internal Controls for Complete Beginners*. Amazon Digital Services, New York, 2013.
King, SJ: *The Bible of Internal Controls*. Amazon Digital Services, 2014.
Marcinko, DE and Hetico, HR: *Dictionary of Health Economics and Finance* (http://www.HealthDictionarySeries.com). Springer Publishing Company, New York, 2007.
Marcinko, DE and Hetico, HR: *Healthcare Organizations*. iMBA, Atlanta, GA, 2010.
Moeller, R: *Executive's Guide to COSO Internal Controls: Understanding and Implementing the New Framework*. Wiley, New York, 2013.
Sweet, S: *Department of Health and Human Resources Report to Congress (Manage the People or Manage the Process?)*. FDR, Washington, DC, October 2014.
Tinsely, RE: *Medical Practice Management Handbook*. Aspen Publisher, New York, 2004.
Turner, L and Weickgenannt, A: *Accounting Information Systems: Controls and Processes Accounting for Decision Making and Control*. McGraw-Hill, New York, 2008.
Young, D: *Management Accounting in Health Care Organizations*. Jossey-Bass Public Health, New York, 2008.
Zimmerman, J: *Accounting for Decision Making and Control*. McGraw-Hill, New York, 2008.

Checklist 15.1: Office Internal Controls	**Yes**	**No**
Check that superbills (patient encounter forms) are prenumbered and accounted for on a daily basis.	o	o
Ensure that the person who posts payments to patient accounts does not open the mail or prepare the deposit slip.	o	o
Reconcile the patients listed on the sign-in sheet to the appointment book and either the daily report of charges (computerized system) or the day sheet (pegboard system).	o	o
Review the daily report of payments (computerized system) or the day sheet (pegboard system) to detect any payments by patients that may not have been posted. Be reasonable after taking into account the practice's payer mix.	o	o
Take a sample of patient charges and trace the information on the related explanation of benefits (EOB) to each individual ledger sheet. Trace payment per EOB to the deposit slip. Investigate any discrepancies.	o	o
Review all patients' ledger cards to detect if any balances were written off in their entirety	o	o
	Yes	**No**
Make sure that the practice has a policy in place so that an account cannot be written off as a bad debt without the authorization of a physician.		
Implement a password into the computer system. Supply the password only to authorized practice personnel.	o	o
For a pegboard system, reconcile the accounts receivable balance per the day sheet to the individual ledger cards.	o	o
Are all practice employees bonded?	o	o
Is a physician the only one who is authorized to sign checks?	o	o
Does a physician review and approve vendor invoices before signing checks?	o	o
	Yes	**No**
Review endorsements of canceled checks and investigate any irregularities.		
Compare month-end collections per medical billing software management report to actual amount deposited per monthly bank reconciliation(s). Review related reconciliations.	o	o

Ensure that the person who posts payments to patient accounts does not open the mail or prepare the deposit slip.	o	o
Take sample of daily deposits and compare to computer daily report of posted payments. Investigate differences.	o	o
Review selected sample of cancelled checks for appropriate vendor endorsement.	o	o
Scan list of cash disbursements to identify possible false vendor relationships.	o	o
	Yes	**No**
Review monthly contractual adjustments posting for reasonableness.		
Review monthly practice charges for reasonableness. Investigate decreases in production.	o	o
Take sample of charge tickets and determine if any charge tickets (or charge ticket numbers) are missing. Investigate discrepancies.	o	o
Conduct on-site visit to review cash and disbursement procedures in place, including related employee interviews.	o	o
Review the practice's contractual adjustments for the period and year to date.	o	o
	Yes	**No**
Review adequacy of current accounts payable procedures and related approval for vendor payment system.		
Review sample of petty cash reconciliations.	o	o
Review access controls to medical billing software system.	o	o
Ensure that all patient account statements are prepared and mailed each month.	o	o
Ensure that all available vacation time has been taken by related billing, collection, and management personnel.	o	o
Ensure that all appropriate personnel are bonded.	o	o

Checklist 15.2: Internal Accounts Receivable Control	**Yes**	**No**
Do we check prenumbered patient encounter forms on a daily basis?	o	o
Should employees that post payments to accounts receivable (AR) open invoices?	o	o
Should employees that post payments to ARs make bank deposit slips?	o	o
Do we reconcile patient sign-in sheets to the appointment book and either the daily report of charges or day sheet?	o	o
Do we review daily payment reports or the day sheet to detect any payments that may not have been posted?	o	o
Do we review contractual adjustments to make sure amounts appear reasonable after considering payer mix?	o	o
Do we track patient charge information on explanation of benefits (EOB) to each ledger sheet and deposit slip?	o	o
Do we investigate any discrepancies?	o	o
Do we review patients' ledger cards for written-off balances?	o	o
Do we institute and police an account write-off bad-debt policy with signature authorization?	o	o
Do we issue a computer password to authorized personnel?	o	o
Are all entity employees bonded?	o	o
Is a manager authorized to sign checks?	o	o

Does an AR supervisor approve vendor invoices before signing checks?	o	o
Do we regularly review cancelled-check endorsements and investigate irregularities?	o	o

Checklist 15.3: Accounts Receivable Bad-Debt Expense Internal Control	Yes	No
Do written AR collections guidelines exist for all third-party and self-pay accounts?	o	o
Are AR collection guidelines reviewed annually and revised periodically?	o	o
Are AR collection guidelines clearly detailed to serve as a reference to personnel?	o	o
Do clinic employees receive training on collection guidelines?	o	o
Do clinic employees receive training on collection guidelines after revisions?	o	o
Does management solicit suggestions for changes in policies and procedures?	o	o
Do AR guideline exceptions require the approval of management on a case-by-case basis?	o	o
Do self-pay AR guidelines allow monthly payments?	o	o
Do self-pay AR guidelines specify the maximum number of acceptable payments?	o	o
Do self-pay AR guidelines specify the minimum monthly acceptable payment?	o	o
Do AR collection guidelines specify actions taken if a patient or vendor misses a payment?	o	o
Does management support the AR collection guidelines, even with complaints?	o	o

APPENDIX

Daily Control Spreadsheet

Number of insurance claim forms prepared: ___________
Superbills used (list numbers): [beginning #] to [ending #]

Charges:
  Per claim forms:___________ Office visits:___________ Total:

Payments:
  By mail:___________ By patients in office:___________ Total:
  Total deposit:___________
Petty cash reconciliation:
  Beginning petty cash balance
  Additions
  Disbursements
  Ending balance
Comments:

Co-pay Control Report

Sample population ________________
Sample rate ________________

Date	Patient #	Co-payment Required	Cash/Credit/Check	Accounted for at Bank/Credit Card

Approved By: ______________________________

Approved By: ______________________________

Weekly EMR Payments Received Reconciliation to Bank Deposits

EMR Payments Posted	Posted Deposits in Bookkeeping Software	Accounted for at Bank/ Credit Card

Approved By: ______________________________

Approved By: ______________________________

16 Medical Workplace Violence Issues
Growing Recognition and Impact

Eugene Schmuckler and David Edward Marcinko

CONTENTS

On November 6, 2009, a 39-year-old army psychiatrist named Maj. Nidal M. Hasan, MD (1997 graduate of Virginia Tech University who received a medical doctorate in psychiatry from the Uniformed Services University of the Health Sciences in Bethesda, Maryland, and served as an intern, resident, and fellow at the Walter Reed Army Medical Center in the District of Columbia) went on a savage 100-round shooting spree and rampage that killed 13 people and injured 32 others.

Yet, the impact of workplace violence became widely exposed, more than two decades before, in Edmond, Oklahoma. In August 1986, Patrick Henry Sherrill, an employee of the U.S. Postal Service, angered by perceived injustices against him by his employers, shot and killed 14 people, wounded 6, and then killed himself.

By 2012, the Bureau of Labor Statistics (BLS) reported that the following:

1. Nearly 2 million Americans report they've been victims of violence at work.
2. In 2010, one in nine workplace fatalities were homicides.
3. Homicide is the most common cause of workplace fatalities in women.

4. Workplace violence is one of the gravest occupational hazards for health-care workers.
5. Nearly one-third of nurses are subjected to physical or verbal assaults at least once a month.
6. Geriatric wards and waiting rooms are two of the most frequent sites for hospital violence (along with emergency departments and psychiatric wards).
7. A Detroit hospital began screening with handheld metal detectors—and collected 33 handguns, 1324 knives, and 97 mace-type sprays during a 6-month period.
8. A veteran's hospital in Oregon reduced violent attacks by 91.6% after implementing a database that identified patients with a history of violence.
9. A New York City hospital reduced reported violent crimes by 65% after implementing ID badges and color-coded passes that limited access to hospital floors.

16.1 INTRODUCTION

These shocking events have not only added, and reinforced, the term *going postal* to our lexicon, but also contributed to our almost blasé attitude about them. Want more recent evidence?

A Boston cardiac surgeon was mortally wounded by a gunman at Brigham and Women's Hospital in January 2015. Dr. Michael Davidson, of Wellesley, Massachusetts, was shot twice at a cardiac center after a man demanded to see him. The 44-year-old Davidson died despite frantic efforts of coworkers to save him. The shooter, who turned the gun on himself and committed suicide in an examining room, had some kind of previous relationship with the doctor and was identified as Stephen Pasceri, 55, of Millbury, Massachusetts. Dr. Davidson, a Yale graduate, had worked at the hospital since 2006 and was an assistant professor at Harvard Medical School.

Yet, during Super Bowl XLIX week pregame preparations, the local and national attention seemed only to be riveted on accusations that Coach Bill Belichick and the New England Patriots football team deliberately deflated 11 of 12 of the footballs used in the division championship game (Deflategate).

16.2 ASSESSMENT OF WORKPLACE VIOLENCE IN HEALTH CARE

16.2.1 What Is Workplace Violence?

Workplace violence is more than physical assault—it is any act in which a person is abused, threatened, intimidated, harassed, or assaulted in his/her employment. Swearing, verbal abuse, playing pranks, spreading rumors, arguments, property damage, vandalism, sabotage, pushing, theft, physical assaults, psychological trauma, anger-related incidents, rape, arson, and murder are all examples of workplace violence. The Registered Nurses Association of Nova Scotia defines violence as "any behavior that results in injury whether real or perceived by an individual, including, but not limited to, verbal abuse, threats of physical harm, and sexual harassment." As such, workplace violence includes the following:

- Threatening behavior—such as shaking fists, destroying property, or throwing objects.
- Verbal or written threats—any expression of intent to inflict harm.

- Harassment—any behavior that demeans, embarrasses, humiliates, annoys, alarms, or verbally abuses a person and that is known or would be expected to be unwelcome. This includes words, gestures, intimidation, bullying, or other inappropriate activities.
- Verbal abuse—swearing, insults, or condescending language.
- Muggings—aggravated assaults, usually conducted by surprise and with intent to rob.
- Physical attacks—hitting, shoving, pushing, or kicking.

Workplace violence can be brought about by a number of different actions in the workplace. It may also be the result of non-work-related situations such as domestic violence or road rage. Workplace violence can be inflicted by an abusive employee, a manager, supervisor, coworker, customer, family member, or even a stranger. The University of Iowa Injury Prevention Research Center classifies most workplace violence into one of four categories.*

- *Type I, criminal intent*—Results while a criminal activity (e.g., robbery) is being committed and the perpetrator had no legitimate relationship to the workplace.
- *Type II, customer/client*—The perpetrator is a customer or client at the workplace (e.g., health-care patient) and becomes violent while being assisted by the worker.
- *Type III, worker on worker*—Employees or past employees of the workplace are the perpetrators.
- *Type IV, personal relationship*—The perpetrator usually has a personal relationship with an employee (e.g., domestic violence in the workplace).

16.2.2 Effects of Workplace Violence

The health-care sector continues to lead all other industry sectors in incidents of nonfatal workplace assaults. In 2000, 48% of all nonfatal injuries from violent acts against workers occurred in the health-care sector.† Nurses, nurses' aides, and orderlies suffer the highest proportion of these injuries. Nonfatal assaults on health-care workers include assaults, bruises, lacerations, broken bones, and concussions. These reported incidents include only injuries severe enough to result in lost time from work. Of significance is that the median time away from work as a result of an assault or other violent act is 5 days. Almost 25% of these injuries result in longer than 20 days away from work. Obviously, this is quite costly to the facility as well as to the victim.

A study undertaken in Canada found that 46% of 8780 staff nurses experienced one or more types of violence in the last five shifts worked. *Physical assault* was defined as being spit on, bitten, hit, or pushed (Duncan et al. 2000).

Both Canadian and U.S. researchers have described the prevalence of verbal threats and physical assaults in intensive care, emergency departments, and general wards. A study in Florida reported that 100% of emergency department nurses experience verbal threats and 82% reported being physically assaulted. Similar results were found in a study undertaken in a Canadian hospital. Possible reasons for the high incidence of violence in emergency

---

* Cal/OSHA 1995; UIIPRC 2001.

† Bureau of Labor Statistics 2001.

departments include presence of weapons, frustration with long waits for medical care, dissatisfaction with hospital policies, and the levels of violence in the community served by the emergency department (Lipscomb; Lipscomb and Love 1992; NIOSH 2002).

Similar findings have been reported in studies of mental health professionals, nursing home and long-term-care employees, as well as providers of service in home and community health.

Violence in hospitals usually results from patients, and occasionally family members, who feel frustrated, vulnerable, and out of control. Transporting patients, long waits for service, inadequate security, poor environmental design, and unrestricted movement of the public are associated with increased risk of assault in hospitals and may be significant factors in social services workplaces as well. Finally, lack of staff training and the absence of violence prevention programming are associated with elevated risk of assault in hospitals. Although anyone working in a hospital may become a victim of violence, nurses and aides, who have the most direct contact with patients, are at higher risk. Other hospital personnel at increased risk of violence include emergency response personnel, hospital safety officers, and all health-care providers. Personnel working in large medical practices fall into this category as well. Although no area is totally immune from acts of violence, it most frequently occurs in psychiatric wards, emergency rooms, waiting rooms, and geriatric settings.

Many medical facilities mistakenly focus on systems, operations, infrastructure, and public relations when planning for crisis management and emergency response: they tend to overlook the people (Braverman 2003). Obviously, no medical facility can operate without employees who are healthy enough to return to work and to be productive. Individuals who have been exposed to a violent incident need to be assured of their safety.

The costs associated with workplace violence crises are not limited to health-care dollars, absenteeism rates, legal battles, or increased insurance rates. If mishandled, traumatic events can severely impair trust between patients, employees, their peers, and their managers. Without proper planning, an act of violence can disrupt normal group processes, interfere with the delivery of crucial information, and temporarily impair management effectiveness. It may also lead to other negative outcomes such as low employee morale, increased job stress, increased work turnover, reduced trust of management and coworkers, and a hostile working environment.

Data collected by the U.S. Department of Justice shows workplace violence to be the fastest-growing category of murder in the country. Homicide, including domestic homicides, is the leading cause of on-the-job death for women and is the second leading cause for men. The National Institute of Occupational Safety and Health (NIOSH) has found that an average of 20 workers are murdered each week in the United States. In addition, an estimated 1 million workers—28,000 per week—are victims of nonfatal workplace assaults each year. Workplace attacks, threats, or harassment can include the following monetary costs:

- $13.5 billion in medical costs per year
- 500,000 employees missing 1,750,000 days of work per year
- 41% increase in stress levels with the concomitant related costs

16.3 UNDERSTANDING THE DEEPER RISKS

More assaults occur in the health-care and social services industries than in any other. In 2000, BLS data showed that 48% of all nonfatal injuries from occupational assaults and violent acts occurred in health care and social services. In 1999, 637 nonfatal assaults on hospital workers occurred—a rate of 8.3 assaults per 10,000 workers—and the NIOSH confirmed this ratio in April 2002, reporting that U.S. hospital workers suffer nonfatal assaults at more than four times the rate of overall private sector workers, which is 2 per 10,000 workers. Almost two-thirds of the nonfatal assaults occurred in nursing homes, hospitals, and establishments providing residential care and social services (Toscano and Weber 1995).

Several studies indicate that violence often takes place during times of high activity and interaction with patients, such as at meal times, during visiting hours, and during patient transportation. Assaults may occur when service is denied; when a patient is involuntarily admitted; or when a health-care worker attempts to set limits on eating, drinking, or tobacco or alcohol use.

The issue of assaults against health professionals is not new. Between 1980 and 1990, 106 occupational violence-related deaths occurred among the following health-care workers: 27 pharmacists, 26 physicians, 18 registered nurses, 17 nurses' aides, and 18 health-care workers in other occupational categories (Goodman et al. 1994). Using the National Traumatic Occupational Fatality database, the study reported that between 1983 and 1989, there were 69 registered nurses killed at work. Homicide was the leading cause of traumatic occupational death among employees in nursing homes and personal care facilities.

Of greater significance than these numbers is the likely underreporting of violence and a persistent perception within the health-care industry that assaults are part of the job. Underreporting may reflect a lack of institutional reporting policies, employee beliefs that reporting will not benefit (and may actually harm) them, or employee fears that employers may deem assaults the result of employee negligence or poor job performance (OSHA 1998).

16.3.1 Workplace Violence Risks in Hospitals

NIOSH (2002) summarizes the risk factors for occupational violence to hospital workers. These include the following:

- Working directly with volatile people, especially if they are under the influence of drugs or alcohol or have a history of violence or certain psychotic diagnoses
- Working when understaffed—especially during meal times or visiting hours
- Transporting patients
- Long waits for service
- Overcrowded, uncomfortable waiting rooms
- Working alone
- Poor environmental design
- Inadequate and/or ineffective security
- Lack of staff training and policies for preventing or managing crises with potentially volatile patients
- Drug and alcohol abuse
- Access to firearms
- Unrestricted movement of the public
- Poorly lit corridors, rooms, parking lots, and other areas

Violence occurring in other occupational groups is most often related to robbery. In health-care settings, however, acts of violence are most often perpetrated by patients or clients (Registered Nurses' Association of Nova Scotia 1995). Family members who feel frustrated, vulnerable, and out of control, and colleagues of patients (especially when the patient is a gang member) are also identified as perpetrators of abuse. There are numerous case reports documenting violence in the medical setting, such as the following:

- An elderly patient verbally abused a nurse when she prevented him from leaving the hospital to go home in the middle of the night.
- An agitated psychotic patient attacked a nurse, broke her arm, and scratched and bruised her.
- A disturbed family member whose father had died in surgery at the community hospital walked into the emergency department and fired a small-caliber handgun, killing a nurse and an emergency medical technician and wounding the emergency physician.

However, the presence of coworkers has been identified as a potential deterrent to assault in health care.

Health-care and social service workers face an increased risk of work-related assaults stemming from several factors, including the following:

- The prevalence of handguns and other weapons—as high as 25% among patients, their families, and friends. Handguns are increasingly used by police and the criminal justice system for criminal holds and the care of acutely disturbed, violent individuals.
- The increasing number of acute and chronically mentally ill patients now being released from hospitals without follow-up care, who now have the right to refuse medicine and who can no longer be hospitalized involuntarily unless they pose an immediate threat to themselves or others.
- The availability of drugs or money at hospitals, clinics, and pharmacies, making staff and patients likely robbery targets.
- Situational and circumstantial factors such as
  - Unrestricted movement of the public in clinics and hospitals
  - The increasing presence of gang members, drug or alcohol abusers, trauma patients, or distraught family members
  - Long waits in emergency or clinic areas, leading to client frustration over an inability to obtain needed services promptly
- Low staffing levels during times of specific increased activity such as meal times, visiting times, and when staff is transporting patients. This also includes isolated work with clients during examinations or treatment.
- Solo work, often in remote locations, particularly in high-crime settings, with no back-up or means of obtaining assistance such as communication devices or alarm systems.
- Lack of training of staff in recognizing and managing escalating hostile and assaultive behavior.
- Poorly lighted parking areas.

The guidelines established by the Occupational Safety and Health Administration OSHA 1998 seek to set forth procedures leading to the elimination or reduction of worker exposure to conditions causing death or injury from violence by implementing effective security devices and administrative work practices, among other control measures. Health-care professionals need to be aware that violence can occur anywhere and in any practice settings. In hospitals and clinics, which are more likely to report incidents of violence than private offices, the most frequent sites are the following:

- Psychiatric wards
- Acute care settings
- Critical care units
- Community health agencies
- Homes for special care
- Emergency rooms
- Waiting rooms and geriatric units (NIOSH 2002)

The impact of workplace violence is far-reaching and affects individual staff members, coworkers, patients/clients, and their families. Those who have been affected, directly or indirectly, by a workplace violence incident report a broad spectrum of responses—anger is the most common. There are also reports of the following:

- Difficulty returning to work
- Decreased job performance
- Changes in relationships with coworkers
- Sleep pattern disturbance
- Helplessness
- Symptoms for posttraumatic stress disorders
- Fear of other patients
- Fear of returning to the scene of the assault*

16.3.2 Contributing Factors

A number of factors may contribute to the risk of violence or potentially violent situations in the workplace, including but not limited to the following:

- *Characteristics of patients or clients*: history of aggressive or violent behavior; clinical conditions such as dementia, head trauma, hypoglycemia, and emotional disorders; or substance abuse
- *Environment factors*: inflexible institutional rules and policies; restrictions on activities; noise or lighting levels; busy or high activity times; invasion of personal space; layout of or overcrowding in units or areas housing patients/clients (e.g., emergency department settings)

* Cooper 1995; Ryan and Poster 1991.

- *Staff characteristics*: staff dynamics (i.e., conflict among staff members); staff attitudes, such as anxiety or ambivalence toward the prevention or management of aggression; and staff behavior (e.g., tone of voice, body language, overt aggression)
- *Organizational policies and educational programs*: a lack of policies or programs aimed at preventing and reducing the incidence and impact of workplace violence can in fact lead to increased risks*

OSHA's General Duty Clause requires employers to provide a safe and healthful working environment for all workers covered by the Occupational Safety Health Administration (OSHA) Act of 1970. Failure to implement is not in itself a violation of the General Duty Clause, but if there is a recognized violence hazard in the workplace and employers do not take feasible steps to prevent or abate it, employers can be cited.

Courts have ruled against employers for the dangerous acts of employees if the employer does not use reasonable care in hiring, training, supervising, or retaining employees in the event that such harm was foreseeable. You may be liable for an intoxicated employee or one who otherwise presents a risk to others. As an example, if one of your employees has had to take a restraining order out against a former spouse, boyfriend/girlfriend, or partner, there is an apparent risk.

Employers are expected to use reasonable care in the maintenance of health-care facility premises, including reasonable security precautions and other measures seeking to minimize the risk of foreseeable criminal intrusion (based upon the experience of the employer, or its location in a dangerous area). Failing to take these precautions potentially leads to significant consequences for the victim as well for the organization, including the following:

- Increased costs to cover sick-leave benefits of the individual involved, and of replacement staff
- Decreased quality of care, resulting from reluctance on the part of the staff to care for the perpetrator of the violence
- Increased staff turnover, along with the difficulties of hiring a competent replacement should the victim choose to leave the profession following a violent incident
- Lowered staff morale as workloads and stress increase as a result of the loss of qualified staff†

Whether in a hospital, clinic, or private practice setting, good preemployment screening is essential. A shortage of trained personnel is not a justification for haphazard hiring practices. As part of the screening, it is necessary to conduct criminal history checks; make certain that employees have the degrees and experience listed on the resume; check references; and make certain that the interviewer is skilled and thorough in questioning techniques.

16.3.3 Risk Analysis

Conducting a risk analysis represents the first step in risk identification. Risk represents exposure to the chance of injury or loss. Risks are relative to the observer and have to do with both uncertainty and damages. We can summarize this with the following formula:

---

* NSNU 1995; Whitehorn 1995; Worthington 1993.

† ICN 1994; NASAHO Task Force Report 1993; Ryan and Poster 1991.

Risk = probability of an event occurring × damages

Crisis management efforts following an incident of workplace violence in a medical facility need to recognize the extraordinary impact the event may hold for the survivors and witnesses—your employees. Drawing from the experiences of situations leading to human crises, such as fatal accidents, violence, becoming overwhelmed when having to deal with situations involving mass fatalities, and being overwhelmed by other seriously injured patients, points to several guidelines needing to be considered prior to the establishment of a formal policy statement.

First, understand and plan for the physical and emotional health of employees at all levels. The emotional and behavioral consequences of the event may include a wide range of potentially disabling conditions such as avoidance, concentration problems, depression, and feelings of vulnerability and sadness. Long term, they can lead to substance abuse (resulting from self-medication), mental and physical problems, and marital problems. These then lead to direct costs from absences, health-care expenses, worker's compensation claims, lawsuits, and employee turnover. *The time to identify resources, make policies, and establish delivery systems is prior to, and not during, the actual crisis event.*

Second, prepare to respond to the crisis-related needs of employees by having a mechanism in place by which accurate and credible information can be disseminated to employees and their families. Lack of information can translate into lack of action. For instance, after the explosion at the World Trade Center in 1993, a survey taken the following month found that

- 76% thought something serious had happened.
- 32% did not evacuate by 1 hour.
- 30% decided not to evacuate.
- 36% participated in a previous emergency evacuation (Aguirre et al. 1998).

Third, create a safe haven for those directly and indirectly affected by events. Offering an environment where employees can come together in order to discuss their emotional troubles affords them the opportunity to see that their responses are not unique to them. This locale also offers a venue in which employees are able to talk, grieve, and receive counseling.

Finally, monitor the medium- and long-term effects of the crisis on the health and occupational functioning of individuals and work units. A mistake made by many organizations is that a crisis is considered to be over as soon as the cleanup is complete. They fail to take into account the far-reaching effects of stress on their employees. When employee stress levels are reduced, there is a concomitant reduction in errors. A study of hospitals showed that medication errors declined 50% after stress prevention activities were implemented in a 700-bed hospital. In another study conducted by St. Paul Fire & Marine Insurance, there was a 70% reduction in malpractice claims in 22 hospitals that implemented stress reduction activities and no reduction in the 22 hospitals that did not.

Risk management has long been used in the context of the medical facility. Well-designed and comprehensive risk-management programs reduce the losses of people, equipment, and material due to accidents. Completing the following six-step process can provide direction for risk management.

1. Identify hazards—Determine as much as possible the hazards associated with a department or an area.
2. Assess hazards—Determine a means to measure the severity of risk and probability that an incident will occur. As an example, a shooting in an urban emergency room may be likely, and the severity of the outcome could be catastrophic. The overall risk would be considered extremely high.
3. Determine the types of hazard*:
   a. Frequent—experienced continuously during the day; occurs often
   b. Likely—experienced often, several times during the day
   c. Occasional—experienced sometimes; occurs sometimes
   d. Seldom—possibly experienced; occurrence is remote
   e. Unlikely—improbable; not expected to occur
4. Develop techniques to prevent or mitigate hazards—The organization develops controls and makes decisions for the hazards that have been identified. The goal is to reduce the probability of a hazard turning into an incident and to limit the consequences of an incident if one does occur.
5. Implement those techniques—Put the techniques developed into actual practice. This requires making someone responsible for ensuring that the control is used correctly.
6. Evaluate the process—Ironically, there is a lack of research data dealing with successful intervention programs. As a consequence, the words of Abraham Maslow are directly applicable: "To the man who only has a hammer in the toolkit, every problem looks like a nail." Some programs, however, may be implemented on a universal basis. For instance, to prevent violence in medical settings; employers should develop a safety and health program that includes management commitment; employee participation; hazard identification; safety and health training; and hazard prevention, control, and reporting. As with all other programs in place, this needs to be evaluated periodically.

* Note: Hazard severity can be looked at from the context of four outcome categories: (1) Catastrophic—death or permanent disability, major equipment damage; (2) Critical—permanent partial disability, significant equipment damage; (3) Moderate—minor injury, lost workday, minor equipment damage; (4) Negligible—first aid, little equipment damage.

16.4 DEALING WITH MEDICAL WORKPLACE VIOLENCE

The previous sections have dealt with some of the risk factors associated with workplace violence in a medical setting. The direct and indirect costs, as well as legal and financial implications associated with workplace violence, have been presented. Unfortunately, many practitioners or institutions practice extreme denial when it comes to the issue of workplace violence, maintaining the mind-set of "it can't happen here." Those who have never experienced workplace violence often comment, "I don't need to worry about this." Nothing can be further from the truth. In fact, situations of this type are increasing in number; they do occur, and they cost lives.

16.4.1 Creating a Prevention Plan

A preventative, proactive approach is needed. In 1982, writing in the *Atlantic Monthly*, James Q. Wilson and George L. Kelling presented "The Broken Window Theory." In effect, the theory holds that if a single window is left unrepaired in a building, in fairly short order, the remaining windows in the building will be broken. Fixing windows as soon as they are broken sends a message that vandalism will not be tolerated. In contrast, not fixing the window sends a message that vandalism is acceptable. Worse, once a problem such as vandalism starts, if left unchecked, it flourishes. Consider the situation where one of your employees begins coming in late on a more and more frequent basis. Not dealing with that employee at the outset of this behavior can result in the other employees delaying their start time.

In the context of workplace violence, we are dealing with problem employees and patients, and the same observations are valid. When verbal abuse, threats of assault, or harassment are tolerated in health-care environments, it increases the likelihood that more serious forms of violence will follow. In other words, *ignoring a situation may result in an escalation of the problem.* Morale and productivity are lowered; effective employees leave. However, dealing effectively with situations like hostility, harassment, intimidation, and other disruptive types of conflict will create a more productive workplace.

Obviously, it is incumbent upon every organization to create a safe workplace for its employees. An initial step is to review any history of violence in your own workplace. The purpose of this exercise is not to cast blame but, rather, to prevent or minimize the likelihood of any future occurrence. This review should include the following (Figure 16.1):

- Ask employees about their experiences and whether they are concerned for themselves or others.
- Review any incidents of violence by consulting existing incident reports, first-aid records, and health and safety committee records.
- Determine whether your workplace has any of the risk factors associated with violence.
- Conduct a visual inspection of your workplace and the work being carried out. Focus on the workplace design and layout, and your administrative and work practices.

There are both crisis-prone and crisis-prepared organizations. It is Pauchant and Mitroff's thesis that given the proliferation of human and environmental crises in our current society,

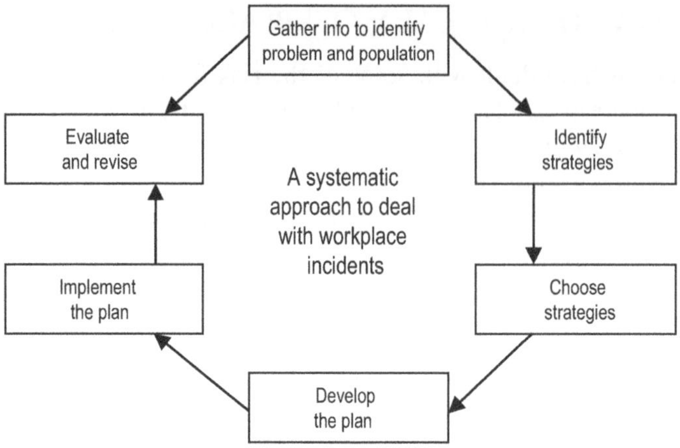

FIGURE 16.1 A schematic plan for dealing with workplace incidents. (From Pauchant, T.C. and Mitroff, I.I., *Transforming the Crisis Prone Organization*, Jossey Bass, San Francisco, 1993.)

those organizations (medical offices, clinics, hospitals) that deny the possibility of crises and do nothing to prevent them or to prepare for them are more likely to experience severe disruption and harm.

A crisis-prone health-care organization does the following:

- Reacts to crises, rather than reading the warning signs that might allow problems to be prevented or mitigated
- Pays lip service to human issues but pays real attention only to bottom-line figures and business interests
- Holds fast to denial, summarily expelling or punishing employees perceived as deviant, rather than confronting their behavior and its causes
- "Delegates" responsibility for programs and policies involving employee welfare to lower echelons while top leadership remains remote, especially during times of change and stress
- Directs communication outward in a crisis (e.g., toward the public and the media) rather than inward, toward employees
- Remains mired in adversarial standoff, thwarting internal communication and problem solving

A crisis-prepared health-care organization does the following:

- Maintains effective systems for collecting, reporting, and analyzing early-stage distress
- Cultivates a sense of mutual interest among stakeholders responding to incipient status
- Develops and fully disseminates a policy for dealing with potential and actual crises
- Encourages a climate in which employees feel free to communicate their distress to management and management feels a responsibility to respond
- Engages in effective problem solving rather than confrontation
- Does not deny problems or avoid dealing with them by expelling or suppressing "deviants"

16.4.1.1 Haddon Matrix for Injury Prevention

An invaluable tool for prevention program establishment is the Haddon matrix. In 1968, William Haddon Jr., a public health physician with the New York State Health Department, developed a matrix of categories to assist researchers trying to address injury prevention systematically. The idea was to look at injuries in terms of causal factors and contributing factors, rather than just using a descriptive approach. It is only recently that this model has been put to use in the area of workplace violence (Runyan et al. 2000).

The matrix (Figure 16.2) is a framework designed to apply the traditional public health domains of host, agent, and disease to primary, secondary, and tertiary injury factors. When applied to workplace violence, the *host* is the victim of workplace violence, such as a nurse. The *agent* is a combination of the perpetrator and his/her weapon(s) and the force with which an assault occurs. The *environment* is divided into two subdomains: the physical and the social environments. The location of an assault such as the emergency room (ER), the street, an examining room, or hospital ward is as important as the social setting in patient interaction, presence of coworkers, and supervisor support.

Subsequent versions of the matrix listed below divide the environment into a physical environment and a social, socioeconomic, or sociocultural environment. Each factor is then considered a pre-event phase, an event phase, and a postevent phase.

Pre-event: Are we psychologically prepared for the event?
Event: What is the level of exposure of the individuals?
Postevent: What will the outcome be?
Results: Distress responses, behavioral change, psychiatric illness.

The Haddon matrix lends itself to a medical setting in that it uses a classical epidemiological framework to categorize pre-event, event, and postevent activities according to the infectious disease vernacular, host (victim), vector (assailant or weapon), and environment. The strength of the Haddon matrix is that it includes the ability to assess pre-events or precursors in order to develop primary preventive measures (McPhaul and Lipscomb 2004).

Table 16.1 shows how the Haddon matrix categorizes influence of the following:

- Human or host behavior
- Agent or vehicle of situation
- Physical and sociocultural environment

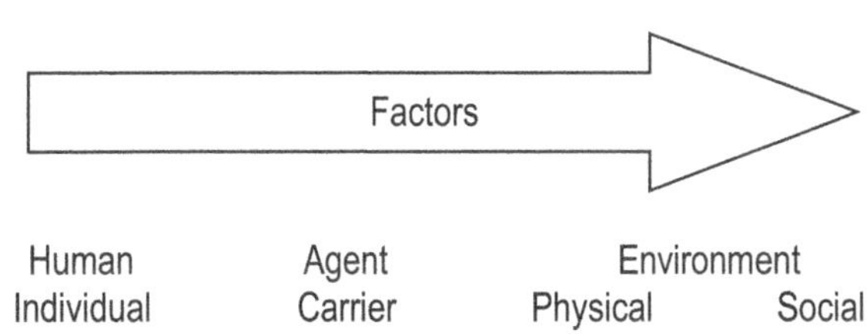

FIGURE 16.2 The Haddon matrix.

TABLE 16.1
Application of Haddon Matrix to Workplace Violence Prevention[a]

Phases	Host	Agent	Physical Environment	Social Environment
Pre-event (prior to assault)	Knowledge, self-efficacy, training	History of prior violence communicated	Assess objects that could become weapons, actual weapons, egress (means of escape)	Visit in pairs or with escort
Event (assault)	De-escalation, escape techniques, alarms/two-way phones	Reduce lethality of patient via increasing your distance	Egress, alarm, cell phone	Code and security procedures
Postevent (postassault)	Medical care/ counseling, postevent debriefing	Referral, law enforcement	Evaluate role of physical environment	All staff must be debriefed and learn, modify plan if appropriate

[a] Home health workplace example.

- Pre-event, event, and postevent
- Gaps and opportunities for improvement

From the perspective of administration, the Haddon matrix does not implicate policy. This means that the matrix does not necessarily guide policy. When implemented, the Haddon matrix can be a "politically" neutral, transdisciplinary or multidisciplinary, objective tool that identifies opportunities for intervention. Furthermore, it outlines sensible "targets of change" for the physical and social environment (Table 16.2).

TABLE 16.2
Haddon Matrix Implementation

Phase	Affected Individual and Population	Agent Used	Environment
Pre-event	Psychological first aid	Communicate efforts to limit action	Have plans in place detailing agency roles in prevention and detection
Event	Population uses skills	Mobilize trauma workers	Communicate that response systems are in place
Postevent	Assessment, triage, and psychological treatment	Communicate, establish outreach centers	Adjust risk communication
End results	Limit distress responses, negative behavior changes, and psychological illness	Minimize loss of life and impact of attack	Minimize disruption in daily routines

16.4.2 Workplace Violence Prevention Guidelines

The federal government and some states have developed guidelines to assist employers with workplace violence prevention. For instance, one of the earliest sets of guidelines for a comprehensive workplace violence prevention program was published in 1993 by California OSHA.* This resulted from the murder of a state employee. In 1996, *Guidelines for Preventing Workplace Violence for Healthcare and Social Service Workers* was published by OSHA.

In its guidelines, OSHA sets forth the following essential elements for developing a violence prevention program:

- *Management commitment*—As seen by high-level management involvement and support for a written workplace violence prevention policy and its implementation.
- *Meaningful employee involvement*—In policy development, joint management–worker violence prevention committees, postassault counseling and debriefing, and follow-up are all critical program components.
- *Work site analysis*—Includes regular walk-through surveys of all patient care areas and the collection and review of all reports of worker assault. A successful job hazard analysis must include strategies and policies for encouraging the reporting of all incidents of workplace violence, including verbal threats that do not result in physical injury.
- *Hazard prevention and control*—Includes the installation and maintenance of alarm systems in high-risk areas. It may also include the training and posting of security personnel in emergency departments. Adequate staffing is an essential hazard prevention measure, as are adequate lighting and control of access to staff offices and secluded work areas.
- *Preplacement and periodic training and education*—Must include educationally appropriate information regarding the risk factors for violence in the health-care environment and control measures available to prevent violent incidents. Training should include skills in aggressive-behavior identification and management, especially for staff working in the mental health and emergency departments.

On May 17, 1999, Governor Gary Locke signed the New Workplace Violence Prevention Act for the state of Washington.† This act mandates that each health-care setting in the state implement a plan to reasonably prevent and protect employees from violence. According to this act, prevention plans need to address security considerations related to the following:

- Physical attributes of the health-care setting
- Staffing, including security staffing
- Personnel policies
- First-aid and emergency procedures
- Reporting of violent acts
- Employee education and training

---

* See California Health & Safety Code §§ 1257.7 and 1257.8. These provisions have been amended several times.

† See Revised Code of Washington §§ 49.19.005–49.19.070.

Prior to the development of an actual plan, a security and safety assessment needs to be conducted to identify existing or potential hazards. The training component of the plan must include the following topics:

- General safety procedures
- Personal safety procedures
- The violence escalation cycle
- Violence-predicting factors
- Means of obtaining a patient history form from a patient with violent behavior
- Strategies to avoid physical harm
- Restraining techniques
- Appropriate use of medications as chemical restraints
- Documenting and reporting incidents
- The process whereby employees affected by a violent act may debrief
- Any resources available to employees for coping with violence
- The health-care setting's workplace violence prevention plan

The act further mandates that any hospital operated and maintained by the state of Washington for the care of the mentally ill is required to provide violence prevention training to affected employees identified in the plan on a regular basis and *prior* to providing patient care.

16.5 ASSESSMENT

If you work in a home health-care environment, the U.S. Department of Health and Human Services (HHS) provides information highlighting the need to address workplace violence in your setting, through the pdf publication "Home Healthcare Workers: How to Prevent Violence on the Job." It is available from the DHHS, NIOSH publication no. 2012-118 (February 2012).

16.6 CONCLUSION

Medical workplace violence (MWPV) is a recognized hazard in the health-care industry. MWPV is any act or threat of physical violence, harassment, or intimidation, or other threatening disruptive behavior that occurs at the work site. It can affect and involve workers, clients, customers, and visitors. MWPV ranges from threats and verbal abuse to physical assaults and even homicide. Its most extreme form, homicide, is the fourth-leading cause of fatal occupational injury in the United States, according to the BLS Census of Fatal Occupational Injuries (CFOI).

16.7 COLLABORATE

Discuss this chapter online with others at http://www.medicalexecutivepost.com.

ACKNOWLEDGMENT

To W. Barry Nixon, MS, SPHR, National Institute for Prevention of Workplace Violence, Inc., Woodlake Lane, Lake Forrest, California.

BIBLIOGRAPHY

Aguirre, Wagner, and Vigo. "Peace and Conflict: Journal of Peace Psychology," in *Handbook of Community Psychology*, Springer Publishing, New York, 1998.

Braverman, M. "Managing the Human Impact of Crisis." *Risk Management.* 59(5) (2003): 10–14.

Buba, V. "Sexual Harassment Risks in Medical Practice," in Marcinko, D.E. (editor): *Risk Management and Insurance Planning for Physicians and Advisors.* Sudbury, MA: Jones and Bartlett, 2004.

Bureau of Justice Statistics. *Special Report on Violence in the Workplace*, FDR, Washington, DC, December 2001.

Colling, M.S. and Russell, L., *Security—Keeping the Healthcare Environment Safe.* Joint Commission on Accreditation of Healthcare Organizations, Chicago IL, 1996.

Dana, D. *The Dana Measure of the Financial Cost of Organizational Conflict: An Interpretive Guide.* Dana Mediation Institute, Inc., Kansas City, MO, 2001.

Duncan, S., Estabrooks, C.A. and Reimer, M. "Violence against Nurses." *Alta RN.* 2 (2000): 13–14.

Goodman, R.A., Jenkins, E.L. and Mercy, J.A. "Workplace Related Homicide among Health Care Workers in the United States, 1980 through 1990." *JAMA.* 272(21) (1994): 1686–1688.

Health Policy and Economic Research Unit. *Violence at Work: The Experience of UK Doctors*, British Medical Association (BMA) London, October 2003.

http://www.bma.org.

http://www.mediationworks.com.

http://www.ojp.usdoj.gov/bjs.

http://www.osha-slc.gov.

http://www.workplaceviolence911.com.

Joint ILO/ICN/WHO/PSI Research. *Workplace Violence in Health Services*, BMA London, 2002.

Levin, P.F., Beauchamp Hewitt, J. and Misner, S.T. "Insights of Nurses about Assault in Hospital-Based Emergency Departments." *The Journal of Nursing Scholarship.* 30(3) (1998): 249.

Lipscomb, B.B. "Healthcare Workers," in Levy, B. and Wegman, D. (editors): *Occupational Health: Recognizing and Preventing Work-Related Disease and Injury* (4th ed.). Philadelphia, PA: Lippincott, Williams & Wilkins, 767–778, 2000.

Lipscomb, J. and Love, C. "Violence toward Healthcare Workers—An Emerging Occupational Hazard." *AAOHN Journal.* 40(5) (1992): 219–228.

Marais, S., Van Der Spuy, E. and Rontsch, R. "Crime and Violence in the Workplace—Effect on Health Workers Part II." Crime, Violence & Injury Lead Programme, MRC and Institute of Criminology, UCT, 1999.

McPhaul, K.M. and Lipscomb, J.A. "Workplace Violence in Healthcare: Recognized But Not Regulated." *Online Journal of Issues in Nursing.* 9(3) (2004): Manuscript 6.

NIOSH. "Violence: Occupational Hazards in Hospitals." Pub. No. 2002-101. CDC/NIOSH, Atlanta, GA, 2002.

Nixon, B. "Medical Office Workplace Violence Risks," in Marcinko, D.E. (editor): *Risk Management and Insurance Planning for Physicians and Advisors.* Sudbury, MA: Jones and Bartlett, 2004.

OSHA. *Guidelines for Preventing Workplace Violence for Healthcare and Social Service Workers*, FDR, Washington, DC, 1998.

Registered Nurses' Association of Nova Scotia. "Violence in the Workplace: A Resource Guide." Cruickshank, Nova Scotia, BC 1995.

Richard H. "Gamble: Apocalypse Maybe." *Controller Magazine*, June 1998.

Runyan, C.S., Zakocs, R.C. and Zwerling, C. "Administrative and Behavioral Interventions for Workplace Violence Prevention." *American Journal of Preventive Medicine.* 18(4 Suppl.) (2000): 116–127.

Schmuckler, E. "Relinquishing the Leadership Role of Physicians," in Marcinko, D.E. (editor): *The Business of Medical Practice.* New York: Springer, 2000.

Schmuckler, E. "Professional Career Development," in Marcinko, D.E. (editor): *Financial Planning for Physicians and Healthcare Professionals*. New York: Aspen Publishers, 2003.

Schmuckler, E. "Bridging Financial Planning and Human Psychology," in Marcinko, D.E. (editor): *Financial Planning for Physicians and Advisors*. Sudbury, MA: Jones and Bartlett, 2004.

Schmuckler, E., Marcinko, D.E. and Hetico, H.R. *Healthcare Workplace Violence Prevention. Hospitals and Healthcare Organizations*. Boca Raton, FL: Productivity Press, 2014.

Smith, M.H. "Legal Considerations of Workplace Violence in Healthcare Environments." *Nursing Forum*. 36(1) (2001): 5–14.

Toscano, G. and Weber, W. *Violence in the Workplace*, Table 11. Washington, DC: Bureau of Labor Statistics, 1995.

U.S. Department of Labor, Bureau of Labor Statistics. "Fatal Occupational Injuries by Event or Exposure," Census of Fatal Occupational Injuries, FDR, Washington, DC, 1991–2002.

17 Accountable Care Organizations, Global Payments, and Capitation Reimbursement

Eliminating Fee-for-Service Physician Compensation

David Edward Marcinko and Hope Rachel Hetico

CONTENTS

There is increasing recognition that the prevailing model of primary care practice that evolved in the United States under the current fee-for-service (FFS) reimbursement system is dysfunctional. Models of enhanced primary care such as the patient-centered medical home (PCMH), and the models discussed in this chapter, are being introduced nationally and are considered a foundational element of new global payment arrangements. Under these types of arrangements in particular, but in primary care more broadly, primary care practices are expected to reorient toward providing enhanced services designed to optimize both patient experiences and health, which requires a fundamental change in the way primary care practices are reimbursed for their services.

After dismissing FFS payment as antithetical to meaningful payment reform, we must now recognize that global payment that covers all medical, coordinating, as well as non-physician services of the PCMH is tantamount to old-fashioned capitation.

Yet, various medical capitation reimbursement systems have been used for centuries. On the other hand, global reimbursements in the form of pay-for-performance (P4P) initiatives have been used for the last 20 years. And, accountable care organizations (ACOs), using modifications of these two reimbursement machinations, have been in force for less than a decade.

- So, how are these issues related?
- How do we unite them; can and should we unite them?
- What implications exist for medical malpractice insurance entities?
- How about for professional liability policy premium-setting purposes and economic risk management of medical providers?

Most importantly, are some medical providers paying too much for professional liability protection, in the rapidly changing insurance ecosystem, and are others paying too little? So, to contain liability overhead expense costs, the physician executive should understand the dynamics of the insurance industry and agent selling process; insurance is generally sold through one of three agency avenues:

- Direct insurance agents
- Captive insurance agents
- Independent insurance agents

17.1 BRIEF HISTORY OF ACCOUNTABLE CARE ORGANIZATIONS

According to the *Health Dictionary Series* of administrative terms, valuation expert and colleague Robert James Cimasi, MHA, ASA, AVA, CMP, of http://www.healthcapital.com, an ACO is a health-care organization in which a set of providers, usually large physician groups and hospitals, are held accountable for the cost and quality of care delivered to a specific local population. ACOs aim to affect a provider's patient expenditures and outcomes by integrating clinical and administrative departments to coordinate care and share financial risk (personal communication).

Since their four-page introduction in the Patient Protection and Affordable Care Act (PPACA) of 2010, ACOs have been implemented in both the federal and commercial health-care markets, with 32 pioneer ACOs selected (on December 19, 2011), 116 federal applications accepted (on April 10, 2012 and July 9, 2012), and at least 160 or more commercial ACOs in existence today.

17.1.1 Federal Contracts

More recently, Donna Marbury, writing in *Medical Economics*, revealed that federal ACO contracts are established between an ACO and Centers for Medicare and Medicaid Services (CMS), and are regulated under the CMS *Medicare Shared Savings Program* (MSSP) *Final Rule*, published November 2, 2011. ACOs participating in the MSSP are accountable for the *health outcomes*, represented by 33 quality metrics, and *Medicare beneficiary expenditures* of a prospectively assigned population of Medicare beneficiaries. If a federal ACO achieves Medicare beneficiary expenditures below a *CMS established benchmark* (and meets quality targets), they are eligible to receive a portion of the achieved Medicare beneficiary expenditure savings, in the form of a *shared savings payment.*

17.1.2 Commercial Contracts

Commercial ACO contracts are not *limited* by any specific legislation, only by the contract between the ACO and a commercial payer. In addition to *shared savings models*, which may not be in effect for another 3–5 years, commercial ACOs may incentivize *lower costs* and *improved patient outcomes* through reimbursement models that share risk between the payer and the providers, i.e., *P4P compensation* arrangements and/or *partial to full capitation.* Although commercial ACOs experience a greater degree of flexibility in their structure and reimbursement, the principles for success for both federal ACOs and commercial

ACOs are similar. And, although nearly any health-care enterprise can integrate and become an ACO, larger enterprises may be best suited for ACO status.

Larger organizations are more able to accommodate the *significant capital requirements* of ACO development, implementation, and operation (e.g., *health-care information technology*), and sustain the sufficient number of beneficiaries to have a significant impact on *quality* and *cost metrics.*

17.2 CAPITATION REIMBURSEMENT HISTORY

According to Richard Eskow, CEO of Health Knowledge Systems of Los Angeles, capitated medical reimbursement has been used in one form or another, in every attempt at health-care reform since the Norman conquest. Some even say an earlier variant existed in ancient China (personal communication).

Initially, when Henry I assumed the throne of the newly combined kingdoms of England and Normandy, he initiated a sweeping set of health-care reforms. Historical documents, though muddled, indicate that soon thereafter, at least one "physician," John of Essex, received a flat payment honorarium of one penny per day for his efforts. Historian Edward J. Kealey opined that that sum was roughly equal to that paid to a foot soldier or a blind person. Clearer historical evidence suggests that American doctors in the mid-nineteenth century were receiving capitation-like payments. No less an authoritative figure than Mark Twain, in fact, is on record as saying that during his boyhood in Hannibal, Missouri, his parents paid the local doctor $25 per year for taking care of the entire family regardless of their state of health.

Later, Sidney Garfield, MD (1905–1984), noted as one of the great underappreciated geniuses of twentieth-century American medicine, stood in the shadow cast by his more celebrated partner, Henry J. Kaiser. Garfield was not the first physician to embrace the notion of prepayment capitation, nor was he the first to understand that physicians working together in multispecialty groups could, through collaboration and continuity of care, outperform their solo-practice colleagues in almost every measure of quality and efficiency. The Mayo brothers, of course, had prior claim to that distinction. What Garfield did was marry prepayment to group practice, providing aligned financial incentives across every physician and specialty in his medical group, as well as a culture of group accountability for the care of every member of the affiliated health plan. He called it "the new economics of medicine," and at its heart was a fundamentally new paradigm of care that emphasized prevention before treatment and health before sickness. Under his model, the fewer the sick, the greater the remuneration. And, the less serious the illness, the better off the patient and the doctors.

Such ideas were heresy to the reigning FFS, solo-practice ideologues of the mainstream medical establishment of the 1940s and 1950s, of course. Throughout the period, Garfield and his group physicians were routinely castigated by leaders of the American Medical Association (AMA) and county medical associations as socialistic and unethical. The local medical associations in Garfield's expanding service areas—the San Francisco Bay Area, Los Angeles, and Portland, Oregon—blocked group-practice physicians from association membership, effectively shutting them out of local hospitals and denying them patient referrals or specialty society accreditation. Twice in the 1940s, formal medical association charges were brought against Garfield personally, at one time temporarily succeeding in suspending his license to practice medicine.

Of course, capitation payments made a comeback in the first cost-cutting managed care era of the 1980–1990s because FFS medicine created perverse incentives for physicians by paying more for treating illnesses and injuries than it does for preventing them—or even for diagnosing them early and reducing the need for intensive treatment later. Nevertheless, the modern managed care industry's experience with capitation wasn't initially a good one. The 1980–1990s saw a number of HMOs attempt to put independent physicians, especially primary care doctors, into a capitation reimbursement model. The result was often negative for patients, who found that their doctors were far less willing to see them—and saw them for briefer visits—when they were receiving no additional income for their effort. Attempts were also made to aggregate various types of health providers—including hospitals and physicians in multiple specialties—into "capitation groups" that were collectively responsible for delivering care to a defined patient group. These included health-care facilities and medical providers of all types: physicians, osteopaths, podiatrists, dentists, optometrists, pharmacies, physical therapists, hospitals and skilled nursing homes, etc.

However, the health-care industry isn't collective by nature, and these efforts tended to be too complicated to succeed. One lesson that these experiments taught is that provider behavior is difficult to change unless the relationship between that behavior and its consequences is fairly direct and easy to understand. Today, the concept of prepayment and medical capitation is to uncouple compensation from the actual number of patients seen, or treatments and interventions performed. This is akin to a fixed-price restaurant menu, as opposed to an *à la carte* eatery.

17.2.1 Global Capitation

As we have seen, an ACO is a provider-led company willing to be accountable for the full continuum of care for its patients. Global capitation will be used. A report by the Dartmouth Institute for Health Policy & Clinical Practice and the Engelberg Center for Health Care Reform at Brookings Institution outlines how providers in an ACO would be paid: "Spending benchmarks must be projected with sufficient accuracy based on historical data (or other comparison groups) and savings thresholds to provide confidence that overall savings will be achieved. Sufficient measures of quality to provide evidence of improvement are also essential."

In other words, if the costs for treating the entire population of primary care patients assigned to the physicians in the ACO are expected to increase 5% next year in a specific geographical area, and the ACO keeps that hike to 2%, the providers get to keep some portion of the extra 3%.

17.2.2 Episodes of Care

Treatment in an ACO is a departure from the way things are done today. In an ACO, or a virtual ACO, the entire team will be paid for the episode of care. The care team has incentives to follow every checklist to prevent infection and error, for example. It is an entirely cooperative approach.

Princeton University economist Uwe Reinhardt, PhD, believes that ACOs are a good idea "as ideas go." However, "it is not at all a new idea. It's the Kaiser model, the Ellwood–Enthoven Model." In fact, Jan Berger, MD, president and CEO of Health Intelligence Partners and a member of MANAGED CARE's editorial advisory board, said, "As much as many say that this is different from old capitation models, I do not clearly see the difference." Again, it will depend on the details (personal communication).

17.2.3 Capitation Market Dynamics

Continuing changes in the Health 2.0 marketplace today make evaluating capitated contracts both difficult and vital to the success of a physician's practice. Market dynamics have shifted to a less restrictive form of managed care arrangements. This shift has resulted in the prevalence of more PPO products rather than more restrictive HMO coverage. The shift in insurance coverage initially appears to favor the physician's ability to remain in FSS contract arrangements (albeit at reduced rates); however, it also makes remaining capitated contracts more critical to evaluate. The fewer patient members there are under capitated arrangements, the more financial risk the physician may incur. And, the emergence of a new machination, known as microcapitation, illustrates the fluid nature of this concept.

17.2.4 Capitated Reimbursement Contracts

For physicians in solo practice or in small group practices, the common path to capitated contracting comes through membership in an independent practice association (IPA) or similar affiliation, which has the legal authority to secure health plan contracts on behalf of its members. Even though the individual members of the IPA may not be involved in negotiations with the health plans, it is important for them to understand the terms of each contract. The key areas of concern are as follows:

- Patient mix
- Capitation rate and contract terms
- Service responsibility
- Stop-loss coverage

17.2.4.1 Patient Mix

Health plan contracts are marketed to specific population groups, and the demographic characteristics of the patient populations will vary accordingly. Typically, the target population is identified in terms of the health plan's product—commercial private plan, Medicare plan, or Medicaid plan. It is important for the physician to know about the population that is covered by the contract, in anticipation of the types of services that those patients will require. Physicians should inquire about the age/sex/health status characteristics of the population the health plan expects to enroll, and compare those to the current profile of the practice.

17.2.4.2 Capitation Contract Questions and Responsibilities

The most important considerations are the actual capitation rate and the factors that can affect that rate, either up or down. It is also important to have a sense of *market comparison* on the capitation rate provided under the contract. Here is a list of specific questions physicians should ask.

- Which health plans can access this contractual arrangement? Is the health plan limited to just the one negotiating the contract, or are there silent or affiliated plans that can access the agreement? This will impact the number of lives covered under this agreement.
- What is the monthly capitation rate paid to the physician? What is the IPA keeping from the health plan's payments to cover the cost of their services?

- Is the capitation rate a fixed amount per member per month, or will it be age/sex adjusted based on the actual blend of patients who are assigned to the physician?
- What day of the month will the capitation payment be given? Does the contract stipulate that the IPA must pay interest charges for late payments?
- Are there any "low enrollment guarantees" built into the contract to provide for minimum payment amounts in the early stages of contract enrollments? Some contracts provide for FFS payments until enrollments reach an effective level for capitation, such as 500 members.
- Are there provisions for retroactive changes in the enrollment assigned to the practice, and are there specific time limits on those provisions, such as 30, 60, or 90 days? Failure to include time limits on retroactive enrollment adjustments may result in disruptions to cash flow and increased administrative paperwork.
- How are bonuses, if any, earned and paid? What are the specific measures if bonuses are based on performance?
- What penalties and deductions from the capitation payment can be imposed for actions such as "inappropriate referrals" or for referrals to noncontracted providers?
- How often can the capitation rates be renegotiated?
- What are the physician's financial obligations upon termination of the contract? Does the contract convert to an FFS agreement, or is continuing care for the patient covered under the existing capitation rate? If so, what is the contract time limit for providing continuing care?

17.2.4.3 Contract Service Responsibilities

Physicians should ask for a copy of the list of the services that are included in the capitation payment. All rendered services should be defined by current procedural terminology (CPT) or a similar billing code. Physicians who take primary care contracts and who also practice in specialty fields, such as allergy, cardiology, gastroenterology, or pulmonology, should have a clear understanding of how these services are managed under the contract—whether they are included or excluded in the capitation payment and whether these services can be billed separately. Other key questions about service responsibilities include the following:

- What are the restrictions or limitations on billing patients for services that are not covered by the responsibility matrix? If it is permissible to bill for these services, are there restrictions on the billing rates?
- How is the physician reimbursed for nonphysician services, such as supplies, lab tests, and injections? This is particularly important if the practice has a high number of pediatric patients or provides allergy shots.
- What are the financial responsibilities of the practice for call coverage? Does the contract require that the physician pay for call coverage out of the capitation payment? If so, how is this payment handled—physician to physician, or as a deduction from the capitation payment?

17.2.4.4 Stop-Loss

Another critical factor is reinsurance for high-cost cases—stop-loss coverage. Physicians should know if the contract has stop-loss provisions, what the costs are for coverage, and the effect on the capitation rate once the stop-loss level has been reached. In some cases, the contract may convert to a new capitation rate. In others, payment may be on a predetermined FFS arrangement. It is also important to know who is responsible for identifying cases when they reach the stop-loss limit and whether there is a time limitation when filing a stop-loss case.

In addition to these key points in capitation contracts, physicians should also anticipate that there will be "administrative burdens" related to new contracts. In most situations, the IPA or other physician organization will take responsibility for credentialing for the provider network, for utilization management and quality management programs required by the health plans, and for claims administration. Each physician, however, will be required to submit encounter data and respond to various queries and requests for information. In some cases, health plans or IPAs may stipulate financial penalties for failure to comply, for poor timeliness, or for administrative burdens.

17.3 FIXED PAYMENTS REEMERGING

Today, the national conversion to a modified form of capitation financing is again reemerging in the era of the employed-physician business model, hospitalist, and PPACA as a marketing force and not merely a temporary health-care payment trend. More than 40% of all physicians in the country are now employees of a managed care organization (MCO) that uses, or is reconsidering, actuarially equivalent P4P, global reimbursement schemes, or medical capitation.

17.3.1 The Promise?

Has medical capitation reimbursement finally fulfilled its promise as a quality-improving and revenue-enhancing machination, or is it just another managed care and PPACA cost reduction strategy that financially squeezes doctors and hospitals, and limits patient care and choice? To answer this query, one needs to review the Stark laws.

17.3.2 Wholesale Medicine

Curiously, Stark laws I, II, and III were created to eliminate self-referral concerns potential leading to excessive medical care and FFS payments. Ironically, these types of economic enriching paradigms of less care were perfectly acceptable. Many also never understood how a commitment to treat an entire patient population cohort could be made with little or no actuarial information. Hence, frustration was the initial exposure of many medical providers to capitated reimbursement, also known as "wholesale medicine."

17.3.3 Aligned Incentives

But, since inception, more modern medical cost accounting endeavors have gradually demonstrated that capitation has some advantages over traditional FFS care. For example, it can create and align incentives that help patients, providers, and payers by limiting their contingent fiscal liabilities. So, capitation in the current credit-deprived national economy is increasingly being viewed in a more positive way. More importantly, those health-care organizations and providers that embrace it may thrive going forward, while those opposed may not!

17.3.4 Global Physician Capitation Payments Making a Comeback

Since passage of the PPACA, many insurance carriers are making a major change in the way they pay physicians. They're moving from (discounted) FFS pay to per-patient per-year capitation rates, adjusted for age and sickness (severity adjustments), plus a bonus for those MDs who improve patient health status. No definition of this term was given, however. Under the new "incentive" plan, these plans hope to transfer risk to primary medical care groups.

Typically, capitation will cover all primary care, specialist, counselor, and hospital costs. Interestingly, Blue Cross Blue Shield (BCBS) has publicly denied that this system is capitation, and assured the public that it has safeguards in place to make sure patients won't be undertreated and doctors won't be underpaid. Yet, BCBS for the state of Massachusetts hopes to cut the growth in medical costs in half in 2–4 years among providers who accept this cloaked *global capitation redux*.

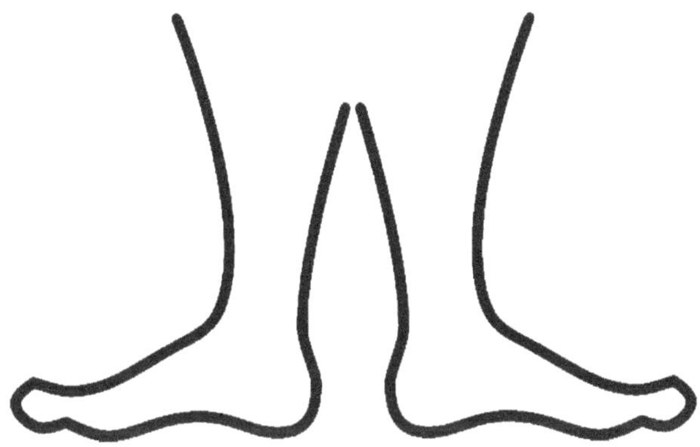

17.4 ECONOMICS OF SHIFTING TO AND FROM CAPITATION REIMBURSEMENT

Shifts in payor mix can cause dramatic impacts to the financial performance of a medical practice. While it is important to try to evaluate the impact before taking on capitated business, similar principles apply as physician practices shift back to FFS business from capitation. Before taking capitated contracts, physicians should answer three questions:

1. How much capitation should I accept as a percentage of my total business?
2. How will the shift to capitation affect my practice financially?
3. By how much will I need to reduce operating expenses in order to break even or profit from capitation?

As physicians' practices shift back to FFS from capitation, two additional considerations must be addressed:

1. How much capitation is too little?
2. How will another shift in payer mix impact my practice cost structure?

Whether shifting to or from capitation, it is important to understand the factors that contribute to overall practice economics. The following examples can help a physician answer these questions by demonstrating the effect of changes in payor mix on a solo primary care physician practice. The methods described may also apply to other medical specialties or group practices.

17.4.1 The Shift to Capitation

To determine the impact that a capitated contract might have on a practice, it is necessary to analyze the economics of that practice. In traditional FFS practices, there are three key financial measures:

1. Net revenue and net revenue per patient visit
2. Office expenses including fixed expenses, such as rent, and those that vary with patient volume, such as medical supplies
3. Net income, the amount remaining to be paid as physician compensation or reinvested in the practice

By adding capitation to the practice, a physician must consider two additional factors:

- The capitation rate per member per month
- The estimated number of visits for each capitated patient

It is often difficult to isolate the financial performance related to one specific payor contract because the same resources are used to care for all the practice's patients. One way to evaluate the impact of a new contract is to determine what the practice's breakeven volume level is before and after the shift to capitation. Breakeven can be described as the level of patient volume required to cover all practice expenses. It is an important measure because once a practice achieves breakeven volume, each additional visit contributes to practice net income. Two variables that impact breakeven are revenue per visit and variable cost per visit.

$$\text{Breakeven volume} = \text{total fixed expenses} \times (\text{net revenue per visit} - \text{variable expenses per visit})$$

In some cases, the impact of a shift in payer mix on breakeven volume can be dramatic. This is illustrated in the following examples.

17.4.2 Baseline Example

The baseline example is an internal medicine physician in solo practice. Currently, payment for services is from traditional FFS sources including indemnity insurance, some discounted-rate plans, self-pay patients, and Medicare. To analyze the potential financial impact of a shift in payor mix to or from capitation, it is necessary to establish a few key statistics from the practice's most recent 12-month period. Total net patient revenue and total operating expenses can be easily identified. Next, identify fixed operating expenses, which are those costs that generally do not change with volume within a defined range of capacity, such as space, most staffing, and utilities. Subtracting fixed expenses from total operating expenses provides total variable expenses, or those costs that are directly related to patient volume, such as medical supplies. Average variable expense per visit is calculated by dividing total variable expenses by the number of patient visits. The baseline practice profile is shown in Table 17.1.

TABLE 17.1
Baseline Practice Profile

	Total Annual	Average per Visit
Patient visits FFS	4800	
Total net revenue	$480,000	$100.00
Fixed expenses	$165,000	$34.38
Variable expenses	$89,400	$18.62
Total practice expenses	$254,400	$53.00
Net income	$225,600	$47.00
Breakeven visits	2028	
Contribution to net income after breakeven		$81.38

In the baseline example, the practice needs 2028 annual visits to break even. Any additional visits contribute $81.38, or the difference between net revenue and variable expenses, to net income.

17.4.3 Payer Mix Scenarios

We can now develop scenarios to help evaluate the impact of changes in payor mix. Computerized spreadsheets are ideal for analyzing these what-if scenarios. In each scenario, assume that the practice is at capacity with 4800 visits, so new capitated patients represent a shift from FFS business and are not incremental business to the practice.

17.4.3.1 Scenario 1

Let's assume that 333 of the practice's patients shift to a capitated plan and that on average, a capitated patient has three visits per year, for 1000 total visits. The physician receives a capitation payment of $12 per member per month. The average revenue per visit under the capitated agreement is $48 ($12 per month times 12 months, divided by three visits), a substantial reduction from the FFS average of $100. Therefore, the breakeven number of visits for the practice increases to 2339 as the overall average net revenue per visit decreases to $89.17. In order to maintain the FFS breakeven level of 2028, the practice would need to reduce total costs significantly. However, even modest reductions in operating expenses can help to compensate for the downward pressure of capitated contract rates on net revenue. In scenario 1, total expenses are reduced by 10% through a combination of fixed and variable cost reductions. Scenario 1 is shown in Table 17.2.

As a medical practice shifts back from capitation to better-paying FFS business, it is important to remember two things:

1. Increasing revenue per visit does not mean costs should increase.
2. Be careful to maintain enough capitated business to average out the effect of a few high utilizers, or get out of capitation entirely.

17.4.3.2 Maintain Practice Cost Savings

Let's assume that the practice was able to decrease operating expenses by 10%. With the shift to capitated business, the practice's net income is $199,060. What happens if the practice's business shifts back to FFS? If the costs revert back to the levels before cost savings

TABLE 17.2
Payer Mix Scenario 1: Shift to Capitation

	Total Annual w/ No Expense Reductions	Avg. per Visit w/ No Expense Reductions	Total Annual w/ Expense Reductions	Avg. per Visit w/ Expense Reductions
Patient visits—FFS	3800		3800	
Patient visits—capitation	1000		1000	
Total net revenue	$428,000	$89.17	$428,000	$89.17
Fixed expenses	$165,000	$34.38	$148,500	$30.94
Variable expenses	$89,400	$18.62	$80,440	$16.76
Total practice expenses	$254,400	$53.00	$228,940	$47.70
Net income	$173,600	$36.17	$199,060	$41.47
Breakeven visits	2339		2051	
Contribution to net income after breakeven		$70.55		$72.41

TABLE 17.3
Shift from Capitation to Fee for Service

	with Old Cost Structure	with New Cost Structure
Total visits	4800	4800
Net revenue	$480,000	$480,000
Total expenses	$254,400	$228,940
Net income	$225,600	$251,060
Breakeven visits	2028	1784
Contribution to net income after breakeven	$81.38	$83.24

were implemented, the practice's net income and breakeven volume are the same as they were originally under the baseline scenario. But if the practice is able to maintain the cost savings it experienced, net income increases by $25,460, breakeven volume decreases by 244 visits, and each visit above breakeven contributes $83.24 to the bottom line. This is shown in Table 17.3.

17.4.3.3 Manage the Level of Capitated Business

Physicians are paid a fixed amount per member per month to care for capitated patients. Capitation rates paid to the practice are determined actuarially based on demographics of the patient population covered, including their anticipated utilization of resources. When a practice has a significant number of capitated patients, the effects of a few high utilizers are usually offset by the utilization patterns of the rest of the population.

For example, if the average number of visits per year for a capitated patient is three, it is likely that a few patients will have more visits but that most patients will visit the physician

TABLE 17.4
Shift from Capitation to Fee for Service

	333 Capitated Patients	50 Capitated Patients	15 Capitated Patients
Capitated patient visits	1000	220	115
Average visits per capitated patient	3.00	4.40	7.67
Annual capitation revenue	$48,000	$7200	$2160
Capitation revenue per visit	$48.00	$32.73	$18.78
Variable expense per visit	$16.76	$16.76	$16.76
Contribution to net income after breakeven	$31.24	$15.97	$2.02

less frequently. In a practice with a large capitated population, those patients offset the additional use of resources (cost) required to care for the higher utilizers.

Assume that the practice's capitated enrollment shifts mostly back to FFS, so that only 50 capitated patients remain. Of those 50, 10 are high utilizers, requiring 10 visits per year. The contribution to net income drops by nearly half, from $31.24 to $15.97. As an extreme example, assume that only 15 capitated patients remain and that 10 of them are high utilizers. The contribution drops to only $2.02 per visit, barely enough to cover variable costs. The impact of this is shown in Table 17.4.

17.5 SUBCAPITATED CONTRACTS

The often contentious dilemma of "carve-outs" from capitated managed care contracts is abating in some parts of the country, just as it is accelerating in others. Under this scenario, medical services or products such as surgery, trauma, physical therapy, eye care, immunizations, certain tests, wound care, or prosthetic devices may be excluded from a managed care contract in favor of another, often subcapitated, provider. However, if you or your health-care organization is contemplating a subcapitated contract, consider the following example.

17.5.1 Primary Care Example

A primary care group notes that allergy testing, and related services, are included in their contract proposal. Since these services are not in their area of expertise, they negotiate to have them deleted, reducing the capitation rate accordingly.

Thus, the following are conditions considered important for carved or subcapitated risk contracts:

- Equivalent risk for the provider and subcapitated specialist
- Fixed expenses for the subcapitated specialist
- Predictable and low cost of care, per specialty episode
- High episodes of specialty care (not unusual or unpredictable events)
- Definable and understood responsibilities of the specialist
- Profit and cost-savings potential for both the referring and specialty provider
- Existence of reinsurance

17.5.2 Orthopedic Specialty Example

An orthopedic group notes that foot surgery is listed in a new capitation contract that it is considering. The group is not comfortable with such surgery, and they ask that these services be excluded. Since the contract provider will not exclude the surgery, the orthopedist group has to either accept it and perform unfamiliar surgery, or reject it.

17.6 MICROCAPITATION

More than a few medical providers and health-care facilities have developed natural aversion to capitated reimbursement. Almost since inception, it has always been associated with the worst components of managed care: hurried office visits and soulless physicians.

A decade ago, astute physician executives and health-care administrators were averse to the idea that they should accept prepayment for unknown commitments to provide an unknown amount of services. It seemed to create an unnatural and difficult set of incentives where fewer patients were seen and less care was rendered for more compensation. Curiously, Stark laws I, II, and III were created to eliminate concerns that self-referral could lead to excessive care and FFS payments, though this system had long been perfectly acceptable. Many also never understood how a commitment could be made with little or no actuarial information. Hence, frustration was the initial reaction of many medical providers to capitated reimbursement.

17.6.1 Medical Care Packages

When capitation is focused on discrete medical conditions, or subsets of clinical conditions, rather than through CPT or Medicare Severity Diagnosis-Related Groups (MS-DRG) activities, it is delivered in more discrete "medical care packages." This creates a true health-care marketplace where price, quality, and medical outcomes can be compared side by side, or provider by provider, or facility by facility.

The discrete services provided by vertically or virtually integrated medical teams would enable a new level and degree of expertise. High-volume providers would develop additional experience, which would enable them to introduce innovations and efficiencies in a classic economies-of-scale cycle. With the additional delivery and outcomes experience, providers would be much more willing to put out a set fee for a set grouping of clinical services, because they would have some confidence in their ability to deliver care for that price. Philosophically, this is still capitation, but it is a finer microcapitation at the medical-condition level (*lowest common unit of care delivery that can be measured*), not the gross CPT code or MS-DRG level.

To emphasize the concept, the term *microcapitation* was coined by Dr. Scott L. Shreve in 2008 (personal communication). It makes some sense because it is for a definable, controllable, and limited set of clinical activities in which providers can, with confidence, provide services for a set fee. Microcapitation delivered in smaller care packages will be a critical new clinical service product as we transition toward a futuristic competitive marketplace.

Microcapitation around specific medical conditions, or acute episodes of care, also provides a manageable unit of health-care delivery in which we can develop the appropriate

TABLE 17.5
Sample Allocation Formula for Comprehensive Payment System

25%	Primary care physician reimbursement: $250,000 before bonus/fringe benefits
60%	Staff, fringe, rent, office expense (assumes hiring of multidisciplinary office team charged with timely delivery of personalized comprehensive care): $600,000 • Nurse practitioner: $100,000 • Medical assistant: $50,000 • Nurse: $90,000 • Rent: $40,000 • 0.5 FTE nutritionist: $35,000 • Office expenses: $50,000 • 0.5 FTE social worker: $35,000 • Insurance: $50,000 • Receptionist: $60,000 • Physician FBs: $75,000–90,000
10%	Information technology/patient safety/quality monitoring: $100,000 Purchase/lease/setup of electronic health record and quality monitoring system: $35,000; data manager: $35,000
5%	Performance bonus, annual meeting for mutually established goals: $50,000

Source: Goroll, A.H. et al., *J. Gen. Intern. Med.*, 22, 410–415, 2007.

Note: Example assumes an average comprehensive payment of $800 per year per patient, an average panel size of 1250 patients per full-time primary care physician and team, 30% fringe benefit unless otherwise specified, and gross revenue of $1 million per full time equivalent primary care physician and team. FB, fringe benefits; FTE, full time equivalent.

care linkages across all provider lines, and form a team to deliver a full episode of care. It represents a properly sized clinical bite in which the appropriate health-care infrastructure allows for better outcomes measurement, monitoring, comparison, and ultimately, consumption in a competitive health-care marketplace. The marketplace today is taking a fresh look at capitation exposure and attempting to control economic risk by moving to discrete microcapitated care packages or bundles that can be understood, measured, and marketed (Table 17.5).

17.7 INSURANCE AGENTS AND THE LIABILITY INSURANCE INDUSTRY

An agency relationship is defined as the ability to solicit, create, modify, or terminate a property and casualty malpractice insurance policy. Under this *law of agency*, the agent and insurer are one and the same, and the acts and knowledge of the agent are deemed to be acts and knowledge of the insurer, regardless of whether the insurer has actually authorized the agent to do business. The insurer is bound by acts of its agent, if a relationship has been established through express, implied, or apparent authority.

The first two agents have little incentive to promote any company other than the one they represent. The later agent type brings a different set of complexities to the choice arena.

For example, they often receive bonuses or incentives or are held to production quotas as a requirement of employment. Commission structures are the most important incentives at work on the selling side of the process since different companies pay varying percentages of total premium dollars sold. This can work against the doctor because the agent has an incentive to sell the highest-priced product in order to earn the greatest commission. Upon request, however, a reputable insurance brokerage house will provide in writing a detailed market comparison that demonstrates the major options available to the practitioner. This is because, in contrast to agents, an insurance broker is an independent contractor who examines the malpractice needs of the client and then shops for coverage to best fill those needs. Moreover, group insurance purchasing usually nets a better deal than a practitioner could negotiate individually. Thus, if capitated medicine as demonstrated by many MCOs continues, the potential for reduced operational costs through lower medical malpractice premiums could be significant.

17.7.1 The Capitation Liability Theory

The major thrust of the capitation liability theory (CLT) suggests that a fixed-rate reimbursement system (global reimbursement; ACOs; P4P; and/or full capitation, partial capitation, or microcapitation) reduces the incidents of malpractice because of a reduction in the total number of patient–physician encounters and the acuity of those encounters, particularly for invasive procedures such as surgery and for procedural specialists. Consequently, some providers may be paying too much for professional liability protection in the presently changing health-care industrial complex, and others, too little.

17.7.2 The Liability Premium-Setting Process

Most liability insurance companies and their associated underwriters and actuarial advisors have limited interest in the nuisances of patient care and tend to focus economic factors such as income/loss ratios, market forces, and trend analysis as a basis for a continuing line of insurance coverage. Their bottom-line concern is financial and typically considers only those factors that can be altered to realize projected growth, profitability, and return on capital projections. Carriers have considerable latitude in how they function as a business, whom they insure, how they align their members, in what manner they allocate reserves, and how they mange cost/income factors and determine market variations for the purpose of setting premium levels. If their cost trend is downward and their profit trend is upward, efficiency is confirmed. To this end, underwriters and actuaries strive to make the premium pricing process a scientific discipline, but ultimately, the process is still a decidedly heuristic one.

As the liability premium pricing process arrives at the bottom line of corporate fiscal responsibility, the stability of the individual company and national market forces determine premium structure on a comprehensive basis. Managed care entities may be national in scope, but the delivery of health-care services is a local business. The potential negative effect of national pooling on individual premium pricing is significant as the CLT is confirmed. Unfortunately, liability underwriters are reluctant and even secretive about sharing confidential experience data. These professionals are skilled at data collection, information management, manipulation, and trend analysis to justify and defend their own charges. Challenging such cost projects and making a case for premium reductions is not easy but can be addressed with adequate knowledge, information, and constant persistence, as described herein.

17.7.3 CLT Areas of Interest (Litigation Equation)

The CLT considers four primary areas of potential significance in malpractice liability management and premium costs. This is known as the litigation equation and includes (1) patient communication factors, (2) provider health-care delivery systems and reimbursement factors, (3) payer factors, and (4) revised liability legislation and patient encounter data factors.

Patient communication factors include reduced economic and financial fear, consideration of cultural barriers, improved medical awareness through continuing education, concern for geographic access, focused primary and specialty care availability, management information systems, and the frequency and duration of utilization.

Provider reimbursement factors and health-care delivery systems include both soft and hard varieties. Soft provider factors include increased patient availability to services, accessibility to timely appointments, office and quality-care satisfaction surveys, communication assessments, known fixed costs, and technical information interchanges. Hard factors include managed operational procedures, reduced illness severities, defined treatment options, reduced clinical variations, outcomes measurements and quality monitoring, performance quotas, aligned financial incentives, and predictable reimbursements.

Payer factors include practitioner screening and shifting, quality assessment, behavioral modification and team care, provider discipline, complaint management, cost and call economic considerations, and adequate capitalization rates. Liability factors include allegation frequency and severity, standards of care, defensibility, risk management, premium pricing, loss adjustment, settlement losses, and administrative costs.

To fully understand the CLT, all four parts of the litigation equation must be recognized. These factors, when integrated with underwriter data and experience, determine the level of liability risk and the ultimate cost of malpractice coverage. If capitated medical care is deemed to involve less risk than seen in the indemnity environment, the cost of liability coverage should gradually decrease as the percentage of capitated managed care increases, in a particular office setting. In actual terms, the CLT suggests that capitated insurance and patient care risk are inversely, but not necessarily proportionally, related since experiential data will determine the percentages.

17.7.4 Premium Structures and Models

Collectively, liability claim managers suggest that financial issues are a secondary, albeit precipitating, factor in 15–25% of all malpractice allegations. Adjudicators further state that aggressive attempts to collect account balances, deductibles, co-payments, and noncovered services are a significant causative factor in litigious individuals. The liability factor is compounded if the medical outcome is less than desirable. The theory also does not discount the significance of contingency legal arrangements prevalent in the litigation process. Correspondingly, the following four reimbursement structures and models can be reviewed in light of this information.

The "FFS reimbursement model" was the bedrock of health-care financing until recently and was the dominant model of paying for medical services. This insurance-driven and technology-motivated approach was powered by utilization and consumption with limited concern for the total cost of care or economic consequences. While indemnity providers continue to be forgiving in the management of patient indebtedness, the incidence of financial hardship and subsequent litigation is believed to be the most frequent in this system. A recent review of provider-owned insurance carriers generally supports this conclusion.

Conversely, a "capitated-model" reimbursement system views the patient and the services they require as a cost driver to be debited against a fixed-rate or constant reimbursement scheme. Utilization is controlled, referrals managed, and technology limited as well as creating a new set of behavioral problems, stress, frustration, and liability. However, patient indebtedness and personal financial hardship is substantially reduced and so is a precipitating liability factor.

The "quasi-socialistic model" is powered by entrepreneurs who believe that health care is immune to market forces, such as competition or accountability. Reformer–change agents suggest that consumer needs and social welfare in general will prosper through structured business systems with quantifiable and measurable processes. This top-down management structure embraces the general public opinion that affordable health care is a right and that managed markets are the best model for this philosophy. Although results remain uncertain, the market trend is irreversible.

A "mixed model" or transitional reimbursement system represents the best, or perhaps the worst, of both payment options and is a major administrative challenge for the healthcare provider. Services may be classified as a profit or debit depending on the payer arrangement, and all care must be performed with equal concern for quality, medical, necessity and appropriateness. Gatekeepers manage the capitated care, control referrals, and provide care for at-risk for reimbursement, with the ultimate payer intent of a 50/50 provider mix of primary care and specialists. Frustration is significant for all participants, but the number of malpractice allegations is believed to be reduced.

A preliminary evaluation of these four reimbursement methodologies suggests that the level of malpractice risk, and associated litigation, is decreasing as the volume of capitated managed care increases.

17.7.4.1 Insurance Legislation Implications

The current malpractice insurance market has evolved as a result of legislative action, in response to the liability crisis of the early 1980s, with the introduction of the Liability Risk Retention Act (LRRA). This act, of 1986, turned a hard market for malpractice insurance soft, as legislative action expanded the definition of liability and preempted state regulations that restricted small groups from underwriting for commercial insurance buyers engaged in similar or related business activities.

The LRRA permitted the formation of risk retention groups (RRGs) and purchasing groups (PGs) to qualify as insurance companies and retain certain layers of risk while transferring higher layers to reinsurers. In essence, the LRRA flipped the insurance industry upside down and returned the decision-making process and control back to the consumer.

The fundamental difference between RRGs and PGs is that RRGs retain risks, and PGs do not. In enacting the LRRA, Congress provided two ways for insurance buyers to obtain liability coverage. These included becoming owners of their own liability insurance company (RRG) or becoming members of a PG that purchased insurance from a commercial carrier, usually at a substantial discount. The homogeneity requirement states that both RRGs and PGs must be engaged in a similar or related business, but there are no group size requirements, representing a significant marketing factor. PGs can evolve into RRGs if growth, profitability, and actuarial data are favorable. The advantages can be summarized by the following benefits:

- Tailor-made coverage and favorite premium rates
- Better policy terms and ownership of the loss experience

- Segregation of loss data and reward for good experiences
- Risk-management and loss-prevention programs
- Long-term commitments from insurers

As the health-care delivery system is transformed by consolidations, mergers, and acquisition, so goes the liability need of the individual, group, or institutional provider. Traditional insurance solutions are no longer suitable for the medicine of the new millennium as hospitals are combined into larger systems, and large systems are merged into even larger organizations with ownership of, or in partnership with, physicians and alternative treatment centers. Risk factors and pricing models of the past become inappropriate for contemporary providers who function within a corporatized structure.

As these larger organizations develop, their malpractice insurance needs change, and so must the companies that supply those needs. Larger groups can afford to take on attrition or frequency risks, internal to their own capital base and organization structure. As systems grow, groups become increasingly interested in risk layering, reinsurance, and loss-sensitive pricing options.

Larger systems can institute and provide their own internal risk prevention, quality monitoring, and incident management processes. Medical malpractice premium pricing ceases to be a one-dimensional market, even in the same geographic community or specialty provider class. Regulatory management and capitated reimbursement price controls are thus redefining the industry at all levels, and liability pricing and pricing flexibility are no exception.

Moreover, frequency, severity, and average indemnity payments are not necessarily reflective of the entire medical liability industry or specialty underwriters. The significance of risk-based, capitated reimbursement systems in the stability of the current professional liability market is not identifiable from current data but believed to be a factor. Additionally, liability data from the several closed-panel capitated reimbursement systems suggest support for the stability trend. As interesting as this may be, staff-model HMOs, which are a shrinking type of delivery option, are not necessarily reflective of other vertically integrated and at-risk delivery systems more prevalent in the emerging health-care marketplace.

Therefore, the following six processes can be used to support reduced professional liability costs in an ever-evolving reimbursement system:

- Knowledge of the local medical malpractice market environment and provider position in it.
- Clarity on how and by whom medical service payment is provided, as well as payment mix, percentages, and trends.
- Reticence to accept quoted liability rates as the only possible option since further inquiries, comparisons, evaluations, and alternatives may be available.
- Implementation of a data tracking system with risk management and risk education.
- Features, technology-driven proprietary information, and specific data for each medical specialty.
- Familiarity with the concept of clash coverage or multiple coverage for a given exposure incident. A single policy covering all entities is always less expensive than multiple policies covering multiple entities.
- Dissemination of risk and the transfer of professional liability to corporate medicine (i.e., physician practice management companies [PPMCs], IPAs) enterprise systems and managed care structures, thereby layering risk and coverage.

Consequently, doing nothing to reduce professional liability costs in an increasingly integrated delivery system environment with capitated reimbursement is a guaranteed financial drain on medical office net income after expenses.

17.7.4.2 Indemnification Concerns

An indemnification or hold-harmless clause in a managed care contract is quite specific about the legal relationship between the medical provider (agent, servant, or employee) and the managed care entity, should a medical malpractice issue occur. In the strongest possible language, most MCOs will attempt to shield or indemnify themselves from the actions of their providers, according to the vicarious-liability concept of *respondeat superior* under the normal laws of agency.* Furthermore, according to attorney Richard W. Boone, JD, of Vienna, Virginia, "What we are really recognizing is that although there may be two entities being sued, there is really a single event." It then makes legal and economic sense to known in advance which entity will be providing the defense and indemnification and price the capitated contract accordingly. Applying this advice may necessitate additional negotiations, but it does suggest another reason to rethink risk-based reimbursement and liability protection in a managed care environment.

17.7.5 Liability Coverage Forms

Over the past decade, medical liability was one of the most profitable and exciting segments of the insurance industry, producing returns averaging 30% over the 5 years from 1989 to 1993 and well above the financial sector industry average. Specialists, underwriters, and provider-owned mutual companies or health-care associations now underwrite about 70% of the U.S. medical malpractice market, with 73% being claims-made policies.

Under traditional insurance policies, there was an occurrence form that was maintained even if a negligence claim was made several years later, and a claims-made form developed to prevent the stacking of claims. By definition, occurrence is the repeated stacking of risk exposures, and a loss that occurs during two or more policy periods means that two or more sets of policy limits apply on top of each other. By contrast, a claims-made policy covers claims that are first made during the policy period. Other features of the claims-made form are that it reduces the time medical records must be kept for future claims and that it is more inflation-proof than occurrence coverage. Most other provisions of the two forms are identical, and the only real difference is what triggers the coverage. Occurrence coverage applies to the injury that occurs during the policy period, while the claims-made form states that insurance applies only if a claim is made during the policy period. Another departure from the occurrence form is that the claims-made agreement states that insurance does not apply if the claim occurred before the retroactive date or after the policy period. Usually, when an occurrence policy is renewed by a claims-made policy, the retroactive date is the effective date of the claims-made policy, thus eliminating overlapping coverage. Once established, the retroactive date may be advanced only with the written consent of the insured doctor and after being informed of the right to buy a supplemental extended reporting (SERP), or tail coverage, policy. Otherwise, a gap would result if the coverage were to be renewed on an occurrence form, or if the coverage were permanently terminated. Once in effect, SERPs of unlimited duration cannot be canceled and can be purchased for an endorsement

* See http://www.law.cornell for further information on the law of agency.

charge of about 200% of the annual coverage premium. SERPs effectively then become the transitional opposite of the retroactive date, as the latter excludes coverage for earlier occurrences because other insurance applied. It is also import to note that claims-made policies are initially less costly since the SERP is purchased later, while tail coverage is initially included with an occurrence policy, making it more costly.

More recently, however, health care has become a claims-made market of change with intensified financial challenges and consolidation driven primarily by the evolving managed care industry and risk-shifting capitated reimbursement environment. The capitation liability theory can be considered one result of this paradigm shift.

17.7.6 The Contrarian Viewpoint

The paradigm shift in health-care reimbursement models may signal a decrease in medical liability risk, or it may actually increase the risk. Errors of commission, which may be more likely in a fee-based system, are easier to prove than errors of limited treatment and omission. Nevertheless, the changes in health-care reimbursement may actually be setting the stage for increased medical liability costs, going forward in the new millennium, as described in the three models below.

17.7.6.1 Pure at-Risk Capitation Model

Under the pure at-risk capitated model, the health-care provider receives a sum certain each period in return for treating a certain pool of patients. The provider must provide care to all patients that request it during the specified time period. The fewer patients that the provider treats, and the fewer treatments rendered per patient, the lower the cost per patient, and the greater profit during that time period. Obviously, this model creates a powerful incentive for the provider to treat fewer patients and to provide fewer services to each patient. The incentive is to undertreat. Under this scenario, the number of liability claims made is likely to decrease because fewer patients are treated, and fewer at-risk procedures are performed. However, the likelihood is great that claims that are presented will result in a larger payout. This is because by undertreating a patient, the adverse condition may have significant time to worsen until definitive treatment is undertaken, and damages will be much greater.

For example, if an MCO limits the provider's ability to provide mammogram screenings, far fewer women will be diagnosed at the earlier stages of breast cancer. By the time a woman falls within the age parameters of the MCO to be eligible for the mammogram, a small surgical lesion may have progressed to a large metastasized lesion. The eventual liability would become much greater. This model is more common with primary care provider (PCP) medical groups. In the current trend, PCPs are seeing more patients while the specialists are seeing fewer patients. The gatekeeper concept and the plans that require the PCP group to pay specialists all seek to encourage treatment by PCPs and limit referrals. The incentive for this outcome is the real or perceived increased cost of specialist treatment. Not only are PCPs seeing more patients; they are also treating more conditions and performing more procedures that, a decade ago, were more often under the purview of a specialist. The result is that PCPs may end up treating conditions, and performing procedures, for which they are not suited by training or experience. As PCPs venture into these areas, the likelihood of incompetence, patient injury, and liability claims increase.

In this model, specialists also see more patients that are likely to increase the specialist's risks. The patient may have had previous treatment by the PCP, and the specialist's treatment may be more advanced. In the past, the chances were that a specialist may have initiated conservative treatment, but now, he/she gives more advanced treatment and increases his/her risk. The prior treatment by the PCP may not only have been ineffective, but the patient may actually be worse. Consequently, a sicker patient increases the risk for the specialist. Finally, the pure at-risk capitated model may increase risks for greater injuries and greater awards/settlements.

17.7.6.2 Reduced Fee-for-Service Model

Under the reduced FFS model, the provider receives a fee for every patient treated and a fee for every procedure performed. The provider can increase revenue by increasing the number of patients treated and the amount of procedures performed. Under this scenario, there is no decreased liability risk, or it may actually increase for several reasons.

First, more patients are treated, and more procedures are performed. Each individual patient encounter carries with it a degree of risk. By increasing the number of encounters, the risk is increased. It would appear that the risk would increase arithmetically, but in fact, it has the potential to increase exponentially. The reason is that the provider only has a certain amount of time in which to provide the service. In the current environment, the provider must squeeze more encounters into the same time period than a decade ago. The increased workload may increase stress and fatigue for the provider. With increased stress and fatigue, mistakes are more likely. Therefore, the increased liability risk is due to not only the increased number of patients but also the increased fatigue levels that may result in medical error. Under the reduced FFS model, there is also the possibility of undertreatment. The provider may determine that the reimbursement for certain procedures is unreasonably low and avoid such procedures. To the extent that the provider performs a lesser procedure, the possibility of increased liability exists.

17.7.6.3 Hybrid Capitation/Reduced Fee-for-Service Model

This hybrid capitated/reduced FFS model is commonly employed with a group of specialists, as opposed to primary care physicians. An entire group of specialists will be capitated with a fixed dollar amount (risk pool). The allocation to the individual specialist will be based on a function of the allowed rate of all procedures performed by the individual, compared with the allowed rate of all procedures by the group. Although the entire group of specialists is capitated such that the MCO's liability is limited, each individual provider still acts on a (reduced) FFS basis. Unless there are disincentives, this forces each provider to compete for a smaller share of the monetary disbursement. By performing more services/procedures, the individual provider can increase the share of the total allocated capitation. However, by increasing the number of services performed, in aggregate, the total reimbursement per service/procedure is reduced.

Unlike the pure at-risk capitation model, which gives incentive to reduce the number of services/procedures, this hybrid capitated/FFS model actually creates incentives, up to the point of diminishing marginal (marginal cost > marginal benefit) returns, for the individual to increase the number of services. The increase in services will continue until the individual perceives that the per-procedure reimbursement has fallen to levels that make the addition or continuation of certain services/procedures unprofitable.

This model has several advantages for the MCO. First and foremost, the MCO's liability is limited and definite. Second, specialists will individually seek to increase the number of patients treated. Consequently, MCO patients have access to needed specialist care. Finally, this model also has the potential to incite the drawbacks of both the at-risk capitated model and the reduced FFS model. There is incentive both for undertreatment in certain instances and for increased patient encounters, in other instances.

17.7.7 Miscellaneous Liability Factors

The current managed care environment also poses several other threats that may work to increase the number and severity of claims. These factors relate mostly to the depersonalization of modern medicine and create forces that can increase the likelihood of a lawsuit.

Unlike prior decades, there is a significant decrease in the patient loyalty factor. Patients are driven by MCO and PPACA plans, and providers are driven by costs and revenues. Patients perceive physician services to be interchangeable and medically equivalent. Currently, most have no loyalty to any one individual provider. Patients select PCPs based on a list in an insurance book. When they change plans (either by employer substitution or by change of employer), they often are required to select a new PCP from a new list of options. Patients consider the PCP to be the "insurance company's doctor," and the idea of "my personal doctor" departs with bygone days. Loyalty to medical specialists is especially strained since, in the past, patients often chose specialists based on reputation. Now, it is just as likely that the patient will be referred to an unknown specialist and have no input into the selection process. This factor, combined with less time for the specialist to develop patient rapport, leads to the patient viewing the specialist more impersonally, when considering whether to file a malpractice claim.

Additionally, with patients changing MCO and ACA plans and being subjected to narrow ("skinny"), less comprehensive, and different medical providers, treatment facilities, and hospital panels (outpatient and ambulatory clinics etc.), there is the increased likelihood that one provider may start a treatment plan and may not finish it. With patients switching providers, the provider will lose control of the patient. Subsequent treating physicians may find fault with the prior treatment and cause the patient to seek redress. This also may increase the likelihood of claims.

THE MEDICAL AND HEALTH-CARE ACTUARY

Health actuaries analyze potential risks, profits and trends that will affect their employers, which are often in the health insurance, government health services and medical provider industries. They advise companies on issuing policies to consumers based on risks, calculated premiums and upcoming changes in health-care costs. It's common for an actuary to have a bachelor's degree or higher in actuary studies, mathematics or statistics. Coursework on medical terminology and hierarchy of the medical field is also beneficial. In addition to academic education, certification is also necessary to reach "professional status," which is required by most employers. The professional organization Society of Actuaries certifies actuaries in the health and medical field. Their statistical work is commonly done with predictive tables, probability tables and life tables that are created on customized statistical analysis software such as Stata or XLSTAT. The actuary field as a whole is growing faster than other fields, according to the Bureau of Labor Statistics. By 2020, it is expected to expand by 27%. The average annual salary for an actuary in 2010 was $87,650. Specifically in the health insurance field, the salary was slightly higher at $91,000.

17.8 ASSESSMENT

Given emerging new payment mechanisms of the modern era (global reimbursement through the American College of Surgeons [ACS], medical homes, P4P, and capitation), are some medical providers paying too much for professional liability protection in the presently changing health-care industrial complex, and are others paying too little? More time, data, and research are needed for a definitive answer. But, the time for provoking the question has arrived.

17.9 CONCLUSION

Liability underwriters and actuarial advisors are risk averse by education and training. They react slowly, cautiously, and incrementally to shifting risk factors, especially toward trends that suggest reduced underwriter income and liability premiums. Physicians and medical group

CASE MODEL 1 TO JOIN OR NOT TO JOIN AN ACO *(EVALUATING A MODERN PPACA CONTRACT PROPOSAL)*

A new accountable care organization network wanted a multispecialty medical group to contract with them to provide medical services to all subscribers. Compensation would be in the form of a fixed-rate capitated payment system, also known as (aka) per member per month (PMPM).

The medical group practice administrator reviewed their request for proposal (RFP) very carefully but is still not sure what to do.

KEY ISSUES

Facts to know for an informed PMPM capitated reimbursement decision:

- Annual frequency (office visits) or service rate per 1000 patients
- Unit cost of medical services per unit-patient
- Co-payment dollar amount per patient
- Co-payment frequency rate per 1000 patients
- Variable cost per patient
- Undercapacity medical group office utilization rates
- Fixed overhead office-cost coverage (+/–)

SOLUTION

There are several issues to resolve:

1. Be sure that all office fixed costs are paid, since revenues are fixed, and costs vary with patient volume.
2. Be sure there is sufficient unused office capacity for the additional patients. Additionally, one must determine the maximum amount of services provided under the PMPM rate that will make it possible to still break even.
3. Expected costs per patient must be estimated. If total PMPM cost is less than the PMPM compensation premium, the capitated contract might make economic sense for the medical group. If not, it should be rejected or renegotiated.

CASE MODEL 2 MICROCAPITATION: A CHRONIC DIABETIC CARE PACKAGE IN DUBUQUE, IOWA

A family practice doctor in rural Dubuque, Iowa (population ~5000) cared for a fairly sizable population of diabetic patients. Dubuque is the county seat, nestled at an elevation of 6200 ft. in an incorporated area of more than 500 acres.

In reviewing several paper charts, and electronic health records (EHRs), the doctor recognized that many patients were not getting the care they needed. In questioning these patients, he learned that it was difficult for them to receive proper care because busy schedules created seasonal encounter difficulties. The physician determined to bolster his sparsely attended diabetic clinic by creating a new microcapitated diabetic care package (DCP).

COORDINATION OF CARE

In order to deliver this DCP, the family practice physician entered into conversations with other medical providers to determine a pricing schedule, how care was to be coordinated, and how the virtual team would work together to deliver care. They agreed to revenue splits, performance metrics, and a mechanism to market the microcapitated service. Contingencies were even made for patient needs that extended beyond the initial DCP provider agreement.

MEDICAL CARE VALUE ADDED

Because an entire year of routine care was included for a single discounted fee, given the efficiencies gained through care coordination, patients saw the clinical and financial value added. The physician signed up 50% of his current patient population immediately (250 people). An additional 100+ patients signed up within the first 90 days, as word-of-mouth marketing and positive local press reports made the program more widely known.

KEY ISSUES

1. Coordination: A single program coordinator would help schedule appointments and provide outcomes measurements.
2. Staffing: All participating medical providers were staffed and organized to deliver their component services, and because they were all working at under-capacity, no new equipment or staffing would be required.

SOLUTION*

The DCP included the following medical services:

- Four routine medical office visits
- A biannual podiatric visit for foot care
- An annual optometric eye examination
- Four additional in-home nutritional/medication consultations

* Modified from Scott L. Shreve, MD, personal communication.

Multiple side effects emerged from initiation of the DCP, including a spontaneous patient support group that met bimonthly to discuss nutrition, insulin regimens, and related diabetic health-care issues. The program coordinator participated actively with the group and recognized the opportunity for the various component providers to present the latest treatment options on a monthly basis. These meetings built additional rapport and patient confidence, and served as a recruiting mechanism for other diabetics in the community.

Within 2 years, three other physicians began selling modified versions of the DCP with new features, functions, and capabilities. The average community A1C metric, which was assembled by the patient support group, dropped from 9.5 to less than 7.0, for the known 472 community diabetic patients.

administrators must therefore develop their own strategies for evaluating liability risk factors and lead the trend toward reduced operational expenses through managed liability costs. This is accomplished by exploring new medical payment models and the advantages/disadvantages of Limited Liability Retention Association (LLRAs), as presented in the CLT of this chapter.

17.10 COLLABORATE

Discuss this chapter online with others at http://www.MedicalExecutivePost.com.

17.11 THE NEGOTIATION PROCESS

Once the numbers are crunched, the formal negotiation process with the MCO consists of a five-step sequence, according to Professors Bruce Patton and William Ury, of the Harvard Business School.

1. Don't bargain over positions. Taking them only makes matters worse since egos often become identified with positions. Is it harder to rob a friend or a stranger?
2. Separate the people from the process before considering the substantive problem. Figuratively, if not literally, both parties should come to see each other as working side by side, attacking the problem, not each other.
3. Invent options for mutual gain since having a lot at stake narrows your vision and inhibits creativity. Brainstorm possible solution options that advance shared interests and creatively reconcile differences.
4. Insist on using objective criteria rather than discussing what the parties are willing, or not willing, to accept. These standards can be a matter of custom, law, informed opinion, or market value.
5. Know your bottom-line limit, and recognize that you do not have to come to an agreement in each and every situation. Therefore, you must know your best alternative to a negotiated agreement (BANTA) and be prepared to say "no," and walk away.

Furthermore, financial steps to successfully negotiating capitated medical contracts will involve the following key elements: developing a pricing model; using effective negotiation skills; incorporating protective contract clauses; and monitoring, implementing, and renegotiating the contract as needed.

17.11.1 Use Effective Negotiation Skills

The general negotiation skills advocated by the Harvard Business School (above) are very effective when beginning to negotiate an MCO contract. The following skills are also excellent tips for how to effectively negotiate payment agreements.

- *Do not get emotional, upset, or angry...Stay cool!*—Although financial negotiations are a vitally important matter to you, it is probably just another job to your MCO opponent. He/she will likely negotiate with many doctors, and you are not important enough for him/her to get upset about. Do the same with him/her, and stay cool.
- *Do not get personal or lose your dignity*—No one will respect an angry, loud, or abusive doctor. This type of behavior will not only *not* get you an increase, but you may be delisted from the plan because one can reasonably infer that your patients might get treated in the same impolite manner as your MCO opponent.
- *Do not share your information*—If you have good results or outcomes with a particular treatment protocol, do not share them with the plan unless they sign a nondisclosure, noncompete, or no-sale agreement with you. Get information before you give information that might later be used against you.
- *The first offer should not be the last offer*—Even if you split the price difference, you might not receive a better financial deal. On the other hand, the initial offer was likely so low that even a split would benefit the MCO, so be careful. Splitting the difference is not negotiation.
- *Stand firm and await counteroffers*—Once you have performed the calculations to determine your bottom line, don't settle for less. You will only be offered less next time. Be aware of your best alternatives.
- *Leave something on the table*—If you give something in return for getting something, you will foster a continuing relationship with your MCO plan. For example, you might accept a slightly lower per-member per-month (PMPM) rate in exchange for a "diabetic carve-out." In an older geographic neighborhood, this might be a better deal for you since wound or ulcer care is expensive. Your opponent can then go back his/her supervisor and brag about putting one over on you, by getting a lower capitation rate! In other words, you both get bragging rights.
- *Do not be afraid of calculated risks*—Partial- or full-risk, fixed-based medical capitation is the wave of the future. So is the corporate practice of medicine seen in professional practice management corporations (PPMCs). Do not be foolhardy, but those who take calculated and informed risks will prosper, while conservative types will not.
- *Do not give your MCO opponent too much credit*—Your opponent may know nothing about your area of medical specialty, so do not give him/her information about your practice or profession to use against other colleagues. You might just know more about managed care than he/she does.
- *Take your time; it's usually on your side*—Unless you have no practice accounts receivable reserve, are a new practitioner, cannot get a line of credit, or are really destitute, you probably have time on your side to negotiate a deal in your favor. Often, simple procrastination will increase your capitation or fee rates.
- *Use a professional negotiator or Certified Medical Planner if you are uncomfortable*—Although professional negotiators and business specialists may

be expensive in the short run, you may gain much more by using them in the long run, especially if they are knowledgeable. If you have been unhappy with your own results to date, by all means get professional assistance.

17.11.2 Incorporate Protective Contract Clauses

Protective or "safe-harbor" contract clauses are designed to help clarify the appropriateness of percentage-based MCO contract arrangements, and they include termination, renegotiation, catastrophic, solicitation, nondisclosure, noncompete, gag-order, and solicitation clauses. The (Stark I, II, and III) antikickback or safe-harbor clauses make it a criminal offense to knowingly and willfully offer, pay, solicit, or receive any remuneration to induce the referral of business covered by a federal health-care program (Medicare and Medicaid).

According to the Office of the Inspector General (OIG), in Opinion 98-4, a percentage-based MCO contract would only qualify for the safe harbor of personal services and management contracts, and would be suspect if it did not meet *all* six of the following safe-harbor regulations:

1. The agreement is set out in writing and signed by the parties involved.
2. The agreement specifies the services to be performed.
3. If the services are performed on a part-time basis, the schedule for performance is specified in the contract.
4. The agreement is for not less than 1 year.
5. The aggregate amount of compensation is fixed in advance, based on fair market value in an arms-length transaction, and not determined in a manner that takes into account the volume or value of any referrals or business otherwise generated between the parties for which payment may be made by Medicare or a state health-care program.
6. The services performed under the agreement do not involve the promotion of business that violates any federal or state law.

Other important clauses to consider include indemnification clauses, procedural carve-outs, low enrollment guarantees, utilization rate "kick-outs," drug or formulary clauses, risk-pool limitation clauses, MD/member ratio requirements, "all or none" group clauses, stop-loss reinsurance, as well as arbitration and mediation clauses in your home state.

Note: Opinion 98-4 was generated by a request from a single physician. All medical practitioners are entitled to seek an OIG opinion on individual contract arrangements.

17.11.3 Monitor, Implement, and Renegotiate the Deal

Ongoing total quality improvement and management (TQIM) evaluation, payment schedules, medical and economic credentialing, as well as financial ratio analysis should be done quarterly with MCO administrators to ensure that the contract you originally signed is meeting the expectations of all concerned. For example, the following scheme may be used to assess your contract(s) utilization and net revenue(s).

As HMOs are themselves increasingly coming under their own cost pressures, many are willing to negotiate complementary or alternative health-care modalities as part of a benefits program (i.e., weight and stress management, nutritional services, biofeedback, herbal medicines, meditation, and yoga).

NEGOTIATING A BETTER PHYSICIAN FEE SCHEDULE

It is known that most health plans operate with fixed fee schedules. While these fee schedules have little or nothing to do with a resource-based relative value scale (RBRVS), and most are based on a percentage of what Medicare pays, the question is "are they tied to levels that are more than 3 or 4 years old?" Physicians who have no negotiating tools or a plan in place, and who question the methodology that the payers are using, are too casual, left with a "take it or leave it" response from the health insurance provider. Accordingly, a good solid foundation of data, and the above information, is necessary to negotiate better reimbursement rates successfully. The practice administrator or accountant (not 1 in 100 accountants can actually do this) should have this information readily available, especially if the office has an automated billing system.

Steps to Preparing a Fee Analysis

First and foremost, the medical management team in charge of this project will need to determine the most commonly used CPT codes for the practice. The bulk of primary care or family practice physician fees should be derived from the revenue of the office visit, hospital, and preventive medicine codes. This, in turn, may limit the number of codes for the study. The frequency of each CPT code should be listed over a 12-month period. If applicable, laboratory fees should also be included to see if there are fluctuating reimbursement schemes for these services. The codes on the list should account for at least 75% of the total practice charges.

Determining Top Payers and Reimbursement by Payer

It is known that Medicare and Medicaid use established fee schedules and do not negotiate; therefore, the focus should be on the other major payers that make up the bulk of the reimbursement. In this process, make sure that the payers in the report are the practice's top payers. The practice administrator will also need to determine the reimbursement for each code that is sent to the various payers' list in the report. For this project, we can use the explanation of benefits (EOB) that is received from each payer that has been selected for the report. When including these data, make sure the allowed amount, not the paid amount, is referenced. After this information has been gathered, each payer's reimbursement rate will need to be calculated as a percentage of Medicare's reimbursement rate. Medicare's current rates for any geographical area can be found in the Medicare Physician Fee Schedule lookup tool on the CMS website. The site also provides a reference to the relative value unit (RVU) that Medicare assigns to each code.

RVU Conversion Factors

It is important for the practice administrator, physician or manager, to understand the RVU conversion factors and how they work, simply because most payers are in the beginning stages of using this method. To calculate a payment for service, you multiply a particular CPT code by the Medicare conversion factor for that code. For an example, we will use the code 99214—office visit. The RVU for that code is 2.2. The

Medicare conversion factor for the same code is $37.34. The calculation would result in a rate of $82.15. Geographical adjustments must be taken into account when performing these calculations. The next step in this process would be to review the fees for each code listed in the report. Calculate each fee as a percentage of Medicare's rates. You will find different statistics for each payer.

Apply the Rules

Follow these basic rules when applying this new process:

- If the charges are being reimbursed at 100%, the fee may be too low. At this point, raising the fee for that code would be acceptable (usually not the case).
- If several fees are in this category, the practice should just set all its fees to a percentage of Medicare reimbursement across the board, such as 125% (many managed care plans pay at less than marginal cost [MC], i.e., 80% MC).
- A tiered fee schedule would be applicable if the payers seem to pay more for certain procedures or diagnostic studies. That would set evaluation and management codes at 125% of Medicare reimbursement while charging 150% of Medicare reimbursement for other procedures and diagnostic tests.

The doctor or medical practice administrator should make sure that no matter which fee schedule is best suited for the practice, it is updated annually to prevent loss of any increases that may occur per payer.

Physician Fee Schedule Augmentation

After all medical practice management data have been gathered, organize them onto a spreadsheet or chart. This analysis report will help to determine the codes and/or health plans that should be targeted for process improvement.

Focus Like a Laser Beam

The focus should be on the highest volume and dollar value codes. Does this mean that patients with unusual conditions or low-dollar-value codes are not treated? Hopefully, it will not, but it will push this process forward, and the practice will see the greatest benefit from these categories. When you review the report and find that a fee is being paid at a much lower rate, this would be indicative of a necessary negotiation with the payer for an increase for that procedure. Most health plans are committed to preventing disease. Maybe, but they are still actually aimed at treating diseases, not preventing them. If this is true of many payers, then they should be willing to provide the incentives for those services to be carried out. You will find that some payers' fee schedules are very much out of line with a percentage of Medicare payments;

therefore, the practice administrator should focus on those payers and bring evidence of the inadequacies to their attention.

Specialists versus General Practitioners

Specialists are, for the most part, paid at a higher rate than primary care physicians for a similar service! But, with GPs as gatekeepers in the early managed care era, specialty-doctor income was actually poised to decrease in some instances, while GP income increased briefly. Unfortunately, this may no longer be true today, according to blogger Scott Shreeve, MD, whose criticism of the specialty-laden American Medical Association (AMA) coding CPT commission is legendary. There was a time when Medicare had two conversion factors, and this was the result. This inequity could also be used as a tool for better reimbursement rates (personal communication).

Finalizing the Fee and Revenue Analysis

When the final preparations of the fee analysis have been completed, it is time to react to the results of the findings. There are several options to choose from when it has been determined that a health plan's fee schedule is not in tune with the practice's financial growth. The practice should act on these results as soon as they are discovered, to avoid the loss of any more revenue.

When No Longer Accepting Health Plans

During the analysis phase, you may determine that a health plan's payment levels are extremely low. You will have to determine whether the plan is worth negotiating or the practice administrator should consider dropping out of the plan altogether at the end of the contract period. It will have to be carefully determined by the local market. If the practice is in a highly competitive market, this process should not be considered as the first choice. However, if the market is very slim, the health-care purchaser will be responsible for complaining to the health insurance plan provider that there is simply not enough physician coverage for their employees for the area. This could be a very effective way to force a negotiation with the health-care company. If this were the case, the area would have less managed care and more MCs/MDs.

When Not Accepting New Patients from Low-Paying Health Plans

One option would be to not accept any more patients from the health plan that is reimbursing the practice with low rates. Although this may initially lower your patient count, over time, the practice will benefit from new patients with health plans that have a better reimbursement policy. Include a snapshot of what the final analysis or report should look like and the details of what it should include. This can be used in any specialty to assist in putting together the individual practice analysis to achieve the same results. But is it noble or ethical? What about any-willing-provider laws?

FURTHER READINGS

Cimasi, RJ: *Accountable Care Organizations: Value Metrics and Capital Formation*. Productivity Press, Boca Raton, FL, 2013.

Congressional Budget Office: "Budget Options Volume 1: Health Care," December 2008. Available at: http://www.cbo.gov/doc.cfm?index=9925.

Dartmouth Institute for Health Policy & Clinical Practice, and the Engelberg Center for Health Care Reform at Brookings: "Reforming Provider Payment: Moving Toward Accountability for Quality and Value," March 2009. Issue Brief. Available at: http://www.brookings.edu/events/2009/0311_aco.aspx.

Diamond, F: "Accountable Care Organizations Give Capitation Surprise Encore," *Managed Care*, Washington, DC, September 2009.

Eskow, R: "A Brief History of Capitation; From Medieval Days to the 21st Century," *Sentinel Effect*, 2007. http://sentineleffect.wordpress.com/2007/04/16/a-brief-history-of-capitation/.

Fisher, ES, McClellan, MB, Bertko, J, Lieberman, SM, Lee, JJ, Lewis, JL, and Skinner, JS: "Fostering Accountable Health Care: Moving Forward in Medicare," *Health Affairs* 2009; 28(2):w219–w231. Available at: http://content.healthaffairs.org/cgi/content/abstract/hlthaff.28.2.w219.

Hackbarth, G, Reischauer, R, and Mutti A: "Collective Accountability for Medical Care—Toward Bundled Medicare Payments," *N Engl J Med* 2008;359(1):3–5.

Irving, F: "Top 10 ACS Cashing on Shared Savings," *Medical Practice Insider*, December 2, 2014.

Landon, B: "Structuring Payments to Patient-Centered Medical Homes," *JAMA* 2014;312(16):1633–1634. doi:10.1001/jama.2014.9529.

Marbury, D: "ACOs Have Three More Years before Sharing Risks with CMS," *Medical Economics*, New York, December 3, 2014.

Marcinko, DE and Hetico, HR: *Dictionary of Health Insurance and Managed Care*. Springer Publishing, New York, 2006.

Marcinko, DE and Hetico, HR: *Dictionary of Health Economics and Finance*. Springer Publishing, New York, 2007.

Marcinko, DE and Hetico, HR: "Analyzing and Negotiating Cost–Volume Profit Medical Contracts," in Marcinko, DE (Editor): *Healthcare Organizations (Journal of Financial Management Strategies)*. iMBA Inc Publishing, Atlanta, GA, 2010.

Marcinko, DE and Hetico, HR: *The Business of Medical Practice* (3rd edition). Springer Publishing, New York, 2011.

Marcinko, DE and Hetico, HR: *Hospitals and Healthcare Organizations: Management Strategies, Operational Techniques, Tools, Templates and Case Studies*. Productivity Press, Boca Raton, FL, 2013.

Marcinko, DE and Hetico, HR: *Financial Management Strategies for Hospitals and Healthcare Organizations: Tools, Techniques, Checklists and Case Studies*. Productivity Press, Boca Raton, FL, 2014.

Marcinko, DE and Hetico, HR: *Comprehensive Financial Planning Strategies for Doctors and Advisors: Best Practices from Leading Consultants and Certified Medical Planners™*. Productivity Press, Boca Raton, FL, 2015.

Medicare Payment Advisory Commission: "Report to Congress: Reforming the Delivery System," June 2008. Available at: http://www.medpac.gov/documents/Jun08_EntireReport.pdf.

Special Commission on the Health Care Payment System: "Recommendations of the Special Commission on the Health Care Payment System," July 16, 2009. Available at: http://www.mass.gov/Eeohhs2/docs/dhcfp/pc/Final_Report/Final_Report.pdf.

Stewart, J: *The Story of Dr. Sidney R. Garfield: The Visionary Who Turned Sick Care into Health Care*. The Permanente Press, San Francisco, 2009.

18 Nondisclosure Agreements and Physician Restrictive Covenants

Practice Valuation and Buy/Sell Agreements

Charles F. Fenton III, David Edward Marcinko, Frederick William LaCava, and Hope Rachel Hetico

CONTENTS

Some of the angriest individuals we have ever met are parties to litigation over contractual covenants not to compete. Not medical malpractice cases, not even divorces, produce the fury, the expense, the feelings of betrayal, and fraud that infect doctors fighting over whether, if, and how a paragraph in what was once a friendly business deal should be interpreted. The anger and grief probably spring from a failure of the parties to achieve mutual understanding at the time that the agreement is negotiated. These covenants are still necessary, but overreaching by one side or the other may lead to terrible legal conflicts.

18.1 RESTRICTIVE COVENANTS DEFINED

The covenants in question are agreements that in certain circumstances, one of the parties is committing himself/herself not to practice his/her profession for a period of time within a geographical area or with members of a defined population or to buy or sell a medical practice. They arise in two sets of circumstances: purchase/sale or fair market valuation of a medical practice or as a term of an employment agreement. The law treats the two types quite differently, favoring agreements as part of the purchase/sale of a practice, and entertaining challenges to covenants in employment contracts.

A covenant not to compete is legally based on preservation of a protectable interest in goodwill. Though goodwill is an intangible property right, it is very much a real one. Accountants and the Internal Revenue Service (IRS) have recognized methods of quantifying it. The federal government's Fraud and Abuse enforcement arm is very interested in it to make sure that it is not, in fact, a disguised kickback, and divorce lawyers love it when divorce prompts an evaluation of marital property. Goodwill is the value attributed to an ongoing practice's name recognition, location, telephone numbers, business names, and all those things that would make a potential patient come to one doctor's office rather than another's. The law recognizes that a practitioner has the right to protect that value from a competitor who unfairly tries to appropriate it.

18.2 COVENANTS FOR THE SALE OF A MEDICAL PRACTICE

Goodwill should be protected in a sale of a practice because much of the value of such a practice is encompassed by the element of goodwill. A practice may include a building or suite of offices, either owned or leased; the equipment, furniture, and supplies on hand; records of patients; and other financial interests. But the biggest value of a practice is the propensity of existing patients to come to that location for medical services, and more recently, inclusion in insurance, hospital, or third-party provider networks. The goodwill has been created by the practitioners who have provided those services in the past. To the extent that patients have liked Dr. Washington and have been satisfied with his medical treatment, they will tend to come to his office after Dr. Adams has acquired the practice. A large part of what Dr. Adams has paid for is the likelihood of transfer of that patient loyalty from Dr. Washington to him. A necessary part of the sale of the practice then is a commitment from Dr. Washington not to compete with Dr. Adams in that location or nearby for some reasonable amount of time. If Dr. Adams were not to require such a commitment from Dr. Washington, Dr. Washington would be free to open a new office across the street from the old one and attract the patients who were loyal to him in the old office to come to the new office. Unless Dr. Adams only bargained for some second-hand equipment and shop-worn office space, he would not have gotten the goodwill he paid for.

Covenants not to compete that are incident to the sale of a practice are favored by the law, almost universally enforced, and play a logical and necessary part of the sale or transfer of goodwill. Disputes and litigation over these covenants arise when the seller tries to find a way to get around the commitment.

For example, "Yes, I signed the covenant not to compete with Dr. Adams, but my wife, Dr. Martha Washington, did not. She can start up a competing practice across the street from the old office. She doesn't use the business name 'Washington Internal Medicine Associates' that I sold to Dr. Adams; she uses 'Dr. M. Washington Internal Medicine, PC.' I don't practice medicine in any way at her office; I just sit out in the waiting room and drink coffee and chat with the patients."

Sellers who try such tactics usually lose. In negotiating the sale of a practice, either as a seller or a buyer, use an attorney who is an expert in the area of covenants not to compete. Don't use a real-estate lawyer, your tax attorney, or your divorce attorney! Don't use your brother's former college roommate just because he would do it cheap! You would never have a psychiatrist set your broken leg, so pay for the appropriate specialist. Make sure that the terms of the covenant are reasonable. A covenant whose terms are draconian may be voided by a court, leaving the purchaser with no protection at all.

18.3 INDEPENDENT CONTRACTOR OR EMPLOYEE

A payer has the right to control or direct only the result of the work done by an independent contractor and not the means or methods of accomplishing the result. By contrast, anyone who performs services for another is an employee if the latter can control what will be done and how it will be done. Employed physicians are usually not compensated as independent contractors.

However, many tasks may be successfully delegated to independent contractors or physician consultants without fear of such characterization. For example, a company does not have to withhold payroll taxes for an independent contractor but must file a 1099-MISC whenever payments exceed $600 a year. To distinguish between the two, there are several factors to consider. In general, the more you have control over a worker, the more the worker looks like an employee. Two brief tables below note a few of the differences:

Employee:

- Works at site of employer
- Uses company tools or equipment
- Cannot delegate or hire others for job
- Method/timing of job specified/controlled
- Expenses reimbursed
- Little invested by worker
- Payment weekly, biweekly, or monthly
- Only works for one employer
- No risk of nonpayment if poor job
- Profit/bonus limited
- No advertising
- Contract states employee relationship
- Position seems permanent
- Work done is essential to business

Independent contractor:

- Works off-site
- Uses own tools and equipment
- Can hire others or delegate
- Method/timing of job uncontrolled
- Expenses borne by worker
- More invested by worker
- Payment by the job or flat fee
- Works for several clients
- Opportunity for profit
- Advertising to general public
- Contract says independent contractor
- Position temporary
- Work done is noncore function

18.3.1 Multifactorial Analysis Needed

No single one of these factors determines status. The IRS has a 20-factor test outlined in Revenue Ruling 87-41 and discussed in publication 1976, "Independent Contractor or Employee." When you have a relationship that is unclear, you should consult with the IRS guidelines and publications. If your intent is to hire an independent contractor, try to make sure the relationship has more of the factors indicative of that status, checking the latest IRS publication for all relevant factors. Because of the large amounts at stake, you should err on the side of employee status, if uncertain. You may wish consult a tax attorney or accountant as well, especially if you have multiple workers in a gray area. In addition, you can request that the IRS make a determination of worker classification by submitting

Form SS-8, "Determination of Employee Work Status for Purposes of Federal Employment Taxes and Income Tax Withholding."

The IRS guidelines on this topic are rather lengthy. And, $600 is still the threshold amount this year unless it is royalties ($10). Nonemployee compensation, rent, royalties, prizes or awards, and services are only a few of the situations giving rise to a 1099-MISC.

18.4 COVENANTS AS PART OF A MEDICAL EMPLOYMENT CONTRACT

A covenant not to compete that is part of a contract of employment (or part of a stockholder's agreement) is far more likely to result in litigation because these covenants are far more likely to be used or avoided unfairly. Many an employer would like the covenant to function to punish an employee who would dare to leave a job with an ongoing practice and compete with it in any conceivable fashion. Many an employee has signed an employment contract without ever giving thought to the possibility that the covenant would not be enforced against him/her, or worse, thinking that the covenant could not be enforced. If the covenant is drafted to be reasonable, it will be enforced, and should be enforced. The reasons are easy to see.

Young associate Dr. Johnson joins elder practitioner Dr. Lincoln, in an ongoing practice with goodwill created by Dr. Lincoln. Dr. Johnson gets to know Dr. Lincoln's patients and impresses them with his own abilities. Dr. Johnson and Dr. Lincoln do not agree on an extension of the employment contract, and Dr. Johnson is notified that he may not practice medicine within the terms of the covenant not to compete contained in his employment contract. Dr. Lincoln has a protectable interest in the goodwill of his practice, which Dr. Johnson should not be allowed to appropriate and use against his former employer as a competitor. If the covenant is reasonably drafted, it will do no more than protect that defined interest belonging to Dr. Lincoln. The problem is defining what interest may be reasonably protected.

18.5 REASONABLE COVENANT TERMS

A covenant not to compete will not be upheld by a court if its effect is to go beyond the interest that Dr. Lincoln has in his goodwill. Current patients who have a current relationship of trust with Dr. Lincoln should be recognized as a legitimate interest. But, what about persons who have never been patients of Dr. Lincoln's, patients who may never have heard of Dr. Lincoln? What about patients who have not seen Dr. Lincoln in years and who may no longer have any tendency to consult with him on a new problem? The courts have struggled with this concept, and decisions can be found that both enforce and strike down covenants that cover future or possible patients.

The covenant must be for a reasonable amount of time. How long is there a reasonable expectation that a patient would come back to a doctor who treated him/her earlier? Covenants up to 2 years have been almost uniformly upheld, while covenants longer than that period have had varying fates.

The covenant must extend over no more than a reasonably necessary geographical area to effectuate protection of the legitimate interest. That geographical area may be far wider in a rural area than within a metropolis. The size of the geographical area may also vary with the kind of business interest being protected. In some cases, an area of a whole county is too big, while in others, an area of 12 states is deemed reasonable. The definition of the geographical area is, many times, given little review by a court, and instead, another covenant with protection of one county or a 50-mile radius is cited with a conclusion that a similar-sized area is also reasonable. A more particular examination of the facts of the particular case may distinguish it from another case.

An alternative to a geographical limitation is a specification of certain persons whose business may not be solicited by the former employee, usually a designation of "current" patients (customers), contracts, or networks who have been served by the employer within the time of the associate's employment. In these cases, there is no geographical area of coverage, and the patient or customer may reside anywhere. Courts approve of these current customer limits.

A covenant may be declared unenforceable if one of its terms is unreasonable and cannot be separated from the remainder of the covenant. The law will not apply a blue pencil to rewrite the terms of a covenant to bring it within the scope of reasonability, but it will strike down a term that is unreasonable that can be isolated from the other terms of the covenant. However, a covenant may contain a *cy pres* clause (medieval French for "as close"), which directs the court to enforce the covenant within the limits of the law as closely to the meaning of the parties as possible.

18.6 REMEDIES COVENANT BREACH (THE LEGAL Rx)

No, a "remedy" at law is not a medical prescription but the things that courts can do to protect or compensate a person who has been harmed by violation of a covenant not to compete. The possible remedies are (1) an award of actual damages proven after the fact, i.e., how much monetary loss can be attributed directly to the unfair competition of the former employee; (2) liquidated damages calculated in advance at the time the covenant was drafted; and (3) injunction, i.e., a court order that the former employee stop violating the covenant immediately. The first remedy is almost never used and is included in this analysis to show why the other two remedies are used instead. Actual damages after the fact requires that the whole period of the covenant run before any remedy can be considered. Employers argue that they could be put out of business before they ever get to be heard in court. Employers also argue that it would be so difficult as to be impossible to calculate. We have doubts about how impossible it would be, but it is not very practical, and we will come back to liquidated damages and why they are far more appropriate for physicians later.

An injunction is an order by the court, i.e., the government, that a doctor not practice his/her area of medicine within the area and time limits of the covenant. In order for a court to issue an injunction, the court must find that the damages that may be done to the former employer are irreparable, i.e., that no amount of money that can be reasonably calculated can compensate the former employer for the harm done by the former employee's competition. Further, the court must determine that it is in the public interest to issue the injunction. Very, very frequently, an employment agreement with a covenant not to compete in it will have recitations in it that the parties agree that damages to the employer would be irreparable and that it would be in the public interest that an injunction be issued to enforce the covenant, i.e., that the covenant tries to supply these necessary areas of proof by incorporating them into the language of the covenant. No court is bound by such recitations. It is only the court that determines the public interest, not the parties, and it is only the court that can determine that an alleged damage is or is not irreparable.

There are a million arguments and counterarguments between medical practitioners over whether the financial damages that may be done between them can or cannot be calculated. Once a court turns, however, to damages that may be done to patients, arguments tend to be more one-sided. With passage of the Patient Protection and Affordable Care Act (PPACA), and the prevalence of medical provider networks, the courts are beginning to pay serious attention to the public interest, which may be affected by the issuance of an injunction in circumstances in which it may be shown that an injunction would endanger members of the public who may need a particular specialty of medicine or even the ability to perform a specific procedure within that area of specialty, for example, by having physicians available to make full use of a particular facility in a community hospital that would otherwise suffer.

Arguments have also been made that a covenant between doctors is or should be against public policy because the enforcement of such an agreement forbids a patient from seeing the physician whom he/she prefers without allowing the patient any say in the matter. The Opinions of the Council on Ethical and Judicial Affairs of the American Medical Association (1986, 1994, 1996) section 9.02 provides for agreements restricting medical practice.

18.7 AGREEMENTS RESTRICTING THE PRACTICE OF MEDICINE

The Council on Ethical and Judicial Affairs discourages any agreement between physicians that restricts the right of a physician to practice medicine for a specified period of time or in a specified area upon termination of employment, a partnership, or a corporate agreement. Such restrictive agreements are not in the public interest.

Yet, we are unaware of the American Medical Association giving any practical support against covenants not to compete. Courts in some states have taken the position that the covenants are void as against public policy. You must consult with an attorney to find out the legal handling of covenants not to compete between physicians involving injunctions.

Liquidated damages are specifications within a contract, in advance of any breach, which reasonably determine what monetary damages are likely to result from a breach of the covenant not to compete. The liquidated damages may set a specific figure or provide a certain formula for calculating the damages based on specified elements such as collections at a particular office etc. If the covenant is for longer than a year, the contract may provide that liquidated damages for breach during the first year will be this amount, and a breach after 1 year would be that amount. The law highly favors liquidated damages because the two parties have calculated the amount in advance and relieve the court of having to determine damages from the many different ways by which they can be calculated.

It is our position that a specification of liquidated damages in a contract eliminates the claim for injunctive relief as well. The basic argument for injunctive relief is that a monetary award cannot compensate for the injuries done. Liquidated damages specify that amount and eliminate that claim. Some courts have, however, granted both damages and injunctive relief, perhaps because the parties did not raise the logical conflict before the court. We personally suggest that clients seek or offer provisions for liquidated damages because we personally find it repugnant to use the power of the state to tell a patient that he/she may not seek medical treatment from Dr. Kennedy or Dr. Nixon. The patient's choice is not to be sacrificed for a business concern, while the monetary damages will protect the loss of any goodwill that may be suffered.

Liquidated damages, however, have their own set of abuses. The amount of the damages may not bear a logical relationship to any reasonable way to calculate damages. An amount that is obviously in excess of such an estimate is legally a penalty on the person violating the covenant rather than compensation of injuries sustained by the complaining party. The law will not enforce a penalty or private punishment. An employer who overreaches may find himself/herself with no protection at all.

18.8 MEDICAL PRACTICE BUY/SELL AGREEMENTS

All medical practice and other business agreements that dictate what happens to a physician's property should be addressed in a document called a *buy/sell agreement.*

18.8.1 Definition

A buy/sell agreement stipulates what would happen to your medical practice should you die, become disabled, leave, or wish to retire. It is also a useful adjunct for a buy-in or buyout arrangement for a new or retiring practitioner.

The agreement states that your partner or partners will buy your interest upon death (sales, buy-in, buyout, merger, acquisition, or other disposition) and stipulates that your estate will sell your interest. It is a binding agreement to both parties. Its structure with differing model types is addressed below by Lawrence E. Howes, MBA, CFP®, and Joel B. Javer, CFP (Sharkey, Howes & Javer, South Denver, Colorado, personal communication).

The agreement will have a valuation method or will name a future valuator agreed upon by all parties, which might be a stated fixed price or a formula. If a fixed price is selected, then a procedure should be in place to ensure at least an annual revaluation of the practice. In the past, economic formulas provided an adequate representation of the value of the practice. However, the dynamic health-care environment today warrants a more detailed review of the validity of your existing formula and/or the retention of a medical practice valuation specialist. If the practice is valued highly, then having an expert valuator/practice appraiser and sufficient cash to buy out a deceased partner might be a difficult—and possibly an overwhelming—financial burden. Hence the various buy/sell agreement structure types.

18.8.2 What to Include in a Buy/Sell Agreement or Practice Sale

A buy/sell (sales) agreement, or practice purchase/sale, must disclose the items that are being transferred and the items that are/are not considered part of the agreement. This section should be crystal clear, so that anybody reading the contract (and hence a court that may be called upon to enforce the contract) and not privy to the preliminary negotiations will know what is part of the agreement and what is not part of the agreement.

18.8.2.1 Sale of Stock versus Sale of Assets

In most cases, well-informed doctors and their consultants will recommend that the buyer solely purchase the assets of the practice and not the stock of the practice. By purchasing selected assets, the buyer is ensured that he/she will not become responsible for the known or unknown liabilities of the corporation. In prior days, avoiding purchasing the stock of the corporation was a wise recommendation. However, with the advent of managed care and health reform, the purchase of the stock of the corporation can provide the new practitioner with certain competitive advantages. It may take a new practitioner 3–9 months to get onto enough managed care panels to make the practice profitable. Purchase of the stock of the corporation ensures the new practitioner of acquiring the federal tax identification number (TIN), personal identification number (PIN), Drug Enforcement Agency (DEA), Centers for Medicare and Medicaid (CMS), Global Location Number (GLN), National Provider Identifier (NPI), Health Information Exchange (HIE) Form 834 transmission number, durable medical equipment number (DME), etc. of the corporate entity. Since most managed care corporations identify providers by the federal TIN, purchase of the stock of the corporation should allow the new practitioner to be enrolled on managed care panels in a shorter period of time.

18.8.2.2 Items Purchased

Items purchased in the agreement, or purchase/sales contract, often include the tangible and intangible property of the seller that will be transferred to the buyer. Such items often include the following:

1. A detailed inventory of the tangible assets to be purchased
2. A detailed listing of the inventory of the practice
3. The names and addresses of all of the patients of record treated by the seller
4. The patient medical records/electronic health records (EHRs) maintained by seller
5. The computer records maintained by seller
6. All licenses, permits, accreditation, and franchises issued by any federal, state, municipal, or quasi-government authority relating to the use, maintenance, or operation of the practice, running to or in favor of seller, but only to the extent that they are accepted by buyer

7. All of seller's right, title, and interest in and to all real-estate and equipment leases, if any; service agreements; employment and professional service contracts relating to the practice but only to the extent that the foregoing are accepted by buyer
8. Assignment of lease should be attached and be incorporated to the agreement
9. All existing telephone numbers used in connection with the operation of the practice and all yellow page advertising of the practice
10. The goodwill of the practice, which includes seller's assistance and cooperation in transfer of all seller's rights and interests in the practice, and any other intangible assets of the practice not listed in any other category, to buyer

Certain items purchased, such as (paper or electronic) medical records, governmental licenses, fax, e-mail, website, and telephone numbers, have special considerations, as discussed below.

18.8.2.3 Medical Records

The seller should protect its future need to use the transferred patient medical records. In the current managed care environment, providers are subject to strict scrutiny. Even after leaving a practice, a provider may find himself/herself subject to a government or third-party audit or to a medical malpractice lawsuit. Therefore, the provider should ensure that the contract allows for him/her to take future possession of the specific medical record(s) of the practice in order to mount an appropriate defense.

18.8.2.4 Governmental Licenses

Certain government licenses and permits may be nontransferable. These would include items such as the federal and state employer identification numbers, as these are unique to the seller as a corporate entity. Likewise, other items unique to the seller include Medicare identification numbers, Medicaid identification numbers, NPIs, and Unique Provider Identification Numbers (UPINs). The buyer would have to purchase the stock of the corporation in order to acquire such items, which is another advantage of a stock transaction versus an asset transaction. Likewise, some local business licenses may or may not be transferable.

18.8.2.5 Telephone and Fax Numbers, Website URLs, Blogs, Facebook, Instagram and Twitter Accounts, etc.

Transference of telephone numbers often requires that a special local telephone company form an authorizing transfer of the telephone numbers to the buyer. Often, the new owner of the telephone number will also become liable for any current yellow page advertisement monthly fees. It is the same with an URL or website address, office Twitter account, etc.

18.8.2.6 Items Not Purchased

Items not purchased or "excluded items" often list the personal items of the parties or of the employees of the parties. Such items would often include the following:

1. All cash on hand or on deposit
2. All accounts receivable (ARs) generated prior to the closing date
3. All prepaid expenses, utility deposits, tax rebates, insurance claims, credits due from suppliers and other allowances after Closing Date

4. Personal effects, including but not limited to photographs, diplomas, uniforms, books, mementos, memorabilia, personally owned art, and any personal property owned by them
5. Life insurance, disability insurance, and disability buyout insurance on seller
6. Motor vehicles used in connection with the practice
7. Any or all tangible and intangible assets used in conjunction with another practice of seller
8. All other assets owned by seller other than those specifically described as items purchased

The exact items transferred will often depend upon the prior negotiations of the parties. For example, the parties may have agreed that the ARs will be transferred with the practice. In such an instance, the ARs will be listed as an item to be purchased.

18.8.3 Medical Practice Worth

Medical practice worth and value isn't an absolute number; it is a price range. And, a medical practice's tangible and intangible assets can be grouped into two broad categories:

- *Physical assets*: Examples are real estate, medical records, leaseholds, medical equipment and furnishings, and ARs.
- *Nonphysical assets*: These include goodwill, restrictive covenants, buy/sell agreements, managed care contracts, and an assembled workforce.

Estimates of value differ markedly, depending on the purpose of the appraisal, the acumen of the appraiser, etc. To help determine the value, some important questions to consider are the following:

- What is the value of the practice for purchase or sale?
- What is the value of a practice for merger?
- What is the value of practice assets for joint venture with a corporate partner?
- What is the value to establish buy-in or buyout arrangements for partners?
- What is the value of practice assets for purchase or sale, apart from ongoing operations?

To answer these questions, physicians (buyers and sellers) must understand how practices are valuated—beginning with the following informal, and then more formal, definitions:

18.8.3.1 Informal Terms of Valuation

- The *asking price* is often arbitrary and difficult to substantiate, and typically is reduced 25–50% after negotiations.
- The *creative price* is derived by way of creative financing. For example, the practice may provide the down payment.
- The *emotional price* may involve either a motivated buyer or seller, who pays an underinflated or overinflated price for the practice.
- The *friendly price* is reserved for associates, partners, or other colleagues.
- The *realistic price* is one that both buyer and seller believe is fair.

18.8.3.2 Formal Terms of Valuation

- Most appraisers use *fair market value* (FMV) as the standard to derive a reasonable value for a practice. FMV means an arm's-length transaction between an unpressured, informed buyer and an unpressured, informed seller (IRS Revenue Ruling 59-60).
- The *business enterprise value* of a practice equals a combination of all assets (tangible and intangible), and the working capital, of a continuing business.
- The value of *owner's equity* equals the combined values of all practice assets (tangible and intangible), less all practice liabilities (booked and contingent).
- The *working capital value* equals the excess of current assets (cash, ARs, supplies, inventory, prepaid expenses, etc.) over current liabilities (accounts payable, accrued liabilities, etc.).

Realizing that there is no absolute sales price is the essence of FMV. When determining valuation, look for a price range with a reasonable floor and ceiling.

18.8.4 The Valuation

The following steps should occur before the practice appraisal process begins:

- Retain an appraiser (for each side), or mutually agreed upon intermediary, who understands the changing health-care industry.
- Aggregate historic practice business information and consolidated financial statements, ARs, operating statistics, payer mix, Current Procedural Terminology (CPT) utilization, acuity rates, etc.
- Eliminate one-time, nonrecurring expenses, adjusted or normalized for excessive or below-normal expenses.
- Understand key assumptions used in financial projections.

To determine value, appraisers should follow the American Society of Appraisers' Principles of Appraisal Practice and Code of Ethics. The IRS issued guidelines in 1995 further suggesting that appraisers use the general methods of the Uniform Standards of Professional Appraisal Practices (USPAP), which recognizes three approaches to medical practice valuation, discussed as follows.

18.8.4.1 Income Methods

There are two methods to value a practice by income:

1. *Capitalization method*: The excess earnings or capitalization method estimates value by dividing normalized historical or current income by an appropriate rate of return for the buyer. This method does not require assumptions.
2. *Discounted method*: Discounted cash flow (DCF) analysis requires assumptions to estimate practice value by discounting future net cash flows to their present worth based on market rates of return required by an investor. Understanding the key assumptions produces a meaningful estimate of practice value. These assumptions may include the following:
   - Projections of future practice revenue, productivity, reimbursement trends, and shifts in payer mix
   - Projections of practice cost structures and projected physician compensation

- After-tax practice cash flows
- Reinvestments to replace equipment or other assets
- Residual practice value at the end of the forecast period
- Discount rate based on the practice-specific weighted average cost of capital
- Practice efficiencies, operations, and competitive market conditions

The DCF analysis consistently produces higher values than other methods of estimating practice value because there may be supportable reasons to forecast improvements in future practice performance.

18.8.4.2 Marketplace Multiples

Market transaction multiples are ratios developed by correlating actual practice sale prices to key practice performance measurements. Common multiples include comparisons of sale price to revenue; sale price to earnings before interest and taxes (EBIT); sale price to earnings before interest, taxes, and depreciation allowance (EBITDA); gross revenue; net revenue; and sale price to number of physicians. Market transaction multiples are typically limited to serving as a benchmark for testing the reasonableness of the other approaches. They are becoming less common and less useful.

18.8.4.3 Cost Approach

The cost approach calls for identification and separate valuation of all the practice assets, including goodwill, depreciated over 15 years. The cost approach is more labor-intensive than using enterprise analysis to estimate practice value, especially for a new practice, which typically includes the expenses for acquiring space, office furnishings, equipment, marketing, advertising, staff development, and losses incurred during the startup period. This estimate of "replacement cost or cost avoidance" value represents an upper limit (or ceiling) of value and generally is not considered useful in estimating the value of an established medical practice.

18.8.5 Net Income Statement Adjustments

When analyzing a set of financial statements to determine practice value, adjustments (normalizations) generally are needed to produce a clearer picture of likely future income and distributable cash flow. It also allows more of an apples-to-apples line-item comparison. This normalization process usually consists of making three main adjustments to a medical practice's net income (profit and loss) statement.

1. *Nonrecurring items*: Estimates of future distributable cash flow should exclude nonrecurring items. Proceeds from the settlement of litigation, one-time gains/losses from the selling of assets or equipment, and large write-offs that are not expected to reoccur each represent potential nonrecurring items. The impact of nonrecurring events should be removed from the practice's financial statements to produce a clearer picture of likely future income and cash flow.
2. *Perquisites*: The buyer of a medical practice may plan to spend more or less than the current doctor-owner for physician-executive compensation, travel and entertainment expenses, and other perquisites of current management. When determining

future distributable cash flow, income adjustments to the current level of expenditures should be made for these items.

3. *Noncash expenses*: Depreciation expense, amortization expense, and bad-debt expense are all noncash items that impact reported profitability. When determining distributable cash flow, you must analyze the link between noncash expenses and expected cash expenditures.

The annual depreciation expense is a proxy for likely capital expenditures over time. When capital expenditures and depreciation are not similar over time, an adjustment to expected cash flow is necessary. Some practices reduce income through the use of bad-debt expense rather than direct write-offs. Bad-debt expense is a noncash expense that represents an estimate of the dollar volume of write-offs that are likely to occur during a year. If bad-debt expense is understated, practice profitability will be overstated.

18.8.6 Balance Sheet Adjustments

Adjustments also can be made to a practice's balance sheet to remove nonoperating assets and liabilities, and to restate asset and liability value at market rates (rather than cost rates). Assets and liabilities that are unrelated to the core practice being valued should be added to or subtracted from the value, depending on whether they are acquired by the buyer. Examples include the asset value less outstanding debt of a vacant parcel of land, and marketable securities that are not needed to operate the practice. Other nonoperating assets, such as the cash surrender value of officer life insurance, generally are liquidated by the seller and are not part of the business transaction.

18.8.7 Life Insurance as Cash Vehicle

Life insurance is commonly considered the best vehicle to provide the cash when it is needed the most, and there are a number of keys to creating a successful buy/sell agreement:

- It must be decided who will buy the practice from the disabled proprietor or partner, or his/her heirs upon death. It may be the remaining partner(s), the practice entity itself, or, in the case of a sole doctor proprietor, a key physician employee.
- The buy/sell agreement must be stipulated as mandatory. According to the IRS, if the agreement is not mandatory, the value of the practice is not considered fixed. As a result, the IRS might not consider the agreement binding in determining the value of the practice for estate tax purposes.
- The most important key is determining the correct value for the practice or share in question. The IRS will rarely challenge a value for being set too high but will challenge those deemed valued too low.

18.8.8 Buy/Sell Agreement Types

There are also a number of different forms of buy/sell agreements. The following is a quick overview of four different variations.

18.8.8.1 Sole-Proprietor Buy/Sell Agreement

Since a sole medical proprietor does not have a partner, other than a spouse, he/she usually must look elsewhere for a buyer. Therefore, the sole proprietor is likely to turn to either a valued physician employee or a competitor to continue the business. In this case, a life insurance policy is purchased on the life of the proprietor, and the agreement is signed between the current and the future owners providing the guidelines for the future practice transfer. In addition to being the owner of the policy, the future doctor-owner typically names himself/herself beneficiary, as well.

18.8.8.2 Cross-Purchase Buy/Sell Agreement

This type of buy/sell is normally used for any practice with multiple owners, although it is best used for agreements with only two owners. In this arrangement, each owner purchases insurance on each of the others' lives. Again, the owner of each policy names himself/herself beneficiary as well. Upon the death or disability of one partner, the remaining partner(s) is provided the funds to purchase a *pro rata* share of the deceased or disabled individual's practice interest.

18.8.8.3 Entity Purchase Buy/Sell Agreement

This form is used for multiple owners, and/or when the owner(s) of the practice wants to use the assets of the business to fund the insurance policies. In this arrangement, the practice owns the policies on each partner or shareholder and is also listed as the beneficiary of each policy. Upon the death or disability of the physician partner, the business would be able to purchase the shares from the disabled partner or the deceased's heirs.

18.8.8.4 Optional Purchase/Wait-and-See Buy/Sell Agreement

This type of agreement allows either the practice or the individual partner(s) the option of purchasing the deceased or disabled partner's interest in the practice. Normally, if the practice does not initially exercise its option to buy within a set period, the remaining partners would then have a period in which to exercise their option. If they do not buy the outstanding interest, the practice would then be forced to purchase the shares.

18.8.9 Trustee

Often, a trusteed agreement is advisable. It is not unusual to find situations where the practice partners work together smoothly and efficiently. Their spouses, however, are another story. So, in order to remove personalities from the transfer of ownership interests for money, especially at a very stressful point in their lives, it is often a good idea to let a disinterested third party (a trustee) conduct the transfer.

Example

Dr. May has been the sole owner of the Family Physician Group, which includes 6 other physicians and 12 other employees, for over 10 years. He has often thought about who will continue this successful practice. In the past month, he has decided that Dr. Roy is the best candidate for the job. She has also expressed an interest in becoming the successor to Dr. May.

As a result, they have decided to set up a trusteed sole-proprietor buy/sell agreement that would provide for the smooth, mandatory transfer of the practice in the case of the death or disability of Dr. May. Once the practice is correctly valued, Dr. Roy plans to purchase a life insurance policy on the life of Dr. May, which will be owned by a third-party trust, who will also be the beneficiary. Upon the death or disability of Dr. May, the agreement is executed by the trustee, and Dr. Roy becomes sole owner of the Family Physician Group.

18.8.10 A Checklist Approach

The following checklist is submitted for consideration, as this very personal document is created after reviewing the following issues, and more:

- Death of doctor.
- Disability of doctor.
- Retirement of doctor.
- Voluntary or involuntary termination of doctor.
- Number of disability-months required for physician to give up ownership in the practice.
- Age requirements to retire from the group (for example, to qualify for retirement, a physician must be at least 62 years old; otherwise, the withdrawal is considered voluntary).
- In the case of a voluntary withdrawal, agreement specifies how much notice is required.
- In the case of a voluntary withdrawal, agreement specifies whether there will be penalties to the buyout price if the owner forms a competing practice, joins a competing practice, or violates the employment contract.
- In the case of an involuntary withdrawal, agreement specifies how much notice is required.
- Agreement specifies the required vote to admit a new physician into the group.
- Reasonableness of the buyout price of an ownership interest has been reviewed.
- If the buyout price is to be based on an appraised value, the qualifications of the appraiser have been assessed.
- Agreement specifies, based on the current practice environment, whether goodwill should be paid to a departing owner.
- The manner in which the buyout price will be paid has been established and reviewed.
- The tax consequences of the buyout provisions have been reviewed.
- The buyout amount has been calculated for each owner using the current formula in the agreement.
- Each owner has reviewed the calculations.
- All parties agree to the reasonableness of the buyout amounts.

Overheard in the Doctor's Lounge

Dental/Medical Antidefamation Contracts

If you were to walk into my dental office with a toothache, and I told you that before I relieve your pain, you have to agree not to say bad things about me on the Internet, how badly would the tooth have to be hurting to keep you from walking out the door? Well, the article "Toothache Lawsuit May Stifle Medical Gag Orders against Online Rants," by JoNel Aleccia, was posted a few years ago on http://www.msn.com. Patient "[Robert Lee, 42] who had a bad toothache filed a class-action lawsuit against his New York dentist after she required him to sign a contract promising not to trash-talk her online—and then fined him thousands of dollars trying to enforce it."

Aleccia adds: "[Dr. Stacy Makhnevich] was among hundreds of medical professionals nationwide in recent years that refused to care for patients unless they signed antidefamation contracts. In the contracts, the doctors and dentists promised not to evade federal patient privacy protections in exchange for patients' agreeing not to post public comments about them."

THE DENTIST

Other than its obvious ineffectiveness for this particular dentist, what's wrong with this business plan?

First of all, aside from the insult, if a dentist required you to sign a contract forfeiting your right to express your opinion about the quality of care even before being seen, how confident would it make you feel about the doctor's abilities? Then there's Health Insurance Portability and Accountability Act (HIPAA). It's sad that health-care providers would take advantage of vulnerable Americans who don't understand that their right to privacy isn't something that can be withheld—even as part of a twisted "copyright" deal intended to enable a dentist to dodge accountability. It seems to me like the Office of Civil Rights as well as the attorney general should be alerted. How is threatening a patient's privacy in return for direly needed treatment different than extortion?

THE GOTCHA!

Mr. Lee had forgotten the contract until months later, when he allegedly discovered that Dr. Makhnevich had overcharged him by about $4000, allegedly filing an improper insurance and then allegedly refusing to provide him with the documents he needed to file the claim himself. That's when he started posting rants on sites like Yelp and DoctorBase, such as "Avoid at all cost! Scamming their customers!" and "Honestly, how do you live with yourself? Just try being a decent human being." "Within days, Makhnevich demanded that the sites remove the comments and threatened to sue Lee. She also said he was infringing on her copyright provisions and started sending invoices for fines of $100 a day. By October, the total topped $4600, he said."

THE SERVICE

Since the dentist purchased the right to use *Medical Justice Inc.* antidefamation contracts to prevent complaints from unsatisfied customers from being discussed on the Internet, I say she is due a refund. What's more, if she's given any trouble about it, she should get on the Internet and complain—if she didn't forfeit that right as part of the agreement.

THE ADA?

So where did Dr. Stacy Makhnevich learn about Medical Justice Inc.'s ineffective, unethical, and probably illegal antidefamation contract service? Of all places, it may well have been in ADA headquarters. Dr. Jeffrey Segal, MD, JD, the neurosurgeon and founder of Medical Justice Services Inc., which sold providers like Dr. Makhnevich the right to use his company's contracts, was a featured speaker at the American Dental Association's (ADA) annual benefits conference a few years ago. The ADA leadership's decision to invite Dr. Segal to advertise his product at a benefits conference(?) reveals the old-timers' underlying paranoia that makes them prefer silence from members as well as their own dental patients.

From http://vitals.msnbc.msn.com/_news/2011/11/30/9124107-toothache -lawsuit-may-stifle-medical-gag-orders-against-online-rants

18.9 ASSESSMENT

When faced with the prospect of drafting or of signing a restrictive covenant, practice purchase, buy/sell agreement, nondisclosure agreement, etc., consult a health law attorney experienced in contract negotiations and assisted by an experienced medical practice valuation consultant, risk manager, trusted insurance agent, and/or counselor.

18.10 CONCLUSION

The various restrictive covenants discussed in this chapter are reasonable and appropriate protections for the legitimate rights of doctors and physician executives. But, such covenants will lead to bitter conflict if they attempt to restrict beyond what is legitimately protectable.

18.11 COLLABORATE

Discuss this chapter online with others at http://www.medicalexecutivepost.com.

ACKNOWLEDGMENTS

Robert James Cimasi; MHA, ASA, FRICS, MCBA, AVA, CM&AA, CMP™, Health Capital Consultants, LLC, St. Louis, Missouri.

FURTHER READINGS

Babitsky, S and Mangraviti, J: *Legal Mistakes Physicians Make and How to Avoid Them*. SEAK, Inc., Falmouth, MA, 2005.

Fenton, CF: Medical Risk Management Issues. In Marcinko, DE (editor): *Insurance Planning and Risk Management for Physicians*. Jones and Bartlett Publishing, Sudbury, MA, 2006.

Fenton, CF: Sales Contracting for Medical Practice Succession Planning. In Marcinko, D and Hetico, HR (editors): *Comprehensive Financial Planning Strategies for Doctors and Advisors: Best Practices from Leading Consultants and Certified Medical Planners*. Taylor & Francis Group, Productivity Press, Florence, KY, 2015.

LaCava, W: Risks of Medical Practice Non-Compete Agreements. In Marcinko, DE (editor): *Insurance Planning and Risk Management for Physicians*. Jones and Bartlett Publishing, Sudbury, MA, 2006.

Marcinko, DE: Medical Practice as a New Asset Class. In Marcinko, D and Hetico, HR (editors): *Comprehensive Financial Planning Strategies for Doctors and Advisors: Best Practices from Leading Consultants and Certified Medical Planners*. Taylor & Francis Group, Productivity Press, Florence, KY, 2015.

Wilensky, SE and Teityelbaum, J: *Essentials of Health Policy and Law*. Jones and Bartlett Learning, Sudbury, MA, 2014.

Checklist: Reimbursement Issues in Health-Care Valuation	**Yes**	**No**
Checklist main statement:		
Have you considered the contribution of margins from technical component services?	o	o
Have you reviewed the impact of the shift from defined benefits to defined contribution?	o	o
Have you considered the importance of physician supply?	o	o
Have you relied on historic reimbursement data?	o	o
Have you assumed that the federal government reimbursement (Medicare) will always increase?	o	o
Have you looked at state reimbursement (Medicaid) practices?	o	o
Have you considered the payor mix?	o	o
Have you examined incurred but not reported (IBNR) liabilities in capitated contracts?	o	o

Checklist: Regulatory Issues in Health-Care Valuation	**Yes**	**No**
Checklist main statement:		
Have you underestimated the risk of regulatory change, e.g., specialty hospital moratorium?	o	o
Have you assumed the regulatory environment of the health-care industry to remain the same?	o	o
Have you fully assessed the implication of regulations on competition?	o	o
Have you reviewed both federal and state regulations?	o	o
Have you assessed the regulations affecting the subject entity and competitors?	o	o
Have you considered regulatory barriers to entry, e.g., certificate of need?	o	o
Have you assessed the costs of regulatory mandates, e.g., Health Insurance Portability and Accountability Act (HIPAA), Clinical Laboratory Improvement Amendments (CLIA), Occupational Safety and Health Administration (OSHA)?	o	o
Have you taken into account the significant costs associated with the movement to electronic medical records systems?	o	o

Checklist: Typical Preengagement Steps in the Health-Care Business Valuation Process	**Yes**	**No**
Checklist main statement:		
Preengagement:		
Have you determined if there is a conflict of interest before signing the agreement?	o	o
Have you provided the appraiser with your detailed description of the appraisal subject including the specific definition and description of the entity and the specific definition and description of the type and size of the entity?	o	o

Project parameters:		
Have you worked with the appraiser to determine the amount of time required to complete the assignment?	o	o
Has the appraiser developed and discussed with you a list of assumptions and limited conditions that are expected to be part of the report?	o	o
Engagement fees and agreement:		
Has the appraiser developed a budget to estimate the required chargeable hours and fees?	o	o
Has the appraiser submitted a proposal letter and engagement agreement that includes consultant and client responsibilities, a schedule of professional fees, a retainer, and expense requirements?	o	o

Checklist: Typical Steps during the Health-Care Business Valuation Process	**Yes**	**No**
Checklist main statement:		
Has the appraiser given you a detailed work program including an appraisal staff assignment and identified the project milestones?	o	o
Does the general industry research collected include information relative to economic, demographic, industry, competition, health-care industry, and medical specialty trends?	o	o
During the analysis of the data that were gathered, did the appraiser conduct a thorough financial analysis, assessment of risk, and forecasting of future performance?	o	o
Did the appraiser explain the selection of valuation methods depending on factors such as the purpose of the valuation report, the availability of data for each method, and the specific characteristics of the subject entity?	o	o
Did the appraiser communicate the valuation process and provide a discussion draft of the report?	o	o
Did the appraiser complete the engagement within a reasonable time frame once all of the required data were received?	o	o

ABBREVIATED NONDISCLOSURE STATEMENT TEMPLATE

The undersigned acknowledges that Hamilton Family Clinic (HFC) has furnished to the undersigned potential investor ("Investor") certain proprietary data ("Confidential Information") relating to the business affairs and operations of HFC for study and evaluation by Investor for possibly investing in HFC.

It is acknowledged by Investor that the information provided by HFC is confidential; therefore, Investor agrees not to disclose it and not to disclose that any discussions or contracts with HFC have occurred or are intended, other than as provided for in the following paragraph.

It is acknowledged by Investor that information to be furnished is in all respects confidential in nature, other than information which is in the public domain through other means, and that any disclosure or use of same by Investor, except as provided in this agreement, may cause serious harm or damage to HFC, and its owners and officers.

Therefore, Investor agrees that Investor will not use the information furnished for any purpose other than as stated above, and agrees that Investor will not, either directly or indirectly by agent, employee, or representative, disclose this information, either in whole or in part, to any third party; provided, however, that (a) information furnished may be disclosed only to those directors, officers, and employees of Investor and to Investor's advisors or their representatives who need such information for the purpose of evaluating any possible transaction (it being understood that those directors, officers, employees, advisors, and representatives shall be informed by Investor of the confidential nature of such information and shall be directed by Investor to treat such information confidentially), and (b) any disclosure of information may be made to which HFC consents in writing. At the close of negotiations, Investor will return to HFC all records, reports, documents, and memoranda furnished and will not make or retain any copy thereof.

____

Signature and date

19 Operational Risks and Financial Impact of the Health Insurance Portability and Accountability Act

Privacy, Security, and Health Information Technology for Economic and Clinical Health Act Implications

Carol S. Miller

CONTENTS

This chapter will review the changes in the Health Insurance Portability and Accountability Act (HIPAA) and Health Information Technology for Economic and Clinical Health (HITECH) Act as they relate to security and privacy; their impact in today's health-care marketplace; the associated cost for complying with regulations and/or the cost of noncompliance; the risks involved with new mobile technology; and recommendations to assist physicians, medical clinics, and hospitals with understanding and complying with the regulations. It will also provide an overview of HIPAA and the HITECH regulations.

19.1 INTRODUCTION

The health-care system consists of countless individuals who have access to a person's health data, including doctors, nurses, technicians, clerical workers, and administrative staff, as well as third-party personnel involved in health care such as health plans, medical supply companies, billing and coding companies, pharmacies, and researchers. All of these individuals have a need to use systems and devices to access personal health information at different levels and authorities. With the introduction of security and privacy regulations, hospitals have had to expand staff roles and responsibilities and spend dollars on systems and processes to implement, adapt, monitor, and maintain compliance. Whatever one thought initially about the HIPAA, it is clear today that HIPAA has had a vast impact on patients, the health-care industry, and many others and will continue to be a presence and to impact the daily operations and HIPAA-aligned budgets of facilities and providers for many years to come.

Regardless of HIPAA regulations and compliance requirements, health-care organizations, large and small, are susceptible to information breaches, which can negatively impact the privacy and security initiatives that have been set forth in HIPAA. Vulnerabilities are inevitable, and the cost of breaches is growing significantly, with HIPPA fines representing only a fraction of the financial impact. Many of these breaches are caused by human error and/or accidental data or device loss, while other breaches are more insidious and involve organized efforts to implement medical identify theft. Keeping protected health information (PHI) private and secure is a massive task with ever-increasing cost—in time and dollars—and is even greater when there is a failure to adhere to the HIPAA requirements. Successful compliance requires diligence and continuous improvement, especially with the final omnibus HIPAA and HITECH rule released and adopted by the Department of Health and Human Services (HHS) in early 2013.

19.2 HEALTH INSURANCE PORTABILITY AND ACCOUNTABILITY ACT

The original HIPAA was signed into law by President Clinton in 1996 to be an adjunct to health-care reform. The intent was

- To curtail health-care fraud and abuse
- To enforce standards for health information

- To guarantee the security and privacy of health information
- To ensure health insurance portability for employed persons

HIPAA regulations apply to group health plans, health maintenance organizations, physicians, hospitals, pharmacies, and any organization that offers health, dental, and/or insurances. Title I of the HIPAA regulates the availability and breadth of group health plans and certain individual health insurance policies. Title I also limits the restrictions that group health plans can place on benefits for preexisting conditions and requires insurers to issue policies without exclusion to those leaving group health plans with creditable, continuous coverage. Title II of HIPAA defines policies, procedures, and guidelines for maintaining the privacy and security of individually identifiable health information as well as outlines numerous offenses relating to health care and the associate sets of civil and criminal penalties for violations. Title II also creates several programs to control fraud and abuse within the health-care system. The most important aspect included in Title II was the Administrative Simplification rules, which were aimed at increasing the efficiency of the health-care system by creating standards for the use and dissemination of health-care information.

In 2002, HHS published amended recommendations to HIPAA governing standards of privacy of individual identifiable health information. In 2003, the privacy regulations went into effect, which controlled the use and disclosure of PHI. PHI includes the past, present, or future physical or mental condition of an individual and information about payment for health care for that individual, either in an electronic, written, or oral format. Finally, in 2013, the Final Omnibus Rule was released, which included updates to the Security Rule and Breach Notification portions of the HITECH Act that affected business associates, provided added protection of PHI, and included more severe penalties for violation of PHI privacy requirements.

The following paragraphs provide an overview of the requirements and regulations within HIPAA that pertain to the security and privacy. In addition, a more detailed overview is included in the newer regulations from the HITECH Act.

19.2.1 Privacy Regulations

Privacy is a necessary foundation for delivery of high-quality health care—the entire health-care system is built upon the willingness of individuals to share the most intimate details of their lives with their health-care providers, insurers, lawyers, and other entities. At the same time, there is increasing public concern about loss of privacy in general and health privacy in particular. The continued use of interconnected electronic medical records both for the business entity (hospitals, provider offices, clinics, and others) and for personal health records; the evolution of mobile connectivity through social media, iPads, iPhones, texting, and other devices; the movement toward obtaining and storing genetic make-up; and the increasing complexity and interconnectivity of the health system bring the potential for tremendous benefits to individuals, providers of care, and society but also bring new potential for invasions of our privacy—all at an associated cost and risk. The ramifications can be far-reaching. End results can be disastrous to individuals when there is a breach of PHI, such as a loss of employment, loss of insurance coverage, public humiliation, or alienation of family and friends. The cost of information is a significant factor, for many times, firms/employers, insurers, and/or providers know far more than the patient about how PHI will be used. Secondarily, these same individuals often know many details about how PHI may be generated, combined with other databases, or sold to third parties. Even outside firms not affiliated with the health-care system may know where and what is included in databases, can access the data, and can use it for their own personal gain. Any loss of PHI information creates a significant risk to the patient and a potential liability to the hospital.

Under the privacy regulations, even patients face a cost in time and dollars in learning about how their information is used. First, patients face the challenge of trying to understand technical medical terminology and practices. A patient generally will have difficulty understanding medical records, billing codes, and the implications of transferring health information from one party to another. Second, patients may face significant costs in trying to learn and understand the nature of hospital, provider, insurer, or even their employer's privacy policies. With that said, patients still have issues of trying to understand whether the hospitals or providers are really complying with the official policies set in place. Today, PHI must often flow legitimately among multiple entities for purposes of treatment, payment, health-care operations, and other necessary uses. If the information is leaked or stolen, the patient cannot easily tell which provider was the source of the leak or which of those multiple entities inadvertently or directly transferred his/her information. The cost and ineffectiveness of monitoring thus leads to less-than-optimal protection of individually identifiable health information!

Privacy rules will become more critical to prevent unanticipated, inappropriate, or unnecessary uses or disclosures of individually identifiable health information without patient consent. In terms of market failure, it will become more difficult for patients to know how their health-care provider or hospital is using health information about them. Further, it will become more difficult to monitor the subsequent flows of individually identifiable health information, as the number of electronic flows and possible points of leakage increase. Overall, measuring the costs and benefits of health information privacy is difficult.

19.2.2 Security Regulations

With the continued implementation and enforcement of electronic health records, Internet access, intranet availability throughout the hospital and physician complexes, virtual access from home or other locations, and mobile wireless devices (such as cell phones [texting and social media], iPads, and laptops), all of these applications have the potential for security violations and associated vulnerabilities. Each may cause serious harm to hospitals, providers, patients, or information technology (IT) firms managing devices. In addition, patients are being given a front seat to their data, as they store information from multiple sources on their own personal health system. There are associated vulnerabilities with the use of simple passwords, lost portable equipment, unencrypted and unprotected data, and/or inappropriately approved accesses, that result in security violations, from very small to significant. Recently, one of the latest incidents was a breach of data from Anthem Blue Cross and Blue Shield where over 80 million individuals had their personal patient data leaked through cybersecurity invasion techniques. The simple fact is that security is a problem that could have a catastrophic effect on any hospital at any given time if any "guards" or security channels are breached.

The HIPAA security standards are part of the Administrative Simplification provisions, just like the privacy standards. These rules enforce the security of electronic patient health information applicable to cover entities. Security and privacy are closely linked. The privacy protection of any information is heavily dependent on the steps taken for its security.

The HIPAA security standards include the following, which each hospital and facility must adhere to. These standards require that covered entities put in place basic safeguards necessary to protect electronic PHI (ePHI) from "unauthorized access, alteration, deletion, and transmission."

- *Administrative safeguards*—Policies and procedures designed to clearly show how the entity will comply with the act. Risk analyses and training are also included under administrative safeguards.
- *Physical safeguards*—Controlling physical access to protect against inappropriate access to protected data. Examples of this safeguard include a locked location for network servers and shielding screens from unauthorized viewers.
- *Technical safeguards*—Controlling access to computer systems and enabling covered entities to protect communications containing PHI transmitted electronically over open networks from being intercepted by anyone other than the intended recipient. Examples include encryption and the use of secure passwords.
- *Organization safeguards*—Includes access to information, training of staff, and privacy and security officers.

The following list provides examples of typical questions related to security of information stored on either laptops or other media that should be addressed as part of the security requirements. All of these questions relate to additional time and expense in having an assigned individual monitor all aspects of this tracking process.

- Is there an accurate record or log of each piece of equipment referenced at the hospital?
- Do I know how many of the laptops are taken out of the hospital and used at other locations?
- Are all laptops, iPads, and other mobile devices encrypted, and is the employee required to change passwords frequently?
- Do I know if any of the laptops are used by family members?
- Do I know how secure the portable systems are?
- Do I know if they are just password protected or whether other security measures are in place?
- Is every piece of equipment accounted for when an employee terminates employment?
- Do I know who can access PHI from a remote location?
- Is there a defined process for discarding laptops and other devices?
- Do employees know the hospital's reporting process if their laptop is stolen or hacked?
- Is virus and spyware software placed on all computers, and is it updated frequently?
- Are employees provided with information on how to secure their laptops, iPads, or other devices?
- Do employees know what to do when attachments from unknown sources are sent and/or downloaded?
- Is the system backup maintained by every employee, and how often is backup done?
- Do employees know to log off when leaving their desktop, or is there an automatic log-off capability within the system?
- Has the hospital considered single-sign-on and card access?

Today, as in the past, it is important for all hospitals to focus on contingency plans and disaster recovery to prevent any arbitrary loss of patient information. Many hospitals provide routine reviews and system maintenance and updates to combat potential security problems or concerns with regard to confidential patient information. However, inadvertent or even intentional changes to systems can cause serious data problems as the data integrate throughout the hospital IT environment. Security breaches at this level can come from inside or outside of the hospital. They can be malicious or accidental, and they can be related to system function disruption or data degradation. They can relate to potential failures to properly share data and coordinate information. They can also be the cause of major patient clinical errors; physician dissatisfaction; inaccurate record information; duplication of records; and as always, additional cost to the hospital, which must identify the potential breach, develop a solution, and correct the issue at hand.

Direct access to information is probably the biggest security issue. It affects personnel access to the systems they need in their daily jobs and tends to be poorly controlled. Because hospitals need to provide access to information, they are sometimes lax about who has that access. As an example, ask any hospital to not only identify each access user on the system but also identify who uses each specific application. Few hospitals have that capability. Hospitals would need additional resources not only to develop a major computerized index but also for the time and attention to monitor and change users' right to access. Many hospitals routinely request that the business or IT manager provide access for new employees that is similar to what another comparable staff member has—not really addressing the particular "right to know" or determining whether the new employee really needs a particular level of access. Experience within the hospital environment also shows that many of the staff still have the same access to systems that they have had for years, even though they may have changed positions several times. Finally, many staff members have access to confidential patient information, yet few of the hospitals have ever linked this "right of access" to a background check. Access to the hospital system is given to employees to perform a job. In turn, the hospital is widely opening its doors to access to a wide range of financial or confidential information, or even competitive information. Many of these hospitals have employed designated staff to change and delete access rights, or allow read-only access or read/write access; however, vulnerability still can exist. Security is a trade-off between control and flexibility, and there will always be weak points. For those hospitals that have in place comprehensive security review processes, policies and procedures, and a contingency plan, the risk and liability can be limited.

Regardless of the cost, HIPAA security and privacy regulations have changed the hospital environment. The hospital and its IT and security staff need to be proactive. There is simply too much at stake, and there are potentially too many issues where mistakes could cause the hospital a serious system problem or result in a large fine. HIPAA and the responsibility to provide reasonable patient-care risk reduction mandate secure health-care IT operations. To do less simply allows patient-care and health-care delivery outcomes to be exposed to unacceptable levels of unnecessary risk.

19.2.3 Implications of the Health Information Technology for Economic and Clinical Health Act

One of the most important set of changes in privacy standards was brought about in the HITECH Act, which was signed into law as part of the American Recovery and

Reinvestment Act (ARRA) of 2009. The HITECH Act adds notification requirements for health-care-related information and any security breach of unsecured PHI data; implements new data security standards for electronic health records; and expands security and privacy provisions beyond HIPAA. While HIPAA addresses health information security and privacy issues, the HITECH Act extends the HIPAA security and privacy rules to non-HIPAA-covered entities, holding them to the same privacy and security standards as covered entities. For example, under HITECH, health-care providers, pharmacies, and other business associates of a covered entity will now be subject to privacy and security provisions in HIPAA. This extends beyond the health-care provider to include even the vendors of personal health records.

HITECH thus includes provision that are designed to protect patient health information by calling for health-care organizations, their business associates, and service providers to fully disclose breaches, including a description of the incident, when it occurred, what was discovered, what types of information were involved, and what was done to investigate and prevent future incidents. This act will likely force health-care providers, vendors, and caregivers to implement stronger access security to truly protect patient data and avoid multi-million fines similar to those levied against many of the larger facilities for noncompliance. Additionally, HITECH requires all health-care organizations and their business associates, regardless of size, to be audited. Hospitals should be prepared with an internal committee and/or software that can greatly simplify and streamline the task of automating the process of achieving compliance.

The key compliance tasks for covered entities related to the Final Rule are as follows:

- Revise and redistribute notices of privacy practices to patients
- Revise policies and procedures and train workforce on new requirements
- Update breach definition and breach assessment tools to comport with the new "objective" breach standard
- Evaluate all business associate relationships to ensure that business associate agreements are in place as required under the expanded definition of *business associate*
- Revise business associate agreements by September 2014

While the Final Rule contains many provisions that amplify penalties for HIPAA violations, the Office of Civil Rights must first consider four factors that may be mitigating or aggravating, before determining the amount of a penalty—(1) the nature of the violation, (2) the extent of the harm caused, (3) past HIPAA compliance, and (4) the financial condition of the facility or covered entity. Each facility is reviewed and evaluated before determining whether a simple education session is needed or a fine should be imposed.

19.2.4 Summary of Cost Impact to Hospitals

Business and hospital costs are increasing to keep pace with technology. It is estimated that hospitals and health-care providers are likely to spend more than millions of dollars over the next decade to continue to convert records to electronic format and to enable physicians and hospital staff to use wireless handheld smart phones, tablets, or phablet devices, or cloud capabilities to easily access and input "real-time medical information on any given patient." Costs extend to interfacing legacy systems or existing clinical systems with more automated systems that integrate the current privacy and security requirements. The overall intent of electronic records is to readily improve access to patient information, improve the quality of patient care, reduce the number of medical errors, and improve the safety. If this is not accomplished, there is the potential for ineffective, noninterfaced technologies, silo data, and unsuccessful outcome that could result in lawsuits related to malpractice or inadvertently releasing confidential information without permission.

When calculating and understanding cost related to HIPAA, there are several factors to evaluate.

- Type of facility—hospital, clinic, health plan, or clearinghouse
- Size—large health-care system or small provider practice
- Culture—conservative about patient privacy and views HIPAA as an opportunity to improve, or liberal and views HIPAA as another compliance issue
- Environment—high-tech with good security controls in place or low-tech with minimal security controls in place
- Risk tolerance—high risk taker or low risk taker

Within a facility, the budget projected for HIPAA can be divided into three general categories—*labor, expense*, and *capital*. For most facilities, the greatest cost of HIPAA compliance is *labor*, which includes an individual(s) who oversees privacy and/or security, such as a privacy or security officer, and administrative staff who support the multitude of work associated with implementing and reviewing HIPAA compliance. A good 75% fall into the latter category of administrative support, where staff spend time reviewing, revising, and updating or creating new policies; covering organization process changes; hiring new staff and training and reevaluating the follow-up on gap analyses. All these processes are done to ensure that compliance efforts are successful and business continuity plans like backup and recovery facilities are maintained. In addition, the same staff need to inventory how PHI flows out of the facility, say, to business associates, insurers, attorneys, or patients, and these same staff might also be responsible for chain-of-trust agreements. Further, the inventory includes an accounting of all biomedical equipment that processes and stores PHI, especially if it is computerized and connected to the network.

Expenses can be a one-time expense or a recurring cost and include consultants who prepare readiness assessments and implementation plans; lawyers to write new contracts and review policies and procedures and other documentation; vendors who need to test network vulnerabilities and provide disaster planning and recovery; and temporary employees, who may be used to write new policies and procedures. Expenses include such items as collection of confidential trash for shredding; disaster recovery services and/or off-site storage for backup media; printing and mailing costs of notice of practices to patients; privacy screens for computer workstation monitors; and training and awareness items, such as computer-based training (CBT) modules, videotapes, posters, and giveaway items such as mouse pads with security reminders printed on them.

With investments in new technology comes the need to spend *capital*. Because the HIPAA regulations say what has to be done but is technology neutral, a facility may spend little or large amounts of capital depending on its current environment, level of risk, and how HIPAA fits within its strategic plans. As an example, a facility may choose to implement an electronic medical record to improve audit capability and the ability to flag privacy restrictions and disclosures as both a strategic decision and part of its

HIPAA compliance plan. In addition, cost considerations for capital need to also address the following:

- Information system upgrades for processing standard transactions and audit trails, and flags for when patients or health plan members choose to exercise their privacy rights.
- Physical security upgrades to create physical privacy safeguards of patient data, such as electronic "door locks," surveillance equipment, facility remodeling, shredders, and backup generators.
- Secure fax machines or fax servers.
- Network upgrades or enhancements, including intrusion-detection systems, virtual private networks or encryption software, and stronger authentication methods such as tokens, biometrics, digital signature, and public/private key informatics/ infrastructure Public Key Infrastructure (PKI).
- Smart cards—Portable and secure, smart cards are becoming an increasingly popular tool for safeguarding physician security and ensuring the privacy of sensitive electronic information in hospitals. Contact or contactless smart card technologies provide an opportunity for security administrators to implement one badge that serves as workplace identification, a physical security access card, and a strong authentication token for network access.
- Tools for evaluating audit trails.

It is important to remember that lack of adequate security may result in unauthorized access to confidential information, while too much security could hinder health care. Each facility, depending on its requirements, needs to develop a balanced approach and an acceptable risk tolerance.

19.2.5 Cost of HIPAA Breaches

Part of the HITECH Act includes the Breach Notification Rule, which mandates that affected individuals be notified of any breach of their PHI. As of March 2013, HHS has

COST OF BREACH NOTIFICATIONS

- E-mail and First-Class Mail—$3,467,122
- Substitute notices: media notice—$571,200
- Substituted notices: toll-free number—$1,816,379
- Inputted cost to affected individuals who call the toll-free line—$2,042,665
- Notice to media of breach: over 500—$15,420
- Report to HHS: 500 or more—$15,420
- Investigation costs: under 500—$5,277,456
- Investigation costs: 500 or more—$837,500
- Annual report to the secretary: $422,438

From Diaz, L., and Crapo, D., The Cost of a Data Breach: The Health Care Perspective, *Metropolitan Corporate Counsel (MCC)*, November 18, 2013.

investigated over 19,306 cases that have been resolved by requiring changes in privacy practice or by corrective action and 9146 cases where HHS investigation found that HIPAA was followed correctly. In addition, there were 44,118 cases where HHS did not find eligible cause for enforcement, for example, a violation that started before HIPAA started, cases withdrawn by the pursuer, or an activity that does not actually violate the Rules.*

Most of the issues are related to: misuse and disclosure of PHI are lack of protection in place for health information, patients being unable to access their health information, using or disclosing more than the minimum necessary PHI, and a lack of safeguards of ePHI. The most common violators, in order of frequency, were providers, hospitals, outpatient facilities, group plans such as insurance groups, and pharmacies. HHS stated in the preamble to the Omnibus Rule that an estimated breach notification compliance cost would total $14,475,600. A breakdown of those costs is listed below.

Civil monetary penalties for HIPAA-related breaches are now being enforced more vigorously with HITECH and the Omnibus Rule. Penalties have been tiered base on culpability as follows:

- The entity did not know and could not have known of the HIPAA violation: not less than $100 nor more than $50,000 per violation.
- There was reasonable cause for the HIPAA violation: not less than $1000 nor more than $50,000 for each violation.
- The HIPAA violation resulted from willful neglect on the part of the entity but was corrected within 30 days of the date the entity became or should have become aware of the violation: not less than $10,000 nor more than $50,000 per violation.
- The HIPAA violation resulted from willful neglect, and violation was not corrected: not less than $50,000 per violation.

The penalty is capped at $1,500,000 for identical violations during a calendar year. Above and beyond these costs are the legal fees, which can amount to $4–5 million.

Even though HIPAA, the HITECH Act, and the Omnibus Rule do not provide for private cause of action, litigation has continued, and multiple cases have been presented before the courts. Several examples of cases are as follows:

- Affinity Health Plan, Inc., returned a number of photocopiers to leasing agents without erasing PHI from their hard drives.†
- Advocate Health and Hospital Corporation housed four laptops that were not encrypted and were stolen, with more than 4 million individuals being compromised.†
- Anthem Blue Cross and Blue Shield experienced a cyber attack in which over 80 million health-care customers' personal information (not medical data) was hacked.‡
- Women & Infants Hospital of Rhode Island allegedly failed to safeguard patient information. The hospital notified 14,000 of its patients—some 12,000 from Massachusetts—that the hospital had lost 19 unencrypted backup tapes containing

* From HIPAA Wikipedia.

† From Diaz, L., and Crapo, D., The Cost of Data Breach: The Health Care Perspective.

‡ From the *Washington Post*, January 2014.

DATA BREACH RESULTS IN $4.8 MILLION IN HIPAA SETTLEMENTS

Two health-care organizations have agreed to settle charges that they potentially violated the Health Insurance Portability and Accountability Act of 1996 (HIPAA) privacy and security rules by failing to secure thousands of patients' electronic protected health information (ePHI) held on their network. The monetary payments of $4,800,000 are the largest HIPAA settlement to date.

The U.S. Department of Health and Human Services (HHS) Office for Civil Rights (OCR) initiated its investigation of New York and Presbyterian Hospital (NYP) and Columbia University (CU) following their submission of a joint breach report, dated September 27, 2010, regarding the disclosure of the ePHI of 6800 individuals, including patient status, vital signs, medications, and laboratory results.

NYP and CU are separate covered entities that participate in a joint arrangement in which CU faculty members serve as attending physicians at NYP. The entities generally refer to their affiliation as "New York Presbyterian Hospital/Columbia University Medical Center." NYP and CU operate a shared data network and a shared network firewall that is administered by employees of both entities. The shared network links to NYP patient information systems containing ePHI.

The investigation revealed that the breach was caused when a physician employed by CU who developed applications for both NYP and CU attempted to deactivate a personally owned computer server on the network containing NYP patient ePHI. Because of a lack of technical safeguards, deactivation of the server resulted in ePHI being accessible on Internet search engines. The entities learned of the breach after receiving a complaint by an individual who found the ePHI of the individual's deceased partner, a former patient of NYP, on the Internet.

In addition to the impermissible disclosure of ePHI on the Internet, OCR's investigation found that neither NYP nor CU made efforts prior to the breach to assure that the server was secure and that it contained appropriate software protections. Moreover, OCR determined that neither entity had conducted an accurate and thorough risk analysis that identified all systems that access NYP ePHI. As a result, neither entity had developed an adequate risk-management plan that addressed the potential threats and hazards to the security of ePHI. Lastly, NYP failed to implement appropriate policies and procedures for authorizing access to its databases and failed to comply with its own policies on information access management.

NYP has paid OCR a monetary settlement of $3,300,000 and CU $1,500,000, with both entities agreeing to a substantive corrective action plan, which includes undertaking a risk analysis, developing a risk-management plan, revising policies and procedures, training staff, and providing progress reports.

From Hospitals Fined $4.8M for HIPAA Violation, *HIPAA Journal*, May 2014.

social security numbers, dates of birth, and medical information. The settlement was $150,000. The box on the previous page is a case study of the largest data breach at a hospital setting.*

Hospitals today still have to absorb costs for work supporting HIPAA. Several examples include the following:

Privacy or security officer cost—The primary cost associated with this requirement is the cost of a new hire or, if the role is to be handled by an existing employee, the personnel hours for training and developing and updating the policies and procedures, as well as the costs of oversight management, such as coordinating between departments, evaluating procedures, and assuring compliance. The cost is associated with the security or privacy officer salary and staff administrative support.

Internal complaint cost—The privacy regulations require that each hospital have an internal process to allow an individual to file a complaint concerning the covered entity's compliance with privacy policies and procedures. Even though a form response is not required, it will still take around 10–15 minutes to discuss, document, and forward the complaint to the appropriate resource for handling. The most frequent complaints still come from disclosure of more information than is minimally necessary and impermissible disclosure of an individual's PHI, which can be due to curiosity or accidentally obtained.

External complaint cost—External compliance reviews can be conducted when the government feels there may be an issue with a hospital's HIPAA compliance. The hospital must utilize key and administrative staff to review the request, obtain the appropriate documentation, respond to questions from the reviewers, update policies or procedures based on the findings, and provide other support during the review—all at their own cost. Examples include a breach occurring but not being processed, computer equipment that is discarded without PHI data being adequately removed, and not maintaining updates to security controls and patches.

Disclosure tracking and history costs—The privacy regulations require that hospitals and providers produce a record of all disclosures of PHI, for treatment, payment, health-care operations, or disclosures to patients. This task may average around 2 minutes per disclosure as to when, to whom, and purpose of disclosure.

De-identification of Certain Information Costs—Hospitals and providers are required to assess what information needs to be deidentified, such as information related to age, social security number, driver's license numbers, research data, and other information. This requires hospitals to review and modify existing agreements and/or reprogram automated systems to remove key information that needs to be excluded. It is impossible to gauge a time or associated cost for this effort, for it varies by hospital.

Policy and procedure update costs—With HIPAA and HITECH regulations, most hospitals have developed internal policies and procedures; however, many hospitals have let time pass where updates are not occurring on a regular basis. In addition, some hospitals, even though they have policies and procedures, do not reference or enforce them as they should.

* From McCann, E., Hospital Hit with $100K HIPAA Bill, *Healthcare IT News*, November 2014.

Training costs—The privacy regulations provide each hospital with a great deal of flexibility in developing training programs for its staff as well as how often training should be repeated. Most hospitals have established time frames for update sessions, and new employees are required to take HIPAA training classes. On average, a new employee joining a hospital would need around an hour of training time if provided in person; however, most facilities have automated the training through a web training program.

Consent costs—The patients have the right to elect or not elect to have their information disclosed. Patients must be informed about how their PHI will be used and given the opportunity to object to or restrict the use or release of their information. Hospitals still have the right to use and disclose PHI without the patient's consent for purposes of treatment, payment, and health-care operations. This effort requires a minimum amount of time by an administrative person. Examples of patients' rights include the following: (1) HIPAA has limitations on releasing confidential patient information, such as behavioral health or HIV/AIDS status; however, state and federal laws may impose more specific limitations. (2) For minor children, information may be released with the consent of a parent or legal guardian.

Business associate costs—The privacy regulations require a written contract that documents satisfactory assurance that business associates will appropriately safeguard PHI. Hospitals will continue to modify business associate agreements based on changes in regulations or as new associates are added.

Inspection and copying costs—This will continue to be a cost to all hospitals. The degree of inspection and copying of medical records is not expected to change: attorneys and patients, and third-party insurers will continue to request this information. Hospital cost vary based on facility cost for xeroxing and the number of pages to xerox.

Finally, there are also hidden costs that cannot be easily quantified, such as reputational damage, unfavorable media attention, loss of productivity due to individuals being reassigned to support the investigation, potential cost of securing credit monitoring services for affected individuals, outsourcing hotline support, hiring an external investigation expert, and eroding patient and public trust.

19.2.6 New-Wave Technology

To help hospitals and health systems comply with HIPAA regulations, best practices are emerging for securing all electronic communication—cloud, wireless, and texting—of PHI. These new technologies will continually be evolving as hospitals, providers, and patients move to new means of communication. Below is a description of how each is impacted by HIPAA.

19.2.6.1 Cloud Solutions

Cloud solutions are becoming a needed commodity in treating patients today but also present a risk to privacy and security violation. Despite the advantages of cloud computing, organizations are often hesitant to use it because of concerns about security and compliance. Specifically, they fear potential unauthorized access to patient data and the accompanying liability and reputation damage resulting from the need to report HIPAA breaches. While these concerns are understandable, a review of data on HIPAA breaches published by the HHS shows that these concerns are misplaced. In fact, by using a cloud-based service with an appropriate security and compliance infrastructure, a facility can significantly reduce its compliance risk.

Because HIPAA compliance involves stringent privacy and security protections for electronic health information (PHI), many cloud providers are balking at signing new business associate agreements. Most cloud-technology providers, such as *Box* and *Dropbox*, do not include the built-in privacy protections that guarantee HIPAA compliance. Because many cloud storage companies store plaintext data on their servers, PHI is especially vulnerable to breaches and compliance violations.

19.2.6.2 Mobility Solutions

The recent launches of Apple Health and Google Fit have stirred a lot of interest in health application development. It is important that hospitals and providers understand the laws around PHI and HIPAA compliance for any health-care-focused mobile application or software. While not all health-care applications fall under HIPAA rules, those that collect, store, or share personally identifiable health information with covered entities (such as hospitals and providers) must be HIPAA compliant.

For years, hospitals have wanted to bring computers into exam rooms, waiting rooms, and treatment rooms to eliminate hard-to-read patient charts, making sure everyone treating the patient was seeing the same information; assuring that everything was recorded as it occurred; and enabling doctors, nurses, and technicians to stay connected to vital information and services wherever they were throughout the hospital. Many hospitals have adopted computers on wheels (COWs) or tablets, but many of these are hard to use, have a poor touch-screen interface, and do not last long on a battery. iPads seem to be the logical replacement as long as they can comply with HIPAA rules.

HIPAA was written nearly 20 years ago, before mobile health applications were ever envisioned. Because of this, some areas of the law make it hard to determine which applications must be HIPAA compliant and which are exempt. Considering the numerous ways security breaches can occur with a mobile device, it is no wonder that HHS is very leery about how PHI is handled on smartphones, wearables, and portable devices.

If the applications are going to send or share health data to a hospital, doctor, or other covered entity, it *must* be HIPAA compliant. Adhering to the privacy and security rules of HIPAA is essential, especially considering the dangers that come with handling protected health data on a device. Examples include the following:

- Phones, tablets, and wearables can be easily stolen and lost, meaning PHI could be compromised.
- Social media and e-mail are easily accessible by the device, making it easy for users to post information that breaches HIPAA privacy laws.
- Push notifications and other user communications can violate HIPAA laws if they contain PHI.
- Users may intentionally or unintentionally share personally identifiable information, even if the application's intended use doesn't account for it.
- Not all users take advantage of the password-protected screen-lock feature, making data visible and accessible to anyone who comes in contact with the device.
- Devices like the iPhone do not include physical keyboards, so users are more likely to use basic passwords that are not as safe as complex options.

This PHI can include everything from medical records and images to scheduled appointment dates. Regardless of the device, it is important to take all the steps possible to comply with HIPAA guidelines.

19.2.6.3 Texting

Text (or SMS) messaging has become nearly ubiquitous on mobile devices. According to one survey, approximately 72% of mobile phone users send text messages. Clinical care is not immune from the trend, and in fact, physicians appear to be embracing texting on par with the general population. Another survey found that 73% of physicians text other physicians about work.*

Texting can offer providers numerous advantages for clinical care. It may be the fastest and most efficient means of sending information in a given situation, especially with factors such as background noise, spotty wireless network coverage, lack of access to a desktop or laptop, and a flood of e-mails clogging in-boxes. Further, texting is device neutral—it will work on personal or provider-supplied devices of all shapes and sizes. Because of these advantages, physicians may utilize texting to communicate clinical information, whether authorized to do so or not.

All forms of communication involve some level of risk. Text messaging merely represents a different set of risks that, like with other communication technologies, needs to be managed appropriately to ensure both privacy and security of the information exchanged.

Text messages may reside on a mobile device indefinitely, where the information can be exposed to unauthorized third parties due to theft, loss, or recycling of the device. Text messages often can be accessed without any level of authentication, meaning that anyone who has access to the mobile phone may have access to all text messages on the device without the need to enter a password.

Texts also are generally not subject to central monitoring by the IT department. Although text messages communicated wirelessly are usually encrypted by the carrier, interception and decryption of such messages can be done with inexpensive equipment and freely available software (although a substantial level of sophistication is needed). If text messages are used to make decisions about patient care, then they may be subject to the rights of access and amendment. There is a risk of noncompliance with the privacy rule if the covered entity cannot provide patients with access to or amend such text messages.

According to 2012 data from CTIA–The Wireless Association, U.S. citizens alone exchange nearly 200 billion text messages every month. So it's not surprising that an increasing number of clinicians are using text messaging to exchange clinical information, along with a wide range of other modes—smartphones, pagers, computerized physician order entry, e-mails, etc. Electronic communication is certainly faster, can be more efficient, enhances clinical collaboration, and enables clinicians to focus on patient care. But with these benefits comes an increased risk of security breaches.†

Unfortunately, vendor hype about the HIPAA is causing many hospitals and health systems to implement stop-gap measures that address part—but not all—of a problem. To identify all vulnerabilities, health-care leaders need to consider not only text messaging but all mechanisms by which PHI in electronic form is transmitted—as well as the security of those mechanisms.

---

* From Green, A., HIPAA Compliance for Clinician Texting, *Journal of AHIMA*, April 2012.

† From Hardiman, M., and Edwards, T., Clarifying the Confusion about HIPAA—Compliant Texting, *American Health Information Management Association (AHIMA)*, May 2013.

Mobile device-to-mobile device SMS text messages are generally not secure, because they lack encryption. The sender does not know with certainty that his/her message is indeed received by the intended recipient. In addition, the telecommunications vendor/wireless carrier may store the text messages. Recent HHS guidance indicates that text messaging, as a means of communicating PHI, can be permissible under HIPAA depending in large part on the adequacy of the controls used. A hospital or provider may be approved for texting after performing a risk analysis or implementing a third-party messaging solution that incorporates measures to establish a secure communication platform that will allow texting on approved mobile devices.

A study reported in *Computer world* in May 2013 by the Ponemon Institute with 577 health-care and IT professionals in facilities that ranged from fewer than 100 beds to over 500 beds stated that 51% of the respondents felt that HIPAA compliance requirements can be a barrier to providing effective patient care. Specifically, HIPAA reduces time available for patient care (85% of the respondents), makes access to electronic patient information difficult (79% of the respondents), and restricts the use of electronic mobile communications (56% of the respondents). The study stated that "respondents agreed that the deficient communications tools currently in use decrease productivity and limit the time doctors have to spend with patients." They also stated that "they recognized the value of implementing smartphones, text messaging and other modern forms of communications, but cited overly restrictive security policies as a primary reason why these technologies were not used." Clinicians in the survey stated that only 45% of each workday is spent with patients; the remaining 55% is spent communicating and collaborating with other clinicians and using the electronic medical record and other clinical IT systems.

Several other statements made were the following:

- Because of the need for security, hospitals and other health-care organizations continue to use older, outdated technology such as pagers, e-mail, and facsimile machines. The use of older technology can also delay patient discharges—now taking an average of 102 minutes.
- The Ponemon Institute estimated that the lengthy discharge process costs the U.S. hospital industry more than $3.189 billion a year in lost revenue, with another $5 billion lost through decreased doctor productivity and use of outdated technology. Secure text messaging could cut discharge time by 50 minutes.*

Several suggestions offered for these preferred mobile devices are as follows: (1) ensure encryption and access to individuals who need to have access; (2) use secure texting applications; and (3) even consider alerting employees with warnings before they send an e-mail or share files that let them know they are liable for the information sent.

19.2.7 Risks

A HIPAA risk analysis is the foundation for safeguarding ePHI and leads to an overall risk-management strategy. The HIPAA rules do not mandate a one-size-fits-all approach to risk analysis. Methods will vary dependent on the size, complexity, and capabilities of the

* From Mearian, L., HIPAA Rules, Outdate Tech Cost U.S. Hospitals $3.38 B a Year, *Computer World*, May 2013.

organization; however, all affected organizations, regardless of size, are expected to conduct an appropriate risk analysis.

The following questions adapted from National Institutes of Standards and Technology (NIST) Special Publication (SP) 800-665 are examples an organization could consider as part of a risk analysis.

- Has the organization identified the ePHI within the organization? This includes ePHI that the organization creates, receives, maintains, or transmits.
- What are the external/third-party sources of ePHI? For example, do vendors or consultants create, receive, maintain, or transmit ePHI?
- What are the human, natural, and environmental threats to information systems that contain ePHI?
- What are the potential threats and vulnerabilities to ePHI? This would include determining the likelihood of threat occurrence, the level of risk, and the mitigation or correction strategy.
- Are the current security measures in place sufficient?

As with any device, the key risks associated with any mobile device, including laptops, are the risk of loss, theft, or improper disposal of devices containing unsecured PHI. Another risk is that individuals other than the intended recipient may gain access to PHI stored in any mobile device or communication via social media or texting. In addition, PHI could be intercepted by unauthorized persons or telecommunications vendors or wireless carriers.

Based on the hospital's risk analysis, the hospital must develop a risk-management plan that addresses its needs and vulnerabilities and manages its anticipated risks to a reasonable and appropriate level. Some examples of safeguards that may form part of a risk-management plan are as follows:

- Banning the texting of ePHI entirely, or limiting the texting of identifiers, diagnosis, and other information
- Requiring the deletion of texts (policies also need to address circumstances where HIPAA requires that ePHI in texts be included in the medical record to address individual patient rights)
- Passcode protection
- Encryption
- Secure disposal of devices
- Registration of devices, including personally owned devices
- Use of third-party secure messaging solutions
- Staff training requirements

Risk management is a process. To ensure continued compliance with security standards, organizations must conduct ongoing monitoring of their information security risk to determine whether it is being effectively managed by existing safeguards or whether those safeguards need to be strengthened. Changes in the regulatory environment, such as enforcement actions or the issuance of additional guidance, also need to be monitored. Senior leadership of the hospitals and provider practices need to ensure that the risk analysis is updated regularly as technology and health-care delivery change.

19.2.8 Research

HIPAA has hampered health research and patients' ability to participate in such research mainly by its effects on the patient informed-consent and authorization process, and the internal review board (IRB) process. These effects include deterring patients from participating in research; fostering research findings with limited relevance to patients; hampering personalized medicine research dependent on biospecimens and stored clinical data; fostering rejection or abandonment of clinical studies; and hampering and increasing the time and cost of large, clinical studies.

There are numerous explicit and implicit costs due to the original Privacy Rule. These costs include increased cost of staff time and additional resources needed to implement and carry out long and more labor-intensive studies due to increased paperwork and/or the inability to reuse clinical data and specimens. The substantially increased expenses tied to complying with HIPAA have made health research less efficient and affordable, closing some research avenues and ultimately impeding progress in delivery of better care of patients.

In addition, the HIPAA Privacy Rules have imposed barriers to researchers, including selection bias, inefficiency, procedural burdens, increased costs, and abandoned studies. Translating these barriers into a patient perspective, the selection bias driven by HIPAA creates challenges to finding treatments applicable to all types of patients, thereby perpetuating health disparities. HIPAA delays comparative effectiveness studies, which can identify the most effective therapies more rapidly for patients. The consent process makes the patient experience more complicated, time-consuming, and unpredictable.

Under HHS's modified interpretation in the Final Rule, an authorization for the use or disclosure of PHI for research purposes does not have to be study specific. Rather, in order to satisfy the requirement that an authorization include a description of each purpose of the requested use or disclosure, an authorization for uses and disclosures of PHI for future research purposes must describe those purposes in a manner such that it would be reasonable for the individual to expect that his/her PHI could be used or disclosed for such future research. The Final Rule gives covered entities, researchers, and IRBs flexibility to determine how to adequately describe the purpose of future purpose research, the information to be used or disclosed for the future research, and the recipients of the PHI for the future research. In addition, HHS specifically noted that a description of the PHI to be used for the future research may include information collected beyond the time of the original study. Finally, HHS stated that covered entities and researchers may rely on IRB-approved consent obtained prior to the effective date of the Final Rule that reasonably informs individuals about future research, as long as the informed consent is combined with a HIPAA-compliant authorization. HHS may issue additional guidance with respect to revocations of authorizations for future research uses.

In addition, there is no question that the resources required to process, analyze, and manage petabytes of genomic information represent a huge burden for even the largest academic research facility or health-care institution. That burden becomes even greater when one factors in the need to handle these data in compliance with an alphabet soup of regulatory regimes, one of which is HIPAA data privacy laws. In this context, the use of cloud-based solutions to manage, analyze, store, and share data can provide some relief. Computer and storage resources are instantly available on demand. There is no need to lease brick-and-mortar facilities, purchase equipment, or hire staff to maintain them. However, HITECH states that it protects "individually identifiable health information," which the rule calls "protected health information," or "PHI." Opinions differ as to whether a human genome, stripped of identifiers such as name or social security number, constitutes PHI. Whether these data constitute PHI depends on whether there are sufficient publicly available reference data sets to create a "reasonable basis to believe" that a genome can be associated with an identified individual. Recent publications suggest that if these data are not currently classified as PHI, they will be soon. As a consequence, organizations that handle genomic data are well advised to implement systems that treat a whole genome as PHI, even if public reference data sets are not yet common enough to make it PHI today.

19.2.9 Recommendations

HIPAA compliance can be time-consuming and costly. There are ways to achieve compliance by being cognizant of the requirements, educating the staff, and adhering to defined policies and procedures. Even though the health-care industry is investing in electronic health records, mobile medicine, cloud solutions, and other information-sharing opportunities, the hospital industry still has little understanding of the business and clinical repercussions in terms of data security HIPAA compliance and patient safety. To be compliant, the health-care industry does need to invest time and human capital to achieve HIPAA compliance; if not, they will ultimately pay a cost from violating standards.

The final HIPAA omnibus ruling emphasizes securing the risk-management process, rather than the technologies used to manage risk. So, for hospitals and health systems, safeguarding communication of ePHI is part of an overall risk-management strategy. Ideally, this involves forming a security committee that spans the entire organization; the committee should include representatives from IT, operations, the medical staff and nursing, as well as legal counsel. It also may be appropriate to hire an external security firm, depending on the security expertise of the committee members. Below are six steps to achieve HIPAA compliance.

19.2.9.1 Step 1: Complete a Risk Assessment

A risk assessment equips your facility with an accurate blueprint of where you stand with regard to HIPAA compliance so you can make wise decisions about next steps and the risk level that's acceptable to you. A risk assessment also reveals steps you can take toward compliance, which may be as simple as changing your easy-to-recognize password. This analysis should break down the types of technology used for electronic communication (that generate, store, maintain, or transmit ePHI) within the entire hospital or health systems as well as the transmission routes for all ePHI. These can be devices that are not part of the network, such as a freestanding portable x-ray machine, or those devices that are connected. To ensure HIPAA compliance, ePHI transmitted through all communication channels (phone, text, e-mail, etc.) must be "minimally necessary," which means it includes only the PHI necessary for that clinical communication. This layer of complexity, which is common in clinical communication processes, underscores the need for a comprehensive security assessment.

An often ignored or underutilized document that can help you understand the risks of a medical device that maintains or transmits ePHI is the Manufacturer Disclosure Statement for Medical Device Security. This form, developed by the Health Information and Management Systems (HIMSS) Medical Device Security Group, is designed to be completed by the device manufacturer and provide the reader with device-specific elements of the information needed to start the risk assessment of the covered medical device.

Not all deficiencies need to be addressed immediately. What you need to develop from this risk assessment is a plan and a timeline.

19.2.9.2 Step 2: Collaborate with Stakeholders

Involving decision makers is essential for successful and lasting alterations to privacy and security policies, since a buy-in is more likely when people have an opportunity to contribute opinions and ideas. Giving a voice to people across different departments also safeguards against inadequate or unrealistic policies, especially those affecting patient care. Regardless of whether it is the IT department, nurses, physicians, technicians, or others, each department provides valuable input to choosing the right device for your organization and revealing all the risks that can exist with the data being shared by these devices.

Choosing medical devices that meet HIPAA standards is not the responsibility of just one department. Bringing all departments together enables better decisions—sooner—that will result in HIPAA compliance for the long term. It also brings an "accountability factor" into play. If patient records are compromised through a breach, departments are less likely to point fingers when all have been consulted regarding security and privacy precautions.

19.2.9.3 Step 3: Craft Policies That Reflect What You Want to Accomplish, and Train Staff

This is perhaps the most critical step in ensuring HIPAA security and compliance, especially because a substantial portion of reported HIPAA security breaches are due in part to insufficient training. When discussing policies related to HIPAA compliance, they must be system-wide, not department specific. This effort is a joint effort across multiple hospital departments that are different and unique from each other. What policy might be necessary for one department may not be necessary for another, depending on their patient activity and ability to view other individuals' records. Collaboratively with all the departments, the hospital or hospital system can develop a comprehensive hospital-wide policy that will meet everyone's needs.

The hospital should develop a risk-management strategy that's specific to the needs and vulnerabilities of the organization. This strategy should manage the risk of an information breach to a reasonable level. Of course, HIPAA does not specifically define "reasonable," but the risk-management strategy should include policies and procedures that ensure the security of data during transmission, routing, and storage. For example, it may be appropriate to implement two-factor authentication, which requires anyone logging into an ePHI platform, or opening a message that may contain ePHI, to provide two means of identification. Whatever the strategy, health-care organizations should develop specific safeguards for administrative, physical, and technical teams.

When crafting hospital security and privacy policies, it's important to consider *easy to address issues* specifications, such as encryption, versus *required* specifications, meaning those requiring appropriate assessment and safeguards, and mandatory implementations as stated in the HIPAA Security Rule, respectively. *Easy to address*, however, does not mean *ignorable*. Each item to address must be evaluated as to whether the policy applies to your hospital and/or whether the policy may be determined not to be necessary to reduce your risk. Don't impose impossibly strict self-regulation when your privacy policies are adequate at a lower level. If there is a privacy breach, HIPAA officials may judge your institution based on your own policies if they're stricter than federal regulations require.

19.2.9.4 Step 4: Review Purchases of IT and Medical Equipment from a Risk-Management Perspective

When making capital purchasing decisions, it's important to consider factors like purchase price and total cost of ownership (cost to operate over time, total revenue generated, maintenance costs, parts procurement, etc.), but it's also crucial that you consider security standards.

Ask yourself the following questions:

- Are the security features that you need already built into the product?
- What antivirus product should be used?
- How should the device be connected to your network?
- Does the device need to be retrofitted after it's installed to make sure it's HIPAA compliant?
- How much will the retrofit cost?
- Is the software up to date, or already outdated, making the device harder to secure?

19.2.9.5 Step 5: Develop a Culture of Accountability

The staff need to be encouraged to report problems and/or be held accountable to HIPAA compliance. If there is a breach, accountability means learning how to improve the next time around, not point fingers. With multimillion-dollar fines and patient data vulnerabilities at stake, you can't afford not to do so. The ultimate goal is to minimize the number of mistakes by preplanning and collaborating ahead of time and not repeating the same mistake again.

19.2.9.6 Step 6: Monitor Risk on an Ongoing Basis

As technology and health-care delivery change, it is necessary to conduct ongoing monitoring of ePHI risks to ensure continued compliance with security standards. The committee or persons responsible for ensuring HIPAA compliance should provide health-care leaders with regular trend reports on ePHI security at the organization. This insight is critical in supporting the ongoing assessment of security needs in a hospital or health system and can prompt changes to the policies and procedures as they become necessary.

In an increasingly complex health-care environment, assessing the security of ePHI and creating and implementing policy for security across all forms of electronic communications—rather than focusing on any one mode of communication in isolation—needs to be a key focus for hospitals and health systems. Following these steps will help any health-care organization to avoid and mitigate the risk of financial and other repercussions caused by preventable information security breaches.

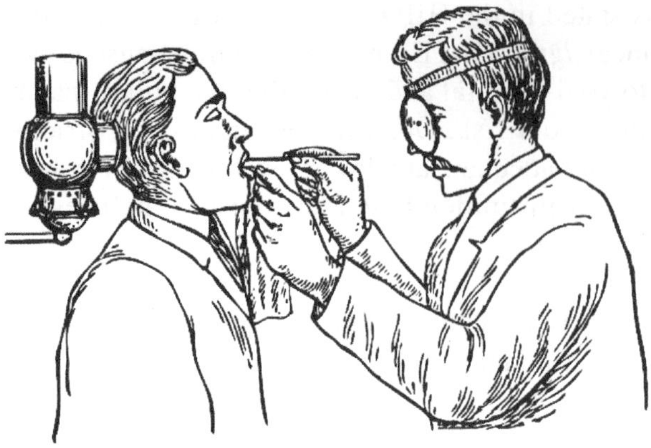

19.3 CONCLUSION

With the implementation of the HITECH regulations, a new era is expected that will increase the number of HIPAA audits that will include business associates. The best advice is to implement HIPAA compliance efforts that include risk assessments, updating privacy and security policies and procedures, security incident planning, and workforce training. Breaches will continue to occur, but hospitals and providers need to do a better job of protecting PHI and security monitoring to prevent future breach incidents and potential theft of data. As an example, HHS, in January of 2013, stated that there were over 274 reported breach incidents due to theft—the top breach cause, accounting for 52% of incidents.

The future holds new and emerging technology that requires special consideration as it relates to HIPAA. Social media in itself has exploded in usage and sharing of information and probably possesses the greatest challenge to patient privacy. How does the government, hospitals, providers, insurers, or any other health-care entity monitor and curtail the exchange of PHI? Mobile devices and unencrypted laptops also remain a challenge to health-care privacy and security. Technology is constantly changing. The various modalities used in sharing and connecting health-care data and the multiple entities that handle the data will continue to pose challenges in the future. The whole process may require new thinking on how the future generation of data sharing will be able to protect health information.

Regardless of the critics of HIPAA and the barriers applied to the new mobile technology, HIPAA is here to stay and will grow stronger and more influential throughout the forthcoming years. HIPAA compliance is an ongoing process, which will only continue to change as the environment adapts to medical advances, government regulations, and technological developments. Despite our focus on costs, we believe that it is paramount for privacy and security directors, health information managers, and all other medical professionals to always keep in mind that HIPAA was drafted to better the privacy and care of patients. Health care is about saving and improving lives, oftentimes regardless of what the cost will be.

Prevention is still the best medicine for reducing the risk of information breach and ensuring HIPAA compliance. The human-error aspect of breaches is solvable only through awareness and education. Executive supervision and active participation are key and absolute necessities to the entire security and privacy requirement. With procedures and processes in place, hospitals will continue to improve and fine-tune its operations, documentation, and reporting, thereby decreasing the possibility of fines and penalties, saving staff time, and reducing costs attributed to supporting the requirements.

19.4 COLLABORATE

Discuss this chapter online with others at http://www.MedicalExecutivePost.com.

ACKNOWLEDGMENT

To Pati Trites, PhD, MPA, CHBC, CPC, of Compliance Resources, LLC, Waterloo, Indiana.

BIBLIOGRAPHY

Bowen, R, "Privacy and HIPAA: What Executives Need to Know Now," *Health IT & CIO Review*, April 2013.

Carmell, H and Bushee, M, "HIPAA Compliance: 5 Key Considerations for Hospitals and Other Larger Providers," *Health IT & CIO Review*, April 2013.

Crouch, S, "Ensuring Patient Privacy in Cyberspace," *Hospitals and Health Networks*, September 2013.

Currier, B, "HIPAA Compliance: What Has Changed and How Will It Impact Healthcare Providers," *Health IT & CIO Review*, November 2012.

Daily Briefing, "Achieving Compliance under the HIPAA Final Rule," April 2013.

Diaz, L and Crapo, D, "The Cost of a Data Breach: The Health Care Perspective," November 2013.

Green, A, "HIPAA Compliance for Decision Texting," *Journal of AHIMA*, April 2012.

Gruman, G, "The iPad Revolution is Coming to a Hospital Near You," January 2013.

Hardiman, M and Edwards, T, "Clarifying the Confusion About HIPAA–Compliant Texting," *American Health Information Management Association (AHIMA)*, May 2013.

Health Information Technology for Economic and Clinical Health Act: http://www.hitech.gov.

Health Insurance Portability and Accountability Act: http://www.hipaa.gov and HIPAA Wikipedia.

Healthcare: HIPAA and HITECH Compliance: http://www.duosecurity.com/solutions/healthcare.

HHS Press Release, "Data Breach Results in 4.8M in HIPAA Settlements," May 2014.

"HIPAA Violation and Data Breach Results in $4,8M Fine," *HIPAA Journal*, May 2014.

McCann, E, "Hospitals Fined $4.8M for HIPAA Violation," *Healthcare IT News*, May 2014.

McCann, E, "Hospital Hit with $100K HIPAA Bill," *Healthcare IT News*, November 2014.

McNeal, M, "What New HIPAA Regulations Mean for BYOD in Hospitals," October 2013.

Mearian, L, "HIPAA Rules, Outdate Tech Cost U.S. Hospitals $8.3B a Year," *ComputerWorld*, May 2013.

O'Neil, L, "Best Practices for Building and Maintaining HIPAA-Compliant Cloud Applications," *Health Management Technology*, July 2012.

Patlak, M, Smith, A, Cox, K, Shah, P, and Young, R, "The Costs of HIPAA," *Int. J. Business Info Systems*, 2012.

Reber, E, "Five Steps to Achieving HIPAA Compliance," *Int. J. Business Info Systems*, April 2012.

Solove, D, "HIPAA Turns 10: Analyzing the Past, Present and Future Impact," *Journal of AHIMA*, 84(4):22–28, 2013.

The Washington Post, Article on Anthem Blue Cross and Blue Shield Loss of Data, January 2014.

Van Dyke, D, "How Much Could a HIPAA Breach Cost You?": http://www.Bridgellc.com, September 2014.

Walsh, T, "What Will HIPAA Cost? And HIPAA Privacy and Proposed Security Standards: A Tandem Approach to Compliance," *Advanced Healthcare Networks*, 2001.

Weeng, J, "HIPAA Compliance: What Every Developer Should Know," *Information Week*, July 2014.

20 How to Conduct a Health-Care Environment Electronic Risk Assessment

Mitigations for the Digital Health Era

Shahid N. Shah

CONTENTS

In health care, keeping patient records and other sensitive data private is of utmost importance. A flaw in an application or system could lead to unauthorized data access or loss, a serious event that can turn fatal. By performing periodic security assessments of the system and mitigating its risks and flaws, it's possible for the medical practice, clinic, or health-care entity to improve safety and meet various compliance requirements such as those found in the Health Insurance Portability and Accountability Act (HIPAA).

20.1 INTRODUCTION

The following steps show how a systematic and well-defined process can be implemented to understand the environment, identify risks, perform mitigation, and carry out continuous monitoring. There are many tools, such as Netspective's Opsfolio,* that help with the full cybersecurity life cycle.

20.2 PERFORM A SECURITY ENVIRONMENT SURVEY

Scan the client environment for relevant information technology (IT) assets, their connection points and configuration, and compliance requirements.

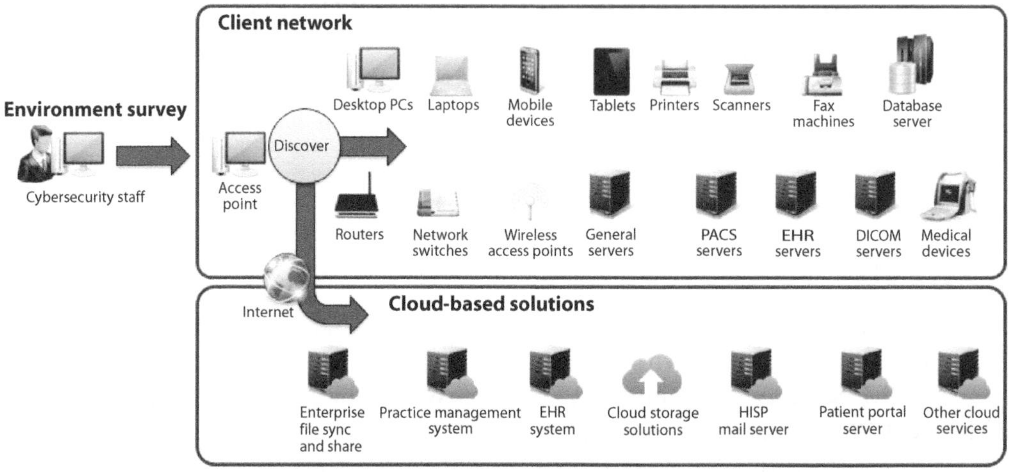

Note: Picture Archive Communication System (PACS), Digital Imaging and Communication Medicine (DICOM), Health Information Systems Program (HISP)

20.2.1 Security Environment Assessment Work Flow

1. Identify IT assets such as servers, databases, network devices, printers, mobile devices, and medical devices.
2. Identify connection points such as the Internet, interpartner private networks, and wireless LAN access points.
3. Gather information about IT assets, connection points, etc. with inventory management tools.
4. Identify detailed information about existing asset configurations and existing connection point configurations.
5. Identify compliance requirements and related policies and procedures.
6. Create an environment assessment report by organizing information gathered in steps 1 through 5.

After the security environment survey is completed, a detailed risk analysis will give an idea of how secure the environment is.

---

* http://www.opsfol.io enables health-care organizations to redefine strategic business goals, streamline internal processes, and leverage the latest technology to create cost-effective solutions that focus on improving patient care and developing customer intimacy while maintaining security, privacy, HIPAA, and related regulatory compliance mandates.

20.3 RISK ANALYSIS

The risk analysis step includes information gathering, security assessment, risk analysis, and testing steps. This assessment should be performed from, within, and outside the network.

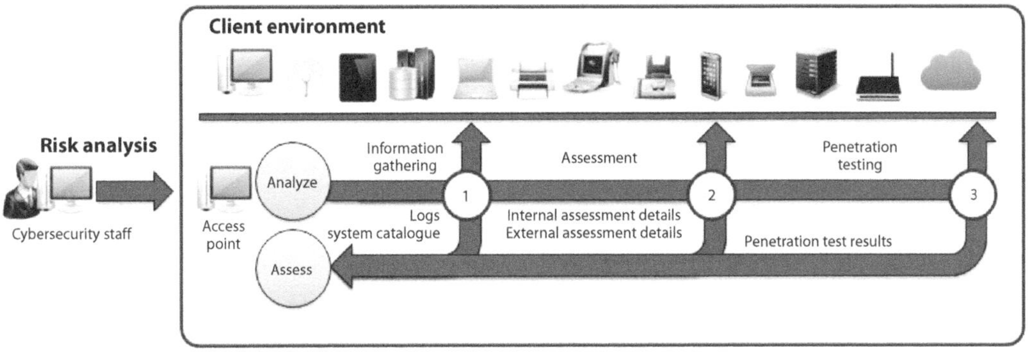

20.3.1 Risk Analysis Work Flow

1. Information gathering
   - Inventory management tools should be used to gather logs and other information.
   - Log aggregation tools can compile log data from all assets and connection points.
   - Vulnerability test tools should be used to scan for security weaknesses.
2. Internal penetration tests
   - Use tests to simulate attacks originating within the environment (preferably with an authenticated user).
   - Make internal intrusion attempts to assess the security environment within the corporate firewall.
3. External penetration tests
   - Use tests to simulate attacks originating from outside the IT environment (preferably with an anonymous user).
   - Make external intrusion attempts to assess the security environment outside the corporate firewall.

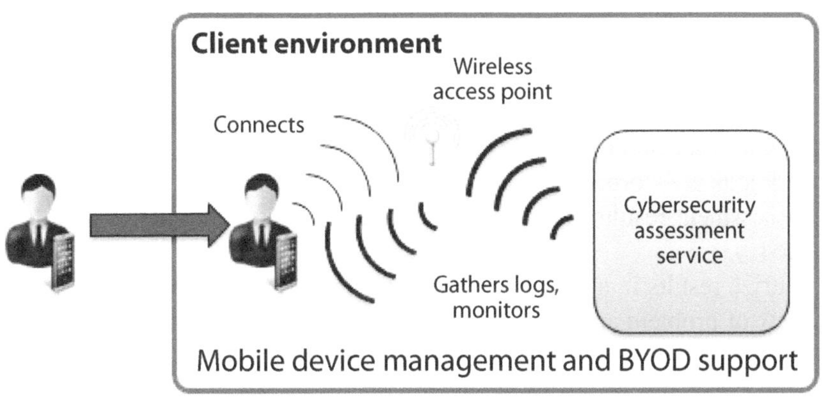

4. Mobile devices connected to the network to enable Bring Your Own Device (BYOD) usage need to be monitored with mobile device management (MDM) tools.
5. Check all connected devices for data encryption.
6. Check all BYOD device passwords against current policies.
7. Perform a gap analysis to compare compliance requirements with existing company policies and procedures.
8. Generate a report, including penetration test results and the security process analysis.

The next step, a detailed risk assessment, analyzes all data and test results gathered so far.

20.4 SECURITY RISK ASSESSMENT

Gather, summarize, assess, and present log data used in the risk analysis phase. Create a detailed report of the risk assessment tasks performed and vulnerabilities.

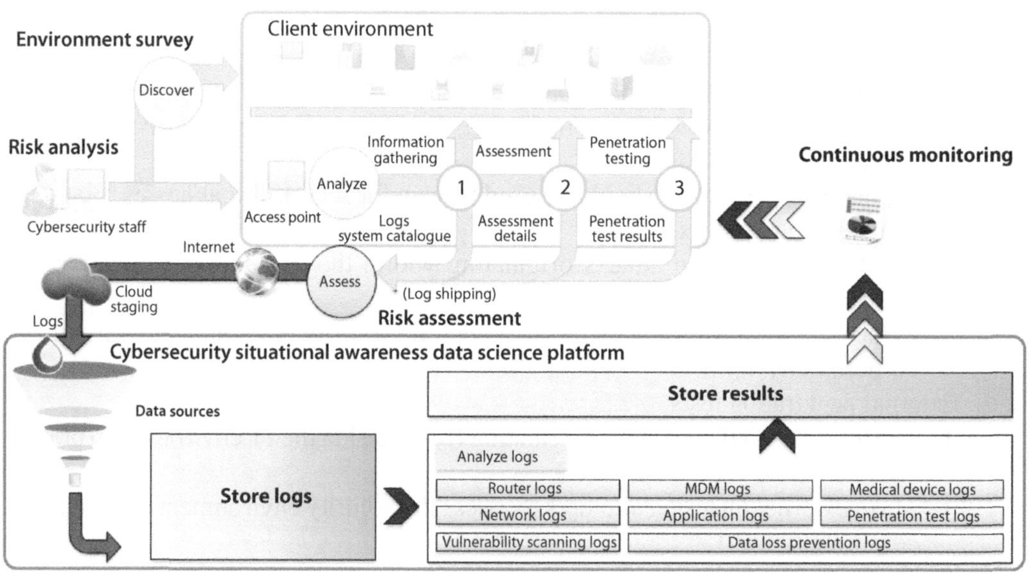

20.4.1 Security Risk Assessment Work Flow

1. Detailed log data and results of penetration tests and security analysis are provided.
2. Security logs are stored in a secure cloud environment.
3. Risk assessment results (security threat levels and vulnerability impact levels) are provided.
4. Summarize results in a cybersecurity resiliency scorecard (below) for an itemized overview of problem areas.

		Score on a scale of 0–10
Presence of virus scan software		9
Virus scan updated		6
Open port(s) accessible to external environments		5
Network share security		3
Password policy adherence		9
Security policy adherence		8
Privilege escalation		4
Cybersecurity resiliency score		6.29

Score and security are directly proportional

In the final step of the assessment process, security risks should be mitigated after they are identified and measured.

20.5 RISK REMEDIATION AND ONGOING MONITORING

After the risk assessment is complete, corrective measures need to be implemented and documented.

20.5.1 Continuous Monitoring

After all four steps in the assessment are complete, the environment needs to be monitored to track changes and to identify and prevent newly introduced risks. Netspective Opsfolio* is an example of a tool that can continue to look for ongoing security threats by collecting log data and monitoring changes in the client environment.

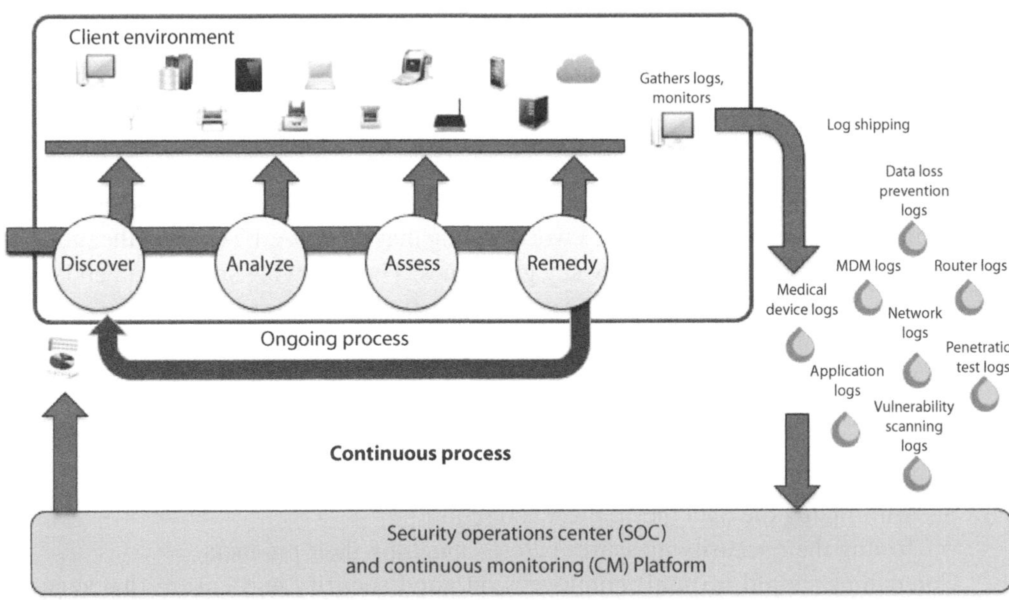

20.6 SAMPLE RISK ASSESSMENT: SMALL PHYSICIAN'S OFFICE

This section provides an example of a cybersecurity assessment process in action. The following graphic describes end users and IT assets that are part of a small practice of a doctor and her medical staff.

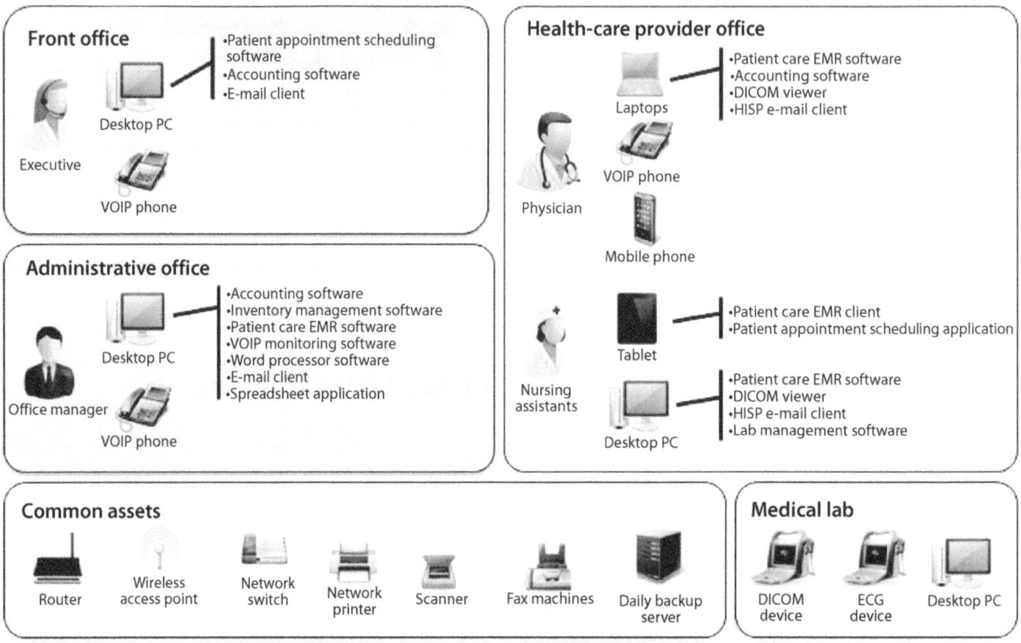

Note: Voice Over Internet Telephony (VOIP).

20.7 SPECIAL CONSIDERATIONS FOR MEDICAL DEVICES

In 2013, the Food and Drug Administration (FDA) issued its first cybersecurity safety communication, followed in 2014 by final guidance. It struck a reasonable balance between new regulations (almost none) and guidance (in the form of nonbinding recommendations).

In 2015, the Federal Trade Commission (FTC) released a staff report entitled *Internet of Things: Privacy & Security in a Connected World*, in which it recommended that Internet of Things (IoT)–style devices, which of course include medical and clinical devices, need to maintain a good security posture. It's worth noting that the FDA, FTC, and other government regulators are centering on a few key guidelines. The following six recommendations come directly from the FTC report:

1. Companies should build security into their devices at the outset, rather than as an afterthought. As part of the security by design process, companies should consider the following:
   - Conducting a privacy or security risk assessment
   - Minimizing the data they collect and retain
   - Testing their security measures before launching their products
2. Companies should train all employees on good security and ensure that security issues are addressed at the appropriate level of responsibility within the organization.

3. Companies should retain service providers that are capable of maintaining reasonable security and should provide reasonable oversight for these service providers.
4. When companies identify significant risks within their systems, they should implement a defense-in-depth approach, in which they consider implementing security measures at several levels.
5. Companies should consider implementing reasonable access control measures to limit the ability of an unauthorized person to access a consumer's device or data, or even the consumer's network.
6. Companies should continue to monitor products throughout the life cycle and, to the extent feasible, patch known vulnerabilities.

The FTC report and FDA guidelines are remarkably consistent. When thinking of cybersecurity and data privacy, engineers tend to think about authentication, authorization, and encryption. Those are the relatively easy topics. For safety-critical devices, however, things are much more difficult and need to encompass a larger surface of questions, including but not limited to the following:

- *Asset inventory*: Is the device discoverable, and can it associate itself with standard IT inventory systems so that revision management, software updates, and monitoring can be automated?
- *Cyber insurance*: Does the device have enough security documentation to allow it to be insured by standard cyber insurance riders?
- *Patching*: How is the firmware, operating system (OS), or application going to be patched by IT staff within hospitals (or the home for remote devices)?
- *Internal threats*: Has the device been designed to circumvent insider (hospital staff, network participants, etc.) threats?
- *External threats*: Has the device been designed to lock down the device from external threats?
- *Embedded OS security*: Is the device sufficiently hardened at the OS level, such that no extraneous software components, which increase the attack surface, are present?
- *Firmware and hardware security*: Are the firmware and hardware components sourced from reputable suppliers and free of state-sponsored spying?
- *Application security*: Is the Microsoft Security Development Lifecycle (SDL) or similar software security assurance process integrated into the engineering process?
- *Network security*: Have all network protocols not in use by the device been turned off so that they are not broadcasting?
- *Data privacy*: What data segmentation, logging, and auditing is being done to ensure appropriate data privacy?
- *HIPAA compliance*: Have proper steps been followed to ensure HIPAA compliance?
- *FISMA compliance*: If you're selling to the federal government, have proper steps, such as the use of Federal Information Processing Standard (FIPS)–certified encryption, been followed to ensure Federal Information Security Management Act (FISMA) compliance?
- *Data loss prevention (DLP)*: Is there monitoring in place to ensure that data leakage outside of the device doesn't occur?

- *Vulnerabilities*: Have common vulnerabilities such as the Open Web Application Security Project (OWASP) Top 10 been reviewed?
- *Data sharing*: Are proper data-sharing agreements in place to allow sharing of data across devices and networks?
- *Password management*: Are passwords hard-coded into the device or made configurable?
- *Configuration protection*: Are configuration files properly checksummed and protected against malicious changes?

20.8 ASSESSMENT

It is vital to perform a security assessment on a health-care practice to understand the environment, identify risks, and perform risk mitigation. A one-time security assessment with risk mitigation is not sufficient. This is a continuous process that needs to be performed religiously to maintain a secure and compliant practice.

20.9 CONCLUSION

This chapter illustrates how to conduct a health-care environment risk assessment for a medical practice or clinic, in order to mitigate or even eliminate risk to secure electronically protected health information (ePHI). The process is not perfect, however, due to the fluid nature of modern cybersecurity risks.

20.10 COLLABORATE

Discuss this chapter online with others at http://www.medicalexecutivepost.com.

21 Topical *A* through *M* List of Emerging Medical Practice 2.0 Risks
The Too Numerous to Count Syndrome

David Edward Marcinko, Charles F. Fenton III, and Hope Rachel Hetico

CONTENTS

Defensive medicine and risk management were often synonymous terms. However, limiting medical risk management concerns to these customary issues is completely misplaced in modernity, for the medical practitioner and his/her financial advisor, attorney, health-care information technology (HIT), and/or risk management consultant.

21.1 INTRODUCTION

In today's medicolegal environment, the physician faces risks from many directions, almost *ad naseum* or *too numerous to count.* And so, here is an alphabetized list, *A* through *M*, of some modern perils and emerging risks that may defy formal definition, chapter inclusion, or even classification, but are nevertheless important considerations.

21.2 -A-

21.2.1 Abusive Treatment or Services

According to the *Dictionary of Health Insurance and Managed Care*, health-care abuse is the activity where someone overuses or misuses services. And the Center for Medicare and Medicaid Services (CMS) states that, "although some of the practices may be initially considered to be abusive, rather than fraudulent activities, they may evolve into fraud." In the case of health-care abuse, this may occur when a physician sees the patient for treatment more times than deemed medically appropriate. If there are reported issues or actions from other sources, such as the National Practitioner Data Bank (NPDB) or a medical board, a health insurance program can take that opportunity to review health-care providers' activities. Most insurance or managed care participation agreements allow for this type of scrutiny.

21.2.2 Accountable Care Organizations

Since their four-page introduction in the PPACA of 2010, accountable care organizations (ACOs) have been implemented in both the federal and commercial health-care markets, with 32 pioneer ACOs selected (on December 19, 2011), 116 federal applications accepted (on April 10, 2012 and July 9, 2012), and at least 160 or more commercial ACOs in existence by 2014. Federal ACO contracts are established between an ACO and CMS, and are regulated under the CMS *Medicare Shared Savings Program* (MSSP) *Final Rule*, published November 2, 2011. ACOs participating in the MSSP are accountable for the *health outcomes*, represented by 33 quality metrics, and *Medicare beneficiary expenditures* of a prospectively assigned population of Medicare beneficiaries. If a federal ACO achieves *Medicare beneficiary expenditures* below a *CMS established benchmark* (and meets quality targets), they are eligible to receive a portion of the achieved *Medicare beneficiary expenditure* savings in the form of a *shared savings payment*.

Yet, by January 2016, three ACOs dropped out of Medicare's Pioneer program, which was designed to test the payment and delivery model with a small group of elite providers deemed best prepared to handle the operational demands and financial risks. The Franciscan Alliance, Genesys PHO, and Renaissance Health Network exited the program, which is now in its third year. A few months earlier, Sharp HealthCare, San Diego, announced its decision to pull out after determining that "the model was financially detrimental," despite the ACO's performance managing quality and health-care use. Medicare's ACO programs so far have produced inconsistent results, some of which policy experts and ACO executives have blamed on how Medicare calculates how much ACOs potentially saved the program. In December 2014, CMS announced that the initiatives saved Medicare $817 million through 2013. Dozens of participants shared $445 million of that amount, but three quarters of ACOs saw nothing after failing to do sufficiently well against the financial benchmarks.

Commercial ACO contracts, on the other hand, are not *limited* by any specific legislation, only by the contract between the ACO and a commercial payer. In addition to *shared savings models*, Commercial ACOs may incentivize *lower costs* and *improved patient outcomes* through reimbursement models that share risk between the payer and the providers, i.e., *pay for performance compensation* arrangements and/or *partial to full capitation*. Although commercial ACOs experience a greater degree of flexibility in their structure and reimbursement, the principles for success for both federal ACOs and commercial ACOs are similar.*

21.2.3 Adverse Events

Aggregated experience from the *Doctors Company* and other malpractice insurers has shown that adverse medical events tend to fall into three categories.

21.2.3.1 Medical and/or System Error

Error is defined by the National Quality Forum Consensus report titled *Standardizing a Patient Safety Taxonomy* as "the failure to perform a task satisfactorily against customary standards and the failure cannot be attributed to causes beyond the patient or provider." When the investigation (including a sentinel event root cause analysis) is complete and the cause is determined to be medical and/or system error, a disclosure meeting should take place with the patient or family.

21.2.3.2 Known Risk/Complication or Unforeseeable Event

The key factor in this category is preventability. Disclosure communications following unpreventable complications or unforeseeable events need to be forthright, open, and compassionate, though they differ qualitatively from apologies after preventable errors.

1. Review the known facts surrounding the adverse outcome.
2. Determine if the event was preventable.
3. Review your process of informed consent to determine if the known risk or complication was discussed.
4. Proceed to the disclosure meeting with the patient or family. Focus on discussing the cause(s) of the known risk or complication. Review the informed consent if appropriate.

21.2.3.3 Unexplained Change in Patient Status or New Diagnosis of Late-Stage Disease

1. The main challenge in communicating after a Category C event is the avoidance of a premature conclusion that a severe and surprising outcome must be due to a negligent error. It is especially important in these circumstances to limit the information conveyed to the confirmed details and to provide ongoing updates as new information becomes available. These cases are particularly vulnerable to retraction and correction cycles that render all subsequent communications with the patient and family questionable.
2. Conduct an internal review of the medical records to determine exactly what happened and to determine if the status change was preventable or if the new diagnosis could have or should have been made earlier.
3. If appropriate, initiate an external expert review. Peer reviews of the medical care with the outcome blinded can lend unique insight into these events.
4. If a sentinel event occurred, a root cause analysis is appropriate.

* From Melanie Evans, *Modern Healthcare*, September 25, 2014.

5. Proceed to the disclosure meeting. Review the findings of your medical record review and investigation. Explain the implications of the change in the patient's health status and how this will affect his or her subsequent disease management. Discuss the prognosis and management of the newly diagnosed late-stage disease.

21.2.4 Antitrust Risks

- *Monopolistic* risks are reduced when more than a few networks or contracts are available in the local area for excluded providers to join.
- Fee schedule MCO contracts, *per se*, are not generally considered price fixing, provided the providers have not conspired with one another to set those prices. Moreover, network pricing schedule should not spill over into the non-network patients.
- Individual providers may be excluded from a network if there is a rational reason to do so. It is much more difficult to exclude a *class* of providers than it is to exclude an *individual* provider.
- A *safety zone* can be created if networks or other contractual plans require a substantial amount of financial risk-sharing among plan participants, since Stark II laws have been relaxed. Such zones have been created by the *Department of Justice (DOJ)* and *Federal Trade Commission (FTC)* in recent policy statements.
- The FTC and DOJ are not likely to challenge an exclusive provider IPA that includes no more than 20–25% of the doctors within the panel who share financial risk. Such panels are likely to fall within a *Safe Harbor.*
- *Tying arrangements* (e.g., the requirement to buy one item/service in order to buy another item/service) are suspect if not reasonably justified. For example, a patient should not be required to obtain a brace prescription from a specific provider in order to purchase the device from a laboratory that the doctor owns.
- *Nonexclusive* provider panels will not usually be challenged if no more than 30% of the providers are included (another Safe Harbor provision).
- Physician networks are often analyzed according to *four criteria*: (1) anticompetitive effects, (2) relevant local markets, (3) procompetitive effects, and (4) collateral agreements.

Further antitrust considerations consist of analyzing *market power.* This consists of two factors: (1) geographic power and (2) product power.

Geographic power is difficult to define in today's environment. In the past, the geography that was analyzed when medical practices merged was the immediate neighborhood. Currently, the geographical area could consist of an entire metropolitan area. In the past, individual patients would often seek a physician whose office was close to work or home. Now they seek a physician based on inclusion in a health plan. Now, health plans choose physicians based on needs within an entire metropolitan area.

Product power relates to the specific service being performed. There are two products in today's environment: (1) primary care and (2) specialty care. Since there are so many primary care physicians in practice, it would be difficult for all but the largest group to acquire product power.

It is easier for specialists to develop product power. However, certain specialists may never be able to obtain product power. For example, foot care is provided by many types of physicians. Primary care physicians, emergency physicians, chiropractors, physical therapists, orthopedic surgeons, nurse practitioners, and podiatrists all provide foot care. Therefore, it would be difficult even for a large group of podiatrists to obtain significant product power.

21.2.5 Apology Programs

To deal with the aftermath of medical errors, an increasing number of providers are encouraging injured patients to participate in *medical apology programs*. The idea, proponents say, is for patients to meet with facility representatives to learn what happened and why. It gives the patient a chance to ask questions, and it gives providers a chance to apologize, and as appropriate, offer compensation. These programs are promoted as humanitarian, and, at least in terms of providing an emotional outlet for patients, they are.

The evidence also suggests that they are about something else: money. Every aspect of how they operate—from who risk managers involve to what those involved are told to say—suggests that a key goal is to dissuade patients from seeking compensation by creating an emotional connection with them. The data establish that it works, too. A 2010 study found that at one major facility, apology programs resulted in fewer injured patients making claims and, among those that did, they accepted a fraction of the amount in settlement compared to patients who made claims before the program was instituted. For minor injuries, no real harm is done by this; but the outcome can be cataclysmic for seriously injured patients who accept an apology in lieu of compensation.

Doug Wojcieszak, owner of the advocacy group *Sorry Works* (http://sorryworkssite.bondwaresite.com), often receives requests to teach doctors how to communicate after a problem. He became interested in the topic when his older brother died at age 39 from a medical error. While losing his brother was awful, the experience was compounded by a total lack of communication and accountability afterward.

Curiously, when an attorney suspects that he/she has committed legal malpractice, he/she must disclose it to the client and recommend that the client seek outside counsel to get objective legal advice on how to proceed. By contrast, when a doctor suspects that he/she has committed medical malpractice, at many facilities he/she is expected to employ a set of protocols that discourage the injured patient from considering the need for compensation. Yet, while an attorney could be disbarred for this sort of behavior, medical apology programs widely receive praise.*

21.2.6 Artificial Intelligence

Machines beat humans at chess. Machines can pilot airplanes to land at O'Hare airport in Chicago or on the planet Mars. There is now a machine that beats the best of us at Jeopardy. Many predict that an artificial intelligent (AI) medical clinician is 10 years away. And few will use a biological doctor in 25 years. Then, the *singularity!* So, if you think *ROBO-MDs* won't impact patients and the industry… think again!

---

* From Gabriel H. Teninbaum JD: Suffolk University Law School-Chapman Law Review Research Paper, 11–30.

21.3 -B-

21.3.1 Billing Company Risks

Particular attention should be paid to issues of appropriate diagnosis codes, CPT, DRG, and MS-DRG coding, individual Medicare Part A and B claims (including documentation guidelines for evaluation and management services), and the use of patient discharge codes. The billing company should also institute a policy that all rejected claims pertaining to diagnosis and procedure codes be reviewed by the coder or the coding department. This should facilitate a reduction in similar errors. Among the risk areas that some billing companies who provide coding services should address are

- Internal coding practices
- *Assumption* coding
- Up-coding and down-coding
- Alteration of medical records and documentation
- Coding without proper documentation of all physician services
- Billing for services provided by unqualified or unlicensed clinical personnel
- Availability of all necessary documentations at the time of coding
- Employment of sanctioned individuals

21.3.2 Biological and Chemical Attacks

Title X of the USA PATRIOT Act contains several calls for strengthening the public health system. Section 1013(a)(4) calls for "enhanced resources for public health officials to respond to potential bioterrorism attacks." Section 1013(a)(6) calls for "greater resources to increase the capacity of hospitals and local healthcare workers to respond to public health threats." Prior to September 11, 2001, the capacity of health-care entities to respond to biological and chemical attacks by terrorists was quite limited. Strictly speaking, however, health-care organizational preparedness plans are not as directly encumbered by the USA PATRIOT ACT, or by the Department of Homeland Security's (DHS's) Chemicals of Concern (COC) List, or the various steps of its Section 550 Program as some other industries. Nevertheless, health-care organizations may have their sources of contaminants, such as *mercury, dioxin*: *DEHP* (2-ethylhexyl), *volatile organic compounds*, and *glutaraldehyde*. For some time now, the Joint Commission (formerly the Joint Commission on Accreditation of Healthcare Organizations) has also required hospitals to have a disaster preparedness plan mimicking the USA PATRIOT Act (Kenneth A. Powers, Media Relations Manager, TJC, personal communication).

After September 11, 2001, *disaster preparedness* evolved into something that could more accurately be described as *emergency preparedness*. Experience in New York and Virginia has shown that there will be spillover outside the immediate geographic areas affected by a terrorist attack, which will affect suburban and rural hospitals. Thus, the emphasis in emergency preparedness is on the coordination and integration of organizations throughout the local system. Hospitals and health-care entities therefore need to revise existing plans for disaster preparedness to reflect the realities of potential terrorist threats. Mitigation against risk is essential to safeguard the financial position of an entity. Medical practices and health-care entities can mitigate risks by developing an emergency preparedness plan.

The entity should start by identifying possible disaster situations, such as earthquakes and biological or chemical attacks that could affect the facility. Next, the entity should identify the potential damages that could occur to structures, utilities, computer technology, and supplies. After that, the entity should use resources currently available to safeguard assets, and then budget to acquire any additional materials or alterations required to secure the facility. Practices can take several steps to mitigate even in the absence of significant funding:

- First, establish links with *first responders* such as local law enforcement, fire departments, state and local government, other health-care organizations, emergency medical services, and local public health departments.
- Second, establish training programs to educate staff on how to deal with chemical and biological threats.
- Third, make changes in their information technology (IT) to facilitate disease surveillance that might give warning that an attack has occurred. IT may be useful in identifying the occurrence syndromes such as headache or fevers that might not be noticed individually but in the aggregate would signal that a biological or chemical agent had been released.
- Fourth, acquire access to staff and equipment to respond to biological and chemical attack through resource sharing arrangements in lieu of outright purchases.

In addition to preparedness for an attack within its catchment area, a health-care organization must be prepared for an attack on its own facility or office. They should assess the vulnerability of the heating, ventilation, and air conditioning (HVAC) systems to biological or chemical attack. The positioning of the air intake vents is especially important because intakes on roofs are fairly secure as compared to intakes on ground level. One way to increase security is to restrict access to the facility. Some facilities are using biometric screening to restrict access to their facilities. Biometric screening identifies people based on measurements of some body part such as a fingerprint, handprint, or retina. The advantage of this approach is that there are no problems with forgotten badges, and biometric features cannot be shared or lost like cards with personal identification numbers (PINs). In preparing for a possible attack, health-care entities should also examine the federal, state, and local laws that might affect their response to a biological or chemical attack. Unfortunately, there is no central source of legislation, and an extensive search of many sources might be required to determine the legal constraints.

21.3.3 Blogging Doctors

According to http://www.npr.org, there are more than 120,000 health-care forums on the Internet with opinions ranging from pharmaceuticals, to sexual dysfunction, to acne. The same goes for commercial doctor blogs that promote lotions, balms and potions, diets and vitamins, minerals, herbs, drinks and elixirs, or various other ingest-ants, digest-ants, or pharmaceuticals, etc. And to other doctors, the blogging craze is a new novelty where there are no rules, protocols, standards, or precise figures on how many medical doctor or related physician blogs are out there. Unfortunately, too many recount gory ER scenes, or pictorially illustrate horrific medical conditions or serious and traumatic injuries. Of course, others simply are medical practice websites, or those that entice patients into more lucrative plastic surgery or concierge medical practices. Some are from self-serving/credible plaintiff-seeking attorneys wishing to assist patients.

Not all physician blogs are geared toward practice information, marketing, or medical sensationalism. In fact, just the opposite seems to be the case in extremely candid blogs, like "Ranting Docs," "White Coat Rants," "Grunt Docs," "Cancer Doc," "The Happy Hospitalist," "Mom MD," "Cross-Over Health," "Angry Docs," and "M.D.O.D.," which bills itself as "Random Thoughts from a Few Cantankerous American Physicians" (link: http://www.thehappyhospitalist.blogspot.com). According to some of these, they are more like personal journals, or public diaries, where doctors vent about reimbursement rates, difficult cases, medical mistakes, declining medical prestige and control, and/or what a "bummer" it is to have so many patients die, not pay, or who are indigent or noncompliant. We call these the *disgruntled doctor sites*. Some even talk about their own patients, coding issues, or various doctor–patient shenanigans.

But, according to psychiatrist and blogger Dr. Deborah Peel and others, the problem with blogging about patients is the danger that one will be able to identify themselves—the doctor—or that others who know them will be able to identify them. Her affiliation, *Patient Privacy Rights*, rightly worries that patients might tracked back to the individual and adversely affect their employment, health insurance, or other aspects of life (link: http://www.patientprivacyrights.org). And, according to Dr. Jay S. Grife, MA, Esq., it is certainly true that if a doctor violates a patient's privacy, there could be legal consequences. Under the Health Insurance Portability and Accountability Act (HIPAA), physicians could face fines or even jail time. In some states, patients can file a civil lawsuit if they believe a doctor has violated their privacy. Still, Internet privacy issues are an evolving gray area where even if something is not wrong if may still be morally and ethically questionable (personal communication).

Our colleague Robert Wachter, MD, author of the blog called "Wachter's World," says it's important for doctors to be able to share cases as long as they change the facts substantially. On the other hand, this leading expert on patient safety alternately suggests, "You might say we as doctors should never be talking about experiences with our patients online or in books or in articles." But, he says that "patients shouldn't take all the information on blogs at face value. Taken for what they are—unedited opinions, and in some cases entertainment—blogs can give readers some useful insight into the good, the bad and the ugly of the medical profession" (link: http://www.the-hospitalist.org/blogs). Well, fair enough! But, doctors unhappy with their current medical career choice, or its modern evolution, should probably consider counseling or even career change guidance, reeducation, and reengineering. It is very inappropriate to vent career frustrations in a public venue. It's far better for the blog to be private and/or by invitation only, if at all (personal communication).

We believe that a hybrid mash-up of both views can be wholly appropriate or grossly inappropriate in some cases. Of course the devil is in the details, linguistics and semantics aside. Nevertheless, what is not addressed in electronic physician *mea culpas* are the professional liability risks and concerns that are evolving in this quasi-professional, quasi-lay, communication forum. For example, we have seen medical mistakes, and liability admissions of all sorts, freely and glibly presented. In fact,

> Some physicians find that the act of liability blogging is a professional confession that is useful in moving past their malpractice mistakes. And, it is also a useful way to

begin a commitment to a better professional life of caring in the future. It helps eliminate the toxic residue and angst of professional liability and guilt. Moreover, as they are unburdened of past acts of omission or commission, doctors should remember to also forgive those who have wronged them. This helps greatly with the process and brings additional peace. (Dr. D.E. Marcinko, MBA, pers. comm.)

However, although some may say that this electronic confession is good for the soul, it may not be good for your professional liability carrier, or you, when plaintiff's attorneys release a legion of IT-focused interns, or automated bots, searching online for your self-admissions and scouring for your self-incriminations. Of course, a direct connection to a specific patient may still not be made and no HIPAA violation is involved. But, a vivid imagination is not needed to envision this type of blind medical malpractice discovery deposition query even now.

Q: "Doctor Smith, I noted all the medical errors admitted on your blog. What other mistakes did you make in the care and treatment of my client?"

And so, the question of plausible deniability, or culpability, is easily raised. If you must journalize your thoughts for sanity or stress release, do it in print. And, don't tell anyone about it so the diary won't be subpoenaed. Then tear it up and throw it away. Remember, with risk management, "It is all about credibility." Don't trash yours! These thoughts may be especially important if you covet a medical career as a researcher, editor, educator, medical expert, or something other than a working-class or employed physician.

21.3.4 Bullies

Every workplace has *microaggressors* or bullies that exhibit disruptive behavior. But, when the workplace is a hospital, it's not just an employee problem. In one reported case, the worker felt threatened: his superior came at him "with clenched fists, piercing eyes, beet-red face, popping veins, and screaming and swearing." He thought he was about to be hit. Instead, his angry coworker stormed out of the room. But, it wasn't just any room: it was in a hospital, adjacent to a surgical area. The screamer was a cardiac surgeon, and the threatened employee was a perfusionist, a person who operates a heart/lung machine during open heart surgery. In 2008, the Indiana Supreme Court ruling in *Raess v. Doescherupheld* was a $325,000 settlement for the perfusionist, who said he was traumatized.*

Overheard in the Doctor's Lounge

Fighting Physician Burnout

Lisa Chu, MD, is a physician, life coach, sound healer, musician, body-worker, and artist, based in Half Moon Bay, California. She is the creator of *The Music within Us*. She inspires, educates, and empowers adults to live more creatively, and more courageously.

---

* From Kim Painter: When doctors are bullies, patient safety may suffer. *USA Today*. April 20, 2013.

She just launched her new offering, *Live Your Medicine*, for physicians facing burnout. Lisa is considered an evolutionary leader being called to create a new definition of medicine for our world.

Ann Miller, RN, MHA
http://www.TheMusicWithinUs.com

21.3.5 Business Practice Litigation Risks

A recent Federal Record (FR) report stated that 25% of all suits filed in *Federal District Court* relate to a growing field of law loosely called *business practices litigation.* That percentage is only likely to grow in the coming years. Business practices litigation encompasses a wide variety of issues, but they mostly resolve around the relationship between a business and its employees and customers. The issues include, for example, racial and sexual discrimination, sexual harassment, wrongful termination, and violations of the *Americans with Disabilities Act.* These claims are not confined to big corporations but can affect the sole proprietor physician.

For example, a Georgia physician recently paid $5000 in settlement of an employment claim. Apparently, the physician would have won the claim, but only after paying over $20,000.00 in legal fees. That $5000.00 settlement was not paid by the malpractice insurance carrier, but was paid by the individual physician himself.

21.4 -C-

21.4.1 Captive Insurance Companies

Medical practices face multiple risks in their daily operations including loss of a medical license or professional certification, legal defense reimbursement, medical/Medicare collections risk, HIPAA violations, and reputational risk. Small-to-medium-sized practices can benefit from risk-management tools that can help them handle such risks more effectively and reduce their overall insurance costs. To that end, the practice may want to consider the establishment of a captive insurance company (CIC) to protect themselves from risks not typically covered by traditional insurance companies.

Captive insurance planning is a strategy for physicians to manage risk through the purchase of a property-casualty insurance policy. Premiums paid by the practice to a properly structured CIC should be tax-deductible to the practice under section 162(a) of the IRS code just like their workers' compensation or malpractice coverage. When the practice forms a CIC, it receives premium income tax-free up to $1,200,000 per year, per captive. Profits that come out of the CIC turn out as a distribution from a C-corp. as qualifying dividends or long-term capital gains, which are currently 15%. Furthermore, the CIC may retain surplus from underwriting profits within reserve accounts, free from income tax. Profits that accumulate within the CIC can be used as a tax-deductible sinking fund in order to save money on malpractice premiums by shifting to a high deductible policy and/or insuring that deductible through the CIC.

There are no hard-and-fast rules regarding the minimum amount of gross revenue from a practice or the minimum amount of insurance premiums paid by a practice before considering the establishment of a CIC. The establishment of a CIC creates immense planning opportunities for physicians because of the flexible ownership of the CIC. The CIC is set up as a C-Corp and someone or some entity owns the shares of the C-Corp. While it's important to keep in mind that the primary business purpose of the CIC is for risk management, some potential financial planning opportunities include the following, according to Guy P. Jones, CFP (personal communication):

- *Wealth accumulation/surplus retirement income*: Physicians own the CIC outside the practice for surplus dollars in retirement.
- *Asset protection planning*: Most physicians have the CIC owned inside an asset protection trust to potentially shield pre-tax dollars and assets from judgment creditors or litigation.
- *Estate planning/wealth transfer*: Physicians who don't need access to this money may be interested in having the CIC owned outside of their estate to also bypass gift and estate taxes with each premium payment.
- *Practice-owner benefits*: By the CIC not being an employee benefit plan, it is not subject to the nondiscrimination rules of ERISA and therefore only benefits the owners of the practice.
- *Nonmandatory participation for practice doctors*: Doctors at smaller levels can join together to create a CIC for economies of scale.

21.4.2 Career Selection Risks

Even as doctors enter a medical field with more paying patients under the Affordable Care Act and unprecedented numbers of job opportunities, 25% of *newly trained physicians* would still choose another field if they could, according to one analysis. More than 60% of doctors-in-training who were in the final year of their medical residency last year received at least 50 job solicitations during their training, according to a survey by physician staffing firm *MerrittHawkins*. Another 46% received at least 100 job solicitations. The 2015 survey of residents in their final year of medical residency, which tallied more than 1200 responses from a sampling of 24,000, indicates that young doctors are ready to enter a world of 9 to 5 employment rather than launching their own private practice. More than 90% said they preferred employment with a salary rather than an "independent practice income guarantee."*

21.4.3 Celebrity Patient Risks

In the wake of Michael Jackson's death more than five years ago, as well as Joan Rivers on September 4, 2014, a recent essay in *American Medical News* summarizes some of the dangers physicians face by taking on celebrities. The piece cites a study that concluded that "celebrities were an average 17% more narcissistic than the general public," and perhaps because of this, some "are extremely manipulative, and there is a lot of drug-seeking behavior." When treating a celebrity, the standard doctor–patient relationship doesn't apply, with the patient's fame upsetting the dynamic: "It is a power issue," said Dr. Turton, a Sarasota, Florida, internist. "In a normal doctor–patient relationship, there is a well-defined power relationship. The doctor has the power to prescribe, and he follows his professional tenets to do that appropriately, and we depend on him for that. But,

* From Bruce Japsen, *Forbes*, January 11, 2015.

if the patient has power over the doctor, then it short-circuits those professional guidelines and safeguards.… That is the conflict of interest—who are you really taking care of here, yourself or your patient?" (personal communication). And, to compound that difficulty, if the doctor takes a stand against a celebrity, he or she can be easily replaced by another who will eagerly fill the role. So, beware when taking on high-profile patients. No doubt Michael Jackson's personal physician, Dr. Conrad Murray, is having some serious second thoughts right about now.*

21.4.4 Certificate of Need Laws

Certificate of Need (CON) was a federal requirement enacted as part of the Health Planning Resources Development Act of 1974. Though the federal law was repealed in 1987, state CON programs still restrict and govern the development and licensure of medical services in approximately 36 states. The original intent of these laws was to prevent any tendency to create overutilization of health-care services by limiting the supply of health-care provider facilities. Nursing homes are the most commonly controlled health-care service under state CON laws. Additionally, over 12 states have enacted moratoriums (freezes) on the total number of nursing home beds in their respective state. In some states, nursing home bed licenses are regularly bought and sold between facilities as transferable assets. Here are the latest counts of state CON programs for various services:

- Nursing home/LTC beds: 36 states/DC
- Hospitals: 28 states
- ASCs: 27 states
- Cardiac cath: 26 states
- Open heart surgery: 25 states
- Rehabilitation: 25 states
- Neonatal intensive care: 23 states
- Radiation therapy: 23 states
- PETs: 20 states
- Substance/drug abuse: 19 states
- MRI: 18 states and DC
- Home health, hospice: 18 states
- Computed tomography: 13 states

21.4.5 Civil Asset Forfeiture

Civil asset forfeiture is a *seize now, ask questions later* activity. This appears on the surface to constitute punishment without due process. However, in civil asset forfeiture, there is due process; it just comes *after* the seizure. Civil asset forfeiture is to property like an arrest is to the person. A warrant is issued stating in essence that the property did something wrong. The property is *arrested* (i.e., seized), and then a hearing or trial will follow at some later date to determine the facts. But, in February 2015, Attorney General Eric Holder reduced a related national policy called *equitable sharing*—a policy that for decades allowed law enforcement to seize billions of dollars from criminal activities.

* Available at http://www.amednews.com/article/20090713/profession/307139981/2/.

21.4.6 Collateral Consequences Risks

Many risks inherent in medical practice also have collateral consequences. For example, making a payment in response to a medical malpractice claim requires reporting to the NPDB. Often such a report instigates an investigation by state boards and hospital staffs. The result is that the medical license of staff privileges can be placed in jeopardy.

21.4.7 Concierge Medical Practice

Concierge medicine firm found liable for doctor's negligence. MDVIP is the nation's largest concierge medicine practice promising *exceptional care* and quick access to doctors in exchange for a $1500 annual membership fee. But, it took a big hit in 2015 when a Palm Beach County, Florida, jury returned an $8.5 million malpractice verdict against the company, which has nearly 800 affiliated physicians in 41 states. It was the first malpractice verdict against MDVIP and is believed to be the first against any concierge management firm. The companies offer such perks as same-day appointments and more personalized care with contracted doctors in return for a retainer. The jury found that MDVIP was liable for the negligence of one of its physicians, who was sued for misdiagnosing the cause of a patient's leg pain, leading to its amputation. The jury also found that the firm had falsely advertised its exceptional doctors and patient care. Industry experts say the ruling is significant because it shows that concierge companies can be held liable for the care provided by their contracted doctors.*

21.4.8 Contract Cohort Pitfalls

There are several key pitfalls to watch out for when evaluating an ACO, HMO, managed care organization, or related cohort contract or book-of-business, as medicine migrates from a retail model to a wholesale cohort contract business model:

- *Profitability*—Less than 52% of all senior physician executives know whether their managed care contracts are profitable. "Many simply sign up and hope for the best."
- *Financial data*—90% of all executives said the ability to obtain financial information was valuable, yet only 50% could obtain the needed data.
- *Information technology*—IT hardware and sophisticated software is needed to gather, evaluate, and interpret clinical and financial data; yet it is typically "unavailable to the solo or small group practice."
- *Underpayments*—The rate is typically between 3% and 10% and is usually "left on the table."
- *Cash flow forecasting*—MCO contracting will soon begin yearly (or longer) compensation disbursements, "causing significant cash flow problems to many physicians."
- *Stop-loss minimums*—SLMs are one-time up-front premium charges for stop-loss insurance. However, if the contract is prematurely terminated, you may not receive a pro rata refund unless you ask for it!

---

* From Phil Galewitz, *Kaiser Health News*, February 13, 2015.

- *Automatic contract renewals*—ACRs or *evergreen* contracts automatically renew unless one party objects. This is convenient for both the payor and payee, but may result in overlapping renewal and renegotiation deadlines. Hence, a contract may be continued on a sub-optimal basis to the detriment of the providers.
- *Eliminate retroactive denials*—Eliminate the rejection of claims that were either directly or indirectly approved, initially. For example, "MCO reserves the right to perform utilization review [prospective, retrospective and/or concurrent] and to adjust or deny payments for medically inappropriate services."
- *Define "clean" and "dirty claims"*—Eliminate the rejection of standard medical claim formats like newer or updated CMS-1450, CMS-1500, or UB-92 for non-material reasons. Make payment of appropriate clean claims within some specific time period, like 30 days, in order to enhance free cash flows.
- *Reject silent or faux HMO or PPs, etc.*—Eliminate leased medical networks or affiliates and reject further payment discounts to larger subscriber cohorts than originally anticipated.
- *Include terms for health IT*—Eliminate the economic risk of leading-edge electronic advancements like electronic medical records (EMRs), PHRs, CPOEs, and so on.
- *Establish ability to recover payments after contract termination*—Eliminate financial carry forward for an excessive period of time.
- *Preserve payment ability*—Provide medical services if requested by patients, who are then billed directly.
- *Minimize differentials*—Establish a standardized rate structure (fee schedule) for all plans and then grant discounts for administrative or other efficiencies, rather than have different schedules for each individual plan.

21.4.9 Contract Capitulation Dilemma

The dilemma that a medical provider will have to consider when facing the adverse effects of a *Hold Harmless Clause* is the prospective detriment to his/her practice if he/she does not capitulate to the managed care company's demand to provide indemnification for a settled case. The provider has the option to fight the issue in court. In some cases, the provider may prevail, but it is likely to be a futile and expensive effort in most scenarios. In any event, if the provider does not indemnify the managed care company, most likely, he/she will find himself/herself deselected from the panel. Such a deselection is likely to create a domino effect of deselection from other panels. Such events could destroy the provider's practice.

21.4.10 Controlled Substances Risks

The Drug Enforcement Agency (DEA) controls the issuance of DEA numbers that permit physicians to prescribe controlled substances to their patients. The use of controlled substances is important to almost all medical specialties. Family practitioners use codeine to treat coughs and surgeons use narcotics to manage pain. The spectrum of use is wide. Unfortunately, there will always be a rogue physician willing to sell narcotic prescriptions. These physicians cause the DEA to cast a jaundiced eye toward all physicians. However, the dilemma may be that there are simply too many stories of physicians who *overuse* controlled substances in a practice designed to ease the suffering of their patients, or not? And how do we differentiate among them all? The physician never knows when a patient coming into the office complaining of pain and asking for pain medication—whether that patient is truly in pain or not—is an undercover agent for the DEA. Has it come to *prescriber beware*? This peril and paranoia (combined with the risk of a malpractice claim of *hooking* the patient) cause some physicians to actually underprescribe pain medication. The U.S. Department of Veterans Affairs may be at particular risk (*Chicago Tribune*, January 9, 2015).

21.4.11 Corporate Practice of Medicine Laws

Approximately half of the states in the United States have made it unlawful for practicing physicians to be employees of corporations. This ban on the *corporate practice of medicine* (CPM) is intended to keep medical professionals independent and free from financial pressures and influence. Most states have made exceptions allowing physicians to become employees of not-for-profit organizations and sometimes hospitals. States such as California, Iowa, and Texas have declined to allow hospitals to employ physicians, although even those states have special exceptions. Iowa hospitals may employ pathologists and radiologists, and Texas public hospitals and California teaching hospitals may employ physicians. Ohio has no ban on the CPM. Anyone can own a physician practice in Ohio.

21.4.12 Correctional Care Risks

Most primary care doctors, psychologists, and psychiatrists who work in corrections long enough will end up being named in a lawsuit or having a complaint filed against them with their licensing board. It is a fact that physicians who treat inmates are at greater risk of litigation. According to the 2011–2012 National Inmate Survey conducted by the Bureau of Justice Statistics:

- Half of state and federal prisoners and jail inmates reported a history of a chronic medical condition.
- About 2/3 of females in prisons (63%) and jails (67%) reported ever having a chronic condition.
- An estimated 40% of prisoners and inmates reported having a current chronic medical condition.
- About 1 in 5 (21%) of prisoners and 14% of jail inmates reported ever having an infectious disease.
- Approximately 1% of prisoners and jail inmates reported being HIV positive.

- High blood pressure was the most common condition reported by prisoners (30%) and inmates (26%).
- Nearly a quarter (24%) of prisoners and jail inmates reported ever having at least two chronic conditions.
- 66% of prisoners and 40% of jail inmates with a chronic condition reported taking prescription medication.

And, although specific figures are not available, malpractice carriers are quite aware of this risk. Yet, according to colleague Eric A. Dover, MD, and Jeffrey Knuppel, MD, a psychiatrist who blogs at *The Positive Medical Blog*, the risk of litigation should not be a deterrent to working as a health-care professional in correction facilities if

1. You truly like working in the correctional setting. This work is not for everyone. If you don't really like it anyway, then the thought of getting sued is just likely to decrease your career satisfaction further.
2. You have ability to be assertive yet get along well with most people. If you frequently find yourself in power struggles with people or cannot politely set limits, then do not work in corrections. If you let your ego get involved in your interpersonal interactions very often, then you're likely to irritate many inmates, and you probably will become a target for lawsuits and complaints (personal communication).

21.4.13 Credentialing Delays

Delegated credentialing is the process by which a health plan (or any other entity responsible for credentialing) agrees to turn over a portion of their credentialing review process to a qualified entity and must provide oversight over the delegate for ongoing adherence to program requirements. Delegated credentialing involves three key components. The delegation agreement outlines the responsibilities of both the plan and the delegated entity, the assessment and evaluation of the credentialing program provides the plan all information required to determine whether the proposed entity meets plan standards, and ongoing oversight insures that the delegated entity continues to operate in a compliant manner. The delegation process is repeated with each plan.

21.4.14 Crowd-Sourced Funding Ethics for Medical Care

If we use crowd-sourcing for healthcare costs as a way to replace what a good insurance policy or healthcare system might do, then are we really creating a new health disparity?

So, is it fair to ask the blog-o-sphere to help pay medical and hospital bills? Is the Internet a moral hazard in this case?*

21.4.15 Crowd-Sourced Medicine

Do-it-yourself health care, in the guise of http://crowdmed.com, harnesses the wisdom of crowds to collaboratively solve even the world's most difficult medical cases quickly and accurately online. The company offers individuals, insurance providers, and self-insured

* From Cari Romm, *The Atlantic*, March 15, 2015.

corporate customers the ability to more quickly diagnose medical conditions and reduce health-care costs without compromising care. Founded by veteran technology entrepreneur Jared Heyman and based in San Francisco, California, CrowdMed has received more than $2.4 million in funding from some of Silicon Valley's top venture capital firms including NEA, Andreessen Horowitz, Greylock Partners, SV Angel, Khosla Ventures, and Y Combinator. The company's advisors have founded and run some of the world's most successful online health-care companies including WebMD. CrowdMed graduated from Y Combinator's Winter 2013 class and was officially launched during the TEDMED 2013 conference in Washington, District of Columbia. So, U.S. physicians and consumers may be ready to embrace a dramatic expansion of the high-tech, personal medical kit. And, wearable technology, smartphone-linked devices and mobile apps will become increasingly valuable in care delivery. Furthermore, other firms like 23andMe, Navigenics, DeCodeMe, CollabRx, and Cure Together hope that genomics and aggregated patient experiences will advance fast enough so the current epidemic of "more diagnosis with less ability to change outcomes" will morph into one where knowing your future averts adverse medical consequences.

21.5 -D-

21.5.1 Database Breaches

While not a new risk, the higher prevalence is new. The risks of being fined by Office Civil Rights (OCR) due to the privacy rules of HIPAA because a practice had a data breach with their EHR are becoming more common and very expensive. The three classic components of information security and data integrity are confidentiality, integrity, and availability. iMBA Inc., colleague Richard J. Mata, MD, MS-CIS, CMP (Hon), and Donna B. Parker, a pioneer in the field of computer information protection, added possession, authenticity, and utility to the original three. These six attributes of information that need to be protected by information security measures are defined as follows:

1. *Confidentiality*: The protection and ethics of guarding personal information—for example, being cognizant of verbal communication leaks beyond conversation with associated health-care colleagues.
2. *Possession*: The ownership or control of information, as distinct from confidentiality—a database of protected health information (PHI) belongs to the patients.
3. *Data integrity*: The process of retaining the original intention of the definition of the data by an authorized user—this is achieved by preventing accidental or deliberate but unauthorized insertion, modification, or destruction of data in a database. Make frequent backups of data to compare with other versions for changes made.
4. *Authenticity*: The correct attribution of origin—such as the authorship of an e-mail message or the correct description of information such as a data field that is properly named. Authenticity may require encryption.
5. *Availability*: The accessibility of a system resource in a timely manner—for example, the measurement of a system's uptime. Is the intranet available?
6. *Utility*: Usefulness; fitness for a particular use—for example, if data are encrypted and the decryption key is unavailable, the breach of security is in the lack of utility of the data (they are still confidential, possessed, integral, authentic, and available).

21.5.2 Debt Collection Agencies

According to the U.S. Department of Health & Human Services, "The Privacy Rule permits covered entities to continue to use the services of debt collection agencies; like doctordefender.com; for example. Debt collection is recognized as a payment activity within the 'payment' definition (See the definition of 'payment' at 45 CFR 164.501). Through a business associate arrangement, the covered entity may engage a debt collection agency to perform this function on its behalf. Disclosures to collection agencies are governed by other provisions of the Privacy Rule, such as the business associate and minimum necessary requirements. The Department is not aware of any conflict between the Privacy Rule and the Fair Debt Collection Practices Act. Where a use or disclosure of protected health information is necessary for the covered entity to fulfill a legal duty, the Privacy Rule would permit such use or disclosure as required by law" (FDR, Washington, DC).

21.5.3 Deselection Contract Risks

In the current medical environment, a physician's practice does not consist of a collection of individual patients or of the *charts*. A physician's practice consists of a number of managed care contracts, cohorts, or *book-of-business* that allow the physician to be a member of a panel and listed in the individual subscriber's insurance book. The patients merely flow from these contracts. Without the contracts, there will be no patient flow. Therefore, the physician faces the risk of being deselected from an individual, or several, managed care panels. Each deselection will have an adverse effect on the physician's practice. In actuality, the revenue lost from deselection will come disproportionally from the net revenue of the practice. Often, one deselection will snowball into several deselections, until the physician barely has a practice remaining. Therefore, in order for you to appeal the decision, the following guidelines are suggested in any request for a reconsideration process:

- Obtain a letter of explanation from the medical or clinical executive director.
- Ensure your initial application went through the proper channels of consideration.
- Contact your local plan representative, in person, if possible.
- Make sure your state and national medical affiliations are current, as well as hospital and surgical center staffing applications and credentials.
- Write a letter to the medical director and send it return receipt (U.S. mail) or by private carrier.

Inform the director of the actions you are taking (in writing) to become more attractive to the plan or what you have done to correct the deficiencies that caused your non-inclusion initially.

21.5.4 Digital Asset Protection

21.5.4.1 Facebook

In Facebook's settings since 2015, people can now appoint a friend or family member to be in charge of their legacy. The person gets to make one last public post, download all the loved one's photos, and respond to friend requests. The decision was applauded by asset protection attorneys and estate planners—especially because it gets around the issue of needing a password to get into people's accounts.

21.5.4.2 Apple

If you die, you can't designate anybody else to get into your account. "Any rights to your Apple ID or content within your account terminate upon your death," Apple's iCloud terms in the United States say. "Upon receipt of a copy of a death certificate your account may be terminated and all content within your account deleted."

21.5.4.3 Yahoo!

Cancelling bills, many of which are now autopaid online or arranged through e-mail, may be difficult. Some cable or Internet providers that don't have the right passcodes or account information can require mailing a death certificate and a legal cover letter. E-mail accounts may also give clues or avenues to other revenue streams, such as blogs with regular advertising revenue or Bitcoins, which may not otherwise be discovered.

21.5.4.4 Google

Like Facebook, Google allows someone to decide whether his or her profile should be deleted after death or to create an *inactive account manager*. Once that person has died, the account manager can complete a questionnaire to request data or shut it down, among other options.*

21.5.5 Direct Patient Access to Laboratory Results

According to Patricia Salber, MD (personal communication), there are a number of reasons why direct patient access to laboratory results is a good idea:

- Between 8% and 26% of abnormal test results, including those suspicious for cancer, are not followed up in a timely manner. Direct access could help reduce the number of times this occurs.
- Self-management, particularly of chronic illness, has known benefits. Just like the QS people, many folks with chronic illness obtain and manage to self-acquire lab results every day via glucometers, home pulmonary function tests, blood pressure measurements, and so forth. Direct access to laboratory-acquired data, one could argue, is a continuation of that personal responsibility.
- Patients want to be notified about their results in what they perceive as a timely fashion. In one study, patients who received direct notification of their bone density test results were more likely to perceive that they had timely notification compared to usual care, even though there was no measurable effect on actual treatment received after 3 months.
- Being more responsible for test results could encourage consumers to try to learn more about the meaning of the test results, conceivably increasing their health literacy.

But, the arguments against direct access discussed include the following:

- Patients prefer their physicians contact them directly when they have abnormal test results, although the major studies published in 2005 and 2009 preceded the extraordinary use of the Internet to access health information that exists today.

* From Sarah Frier, *Bloomberg*, February 2015.

- There is concern over whether patients will know what to do when they receive the results—will they make erroneous interpretations or fail to contact their docs? This could be, but the intent of the proposed rule is shared access to the results. We suspect that if the rule becomes law, docs will develop better notification mechanisms so that they reach the patient before the patient directly accesses the results *or* lab companies will design better lab test notifications with easy-to-understand interpretations *or* a whole new industry will appear that can provide instantly available individualized lab interpretation…*or* maybe all three of these would happen and that would be a very good thing.
- Unknown impact of dual notification (doctors and patients) of lab test results on physician behavior…would docs simply shift responsibility for initiating follow-up care from themselves to their patients?
- Would direct access of life-changing lab tests, such as HIV or malignancy, lead to unnecessary patient anxiety—or worse? (Conversely, is there less anxiety, desperation, or suicidal ideation if the bad news is delivered face to face?)
- Individuals likely may contact their physicians immediately after getting the lab results asking for a telephonic or face-to-face interpretation… it is not known how this would impact physician workload and/or potential for reimbursement (Richard Hudson, DO, Atlanta, Georgia, personal communication).

21.5.6 Direct Pay Medical Provider Risks

A cash-based medical practice or direct care provider has these basic duties:

- To comply with statutory duties such as the drug laws
- To obtain proper consent for medical care
- To render care that is not substantially inferior to that offered by similar providers

A breach of any of these duties that causes harm to a patient can result in a malpractice suit. While the first two duties are important, it is the duty to render good-quality medical care that is the basis for most malpractice lawsuits. The breach of this duty is most likely to result in a serious patient injury. The prevention of such negligent injuries is the responsibility of the individual provider, but it is also basic to the institution's quality control program. From the individual provider's point of view, quality control involves continuing education, attention to detail, and retrospective review of the course of the provider's patients. The process is only loosely structured and is usually poorly documented. This lack of formal structure is less important for the individual provider because the provider's actions are judged only within the context of the injured patient in question (although previous actions may be used to negate claims of accidental injury). The legal question is whether the care rendered the injured patient was negligent. It is not relevant to the case if the provider carried out an effective personal quality control program.

21.5.7 Duty to Treat Risks

The simplest example of a duty to render care is the duty owed to a patient already under the health-care provider's care. If a patient is under the care of a physician for an acute illness, the physician cannot quit treating that patient (unless released by the patient) if it would compromise the patient's recovery. The physician may arrange to transfer the patient to the care of another physician, but this cannot be done without the patient's permission. If the transfer is done without the patient's permission, the referring physician must ensure that the new physician is equally skilled, will accept the patient, and will be equally accessible to the patient. The patient cannot be referred to a physician 100 miles away, nor can the duty to continue treating the patient be obviated by referring the patient to a physician who refuses to treat the patient. The physician has a responsibility to transfer the patient if the patient needs special care that the physician is unable to render. And, the doctor must still ensure that the patient will receive proper care as a result of the transfer. If the patient's only choice is limited care from the original physician or no care because the receiving physician will not accept the patient, it would be legally risky to force the patient to accept the no-care alternative.

The continuing duty to treat is fairly limited in chronic conditions. If the patient has a chronic condition, such as diabetes, the physician may terminate the physician–patient relationship during a stable period of the patient's illness. The patient must be given notice of the provider's intention to end the relationship so that the patient may seek care elsewhere. This notice should be in writing, and there should be a receipt indicating that the patient received the notice. If the patient is not due for an appointment or has ceased coming to the physician, the most effective way to give notice is to send a letter by certified mail. A return receipt should be requested, with delivery restricted to the addressee. When the return receipt is received, it should be clipped to a copy of the letter and placed in the patient's medical record. If the letter is returned as undeliverable, it should be placed, unopened, in the patient's record as evidence of a good faith effort to contact the patient. The physician does not owe the patient a legal duty to recommend alternative sources of care; but it is good practice to do so, and it may defuse potential disputes with the patient.

No matter how effective the notice is, it would be questionable, from a quality control point of view, if the physician should ever knowingly refuse care to a former patient who presents to the physician needing emergency care. If the patient is injured because of a delay caused by the physician refusing to render care, the physician may be sued and may have to defend the decision to refuse care. The law may be on the physician's side, but this will not prevent the expense and trauma of litigation.

21.6 -E-

21.6.1 Emergency Room (Department) Risks

In the emergency room, or department setting, indemnification means that some third person, either the physician or the emergency room service company, contracts with the hospital to pay the hospital for any losses the hospital incurs due to the negligent actions of the emergency room physician. The two requisites for indemnification are (1) that the third party be legally obligated to pay the losses and (2) that the third party has sufficient assets to cover the potential losses. The third party is usually required to carry insurance to cover any expected losses, although this is not essential if the third party has sufficient liquid (and nonexempt) assets. Indemnification is widely used in business contracts, but it is seldom found in medical service agreements.

21.6.2 Employee Office Risks

Medical practice employees have *inside information* concerning the practice and the physician's patterns of practice. In most cases, the staff is trained by the doctor. The staff's frame of reference is thereby limited to what they have been taught. However, more credit should be given to the office staff. Staff members deal everyday with insurance companies (including Medicare), and they field a wide array of patient questions and complaints. An astute staff member will soon realize if the physician is miscoding insurance submission.

An informed, irate employee can be your biggest risk. Many medical malpractice lawsuits have been brought by patients because terminated employees have informed the patient that "something was wrong" with their treatment. Likewise, Occupational Safety and Health Administration (OSHA) investigations have been instituted by disgruntled employees. In these cases, the employee had nothing to gain but revenge against real or perceived injustices from their former employer. Now, an employee also has a financial incentive to bring health-care fraud charges against his or her former physician employer.

21.6.3 Employment Crisis Management

Sooner or later, the employed medical professional, or hospitalist, will be terminated or reduced in force due to the current health reform care crisis. In the future, it will not be unusual to have a career with several different companies throughout a lifetime. This form of employment crisis management encompasses two different perspectives. If you become aware that you may lose your job, the following proactive steps will be helpful to your financial condition:

- Decrease retirement contributions to the minimum required to get the company match. Place the difference in your after-tax emergency fund.
- Eliminate unnecessary payroll deductions and deposit the difference to cash.
- Replace group term life insurance with personal term or universal life insurance. Take your old group term policy with you, if possible.
- Establish a home equity line of credit to verify employment.
- Borrow against your pension plan only as a last resort.

After you have lost your job, negotiate your departure and get an attorney if you believe you lost your position through breach of contract or discrimination. Then, the following retroactive steps will be helpful to your financial condition:

- Prioritize fixed monthly bills in the following order: rent/mortgage, utility bills, minimum credit card payments, and restructured long-term debt.
- Consider liquidating assets to pay off debts, in this order: emergency fund, checking accounts, investment accounts, or asset held in your children's names.
- Review insurance coverage. Increase deductibles on homeowner's and automobile insurance for needed cash.
- Then, sell stocks or mutual funds; personal valuables, such as furnishings, jewelry, and real estate; and finally assets not in pension or annuities, if needed.

- Keep or roll over any lump sum pension or savings plan distribution directly to your new company, if possible, when you get rehired. Pay taxes and penalties, and use the money only as a last resort.
- Apply for unemployment insurance.
- Review your medical insurance, COBRA coverage, and the PPACA.
- Eliminate unnecessary variable, charitable, and/or discretionary expenses.
- Become very frugal.

21.6.4 EMR Risks

EMRs can increase malpractice risk in documentation of clinical findings: copying and pasting. This was first noted more than 30 years ago by Dr. William P. Scherer, MS, of the Department of Radiology at Barry University, in Miami, Florida (personal communication). As a pioneer of digital health records, he noted that previously entered information can perpetuate any mistakes that may have been made earlier. Incorrect information is the most common user-related contributing factor in malpractice cases involving EMRs, according to a study by *The Doctors Company* of EMR-related closed claims from 2007 to 2013 (personal communication). In the study, 15% of cases involved prepopulating/copy-and-paste as a contributing factor. Copy-and-paste is a necessary evil to save time during documentation of daily notes, but whatever is pasted must also be edited to reflect the current situation. Too often, the note makes reference to something that happened *yesterday*. For example, the sentence "Patient presented to ED with chest pain yesterday…" is pasted over the next 2 weeks in the daily progress note. An even more telling example is a sentence like "Patient's admitting lab is normal…" being perpetuated while the actual creatinine levels rise every day. In one case, the judge commented about copy-and-paste issues: "I cannot trust any of the physician notes in which this occurred and the only conclusion I can reach is that there was no examination of the patient… it means to me that no true thought was given to the content that was going into 'the note.'"

Checkboxes, particularly those that prepopulate, can be a physician's nemesis. It's easy to click on checkboxes, and often they are prechecked in templates. EMRs have been presented in court that show, through checkboxes, daily breast exams on comatose patients in the ICU, detailed daily neurological exams done by cardiologists, and a complete review of systems done by multiple treating physicians on comatose patients. Questioning in court as to how long it takes to do a review of systems and a physical examination, the patient load of the physician for that day, and how many hours the physician was at work cast doubt on the truthfulness of the testifying physician. A time analysis showed that there was no way the physician could have accomplished all that was charted that day. The fundamental mantra when writing a note in an EMR is to show that you put thought into the record. Discrete data, though strongly favored by IT professionals and insurance companies, do not accomplish this. Free-text entry of three or four sentences can convey far more information than several pages of template-driven notes and will reflect that you saw the patient and put thought into the note.

All these common EMR issues—incorrect information, copy-and-paste, and poor note-taking—cast doubt on the integrity of the doctor and the medical record. While the doctor may not have committed a clear-cut act of malpractice, these types of issues in the medical record cast the doctor in an unfavorable light in front of a judge or jury.*

21.6.5 Environmental Protection Agency Risks

The practitioner may not think about the *Environmental Protection Agency* (*EPA*) when thinking about the possible risks of practicing. But, that agency could be a nightmare for the unsuspecting physician. For example, a doctor who improperly disposes of developing fluid, silver wastes, bodily fluids or biohazardous materials, and/or other wastes may become a target of the EPA.

21.6.6 Evidence-Based Medicine

A disconcerting component of the health-care reform debate in 2010 was the opposition by many to research into and use of *evidence-based* practices as a means to reduce the cost of care while improving its effectiveness. Numerous studies have shown wide variability in treatment methodologies and associated costs, often on a regional basis, and have called on adoption of those practices that have shown to have positive outcomes at lower costs. Opponents have condemned such proposals as *cookbook medicine* that strips away professional judgment and discretion, while supporters argue that physicians should be advocates for widespread application of such *best practices* when proven to provide more effective outcomes. This debate will continue so long as organized medicine fails to acknowledge that widespread variation in treatments increases the cost of care without contributing to optimal outcomes.

21.6.7 Exclusion from Medicare (CMS) Program Risks

Medicare rules provide for a mandatory exclusion of a provider who has been convicted of certain crimes. For example, a physician who is convicted of insurance fraud (unrelated to the Medicare program) could also be excluded from Medicare participation during a 5-year period.

21.6.8 Exit Fee-for-Service Medicine

Continuing the health insurance industry's march further away from fee-for-service medicine, UnitedHealth Group (UNH) will increase value-based payments to doctors and hospitals by 20% in 2015 to "north of $43 billion." UnitedHealth, considered a barometer for the health insurance industry given its size, is rapidly departing from the traditional fee-for-service approach that can lead to overtreatment and unnecessary medical tests and procedures. Value-based pay is tied to health outcomes, performance, and quality of care provided. UnitedHealth's pronouncements are in keeping with its previously stated commitment to increase payments that are tied to value-based arrangements to $65 billion by the end of 2018. Value-based payments come in a variety of forms. They include pay-for-performance

* From Keith L. Klein, MD, clinical professor of medicine, David Geffen School of Medicine, University of California, Los Angeles.

programs, patient-centered medical homes, and ACOs, a rapidly emerging care delivery system that rewards doctors and hospitals for working together to improve quality and rein in costs.*

21.6.9 Experimental Medical Treatment Risks

What is a medical experiment? Physicians conduct experiments when they try a treatment that is different from the accepted practice in their specialty. Are experimental treatments always more dangerous than conventional treatments? No. In many cases, the experimental treatment is being tried because it is believed to be safer or less painful than the conventional treatment. As a patient, can one be experimented on without any consent? No. There are very strict ethical requirements that the doctor must fulfill to obtain consent for experimental treatment. Additionally, there are legal standards that the physician must meet to ensure that your consent is informed. So, here are some of these requirements:

- Patients must be told the details of the proposed treatment, its risks, its possible benefits, and how it differs from the conventional treatment.
- Patients are entitled to know how the experimental treatment was developed and the basis for any claims that are made about its safety or effectiveness.
- Patients have the right to end the experimental treatment at any time and to be given conventional treatment.
- All possible efforts must be made to protect patients from any unnecessary mental or physical suffering or injury.

And, as a charity patient, may one be required to participate in medical experiments? No. A patient cannot be required to participate in medical experiments to get medical care, charitable or otherwise.

21.6.10 Expert Witness Risks

In the past, a physician expert witness for the plaintiff was merely an opposing opinion by a learned and/or like colleague. But today, it is becoming a risk management minefield; but why? Allen Frances, MD, a psychiatrist and professor emeritus of Duke University, suggests that many factors contribute to experts generating heat, not necessarily light (personal communication).

- First, some alleged experts are simply not really all that expert and say things that are just dead wrong. The filters meant to eliminate errant opinion and junk science don't work.
- Second, the adversarial system cultivates expert allegiance bias. Consciously or unconsciously, expert opinions are strongly influenced by who is paying the bill.
- Third, juries often have to decide questions that are far beyond their competence. And, which dueling expert to believe is more often determined by presentation skills and likability than the technical accuracy of medical testimony.

* From Bruce Japsen, *Forbes*.

- Finally, the adversarial quality of the legal system demands that experts give black-and-white, yes-or-no answers to questions that often require a shades-of-gray, nuanced response. Even wise and unbiased experts mislead when they are forced to choose a yes or no when the best answer would be maybe or a little bit of both. As it stands now, the expert testimony in some trials is pretty worthless. Each side presents an extreme set of opinions that in opposite ways distort the complex reality. The jury cancels them out or makes a pretty blind choice between them.

The American Medical Association (AMA) and other groups are urging state medical licensing boards to police expert witnesses, which might require that expert testimony be considered the practice of medicine. This seems especially true with the Illinois-based American Association of Neurological Surgeons (AANS). Currently, a member of the AANS can file a complaint against any fellow member for testimony as either an expert witness for the plaintiff, or defense witness for the doctor. A committee then reviews the court records and requires the accuser to face the accused in a formal review. Sanctions range from 3 months to a year to complete expulsion from the association. Since 2001, the courts are beginning to take the AANS process seriously. So always remember, if you testify falsely, or too far from the norm, you may be at risk.

21.7 -F-

21.7.1 Facility Fees

Increasingly, it seems that patients are being caught off guard by new *medical facility fees* for visiting doctors who are based in a hospital-owned building. The issue is not exactly new, but it is expected to become more contentious as patients use the PPACA's high deductibles, and/or those insurance plans imposed by consumer-directed health-care plans (HD-HCPs). Those facilities, like Milwaukee's Froedtert & Community Health that charges the fees, usually post warning signs, although their patients often end up arguing with insurance companies over payment. Making the financial sting even worse, some insurance companies treat the facilities fee at the doctor's office as the first dollar of what can be a high hospital deductible, rather than applying it to a physician deductible. And, the fees vary widely, from a relatively small $20 or $30 to a few hundred dollars. What's even more insidious is that some hospitals are already charging patients not only for professional medical services but also a facilities fee for physical use of the building.

21.7.2 *Faster Medicine* Risks

Our colleagues Darrell K. Pruitt, DDS, and blogger Kent Bottles, MD, are opining and posting about the emerging philosophy of *slow medicine*. Of course, health economists realize how complex and difficult it is to transform American health care so that we will enjoy lower per-capita costs along with increased medical care quality in our lives. Unfortunately, grassroots practitioners have done just the opposite these last two decades or so, in other words, practicing *faster medicine* with assembly line efficiency and relegating office visits to 15, 10, or even 7 minute increments, etc., in order to compensate for diminishing MCO/HMO reimbursement. And, this may have been a financially acute perspective for modernity, until now! The risks and need for speed are great (personal communication).

21.7.3 *Fatigued Medicine* Risks

Fatigue matters, even when it comes to doctors. Especially when it comes to doctors! Clinicians make many patient care decisions each day. The cumulative cognitive demand of these decisions may erode clinicians' abilities to resist making potentially inappropriate choices. Psychologists, who refer to the erosion of self-control after making repeated decisions as *decision fatigue*, have found evidence that it affects medical as well as nonmedical professionals alike.*

21.8 -H-

21.8.1 Hierarchy of Needs

Everyone, it seems, aspires at some point in their lives to become a doctor. It's somewhat of a dream job to most people: high pay, respect, prestige, authority. Nevertheless, for those who never made the dream come true, there's some comforting news.

Doctor is the most overrated profession there is, according to a website that analyzes careers. On a list of the 12 most overrated jobs compiled by Career Cast, doctors—specifically surgeons, physicians, and psychiatrists—occupy three of the top five spots. Only a corporate executive is more overrated. Career Cast analyzed pay, stress, physical demands, and the current and future employment outlook in compiling its list. And, Wall Street's stockbrokers, vilified on Main Street, average a little over $67,000 a year, less than some teachers.[†,‡]

21.8.2 Head-Hunter Risks

Any time an executive search firm makes the following claims, you should push back and try to get more information before assuming it's the truth. While some can deliver, others can't—and it's up to you to figure out which ones are sincere. So, here are some potential misleading statements and/or lies told to physician executives in the hiring process:

1. There's great opportunity for advancement.
2. Our bonus structure will double your income.
3. Your job and schedule is protected and won't change.
4. You'll get extensive on-boarding and training.
5. We'll hire you some help when it gets busy.
6. Once you fix this problem/department/project, etc., you'll get to work on something new and exciting.

---

* From Jeffrey A. Linder, MD, MPH; Jason N. Doctor, PhD; Mark W. Friedberg, MD, MPP; Harry Reyes Nieva, BA; Caroline Birks, MD; Daniella Meeker, PhD; Craig R. Fox, PhD. Time of Day and the Decision to Prescribe Antibiotics. *JAMA Internal Medicine* 174 (12): 2029–2031, 2014.

† Maslow's hierarchy of needs is a theory proposed by Abraham Maslow in his 1943 paper "A Theory of Human Motivation." Maslow subsequently extended the idea to include his observations of humans' innate curiosity. His theories parallel many other theories of human developmental psychology, some of which focus on describing the stages of growth in humans. Maslow used the terms "physiological," "safety," "belongingness," "love," "esteem," "self-actualization," and "self-transcendence" to describe the pattern that human motivations generally move through.

‡ Available at http://www.careercast.com/jobs-rated/most-overrated-jobs-2011.

21.8.3 Health Economics Outcome Research

New draft guidelines recently issued by the federal Office for Human Research Protections (OHRP) regarding the evaluation and disclosure of risks in comparative-effectiveness research (CER) fail to clarify current federal policy. If adopted, the result of this approach will be consent forms that make research seem riskier than it truly is and make existing practices seem safer than they truly are.*

21.8.4 Health-Care Licensing Laws

Every state has its own licensing laws and standards for health-care facilities, services, and professionals. State departments of health usually have a licensing division that processes new applications and renewals, performs site survey inspections, and revokes licenses when deemed appropriate. State licensure, accreditation, and Medicare certification are separate credentials, yet they are sometimes related by state law. Some states require businesses to achieve accreditation (e.g., The Joint Commission, AAAHC) as a requirement for state licensure. Some states perform Medicare surveys on behalf of the federal government. To further complicate things, different versions of health-care building life safety codes and AIA building guidelines are required for different state licensures, and those versions of the standards may differ from those required by accreditation organizations. In one unique example, California has no state licensure requirement for ASCs that have partial or total physician ownership. So in California, all nonphysician-owned ASCs pursue state licensure, while physician-owned ASCs must instead become accredited through an accreditation organization or become certified by Medicare to satisfy California's requirements.

21.8.5 Historic Bars to Managed Care Risks and Lawsuits

Historically, managed care companies have been afforded immunity from negligence and malpractice lawsuits. Several state and federal bars, including *Employee Retirement Income Security Act of 1974 (ERISA)*, have insulated managed care companies from liability relating to the treatment of patients. Likewise, managed care companies have historically been immune from malpractice committed by a health-care member of its panel of providers. On a state law basis, the *Corporate Practice of Law* often insulated managed care companies from such liability. The theory underlying this protection was essentially uncomplicated; since corporations are prohibited under the Corporate Practice of Law Doctrine from practicing medicine, they should not be held liable for medical negligence and malpractice. However, in recent years, it has become apparent that managed care companies do in fact *practice medicine*. These companies tell their panel of providers how to practice, whether it is in a generalized or specific field of medicine. They establish a formulary of approved drugs, limiting those medications available to their subscribers. They review and then approve or deny needed medical care. They create economic incentives for patients to be undertreated or treated in a predetermined manner. They effectively minimize referrals to specialists, often at the peril of the patient subscriber and the health-care provider seeking that consultation.

In the federal arena, ERISA has been the primary deterrent to suits against managed care companies. Under the theory of federal preemption, even the lowest federal regulation

* From *The New England Journal of Medicine*, November 19, 2014.

takes precedence over any and all state laws. ERISA has, however, been described as possessing *Super-preemption*. That term was coined to evince the special deference that courts have displayed to potential defendants who allege defensive protection based upon ERISA. In the past, most providers ran into the ERISA preemption when a health plan governed by ERISA was contrary to a state law, such as state antidiscrimination law (i.e., a state law prohibiting insurance payment discrimination based on degree). In the context of this chapter, the reader should understand that liability claims, such as medical malpractice claims, are a state cause of action. Since the federal ERISA law trumps state laws, bringing a medical malpractice action against an ERISA entity is almost impossible.

21.9 -I-

21.9.1 Identity Theft Concern

Along with a rise in health-care breaches, medical identity theft remains a top concern among patients and consumers as cyber-criminals look to capitalize on the bigger payout for PHI on the black market. Industry reports reveal that medical identity theft has now claimed more than 1.8 million U.S. victims, granting hackers the ability to gain medical services, procure drugs, and defraud private insurers and government benefit programs. Health-care organizations face the challenge of securing a significant amount of sensitive information stored on their networks, which combined with the value of a medical identity string makes them an attractive target for cyber-criminals.

21.9.2 Improper Medical Supervision

A major class of risks involving nursing and medical students involves injuries resulting from improper supervision. These injuries may occur because of improper delegation of authority by the staff physicians, or they may occur because of unauthorized care rendered at the initiative of the student. In the first situation, the staff would be legally liable because they authorized the medical student's overreaching behavior. The student would also be liable if it could be shown that the student knew or should have known that the actions were improper. In the second situation, the staff would be liable for failing to supervise the student properly, and the student would be liable for taking unauthorized initiatives. In both situations, the student's actions would precipitate the lawsuit, but students are seldom named as defendants. The hospital and the supervising physicians are the usual defendants in these lawsuits.

Most medical malpractice suits are pieced together from the medical records after the charts have been *completed*. At this point, all the student's orders will have been cosigned, and the entries will be legally attributed to the supervising physician. The supervising physician will be *estopped* from denying the validity of these orders because the countersignature legally shifts the liability from the student (and the nursing personnel who take the orders) to the staff member. The countersignature process is routine and often lags the execution of the student's orders by the nursing staff. This puts the hospital in the legal position of depending upon after-the-fact ratification of the student's orders. This can be very risky if the order causes immediate harm and the supervising staff member refuses to countersign it. The liability for the injury will then lie with the nurse for carrying out the unauthorized order and with the hospital for failing to supervise the nurse properly.

All nonphysician medical personnel—whether in a hospital, clinic, or individual practice—must be cautioned never to accept orders from a medical student without specific authorization by a licensed physician. If the authorization is verbal, it should be entered into the medical record as a voice order that, "1 grain codeine by mouth, [verbal] voice order Mr. Smith, confirmed by Dr. Jones." Dr. Jones will then cosign the order as required by the applicable hospital or practice protocol. All members of the medical and nursing staffs should be apprised of the legal problems associated with the exercise of medical judgments by medical students. The students themselves should be warned that although the hospital and supervising physicians will usually be the defendants, plaintiffs' attorneys are beginning to name students as parties to lawsuits. This is especially true when the injury occurs because of an unauthorized action initiated by the student.

21.9.3 Information Distrusting Patients

With the ubiquity of medical information on the Internet, the risks incurred by a medical practice in properly dealing with the newly informed patients with medical degrees from the *University of Google* or *Bing Medical School* are on the rise. Physicians must refine their bedside manner and improve their communication skills in order to deal with a more questioning patient population. Clinicians should actively discuss what patients have read on the Internet when patients refer to their Internet diagnoses.*

21.9.4 Informed Consent in Malpractice Cases

Evidence that a patient affirmatively consented to treatment after being informed of the risks of that treatment generally is irrelevant to a claim of medical negligence, a state high court said (*Brady v. Urbas*, 2015 BL 82413, Pa., No. 74 MAP 2014, 3/25/15). The Pennsylvania Supreme Court affirmed an appeals court decision that vacated a judgment for podiatrist Dr. William Urbas in a medical malpractice action brought by Maria Brady. The two higher courts held that the trial court erred by allowing the jury at trial to see a consent form Brady signed prior to her treatment by Dr. Urbas. The state Supreme Court, however, didn't go as far as the intermediate appeals court, which had adopted a bright-line rule that informed-consent evidence is never admissible in a medical negligence case. Such evidence might be relevant, the Supreme Court said, if the standard of care required a physician to discuss certain risks with a patient and might be relevant to establish the standard of care itself. The consent to treatment doesn't amount to a consent to negligence—regardless of the risks—of which the patient was made aware of, it said.†

21.9.5 Informed Consent Risks

According to the *Dictionary of Health Insurance and Managed Care*, informed consent is the oral and written communication process between a patient and physician that results

* From Lam-Po-Tang, John, and Diana McKay. "Dr. Google, MD: A Survey of Mental Health-Related Internet Use in a Private Practice Sample." *Australasian Psychiatry* 18.2 (2010): 130–133. *Academic Search Complete*, Web, April 27, 2012.

† From BNA's Health Care Daily Report May 20, 2015.

in the agreement to undergo a particular procedure, surgical intervention, or medical treatment. Unfortunately, a lack of standardization surrounding this process represents a major risk for patients and surgeons, and may lead to inaccurate patient expectations, lost or incomplete consent forms, missing encounter documentation, and delays in critical surgeries and procedures.

Render S. Davis, MHA, CHE, of Emory University (2008 recipient of the *Health Care Ethics Consortium's Heroes in Healthcare* Ethics Award) writes in the *Business of Medical Practice* (third edition) that the concept of informed consent is rooted in medical ethics and codified as a legal principle (personal communication). It is based on the assertion that a competent person has the right to determine what is done to him or her (self-regulated autonomy). And, the AMA recommends that its members disclose and discuss the following with their patients:

- The patient's diagnosis, if known
- The nature and purpose of a proposed treatment or procedure
- The risks and benefits of a proposed treatment or procedure
- Alternatives (regardless of cost or health insurance coverage)
- The risks and benefits of the alternative treatments
- The risks and benefits of not doing the procedure

The requirements for informed consent are spelled out in statutes and case law in all 50 states. It is a necessary protocol for all hospitals, medical clinics, dental, chiropractic, podiatry, and related health-care practices and ASCs. Now, as a patient, may you decline to be informed about your condition, or the risks of treatment? Yes, but you should put this in writing because your physician is legally required to inform you and needs proof that you decline this information. May an adult refuse treatment, even if this means certain death? Yes. You may refuse any treatment, although the physician or hospital may ask the court to intervene. The courts have shown a strong tendency in favor of taking all steps necessary to preserve human life and will often direct treatment when a patient refuses. The right to refuse treatment is very important for certain religious groups. If you plan to refuse some or all medical care, you should fill out an explanation form before you need care, preferably with the advice of an attorney.

May a minor refuse care? Only when the minor falls into one of the categories (described above) allowing consent by a minor. However, an older minor may have the ability to veto some care that could have a severe impact, such as a therapeutic hysterectomy for a 16-year-old minor. What if a minor and the minor's parent, or guardian, disagree over nonemergency care? If the minor falls into one of the exempt categories, the minor may refuse care even if a parent or guardian requests the care. If the health-care provider has any doubts about the minor's capacity to consent, a court ruling should be obtained.

Finally, may medical care be rendered without a valid consent? Medical care may be rendered without a valid consent only in emergency situations, or when a child is apparently the victim of neglect or abuse. What recourse is there if I am being treated without proper consent? You should bring this to the attention of your physician with a written complaint, stating clearly that you do not consent to such treatment. You should keep a copy of this complaint for yourself.

21.9.5.1 Emergency Treatment Informed Consent

What is an emergency? An emergency exists when treatment is needed at once to preserve the patient's health or life. Although this may be self-evident, in some situations, an *emergency* can be determined only by a physician.

Is consent needed in an emergency? In an emergency, consent to necessary treatment is implied; it does not need to be given expressly. What must be done if an adult patient is unconscious but there is no emergency? Unless someone has already been legally authorized to consent for the patient, a guardian must be appointed to give consent to treatment. As indicated before, although doctors and hospitals often furnish treatment to such patients, they should insist upon the appointment of a guardian if a dispute arises as to the proper care.

21.9.5.2 Inadequacy of Traditional Consent Forms-to-Date

The typical informed consent process, particularly one that relies solely on traditional generic consent forms, is often inadequate or incomplete or offers the potential for not fully explaining and documenting a particular procedure to a given patient. Traditional consent forms are subject to errors and omissions, such as missing signatures (patient, provider, or witness), missing procedure(s), and missing dates that place the validity of consent at risk. Lost or misplaced forms may result in delayed or postponed procedures often at the expense of costly operating room time. Moreover, far too many forms are generic in nature and wholly unsuited for a specific patient or increasingly sophisticated procedures.

According to the Institute of Medicine's (IOM) report, *To Err is Human*, more than 1 million injuries and nearly 100,000 deaths occur annually in the United States due to mistakes in medical care. Wrong-patient, wrong-side, wrong-procedure, and wrong-toe surgery are particularly egregious. In fact, these are among several other *never-events* that Medicare and an increasing number of private insurance companies are refusing to reimburse. Based on the need to make health care safer, the Agency for Healthcare Research and Quality (AHRQ) undertook a study to identify patient safety issues and develop recommendations for *best practices*. The AHRQ report identified the challenge of addressing shortcomings such as missed, incomplete, or not fully comprehended informed consent as a significant patient safety opportunity for improvement. The authors of the AHRQ report hypothesized that better informed patients "are less likely to experience errors by acting as another layer of protection." And, the AHRQ study ranked a more interactive informed consent process among the top 11 practices supporting more widespread implementation. A General Accounting Office report found that malpractice insurance premiums were relatively flat for most of the 1990s, but projections began to increase dramatically by 2016.

Failure to obtain adequate informed consent, depending on state law, may place surgeons, residents, fellows, ambulatory and office surgery centers, medical clinics, and hospitals at risk for litigation ranging from medical negligence to assault and battery. And, allegations of a lack of informed consent are often a secondary factor in medical malpractice litigation. Some attorneys note that physicians are liable, and that plaintiffs may be able to recover damages, in cases involving improper informed consent, even if the procedure is successful.

The AMA advises its membership of the following regarding informed consent and liability reduction:

To protect yourself in litigation, in addition to carrying adequate liability insurance, it is important that the communications process itself be documented. Good documentation can serve as evidence in a court of the law that the process indeed took place. A timely and thorough documentation in the patient's chart by the physician providing the treatment and/or performing the procedure can be a strong piece of evidence that the physician engaged the patient in an appropriate discussion.

21.9.5.3 Impact of Comprehensive Informed Consent Forms

One iMBA, Inc., study found that providing informed consent information to patients in written form increased comprehension of the procedure (personal communication). It was also hypothesized that

- Better informed patients are more compliant with medical advice and recover faster.
- Informed consent discussions strengthen physician–patient relationships and increase patients' confidence in their doctor.
- Well-informed patients are more engaged in their own care and are thus less likely to experience surgical errors than more passive or less informed patients.

As a result, a particularly innovative new form for lower extremity surgeons, podiatrists and orthopedists, offering a possible solution to the informed consent dilemma is http://www.epodiatryconsentforms.com. The firm offers a suite of software programs that seem to help solve informed consent problems and enhance the education, discussion, and documentation of the informed consent process for any doctor performing foot, ankle, and leg reconstructive surgical procedures.

21.9.5.4 TV Drama and Reality Shows

Patients caught up in emergencies are now also vulnerable to informed consent problems, posing special issues for reality TV shows. They may not be conscious or be able to speak for themselves; they may be quite literally exposed, as caregivers work to help them. So, the American College of Emergency Physicians opposes "the filming for public viewing of emergency department patients or staff members except when they can give full informed consent prior to their participation," yet show after show returns to the emergency room, drawn by the life-or-death stakes. In an example, the New York Times Co. was sued for invasion of privacy in the early 2000s by a group of patients in New Jersey who appeared in "Trauma: Life in the E.R.," a series produced for Discovery's Learning Channel. One appeals court ruled that the show qualified as news and deserved the same protections under the law. Medical ethicists and groups like the AMA worry that these shows exploit patients' pain for public consumption, but their makers argue that they educate viewers and inspire people to choose careers in medicine.*

21.9.6 Infrastructure Risks

Title X of the USA Patriot Act contains section 1016, entitled "The Critical Infrastructures Protection Act of 2001." It acknowledges that the defense of the United States is based upon the functioning of many networks and that these networks must be defended against attacks of both

* From DE Marcinko. Emerging Medical Informed Consent Dilemma, *Medical Executive Post*, October 14, 2008.

a physical and a virtual nature. Section 1016 specifies that actions necessary to carry out policies designed to protect the infrastructure will be based upon public and private partnerships between the government and corporate and nongovernmental agencies. Further, it specifies that these actions are designed to ensure the continuity of essential government functions under all circumstances. Toward this end, the act establishes a National Infrastructure Simulation and Analysis Center (NISAC) to support counterterrorism, threat assessment, and risk mitigation. NISAC will acquire data from governments and the private sector to model, simulate, and analyze critical infrastructures including cyber, telecommunications, and physical infrastructures. Attacks on the Internet and attacks on the information systems of hospitals have already occurred in significant numbers and are likely to continue. As a result of the USA Patriot Act, agencies to combat IT terrorism have been created, such as the Critical Infrastructure Protection Board and the Critical Infrastructure Assurance Office. An Information Sharing and Analysis Center (ISAC) has been created to gather, analyze, and distribute information on cyber threats and vulnerabilities, provide alerts, and develop response plans. An ISAC for health care that will compile industry best practices, develop security systems, and establish a governance structure to which health systems can turn is under development.

The increasingly complex relationships among layers of hardware and software mean that new avenues for exploitation appear on almost a daily basis. Also, increased connectivity among computers means that the effects of attacks can be far reaching. One interesting consequence of the USA Patriot Act is that some cyber-attacks can now be defined as acts of terrorism. As a practical matter, legal recourse against most attacks is of no use since laws tend to apply only locally and cyber-attacks can come from anywhere in the world. As a result, most organizations concentrate on technical defenses to protect their infrastructure. However, efforts to protect computer systems may not be entirely defensive. One mode of defense is to monitor for intrusions, trace the source of intrusions, and aggressively attack and shut down the server of an intruder.

21.10 -J-

21.10.1 Justice for Student Loans

StudentLoanJustice.Org is a grassroots citizen organization dedicated to returning standard consumer protections to student loans. The group was started in March 2005 and has focused primarily on research, media outreach, and grassroots lobbying initiatives. The group and its members have been featured on 60 Minutes, 20/20, The News Hour, CNBC, and many other television programs; print media including the *New York Times*, *Wall Street Journal*, *Washington Post*, *Fortune Magazine*, *The Chronicle of Higher Education*, and many others; as well as numerous radio and Internet broadcasts. The group is also featured in two documentaries released in the fall of 2010. It was credited as the inspiration for the Student Borrower Bill of Rights and has broken numerous news items in the press with its research findings regarding conflicts of interest in the student loan system, student debt levels, default rates, corporate lobbing, and other areas. Group founder Alan Collinge has written numerous articles and editorials on the topic and also published *The Student Loan Scam* in 2009. He was selected as one of seven *Financial Heroes* by *CNN/Money Magazine* in December 2008. The group is funded entirely by its members (personal communication). Contemporary tips for managing medical school debt in 2016 can be found at http://www.enttoday.org/article/tips-managing-medical-school-student-loans/.

21.11 -L-

21.11.1 Leaving a Job

With the tighter financial medical market and pressures from managed care mounting, hospitals, medical clinics, and private practice employers are less likely to tolerate a non-productive employee. Interoffice or personality conflicts may become intolerable for an unhappy or stressed physician. Leaving a hospitalist system or medical practice is never an easy decision, whether it is made voluntarily or not. A physician terminating a relationship with an employer may face emotionally charged conversations, difficult financial considerations, and long-term legal consequences. Physician turnover is a common occurrence, and if not handled properly, it can be disruptive for all parties involved. So, be aware of these issues and address them proactively with your employer. This can minimize hard feelings and surprises down the road for you, your former employer, and your colleagues.

21.11.1.1 The Employment Agreement

Ideally, physician separation matters are addressed preemptively when the physician enters the employer–employee relationship and executes an employment agreement. Before contemplating a move, you should always start by reviewing the terms of your current employment agreement. A well-drafted employment agreement should specify the grounds for termination, both for cause (i.e., a specific set of reasons for immediate termination) and without cause (i.e., either party may terminate voluntarily, usually after providing notice). The agreement should also specify the parties' rights and obligations following a termination, which will likely vary depending on the basis for termination. Typically, an employer will provide malpractice insurance for its physicians during their term of employment. However, upon termination of employment, physicians may be responsible for the cost of *tail coverage*, insurance that is designed to protect the departing physician's professional acts after leaving the employ of a practice with claims-made coverage. Because this coverage can be quite costly, a good employment agreement will often set forth terms determining whether the employer or employee-physician is responsible for the procurement and payment of tail coverage. You should also review the employment agreement in order to determine the proper method to provide notice of termination, such as first-class mail, overnight courier, or hand delivery. Employment agreements will often include a clause titled *Notice* that outlines the proper delivery method.

21.11.1.2 Termination/Separation

Entering into a termination agreement, sometimes referred to as a separation agreement, may address and resolve many of the outstanding issues that are not otherwise addressed in the employment agreement. A termination agreement may avoid unnecessary problems down the road, including potentially acrimonious and costly litigation. The key elements of a termination agreement often include the following:

- The effective date of the separation, as well as what exactly is ending (e.g., employment, co-ownership, board membership, medical staff privileges).
- Payment terms and any buyout terms.
- If the physician is an owner of the practice, a requirement that he or she be removed from the board, any officer position, and any retirement plan positions. Deferred compensation payments or severance pay may need to be calculated and distributed.

- The employer's obligations, if any, to provide the departing physician's fringe benefits and business expenses, including retirement plan contributions, health insurance, life insurance, and medical dues.
- Explanation of any postdeparture compensation, unused vacation days, bonuses, or expenses due to the leaving physician.
- If previously addressed in the employment agreement, a reaffirmation of obligations regarding medical records, confidential information, noncompetition, and nonsolicitation provisions. Otherwise, the termination agreement should define the physician's competitive and solicitation activities post-termination.
- A noncompetition provision that defines the geographic territory in which, and the time period during which, the departing physician cannot compete with the former employer. Courts will render these provisions unenforceable and invalid if improperly drafted or overly broad.
- Nondisparagement provisions, whereby each party agrees to refrain from making any disparaging or false statements regarding the other. Nondisclosure provisions, detailing what may be disclosed to third parties, are common as well.
- A separation agreement that addresses the return of company property, including office key, credit card, computer, cell phone, and beeper. Patient records and charts should be returned to the practice. Typically, the departing physician will still be allowed reasonable access to patient records post-termination for certain authorized purposes, often at his or her personal expense. The termination agreement may also outline how patients will be notified about the changes in the practice and the circumstances of the physician's departure. If a patient wishes to continue treatment with the departing physician, the medical practice must be ready to transition the patient.
- Mutual releases, as well as any exclusions from the mutual releases, such as pretermination date liabilities, medical malpractice claims resulting from the physician's misconduct, or taxes, interests, and penalties covering the pretermination date.

21.11.1.3 Severance Pay

Depending on the circumstances surrounding the termination and the employment agreement terms, you may be entitled to severance payments on the date of termination or for a period of time post-termination. You should determine whether severance is appropriate or whether you're willing to forgo severance payments in exchange for other benefits. Depending on the dollar amount and your career objectives, it may be worthwhile to sacrifice severance payments for a less onerous noncompetition provision, as an example.*

21.11.2 Licensing Doctors?

Dr. Shirley Svorny is chair of the economics department at California State University, Northridge, and holds a PhD in economics from UCLA. About a decade ago, Dr. Svorny wondered if a medical degree is a barrier—rather than enabler—of affordable health care. As an expert on the regulation of health-care professionals, including medical professional licensing, she participated in health policy summits organized by Cato and the Texas Public Policy Foundation. She argues that licensure not only fails to protect consumers from incompetent physicians, but also, by raising barriers to entry, makes health care more

* Dr. Jay Grife, Esq, MA, personal communication; and Steven M. Harris, Esq., *ENT Today*, March 6, 2012.

expensive and less accessible. Institutional oversight and a sophisticated network of private accrediting and certification organizations, all motivated by the need to protect reputations and avoid legal liability, offer whatever consumer protections exist today. Malpractice attorneys and monetary gain potential—motives, too!

Want an example of the growing wave? On February 25, 2015, the U.S. Supreme Court ruled that the North Carolina state dental board did not have the authority to regulate the teeth-whitening businesses. In a 6–3 decision, the justices found the North Carolina Board of Dental Examiners, which is composed mostly of dentists, illegally quashed competition from nondentists who sought to open teeth-whitening shops in the state. And, momentum grows nationally to establish dental therapists as advocates push hard to get states to enact laws that would open the way for dental therapists to get care to people who might otherwise go without it.

Experienced nurse practitioners in New York also took a step toward greater independence on New Year's Day 2015 when new rules under the *Nurse Practitioner Modernization Act* went into effect. The rules stipulate that nurse practitioners with more than 3600 hours of clinical practice no longer need to work under a written collaborative agreement with a physician. The required clinical experience equates to about 2 years in clinical practice. Nurse practitioners with less than the required amount of experience will still be required to work under a physician, according to the legislation. In addition to rescinding the collaboration requirement, the NPMA frees experienced nurse practitioners from submitting patient charts to a physician for review. The only requirement that remains that will tie experienced nurse practitioners to physicians or hospitals is that they must maintain an established relationship for referral or consultation.

These decisions have the potential to impact other professional licensing boards across the country. And, economists who have examined the market for physician services in the United States generally view state licensing as a means by which to enforce cartel-like restrictions on entry that benefit physicians at the expense of consumers. Medical licensing is seen as a constraint on the efficient combination of inputs, a drag on innovations in health care and medical education, and a significant barrier to effective, cost-efficient health care.*

21.12 -M-

21.12.1 Maintenance of Certification

Doctors complain about onerous rules to get recertified, warning that the demands will force some out of practice at a time when the nation faces a shortage. New requirements have made maintaining certifications a process that never ends. Younger doctors already retake arduous certification exams every 7–10 years to keep their credential, long considered the gold standard of expertise. But, physicians of all ages must now complete a complex new set of requirements every 2–3 years or risk losing their certification. Supporters contend the process will ensure doctors incorporate the latest medical advances into their practices, but critics dismiss it as meaningless, costly, and a waste of time.

To date, the highest-profile pushback to the new rules has come from the Association of American Physicians and Surgeons, which last year sued the American Board of Medical Specialties and accused the organization of restraint of trade. Several other medical

* Available at http://journaltalk.net/articles/5473.

specialty societies (which are separate entities from the certifying boards) have also criticized the requirements. The American Association of Clinical Endocrinologists wrote that they have "no proven benefit to physician or patient," and proposed its own alternative certificate for endocrinologists who engage in ongoing education.*

21.12.2 Malpractice Attorneys Like EHRs

"Lawyers smell blood in electronic medical records—as electronic medical records (EMRs) proliferate under federal regulations; as kludgey workflow processes and patient data entry quality can be problematic! The inherent issues with EMRs—and for the healthcare professionals required to learn them—haven't been lost on lawyers, who see the potential for millions of dollars in judgments for plaintiffs suing for medical negligence."†

21.12.3 Managed Care Contract Risks

Attorneys are becoming more aggressive in suing MCOs, ACOs, HMOs, and other managed care companies. Historical bars to such suits are declining simultaneously with recent federal ERISA protection erosion. The upshot is that more litigations against managed care companies, their affiliates, and their health-care providers are likely. The health-care provider needs to be aware of these trends, needs to evaluate his/her own situation, and may need to take certain steps to limit these new evolving risks and potential liabilities. For example, the usual method of protection for the practicing physician, the use of the corporate form of business, is usually no benefit when signing managed care contracts. Most managed care companies credential the individual physician and hence require that the individual physician and not the professional corporation sign the contract. *This puts all of the physician's personal assets at risk.*

21.12.4 Medical Care Contract Risks

The conversion to managed health-care and capitation financing is a significant marketing force and not merely a temporary business trend. More than 60% of all physicians in the country are now employees of an MCO. Those that embrace these forces will thrive, while those opposed will not. After you have evaluated the HMOs in your geographic area, you must then make your practice more attractive to them, since there are far too many physicians in most regions today. The following issues are considered by most MCO financial managers and business experts, as they decide whether or not to include you in their network.

21.12.4.1 General Standards

- Is there a local or community need for your practice, with a sound patient base that is not too small or large? Remember, practices that already have a significant number of patients have some form of leverage since MCOs know that patients do not like switching their primary care doctors or pediatricians, and women do not want to be forced to change their OB/GYN specialist. If the group leaves the plan, members may complain to their employers and give a negative impression of the plan.

* Roni Caryn Rabin. *Kaiser Health News*, July 24, 2014.

† Lucas Mearian. *ComputerWorld.com*, April 13, 2015.

- A positive return on investment from your economically sound practice is important to MCOs because they wish to continue their relationship with you. Often, this means it is difficult for younger practitioners to enter a plan, since plan actuaries realize that there is a high attrition rate among new practitioners. They also realize that more established practices have high overhead costs and may tend to enter into less lucrative contract offerings just to pay the bills.
- A merger or acquisition is a strategy for the MCO internal business plan that affords a seamless union should a practice decide to sell out or consolidate at a later date. Therefore, a strategy should include things such as strong managerial and cost accounting principles, a group identity rather than individual mindset, profitability, transferable systems and processes, a corporate form of business, and a vertically integrated organization if the practice is a multispecialty group.
- Human resources, capital, and IT service should complement the existing management information system framework. This is often difficult for the solo or small group practice and may indicate the need to consolidate with similar groups to achieve needed economies of scale and capital, especially in areas of high MCO penetration.
- Consolidated financial statements should conform to Generally Accepted Accounting Principles, Internal Revenue Code, Office of the Inspector General, and other appraisal standards.
- Strong and respected MD leadership in the medical and business community is an asset. MCOs prefer to deal with physician executives with advanced degrees. You may not need an MBA or CPA, but you should be familiar with basic business, managerial, and financial principles. This includes a conceptual understanding of horizontal and vertical integration, cost principles, cost volume analysis, financial ratio analysis, and cost behavior.
- The doctors on staff should be willing to treat all conditions and types of patients. The adage "more risk equates to more reward" is still applicable, and most groups should take all the full risk contracting they can handle, providing they are not pooled contracts.
- Are you a team player or solo act? The former personality type might do better in a group or MCO-driven practice, while a fee-for-service market is still possible and may be better suited to the latter personality type.
- Each member of a physician group, or a solo doctor, should have a valid license, DEA narcotics license, continuing medical education, adequate malpractice insurance, board qualification or certification, or hospital privileges; agree with the managed care philosophy; and have partners in a group practice that meet all the same participation criteria. Be available for periodic MCO review by a company representative.

21.12.4.2 Specific Medical Office Standards

ACOs, HMOs, and MCOs may require that the following standards are maintained in the medical office setting:

- It is clean and presentable with a professional appearance.
- It is readily accessible and has a barrier-free design (see OSHA requirements).

- There is appropriate medical emergency and resuscitation equipment.
- The waiting room can accommodate 5–7 patients with private changing areas.
- There is an adequate capacity (e.g., 5000–10,000 member minimum), business plan, and office assistants for the plan.
- There is an office hour minimum (e.g., 20 hours/week).
- 24/7 on-call coverage is available, with electronic tracking and eMRs.
- There are MCO-approved subcontractors.

21.12.5 Medical Fraud and Abuse Statistical Billing Risks

The following actions can be taken by the practitioner in an attempt to limit charges of fraud.

21.12.5.1 Statistical Analysis and Fraud Investigations

The CMS compiles data concerning fee charges and payments by all physicians. These data are broken down into various categories, such as by CPT code, physician specialty, and state. Each and every physician should obtain a copy of this report and review it thoroughly. These data are available through CMS or can be downloaded from its Internet website. The report contains valuable yearly statistical information concerning the rendering of services to Medicare beneficiaries. By comparing the statistics of this report with the statistics of your office, you can determine your risk of an audit. Since the likelihood of an audit is dependent upon *where the money is*, then the nationwide average and the placement of your state in the table can indicate the likelihood of your being audited. Therefore, the risks are that many physicians in high reimbursement states will be audited and few physicians in low reimbursement states will be audited. This is not as arbitrary as it may seem. There must be a reason why the average physician's Medicare charge in one state is higher than that of the national average. Unfortunately only an audit will determine the reason why, whether the reason is due to valid treatments or health-care fraud. These statistics are available to Medicare. Since *knowledge is power*, you should familiarize yourself with the data that Medicare will use in targeting audit candidates. By knowing where a likely audit will take place, the practitioner can alter procedures and documentation to ensure that such has the ability to withstand an audit.

21.12.5.2 Bell-Shaped Normalization Curve

Although a bell-shaped normalization curve will not ensure that you will not be audited, it can go a long way to disprove any intent to defraud a third-party payer. Understanding your options is the first step in visualizing the bell curve.

For example, take these five traditional patient E/M codes (99201, 99202, 99203, 99204, and 99205) and five established patient E/M codes (99211, 99212, 99213, 99214, and 99215). A normal bell curve for most physicians would probably see most of the visits spread fairly evenly over the different levels of codes of each group, with a smaller amount in the level one and five codes. You can use your computer to evaluate whether your CPT codes, especially the E/M codes and the other codes, all fall within a bell curve. If these codes do not fall within a bell curve, then you should consider whether to adjust you coding patterns to bring them into a bell curve. Staying within the bell curve is a prudent defensive step.

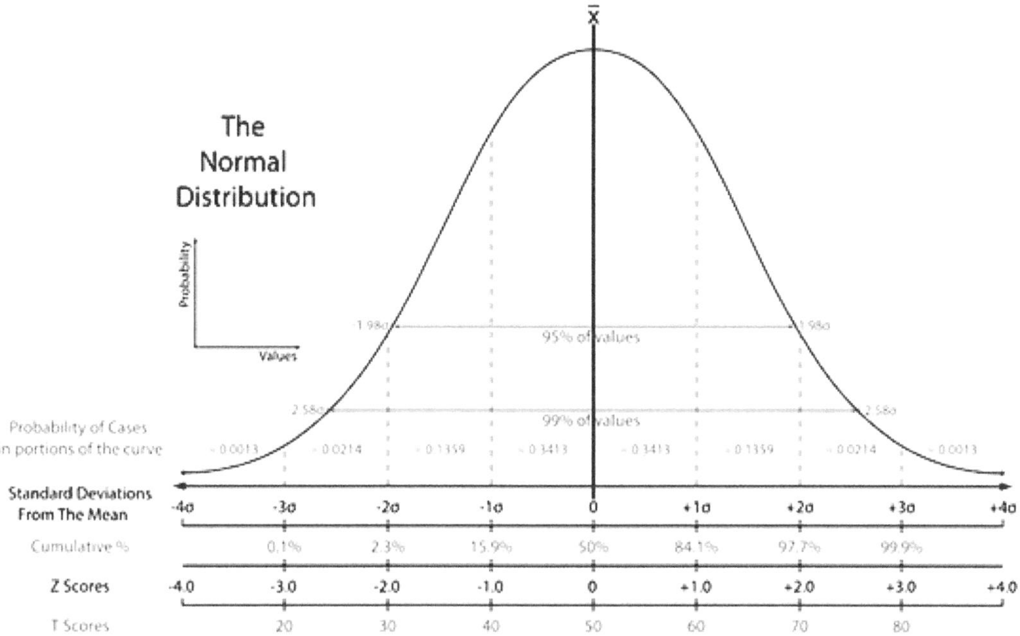

21.12.5.3 Contracts

The provider should read every managed care contract. Most providers simply sign and return every contract that comes across their desk. In recent years, with so much of the population participating in some form of managed care, many providers feel that they have no choice but to sign the contract. Remember that even if the terms are not negotiable, you still have a choice of not signing the contract. If you do sign the contract, you should fully understand the risks that you are undertaking. It is okay to assume a risk, *but* only if you understand the risk you are assuming and are willing to assume that risk. It is often not reasonable to expect that the provider will fully understand the import of many of the clauses in current managed care contract. For that reason, it is prudent to have an attorney review every contract that you intend to sign. Although it costs more initially to pay legal fees to review the contract, it could potentially save a lot of problems and money at a later date. Once you become aware of a risk or a clause in the managed care contract that is contrary to your interests, your first defensive step is to attempt to negotiate the clause out of the contract. Unfortunately, the individual provider has very little leverage in negotiating such contracts and the clause is likely to remain.

21.12.5.4 Practicing Bare

Many providers in practice would not think of *practicing bare*. In the past, the term *practicing bare* meant that the provider did not have malpractice insurance. Current managed care contracts often require that not only the provider has certain limits of malpractice but also that the provider shows evidence of such insurance. Therefore, many providers are under the impression that they are not practicing bare. As can be seen from the example clauses above, most providers are in effect practicing bare. Most providers have no protection from adverse results arising out of a Hold Harmless Clause in an agreement. Most malpractice insurance companies do not provide such coverage. If your malpractice insurance company does not provide coverage for such events, it is incumbent upon you and your associations to lobby the malpractice insurance carriers to provide such coverage. An additional rider, at an additional premium, for Hold Harmless coverage would help the practitioner sleep better at night.

The first question that the provider should ask is, *Would I consider practicing without malpractice insurance?* If the answer to that question is *no,* then the next question that the provider should ask is, *Why am I assuming the risk under the Hold Harmless Clause?* If the provider cannot provide a lucent answer to that question (stating "I have no choice" is not a lucid answer!), then the provider should not sign the managed care contract. Nonetheless, if the provider has signed managed care contracts, then the provider should understand that he/she is practicing bare and should take steps to reduce his/her exposure. In effect, the provider should attempt to become *judgment-proof.* Such a step does present its own risks. Ultimately, the first step for every physician who signs a managed care contract, with hold harmless agreement, is to read the contract and then consult an attorney or other professional. Plaintiff attorneys are beginning to make inroads in suing managed care companies. The managed care attorneys foresaw such events and provided protection for the company in the contracts most providers have signed.

As plaintiffs become successful in suing and recovering from managed care companies, those companies are going to seek indemnity from the provider. Unless the provider protects himself, the provider is likely to become a collateral casualty of events. The current practice of medicine presents risks to the provider. The provider may not be able to insure against these risks and therefore should take defensive steps to avoid future problems.

21.12.5.5 Risky Treatment Elimination

One of the methods most often overlooked in malpractice risk management is an evaluation of the risk/reward ratio of treating certain patients or performing certain surgical procedures. Managed care has effectively reduced the reimbursement of treatments and surgeries across the board. In the past, the physician could demand a reasonable fee for the risk involved. Now, that fee is determined by someone other than the physician. Although the resource-based view values include a malpractice component, sometimes that component does not adequately reflect the risk of certain procedures or the increased risk of certain patients. Therefore, the physician should evaluate their own practice and identify those procedures and those patient types that carry a high risk of malpractice and for which the physician is not adequately reimbursed for that risk. The physician then should tailor his or her practice so that he or she no longer provides those services. The revenue lost will be worth the risk of the malpractice suit and the collateral consequences. This is simply the unintended consequence of insurance company and other managers reducing the physicians' reimbursement. If the reward is high enough, people will take the risk. If the reward is reduced and the risk remains the same, fewer people will be willing to engage in that behavior, simple free market economics. A physician need not feel bad for turning away patients or dropping certain procedures from one's practice. That is simply part of risk management.

21.12.5.6 Staff Education and Training

The medical staff is an extension of the physician. Furthermore, several federal regulations, including HIPAA and OSHA, have specific staff training requirements. Failure to provide the required training subjects the physician to the risk of not only employee transgression but also administrative discipline for failure to conduct proper training of staff.

21.12.6 Medical School Health-Care Services Risks

One area where indemnification may be useful is in the relationship between medical schools and non-university hospitals that are used as teaching hospitals. Past court decisions have usually held the medical school liable for the actions of its students and staff. These decisions usually turned on the close relationship among the students, staff, and the medical school. Since the medical school staff members are also members of the hospital medical staff, the hospital could be held liable if it failed to monitor properly the competence of these medical staff members.

The problem is that the hospital is seldom able to evaluate independently the credentials of the members of the teaching staff. The usual agreement between the medical school and the hospital allows the medical school to decide who will be on the teaching staff, and it allows all members of the teaching staff to oversee the teaching in the hospital. In this type of situation, it would be in the hospital's interest to require the medical school to indemnify it against any judgments arising from the negligence of medical school personnel. Since the assets of the medical school would be large enough to pay any judgment, the indemnity would not even require the medical school to carry additional insurance. The benefits to the medical school of having the hospital accept its students are sufficiently important that the potential risk of the agreement would be offset. This balance of interests is basic to the negotiation of indemnification agreements. The hospital can exact indemnification agreements only if the use of the hospital's resources is sufficiently valuable to offset the potential costs of the agreement to the third party.

In a teaching hospital, there are two factors that mitigate the risk to the medical school of indemnifying the hospital. First, hospitals are seldom held liable for the actions of medical students or residents. Second, in the usual malpractice suit involving a teaching hospital, the plaintiff will sue the student, the medical school, and the hospital. Unless the hospital was in actual control of the student, the hospital will be liable only if it breached its duty to monitor the overall quality of medical care. The hospital can escape liability if it can prove that it did not breach its duty to the patient. The best way to do this is to put all of the blame on the medical school. However, this will seriously compromise the ability of the medical school to defend its actions. It is better for the medical school to risk the potential losses of an indemnification agreement than to force the hospital to aid in making the plaintiff's case. In general, it is the potential infighting between defendants that provides the strongest rationale for indemnification agreements.

21.12.7 Medical Student Debt and Suicide?

Every year, 300–400 physicians commit suicide. More than 10% of doctors are thought to have depression, a frequent precursor to suicide. Rates of depression and suicide among physicians are higher than in the general population. Many reasons including stress, heavy workload, sleep deprivation, lack of autonomy, and lack of outlets for personal care may contribute to higher vulnerability in doctors. Despite the importance of debt and financial worry, few studies have investigated their effect on physician depression and suicide.

A number of studies show that higher debt leads to more burnout, a negative reaction to work-related or interpersonal stress. A study of over 260 radiology residents found that a resident's subjective financial strain was a stronger predictor of burnout than amount of debt. Another study of over 4000 internal medicine residents found that more educational debt was associated with more depressive symptoms and cynicism about medicine. Burnout itself is a risk factor for depression and suicidal behaviors. Concerns about finances likely begin during medical school. Medical students worry most about finances even more than academics. Despite an increase in financial worries during the course of medical school, students with financial worries are less likely to seek counseling.*

21.12.8 Midlevel Provider Risks

While the use of physician extenders can bring added legal risks to a practice, they can also help prevent incidents of malpractice by providing more individualized care for patients. There are several legal theories that may be applied to attach liability to a physician for a Physician Extender's (PE) negligence. First, the physician may be directly responsible for negligent hiring of a PE. Another legal theory is a failure to supervise properly. And, the responsibility for quality assurance, including review and cosigning of charts, is also a common statutory provision. Failure to perform this function may be deemed negligence *per se* such that the supervising physician may be held liable even without proof of negligence by the PE. A physician may also be held vicariously liable for the acts of a PE on the grounds that the PE is acting as an agent of the physician. In some states, statutes create a conclusive presumption of agency so that a physician will always be responsible for the negligence of a PE. In other states, liability will depend on whether the physician has a right to control the work done by the PE. It is also important to be aware, to the extent possible, of the applicable standard of care for PEs. In some states, the PE is held to the standard of care of the supervising physician, on the theory that the PE is carrying out the function of the doctor and the patient is entitled to an equivalent level of treatment regardless of the provider. In other states, the PE is held to the lesser standard of a similarly trained and certified PE, while in still other states, the standard of care has not yet been determined by the courts. In this latter circumstance, it is best to err on the side of caution and assume that the PE will be held to the higher standard of care.†

21.12.9 Mistaken Surgery Risks

While the consent of an individual patient to medical treatment is the responsibility of the treating physician, the monitoring of consent is an important part of the quality control program. Consent should be checked before surgery to ensure that there has been no confusion of patients. Performing the wrong surgery on a patient, or wrong limb, is not easily justifiable, and checking the consent form is good insurance against this type of mistake. The importance of preventing mistaken surgery mitigates against the use of oral consent for surgical procedures. The hospital will share liability for mistaken surgery because it is the hospital's employees (nurses and orderlies) who prepare the patient for surgery and actually deliver the patient to surgery. Because of this shared liability, the hospital must

* Available at http://www.kevinmd.com/blog/2015/03/medical-student-debt-lead-suicide.html.
† Christopher D. Bernard, JD. *Medical Economics*, February 18, 2015.

demand written consent to surgery. This consent should at least describe the intended surgery so that the hospital personnel can determine if the patient is being prepared for the proper operation.

21.12.10 Money Laundering Risks

Charges of money laundering may seem foreign to the practice of medicine. The term *money laundering* evokes visions of a suitcase of drug cash being brought into a legitimate business and being transformed into that business's receipts and later tunneled through legal channels. In medicine, the route begins with receipt of a claim payment check (i.e., a check as opposed to the drug dealer's cash). The check is then deposited into the professional corporation's checking account. The funds are then paid to the physician in the form of wages. Those wages are then deposited into the physician's personal checking account. Those funds and other similarly situated funds are then accumulated until a check is written to pay for a sports utility vehicle. The money received from the alleged fraudulent insurance claim has successfully been *laundered* into a hard asset (e.g., a new SUV).

21.12.11 *Mystery Patient Shopper* Risks

In 2014, the Department of Health and Human Services proposed a *mystery shopper* program to gauge primary-care physicians' timeliness in accepting new patients, according to a notice in the Federal Register. The plan calls for contacting 4185 primary-care physicians—465 in each of 9 as-yet-unnamed states—twice, once by someone pretending to be a new patient who has private insurance and once by someone pretending to be a publicly insured patient. Scenarios will involve patients with both urgent medical concerns and those requesting a routine medical exam. The purpose of this program is to assess the timeliness with which primary-care services could be provided, gain insight into reasons why availability is lacking, and provide current information on primary-care availability and accessibility.

21.13 CONCLUSION

Medical risk management is no longer just about medical malpractice anymore—it has not been for some time now, despite the recent resurgence of liability fears. In fact, since most practicing physicians have malpractice insurance, then a malpractice suit should be viewed as a mere inconvenience, and the practitioner and his financial advisors should realize that the lawsuit is mainly about someone else's money.

A shift in thought paradigm is needed. The medicolegal landscape has changed. The physician in practice today is faced with many legal challenges that have the potential to destroy the medical practice and the individual's personal assets. These have been briefly reviewed in this chapter.

Therefore, every practice, medical clinic, or health-care entity should consider having a qualified attorney, crisis manager, and/or risk management consultant on retainer. Be aware, the risks are only going to increase, going forward!

21.14 COLLABORATE

Discuss this chapter online with others at http://www.medicalexecutivepost.com.

ACKNOWLEDGMENTS

To Edward J. Rappaport, JD, LL.M, Atlanta, Georgia; Dr. Steven D. Chin, MS, MBA, CPHQ, Millbrae, California; Robert James Cimasi, MHA, ASA, AVA, CMP, President of Health Capital Consultants LLC., of St. Louis, Missouri; Dr. Richard Willner of Peer Review Justice Inc.; Rick Kahler, MS, CFP, of Kahler Financial; Eric A. Dover, MD, of Portland, Oregon; and Professor Edward P. Richards, JD, MPH, Program in Law, Science and Public Health, LSU Law Center, LSU.

FURTHER READINGS

Bode, GL: Internal Medical Practice Controls. In Marcinko, DE (editor): *Business of Medical Practice*. Springer Publishing, New York, 2010.

Faden, RR, Beauchamp, TL, and Kass, NE: *N Engl J Med* 2014; Informed Consent, Cooperative Effectiveness and Learning Healthcare, 370:766–768. doi:10.1056/NEJMhle1313674.

Fenton, CF: Medical Risk Management Issues. In Marcinko, DE (editor): *Insurance Planning and Risk Management for Physicians*. Jones and Bartlett Publishing, Sudbury, MA, 2005.

Fenton, CF: Medical Practice Sales Contract. In Marcinko, DE (editor): *Business of Medical Practice*. Springer Publishing, New York, 2010.

Fenton, CF and Marcinko, DE: *Modern Risk Management Issues for Physicians: Comprehensive Financial Planning Strategies for Doctors and Advisors*. Productivity Press, Boca Raton, FL, 2015.

Marcinko, DE and Hetico, HR: *Dictionary of Health Insurance and Managed Care*. Springer Publishing, New York, 2008.

Marcinko, DE and Hetico, HR (eds.): Healthcare Workplace Violence Prevention. In *Hospitals and Healthcare Organizations*. Productivity Press, Boca Raton, FL, 2013.

Pho, K: *Establishing, Managing, and Protecting Your Online Reputation: A Social Media Guide for Physicians and Medical Practices*. Phoenix, MD, Greenbranch Publishing, 2013.

Trites, P: Medical Records, Insurance Billing and Coding Guidelines. In Marcinko, DE (editor): *Business of Medical Practice*. Springer Publishing, New York, 2010.

22 Topical *N* through *Z* List of Emerging Medical Practice 2.0 Risks

The Too Numerous to Count Syndrome

David Edward Marcinko, Charles F. Fenton III, and Hope Rachel Hetico

CONTENTS

Most traditional books for medical professionals limit their discussion of risk management to life insurance planning, occasionally some property casualty issues, usually asset protection management, and perhaps those methods to avoid medical malpractice claims. Defensive medicine and risk management were often synonymous terms. However, limiting medical risk management concerns to these customary issues is completely misplaced in modernity, for the medical practitioner and his/her financial advisor, attorney, health information technicians, and/or risk management consultant.

22.1 INTRODUCTION

In today's medicolegal environment, the physician faces risks from many directions; almost *ad naseum* or *too numerous to count.* And so, here is an alphabetized list (*N* through *Z*) of some modern perils and emerging risks that may defy formal definition, chapter inclusion, or even classification, but are nevertheless important considerations.

22.2 -N-

22.2.1 Never Events

The term *Never Event* was first introduced in 2001 by Ken Kizer, MD, former CEO of the National Quality Forum (NQF), in reference to particularly shocking medical errors (such as wrong-site surgery) that should never occur. Over time, the list has been expanded to signify adverse events that are unambiguous (clearly identifiable and measurable), serious (resulting in death or significant disability), and usually preventable. The NQF initially defined 27 such events in 2002. The list has been revised since then, most recently in 2013, and now consists of 29 events grouped into 7 categories: surgical, product or device, patient protection, care management, environmental, radiologic, and criminal.

Never Events

The National Quality Forum's Health Care *Never Events*

Surgical Events

Surgery or other invasive procedure performed on the wrong body part

Surgery or other invasive procedure performed on the wrong patient

Wrong surgical or other invasive procedure performed on a patient

Unintended retention of a foreign object in a patient after surgery or other procedure

Intraoperative or immediately postoperative/post-procedure death in an American Society of Anesthesiologists Class I patient

Product or Device Events

Patient death or serious injury associated with the use of contaminated drugs, devices, or biologics provided by the health-care setting

Patient death or serious injury associated with the use or function of a device in patient care, in which the device is used for functions other than as intended

Patient death or serious injury associated with intravascular air embolism that occurs while being cared for in a health-care setting

Patient Protection Events

Discharge or release of a patient/resident of any age, who is unable to make decisions, to other than an authorized person

Patient death or serious disability associated with patient elopement (disappearance)

Patient suicide, attempted suicide, or self-harm resulting in serious disability, while being cared for in a health-care facility

Care Management Events

Patient death or serious injury associated with a medication error (e.g., errors involving the wrong drug, wrong dose, wrong patient, wrong time, wrong rate, wrong preparation, or wrong route of administration)

Patient death or serious injury associated with unsafe administration of blood products

Maternal death or serious injury associated with labor or delivery in a low-risk pregnancy while being cared for in a health-care setting
Death or serious injury of a neonate associated with labor or delivery in a low-risk pregnancy
Artificial insemination with the wrong donor sperm or wrong egg
Patient death or serious injury associated with a fall while being cared for in a health-care setting
Any stage 3, stage 4, or unstageable pressure ulcers acquired after admission/presentation to a health-care facility
Patient death or serious disability resulting from the irretrievable loss of an irreplaceable biological specimen
Patient death or serious injury resulting from failure to follow-up or communicate laboratory, pathology, or radiology test results

Environmental Events

Patient or staff death or serious disability associated with an electric shock in the course of a patient care process in a health-care setting
Any incident in which a line designated for oxygen or other gas to be delivered to a patient contains no gas or the wrong gas, or is contaminated by toxic substances
Patient or staff death or serious injury associated with a burn incurred from any source in the course of a patient care process in a health-care setting
Patient death or serious injury associated with the use of restraints or bedrails while being cared for in a health-care setting

Radiologic Events

Death or serious injury of a patient or staff associated with introduction of a metallic object into the MRI area

Criminal Events

Any instance of care ordered by or provided by someone impersonating a physician, nurse, pharmacist, or other licensed health-care provider
Abduction of a patient/resident of any age
Sexual abuse/assault on a patient within or on the grounds of a health-care setting
Death or significant injury of a patient or staff member resulting from a physical assault (i.e., battery) that occurs within or on the grounds of a health-care setting

Source: CMS/National Quality Forum 2013.

Most never events are very rare. For example, a 2006 study estimated that a typical hospital might experience a case of wrong-site surgery once every 5–10 years. However, when *never events* occur, they are devastating to patients—71% of events reported to the Joint Commission over the past 12 years were fatal and may indicate a fundamental safety problem within an organization. Although individual events are uncommon, on a population basis, many patients still experience these serious errors. A 2013 study estimated that more than 4000 surgical never events occur yearly in the United States.

The Joint Commission has recommended that hospitals report *sentinel events* since 1995. Sentinel events are defined as "an unexpected occurrence involving death or serious physiological or psychological injury, or the risk thereof." The NQF's *never events* are also considered sentinel events by the Joint Commission. The Joint Commission mandates performance of a root cause analysis after a sentinel event. The Leapfrog Group recommends that in addition to an RCA, organizations should disclose the error and apologize to the patient, report the event, and waive costs associated with it.

Because *never events* are devastating and preventable, health-care organizations are under increasing pressure to eliminate them completely. The Centers for Medicare and Medicaid Services (CMS) announced in August 2007 that Medicare would no longer pay for additional costs associated with many preventable errors, including those considered never events. Since then, many states and private insurers have adopted similar policies. Since February 2009, CMS has not paid for any costs associated with wrong site surgeries.

Never events are also being publicly reported, with the goal of increasing accountability and improving the quality of care. Since the NQF disseminated its original never events list in 2002, 11 states have mandated reporting of these incidents whenever they occur, and an additional 16 states mandate reporting of serious adverse events (including many of the NQF never events). Health-care facilities are accountable for correcting systematic problems that contributed to the event, with some states mandating performance of a root cause analysis and reporting its results.*

22.2.2 New Age Medicine Risks

The risks of new age medicine practices and their regulation are increasing. For example, *dry needling*, which is like acupuncture, is a growing practice in places like Australia but is unregulated. Physicians should understand all regulatory and other risks when implementing new unregulated practices pushed by our new age society. Home births are on the rise in North America (even in Canada with government-provided hospital delivery), but physicians end up dealing with the disasters and associated risks when they occur.

Alternative medicine is any practice that is put forward as having the healing effects of medicine, but is not founded on evidence gathered using the scientific method. It consists of a wide range of health-care practices, products, and therapies. Examples include new and traditional medicine practices such as homeopathy, naturopathy, chiropractic, energy medicine, various forms of Chinese medicine, Ayurvedic medicine, and faith healing. The treatments are those that are not part of the conventional, science-based health-care system, and are not backed by scientific evidence.

Complementary medicine is alternative medicine used together with conventional medical treatment in a belief, not proven by using scientific methods, that it *complements* the treatment. CAM is the abbreviation for complementary and alternative medicine.

Integrative medicine (or integrative health), on the other hand, is the combination of the practices and methods of alternative medicine with conventional medicine.†

22.2.3 Nonnative Language Perils

Communication risk to immigrants with limited nonnative language proficiency is a growing concern. With today's higher immigrant population in the United States, more medical practices are treating patients with limited English language proficiency. Clinicians now run the risk of not properly communicating medical risk information to these populations.

* AHRQ. Available at http://psnet.ahrq.gov/primer.aspx?primerID=3.

† From Danielle Bochove. "Don't Try This At Home." *Maclean's* 124.33/34 (2011): 68. *MasterFILE Premier*. Web. April 27, 2012; Stephen Adams Janz. "Acupuncture by Another Name: Dry Needling in Australia." *Australian Journal of Acupuncture & Chinese Medicine* 6, no. 2: 3–11. *Alt HealthWatch*, EBSCO*host*. Web. April 27, 2012; With kind permission from Springer Science+Business Media *The Business of Medical Practice* (Third Edition), 2010, DE Marcinko.

A recent study shows that materials that include visual aids are being used by medical practices to effectively communicate with the patient.*

22.3 -O-

22.3.1 Office Crisis Management

The medical professional who remains in practice long enough is sure to undergo some adverse situation that may negatively affect the practice. A patient may die, your hospital may close, or a patient may go ballistic and injure your staff or yourself. When, not if, this scenario occurs, you must have a crisis management business plan in place to deal swiftly and successfully with the matter. Some management experts suggest the following course of actions when tragedy strikes:

- Stay calm and relaxed; act immediately.
- Release detrimental but accurate information as soon as possible. Try to stay neutral.
- Educate your staff about the crisis, then your local community, if relevant.
- Fix the problem or find an alternate solution to minimize recurrence and disruption.
- Continually release information about the crisis if it is ongoing.
- Monitor and report the results of your strategy to all affected parties.
- Thank everyone and turn a negative story into a positive one through good public relations.

Remember, speed and productivity are the keys to adverse public relations fallout. Recall Johnson & Johnson, which recovered beautifully from the Tylenol tragedy a decade ago, and not only recovered lost profits but trust in the marketplace as well.

22.3.2 On-Call and Emergency Department Risks

There is a growing revolt of specialists against hospital on-call duties that threatens to violate federal law and lose status as trauma centers. Specialties most likely to refuse include plastic surgery, ENT, psychiatry, neurosurgery, ophthalmology, and orthopedics. And, refusing to respond to assigned call is a violation of federal law and carries fines as much as $50,000 per case.

In contrast, refusing to sign up for call does not violate the law, and more physicians are taking this option. The opting-out problem is especially acute in California where hospitals are combating issues with compensation, reporting the miscreant docs to the authorities, or threatening to remove them from staff completely. In turn, doctors are fighting back with lawsuits. As an example, essayist Jeff Goldsmith, president of Health Futures Inc., and associate professor of Public Health Sciences at the University of Virginia, opined that

> We can expect intensified conflict with private physicians over the hospital's 24-hour mission and service obligation, specifically providing physician coverage after hours and on weekends. Younger physicians have shown decreased willingness to trade

* From Rocio Garcia-Retamero and K. Dhami Mandeep. "Pictures Speak Louder Than Numbers: On Communicating Medical Risks To Immigrants with Limited Non-Native Language Proficiency." *Health Expectations* 14(2011): 46–57. *CINAHL Plus with Full Text* Web, April 27, 2012.

their personal time to cover hospital call in exchange for hospital admitting privileges as their elders did. Those admitting privileges are either less essential or completely unnecessary in an increasingly ambulatory practice environment. The present solution is for hospitals to pay stipends to independent practitioners for call coverage or to contract with single specialty groups large enough to rotate call internally.*

22.4 -P-

22.4.1 Patient Privacy Rights

Is there anything in your health record that you would *not* want to share with others? Prescriptions for antidepressants, anxiety, cancer, long-ago abortions, AIDS or HIV, testing for the Alzheimer gene, a child's autism or ADD, sexual impotency prescriptions, hospital admissions, or anything else? You assume most personal health information is private, right? *It's not!* According to Deborah Peel, MD, the CEO and founder of PatientPrivacyRights.org, some doctors, many patients, and risk management consultants, like most Americans, probably believe

- What you tell your doctor is totally private.
- If you sign *privacy notices* at a doctor's office, a pharmacy, a hospital, or a lab, your health records will not be used or disclosed without your permission.
- No one can look at your sensitive health records, prescriptions, or tests without your permission.

Yet, none of these assumptions are true. Who can see and use your medical records? Well, PPR estimates that over 4 million businesses can see them, including

- Employers and government agencies
- Insurance companies and billing firms
- Pharmaceutical companies and pharmacy benefits managers
- Marketing firms and data miners

Today, patient consent is no longer required to share health records, no matter how embarrassing or intensely personal the contents may be. While your doctor may wish to protect your information, once the records are sent out of their offices, they can no longer control who sees or uses medical records information (personal communication).

22.4.1.1 What about Electronic Health Records?

Electronic health records (EHRs) are supposed to be progressive, save lives and money. And, in fact, privacy is the key to progress with health information technology (HIT). Yet, the potential benefits of electronic health systems cannot be realized unless Americans have confidence that ironclad privacy protections are in place for online health records, databases, and networks. As Americans realize how open their records actually are, they will avoid treatment and be much more selective about important information they share with their doctors. Patient Privacy Rights applauds the smart use of technology in medicine

* From Jeff Goldsmith. *The Long Baby Boom*. Johns Hopkins University Press, May 2008.

and the health-care industry. *No one should have to choose between privacy and health* (Deborah Peel, MD, personal communication).

22.4.2 Patient Self-Diagnosis Risks

While health care is not *do-it-yourself*, an informed patient can be an asset. A poorly informed patient, on the other hand, clearly complicates treatment. Assume the responsibility of being the primary information source and educator for your patient. To help deal with a self-diagnosing patient, consider the following as suggested by David Troxel, MD, the chief medical officer of The Doctors Company:

- Encourage patients to always check with you about the accuracy of information obtained from external sources. Use the intake time to find out what Internet information the patient has found.
- Directly discuss what the patient has read, even if the patient's external source is a good one in your professional opinion. The exchange enhances your relationship with the patient and can increase treatment compliance. Welcome questions and help put the patient's information in the appropriate context.
- Provide your patient with a list of websites that provide accurate information, such as the Centers for Disease Control and Prevention (http://www.cdc.gov). Make sure the patient understands the limitations of the Internet.
- Document in the patient's chart your diagnosis, your treatment management plan, and medication prescribed, as well as the reasons behind your decisions.

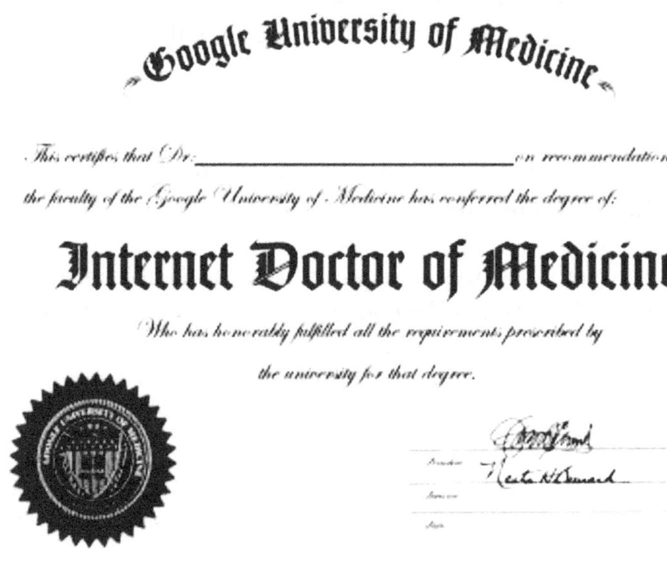

22.4.3 Patterns of Practice Risks

One of the next big areas of risk that will surface in the near future is the *pattern of practice risk*. Pattern of practice refers to the way that a particular physician practices medicine. With computers, eHRs, standardized diagnosis and treatment codes, and the budgetary restraints inherent in medical practice, it is becoming easy to analyze a physician's method of practice. The treatment and diagnosis codes that a physician uses and submits to third-party payers can be quantified and compared with those of his or her colleagues in the same or similar specialties. Statistical *outliers* can be identified. These outliers will then be further audited and required to justify their treatments. If no rational basis exists for the statistical differences, the outlier may find himself the subject of a fraud investigation.

Overheard in the Doctor's Lounge

Fighting for the Rights of Medical Professionals

The Center for Peer Review Justice is a group of physicians, podiatrists, dentists, and osteopaths who have witnessed the perversion of medical peer review by malice and bad faith. Similar to the American Association of Neurological Surgeons (AANS), they have seen the statutory immunity, which is provided to *peers* for the purposes of quality assurance and credentialing, used as cover to allow those *peers* to ruin careers and reputations to further their own, usually monetary agenda or destroying the competition. The group is dedicated to the exposure, conviction, and sanction of doctors, and affiliated hospitals, HMOs, medical boards, and other such institutions, that would use peer review as a weapon to unfairly destroy other professionals. PeerReview.org is a rallying point and resource center for any medical professional that finds himself/herself in the midst of an unfair and bad faith attack by unethical, malicious *peers*.

Dr. Richard B. Willner, DPM
http://www.PeerReview.org
Kenner, Louisiana

22.4.4 Physician Hospital Organizations

A physician hospital organization (PHO) is a blend of private doctors and hospitals, maintaining its concentration and control of surgical rather than medical care. Ownership may be divided by a governing board, according to a pro-rata basis with the larger partner having most organizational strength and bargaining power in the corporate structure. Typically, this favors the hospital. From a strategic standpoint, most MDs are still not currently aligned with many PHOs, since surgical care is increasingly being delivered in private offices, surgical specialty hospitals, or ambulatory care centers. Additionally, PHOs may become potential MD competitors and may often lack managed care contracting experience, may have inflexible provider networks, and may require MD exclusivity in their organization. Nevertheless, the function of a PHO is to

- Negotiate managed care contracts
- Negotiate on all health insurance contracts
- Establish insurance product(s)
- Employ doctors and support staff
- Consolidate and acquire physician practices
- Acquire alternative medical practices

Many believe the "p" in PHO should be lowercase, while an uppercase "H" is a sign of relative strength (i.e., pHO). And so, what do you think?

22.4.5 Physician Service (Third-Party) Company Risks

Indemnification should be requested from corporations with which the office, clinic, or hospital contracts provide physician services, such as the staffing of emergency rooms. These physician service agreements are very profitable, putting the hospital in a good position to require indemnification. This indemnification is especially important for third-party physician groups because of the inability of the hospital to assess the qualifications of those physicians. The hospital is forced to delegate to the third-party provider its duty to select medical staff members, but it cannot delegate its liability if this selection is improperly performed. This leads to the hospital being held liable for the results of decisions that it is unable to participate in. By requiring the physician service corporation to indemnify the hospital against any losses that result from the improper selection of emergency room physicians, the hospital shifts the financial risk of an improper decision to the party that actually made the decision. The benefit to the staffing company is that it is allowed to continue doing business with the hospital, and it is protected from the hospital cooperating with the plaintiff.

If a hospital contracts directly with physicians to staff its emergency room, it is unlikely to be able to negotiate an effective indemnification agreement with physicians. The physicians will seldom have enough available assets to pay a substantial settlement, and the cost of additional insurance may be prohibitive. The same problem may arise if the hospital relies on members of its medical staff to provide emergency room coverage. In these cases, the hospital's only course is to require that the physicians carry personal malpractice insurance. While this does not directly protect the hospital from losses, it does ensure that the physician will have an attorney to protect the physician's interests. A physician without any assets or insurance may agree to help the plaintiff make a case against the hospital in return for being let out of the lawsuit. The insurance will also provide assets for the hospital to reach if it decides to sue for common law indemnity for the physician's actions.

22.4.6 Provider Fraud Schemes (Top Ten in Health Care)

1. Billing for services not rendered
2. Billing for a noncovered service as a covered service
3. Misrepresenting dates of service
4. Misrepresenting locations of service
5. Misrepresenting provider of service
6. Waiving of deductibles and/or copayments
7. Incorrect reporting of diagnoses or procedures (includes unbundling)
8. Overutilization of services
9. Corruption (kickbacks and bribery)
10. False or unnecessary issuance of prescription drugs*

* From Charles Piper. CFE CRT, January/February 2013 ACFE.

22.5 -Q-

22.5.1 *Qui Tam* Federal False Claims Act Risks

A civil war era law, titled the False Claims Act (*qui tam* [in the name of the king]), is increasingly popular with prosecutors who pursue inappropriate billing mishaps by physicians. This act allows a private citizen, such as your patient, your employee, or a competing health-care practitioner, to bring a health-care fraud claim against you on behalf of and in the name of the United States of America. The *relator* who initiates the claim is rewarded by sharing in a percentage of the recovery from the health-care provider. Essentially, this act allows informers to receive up to 30% of any judgment recovered against government contractors (Medicare, Medicaid, TRICARE-CHAMPUS, prison systems, American Indian reservations, or the VA systems). With a low burden of proof, triple damages, and penalties up to $10,000 for each wrongful claims submission, these suits are the enforcement tools of choice for zealous prosecutors pursuing health-care fraud. All that must be proven is that improper claims were submitted with a reckless disregard of the truth. Intentional fraud is irrelevant to these cases, even if submitted by a third party, such as a billing company.

22.6 -R-

22.6.1 Reasonably-Preventable Medical Events

As opposed to *never events*, Medicare recently implemented a new policy of halting payment to hospitals for the added cost of treating patients who are injured in their care. Medicare placed 10 *reasonably preventable* conditions on its initial list, including

- Patients receiving incompatible blood transfusions
- Patients developing infections after certain surgeries
- Patients undergoing a second operation to retrieve a sponge left behind from the first
- Patients developing serious bed sores
- Patients developing urinary tract infections caused by catheters
- Patients suffering injuries from falls

The congressionally mandated Medicare measure is not projected to yield large savings—$21 million a year, compared with $110 billion spent on inpatient care in 2007. But, officials believe that the regulations could apply to several hundred thousand hospital stays of the 12.5 million covered annually by Medicare, while the policy will also prevent hospitals from billing patients directly for costs generated by medical errors. Over the last years, four states Medicaid programs have announced that they will not pay for as many as 28 *never events*, joining some of the country's largest commercial insurers, including WellPoint, Aetna, Cigna, and Blue Cross Blue Shield plans in seven states.

22.6.2 Recoupment Risks from Medicare

Historically, the main risk any physician faced that would place personal assets at risk was the threat of a Medicare recoupment. Although many are surprised upon receipt of a notice of recoupment, the majority of requests were preceded with a request for copies of medical records to determine the necessity of care. Many doctors, upon receiving a request to forward copies of such records, simply assign the task to a clerk and forget about the incident, or attempt to change the records. Both actions are misguided; but it does not mean that you cannot *complete* your medical records. Medical records should be completed according to your office's previously established written medical record policy. But, DO NOT ALTER THE MEDICAL RECORDS!

If unsuccessful at demonstrating medical necessity, and recoupment letter still is received, then the practitioner should retain an attorney to preserve all the legal rights. Generally, there is a right to request a *fair hearing* before a *hearing officer*. At the fair hearing, the practitioner is given the opportunity to present justification of the treatments to the impartial hearing officer. If the fair hearing results are adverse to the practitioner, there is a right to request a hearing before an *administrative law judge*. Even if the practitioner is unsuccessful at that level, there may be additional appeal rights. So, be aware that some malpractice insurance policies may contain an administrative defense rider that might assist you in such an instance.

22.6.3 Recorded Conversations with Physicians

With recent advances in technology, smartphones can become recording devices with the touch of a button. This technological capability gives patients and their families the ability to easily and surreptitiously record conversations with physicians. The frequency of such recordings or whether they even occur is unknown. The ubiquity of smartphones, however, suggests the potential for secret recordings to occur.

As of January 2014, 58% of Americans owned a smartphone, including 83% of young adults. Although recording conversations with physicians may provide some benefit for patients and their families, secret recordings can undermine patient–physician relationships and ultimately affect the provision of health care.*

22.6.4 Referral Risks

Primary care physicians (PCPs) often refer patients to specialists when they face a complicated or perplexing diagnosis, or one that is beyond their purview. But, is that always the right decision for the patient? Some experts say that it absolutely is, but others say knowing the patient is more valuable than being an expert in one specific area. An additional element is the fear of malpractice allegations for a referral or lack of one. Referrals are a growing issue in the United States. A study published in 2012 in the *Archives of Internal Medicine* showed that the incidence of physicians referring patients to other physicians nearly doubled from 1999 to 2009, growing from 4.8% to 9.3%. That represents a jump from 40.6 million referrals annually to 105 million.

However small, there is still a little liability risk in referring to a specialist. Unless the PCP knows the specialist is somehow incompetent, he or she is generally only liable for the care they deliver or oversee directly. Even sending a patient to the *wrong* specialist carries little risk. It all comes down to the physician's medical record for why they are providing that referral. If the differential diagnosis shows it's justified, then the physician has done the right thing. Some experts follow a *rule of three*: if the PCP hasn't figured out a patient's

* Available at http://jama.jamanetwork.com/article.aspx?articleID = 2204226#jvp150030r8; Michelle Rodriguez, JD; Jason Morrow, MD, PhD; Ali Seifi, MD. *JAMA* March 12, 2015. doi:10.1001/jama.2015.2424.

problem within three visits, he or she seeks help either from a colleague in his or her office or an outside referral. Part of his or her rationale is that about 40% of conditions cannot be categorized at the initial presentation. Over time, however, the condition may become clearer. Often, that is the time frame in which the patient is seeing the specialist, making it easier for him or her to diagnose. But, specialists aren't always able to provide answers either, which can be reassuring in a way.

It is also important for PCPs to make referrals to physicians who are in the same networks or with whom they have a relationship. If a specialist delivers poor care to your patient or doesn't send you a note afterward, stop referring to that person. Hopefully, he or she will notice and ask why. Respond with an honest, specific answer if that happens. Since it is incumbent upon PCPs to be sure they get notes back from the specialist, it is equally important to review them. And recall, insurance restrictions may limit who you can refer to, but don't hesitate to appeal a restriction if no one on the *approved* list is right for your patient. You can refer a patient to a specialist, but you cannot force the patient to go. Thoroughly documenting the referral protects you from liability. Next time you see the patient in your office, ask why he or she didn't see the specialist and document the answer. This *closes the loop* on the referral.

Finally, when a patient's problem is urgent, someone on your staff should set up an appointment with the specialist while the patient is still in your office. If the problem is important but not critical, your office can provide the names of several potential specialists and let the patient choose which one to see.

22.6.5 Refusal to Pay

Handling patients with high-deductible health-care plans and/or who refuse to pay in the ACA era is a growing financial risk for private medical practitioners. To help ameliorate the issue, some doctors are using a *credit card on file* program. *Athenahealth* has such a program where, once each year, the doctor swipes the credit card of each patient. Athena's credit card partner (*Elavon*) stores the credit card information securely. The patient signs a 1-year contract that gives permission to bill that card for any outstanding balances. This is the same concept as having a hotel swipe your credit card when you check in but not bill you until you have checked out. Then, as soon as insurance has adjudicated the claim, the patient receives an e-mail informing them that their credit card will be charged for the remaining balance in 5 days. If they have any issue with the bill they can contact the doctor's office in that 5-day period. If not, their credit card is automatically charged for the balance due after 5 days. No work on the doctor's office part is required once the card is swiped. Advantages include no need to send out patient statements, and days-in-AR for patient balances is reduced. And, essentially no staff time is spent collecting patient balances. Another company (http://managemypractice.com) offers helpful online courses on how to set up a credit card on file program regardless of the system used.

22.6.6 Regional Extension Center Risks

The Meaningful Use (three parts) and Certification requirements along with the myriad of government regulations around Medicare and Medicaid reimbursements have proven far too complicated for most physicians to understand and manage on their own. To help out small practices and medical clinics, one of the interesting things funded by the HITECH Act was the creation of the *Health Information Technology Extension Program*. Via that program, the Department of Health and Human Services is required to invest in *Regional Extension Centers* (called *RECs* and pronounced like "wrecks"). RECs are designed to offer consulting and technical support to physicians in order to help accelerate adoption of EHRs.

The purpose of the RECs is to provide guidance on which products to buy, help reduce prices of software through group purchase agreements, and give technical assistance on implementation and deployment. These services will be free of charge to physicians. However, keep in mind that all RECs are nonprofit organizations, and most have little or no inherent knowledge about EMRs, EHRs, implementations, deployments, computer skills, etc.; initially they are groups that responded to the grant request in a manner that fulfilled documentation required by the government and will be provided government money to help physicians become meaningful users (MUs).

In the short run, no RECs will be very good because they will all be inexperienced. Over the long run, some RECs will become very good at their jobs, while other RECs will be mediocre or not good at all; only time will tell which ones will be superb and helpful versus not. Since RECs will be paid by the government for each physician they sign up, they will be very eager to approach and conduct outreach to sign you up. And, it will not cost you anything to sign up and the advice and assistance will be free to MDs.

Keep in mind, though, that whenever something is free to you, always think about why it's free. What does the organization get out of providing you free advice, assistance, knowledge, etc.? In the case of RECs, it's money from the government. The good news is that RECs are being told by the government that you will only be paid if you become a *meaningful user*. Currently, MU is suspect, itself. However, the bad news is that some RECs will not be able to do a good job and may give you bad advice (Shahid N. Shah, MS, personal communication).

22.6.7 Reputation Risks

Online reviews have become a major concern for many doctors, dentists, and health-care practitioners. Patients, people, and clients are posting new content on the Internet every day. Keeping tabs on a personal or professional reputation may be vital to your reputation and/or medical practice success. And the number of platforms to facilitate these reviews is growing rapidly. Review websites such as Google+, Yelp, HealthGrades.com, and Vitals.com are among the ones with the highest visits and traffic. Whether these reviews are positive or negative, you need to take action. The number of new patients will have a direct correlation with your online reputation score.

Still not convinced your patients are checking you out, online? Recall that as of 2012, about one-third of patients who viewed online sites sought out or avoided physicians based on their ratings. The findings come from a nationally representative Internet-based survey of 2137 adults, published February 18th in the *Journal of the American Medical Association*. Fortunately, medical professionals can now get instant online reputation management services. Why you may need Internet monitoring?

- Finds existing posts about *you* online
- Sends alerts whenever new posts appear
- Finds exposed personal info in databases
- Identifies and alerts you to damaging posts

Moreover, no one asks for job references, patient or client referrals, or background information anymore; they ask a search engine. If your name turns up negatively in news, malpractice verdicts reports, patient complaints, messy divorces, bankruptcies, legal filings, embarrassing photos, or other questionable material, you're likely to get passed over.

On the other hand, here's why these negative reviews may really be opportunities in disguise:

1. An online negative review means you actually know when and where your practice has failed a patient. Let's face it; people are chatting about you online. Ten years ago, though, you had absolutely no idea when or what they were saying. Now you do. This means you can correct whatever weaknesses it has because your patients are alerting you about them through their reviews. No longer are you flying blind trying to guess where your patient service weaknesses lie. Online reviews provide you with real-time strengths and weaknesses about your medical practice.
2. A negative review presents a great opportunity to showcase just how good your patient service really is. Let's take this example. Not too long ago a client had a bad experience with a dentist. It was written about on Yelp. Now, here's where the opportunity part comes into play. The doctor could have just ignored this negative review, or he/she could act upon it by proving that he/she really does offer great service. He/she chose the latter by sending a direct message to the disgruntled patient apologizing for the incident. Even if you can't make that one particular patient happy, you let other potential patients know that you will do whatever it takes to ensure satisfaction for all.
3. A negative review builds the credibility and authenticity of positive reviews. No medical practice, clinic, or hospital can satisfy 100% of their patients. Having one negative or slightly negative review among a plethora of positive reviews add to the credibility and authenticity of your positive reviews. Not so perfect reviews mean that the other published reviews are genuine and most likely not fabricated. They establish authenticity.

So, be personally proactive in monitoring and managing your reviews, or check out these resources: http://www.Reputation.com and http://www.MyPracticeReputation.com.*

Overheard in the Doctor's Lounge

Yelp: Real People, Real Reviews… Really?

If Yelp is an honest customer review site—uninfluenced by ad dollars paid by those it reviews—how come its honesty is repeatedly questioned even in the national news? For trustworthy reviews of local dentists, I suggest consumers forget Yelp and turn to DR.Oogle instead (https://www.dr-oogle.com/ftw).†

D. Kellus Pruitt, DDS
Fort Worth, Texas

---

* Available at http://physicianreferralmarketing.com/doctor-reputation-management/.

† From Christopher Zara. "Yelp Fights to Avoid a 'Blackfish' Moment: Documentary Kickstarter Puts Tech Firm on Defense," *International Business*, March 25, 2015.

22.6.8 Resisting Emerging Health-Care Models

As our medical system attempts to evolve to better deal with the modern epidemics of lifestyle-driven chronic disease, much time and attention is being placed on the clinical models for prevention. Rightly or wrongly, various models are popping up with names like lifestyle medicine, preventative medicine, and functional medicine. According to James Maskell, founder of FunctionalForum.com, here are some of the more viable and innovative emerging models:

Community events: More and more doctors are putting on events to teach at scale. Cooking classes (working with other providers), grocery store tours, and evening seminars are all proving popular. A truly remarkable medical experience!

Memberships: By providing a membership, doctors can capture the value of uncovered services while providing a framework that keeps patients coming back after the initial symptoms are resolved. They can spend the rest of their membership time learning how to keep themselves well going forward.

Packages: This provides another way to capture value, adding individual and group experiences into a package that patients commit to when they start their program with the clinic. Engaged patients are committed patients.

Online portals: Peer-to-peer support in a dedicated online portal has been very successful, particularly if they all share a common disease or symptom. Patients really want to hear others' experiences.

Synergistic providers: Health coaches, nurse coaches, and nutritionists are all becoming more and more popular as synergistic team members of a modern practice. Adding those providers into packages also scales down your time.

22.6.9 Resisting Digital Transformation

A majority of executives making tech-purchase decisions report that enterprises are reaching a turning point when it comes to digital transformation—one that will result in a failure to maintain a critical competitive edge if their organizations fall behind. And many hospitals and medical clinics are turning to shared IT services to make this transformation. But, within the next several years, most health-care organizations will appoint a senior executive as their designated digital transformation strategy leader (chief medical information officer). With this, they hope to expand their use of shared services/outsourcing to benefit data analytics, collaboration, and cloud initiatives, among other focus areas.*

22.6.10 Risk Retention Group Risks

Risk retention groups (RRGs) are owner-controlled insurance companies authorized by the Federal Risk Retention Act of 1986. An RRG provides liability insurance to members who engage in similar or related business or activities for all or any portion of the exposures of group members, excluding first-party coverages, such as property, workers' compensation, and personal lines. Authorization under the federal statute allows a group to be chartered

* Available at http://www.cioinsight.com/it-management/slideshows/why-resisting-digital-transformation-is-a-mistake.html#sthash.Zhs8e8jw.dpuf.

in one state, but able to engage in the business of insurance in all states, subject to certain specific and limited restrictions. The Federal Act preempts state law in many significant ways. Purported advantages include

- Avoidance of multiple state filing and licensing requirements
- Member control over risk and litigation management issues
- Establishment of stable market for coverage and rates
- Elimination of market residuals
- Exemption from countersignature laws for agents and brokers
- No expense for fronting fees
- Unbundling of services

Of the 130 new medical malpractice liability insurance companies that entered the market between 2002 and 2006, 65% were RRGs, according to a study conducted for the National Risk Retention Association by the actuarial consulting company Milliman Inc. And, statistics from the *Risk Retention Reporter*, a journal that tracks the industry, showed that through September, 43% of the 23 RRGs formed this year across various sectors are doctor-owned, while in 2001, no new physician RRGs joined the market.

Still, some doctors and industry experts warn about drawbacks of RRGs and question whether the physician-run companies—most of them relatively young—can survive future claims payouts and tough market cycles, while doctors do not have access to state guaranty funds to back up their coverage if an RRG struggles financially or goes out of business. The *Risk Retention Reporter* noted that, anecdotally, physician self-insurance companies have failed at no greater rate than traditional carriers in recent years.

22.7 -S-

22.7.1 Sarbanes–Oxley Act

The Sarbanes–Oxley Act of 2002, enacted July 30, 2002, also known as the "Public Company Accounting Reform and Investor Protection Act" and "Corporate and Auditing Accountability and Responsibility Act" and more commonly called Sarbanes–Oxley, Sarbox or SOX, is a U.S. federal law that set new or enhanced standards for all U.S. public boards, management, and public accounting firms. The bill, which contains 11 sections, was enacted as a reaction to a number of major corporate and accounting scandals, including Enron and Worldcom. The bill covers responsibilities of a public (hospital and health-care entity) corporation's board of directors, and adds criminal penalties for certain misconduct, and required the Securities and Exchange Commission (SEC) to create regulations to define how public corporations are to comply with the law.

22.7.2 Self-Insurance Risks

The high cost of malpractice insurance has caused many providers to seek an alternative to standard commercial insurance. Before discussing these alternatives, it is important to review what is actually being purchased in a malpractice insurance policy.

An insurance policy is more than just an agreement to pay certain types of claims. The insurance company also supplies forms on which to submit claims, personnel to process the claims, adjustors to determine how much should be paid out on the claims, and attorneys to fight unjustified claims. These services require the efforts of a large number of trained personnel. A major part of the premium dollar goes to pay for these administrative services. When a provider considers alternatives to commercial insurance, the total cost of the package must be considered, not just the cost of paying claims. In many situations, a provider will hire an insurance company to provide the administrative services, while retaining for itself the risk of loss. The provider pays all claims that the insurance company determines should be paid, and also pays the cost of processing the claims. In this situation, the provider would realize a net savings only if the level of claims could be reduced below the level used by the insurance company in estimating the premium. The provider usually maintains the ultimate responsibility for deciding to fight a claim. If the provider decides to fight a claim, the entire cost of the legal proceeding will be borne by the provider rather than by the insurance company.

A medical provider who anticipates contesting a large number of unfounded claims may find the legal services provided by the insurance company to be more valuable than the actual dollar limits of the policy. In this situation, the provider may pay the insurance company a premium that exceeds the limits of the policy. It may seem outrageous to pay $100,000 for a $75,000 policy, but the legal services involved in fighting claims may make this a good business decision. The problem arises when the cost of the policy is raised because of unrealistic future claims projections. When this happened in the mid-1970s, health-care providers with good claims experience found themselves paying very large premiums that could not be justified by increased administrative costs or claims paid. These providers were forced into other risk-spreading mechanisms.

The basic risk-spreading alternatives to standard malpractice insurance are own-funded self-insurance, either on a single-provider or multiple-provider basis of funded self-insurance (1) on a single-provider basis, (2) on a multiple-provider basis, (3) with *captive* or limited-purpose insurance companies, or (4) as a combination of any of these with commercial insurance, usually for excess coverage.

22.7.3 Self-Referral Risks

The federal and state governments have enacted several overlapping laws to deal with the issue of financial inducement in the referral of patients. These laws create a virtual maze of laws and regulations, which can easily snare the unwary. The extent of the federal regulation in the area of self-referral includes the *Medicare Anti-Fraud and Abuse Statute*, the *Medicare Safe Harbor Regulations*, and the *Stark Amendment.*

Medicare Anti-Fraud and Abuse Statute: This antifraud statute applies to persons receiving kickbacks for referring Medicare or Medicaid patients. There are many examples of physicians who run afoul of the law. These included chiropractors that were paid *handling fees* for collection and transmission of lab specimens to a certain laboratory. In another case, cardiologists who received *interpretation fees* for referring patients to a certain cardiac lab were found guilty of violating the statute. Additionally, a hospital administrator was found guilty when he received perks from an ambulance company to whom he had referred patients. Succinctly, any benefit given or received in exchange for referral of a Medicare or Medicaid patient will violate the statute.

Medicare Safe Harbor Regulations: The *Medicare Safe Harbor* rules were passed in an effort to identify areas of practice that would not lead to a conviction under the antifraud statute. The Safe Harbor regulations provide for 11 areas where providers may practice without violating the antifraud statute. Areas of safe practice under these regulations are briefly highlighted below:

- *Large entity investments*—Investment in entities with assets over $50 million. The entity must be registered and traded on national exchanges.
- *Small entity investments*—Small entity investments must abide by the 40–40 rule. No more than 40% of the investment interests may be held by investors in a position to make referrals. Additionally, no more than 40% of revenues can come through referrals by these investors.
- *Space and equipment rentals*—Such lease agreements must be in writing and must be for at least a 1-year term. Furthermore, the terms must be at fair market value.
- *Personal services and management contracts*—These contracts are allowable as long as certain rules are followed. Like lease agreements, these personal service and management contracts must be in writing for at least a 1-year term, and the services must be at fair market value.
- *Sale of a medical practice*—There are restrictions if the selling practitioner is in a position to refer patients to the purchasing practitioner.
- *Referral services*—Referral services (such as hospital referral services) are allowed. However, such referral services may not discriminate between practitioners who do or do not refer patients.
- *Warranties*—There are certain requirements if any item of value is received under a warranty.
- *Discounts*—Certain requirements must be met if a buyer receives a discount on the purchase of goods or services that are to be paid for by Medicare or Medicaid.
- *Payments to bona fide employees*—Payments made to bona fide employees do not constitute fraud under the Safe Harbor Regulations.
- *Group purchasing organizations*—Organizations that purchase goods and services for a group of entities or individuals are allowed, provided certain requirements are met.
- *Waiver of beneficiary coinsurance and deductible*—Routine waiver would not come under the safe harbor.

A physician's actions that come under the Safe Harbor Regulations will not violate the Medicare Fraud and Abuse Statutes. However, the provider must still abide by the Stark amendments and must also abide by applicable state law.

The Stark Amendments: The *Stark Amendment* to the *Omnibus Budget Reconciliation Act of 1989* was a step by the federal government to prohibit physicians from referring patients to entities in which they have a financial interest. Originally, the Stark amendment applied only to referral of Medicare patients to clinical laboratories in which the physician had a financial interest. The amendment provides that if a physician (including a family member) has a financial interest in a clinical laboratory, then he or she may not make a referral for clinical laboratory services if payment may be made under Medicare. A financial interest is an ownership interest, an investment interest, or a compensation arrangement.

There are certain *exceptions* to the *Stark I* amendment. They include if a physician personally provides the service or if a physician or employee of a group provides the services. Like the Safe Harbor Regulations, the Stark amendment permits physician investment in large entities and provides an exception for rural providers. Under the Stark amendment, large entities are defined as publicly traded entities with assets greater than $100 million. There are certain other exceptions that are similar to the safe-harbor regulations. They include items such as provision for rental of office space, employment and service arrangements with hospitals, and certain service arrangements. These arrangements must be at arm's length and at fair market value.

Stark II was passed in 1993 to modify and expand the *Stark I* amendment. In particular, it acts to bring numerous other entities, besides clinical laboratories, within the prohibitions of the Stark amendment. Self-referral and overutilization may become less of a problem as managed care makes further inroads in medical practice control and quasi-subrogation. Future legislation is likely to address the concerns of the financial incentives toward underutilization of ancillary medical services.

And, *Stark III* suggests that *under-arrangement* transactions occur when a hospital contracts with a third party (typically a joint venture owned, at least in part, by physicians who may refer) to provide a hospital service, and the hospital then bills and is reimbursed by Medicare for those services and pays the supplier or joint venture. As the *entity* to which the physicians refer patients is the hospital, not the joint venture (i.e., the *entity* is deemed to be the entity that submits the reimbursement claim to Medicare), this type of *arrangement* is permitted under Stark. However, buried in the 2008 Medicare Physician Fee Schedule rules, CMS broadened the definition of *entity* to include the person or entity that performs the designated health services and prohibits space and equipment lease arrangements where per-click payments are made to a physician lessor who refers patients to the lessee. These self-referral prohibitions (as well as arrangements where the physician is the lessee and rents space from a hospital) appeared in the Final Rules of 2008. CMS also passed restrictions related to independent diagnostic testing facility (IDTF) arrangements. For example, IDTFs are no longer allowed to share practice locations, operations, and diagnostic testing equipment with other Medicare-enrolled providers, including leasing and subleasing agreements.

The good news is that "Stark liability does not exist forever. If you are outside the four-year reopening period, you probably have no liability to CMS," according to Bob Wade, who is with Krieg DeVault in Mishawaka, Indiana (personal communication). Wade got the good news when CMS responded to several of his hospital-clients' applications to the self-referral disclosure protocol (SRDP). CMS turned them down, but only because the hospitals didn't have liability under the Stark law because the claims were deemed too old. In letters to Wade, CMS explained that it "uses the time frame established under the re-opening regulations at 42 C.F.R. 405.980(b) as a guide to determine the time frame of the SRDP. As such, the time frame of the SRDP is limited to four years from the date that the disclosing party submits the disclosure to the SRDP, unless reliable evidence of fraud or similar fault exists….Because all of the non-compliance disclosed by [reporting entity] occurred outside of the four-year time frame under the SRDP, CMS is removing [reporting entity] from the SRDP."

22.7.4 *Slow Medicine* Risks

Kent Bottles, MD, and Darrell K. Pruitt, DDS, have been thinking and opining on the emerging philosophy of *slow medicine* for some time (personal communication). Of course, health economists realize how complex and difficult it is to transform American health care so that we will enjoy lower per-capita costs along with increased medical care quality in our lives. Unfortunately, grassroots practitioners have done just the opposite these last two decades or so, in other words, practicing *faster medicine* with assembly line efficiency relegating office visits to 15, 10, or even 7-minute increments, etc., in order to compensate for diminishing MCO/HMO reimbursement. And, this may have been a financially acute perspective for modernity until now! After consulting and serving as a medical expert witness in hundreds of malpractice cases collectively (consulting, chart review, discovery depositions, trial appearances, and sworn testimony)—both directly and indirectly and for plaintiff and through almost 60 years of private practice—the following has been heuristically observed:

Patients do not sue doctors they personally like—they do sue doctors they do not like.

In fact, it may seem axiomatic that great clinical doctors are often sued while their lesser adept souls are not. Moreover, this pleasing reduced liability relationship seems enhanced by more patient face time, not less. This is not a function of competency, but one of human relationships and *connectedness* with one's caregiver. It will not be changed by EMRs, or more diagnostic tests (malpractice phobia), or procedures. It will be improved by intense physical examination, touching, eye contact, sympathy, empathy, and time (aka a *trusting* relationship and pleasing bedside manner forged by *time*). Period! And so, for our business managers, CEOs, and medical executive readers, we compromise on terminology and call it *slow-er medicine.*

Slow-er medicine is practiced by a small, but growing subculture whose pioneer and spokesperson is Dr. Dennis McCullough, author of the book *My Mother, Your Mother.* The downside is economic peril and financial risk.*

22.7.5 Social Media Risks

According to Kevin R. Campbel, MD, social media and the Internet have often been compared to the Wild West at times when it comes to the posting of ideas, opinions, and beliefs. There has been very little regulation of what is posted and how it is utilized—which may actually be a good thing. However, many doctors have learned (often the hard way) that posts on Facebook, Twitter, or other social media sites can be taken out of context and misinterpreted by the masses whom the information may not have been intended for. As physicians who are active on social media, we have even more to consider when talking to the Internet. We must be very careful to choose our words for posts wisely and make sure that we leave very little open to interpretation. We must be mindful of the legal implications of what we say and do online and must be mindful of patient confidentiality issues as well as standards for professional conduct. Medical boards across the country have developed guidelines for physicians on social media, and academic papers have been published on the subject in the *Annals of Internal Medicine*.†

Overheard in the Doctor's Lounge

LinkedIn Ads Will Now Follow You around the Web—Here's How to Opt Out

Because we can't go anywhere online without some social network tracking our data and using them to cash in on targeted advertising, LinkedIn has created its own online ad network that will allow advertisers to follow you around the web based on the information that LinkedIn knows about you.

BusinessInsider reports that the new LinkedIn Network Display service is selling ads not just on the career-oriented networking site but on 2500 other sites, using data on LinkedIn's 347 million registered users to carve out niches of as few as 1000 users for advertisers to target, according to AdAge.

D. Kellus Pruitt, DDS
From Chris Morran
Consumerist, February 19, 2015

* From *Embracing "Slow Medicine," The Compassionate Approach to Caring for Your Aging Loved Ones*, Harper Perennial. 1 Reprint Edition, January 27, 2009.

† From Jeanne M. Farnan, MD, MHPE; Lois Snyder Sulmasy, JD; Brooke K. Worster, MD; Humayun J. Chaudhry, DO, MS, SM; Janelle A. Rhyne, MD, MA; Vineet M. Arora, MD, MAPP; for the American College of Physicians Ethics, Professionalism and Human Rights Committee; the American College of Physicians Council of Associates; and the Federation of State Medical Boards Special Committee on Ethics and Professionalism. Online Medical Professionalism: Patient and Public Relationships: Policy Statement. American College of Physicians and the Federation of State Medical Boards, April 16, 2013.

22.7.6 Special Needs Patient Risks

Once-accepted practices, e.g., jerry-rigging adult medical equipment for a toddler, guesstimating the weight of a patient who exceeds the office scale, or allowing family members to interpret medical discussions, are now vestiges of a less specialized (and less litigious) past. Instead, patients with special needs—and their advocates—have gained traction through the PPACA in obtaining accommodations to reduce their risks of substandard care. Although no profile depicts a *typical* patient—nor a typical plaintiff—a review of 8127 recent medical malpractice cases in a national database indicates that *atypical* patients are common among those who allege they were subject to negligent care. For example, according to Jock Hoffman, MD, the Patient Safety Education Program director for CRICO, the malpractice insurance provider for physicians and hospitals affiliated with Harvard Medical School:

- 520 cases—excluding slips/falls—involved patients over age 75.
- 86 cases involved an issue with a language barrier.
- 48 cases involved ED patients younger than 13 years old.
- Further analysis of 1171 cases asserted against Harvard-affiliated providers from 2005–2010 reveals that 29 involved an obese patient.

This analysis does not reveal which, if any, of these cases were triggered by an inadequate accommodation of the patient's special needs, but it does demonstrate that the population of plaintiffs reflects the diversity of the population of all patients. The extent to which a provider needs to gear up for patients who may require special accommodation depends on the size of the setting, third-party requirements, and the likelihood of such encounters. Full-service hospitals are obliged, or required (e.g., ADA, EMTALA, Joint Commission), to meet the broadest set of special needs with proper equipment and training. A small group practice may not have to be ready for patients at *all* the extremes of age or physical condition or communication impediments, but proper planning for realistic scenarios is prudent (personal communication).

Substandard preparation puts patients at risk of harm and providers at risk of potentially indefensible allegations of negligence. Practitioners and facilities primed and equipped for special needs patients are more likely to avoid the most egregious and damaging errors (and lawsuits).

22.7.7 Staff Selection Risks

The Joint Commission (TJC) Accreditation Manual for Hospitals has established basic guidelines for medical staff selection and monitoring. The responsibility for selecting and monitoring the medical staff rests with the governing body of the hospital. The governing body may delegate the actual process of review to a medical staff committee, but it cannot delegate its responsibility for the decisions that committee makes. The hospital will be liable for allowing an unqualified person to become a member of the medical staff if that person is improperly approved by the medical staff committee. The hospital governing body must ensure that the criteria used in evaluating staff members are sufficient and are followed. While the governing body may not be qualified to judge the professional competence of the potential staff member, it can verify the current status of the applicant's license and determine whether the letters of reference are authentic. These may seem to be simple matters, but they are often neglected, to the great legal detriment of the facility if an unlicensed or incompetent physician is admitted to the medical staff. The application for staff membership should include

- The applicant's full name, date of birth, social security number, driver's license number, current address, and past addresses since being a student or for the last 5 years
- Name of the applicant's medical school, its location, and the date of graduation
- Names, positions, addresses, and phone numbers of references who will vouch for the applicant's professional competence and ethical character
- Type and location of all postgraduate training
- Board certifications or eligibilities
- All places of licensure, whether in force or not, and the identification numbers of the licenses
- All hospital privileges now in effect, those in effect within the past 3 years, and any facilities where privileges were terminated for disciplinary reasons
- All malpractice suits in which the applicant was or is a defendant, including the docket number of the suit, the place of filing, a brief statement of the allegations against the applicant, and the ultimate disposition of inactive suits
- Any current or past challenges to medical or drug licenses
- A statement of the applicant's health
- Any special qualifications or experience that is relevant to the applicant's professional competence

In addition to these items, the applicant should sign a release that will enable the investigating committee to check the validity of the information in the application. There are certain items that must be validated. These include medical school graduation, status of all medical licenses (whether currently in force or not), all disciplinary actions, and personal references. It is especially useful to contact reference by telephone, if care is taken to make a record of any information obtained and its source.

The most important aspect of the application is the history of past disciplinary actions and malpractice suits. Past successful disciplinary action, especially limitation or suspension of a state license, is assumed to be a strong indication of incompetent or unethical practice. The hospital may choose to grant privileges after weighing the offense and the applicant's subsequent behavior, but this is legally very different from granting privileges without exploring disciplinary proceedings. The committee reviewing the application must decide whether the application should be granted and must be able to defend that decision. If a questionable applicant is granted privileges, there should be a formal written statement detailing the investigation of the applicant and the factors relied upon in granting privileges.

The history of past malpractice suits is more difficult to interpret. The loss of a single suit should be reviewed, but this will not usually be a bar to obtaining privileges (unless it turned on intentional or unethical actions). A series of lost lawsuits is a strong indication of both negligence and poor patient relations. The decision is more difficult when there are pending lawsuits or a long string of suits that was settled or won by the defendant.

From a legal point of view, a lawsuit won by the defendant should be treated as if it was unfounded. Practically, however, there are many areas of the country where it is almost impossible for a plaintiff to win a malpractice lawsuit. A physician who attracts litigation but prevail in court may become a threat in an area where plaintiffs' verdicts are more common. If several suits are involved or the charges involve unethical practice, pending litigation should also be reviewed. While civil litigation does not affect licensure in many states, its existence can be used to question the hospital's decision to extend staff privileges to an applicant.

22.7.8 Substance Abuse and Impaired Physicians

According to Eric A. Dover, MD, approximately 10–12% of physicians will develop a drug or alcohol problem at some point during their career. If physicians are impaired, they should be able to seek help from a firm but supportive and fair resource—one that demands sobriety and can determine when physicians are safe to practice (personal communication).

Physicians with substance abuse disorders often seek the assistance of a state physician health program (PHP). Some physicians engage willingly with PHPs, but most are compelled to do so either by their hospital or their board of medicine. PHPs meet with, assess, and monitor physicians who have been referred to them for substance abuse or other mental and behavioral health problems. In most states, physicians who comply with any and all demands of the PHP often may continue to work, provided their sobriety is ensured through drug testing and other means. Many state boards of medicine rely completely on the PHPs for guidance about how to deal with impaired physicians. PHPs are therefore extremely powerful.

The problem with PHPs, though, is that despite their enormous power, they are generally barely known to most physicians and often operate with little oversight and no real means of appealing their recommendations. To compound matters, evaluation/treatment centers and PHPs are often financially dependent on one another: centers depend on referrals from PHPs for their viability and, reciprocally, PHP regional and national meetings are often heavily sponsored by these centers.

Because PHP practices are largely unknown to physicians until they themselves are referred to one, physicians who do register complaints about standard PHP practice are often dismissed as bellyaching. But, some voices of concern have been heard. For example, several years ago, a paper was published in the *Journal of Addiction Medicine* outlining concerns about standard PHP practice, which included the points raised above, along with others. More recently, a group of North Carolina physicians complained about their state PHP to the state auditor. The auditor conducted an investigation and found poor oversight of the PHP by both the state medical society and the board of medicine, a lack of due process for physicians who disputed the PHP's evaluations and/or recommendations, and multiple instances of potential conflicts of interest. And so, some authorities suggest a national federation of PHPs to implement national standards for its members and commence routine audits of its members.

Doctors who are unsafe to practice medicine ought to be prevented from doing so, but every doctor who enters any kind of treatment or monitoring program should be treated respectfully, and fairly, be monitored appropriately, and have legitimate avenues of appealing decisions about their care.

22.7.9 Suicide Risks

The fact is each year we lose over 400 doctors to suicide—that's like an *entire* medical school gone. This year, over 1 million Americans will lose their doctors to suicide. What are the solutions? According to Eric Dover, MD, Michael Lawrence Langan, MD, and Pamela Wible, MD, some come from individuals or institutions inside or outside of medicine (personal communication):

- *Primary prevention*: Actions that prevent healthy medical students or physicians from developing a condition that would lead to suicide
- *Secondary prevention*: Early diagnosis, referral, and rapid initiation of therapy after illness onset or suicide risk factors develop in asymptomatic medical students or physicians
- *Tertiary prevention*: Rehabilitation of suicidal medical students or physicians and return to maximal function with minimal risk for recurrence*

22.8 -T-

22.8.1 Tax Liabilities

Sens. Charles E. Grassley (R-IA) and Charles E. Schumer (D-NY) introduced a bill (S. 626) in 2015 that would prevent Medicaid providers with tax liabilities from receiving full Medicaid reimbursements. The proposed *Helping Ensure Life-and-Limb-Saving Access to Podiatric Physicians* (HELLPP) Act would authorize the secretary of the Department of the Treasury to levy Medicaid reimbursement payments to pay off a tax debt. Currently, Medicaid reimbursement payments can't be garnished to pay a tax debt.†

22.8.2 Team-Based Care Risks

Redundancy occurs when more than one person (or committee) has the responsibility to make a decision or assume a task. Redundancy in a team-based care model becomes a problem when it allows tasks to be overlooked or decisions to be avoided. This happens when a person or committee assumes that someone else with responsibility for the same task will make the necessary decisions. This can be due to a misunderstanding, or it can be due to an intentional dodging of the task or decision.

Redundancy is best avoided by having only one person, lead physician, or committee responsible for each task or decision. Since this is almost impossible in a hospital or large organization, there must be an unambiguous protocol for allocating tasks and decisions among the responsible personnel. The protocol must also establish a system for handling problems that the assigned personnel cannot solve. It is important that such problems be brought to the attention of a supervisor for reassignment to new personnel. Reassignment should not be done by first-level personnel; reassignment at that level will make it impossible to prevent the dodging of unpleasant tasks.

* Available at http://www.idealmedicalcare.org/blog/physician-suicide-101-secrets-lies-solutions. The slideshow is fully transcribed in this link with permission. Every medical student and physician needs this information. Please share widely. You may save a life.

† From James Swann, *BNA*, March 18, 2015.

22.8.3 Telemedicine and Telehealth

As physicians become more technologically enabled in their practice of medicine, some are turning to real-time videoconferencing and other technologies. Some specialties such as psychiatry and radiology are early adopters, but have to make sure they are still employing the same standards of care required by an in-office visit. Also, the telephone can facilitate medical care but also result in adverse outcomes leading to telephone-related malpractice suits.*

22.8.4 Terminating Patient Relationships

Just as it is an acceptable and reasonable practice to screen incoming patients, it is acceptable and reasonable to know when to end relationships. Termination criteria are numerous and varied. Although not exhaustive, the following are situations in which termination is appropriate and acceptable:

- *Treatment noncompliance*—The patient does not or will not follow the treatment plan.
- *Follow-up noncompliance*—The patient repeatedly cancels follow-up visits or is a no-show.
- *Office policy noncompliance*—The patient uses weekend on-call physicians or multiple health-care practitioners to obtain refill prescriptions when office policy specifies a certain number of refills between visits.
- *Verbal abuse*—The patient or a family member is rude and uses improper language with office personnel, exhibits violent behavior, makes threats of physical harm, or uses anger to jeopardize the safety and well-being of office personnel with threats of violent actions.
- *Nonpayment*—The patient owes a backlog of bills and has made no effort to arrange a payment plan.

It is an acceptable practice to end a patient relationship under most conditions. There are a few situations, however, that may require additional steps or a delay of the termination. According to The Doctors Company's Laura A. Dixon, JD, RN, the following circumstances fall into this category:

- If the patient is in an acute phase of treatment, termination must be delayed until the acute phase has passed. For example, if the patient is in the immediate postoperative stage or is in the process of medical workup for diagnosis, it is not advisable to end the relationship.
- If the practitioner is the only source of medical or dental care within a reasonable driving distance, he or she may need to continue care until other arrangements can be made.

---

* From Charles D. Cash. "Telepsychiatry and Risk Management." *Innovations in Clinical Neuroscience* 8.9 (2011): 26–30. *CINAHL Plus with Full Text*. Web. April 27, 2012; Maureen Mondor et al. "Patient Safety and Telephone Medicine." *JGIM: Journal of General Internal Medicine* 23.5 (2008): 517–522. *Academic Search Complete*. Web. April 27, 2012.

- When the practitioner is the only source of a particular type of specialized medical or dental care, he or she is obliged to continue this care until the patient can be safely transferred to another practitioner who is able to provide treatment and follow-up.
- If the patient is a member of a prepaid health plan, the patient cannot be discharged until the practitioner has communicated with the third-party payer to request a transfer of the patient to another practitioner.
- A patient may not be terminated solely because he or she is diagnosed with AIDS/HIV.

When the situation with the patient is such that terminating the relationship is appropriate and acceptable and none of the restrictions mentioned above are present, termination of the patient relationship should be completed formally. The patient should be put on written notice that he or she must find another health-care practitioner. The written notice should be mailed to the patient by regular and certified mail, return receipt requested. Keep copies of the letter, the original certified mail receipt, and the original certified mail return receipt (even if the patient refuses to sign for the certified letter) in the patient's medical record.

22.8.4.1 Elements of the Written Notice

- *Reason for termination*—A specific reason for termination is not required. Under certain circumstances, it is acceptable to utilize the catchall phrase "inability to achieve or maintain rapport" or "the therapeutic practitioner–patient relationship no longer exists."
- *Effective date*—The effective date of termination should provide the patient with a reasonable time period to establish a relationship with another practitioner. Usually, 30 working days from the date of the letter is considered adequate; however, you should follow your state regulations. The relationship can be terminated immediately under the following circumstances:
  - The patient has terminated the relationship.
  - The patient or a family member has threatened the practitioner or staff with violence or has exhibited threatening behavior.
- *Interim care provisions*—Offer interim care. True emergency situations, however, should be referred to an emergency department.
- *Continued care provisions*—Offer suggestions for continued care through local referral services such as medical or dental societies, nearby hospital medical staffs, or community resources. Do not recommend another health-care practitioner by name.
- *Request for medical or dental record copies*—In your written notice, offer to provide a copy of the medical or dental record to the new practitioner by enclosing an authorization document (to be returned to the office with the patient's signature). One exception to this element is the psychiatric record, which may be offered as a summary in lieu of the full copy of the medical record.
- *Patient responsibility*—Remind the patient that follow-up and continued medical or dental care are now the patient's responsibility and that both should be pursued.
- *Medication refills*—Explain that medications will only be provided up to the effective date of termination.

22.8.4.2 Special Circumstances

- *Pregnant patient*—Termination can be safely accomplished during the first trimester with uncomplicated pregnancies and with adequate time for the patient to find another practitioner. Termination in the second trimester should occur only for uncomplicated pregnancies and with transfer of the patient to another obstetrical practitioner prior to actual cessation of services. Termination during the last trimester should occur only under extreme circumstances (such as illness of the practitioner, etc.).
- *Physician or dental groups*—Groups with more than one practitioner may want to consider terminating a patient from the entire practice. This will avoid the possibility that the patient might be treated by the terminating practitioner during an on-call situation.
- *Disabled patients*—The presence of a disability cannot be the reason(s) for termination unless the patient requires care or treatment for the particular disability that is outside the expertise of the practitioner. Transferring care to a specialist who provides the particular care is a better approach.

22.8.5 Tourism and Global Health Care

American businesses are extending their cost-cutting initiatives to include offshore employee medical benefits and facilities like the Bumrungrad Hospital in Bangkok, Thailand (cosmetic surgery), and the Apollo Hospital in New Delhi, India (cardiac and orthopedic surgery), which are premier examples for surgical care. Both are internationally recognized institutions that resemble five-star hotels equipped with the latest medical technology. Countries such as Finland, England, and Canada are also catering to the English-speaking crowd, while dentistry is especially popular in Mexico and Costa Rica. Although this is still considered *medical tourism*, Mercer Health and Benefits was recently retained by three Fortune 500 companies interested in contracting with offshore hospitals, and TJC has accredited more than 100 foreign hospitals through a joint international commission. To be sure, when India can discount costs up to 80%, the effects on domestic hospital reimbursement and physician compensation may be assumed to increase downward compensation.

22.9 -U-

22.9.1 Unauthorized Viewing of Protected Health Information

Early in July 2014, the Department of Health and Human Services Office of Civil Rights (OCR) entered into a settlement for $865,500 with UCLA Health System (UCLAHS) as a result of complaints alleging that UCLAHS employees repeatedly and without permissible reason looked at the electronic protected health information (ePHI) of celebrity patients. Although the complaint was initially made by only two patients, in its investigation, OCR determined that from 2005 to 2008, unauthorized employees of UCLAHS repeatedly looked at the ePHI of numerous other patients as well. In addition to paying the settlement, UCLAHS committed to a correction action plan that includes (1) implementation of policies and procedures; (2) robust training for employees; (3) a commitment to sanction offending employees; and (4) designation of an independent monitor to assess compliance over 3 years. This settlement was the fourth settlement in a year and highlights OCR's increasing enforcement of violations to HIPAA Privacy and Security Rules. Failure to have an effective HIPAA compliance program can result in significant monetary penalties, and therefore, providers and business associates alike should be evaluating their HIPAA compliance programs to ensure that appropriate safeguards are in place.

22.9.2 Unfunded Self-Insurance Risks

The simplest alternative to traditional third-party insurance is unfunded self-insurance, often called *going bare*. While this option has been adopted by many physicians and some hospitals, it can be very risky. There are two areas of potential financial loss when *going bare*. The first is obvious: an adverse judgment with a resulting cash loss. The second is the losses resulting from the cost of litigation. Defending a malpractice claim is expensive and time-consuming. Attorneys are expensive and the cost of having key administrative personnel tied up in court proceedings is high. There are situations where the best economic strategy is to pay the claim rather than to fight it, even if it could be beaten eventually.

Consider the situation where a person is brought in after being badly injured in an automobile accident. The patient is sent to the x-ray department for extensive emergency x-rays. The orderly in the x-ray department inadvertently puts the patient in an x-ray room that has been closed for repairs. The patient is found dead in the room several hours later by a janitor. The subsequent autopsy findings show that the patient suffered a massive intracranial bleed and was probably brain dead before being sent to x-ray. In no event could medical treatment have influenced the patient's death. To win a malpractice case based on these facts, the plaintiff must prove that

- The defendant had a duty to care for the patient properly.
- The defendant violated this duty.
- The patient was injured.
- The patient's injuries were due to the violation of the duty to care for the patient.

Since the patient had been admitted to the hospital, it is clear that there was a duty to care for the patient. While there may be a dispute over who should have cared for the patient, it would have to be a hospital employee or agent. The patient's injuries are also clear. The stumbling block in this malpractice suit is trying to prove that the negligent actions, which violated the duty to care for the patient properly, were the cause of the patient's injuries. In this case, it is clear that the hospital was grossly negligent, but did this cause the patient's death?

In this situation, the hospital could eventually win the lawsuit if it could prove that the patient's death was not caused by its employee's or agent's negligent actions. The plaintiff, however, can prove that the hospital was grossly negligent in the treatment given the patient. If the hospital fights the suit, it will incur large legal costs and very adverse publicity. The adverse publicity may deter patients from seeking care at the facility and may influence potential financial contributors to support other facilities. The hospital thus may decide that settling the lawsuit (usually for much less than the amount sued for) is the best course. Unfortunately, in an unfunded scheme, there is no cash reserve from which to pay a settlement. The hospital may be trapped into fighting the lawsuit because it cannot raise enough cash for a settlement.

The risk of an adverse judgment must not be minimized. A large one-time loss could close the doors of many facilities. If the health-care provider decides to fight a suit and loses, the judgment could be in the millions of dollars. This is the most important reason for a hospital or clinic not to *go bare*. While an individual physician may want to risk bankruptcy, it can be very detrimental to an entire community to have the local hospital become insolvent. Even a facility that can afford to pay the potentially adverse judgment may find that the pending lawsuit hampers the raising of capital. In an unfunded scheme, the pending lawsuit must be mentioned in the bond prospectus for any bond sales. If there is no insurance or trust fund to offset this potential claim, the bond buyers may worry that a judgment against the hospital will impair the ability of the hospital to pay off the bonds.

The precarious nature of single-provider unfunded coverage can be mitigated somewhat by pooling resources with several other providers. This is often done by hospitals with common ownership, whether proprietary chains or religious orders. The hospitals gain financial stability because the pooled resource base makes it less likely that any single claim will bankrupt the system. The hospital can also offset pending claims against the other facilities' assets, making it easier to sell bonds for capital additions. Difficulties arise because these schemes usually require all participating institutions to agree to share in the payment of sizable claims. This can make it difficult for an attorney defending a claim to negotiate effectively. It is particularly troublesome if one of the cooperating institutions is in financial trouble and does not have the cash necessary to pay its share of the claim. If the other facilities do not settle the claim on their own, they may face a much larger judgment that the troubled facility will be even less likely to be able to pay. If they do settle without the authorization of the troubled institution, they must pay more than their fair share of the claim. To recover this extra payout from the uncooperative facility will require litigation and an addition to the expense of the claim and is likely to increase friction among the facilities.

Flexibility in the settlement of lawsuits is increasingly important as jury settlements rise to million-dollar levels. When a jury awards a plaintiff a million dollars, the defendant, after appropriate appeals, must pay the million dollars a single lump sum payment. This lump sum is very difficult for the defendant to raise and often does not serve the needs of the plaintiff. Most million-dollar settlements involve injuries that require continuing medical care and/or persons that require continuing support. In either case, the plaintiff's need is for a continuing source of income over a prolonged period, not a one-time payment. The experience of most people who receive large lump sums, either through judgments or contest winnings, is that the money will be spent in less than 5 years. This may leave medical bills to pay, children to educate, and other continuing expenses unpaid. The plaintiff's need for a steady income, coupled with the defendant's desire to pay out as little cash in present dollars as possible, has led to the development of structured settlements.

A structured settlement usually gives the plaintiff a guaranteed income, payment of any medical bills, and a small lump sum payment. The value of this to the plaintiff is that it provides a tax-free income (usually for life) and protection from rising medical costs. The cost to the defendant is the cost of the annuity. This cost is much less than the lump sum judgment would have been. Like all settlements, however, a structure settlement demands that the defendant have the financial resources to allow the defense attorney to make the plaintiff a fair offer. Unfunded self-insurance, or *going bare*, leaves the defense attorney unable to negotiate effectively when the defendant provider does not have enough available cash to pay a fair settlement. An extrinsic factor that makes *going bare* economically untenable for most institutions is that there is a limit on Medicare/Medicaid reimbursement for the share of overhead attributable to uninsured losses. This is a public policy decision that reflects the importance of keeping hospitals from being driven into insolvency.

22.9.3 Unions

A handful of doctors providing medical services to students at UC San Diego—and their colleagues at nine other University of California campuses—went on strike in late January 2015. It was the first time in 25 years that fully licensed doctors picketed a U.S. employer, according to the *Union of American Physicians and Dentists*, which represents the physicians at the UC schools. The work stoppage began at 7:30 a.m. and lasted 1 day. It involved 150 health center doctors who manage the primary care and mental health needs of students. There are 10 such physicians on its campus.*

22.9.4 USA Patriot Act

The USA Patriot Act is composed of sections covering a variety of topics. Much of the act revises or updates laws already in the United States Code (U.S.C.) in order to better coordinate efforts against terrorism. It is complemented by Executive Order #13224 and U.N. Security Council Resolution #1373, as monitored by the Office of Foreign Assets Control (OFAC) through its Specially Designated Nationals (SDN) list and Terror Exclusion List (TEL). However, several other pieces of legislation applicable to health-care organizations have arisen because of the electronic age. For example, the Internet Spyware Prevention Act of 2005, H.R. 744 (I-SPY Act) passed by the U.S. House of Representatives on May 23, 2005 criminalizes unauthorized spyware, phishing, or other methods of obtaining sensitive personal health or other information without consent; and it forbids the bringing of a civil action under the law of any state if such action was premised in whole or in part on the use of illegally obtained protected information. As is the case with the Health Insurance Portability and Accountability Act of 1996 (HIPAA), protected information defined in the I-SPY Act includes first and last names, home or other physical addresses, e-mail addresses, telephone numbers, social security numbers, tax identification numbers, driver's license numbers, passport numbers, other government-issued identification numbers, credit card numbers, bank account numbers, and passwords or access codes associated with credit card, insurance company, hospital, or bank accounts.

President Bush also signed the USA Patriot Improvement and Reauthorization Act into law on March 9, 2006. This legislation continued the authorization for intelligence and law enforcement officials to share information and use the same tools against terrorists that had been granted in the original act. According to the President:

> The law … will improve our nation's security while we safeguard the civil liberties of our people. The legislation strengthens the Justice Department so it can better detect and disrupt terrorist threats. And the bill gives law enforcement new tools to combat threats to our citizens from international terrorists…†

* From Paul Sisson, UTSandiego.com.

† FDR.

In early 2007, Senator Mark Pryor introduced the Counter Spy Act to make it illegal to implant spyware on a personal computer without consent. Spyware allows one to duplicate websites, including financial, health-care, or retail sites, where personal medical records or financial information like credit card numbers or insurance information is stored. It is usually downloaded without user knowledge during another software download or by simply clicking on a link (*drive-by downloading*). Once downloaded, it is almost impossible to remove. The act also provides that the Federal Trade Commission (FTC) enforce the law as if a violation was an unfair or deceptive practice. The agency would have authority to bring civil and criminal penalties (fines and/or imprisonment for up to 5 years) for violations.

Finally, late in 2007, the Committee on Energy and Commerce passed two additional bills designed to protect Americans from invasive Internet spyware and social security number theft. The first was H.R. 964, the Securely Protect Yourself against Cyber Trespass Act (the Spy Act); and the second was H.R. 948, the Social Security Number Protection Act of 2007.

22.10 -V-

22.10.1 Vicarious Liability Risks

In certain situations, the doctor may be at risk for vicarious fraud charges, even if he or she never submitted a questionable claim. The two classes of practitioners that may have such risk involve physicians who are members of a group practice and employed (or contracted) physicians.

a. *Employed physician*: You may think that as an employed physician, or hospitalist, that you are not at risk. However, in some cases, your risk could be greater. For example, if you work for a physician who employs you to see patients at a contracted nursing home and you either get paid per patient or per day, realize that Medicare is being billed under your name as the provider of services. Although you may never get receipt of the money, since the billing was done under your name, if there is a question of fraud, you would be the one liable! The point is that whether you are a self-employed, a member of a group, or an employed physician, you should personally ensure that the billing being conducted under your name and signature is proper.
b. *Certificates of medical necessity*: Physicians are asked daily to sign certificates of medical necessity (CMNs). Under the new law, you may be liable if you sign a CMN and the product or service is later found to be not medically necessary. In most cases, a physician should have no problem with this rule. The practitioner should be careful in signing CMNs that come into your office unsolicited. For example, you may be asked to sign a CMN for transportation of a Medicaid patient to your office. But, was that transportation or the particular level of transportation medically necessary? Extreme caution should be employed when signing a CMN for transportation. In most cases, transportation to your office will be non-emergency transportation of an ambulatory patient. Unscrupulous transportation companies have been known to bill for stretcher transportation of ambulatory patients. Do not allow yourself to be swept into another's fraudulent scheme. Be careful what you certify as medically necessary!

c. *Group practice*: If you are a member of a group and your income is at all dependent upon the income of another member of a group (e.g., expense sharing or production-based income), then you may be liable for the fraud of another member of your group. The rationale is that if every member of the group benefits financially from the money received secondary to the fraudulent activity. This can put a practitioner in a very difficult position. One must choose whether to continue in practice with a practitioner employing questionable billing techniques or whether to dissolve the group.

22.11 -W-

22.11.1 Weekend Call-Coverage Risks

According to Ann S. Lofsky, MD, and Susan Shepard, MSN, RN, of The Doctors Company, when signing out to a colleague for the weekend, handing off responsibility for patient care call coverage can create liability risks for the physician. The primary objective of a handoff is to provide accurate information about a patient's care, treatment, services, current condition, and any recent or anticipated change. When a handoff occurs, a physician should communicate the following information to the next physician: the patient's previous treatment, current condition, medications ordered to date, and any recent or anticipated changes in his or her condition. Although face-to-face communication is the most effective method, telephone communication can also be efficient. The key elements are setting aside sufficient time to relay the salient information, for the receiver to understand the data, and time for questions and answers. Standardizing the handoff process and content will decrease the omission of critical information.

22.11.2 Whistleblowers

Medical Whistleblower was founded by Dr. Janet Parker, a veterinarian who reported fraud, abuse, and neglect in the medical community (http://medicalwhistleblowernetwork.jigsy.com). The organization is dedicated to advocacy and the emotional support of all medical whistleblowers regardless of their professional background or licensing status. A medical whistleblower is a person who has come forward to report medical fraud, abuse, or neglect to state, federal, or international governmental authorities. A medical whistleblower provides advocacy for all regardless of national origin, religious faith, color, disability, sex, sexual orientation, or age. Anyone with access to information related to medical fraud, abuse, and neglect can be a medical whistleblower. A medical whistleblower advocates for those who have already made that choice and those still considering their future path. There is no cost to request support from a medical whistleblower. A medical whistleblower is not a counseling service and does not provide legal advice or representation. Rather, he or she is an advocate for change and provides meaningful information related to the medical whistleblower's experience and networking contacts for further support.

22.11.3 Wrong Profession or Medical Specialty Risks

As private, state, and federal health reform initiatives are increasing, and professional malaise and discouragement is expanding, medical providers may be facing the ultimate personal contingent liability by selecting the wrong profession (specialty), as suggested by Yale University economist Robert J. Shiller, PhD. In his popular book, *The New Financial Order: Risk in the 21st Century*, Shiller states that a new risk-sharing paradigm to protect us from "gratuitous random and painful inequality" is required. His solution? Livelihood insurance, framed as a risk management contract!

22.12 CONCLUSION

Medical risk management is no longer just about medical malpractice anymore—it has not been for some time now, despite the recent resurgence of liability fears. In fact, since most practicing physicians have malpractice insurance, then a malpractice suit should be viewed as a mere inconvenience, and the practitioner and his or her financial advisors should realize that the lawsuit is mainly about someone else's money.

A shift in thought paradigm is needed. The medicolegal landscape has changed. The physician in practice today is faced with many legal challenges that have the potential to destroy the medical practice and the individual's personal assets. These have been briefly reviewed in this chapter.

Therefore, every practice, medical clinic, or health-care entity should consider having a qualified attorney, crisis manager, and/or risk management consultant on retainer. Be aware, the risks are only going to increase, going forward!

22.13 COLLABORATE

Discuss this chapter online with others at http://www.MedicalExecutivePost.com.

ACKNOWLEDGMENTS

To Dr. Barbara S. Schlefman, MS, Norcross, Georgia; D. Kellus Pruitt, DDS, Fort Worth, Texas; Dr. William P. Scherer, MS, Barry University School of Medicine, Miami, Florida; Robert James Cimasi, MHA, ASA, AVA, CMP, president of Health Capital Consultants LLC., St. Louis, Missouri; John Kelley, DO, Atlanta, Georgia; Marcia Lee, DO, Norcross, Georgia; and Professor Edward P. Richards, JD, MPH, Program in Law, Science and Public Health, LSU Law Center, LSU, Baton Rouge, Louisiana.

FURTHER READINGS

Boyd, W: Managing risk to reputation. *Clinical Risk* 15(6) (2009): 221–223. *CINAHL Plus with Full Text*, Web, April 27, 2012.

Boyd, JW: Help for doctors with substance use disorders. *Psychology Today*, June 9, 2014.

Fenton, CF and Marcinko, DE: *Modern Risk Management Issues for Physicians: Comprehensive Financial Planning Strategies for Doctors and Advisors*. Productivity Press, Boca Raton, FL, 2015.

Gawande, A: *The Checklist Manifesto: How to Get Things Right*. Picador, New York, 2011.

Gawande, A: *Complications: A Surgeon's Notes on an Imperfect Science*. Picador, New York, 2013.

Gawande, A: *Being Mortal*. Metropolitan Books, New York, 2014.

Jauhar, S: *Doctored: The Disillusionment of an American Physician*. Farrar, Straus and Giroux, New York, 2014.

Leifer, J: *The Myths of Modern Medicine: The Alarming Truth about American Health*. Rowman & Littlefield Publishers, New York, 2014.

Manion, K: *Finding Physician Fulfillment.* Physician Executive, New York, 2005.

Marcinko, DE: *The Status of Physician and Medical Unions: Financial Planning for Healthcare Professionals.* Aspen Publishers, New York, 2003.

Marcinko, DE and Hetico, HR: *The Business of Medical Practice* (third edition). Springer Publishing, New York, 2011.

Marcinko, DE and Hetico, HR: *Hospitals and Healthcare Organizations: Management Strategies, Operational Techniques, Tools, Templates and Case Studies.* Productivity Press, Boca Raton, FL, 2013.

Marcinko, DE and Hetico, HR: *Financial Management Strategies for Hospitals and Healthcare Organizations: Tools, Techniques, Checklists and Case Studies.* Productivity Press, Boca Raton, FL, 2014.

Marcinko, DE and Hetico, HR: *Comprehensive Financial Planning Strategies for Doctors and Advisors: Best Practices from Leading Consultants and Certified Medical Planners™.* Productivity Press, Boca Raton, FL, 2015.

Pho, K: *Establishing, Managing, and Protecting Your Online Reputation: A Social Media Guide for Physicians.* Greenbranch Publishing, Atlanta, GA, 2013.

Wible, P: Physician Suicide 101: Secrets, Lies and Solutions. KevinMD, November 13, 2014.

23 Creating a Medical Practice Compliance Program

Part One: Accountability, Processes, and Implementation

Carol S. Miller

CONTENTS

In general terms, health-care entity or medical practice compliance is the organization's adherence to rules, regulations, guidelines, and specifications relevant to performing its day-to-day operations. This includes the observance of all applicable Medicare billing guidelines; state, local, and federal regulations impacting the practice; ethical, privacy, and security requirements; and the steps and processes to avoid potential fraud and abuse. Due to the increasing number of regulations placed on medical practices and the need for operational transparency, provider offices are adopting the use of consolidated and harmonized sets of compliance controls to ensure that all necessary governance requirements can be met without unnecessary duplication of effort or too-extensive processes that could take away from patient care.

This chapter will provide an in-depth understanding of medical practice compliance and the specific risk-management activities that should be included in a successful compliance program.

23.1 WHAT IS A MEDICAL PRACTICE COMPLIANCE PROGRAM?

A compliance program, whether formal or informal, is a process or system to ensure that all regulatory requirements are being followed. Annual financial audits are a customary part of any ongoing compliance program whether it is a business, office practice, hospital, or other entity. Compliance programs for medical practices also have a wide array of services, including support services. Several of these areas are

- Proper Medicare, Medicaid, managed care, and private insurance coding and billing practices
- Compliance with various laws and regulations, such as the Health Insurance Portability and Accountability Act (HIPAA) and Health Information Technology for Economic and Clinical Health (HITECH) Act, Stark III rules, False Claims Act, Clinical Laboratory Improvement Act (CLIA), Emergency Medical Treatment and Active Labor Act (EMTALA), and others, which will be discussed in Chapter 24.
- Requirements imposed by the Environmental Protection Agency (EPA), Department of Transportation (DOT), Occupational Safety and Health Administration (OSHA), and others
- Safety guidelines, Joint Commission on Accreditation, and contracting of managed care services
- Audits including financial audits, the Medicare Recovery Audit Contractor (RAC) program, Medicare Administrative Contractors (MAC), Medicaid Integrity Contractors (MIC) programs, Zone Program Integrity Contracts (ZPIC), and Audit MICs

Health-care compliance programs have been in existence for quite some time. Typically, they are the result of governmental agency requirements in response to civil or criminal actions or from an audit of significant abuse or fraud. In the event of some fiscal irresponsibility or irregularity, the federal government can require the provider and/or organization to submit to an outside review. The entity that performs this review/audit has to report its findings to the governmental agency in order for the provider to continue doing business with the federal health-care programs. These reviews can apply to hospitals, clinics, large and small provider practices, and any other health entity operating in a state. Dependent on the results of these audit reviews, the end result could be no negative outcome; require training of staff to change processes; or escalate to higher levels of review and audit such as through the Office of the Inspector General (OIG) or Federal Bureau of Investigation (FBI), and/or federal trials, monetary penalties, loss of provider's license to practice, and/or incarceration.

Many of these external audits can result in significant risk to legitimate revenue and profit margins for health-care providers. These audits typically include very complex appeals processes with strict penalties such as the automatic recoupment of funds if appeals deadlines are missed. Leading the list of outside reviewers are the Medicare RAC, MAC, and the newly revived Medicaid RAC program. The latter provides an even further layer of complexity, for state Medicaid agencies are permitted to use their current appeals process, modify their existing process, or devise an entirely new process, *and* each state operates differently.

23.2 WHY SHOULD A PROVIDER COMPLY WITH MEDICAL PRACTICE COMPLIANCE?

The typical practice of providing care has substantially changed with the advent of laws, regulations, electronic medical health records, and patient health records—all leading to a very complex health-care system that includes a host of business and administrative functions to support the level of documentation. Further complicating the already complicated practice are the various nuances and guidelines from not just one insurer but multiple insurers, necessitating additional understanding, documentation, and compliance. Additionally, practices are being faced with a dual competing environment where overutilization of tests and procedures may be rejected for being nonmedically necessary, yet the practice is still subjected to patient complaints, adverse incidents, risk, investigations, and settlements in which the practices feel compelled to order more versus fewer tests. To justify what are *best practices* that comply with the rules and regulations at hand, providers are looking to compliance programs to justify and support their level of care.

By implementing and following a compliance program, providers reduce the overhead and risks of regulatory reviews and audits, enabling the providers and their staff to focus on the core business of providing quality health care. In every provider's office, small or large, there is a greater need today to make sure that the practice is meeting all of the necessary obligations.

23.3 BENEFITS OF A HEALTH-CARE COMPLIANCE PROGRAM

There are many associated benefits of a health-care or medical practice compliance program, some of which are only perceived, whereas others are very definitive. Most providers try to comply with the rules and regulations and what is or is not covered by different insurance programs. Regardless of their ethical and quality processes in their office practice, the decision to develop and implement a compliance program still is an important and needed business decision. The processes involved in a compliance program can help improve the organization's performance by providing basic principles in quality improvement, which can help improve the provider's bottom line. Several benefits of a compliance program are

- Improving the quality of patient care
- Serving as a resource for information about compliance-related issues
- Saving time, money, and associated apprehensions during audits or reviews

- Preventing or identifying improper conduct with systems for evaluation and correction
- Providing training for employees and contracted services to recognize fraud and abuse
- Providing a way for employees to report potential problems
- Demonstrating to staff and community that the practice is committed to honesty and appropriate conduct
- Minimizing loss associated with false claims through early recognition and reporting, and decreasing the provider's exposure to civil penalties, sanctions, and other administrative actions, such as exclusion

The OIG has developed a series of voluntary compliance program guidance documents directed at various segments of the health-care industry, such as hospitals, nursing homes, third-party billers, durable medical equipment suppliers, clinical laboratories, home health agencies, hospices, nursing facilities, ambulance suppliers, pharmaceutical manufacturers, physician practices, and others, to encourage the development and use of internal controls to monitor adherence to statutes, regulations, and program requirements. The documents provide principles to follow when developing a compliance program that best suits the organization's needs. The OIG documents also identify fraud and abuse risks to watch out for when creating a program.

23.4 DEVELOPING A MEDICAL PRACTICE/CLINIC/HEALTH-CARE ENTITY

23.4.1 Compliance Plan

The Affordable Care Act (ACA) mandated individual health insurance coverage for everyone; however, for the providers who accept both Medicare and Medicaid, the ACA included provisions for more administrative requirements and the potential for regulatory risk. Among its many provision, initiatives, and amendments, the reform law dramatically broadened the scope of the False Claims Act—the federal law that allows the government to recover overpayments to its contractors, including health-care providers, and to pursue allegations of fraud. Specifically, physician practices and other providers who take more than 60 days to report and return overpayments from Medicare and other federal health programs can face civil charges, even if the overpayment was caused by error. With that said, providers are very uneasy about the potential for prosecution. It is critical that physician practices work credit balances promptly, monitor for correct coding, keep an eye out for overpayments, and report issues to their insurers promptly.

An important step to reduce the risks in a provider's practice is the implementation and adherence to a comprehensive compliance program. Eventually, every health provider receiving payments from Medicare, Medicaid, and other federal health-care programs will be required to have a compliance plan in place. The law also authorizes the Department of Health and Human Services (DHHS) to devise required core elements for compliance programs. While DHHS has not enacted a compliance program for providers, rest assured, DHHS will reflect on the OIG's seven elements for an effective compliance program. In summary, without a compliance plan in place, the law and its continual expansions and clarifications can easily expose any practice to more risk.

Prior to implementing the elements of a compliance plan, it is recommended that the provider's practice develop the following items as a base:

- Code of ethics
- Code of conduct
- Mission and vision statements
- Employee handbook or office manual
- Rights and responsibilities of patients
- Job descriptions
- Performance evaluations
- Office protocol for addressing compliance issues

As mentioned, the OIG compliance program consists of *seven key parts*, called Seven Fundamental Elements of an Effective Compliance Program (https://oig.hhs.gov/authorities/docs/physician.pdf). The Work Plan gives health-care providers visibility into the issues that will receive particular attention from the OIG and provides the necessary guidance to address the related requirements. The Work Plan also serves as a road map to future government enforcement activity. Each of these seven parts is further defined below. These recommendations were developed from experiences with for-profit health-care corporations that have attracted significant media attention. Each of these parts could be adapted to fit a health-care organization, such as a large or small medical practice, surgery centers, freestanding clinics, or other centers servicing health care.

In addition, the OIG can also impose a Corporate Integrity Agreement (CIA) on any health-care provider that participates in one of the federal health programs. This program generally creates significant risk and compliance overhead costs associated with the reviews. The CIAs generally last for 5 years and include specific compliance stipulations that must be enacted within specific time frames, which can be as short as 90 days. These stipulations frequently include verifiable code-of-conduct attestations and training certifications from all covered persons associated with the practice as well as verifiable distribution of relevant policies and procedures to all appropriate covered persons. CIAs also mandate specific claims review criteria and reporting of findings as well as the practice of establishing processes for managing and reporting any events.

23.4.1.1 OIG Compliance Plan Item No. 1—Implement Standards and Procedures

Even when starting from a template plan, it is important to modify and expand the plan to the unique and potential risks associated with the practice. The standards, procedures, and completed templates should be living documents that are adhered to throughout the practice and updated periodically.

Employees and independent contractors should know what is expected of them in terms of compliance. A written program can help set the guidelines for any new and existing employee. Having written procedures helps personnel comply with parameters and increases the awareness of how to meet expectations. Many practices have a code of ethics that employees are required to read and to sign to indicate that they have read and understood it. The act of signing this document can be a declaration to employees of the organization's expectations and their obligations.

It is encouraged in order to obtain buy-in that the development of a compliance program be accomplished in collaboration with not just the providers but also all members of the staff. By actively participating in the creation of the compliance program, the staff fully recognizes the importance and benefit of the plan, especially since they have been instrumental in its creation. Staff also recognize that it is not just a plan that is set on the shelf that will become dormant over time, but it is a plan in which the staff reviews and tracks any undesirable outcomes; and play a significant role in documentation, issue resolution, and performance improvement. No individual has complete responsibility for any errors, and subsequently, the entire organization is responsible for any potential errors or failures. Staff resources along with an oversight compliance officer will address issues that are persistent or high risk. Performance improvement aims to prevent catastrophes before they occur.

23.4.1.2 OIG Compliance Plan Item No. 2—Designate a Compliance Officer

A practice needs to empower a person to educate other employees; update physicians on changes in rules, regulations, and guidelines; call meetings; review the compliance plan and address any updates; review any potential risk; and if needed, initiate corrective actions if there's a deviation from the plan or a violation. Nurses, administrators, billing and office managers, and others with elevated responsibilities in the practice are good compliance officer candidates but, in order to fill that position, still need to receive documented health-care compliance training. The individual selected for this position should have knowledge and skills in modifying behavior and understanding organizational dynamics. It is not in the organizations' best interest to have an individual who is prone to questionable behavior assume the role of compliance officer. Whether the compliance officer is someone appointed from within the organization or hired specifically for the role, certain prerequisites should be required, such as a background check of any past history of Medicare or Medicaid violations, reference checks, and previous experience. The compliance office should have knowledge in many areas, including business administration, clinical activities, coding, billing, reimbursement, risk management, and a general knowledge of laws and regulations applicable to the health-care organization environment. In addition, the person should have a variety of skills that include good judgment, and the ability to prioritize and be respected by not only the firm's leadership but also the staff.

The best way to choose a compliance officer is through rigorous interviewing and training, as there is no single answer to finding the right person for the job. There needs to be a check-and-balance system in place with anyone selected internally to avoid any perceived or real conflicts of interest. As an example, the individual should not have dual roles in being a compliance officer while also being assigned the responsibility of overseeing the coding and billing function of the practice where there may be potential bonuses tied to increased practice revenue. Typical responsibilities of a compliance officer are as follows:

- Overseeing and monitoring the implementation of the compliance program
- Reporting monthly/quarterly to the practice's responsible body on the progress of implementation and assisting the practice in establishing methods to improve efficiency and quality of services to reduce the vulnerability to allegations of fraud, waste, and abuse
- Developing and distributing all written compliance policies and procedures to all employees

- Periodically revising the program in light of changes in the needs of the organization, changes in the law, or changes in government and private payor health plans
- Developing, coordinating, and participating in multifaceted educational and training programs that focus on the elements of the compliance program and seek to ensure that all staff are knowledgeable of and comply with the pertinent federal, state, and payor standards
- Ensuring that all physicians are informed of the compliance program standards with respect to coding, billing, documentation, and marketing
- Assisting in coordinating internal compliance review and monitoring activities, including annual or as-needed reviews of policies
- Independently investigating and acting on matters related to compliance, including the flexibility to design and coordinate internal investigations
- Developing policies and programs that encourage managers and employees to report suspected fraud and other improprieties without fear of retaliation

The compliance officer has the authority to review all documents and other information relative to compliance activities including, but not limited to, requisition forms, billing information, claims information, and records concerning marketing efforts and arrangements with clients.

Larger or multispecialty practices may also consider the development of a compliance committee that will work in collaboration and advisement to the compliance officer. The functions of a compliance committee include the following:

- Analyzing the practice's regulatory environment, the legal requirements with which it must comply, and specific risk areas
- Assessing existing policies and procedures that address risk areas for possible incorporation into the compliance program
- Working within the practice's standards of conduct and policies and procedures to promote compliance
- Recommending and monitoring the development of internal systems and controls to implement standards, policies, and procedures as part of the daily operations
- Determining the appropriate strategy/approach to promote compliance with the program and detection of any potential problems or violations
- Developing a system to solicit, evaluate, and respond to complaints and problems

Regardless of the size of the practice, a compliance officer should be appointed to provide the oversight needed and assure the practice that compliance issues are being addressed.

23.4.1.3 OIG Compliance Plan Item No. 3—Train and Educate

In order to modify or establish compliant behavior, education on the compliance program and plan should be provided to every existing employee and all new staff, and include annual refresher courses. This training needs to address the role that each individual of the organization has in ensuring that the compliance program is operational and effective. Files with dates and content should be maintained on each staff member's training session as well as how it was conducted—webinar, classroom training, or self-training with testing. Each staff person should further sign and certify that he/she attended the course, read the material, and understood the content.

Training should start immediately upon hire. The orientation should consist of what the expectations of the employee are and what the employer has done to promote the culture of compliance. Ongoing education may be completed through weekly staff meetings or monthly business meetings. Outside seminars are another way to educate staff on compliance or proper and accurate coding and billing. Outside consultants can also provide either on-site or off-site services to educate staff on how to review claims and internal processes. Journals, newsletters, and online services provide another method of obtaining information on compliance. Participation of the clinical staff is just as important, as the business staff for the providers are the responsible parties for the overall practice, including its compliance and accuracy of documentation and billing. Although some of the billing and coding functions can be delegated to other staff, it is ultimately the provider whose name, number, and signature appear on the insurance claim form.

Educational topics may include the following:

- Medical record keeping
- Current Procedural Terminology® (CPT®) professional coding
- International Classification of Diseases (ICD-9-CM) and, coming soon, International Statistical Classification of Diseases and Related Health Programs (ICD-10)
- Use of modifiers and Healthcare Common Procedure Coding System (HCPCS)
- Internal auditing practices
- Evaluation and management guidelines
- OIG policies and procedures
- Laws, regulations, guidelines and policies impacting the health-care practice
- Continuous process improvement
- Government and private payer reimbursement principles
- General prohibitions on paying or receiving remuneration to induce referrals
- Proper translation of narrative diagnoses
- Duty to report misconduct

When issues arise as part of a compliance program, education becomes crucial to modify the behavior of the entire organization.

An educational curriculum works well if the program is planned over a period of time, such as a year. This curriculum could use internal staff meetings and outside programs sponsored by professional associations, the insurance firms, or private firms to educate all members of the staff. The education should focus on the issues that have the largest or most significant impact on the practice itself, such as using higher levels of evaluation and management office visits instead of a lower code or fragment billing or unbundling services that are part of a global code. A curriculum will evolve based on issues that the organization identifies as well as information that is disseminated from the Centers for Medicare and Medicaid Services (CMS), other insurance companies, and other entities.

23.4.1.4 OIG Compliance Plan Item No. 4—Monitor and Audit

Periodic chart audits, at least yearly or every 6 months if risk areas have been identified, can help ensure that documentation supports the levels of service billed. There is always a concern from the government, such as CMS, or private insurers that services billed may be unnecessary. CMS has invested significant funding to have programs like Medicare and

Medicaid RAC programs, ZPICs, and MACs conduct reviews and audits of their claims billing practices. Their reviews and targeted risks include items such as provider eligibility, billing for services not provided, reimbursement of unapproved drugs, duplicate billing, services that may compromise quality of care, up-coding, services provided by an unlicensed or untrained personnel, excessive administrative costs, and providing false certifications in claims processing.

Health-care providers need a solution that can help them take control of the entire audit process, including their initial response to record requests, determining if and when to appeal denied claims, and ensuring timely replies throughout the complex appeals process. With that said, a compliance plan that documents audit results, as well as takes any corrective actions and education of staff as a result of the audits, becomes a way for the practice to justify the level of service and compliance. With external reviews, providers need to take control of the audit process to minimize the risk of losing revenues, document and substantiate work flow and services performed, make well-informed decisions throughout the complex external audit, process and incorporate medical claims audit management into the broader compliance and risk-management programs within the practice.

There are several ways to monitor compliance. Although most organizations operate at a fairly high compliance rate, audits offer health-care entities a chance to evaluate progress. Audits can be unannounced or random reviews that test the integrity of the billing or collection processes between regular audits. The auditing and monitoring function accomplishes the following objectives:

- Evaluates compliance with all federal laws and regulations
- Minimizes financial and legal risks to the organization
- Empowers the organization to maintain/implement a compliance program

Risk areas can be determined by reviewing the OIG annual Work Plan, Medicare and Medicaid bulletins and publications, and other communication programs.

23.5 COMPLIANCE AUDITS

An external audit and, sometimes, even an internal audit occur primarily for one of four reasons, outlined below.

1. *Suspicion of fraud and/or abuse.* Medicare and Medicaid fraud is the intentional deception or misrepresentation of services that an individual knows to be false and could result in an unauthorized reimbursement to a practice. The following are common examples of fraud.
    - *Phantom billing* is where the provider bills Medicare for unnecessary procedures, medical tests, or procedures that were never performed. This could include unnecessary equipment or equipment that was billed as new but in fact was used.
    - *Patient billing scams* can include the patient providing his/her Medicare number to others in exchange for kickbacks or can include a collaborative effort with the provider in which the patient attests that tests, procedures, or services were performed when they were not.
    - *Up-coding and unbundling schemes* include inflating bills by using a billing code that indicates that the patient needs a more expensive procedure.

SPECIFIC EXAMPLES OF FRAUD

- A physician solicits a new patient by offering a waived co-payment.
- A practice bills for an office visit when the patient was a no-show or cancelled the appointment.
- The provider falsifies the medical necessity of a procedure in the medical records and on the submitted claim to justify the service being paid.

SPECIFIC EXAMPLES OF ABUSE

- Questionable billing patterns and practices, which may result in unnecessary reimbursement.
- Overuse of medical and health-care services, such as scheduling unnecessary multiple visits for a patient in order to receive more reimbursement.
- Billing different insurance companies different rates.

Medicare and Medicaid abuse is defined as incidents or practices inconsistent with accepted and sound medical, business, or fiscal practices. Abuse is considered a lesser offense, happening when practices do not follow proper coding and billing guidelines. Examples of abuse are as follows:

- Unnecessary costs to the health-care system, including the Medicare and Medicaid programs
- Improper payment for services
- Payment for services that fail to meet professionally recognized standards of best practice

Suspected fraud and abuse investigations can be initiated through their medical board, a health insurance program's review of their submitted data, another provider, or even a patient complaint. The preliminary review will usually request a sampling of specific medical records, which may progress to an on-site review and audit of all medical records of that patient or the entire practice.

2. *Comparative practice data.* Most insurance firms and even those firms that contract with the insurance firms have developed sophisticated data algorithms that can track, analyze based on selected parameters, and statistically evaluate aberrancies in billing practices. Insurance firms have developed benchmarks that will trigger a review. An example is when a provider's visit hours to multiple patients in a given day excessively exceed typical office hours of operation or collectively exceed the hours in a day (i.e., 24 hours). Another example would be the use of narcotics like Oxycontin in which the provider prescribed the drug for a very high number of patients in his/her practice repeatedly and above the standard norm of practice. Even physicians who change their pattern of practice and increase the use of a specialty service more frequently than in the past are subject to review.
3. *Random insurer reviews.* CMS, the largest insurer within the government, is mandated and has internal policies in place that state that a percentage of particular claims must be reviewed; many other larger insurance firms follow similar processes. These programs are performed on a regular basis to ensure program

integrity. In addition, the DHHS OIG's 2013 Work Plan focuses on a wide variety of compliance issues in order to protect the integrity of the DHHS programs and operations and the well-being of the beneficiaries by detecting and preventing fraud, waste, and abuse; improving program efficiency and effectiveness; and holding those who do not meet program requirements accountable. Example focus areas include the following:

- Medical necessity of high-cost radiology procedures
- Place of service coding errors
- Noncompliance with assignment rules and excessively billing patients directly for fees not owed
- Payments for deceased or incarcerated patients
- Continued monitoring of coding of evaluation and management services and use of modifiers in physician reimbursement
- Electrodiagnostic testing questionable billing

4. *Complaints.* This is the most common way that an audit can be triggered. Anyone can call to register a complaint. Physicians can report their colleagues, whether competitors in the same practice or colleagues at the same hospital. A vulnerable group that experiences potential fraud and abuse schemes is the senior population, who unknowingly may be subject to unnecessary services or aberrant practices.

THE COST OF HEALTH FRAUD

There is no question that real fraud, waste, and abuse exist in health-care today. The Office of the Inspector General (OIG) of the Department of Health and Human Services (DHHS) saved American taxpayers a record $21 billion a dozen years ago, according to Inspector General Janet Rehnquist. Savings were achieved through an intensive and continuing crackdown on waste, fraud, and abuse in Medicare and over 300 other DHHS programs for which the OIG has oversight responsibility.

More recently, according to the Centers for Medicare and Medicaid Services (CMS) and under the tenure of Eric Himpton Holder Jr., 82nd attorney general of the United States, and more recently, Loretta Lynch, recovery audit contractors (RACs) collected almost $1 billion in improper payments during their beta-testing period in 2009–2010. Of these payments, 96% were overpayments, and 4% were underpayments; 77% of providers failed to appeal, 7% appealed successfully, and 15% appealed unsuccessfully. And, by fiscal year 2016, recovery auditors collectively identified and corrected more than 1,532,249 claims for improper payments, which resulted in more than $3.75 billion in improper payments being corrected. The total corrections identified include more than $3.65 billion in overpayments collected and $102.4 million in underpayments repaid to providers and suppliers.

After taking into consideration all fees, costs, and first-level appeals, the Medicare Fee-For-Service (FFS) Recovery Audit Program returned over $3.0 billion to the Medicare trust funds. These savings did not take into account program costs and administrative expenses incurred at the third and fourth levels of appeal (Office of Medicare Hearings and Appeals [OMHA] and Medicare Appeals Council within the Departmental Appeals Board [DAB], respectively), as these components do not receive Recovery Audit Program funding for those appeals.

Extensive literature is produced by Medicare to encourage not only the senior population but also their families to be aware of and to report any inappropriate billing activities. The Medicare program relies on patients to be the first party to indicate a problem with an individual practitioner or health-care organization in order to initiate an investigation. The entire system is focused on capturing complaints and evaluating what is true/factual and what is false. Surveys are an excellent way to give feedback on whether or not there is anything inappropriate about the services rendered. Once assessed, the relevant issues can be acted upon accordingly.

23.6 TYPES OF COMPLIANCE AUDITS

There are several types of audits that a health-care organization might need to perform. The starting point is to obtain a baseline audit. Next steps include periodic audits or reviews that are performed after all the information is obtained from the baseline audit. Additional audits can be performed whenever new employees are added or if there are complaints or issues that arise in the course of business.

- *Self-audit.* Routine self-assessments demonstrate proactive measures established to ensure compliance and thus reduce the likelihood of a failed audit.
- *Baseline audit.* Baseline audits are preliminary assessments to develop a reference point. This preliminary audit can help an organization understand where the program is and establish a base to gauge or compare future activities. Without this initial assessment, it is difficult for anyone within the practice or even an external consultant to determine if there are any performance issues.
- *Periodic audits.* Periodic audits are performed on an ongoing basis, based on the decision of the practice. They may occur at random or at a scheduled time, monthly or quarterly.
- *New-employee audits.* New employees require regular training and reviews until there is confidence in their capabilities. Background checks are helpful to find out whether there are any potential conflicts; however, many independent medical practices do not have access to this type of information and may have to rely on other organizations to obtain the information. The OIG and General Services Administration maintain a database of excluded persons and entities, which can be accessed through the Internet. As part of the organization's initial and periodic audits, queries of these two databases should be performed for all employees and any independent contractors.

23.6.1 WHAT TO AUDIT

When selecting what to audit, the sample selected should have statistical significance to a potential problem or risk. A random audit of claims is appropriate in the beginning. The process of selection begins with a determination of the number of claims per provider that need to be identified and reviewed. Based on the size of the practice and volume of business, auditing 100 claims over a year or 25 claims in the past quarter are sufficient sample sizes. If the volume is substantial for a year, you can get a good universal sample; however, if your volume is low, 3 years would be a good benchmark. In addition, the OIG recommends 5 or more medical records per federal payer or 5–10 medical records per physician. Once a problem is found, your next step is to determine the cause, which will vary depending on the problems. One way to determine the cause of a problem found in your audit is to compare data with data from others in the same specialty for similar services. Other issues may have generated the problem as well. Several examples are listed below:

- A physician's encounter form, whether electronic or manual, may be the cause if the provider abbreviates his/her procedures and does not give a complete description, which results in miscoding.
- Outdated ICD-9 codes may still be used by the physicians.
- Multiple physicians in a practice may have varied understanding of how to bill the appropriate evaluation and management code or modifier, resulting in an overall practice inconsistency. Improper evaluation and management coding is a problem that easily can lead to underpayment or overpayment of services. Many practices will routinely bill the lowest level of visit, which may result in lost revenue, whereas other providers overcode the majority of their visits, which can result in potential risk and liability for refunds.
- Billing staff may not have read or attended updated billing seminars and are repeatedly billing the wrong codes for services rendered.

23.6.2 Choosing an Auditor

An auditor needs to have certain core competencies to adequately audit a medical practice. These individuals need to be well versed on coding, billing, and collection protocols; Medicare Part A and B guidelines; and rules and regulations. They must have audit experience with similar practice specialties; a detailed understanding of medical record reviews; and especially, the ability to accurately relate the written description of a service to the appropriate billing code. In addition, the auditors need to have the ability of discerning the presence or absence of appropriate information in the audit process.

The auditor could be a physician, physician extender, business manager, billing manager, coding professional, or accounting or legal person. This individual should have an investigative and inquisitive mind, be a stickler for details and processes, and have the ability to follow through. In addition, this individual should have the ability to determine variations in normal practice patterns compared to norms in a similar practice field. The value of the review process is in bringing in individuals knowledgeable about the nature of the business to evaluate against industry-established standards and to identify good practice and areas for improvement.

23.6.3 OIG Compliance Plan Item No. 5—Respond

Once you have identified a problem, you have to document it and take direct, corrective action, which is also documented. For any future audit or investigation, the practice needs to state that they took legitimate actions to deal with the issue and correct it. When necessary, restitution (refunds) will be made to the appropriate payers, and the organization must be able to implement additional steps to prevent problems from recurring. This is part of performance improvement initiatives. To evaluate a situation, determine what part of the process caused the problem and implement necessary changes to prevent the problem from recurring. A corrective action plan should be developed that would include retraining for all staff and a follow-up plan for a reaudit examination to assure that compliance has been accomplished.

Audits and the associated work entailed with corrective actions require significant time and money to complete. However, once accomplished, a decline will occur with incorrect billing practices. In turn, the staff will have more time to devote their attention to patient care and correct billing practices.

23.6.4 OIG Compliance Plan Item No. 6—Open Lines of Communication

A user-friendly environment needs to be adopted in which staff can report suspicious or potential fraudulent or abusive practice patterns. One of the most important benefits of an effective communication system is that it provides the staff with a means to report suspected or actual noncompliance to someone within the organization. Lack of an effective communication program can contribute to employee reluctance to report inappropriate actions. Many times, communication can get stifled at the level of a provider not willing to review or audit because of the work entailed or because this is his/her billing or documenting pattern. Staff, many times, are reluctant to voice their comments or concerns for fear of losing their job or other types of retaliation. Small-office staff are more vulnerable because everyone knows who said what at any given time.

Whether it is a large medical practice or small, a clinic or a hospital, there are several communication pathways that can be established to communicate issues in a practice. These alternatives can be posted on a compliance bulletin board for all staff to review. Several communication processes are

- Make known to every employee the availability of the compliance officer. In this situation, a staff member with concerns contacts the officer directly and discreetly and presents the issue. The compliance officer conducts a thorough investigation and reports results to the senior management of the practice along with a corrective action plan.
- Establish a toll-free number or suggestion box as a way for a staff to privately communicate with a compliance officer.
- Contract with an outside firm to provide third-party objectivity and anonymity.
- As an alternative, provide staff the names and numbers or regulatory agencies in which a simple report can be filed either via the telephone or through the Internet reporting line. This could include posting the DHHS OIG hotline telephone number in a prominent location.

The most drastic action would be a whistle-blower lawsuit where an employee, at his/her own expense, files a suit in federal court against the health-care entity. This is a more long and drawn-out process, but if the suit goes forward and is settled, the person initiating the suit has the potential to receive 15% or more of the monies recovered.

23.6.5 OIG Compliance Plan Item No. 7—Enforcement through Discipline

The practice should publicize to staff its disciplinary standards, document findings of noncompliant conduct, and be prepared to issue sanctions to violators. Disciplinary actions can include reprimands, probation, demotion, suspension, and even termination and referral for criminal prosecution. The task gets especially hard when a physician is suspected. Regardless of who is involved, the person identifying the aberrancy or noncompliance issue needs to take direct action; otherwise, there is the potential that the person will be seen as a conspirator in a potential False Claims Act suit. Communication on this process needs to be done to all staff and will need to be managed in a consistent manner.

A successful compliance plan sends a message to the staff, physicians, payers, and regulators that the practice is trying to prevent errors. In addition, a good compliance plan not only reduces the risk of costly False Claims Act allegations; it also reduces vulnerability to coding errors generally, as well as Stark violations and other risks. It is best to view compliance plans as "preventive medicine" to minimize mistakes that could end up costing much more than maintaining the plan. Moreover, if the plan helps to increase accuracy in documentation and root out billing and coding problems, it could enhance the delivery of patient care and improve the practice's bottom line.

23.7 IMPLEMENTING A COMPLIANCE PROGRAM

Each physician practice is different—a practice can be a solo practitioner, multiple physicians of the same specialty, a practice of multiple specialties, a clinic, multiple site locations, utilization of part- and full-time physicians and staff, and many more combinations. To create the right compliance plan will include not only an analysis of the practice itself and what is or is not in place, but also cooperation and input from the entire staff. It is extremely difficult to encounter a process that entirely revolves around one individual and that does not affect another individual. A critical success factor will be the ability to determine the processes that involve your billing and collection program and subsequently determine how your compliance program will work. The concept of reengineering is the evaluation of different processes and the determination of how to make the process more efficient.

As stated previously, a compliance officer is key to a successful compliance program. This individual needs to analyze the different factors that affect the organization's processes. It is definitely easier to have one person understand the entire process from the initiation of a scheduled appointment through and including documentation, coding, and the billing and collection process. Even though the process occurring prior to and during the processing of a claim can be straightforward, it can also include various steps and outlier processes that need to be addressed. These can include unforeseen diagnostic outcomes, staff competency, availability of time, capabilities of the information technology (IT) system and electronic health record, physician direction, patient compliance, and/or regulatory requirements. Any of these areas affect the straight line of claims processing, which can cause shortcuts, arbitrary decisions, backlogs, and a multitude of other problems. Processes that have no variables are predictable, but processes with variables can have different end results.

For an efficient and successful compliance program, two things need to be accomplished. First, the organization needs to collectively agree to a compliance program and what the desired outcomes will be, and second, the practice needs to determine what process improvements are needed in order to achieve a more functional process and outcome. Regardless of what is decided, the processes need to be thought out, have built-in checks and balances, and be efficient. Trial-and-error processes are not the best method to implementing change; however, occasionally, these processes need to be used to prove a point as to the validity or nonvalidity of their outcome.

Keep in mind at all times during the development and implementation process that the intent of the compliance program is to protect the health-care entity and its owners and shareholders. The government expects that anyone billing for health-care services will know the rules, and providers cannot claim ignorance as a defense. The expectation is that rules are to be followed constantly. Billing and reimbursement rules and regulations vary according to payer, geographic region, and place of services, and even regions or localities can adopt select guidelines pertinent only to their area. Each health-care provider should have a thorough understanding of the specific rules that apply to his/her practice. This begins with an understanding of each of the contracts or provider agreements that the organization or provider has signed. Because Medicare is one of the principal payers and promulgators of rules that many other insurance companies follow, most practices across the board focus on the Medicare requirements. The following functions need to be considered as part of any start-up compliance plan.

23.7.1 Physician Accountability

The majority of private practices are managed and owned by the practitioners themselves. By providing a service or procedure to a patient, coding and billing the service to the insurance company, and utilizing their own individual provider number, they become the responsible party for that claim. Even though the nurse, billing clerk, and others were involved in the care and office practice, it is the physician who signed the form who is responsible for the accuracy of the claim submitted. The physician or physicians who own and manage the process must agree to proceed, must commit to the elements of a compliance plan and further agree to practice pattern changes that need to be made to be in compliance. This is a critical first step.

Lack of ownership could be translated into lack of interest by the leadership of the organization. If the leaders do not subscribe to the concepts and principles of a compliance program, then the effectiveness of the compliance officer will be seriously hampered. A compliance program that is not working or is ineffective is worse than not having any plan at all.

23.7.2 Risk Management

Risk is an important element in every health organization, and there are two parts. The first is risk prevention, which focuses on reducing the possibility of loss, whether financial, reputation, or market share. The second is risk management, which is the managing of the loss after the event has occurred. The primary focus of a compliance program is the economical and professional risks associated with reimbursement activities.

Risk management includes processes for assessing and monitoring risk, manage the risk response strategy, link the risk-management data to compliance activities, and provide a global view of all risk-related activities through a dashboard. Medical practices will then be able to quickly assess problem areas, proactively adjust processes to respond to issues, and track progress through reports and automated alerts.

23.7.3 Leadership

The person instrumental in implementing a compliance program needs to be able to keep conflicts from getting personal while working with people who are close to a situation. This individual, when the situation arises, needs to have the capability of being an enforcer yet remain pleasant and in charge on continuing forward. Having the practice leadership formalize who this individual is and what his/her role will be will lend credibility to the overall success of the compliance program.

23.7.4 Costs

Costs of implementing a compliance program can vary from several thousands of dollars to over $30,000 depending on the size of the practice, the various locations of the practice, the capabilities of the existing staff, and the training needs. Costs need to include not only the initial implementation and/or the hiring of a dedicated compliance officer, but also the ongoing cost of ensuring that the program continually runs as planned.

An initial recommendation is to assess the current level of staffing, their capabilities, and their roles and responsibilities, to determine what additional costs need to be expended. Do you need more qualified and experienced billers, or do you just need one qualified biller that may eliminate other staff who have been supportive of the function but not fully capable of performing independently? Do you need to develop a training program, or do you need to send individuals for training on compliance; if so, what is that cost? Can you utilize an existing staff person to fulfill the role of compliance officer, or do you need to hire a separately trained individual? Do you need to establish a tracking system internally, and what is that cost? What is the cost of having an outside audit completed? Who will be responsible for correcting policies and procedures, and is that an additional cost? How will the providers be educated on correct billing practices, and is that an associated cost?

These are just several of the questions related to cost that need to be addressed. An initial budget during the design phase needs to be developed and agreed to by all concerned. The budget may also have to be modified as other expenses are identified and addressed.

23.7.5 Boilerplate Documents

Consideration needs to be given as to whether it is effectual or ineffectual to use a boilerplate document or template to develop the necessary forms or manuals for the compliance program. Many times, these forms do not address the uniqueness, size, or specialty of the practice. As an example, below is a sample outline for a compliance plan for physician practices. If you are a large multispecialty practice, this draft outline may save you time in developing a plan; however, if you are a very small practice with limited staff, the extensiveness of this plan may be unnecessary and/or overwhelming to the staff.

SAMPLE OUTLINE FOR A COMPLIANCE PLAN FOR PHYSICIANS

The Seven Elements of a Compliance Plan

1. Commitment to compliance
   a. Standards of conduct—includes adherence to the compliance program; commitment to acts, duties, and laws; due diligence in hiring and reviewing new staff; orientation on compliance policies and procedures and outcomes if noncompliance
   b. Medical necessity—includes a statement assessing that each claim is reasonable and justified based on the patient's treatment, statements on what the major payers will and will not pay for, and the use of signed advance beneficiary notices for services that will not be paid for by an insurer
   c. Billing—includes coding requirements, information on up-coding, and tying codes to medical record documentation
   d. Reliance on standing orders—provides clarification on how to document continued treatment when only standing orders are in place
   e. Compliance with applicable DHHS fraud alerts—states that staff must review and be familiar with all fraud alerts
   f. Marketing—includes that only honest, straightforward, nondeceptive marketing will be used
   g. Antikickback/inducements—discusses what is considered antikickback and what to avoid
   h. Retention of records/documentation—states that the office will abide by all federal and state laws in retaining medical records and discusses the need for minutes, action plans, assessments, and findings
2. Designation of a compliance officer/committee—summarizes the duties of the compliance officer and/or the compliance committee
3. Conducting training and education programs—details the basic training needs upon hire and annually
4. Internal and external communication—provides a detailed discussion on all available avenues to communicate potential issues and problems
5. Disciplinary guidelines—discusses in detail the processes entailed in the disciplinary review process and potential actions such as dismissal of matter, verbal counseling, warning letter, corrective action plan, reduction of privileges, suspension or termination, modification of assigned duties, and/or reduction of salary
6. Auditing and monitoring—reviews all the various audit functions to include patterns and trends in deviations identified by the audit
7. Corrective action—discusses all the corrective action procedures, processes, and documentation that occur with any violations
   a. Response to special agent's visit for the purpose of investigating allegations of fraud and abuse—reviews the detailed steps of what to do and what not to do when an agent is auditing the practice

The concepts behind a business plan or strategic plan and a compliance plan are extremely accurate and detailed; however, a compliance plan needs to be modified and molded into something that is truly reflective of the individual business if it is to be functional.

23.7.6 Correcting the Issues Identified

After the compliance plan is designed, endorsed, and implemented, the next steps are addressing and rectifying the issues found. Examples may include the following:

- *Significant overpayments without justified medical necessity.* The initial audit may quickly uncover repetitive claims with the same issue, necessitating a need for reimbursement back to the insurance company. The end results may entail fines and penalties and will require the compliance program to not only document and report on the massive overpayment but also develop a plan of action of repayment and internal changes in billing patterns. Examples could include routinely billing a comprehensive evaluation and management visit when a problem-focused or brief visit was performed. Another example could be billing separately for every item in an office surgical procedure when the global code encompassed all support services to the surgery. This could include billing separately for the anesthesia, supplies, use of operating room, devices, aftercare, etc. Another example would be billing for each lab test separately when a panel including all of these tests is already priced and has its own procedure code.

  Compliance programs create a much more accurate billing and reimbursement system, which can result in either lowering the practice's overall reimbursement and/or, in some cases, increasing reimbursement to a higher level.
- *Incomplete documentation.* Medical records provide the basis and justification of the patient's condition, the treatment, the outcomes, and the place of service. It is important that the provider's documentation reflect this information for both good patient care and compliance with documentation guidelines. Documentation is the foundation of a successful medical practice because without complete documentation, it is almost impossible to accurately report services and achieve optimal reimbursement.

  Medical records need to be complete and legible and should include the following information:
  - Date of visit, history, physical examination findings, and prior diagnostic tests.
  - Assessment, clinical impression, or diagnosis.
  - Plan for care.
  - Date of visit.
  - Legible identification of which provider performed the care.
  - Rationale for diagnostic and other ancillary services should be referenced.
  - Past and present diagnoses should be accessible to the treating physician.
  - Appropriate health risk factors should be identified.

Many times, the fast pace of a practice causes providers to shortcut their documentation but continue to send to the coder and biller the procedural or diagnostic codes based on what they performed, not what they documented in the medical record. This represents a mismatch of information that can cause a justification problem during an audit. To rectify the situation, the physician may need to refund the government or insurer the difference in dollars between what was documented and what was billed. As part of the compliance plan, the practice needs to correct these deficiencies through education, training, and making sure their internal audits document and substantiate what was actually performed.

In addition, conducting retrospective reviews requires significant time and energy, especially after a claim has been denied and the insurance company is asking for documentation to support the claim. To avoid having to conduct costly retrospective reviews, it is best to complete reviews before the claim leaves the clinical area or physician. If this is not feasible because of time and patient volumes, then a staff member needs to review the documentation compared to the coding before the end of the day and obtain clarification on any discrepancies noted. Utilization of an electronic medical record system provides quicker access to information, and *holds* can be placed on submissions until the information is corrected. As a side precaution, all staff need to understand what needs to be done when an issue is identified during an internal review.

- *Correcting provider numbers.* Each physician is assigned a provider identification number for him/her to use in submitting claims for payment. If the number is incorrect, the provider needs to immediately address the issue with the insurance company and begin using the correct number. If a *locum tenens* physician is billing for an absent physician, he/she may do so for up to 60 days but needs to utilize a modifier, *Q6*, to notify Medicare or another insurer that he/she is temporarily filling in for the provider.

Besides the deficiencies, the practice needs to conform to the following in order to follow the compliance plan now and in the future.

- *Proper coding and billing.* Accurate coding of the procedure(s), service(s), and diagnostic code is critical to proper reimbursement and practice compliance. These codes are updated annually, and the practice is required to update their knowledge and utilize the correct codes. It is also important to make sure that the use of these codes is not contingent upon whether payment will be made for the service but instead reflect the service and the reason for the service that was provided. In addition, providers must select the correct procedure code(s) and ensure that the associated documentation required for each level of service is in the patient's medical record.

  There are also rules associated with selecting the correct diagnosis code. The key issue in determining whether a provider can be paid for his/her services is to show that there was a medically justifiable reason for performing the procedure or service. This is established primarily by looking at the CPT or procedure code that was billed in relation to the ICD diagnosis code that was given as the reason for the encounter, procedure, or hospitalization. If medical necessity can be shown, that the bill will more than likely be paid.

  The basic requirement is that diagnosis must justify the procedure. If the rules listed below are followed, there is a good chance claims will be paid quickly.
  - Code all diagnoses to the ultimate specificity.
  - Use additional codes for any underlying diseases when necessary.

- Code conditions encountered during the service to fully describe the encounter.
- Choose appropriate principal diagnosis and all secondary codes correctly.
- Avoid many of the "catchall" codes that are "otherwise classified."

  Regardless if previous medical records were not documented to their fullest extent, it is not recommended that the medical records be corrected at a later date. This could open the office up to another audit where they look at backdated changes to documentation and adjust previous records in order to get paid. Use this as a lesson learned for all future medical records and coding.
- *Personnel compliance.* Having the staff understand the reason for a compliance plan and comply with its content is probably one of the most important parts of a compliance plan. Staff who do not understand what they are supposed to do or who feel that no one has an interest in their work are more likely to place the organization at risk for potential fines, significant refund events, alienation of patients or other staff members, and/or poor work quality, resulting in lost income. Staff who feel respected and appreciated are usually more productive and convey that same respect and appreciation to their coworkers and patients. This is accomplished through a detailed job description. In addition, the practice should develop, update, and maintain detailed procedure manuals that define how each job function should be accomplished. Clear job descriptions no only aid the person who regularly performs the task(s) but also provide a backup system when that person is temporarily or permanently absent.

Each practice needs to outline and explain, in writing, the expectations and prohibitions that are associated with employment. This can be accomplished through a personnel policy manual.

23.7.7 Policy and Procedure Management

The practice should include not only an initial policy and procedure manual to support compliance but also the ability to monitor activities through version control, audit capabilities, as well as surveys of the staff to ensure they have read and understand each policy. For ease of reference, the policies and procedures should be organized by the regulations that are impacting the practice, enabling physicians and staff to provide real-time evidence of compliance.

23.7.8 Management of Adverse Events/Incidents

Medical practices can experience a wide variety of health-care issues such as slips and falls, needlesticks, audit findings, and legal cases. There are a few other compliance activities that can be as laborious and cumbersome as establishing an effective incident management and reporting process. Whether it is an adverse incident, concern, event, or investigation, a health-care provider's ability to create a consistent and effective intake and resolution process is imperative for proper risk management and proof of compliance. Incidents, in many cases, can be managed across multiple departments, with different approaches, and most certainly arrive from multiple sources (hotline calls, e-mails, verbal communication, handwritten notes, and others). Compliance officers will frequently use this information for the audit committee meetings.

MEDICAL CODERS AND BILLERS

Medical CPT coders document the diagnoses given to a patient as well as the procedures and equipment used to treat them. They then take this list and enter it in a coded form, which makes record keeping easy and consistent across all health-care facilities. Medical coding also helps remove ambiguity from diagnoses, and removes some risk of illegible writing or changes in terminology that might cause problems for patients down the line. It also makes it easy for public health experts to anonymously gather data on the location and frequency of illnesses and injuries. The Certified Professional Coder® (CPC®) credential is the gold standard for medical coding in physician office settings and held by nearly 99,000 coding professionals. CPCs are critical to compliant and profitable medical practices and typically earn 20% more than noncertified coders. CPCs have proven by rigorous examination and experience that they know how to read a medical chart and assign the correct diagnosis (ICD-9, ICD-10), procedure (CPT), and supply (HCPCS level II) code for a wide variety of clinical cases and services. The Bureau of Labor Statistics (BLS) predicts 37,700 new positions for medical coders by the year 2020, not including openings created by older medical coders retiring. Medical coders earn, on average, $32,350 per year, and find employment primarily in hospitals or physicians' offices, although openings exist in other locations, such as nursing care facilities and home health-care centers.

A closely related career is medical billing, so the jobs of billing and coding are often performed by the same person. When a patient undergoes a medical procedure or visit, billers handle payment for that service. Insurance companies and programs like Medicare or Medicaid establish guidelines based on what services they will pay for, and at what rate. By converting the services, medications, and equipment used for a patient's treatment into standard reference codes, medical billers track how much patients owe after deducting the amount that their insurance or program covers.

23.8 ASSESSMENT

Whether the medical practice is large or small, affiliated with a clinic or hospital, a single specialty or multiple specialties, must comply with applicable federal, state, and local laws and regulations and must understand and abide by the health-care insurer guidelines and rules in order to receive reimbursement for services. The medical practice has been developed to treat patients, and with that comes a right to treat, but also, compliance is required.

The practice needs to look at itself to determine whether they are adhering to all the rules and regulations, appropriately coding and billing, and accurately documenting each and every medical record as it occurs. The providers and staff need to document appropriate policies and procedures and address any outstanding issues or problems before they increase in size and dimension. The most effective way we recommend is to develop a detailed medical practice compliance program, plan, and process that keeps the practice sound; accurately reflects services and procedures; and, continually and/or at random, monitors that compliance is being achieved.

23.9 CONCLUSION

Changes in the pattern of practice will occur with a compliance plan. The practice needs to develop mechanisms and processes to implement, seamlessly and easily, a plan to correct any future deficiencies. As stated, we recommend a trained individual to provide the glue between the documenting, coding, and billing practice along with the care provided to patients—that is the compliance officer's role.

Compliance may seem to be associated with more work and documentation, but in the end, compliance results in a safer, more efficient, more effective, and more profitable health-care business.

23.10 COLLABORATE

Discuss this chapter online with others at http://www.medicalexecutivepost.com.

ACKNOWLEDGMENT

To Pati Trites, PhD, MPA, CHBC, CPC, of Compliance Resources, LLC, Waterloo, Indiana.

FURTHER READINGS

American College of Physicians: http://www.acponline.org/running_practice/practice_management/regulatory_compliance.com.

Center for Medicare and Medicaid Services: http://www.cms.gov.

Compliance Guide for the Medical Practice: http://www.amazon.com/compliance-guide-medical-practice.com.

Compliance Manual, Universal Health Services: http://www.uhsimc.com.

Developing a Medical Practice Compliance Plan: http://www.physicianspractices.com, January 2, 2013.

Doctors Management: Simply Compliance, OIG Fraud and Abuse Manual and Training. Knoxville, TN, 2015.

Health Care Compliance Association: http://www.hcca-info.org.

Health Law Partners: http://www.thehealthlawpartners.com.

Healthcare Common Procedure Coding System (HCPCS): http://www.cms.hhs.gov/hcpcsrelease codesets.

McKesson Practice Solutions: http://www.mckessonpracticesolutions.com/reources/editorials/complianceplan.com.

Medical Group Management Association (MGMA): http://www.mgma.com.

Medical Practice Compliance Alert. Decision Health, Gaithersburg, MD, 2015.

Miller, CS: Health Information Technology, Security and Privacy. In Marcinko, DE (editor): *Hospitals and Healthcare Organizations.* CRC Press, Boca Raton, FL, 2013.

Miller, CS and Marcinko, DE: Managing and Improving the Hospital Revenue Cycle Process. In Marcinko, DE (editor): *Financial Management Strategies for Hospitals and Healthcare Organizations.* CRC Press, Boca Raton, FL, 2014.

Office of the Inspector General: http://www.oig.gov.

OIG Compliance Manual for the Medical Practice: http://www.psrbooks.com/oig-compliance-manual-for-the-medical-practice.com.

Physician Practice: http://www.physicianspractice.com/healthcare-reform/developing-medical-practice-compliance.com.

Sanders, DL, Esq.: *Is a Compliance Plan Right for Your Practice?* Kern Augustine Conroy & Schoppman, P.C., New York: http://DRLaw.com, 2015.
Schoppmann, MJ, Esq.: *Medical Practice Audits: Risk Analysis and Prevention.* Kern Augustine Conroy & Schoppman, P.C., New York: http://DRLaw.com, 2015.
Theuns, S: Medical Office Launch, Development and Strategic Operations (3rd edition). In Marcinko DE (editor). Springer Publishers, New York, 2010.
This Medicare Carrier: http://www.aao.org/publications.com.

24 Creating a Medical Practice Compliance Program

Part Two: Rules, Regulations, Laws, and Guidelines

Carol S. Miller

CONTENTS

Health-care or medical practice compliance programs are closely linked to governmental regulations, rules, and laws. With the increase in number and revisions of regulatory and accreditation requirements, combined with contractual agreements, there is a greater need to make sure that every practice meets all of the necessary obligations and that the practice's compliance plan includes or addresses any of the rules and regulations that would have an impact on the practice. As stated in Chapter 23, which addresses the design and implementation of a health-care practice compliance program, noncompliance can result in significant financial penalties as well as potential lawsuits. The same end results could apply to laboratory and x-ray certification for licensure compliance or employee safety requirements.

This chapter will review the rules, regulations, and associated laws that have an impact on the provider's compliance program. The format that follows will include an overview of the rule, regulation, or law; how it affects the practice; and what the practice needs to do to be compliant.

24.1 RULES, REGULATIONS, AND LAWS

24.1.1 Deficit Reduction Act of 2005

The Deficit Reduction Act of 2005 (DRA) requires medical organizations to have policies and procedures in place to detect fraud and abuse as well as train their employees on what is included in the fraud and abuse laws. Part of the act authorized the establishment of a *Medicaid Integrity Program* (MIP) to monitor fraud and abuse in various state Medicaid programs. In addition, the act provided states with an incentive to adopt state false-claims acts that mirror the requirements of the federal False Claims Act (FCA). Specifically, if a state brings an action under its state false-claims law against a Medicaid provider, then the state can be entitled to receive 10% of the federal government's share of any recovery. Effective in 2007, an additional fraud and abuse provision was added that stated that state Medicaid plans are required to ensure than any entity that receives or makes payment under the state plan of at least $5 million per year must provide certain information to its employees, contractors, and agents concerning federal and state false-claims act provisions, penalties, and protections. As a result, entities that are subject to these requirements must review their corporate compliance programs, policies and procedures, and employee handbooks to ensure that the requisite information is being provided to the employees, contractors, and agents. This is the first federal law to explicitly require Medicaid providers to implement a compliance program as a "condition of payment."

24.1.1.1 Impact of DRA on Providers Providing Medicaid Services

Each practice or entity must establish written policies that provide detailed information on the FCA. These policies need to include detailed provisions regarding the entity's or practice's policies and procedures for detecting and preventing fraud, waste, and abuse; a detailed discussion of both federal and applicable state false-claims acts; and whistle-blower protection.

24.1.2 Medicaid Integrity Program

The MIP program is committed to combating Medicaid provider fraud, waste, and abuse and includes the following responsibilities:

- To hire contractors to review Medicaid provider activities, audit claims, identify overpayments, and educate providers and others on Medicaid program integrity issues

- To provide effective support and assistance to states in their efforts to combat Medicaid provider fraud and abuse
- To eliminate and recover improper payments in accordance with the Improper Payments Information Act (IPIA) of 2002

The Comprehensive Medicaid Integrity Plan (CMIP) has been developed as a strategy for addressing the state's fraud and abuse. The following programs and services are included in the Medicaid integrity efforts.

24.1.2.1 Provider Audits

The MIP has procured Audit Medicaid Integrity Contractors (Audit MICs) to conduct provider audits throughout the country to identify Medicaid overpayments and decrease the payment of inappropriate Medicaid claims. The team of auditors, which includes audit investigators, medical claims reviewers, and data analysts, reviews and analyzes claims submitted by all types of Medicaid providers to identify aberrant claims and potential billing vulnerabilities.

- *National Correct Coding Initiative in Medicaid (NCCI).* The Affordable Care Act required state Medicaid programs to incorporate the national correct coding methodologies in order to reduce improper coding, which may result in inappropriate payments. The NCCI contains two types of edits: (1) procedure-to-procedure edits that define pairs of Healthcare Common Procedure Coding System (HCPCS)/Current Procedural Terminology® (CPT®) codes that should not be reported together for a variety of reasons and (2) medically unlike edits (MUEs) that define for each HCPCS/CPT code the maximum units of service (UOSs) that a provider would report under most circumstances for a single beneficiary on a single date of service.
- *Medicaid guidance fraud prevention.* The Centers for Medicare & Medicaid Services (CMS) provides tool kits and training information to states that represent best practice guidelines and performance standards in program integrity. These tools enable staff to more efficiently perform their jobs.
- *State program integrity reviews.* Through these reviews, CMS assesses the effectiveness of the state's program integrity efforts, including its compliance with federal statutory and regulatory requirements. The reviews also assist in identifying effective state program integrity activities that may be considered particularly noteworthy and shared with other states.
- *Provider screening and enrollment.* A critical provision within the *Patient Protection and Affordable Care Act* (PPACA) requires that all participating providers be screened according to their categorical risk level, upon initial enrollment and upon reenrollment or revalidation of enrollment. States must submit a state plan amendment (SPA) to comply with these federal regulations.
- *Medicaid fraud control units (MFCUs).* In conjunction with the Office of the Inspector General (OIG), these units are responsible for detecting fraud and abuse in state Medicaid programs and neglect in health-care facilities or board and care facilities. Although the states are primarily responsible for combating fraud in the Medicaid program, CMS provides technical assistance, guidance, and oversight in these efforts. Fraud schemes often cross state lines, and CMS strives to improve information sharing among the Medicaid programs and other stakeholders. Starting

in June 2013, state MFCUs—financial watchdog offices typically housed under state attorneys general—can use federal funding for Medicaid data mining, which should offer states analytic tools at the same time that Medicaid is being expanded in more than 20 states.

In its final rule, the OIG placed three requirements on the funding change that have to be confirmed in agreements between the MFCUs and state Medicaid agencies, which the OIG will approve in consultation with CMS.

- MFCUs and state Medicaid agencies must "fully coordinate the MFCUs' use of data mining and the identification of possible provider fraud"—i.e., consult with each other on data mining priorities work with auditing organizations like CMS review contractors.
- MFCUs must also confirm their results with state Medicaid agencies and check to make sure any evidence of improper billing or fraud isn't related to policy changes in reimbursement or documentation that weren't taken into account.
- MFCU staff have to be trained in data and statistical analysis and state Medicaid policy. MFCUs, in their annual reports to the OIG, also have to list the costs of data mining and the cases data mining generates, along with their outcomes and any financial recoveries.

The unit's best source of fraud referrals was the state's Surveillance and Utilization Review Subsystem (SURS).

24.1.3 False Claims Act

The FCA takes on many forms, such as overcharging for a product; failing to perform a service; concealing a material fact or making a material false, fictitious, or fraudulent statement in connection with the delivery of or payment for health-care benefits; delivering less than the promised amounts of services; underpaying money owed to the government; and charging for one thing but delivering another. Persons filing under this act stand to receive a portion of any recovered damages. As of 2014, 30 states and the District of Columbia have created false-claims statutes to protect their publicly funded programs from fraud.

The PPACA made amendments to the FCA, including the following:

- *Changes in the public disclosure bar.* The previous version of the FCA stated that private individuals could be barred if it was determined that such cases were based on a public disclosure of information arising from certain proceedings. The amended language allows the federal government to have the final word on whether a court may dismiss a case based on a public disclosure.
- *Original source requirement.* Previously, the original source must have had a "direct and independent knowledge of the information on which the allegations are based." Under PPACA, the original source is one who has "knowledge that is independent of and materially adds to the publicly disclosed allegations or transactions."
- *Overpayments.* Under PPACA, overpayments under Medicare and Medicaid must be reported and returned within 60 days of discovery, or the date a corresponding hospital report is due.

- *Statutory antikickback liability (AKS).* PPACA changed the language of the AKS to provide that claims submitted in violation of the AKS automatically constitute false claims for the purposes of the FCA. Further, the new language of the AKS provides that "a person need not have actual knowledge or specific intent to commit a violation of the AKS." Providers will not be able to successfully argue that they did not know they were violating the FCA because they were not aware the AKS existed.

24.1.4 Health Insurance Portability and Accountability Act Program

The primary goal of the law is to make it easier for people to keep health insurance, protect the confidentiality and security of health-care information, and help the health-care industry control administrative costs. Title I of the Health Insurance Portability and Accountability Act (HIPAA) protects health insurance coverage for workers and their families when they change or lose their jobs. Title II of HIPAA, known as the Administrative Simplification (AS) provisions, requires the establishment of national standards for electronic health-care transactions and national identifiers for providers, health insurance plans, and employers. The intent of this provision is to improve the efficiency and effectiveness of health-care delivery by creating a national framework for health privacy protection that builds on efforts by states, health systems, and individual organizations as well as to protect and enhance the rights of the patients and improve overall quality of care. In addition, Title II defines policies, procedures, and guidelines for maintaining the privacy and security of individually identifiable health information as well as outlining numerous offenses relating to health care and sets civil and criminal penalties for violations. The rules and regulations apply to "covered entities," which include billing services, health-care clearinghouses, health plans, and health-care providers that transmit health-care data in a way that is regulated by HIPAA. The law also provides incentives for informants and increased penalties for those convicted of violations, including exclusion from participation in federally funded health-care programs. HIPAA enacted a new category of "federal health-care offenses," which includes health-care fraud, theft and embezzlement, making false statements, obstruction of criminal investigations, and money laundering. These criminal offenses apply to federally funded and private health-care programs.

Below is a summary of several of the elements of HIPAA impacting the provider's practice, including the Privacy Rule, Security Rule, transaction and code sets rule, unique identifiers rule (National Provider Identifier [NPI]), and Enforcement Rule.

Privacy Rule. This rule regulates the use and disclosure of protected health information (PHI) held by covered entities. PHI is any information held by a covered entity that concerns health status, provision of health care, or payment for health care that can be linked to an individual—which, in essence, can be any information listed in the medical record or payment history. PHI information may, however, be disclosed for law enforcement purposes and to facilitate treatment, payment, or health-care operations without a patient's express written authorization. All covered entities must notify individuals of the uses of their PHI and keep track of disclosures. In addition, as part of their compliance plan, the practice needs to document and abide by the privacy policies and procedures.

Security Rule. This rule compliments the Privacy Rule. Whereas the Privacy Rule pertains to all PHI including paper and electronic, the Security Rule deals specifically with electronic PHI (ePHI). The Security Rule lays out three types of security safeguards—administrative, physical, and technical. For the administrative safeguard, the covered entity must comply with HIPAA requirements and adopt a written set of privacy procedures along with a designated individual who is responsible for implementing set policies and procedures. The administrative policies and procedures should include management oversight, security controls, training, contingency plans, addressing security breaches, and access authorization and/or termination of access. The physical safeguards mainly involve the access and controls to hardware and software, maintenance records, visitor access, training, and proper workstation use. Finally, technical safeguards must be implemented to protect communications containing PHI transmitted electronically over open networks from being intercepted by anyone other than the intended recipient. Regardless of which safeguard, policies and procedures need to be developed and followed as part of the compliance plan, and risks need to be addressed and mitigated to prevent any potential loss of data or PHI information to the wrong individuals.

Unique identifiers rule. Providers must use an NPI when electronically transmitting health-care administrative and financial transactions under HIPAA requirements. The NPI, a 10-digit unique number, replaces all other identifiers used by health plans, Medicare, Medicaid, and other government programs. The NPI does not replace a provider's Drug Enforcement Agency (DEA) number, state license number, or tax identification number.

Enforcement rule. This rule sets the civil money penalties for violating HIPAA rules and establishes procedures for investigations and hearings for HIPAA violations. If noncompliance is determined by Health and Human Services (HHS), covered entities must apply corrective measures. Examples of issues that have been reported according to frequency are as follows (http://www.hhs.gov):

- Misuse of disclosures of PHI
- No protection in place of health information
- Patients unable to access their health information
- Using or disclosing more than the minimum necessary PHI
- No safeguards of ePHI (http://www.hhs.gov/enforcement, 2013)

Transactions and code sets rule. HIPAA added a new part, Part C, titled "Administrative Simplification to Title XI of the Social Security Act." This requires all health plans to engage in health-care transactions in a standardized way. In order for providers to be paid, they need to file their electronic claims using the HIPAA standards.

24.1.5 Health Information Technology for Economic and Clinical Health Act (HITECH Act)

This act is part of the *American Recovery and Reinvestment Act of 2009* (ARRA). ARRA contains incentives related to health-care information technology (IT) and contains specific incentives designed to accelerate the adoption of electronic health record (EHR) systems among providers. The act also was established to improve health-care quality, safety, and efficiency through the promotion of health IT, including EHRs and private and secure electronic health information exchange. Since this act projects a large expansion of ePHI exchanges, the Health Information Technology for Economic and Clinical Health (HITECH) Act also widens the scope of privacy and security protections by increasing the potential legal liability for noncompliance as well as providing more enforcement. Compliance plans and adherence to rules and regulations will be critical to each and every practice. The providers need to document their care in a medical record and demonstrate their adoption and compliance with privacy and security requirements, or they could be fined anywhere from $250,000 up to $1.5 million.

EXAMPLE OF HCFAC SETTLEMENTS IN 2013

"During Fiscal Year (FY) 2013 the Federal government won or negotiated over $2.6 billion in healthcare fraud judgments and settlements and it attained additional administrative impositions in healthcare fraud cases and proceedings. As a result of these efforts, approximately $4.3 billion was deposited with the Department of Treasury and the Centers for Medicare & Medicaid Services (CMS), transferred to other Federal agencies administering healthcare programs, or paid to private persons during the fiscal year. Of the $4.3 billion the Medicare Trust Funds received transfers of approximately $2.85 billion during this period and over $576 million in Federal Medicaid money was similarly transferred to the Treasury."

From HCFAC Program annual report 2013.

24.1.6 Health-Care Fraud and Abuse Control Program

The HIPAA law required the establishment of a national Health Care Fraud and Abuse Control (HCFAC) Program under the joint direction of the attorney general and the secretary of HHS acting through the department's inspector general (HHS OIG). This program is designed to coordinate federal, state, and local law enforcement activities with respect to health-care fraud and abuse. The program is also designed to provide opinions, alerts, and a means for reporting and disclosing final adverse actions against health-care providers.

The act appropriates monies from the Medicare Hospital Insurance Trust Fund to an expenditure account, called the Health Care Fraud and Abuse Control Account, in amounts that the secretary and attorney general jointly certify as necessary to finance antifraud activities. Certain of these sums are to be used only for activities of the HHS OIG with respect to the Medicare and Medicaid programs.

The program's goals are as follows:

- To conduct investigations, audits, inspections, and evaluations relating to the delivery of and payment for health care in the United States
- To facilitate enforcement of all applicable remedies for such fraud
- To provide education and guidance regarding complying with current health-care law
- To establish a national data bank to receive and report final adverse actions against health-care providers and suppliers

With the funding of the HCFAC Program, the HHS OIG has the ability to utilize enhanced data analysis, predictive analytics, trend evaluations, modeling approaches, and mining capabilities for detecting health-care fraud, including tools that allow for complex data analysis. The OIG teams use near-real-time data to examine Medicare claims for known fraud patterns, identify suspected fraud trends, and calculate percentage of allowed services as compared with national averages.

As a result of this act, it behooves practices to educate the physicians and staff on what constitutes fraud and abuse and what penalties (monetary and civil) can occur if there is noncompliance. These areas, along with an agreed upon understanding from the staff, need to be incorporated into the practice's compliance plan and followed throughout the year.

24.1.7 Medicare Integrity Program

Integrity program initiatives are designed to fight fraud and abuse and include processes directed at reducing payment errors as well as activities to prevent, detect, investigate, and ultimately prosecute health-care fraud. This program enables the Department of Health and Human Services (DHHS) to contract with nongovernment private contractors, to perform provider audits, review claims for medical necessity, and conduct investigations. Program integrity includes the following six main activities:

- Conducting provider audits
- Reviewing claims for medical necessity
- Identifying and investigating fraud
- Ensuring that Medicare pays for services for which it has primary responsibility
- Educating providers on Medicare billing procedures
- Identifying improper billing practices that affect both Medicare and Medicaid

There are multiple program integrity contractors to support this area of review, including the following:

- *Medicare Administrative Contractor (MAC).* MACs process and pay claims. In addition, MACs conduct selected program integrity functions including medical review, identification and recovery of improper payments, provider audits, provider education on appropriate billing practices, and screening beneficiary complains of alleged fraud.
- *Program Safeguard Contractor (PSC) and Zone Program Integrity Contractor (ZPIC).* The PSCs were created to detect and investigate potential fraud and abuse in Medicare's Fee-For-Service (FFS) program. The PSCs have been transitioned into ZPICs and will be responsible for benefit integrity activities for Part A (hospital services), Part B (professional services), Part C (Medicare advantage/managed care programs), and Part D (prescription drug program). ZPICs analyze data to identify improper billing patterns, perform provider audits, investigate fraud leads, refer cases to the HHS OIG or the Department of Justice (DOJ) for prosecution, and implement administrative actions to recover improper payments (i.e., prepayment and postpayment claims review, payment suspension, payment denial, or recoupment of overpayments). ZPICs actually do not collect overpayments but instead refer cases over to the appropriately designated regional MAC.
- *Medicare Drug Integrity Contractor (MEDIC).* MEDICs conduct program integrity activities on the Medicare prescription drug benefit program. MEDICs have similar functions as ZPICs for Medicare Parts A and B.
- *Recovery Audit Contractor (RAC).* RACs started out as a CMS demonstration program to review claims already paid and are charged with identifying improper payments made in Medicare Parts A and B and with recouping overpayments. Identifying fraud is not a responsibility of RACs; however, if they assume that fraudulent activity occurred, RACs refer the cases to CMS directly.
- *Comprehensive Error Rate Testing Contractor (CERT).* As a result of the IPIA, federal agencies were required to estimate and report an annual amount of improper payments for all programs and activities. The CERT program was started

to calculate these improper payment rates for its FFS program. There are three types of improper payment rates: (1) contractor-specific improper payments rates, (2) improper payment rates by provider type, and (3) a national improper payment rate.

- *National Supplier Clearinghouse (NSC) contractor.* The NSC is responsible for reviewing enrollment applications from suppliers of durable medical equipment, prosthetics, orthotics, and supplies (DMEPOS) to Medicare beneficiaries. Their enrollment process includes (1) conducing on-site visits to prospective DMEPOS suppliers to determine that they meet required supplier standards, (2) verifying that DMEPOS suppliers have applicable licenses, (3) checking that the DMEPOS suppliers and their principals are eligible to participate in Medicare, and (4) confirming that DMEPOS suppliers meet accreditation and surety bond requirements. NSC also coordinates fraud and abuse efforts with CMS, ZPICs and the HHS OIG, DOJ, and law enforcement officials.
- *Coordination of Benefits (COB) contractor.* The main purpose of the COB contractor is to identify payments that are the responsibility of another or secondary payer. Statutorily, Medicare is the secondary payer to employer-based insurance plans, auto liability insurance, and worker's compensation insurance. Their efforts are accomplished through data-match programs and beneficiary inquiries.

24.1.8 Health-Care Fraud and Abuse Data Collection Program

The Healthcare Integrity and Protection Data Bank (HIPDB) was created to coordinate information with the National Practitioner Data Bank (NPDB). Currently, health plans, health maintenance organizations, and federal state agencies are required to report final adverse actions taken against health-care providers on a monthly basis. This database operates under the auspices of DHHS, the Health Resources and Services Administration, and the Bureau of Health Professions.

Five types of adverse actions against a health-care provider, supplier, or practitioner are reported into this data bank:

1. Civil judgments in federal or state court related to the delivery of a health-care item or services
2. Federal or state criminal convictions related to the delivery of a health-care item or service
3. Actions by federal or state agencies responsible for licensing and certification
4. Exclusions from participation in a federal or state health-care program
5. Any other adjudicated actions or decisions that the secretary of DHHS establishes by regulations

These actions must be reported regardless of whether the subject of the report is appealing the action. Under HIPAA, adverse actions include the following:

- Civil judgments, such as malpractice suits
- Federal or state criminal convictions
- License revocation or suspension
- Reprimand, censure, or probation from health plans or hospital medical staff
- Exclusion from participation in any federal or state health programs

- Any adjudicated actions as determined by DHHS regulations
- Any other federal or state agency negative actions or findings that are publicly available

All Medicare and Medicaid participants are held accountable for complying with CMS guidelines. Any health-care organization that wants a successful review should put into place a solid, well-structured compliance plan.

24.1.9 Stark III Law

Previous to Stark III, there were two other versions of the law. The last version, Stark II, prohibited a physician or his/her immediate family members from referring a Medicare patient to any entity with which the physician or family member has a financial relationship when the referral was for a hit list of "designated health services" (DHSs) unless the transaction met an exception. DHSs include such services as clinical laboratory, physical therapy, radiology or imaging services, radiation therapy, durable medical equipment and supplies, parenteral and enteral nutrients, prosthetics and orthotics, home health services, outpatient prescription drug, and inpatient and outpatient hospital services. A *referral* had a very broad definition that included any request for a service, item, or good paid for under Part B, and any services that flow from such a request and fall within the category of DHSs, including the development of a treatment plan. As a result, the Stark II plan reached directly into the operation of physician practices, primarily in terms of compensation and use of in-office ancillary services.

The Stark III regulations do not establish any new exceptions to the self-referral prohibition but, rather, make certain refinements that could permit or, in some cases, require restructuring of some existing arrangements. Several of the changes include the following:

- Enhanced flexibility in structuring nonabusive compensation arrangements, i.e., enabling physicians to recruit and retain payments to permit recruitment of more physicians in areas where needed
- Relief for inadvertent violations of the self-referral prohibition under certain circumstances, i.e., allowing repayment of excess nonmonetary compensation
- Reduced regulatory burden for compliance, i.e., eliminating the written-notice requirement for an insurer for entities that provide professional courtesy with a reduced coinsurance
- Clarification of existing regulations, i.e., clarifying which provision in an office space and equipment lease agreement may be amended during initial and subsequent terms of the agreements

24.1.10 Federal Trade Commission Red Flags Rule and Regulations

The Red Flags Rule requires businesses and organizations to implement a written identity theft prevention program designed to detect the red flags of identity theft in their day-to-day operations, take steps to prevent the crime, and mitigate its damage. A practice must include the following four basic elements to deal with the threat of identity theft:

- A program must include reasonable policies and procedures to identify the red flags of identity theft that may occur in your day-to-day operation. Red flags are suspicious patterns of practices or specific activities that indicate the possibility of identity theft.

- A program must be designed to detect the red flags you have identified. As an example, you need procedures in place to identify a forged or fake insurance card.
- A program must spell out appropriate actions you will take when you detect red flags.
- A program must detail how you will keep it current to reflect new threats.

Just getting something down on paper won't reduce the risk of identity theft. Practices need to incorporate these plans of actions and traits into their compliance plan as well as include them into their daily operations with their staff. In addition, securing the data they collect and maintain about their patients is important in reducing identity theft.

24.1.11 Preventing and Reducing Improper Medicare and Medicaid Expenditures Act

The Preventing and Reducing Improper Medicare and Medicaid Expenditures (PRIME) Act was introduced into Congress in 2013 and contains a number of provisions that would increase rewards and incentives for those who uncover health-care fraud, as well as heighten penalties for those who commit it. The PRIME Act will enact stronger penalties for Medicare and Medicaid fraud; curb improper or mistaken payments made by Medicare and Medicaid; establish stronger fraud and waste prevention strategies with Medicare and Medicaid to help phase out the practice of "pay and chase" (i.e., recouping monies already erroneously paid to providers instead of detecting problems on the front end); curb the theft of physician identities; expand the fraud identification and reporting work of the senior Medicare patrol; take steps to help states identify and prevent Medicaid overpayments; and improve the sharing of fraud data across state and federal agencies and programs. The law directs the secretary to develop a plan to revise the incentive program under HIPAA for the reporting of fraud and abuse to encourage greater participation by individuals reporting Medicare fraud and abuse. The law also requires the plan to include certain recommendations for ways to enhance rewards for individuals reporting and an extension of the incentive program to the Medicaid program.

24.2 OTHER FEDERAL LAWS AND COMPLIANCE LEGISLATION

The need for health-care organizations to develop and implement compliance programs is further driven by the following federal laws and regulations.

24.2.1 Emergency Medical Treatment and Active Labor Act

Congress enacted the Emergency Medical Treatment and Active Labor Act (EMTALA) to ensure public access to emergency services regardless of ability to pay. Each Medicare-participating hospital that offers emergency services must provide a medical screening examination (MSE) when a request is made for examination or treatment for an emergency medical condition (EMC), including active labor, regardless of an individual's ability to pay. Hospitals are then required to provide stabilizing treatment for patients with EMCs. If a hospital is unable to stabilize a patient within its capability—or if the patient requests—then an appropriate transfer should be implemented.

A hospital may not transfer an individual with an unstable EMC unless:

- The individual or his/her representative makes a written request for transfer to another medical facility after being informed of the risk of transfer and the transferring hospital's obligation under the statute to provide additional examination or treatment.
- A physician has signed a certification summarizing the medical risks and benefits of a transfer and certifying that, based upon the information available at the time of transfer, the medical benefits reasonably expected from the transfer outweigh the increased risks.
- A qualified medical person signs the certification after the physician, in consultation with the qualified medical person, has made the determination that the benefits of transfer outweigh the risks, if a physician is not physically present when the transfer decision is made. The physician must later countersign the certification.

If the patient does not have an EMC, the statute imposes no further obligation on the hospital emergency room (ER).

The 2003 regulations define a *dedicated emergency department* as a state-licensed ER or a place where medical services are provided on an urgent basis, without the need for an appointment, including (significantly) hospital-based ambulatory care centers or freestanding emergency care centers.

24.2.2 Clinical Laboratory Improvement Act

The CMS regulates all laboratory testing (except research) performed on humans in the United States through the Clinical Laboratory Improvement Act (CLIA). The objective of the CLIA program is to ensure quality laboratory testing that includes specimens from humans, such as blood, body fluid, and tissue, for the purpose of diagnosis, prevention or treatment of disease, or assessment of health. CLIA includes accuracy, reliability, and timeliness of patient test results, regardless of where the test was performed. Although all clinical laboratories must be properly certified to receive Medicare or Medicaid payments,

CLIA has no direct Medicare or Medicaid program responsibilities. Any provider, practice, or facility that performs *any* laboratory test is subject to the CLIA regulations, regardless of whether or not they bill for the service. All claims for laboratory services performed in a physician's office must include the laboratory's CLIA number on the claim form submitted to Medicare or Medicaid, as a condition of payment. Those claims submitted without a CLIA number will be returned as incomplete claims. This mandate allows the governmental payers to monitor providers who are billing for laboratory tests that are "outside" or "above" their current certificate.

There are three basic levels of CLIA registrations: waived complexity, moderate complexity, and high complexity. The classification *provider-performed microscopy* is a sublevel of moderate complexity. CLIA specifies quality standards for proficiency testing, patient test management, quality control, personnel qualifications, and quality assurance, as applicable. There are additional requirements for cytology laboratories. Every laboratory that performs tests must register and obtain a CLIA certificate. The only exception is a mobile laboratory, which may utilize the CLIA certificate of a home-based lab.

Physician practices that perform waived tests *only* may apply to obtain a certificate of waiver. Waived tests are those tests that are cleared by the Food and Drug Administration (FDA) for home use, employ methodologies that are so simple and accurate as to render the likelihood of erroneous results negligible, or pose no reasonable risk of harm to the patient if performed incorrectly.

For a monthly updated list of laboratory tests that are classified as waived, see http://www.fda.gov/cdrh/clia. Waived laboratories have no personnel standards or proficiency testing requirements (except those that are part of the testing kit). However, labs performing waived tests are expected to follow good laboratory practices, such as following manufacturers' instructions. Also, tests listed as waived by CLIA on a federal level may not be recognized as waived tests by every state.

Physician practices that are performing provider-performed and/or other moderate tests have increased standards to follow, including the requirement to have a laboratory director. Moderate-complexity labs must establish and follow written quality-control procedures for monitoring and evaluating the quality of the analytical testing process of each testing method to ensure the accuracy and reliability of patient test results and reports. Each laboratory must have a written procedural manual for the performance of all analytical methods used by the laboratory, and the manual must be readily available and followed by laboratory personnel. In addition, all procedures must be approved, signed, and dated by the laboratory or medical director. Any changes in procedure must also get official approval. High-complexity laboratories have even higher standards to document and follow. There are also increased inspection and survey requirements.

24.2.3 Occupational Safety and Health Act

Under the Occupational Safety and Health Act (OSHA), employers are responsible for providing a safe and healthful workplace. The Occupational Safety and Health Administration's (OSHA's) mission is to ensure safe and healthful workplaces by setting and enforcing standards, and by providing training, outreach, education, and assistance. In addition, employers need to keep an inventory of potential safety issues, report accidents and illnesses, keep records, display OSHA posters, and provide safety devices or equipment commensurate with the employee's duties. Employers must comply with all applicable OSHA standards. Employers must also comply with the General Duty Clause of the OSH Act, which requires employers to keep their workplace free of serious recognized hazards.

24.2.4 Drug Enforcement Agency

The DEA controls the issuance of DEA numbers, which permit health-care organizations and licensed independent practitioners to prescribe controlled substances to patients. The use of controlled substances is important to almost every medical practice. For instance, family practitioners use codeine to treat coughs, and surgeons use narcotics to manage pain.

As a side precaution, patients may complain of pain and ask for pain medication. The physician can never know whether that patient is truly in pain, addicted to pain medication and seeking refills, or even an undercover agent for the DEA reviewing the practice patterns of dispensing narcotics. With any new patient, it is always best to explore further before providing a prescription.

24.2.5 Department of Transportation and Environmental Protection Agency

The Department of Transportation (DOT) and the Environmental Protection Agency (EPA) can have an impact on the provider's practice and his/her compliance. These agencies are responsible for assuring that health-care practices and entities properly dispose of and transport fluid, silver wastes, bodily fluids, radioisotopes, biohazardous materials, and/or other wastes. All organizations that generate hazardous waste must be registered with EPA, and waste disposal must be transported by an EPA-certified carrier. All hazardous-waste generators need to produce evidence of the appropriate manifest or receipts of proper disposal, according to DOT regulations. In addition, all employees that perform any function associated with the shipment of hazardous material must be trained in specific areas, and the documentation of training must be retained. This includes the secretary who fills out the shipping form for materials to be mailed or otherwise transported.

Penalties for EPA violations vary based on the severity and/or whether the violation occurred within a state that has its own EPA regulations. Fines can be assessed, and repeat incidents can result in double fines.

24.2.6 Civil Rights Act (Title VI)

The Civil Rights Act provides equal access without discrimination based upon race, religion, or place of origin for all persons in facilities or businesses that receive federal assistance, including health care. In addition, HIPAA legislation expanded to improve access to federally conducted and federally assisted programs and activities for persons who, as a result of national origin, are *limited in their English proficiency* (LEP). HIPAA mandated that all governmental agencies had to develop and disseminate LEP guidance, which has been published and can be found at http://www.hhs.gov/ocr/lep/guide.html. The guidance provides information regarding the obligation of covered entities (as defined by this law) to provide free language assistance to LEP patients. This includes competent oral language translation and, in some cases, written translation of some or all of the practice's written material.

24.2.7 Employee Retirement Income Security Act (ERISA)

The Employee Retirement Income Security Act (ERISA) imposes an obligation on the employer, i.e., the practice, to do the following:

- Operate welfare and/or retirement plans in accordance with the rules
- Inform employees, in writing, of their benefits and how to access them
- Comply with any annual reporting requirements

Although the risk of fines or penalties may be an impetus to follow these rules, better productivity and good morale for the workforce are better motivators for employment and ERISA compliance.

24.2.8 Civil Monetary Penalties

Health-care professional and entities are prohibited from submitting claims that the individual or entity "knows or should have known" were not actually provided and/or were fraudulent. Healthcare insurer policies and procedures as well as State and Federal regulations also prohibit anyone from providing false or misleading information on coverage that could reasonably be expected to influence a decision regarding when to discharge a person from a hospital. Violations may result in civil monetary penalties, which are applicable to any individual who is responsible for providing false or misleading information.

24.2.9 Criminal Penalties for Acts Involving Federal Health-Care Programs

Individuals and entities are prohibited from "knowingly and willfully" making false statements or presentations in applying for benefits or payments under all federal and state health-care programs. Individuals also are prohibited from fraudulently concealing or failing to disclose knowledge of an event relating to an initial or continued right to payments. There is also prohibition against knowingly and willingly soliciting or receiving any remuneration (including any kickbacks, bribes, or rebates) directly or indirectly, in cash or in kind, in exchange for referrals. Violations may result in felony convictions, with penalties including imprisonment and fines.

Individuals or entities can be excluded from Medicare and Medicaid and more than 200 other federal health-care programs for a minimum of 5 years if there is one prior fraud or abuse conviction. The exclusions last for 10 years, and if there are two prior convictions, the exclusion can become permanent. The minimum period of discretionary exclusion is 3 years, unless DHHS determines that a different period is appropriate.

It is just as important to communicate to the employees when laws or regulations do *not* impact your organization, such as the Family Medical Leave Act (FMLA), the employment provisions of the Americans with Disabilities Act (ADA), or continuation of health benefits under the Consolidated Omnibus Budget Reconciliation Act (COBRA). These benefits apply only to organizations with a specific number of employees, so smaller organizations are not necessarily required to offer these benefits.

However, the PPACA provides a slightly different situation for the provider's practice. PPACA mandated coverage, penalizing employers who failed to provide it and creating mechanisms for people to pool risk and buy insurance collectively.

Further, the act stated that (1) all individuals not covered by an employer-sponsored health plan, Medicare or Medicaid, or other public insurance programs such as TRICARE are required to secure an approved private insurance policy or pay a penalty, unless the individual has a financial hardship or is a member of a recognized religious sect exempted by the Internal Revenue Service, and (2) businesses, including larger medical practices that employ 50 or more people but do not offer health insurance to their full-time employees, will pay a tax penalty if the government has subsidized a full-time employee's health care through tax deductions or other means. This is known as the employer mandate. What this means for the provider's practice is that if the provider is offering health-care benefits to their staff, the coverage needs to be comparable with the requirements stated in the PPACA, and if the practice is not offering health-care benefits, then the practice must direct the individual to one of the health insurance exchanges that are offering individual coverage plans.

24.3 CONCLUSION

The health-care or medical practice is similar to any business in having to comply with various rules, regulations, laws, and guidelines, which may affect their day-to-day operations, their staff, their patients, and even their livelihood. Provider practices need to be aware of these laws and regulations and their impact on providing patient care services; if not, consequences in the form of fines, penalties, loss of the ability to bill and collect on federal programs, and/or imprisonment could be the end result. Depending on the type or size of practice, several of these laws and regulations may not apply, but those that do apply should be read, understood by the entire office practice and staff, included in a detailed compliance plan, and referred to and used on a regular basis to demonstrate to anyone (staff, patients, patient families, attorneys, auditors, government review staff, and others) that the office is aware of them and is complying.

To substantiate the activities performed, it is strongly encouraged that each physician practice document issues and reviews; state risks and mitigation to risks; describe action plans and who is responsible for changes; describe the specific patterns of practice that will be modified; develop and update compliance plans; and provide, track, and record training programs or attendance at educational forums. With today's complex governmental requirements, the practice would be in a much stronger position by knowing, doing, and complying.

24.4 COLLABORATE

Discuss this chapter online with others at http://www.medicalexecutivepost.com.

ACKNOWLEDGMENT

To Pati Trites, PhD, MPA, CHBC, CPC®, of Compliance Resources, LLC, Waterloo, Indiana.

FURTHER READINGS

Binder, C: *Medicare Program Integrity: Activities to Protect Medicare from Payment Errors, Fraud, and Abuse*. Analyst in Health Care Financing, Congressional Research Service, July 2011.

Blustein, A and Gulick, S: Deficit Reduction Act Heightens Corporate Compliance Requirements for Medicaid Providers. *New Jersey Lawyer Magazine*, February 2007.

CLIA: http://www.cdc.gov/clia.
CLIA: http://www.cms.gov/reguations.
CLIA: http://www.fda.gov/clia.
DEA: http://www.dea.gov.
Deficit Reduction Act of 2005, Summary of Medicaid/Medicare/Health Provisions, Updated February 3, 2006: http://www.ncsl.org/print/health/sums1932jan3106.pdf.
Fact Sheet: President Bush Signs the Deficit Reduction Act: http://www.georgewbush-whitehouse.archives.gov/news/releases.html.
Federal Trade Commission: Red Flag Identity Theft Rule: http://www.ftc.gov.
Fraud and Abuse Program Control Program: http://www.oig.hhs.gov.
Health Care Fraud and Abuse Control Program Annual Report for Fiscal 2013: http://www.oig.hhs.gov/publications/docs/hcfac/fy2013.pdf.
Health Care Fraud and Abuse Control Program: Indicators Provide Information on Program Accomplishments, but Assessing Program Effectiveness is Difficult. GAO Report, September 2013.
Health Information Privacy, Security and Breach Notification Rules: http://www.hhs.gov/oci/privacy.gov.
Health IT Legislation: http://www.healthit.gov.
HIPAA: http://www.hipaa.com.
HIPAA Summary and Survival Guide: http://www.hipaasurvivalguide.com.
HIPAA Violations and Enforcement: http://www.ama-assn.org.
HITECH Act: http://www.hhs.gov.
HITECH Act Summary—HIPAA Survival Guide: http://www.hipaasurvivalguide.com/hitech-act-summary.
Homeland Security & Governmental Affairs: PRIME Act 2013: http://www.hsgac.senate.gov/media/. http://www.medicaid.gov.
Legal Information Institute: Health Care Fraud and Abuse Data Collection Program: http://www.law.cornell.edu/uscode/text/42/1320a73.
Legal Information Institute: Medicare Integrity Program: http://www.law.cornell.edu/uscode/text 21/1395.
Medicare Integrity Program: http://www.cms.gov.
Office of the Inspector General: Medicaid Integrity Program Report for Fiscal Year 2013: http://www.oig.hhs.gov/reports-and-publications/medicaid-integrity/files/MIP-FY13-final.pdf.
OSHA: http://www.osha.gov.
Patient Protection and Affordable Care Act (PPACA): http://www.en.wikipedia.org/wiki/patient_protection_and_affordable_care_act.
Policy and Medicine Report: DHHS Health Care Fraud and Abuse Control Program Annual Report for Fiscal 2013: http://www.policymed.com/2014/03/dhhs-health-care-fraud-and-abuse-control-program-annual-report-for-fiscal-year-2013.html.
Preventing and Reducing Improper Medicare and Medicaid Expenditures Act of 2013 (PRIME): http://www.congress.gov/bill/113th-congress/house-bill/2305.
STARK Law—Information, Regulations: http://www.starklaw.org.
STARK Phase III Regulations, Health Law Alert: http://www.hallrender.com.
The Deficit Reduction Act: Important Facts for State Government Officials: http://www.cms.gov/regulations-guidance/legislation/deficitreductionact/downloads/checklist1.pdf.
The False Claims Act: http://www.cms.gov.
US Department of Justice: The False Claims Act: http://www.justice.gov.

Appendix 1: Certified Medical Planner™ Chartered Professional Designation and Certification Program Descriptor and Curriculum

Enter the Informed Voice of a New Generation of Fiduciary Advisors for Health Care

Office of the Provost

As the financial planning industry grows, and quality information is available on the Internet, medical professionals have more access to information than ever before. At the same time, the growing number of consulting generalists leads to a troubling countertrend—more financial advisors means less differentiation to being a financial advisor. Perhaps this is the reason for the embarrassing number of valid and specious financial industry certifications in existence today? Enter the Institute of Medical Business Advisors (iMBA) Inc. and its lifelong learning Certified Medical Planner™ initiative.

A1.1 THE INSTITUTE OF MEDICAL BUSINESS ADVISORS INC. FOCUS ON LIFELONG LEARNERS

The iMBA Inc. provides a team of experienced, senior-level educators and consultants, led by chief executive and medical officer *Dr. David Edward Marcinko*, FACFAS, MBA, CMP™, and chief academic officer and dean *Eugene Schmuckler*, PhD, MBA, M.Ed, CTS, to construct individually focused curricula for lifelong learners (LLLs). This curriculum is used throughout all phases of Certified Medical Planner™ program matriculation. iMBA Inc. and its staff of teaching professionals have decades of experience and didactic repute, supported by an unsurpassed inbound research library, to augment knowledge of the integrated health-care and financial services environment. Thus, the iMBA Inc. team provides superior online education in an asynchronous, cost-effective manner by focusing on academic solutions for the unique needs of each adult learner. This vast niche network of cognitive and human resources ensures that the Certified Medical Planner™ instructional team maintains the highest level of current and future competence regarding industry trends to serve as the foundation for each adult-learner e-engagement.

A1.2 CRISIS OF INDUSTRY DIFFERENTIATION IN THE FINANCIAL PLANNING AND SERVICES SECTOR

The outcome of this trend is pressure on advisors to focus and find a niche to establish true differentiation from the competition. Realistically, like doctors, no one advisor can be the best at everything for everyone; but it is possible to be the best for a special group of clientele, with a genuinely unique value proposition (UVP) not provided by other advisors. And, the efficacy of this approach increases as modern Internet search engines become better at helping to match people in need—with the providers who can offer them the best solutions.

By establishing a business focus, financial advisors create a scenario where the size of their targeted universe decreases, but the potential to capture the entire universe increases! This is marketing 101. Ultimately, the point is not to turn away prospective clients who don't fit the niche; it's to have a niche that's so well established that the only clients who contact the advisor are those who seek their advice. And so, there are so many clients seeking you; there isn't time to serve others, anyway!

Doctors and medical and allied health-care professionals are, for like-minded advisors, the perfect niche. *Why?* This space is full of educated and affluent, but often arrogant and challenging, participants who want and even desperately need informed and physician-focused services. And, the space is in flux, which is good for prospecting.

And consider this: medicine is made of specialists. The heart surgeon does not do brain surgery; the dermatologist does not deliver babies; and the podiatrist does not pull teeth. Moreover, the lowest paid physicians are generalists: family practice doctors, internists, gerontologists, pediatricians, general practitioners, etc. Medical niche super specialists earn the most money.

A1.3 STIFFER COMPETITION FOR FINANCIAL PLANNERS

Unfortunately, most financial planners seem to still be operating under the old framework of faux differentiators like service-centricity, technology, and/or experience rather than the real differentiator that comes from deep knowledge and specific wisdom. In marketing, this is known as the perceived *versus* real strategic competitive advantage dichotomy. *Want proof?* It is not unusual for the best/busiest doctors to have a loathsome bedside manner. Sad, but true! Any direction you look, quality but generic financial advice is on the rise and is quickly shifting from being a value-added differentiator to being the expected norm just to have a shot at attracting high-value clients!

A1.4 SPECIFIC INDUSTRY INSIDER KNOWLEDGE—THE NEW DIFFERENTIATOR

So what's the solution in a world where financial planners and their services are increasingly similar to each other (commoditized)? It's time for more advisors to establish a true knowledge-based value proposition (KBVP). Realize; retirement planning is not a niche.

Yes, the UVP marketing buzzword has been around for a long time, but few advisors seem to have truly internalized it. And, just being a financial advisor with sales *credentials* (Million Dollar Roundtable) and years of experience doesn't cut it anymore. Remember, clients appreciate two kinds of experience: good and bad. And, practice does not make perfect; only perfect practice makes perfect. So, experience is not an end point for differentiation anymore; now it's the minimum to get a foot in the door. Didn't 2000 smart but inexperienced Micro-Softies annihilate more than 400,000 experienced but traditional IBMers during the software operating systems (OS) wars three decades ago? "Masses of asses" was the quip from Bill Gates. Instead, the key to differentiating is the education and knowledge you have, and the kind of clientele you work with. In other words, it's all about having a real niche, or a real KBVP; think UVP 2.0 for advisors serving, in our case, colleagues in the health-care industrial complex.

In fact, in 2013, Cerulli Associates opined that financial advisors who keep a narrow niche focus are far better at convincing clients that they bring *incremental* or *quarterback value* to their relationships. "They have a deeper understanding of the client situation and pain points. Such a focus also helps them when competing against generalist advisors."*

What's best in the new age is the increasing ability to build a narrow niche with a broad national clientele, relying on the power of both personal referrals and Internet search engines to help clients find *you*, the one best expert to help solve their problems!

A1.5 UNDERSTANDING MARKET AND NICHE SIZE

Possessing KBVP and a clear niche market means, at least for that subset of clientele, you are the best advisor to offer a solution for their needs. In other words, the market itself might be smaller, but you can have the *whole* market because you're genuinely differentiated as the best provider of solutions for anyone tied to that market. This strategy can actually be far more successful than having a smaller slice of a larger market pie! *Why?* You can actually grow a smaller market niche faster and larger than a huge market. In any event, the bottom line is that as advice and credentials like the CFP® certification become increasingly mainstream, the industry seems to be crossing a tipping point of no return. It is no longer a viable strategy to be a generalist for everyone and letting mere *experience* be your differentiator.

According to Michael E. Kitces, MSFS, MTAX, CFP®, CLU, ChFC, RHU, REBC, CASL, and many others, it is necessary for financial planners to have a niche to survive, flourish, and actually help clients more immensely than ever before (personal communication). A true win-win scenario!

A1.6 INTRODUCTION

The elite Certified Medical Planner™ charter designation program is a 1-year (four academic quarters), 500-hour integrated, *live* and asynchronous, online course-of-study offered exclusively by the iMBA Inc. The program unites personal financial planning topics for health-care professionals with modern medical practice management principles in the post–managed care and PP-ACA era. It is an informed insider niche approach targeting advisors and consultants who wish to enter the ever changing health-care industrial complex ecosystem, which comprises almost 20% of domestic GDP. Adult learners spend 5–10 hours per week reading, writing, and in instructor-led activities in both core topics and elective material.

* From Megan Leonhardt. WealthManagement.com, November 2013.

A1.7 CAREER LAUNCH FOR CERTIFIED MEDICAL PLANNERS™

According to iMBA research, a 47-year-old doctor with $184,000 annual income needs about $5.5 million for retirement at age 65. Although this average monetary corpus sounds daunting, it should serve as a wake-up call to all physicians to cut personal consumption, recognize liability risks, improve practice managerial efficiency, and save and invest more aggressively. And, to financial advisors and consultants, medical practice enhancement knowledge and health economics insight is now an integral part of the personal financial planning equation for all medical professionals. So, we believe the Certified Medical Planner™ program stands alone.

Case Model: As a generic financial advisor, how would you answer this client prospect's inquiry?

Question: I'm a 47-year-old MD—can you help me?

Traditional answer: I am a stockbroker (aka financial advisor) or insurance agent, and I sell financial products and insurance policies on a commission basis. *What do you want to buy?*

Current answer: I am a financial planner, and I charge a percentage amount on the assets I manage for you. But, I have a minimum portfolio amount. *So how much money do you have to invest?*

Niche answer: Yes! I am a fully Certified Medical Planner™ practitioner. I understand holistic financial planning for medical professionals and current health industry tumult. And, as an informed fiduciary—with transparent fees—I can help with your medical practice, business, and/or personal financial planning matters. *When can we meet to discuss your needs?*

A1.8 INDUSTRY HISTORY AND IDENTITY CRISIS

During the 1963–1972 time period, Nobel Laureate Kenneth J. Arrow, PhD, shocked the academe by identifying health economics as a distinct field of study! Yet, the seemingly disparate insurance, asset allocation, econometric, statistics, portfolio management, taxation, and financial planning principles he studied have remained invisible and transparent to most participants. And so, an industry identity crisis was born that continues today. The generalist *versus* the niche health economics expert!

Nevertheless, to informed cognoscenti, this educational dichotomy served as a predecessor to the modern health-care advisory era. In 2004, Arrow was awarded the National Medal of Science for his innovative views, and he is now considered the *father* of health economics.

Now, financial service professionals realize the obvious—that the health-care industrial complex is quickly changing. This milieu has prompted physicians to frantically search for new ways to improve office revenues and grow personal assets. And, the current generation of Health 2.0 savvy young medical professionals is no longer content with traditional *Monte Carlo*, software-driven, or *de-rigueur* financial planning advice for the masses! As medical providers, they seek information like themselves: for *the vital few—not the trivial many.* They want an educated, modern, and accountable advisor, or Certified Medical Planner™, on their side; or many will—and should—do it alone (ME, Inc.). This very text is an attempt to show them the way, not sell them on the traditional FA model.

Moreover, the largest transfer of wealth in U.S. history is taking place as mature doctors sell their practices or inherit parents' estates. Increasingly, the artificial boundary among traditional financial planning, modern health economics, and contemporaneous medical practice management is *blurring.*

This disruption was noted by the iMBA Inc. a decade ago. A research and development program with corpus of work resulted in publications in the Library of Medicine, the National Institutes of Health, and the Library of Congress, along with related trade industry publications, a dozen textbooks, essays, magazine articles, and working white papers.

Note that the Vilfredo Pareto principle (also known as the *80–20 rule*, the *law of the vital few*, or the *principle of sparsity*) states that for many events, roughly 80% of the effects come from 20% of the causes.

A1.9 THE INSTITUTE OF MEDICAL BUSINESS ADVISORS INC.

And so, from 2002 to 2007, the R&D efforts of a governing board of multidegreed and designated physicians–advisors–educators from iMBA Inc. identified the need for integrated personal financial planning and medical practice business management as an effective first step in the business survival and wealth building lifecycle for health-care providers. Now—more than ever—desperate doctors of all ages are turning to financial advisors and medical management consultants for help. Symbiotically, generalist advisors are finding the mutual need for extreme niche knowledge as obvious.

But, there was no established curriculum or educational program; no corpus of knowledge or codifying glossary; no terms of art; no academic accreditation, *gravitas*, or fiduciary accountability; and certainly no identifying professional designation that demonstrates integrated subject matter expertise for the increasingly unique health care–focused financial advisory niche... *until now!*

A1.9.1 Identity Crisis Solved!

Enter a formalized online virtual curriculum and charter designation program that promotes and identifies educated advisors in one of the fastest growing, lucrative, and challenging modern niche markets today.

A1.10 DISTINCTIVE FEATURES OF ONLINE EDUCATION

A1.10.1 The *Electronic Classroom*

The intellectual model for iMBA's online Certified Medical Planner™ program is the *Electronic Classroom* (EC). In the EC, a small group of one to five students interact personally with a living instructor. With this low student/faculty ratio, the environment is intimate, although virtual. Some students/faculty find that they are more comfortable communicating via their computers, tablets, or smartphones than others; but many who try online learning find that they are surprised by the genuinely personal level of communication. This is known as an *Electronic Discussion Activity* (EDA) and represents the core of any online asynchronous learning experience.

A1.10.2 *Asynchronous* Education

The EC is conducted in an *asynchronous* mode, meaning that Certified Medical Planner™ program participants can sign on and access a class whenever it's most convenient to them. Three classes are typically available over the course of a week. This helps busy consultants, FAs, and working adult learners avoid the time-constraint problems they would face with a *real-time* exchange.

A1.10.3 *Live* Interactive Education

Electronic classes can require intense interaction between *live* faculty members and adult learners, often more so than in many traditional on-ground courses and most automated computer-based training (CBT) programs. Students are typically expected to log in and contribute three to five times each week. With this frequency of interaction, students and faculty all get to know one another well. There are few opportunities for passivity. In fact, in the EC of the Certified Medical Planner™ program, students tend to interact with instructors much more than in traditional settings, thus promoting future peer-based discussions and real-world applications. Moreover, in the EC, everyone must write, particularly for the R&D loaded Certified Medical Planner™ program. All assignments are typed, creating a permanent record of each person's contribution. Faculty members find that this promotes careful, reflective submissions from most students. Additionally, instructors can easily monitor student progress and communicate with those who need help or who have trouble keeping up. This is usually done privately by e-mail, Skype, or phone after certain online expectations have been clarified.

A1.10.4 Flexible *Anytime–Anywhere* Education

Because of the extreme flexibility of the iMBA virtual classroom, punctuality is not a problem, and adult learners don't lose valuable class time due to weather, traffic, or unforeseen scheduling conflicts, the bane of all working financial services professionals or medical management consultants. Also, students who travel can log in from anywhere and therefore will not fall behind in their Certified Medical Planner™ class work. This is known as *anytime–anywhere* education. For these reasons and many others, online distance learning is quickly earning adherents among adult learners, faculty, and the profession, both nationally and internationally. Some virtual students may find that they learn even more in this environment, augmenting state-of-the art prestige of the Certified Medical Planner™ program from iMBA Inc.

A1.10.5 Education Model *Not* for Everyone

There are some important caveats to this almost idyllic picture of the online learning model.

First, students and instructors must be fully trained and supported in the use of computer technology. They must be exposed to examples of *good practice* and mentored by colleagues with extensive prior experience in the electronic teaching and learning classroom. Successful online teaching requires much more than simply placing one's lectures online; it mandates the careful rethinking of an entire course and *way* of teaching.

Second, online learning requires much more than simply reading chapter material and answering a few questions. It mandates the careful thinking and the application of learned material to solve real-world problems for future physician clients. All assignments and responses are reviewed and, if necessary, corrected and redesigned. For students, discipline, reading, and writing skills are prerequisites.

For example, like most iMBA faculty members, Dr. Paul Edelson, author of *Complete Book of Distance Learning Schools*, teaches courses online and has determined that for his classes to be successful, each element must be carefully spelled out in greater detail than in courses with conventional syllabi, where ambiguities can be *talked out* in class. He has also discovered that without the visual cues that are commonly taken for granted in the face-to-face classroom, he must pay greater attention to written comments and ask probing questions that require students to respond and follow up in greater detail. In the end, he found that the results of adult learning and teaching online may be comparable to what students experienced in the online classroom. We could not agree more.

Finally, the growth of online learning attests to its increasing acceptance by students, faculty, and the financial, educational, and health-care industrial complex. All groups have discovered that the many positive features of the EC can outweigh the negative effects of not physically meeting in an on-ground class. Hence, the Certified Medical Planner™ program strives to be a leader, not a follower, in contemporary education.

In academic summary, those comfortable with *fill-in-the-bubble-blank* written tests of the past or the *rote-sales training* and *multiple guess* formats of automated CBT programs of the early pioneering years (without critical thinking ability) need not apply for Certified Medical Planner™ matriculation. The revolutionary *live* program is nothing less than exceptional health industry education for professional financial advisors and medical management consultants.

A1.11 Enter the Certified Medical Planner™ Program Curriculum

The Certified Medical Planner™ charter designation program is a *live* instructor-led and online asynchronous educational program. An intimate and personalized team approach is used to increase health industry management experience, business knowledge, and financial advisory affinity for physicians in an honest and ethical fashion. And, as these educated advisors climb their respective career hills, even the most demanding doctors seem attainable and in reach as valued clients!

A1.12 PROGRAM TOPICS AND SUBJECT AREAS*

1. Financial planning strategies for health-care professionals (3 months, 6 class modules)
2. Medical practice management and health-care administration (6 months, 12 class modules)
3. Risk management, liability insurance, and asset protection for health-care professionals (3 months, 6 class modules)

* The program may be *crashed* under special situations and/or delivered *on-ground*, in groups of motivated learners, upon request. The formal curriculum is outlined in course textbooks and may be modified based on prior applicant education and experience. Generally, course topic substitutions, rather than advanced credit, are given for other certification or degree holders. The body of knowledge is just too vast, and changing too fast to omit. So, topics and requirements are subject to change without notice, mirroring modernity.

A1.12.1 Certified Medical Planner™ Program Course Curriculum

The Certified Medical Planner™ curriculum follows these three textbooks and chapter contents for each *chapter-class module* of study. Each chapter module involves two weeks of study with six live instructor-led E-mail Discussion Activities (EDAs). The 48 weeks of study, with 24 topics in the curriculum, are subject to change without notice because of the ever evolving health-care industrial complex and diverse background of each adult learner.

1. *Financial Planning for Healthcare Professionals*
   - The Psychology of Money, Behavioral Economics and Finance
   - Macro and Micro Economics of Healthcare Finance
   - Cash Flow Management and Financial Statement Analysis
   - Personal, Business and Medical Practice Insurance Concepts
   - Medical Office and Personal Income Tax Principles and Reduction Strategies
   - Investing Principles, Vehicles and Asset Allocation—Gen X and Y
   - Malpractice Insurance and Risk Management
   - Modern Portfolio Theory, CAP-M and APM Construction
   - Hedge Funds, M-N Funds, Crypto-Currency and Alternative Investments (AIs)
   - Investment Policy Statement (IPS) Creation and Analysis
   - Retirement Planning
   - Medical Practice Succession Planning
   - Asset Protection and Trust Principles
   - Estate Planning, Wills and Charitable Giving
   - Medical Practice Valuation
   - Fiduciary Responsibility
   - Types of Advisors and Consultants
2. *Medical Practice Management and Healthcare Administration*
   - The Healthcare Industrial Complex
   - Emerging Healthcare Markets
   - Health Economics and Finance
   - Medical Practice Business Panning
   - Office Launch and Development
   - Staffing and Management Human Resources and Outsourcing
   - Patient Resources Management
   - Health Information Technology
   - eMRs, eDRs, eHRs, PHRs and MU
   - Professional Medical Relations
   - Practice Decision Management
   - Medical Clinic Cash Flow Analysis
   - Office Expense Costing and Modeling
   - Accounting for Mixed Practice Costs
   - Medical Activity Based Costing
   - CPT® and ICD9-10 Codes; Capitation Reimbursement Economics
   - Health Law and Policy
   - Negotiating Contract Cost Volume Profit Analysis

- Revenue Cycle Performance
- IBNRs Healthcare Claims
- Internal Controls and Fraud Prevention
- Physician Compensation and Salary
- Financial Accounting, Banking and Practice Benchmarks
- Concierge Practice, Private Pay and Other Medical Business Models
- Appraisals and Business Valuations
- Medical Practice Sales and Contacts
- Patriot Act and SAR-BOX Act
- Physician Recruitment and Retention
- Medical Ethics, Munificence and Sovereignty
- PP-ACA and Health Reform
- Career Development and Leadership

3. *Risk Management for Medical Professionals*
   - Health, HIEs, New Risks, and Life Insurance for Medical Professionals
   - Property and Possession Insurance
   - Medical Practice Business Insurance
   - Non-Competition and Practice Agreements
   - Medical Employment Restrictive Covenants
   - Paper and Electronic Medical Records and Recording Risks
   - Medical Billing and Coding Issues
   - Sexual Harassment in Healthcare
   - Medical Workplace Violence
   - Medical Malpractice, Liability and Tort Reform Risks
   - Capitation Liability Theory
   - Medical Malpractice Trial Risks
   - On Call and Expert Witness Risks
   - Social Media, Twitter, Text Messages, Social Media and Futuristic Risk Management
   - Unrecognized New-Wave and Next-Gen Risk Management Issues
   - Financial and Operative Risks of Divorce and Special Situations
   - Types of Insurance Agents, Advisors and Consultants

A1.13 A GROWING OEUVRE OF TEXT BOOKS AND INDUSTRY STATURE

iMBA Inc. recognized that some adult learners appreciate reading current medical business management theory, health-care economics, technology, or financial planning information privately prior to matriculation. However, there is a virtual information overload out there, little of which addresses the pragmatic concerns of the modern medical provider or health-care industry participant. Little imparts the wisdom to become a better financial advisor or medical management consultant. Most seems designed to sell and motivate the purchase of financial products.

Therefore, as part of the iMBA Research Library for the Certified Medical Planner® program, the following *in-house* produced books (and white papers) are used. Readers may recognize some nationally known contributing authors and Certified Medical Planner™ charter holders.

Required financial planning textbooks:

1. *Comprehensive Financial Planning Strategies for Doctors and Advisors: Best Practices from Leading Consultants and Certified Medical Planners™*
2. *Risk Management, Liability Insurance, and Asset Protection Strategies for Doctors and Advisors: Best Practices from Leading Consultants and Certified Medical Planners™*

Required practice management textbook:

- *The Business of Medical Practice: Transformational Health 2.0 Skills for Doctors, 3rd edition.*

Recommended dictionaries*

1. *Dictionary of Health Economics and Finance*
2. *Dictionary of Health Insurance and Managed Care*
3. *Dictionary of Health Information Technology and Security*

Suggested health-care institution textbooks:

- *Hospitals & Healthcare Organizations: Management Strategies, Operational Techniques. Tools, Templates, Checklists and Case Studies*
- *Financial Management Strategies for Hospitals and Healthcare Organizations: Tools, Techniques, Checklists and Case Studies*

A1.14 PROGRAM OPERATIONS AND LOGISTICS

To maximize development opportunities with the latest technologies, CMP™ books, white papers, and course content are built around three key principles:

1. *Interactivity*—Course content using books, real-world case studies, glossaries, online content, and web blogs to enhance the learner's role as an engaged participant.
2. *Flexibility*—Material offered in short e-learning chapter modules to support professional goals. Content is delivered in print, or electronically, to suit differing learning styles.
3. *Access*—A *live* instructor is available 24/7/365 to minimize time away from job responsibilities, family, or scheduling difficulties, with thrice/weekly virtual classrooms.

A1.15 IDEAL CERTIFIED MEDICAL PLANNER™ CANDIDATES

Matriculation acceptance is selective and a BS/BA degree with background check and/or CRD/FINRA check is required. Typically accepted students include multiple derivations of the following medical degrees and financial industry certifications:

* Designated Doody's Core Academic Titles!

BS/BA
MSHA
CFP®
PhD
MBA/DBA
MS
CFA®
CPA/EA
JD/LLM
CLU/ChFC
MD/DO/MBBS
RN/PA/NP
DDS/DMD
CMO/CIO
MPH/DPH
DPM
CIMA
CXOs
etc.

A1.16 ACADEMIC LEVELS OF THE CERTIFIED MEDICAL PLANNER™ MARK

1. Certified Medical Planner™ (Honorary). Granted to the original Certified Medical Planner™ Board of Director (CMP-BOD) members due to their deep integrated and proven subject matter expertise, ethics, and national notoriety (*grandfathered designation*; without formal course work or testing). This level is no longer available.
2. Certified Medical Planner™ (Candidate). Granted to an adult learner whose course of work is satisfactory and currently *in progress*.
3. Certified Medical Planner™ (Practitioner). Granted to a charter holder who has completed the full course of study (500 hours) and is in current compliance with all continuing Maintenance of Certification (MOC) requirements!

A1.17 HOW TO BECOME A CERTIFIED MEDICAL PLANNER™

A six-step approach is used:

1. *Professional experience*—A successful Certified Medical Planner™ candidate must have 5 to 10 years of financial advisory or management and consulting industry experience within the medical community. One physician or medical client letter of professional recommendation is required.
2. *Coursework*—A candidate must complete the entire online education program in 12 months. An estimated 5–10 hours per week of study, for a total of 500 hours/year, is expected. But, the program may be accelerated or *crashed* to expedite graduation completion in some cases. Group discussions and Skype teleconferences are also possible.

3. *Examination*—Admission and classes matriculation are provided on a rolling monthly basis in an asynchronous fashion *via* secure PC, anytime or anywhere. No multiple-choice tests *or* mega examinations are required for the thrice weekly class format; 2-week courses/6 courses per semester; four semesters per year; 48-week total program length. Instead of *fill-in-the-blank* tests, EDAs are used with 250-word-essay responses for deep subject matter understanding, not just lucky guesses. Class expectations and real-world performance are high. English language, typing, and writing proficiency are required.
4. *Signed ethics statement*—Each CMP™ candidate must sign a *Standard Code of Ethics* to verify an individual pledge to maintain a high standard of conduct, competence, knowledge, professionalism, integrity, objectivity, and fiduciary responsibility in the practice of his/her specialty.
5. *Maintenance of certification*—During each 2-year cycle, a Certified Medical Planner™ designee must write an original peer-reviewed and accepted textbook chapter, published essay, white paper, or related treatise in Modern Language Association (MLA) or American Management Association (AMA) format that is approved by iMBA Press. Editorial assistance is available. No ghost-writing, vanity, self-publications, trade magazine articles, or purchased content is allowed. This innovative requirement allows the academic dean to continually create and update the iMBA library of textbooks, dictionaries, working white papers and handbooks, etc. The iMBA Inc. targeted library stays current and grows in this manner. And, there is *no* recurring CEU fee or required annual dues, a very unique model in the industry. The program seeks insight and cognitive power, not practitioner lucre.
6. *Matriculation application and one-time nonrefundable due diligence fee*—Course acceptance is selective and not automatic, and a telephone interview may be required. An undergraduate (bachelor) degree is required. An educational, criminal, and financial background check is performed. The program is focused, competitive, and selective.

A1.18 ADULT LEARNER EXPERIENCES

The following opinions are from actual Certified Medical Planner™ candidates:

I really like the supportive approach to learning. The limited number of Certified Medical Planner™ students each semester allows the staff to take an evident, genuine interest in the success of learners. I also agree with the program's premise that specialization is necessary for success as a financial advisor, and for providing the best advice to clients. I also appreciate that I had the opportunity to submit my first published work.

The online Certified Medical Planner™ program has shined a harsh light on how much I still have to learn. I would like for part of the program to include suggestions for continued professional development and practice growth.

I would incorporate some form of case study for each semester that examines some particular topic. I envision almost a quarterly thesis that would be based upon a prearranged list of topics. For example, one thesis may involve the analysis of a set of medium-sized practice financials and operating results. As an alternative, the program could incorporate a juried presentation designed to incorporate a wide spectrum of the knowledge gained during the program. Perhaps, this presentation could begin late in the second quarter with subsidiary presentations designed to allow the faculty to gauge progress and suggest revisions? This would likely increase the rigor of the program and make it more difficult for some professionals to undertake it.

You will be more able to talk the talk of physicians if you have completed the Certified Medical Planner™ program.

A1.19 WHITHER THE CMP™ PROFESSIONAL DESIGNATION MARK

The Certified Medical Planner Board of Standards and iMBA Inc. own the terms, copyright, and certification marks CMP™, CERTIFIED MEDICAL PLANNER™, and CMP™ (with license plate design), which they award to individuals who successfully complete the Board's initial curse work and ongoing certification requirements. The copyright, and then trademark, has been confirmed by CACI International. A public company since 1962, CACI is a member of the Fortune 1000's Largest Companies and Russell 1000 index. The Chairman and CEO of CACI Inc. is Dr. JP (Jack) London. All rights reserved, USA. A Federal Registered Mark® is pending.

A1.19.1 How to Use the CMP™ Marks

When used, the CMP™ mark must be displayed under strict use and reproduction guidelines or their value as trademarks could be lost.

- Use either lower case *or* capital letters, but be consistent.
- Never use periods.
- Always use the trademark (™) symbol.
- Always associate with the individual(s) certified by the CMP™ Board.
- If possible, use three components of the design (license plate, "CMP," and ™).
- Always reproduce the logo design from original artwork.
- Always associate with the individual(s) certified by CMP™ Board of Directors.
- Never alter or modify the license plate design.

Overheard in the Advisor's Lounge

On Financial Certifications and Designations

I will rank the designations I have earned or have made progress in earning:

1. CFA: really tough unless you work in securities valuation every day.
2. CPA: this was a very tough exam and required a lengthy process of learning. However, I think that much of the CPA exam was rote—without a full understanding of the content.

3. CFP®: this is a little more difficult than the CMP™ mainly because of the time constraints and structure of the exam. It is less difficult than the CPA because it incorporates some of the knowledge that CPA's typically already possess.
4. CMP™: Certified Medical Planner™ program 12-month course.
5. CLU: these exams were not very difficult but mainly required time and some limited reading.
6. Securities Licensure (Series #7).
7. Insurance Licensure.

Wayne Firebaugh, CPA, CLU, CFP®, CMP™
Private Practitioner-Registered Investment Advisor
Roanoke, VA

A1.20 CERTIFIED MEDICAL PLANNER™ DESIGNATION VERIFICATION AND COMPLIANCE SERVICE*

Sherry Cooper
National Compliance Services, Inc.
Verification Supervisor

Bruce Spates
Director FINRA Investor Education
http://www.finra.org

FINRA does *not* approve of the Certified Medical Planner™ designation nor does it endorse *any* professional designation, such as the more widely known Certified Financial Planner™. Inclusion/omission of the marks in their database implies that FINRA considers the designation to be acceptable for use by a registered representative (stockbroker). Furthermore, state securities regulators may prohibit or restrict the use of certain listed designations by registered persons and investment adviser representatives. *Why?*

Scenario: Bernie Madoff, a past vice chairman of FINRA, wasn't merely a name associated with FINRA; in some sense Madoff was FINRA. Madoff joined FINRA (then NASD) in 1994 and was vice chairman while his Ponzi scheme was under way. Peter Madoff made it to that same office at one point. Mark Madoff was on the National Adjudicatory Council, another regulatory body that reviews disciplinary decisions made by FINRA. It was an appointed position courtesy of CEO Mary Schapiro, who was chairman of the SEC until December 14, 2012. Finally, Shana Madoff, a compliance officer until the firm's collapse, was a member of a compliance advisory committee of FINRA.

Note that iMBA Inc. and the Certified Medical Planner™ program is an educational and academic program, not a state or FINRA/SEC-related affiliate.

* Available at http://www.fpanet.org/journal/CurrentIssue/TableofContents/AskingtheWrongQuestionsofFINRA/.

A1.21 DISCIPLINARY PROCESS

If any medical professional client has a complaint against a *Certified Medical Planner*™ charter holder, they may submit a complaint to initiate investigation on the matter. All *Certified Medical Planner*™ designees should act in accordance with the *Code of Ethics*, along with applicable state and federal governing regulatory bodies. Investigation costs are incurred by the designee. Complaints are submitted in writing, and must include supporting documents, to this address:

The Institute of Medical Business Advisors, Inc.
Peachtree Plantation West–Office Park
Suite #5901 Wilbanks Drive
Norcross, GA 30092-1141
http://www.certifiedmedicalplanner.org

A1.22 THE FUTURE

We imagine a customized network of learning centers electronically linked and globally functioning as academic centers of excellence and operating 24/7/365. For example, MOOC is a *massive open online course* aimed at large-scale interactive participation. In addition to traditional course materials, MOOCs provide interactive user forums that help build a community for doctors and nurses, students and adult learners, professors, instructors, online teaching assistants (TAs), etc.

Why? Medical, business, and graduate schools, and allied health-care educators, are *finally* beginning to identify students who are adept at learning online and reward the top achievers and professors. And, employers and recruiting firms are beginning to troll MOOCs seeking viable job candidates. In fact, when last checked, the nation's graduate students were enrolled in more than 118 online graduate-level programs in business management, IT, and health sciences. MOOCs offer greater access for a larger number of students at significantly lower costs than on-site programs. And, the irony is that traditional health-care management programs have only begun to consider these broader implications.

By the same token, technologies like Blackboard, Cernage, eXplorance, Kalture, and others must be used to full potential. Smartphones, laptops, desktops and tablets, videos, interactive games, simulations, and related apps with Skype-like virtual classrooms and cloud storage are obvious embellishments to our online Certified Medical Planner™ educational initiatives.

We look forward to this didactic journey of the future.

ACKNOWLEDGMENTS

To Mackenzie Hope Marcinko; Ann Marie Miller, RN, MHA; Professor Hope Rachel Hetico, RN, MHA, CHQ, CMP™; Rachel Pentin-Maki, RN, MHA; and Eugene Schmuckler, PhD, MBA, MEd, CTS, Academic Dean, consulting psychologist, and senior psychometrist for the Institute of Medical Business Advisors Inc., and the Certified Medical Planner™ online professional designation and certification education program. To Dr. William P. Scherer, MS, Chief Technology Officer; and Parin Kothari, MBA, Chief Marketing Officer. To the Princeton Review™ modified by iMBA Inc. and adapted from the *Complete Book of Distance Learning Schools* by Dr. Jerry Ice and Dr. Paul Edelson.

FURTHER READINGS

Bowen, WG: *Higher Education in the Digital Age*. Princeton University Press, Princeton, NJ and Oxford, UK, 2013.

Cimase, RJ: *Accountable Care Organizations: Value Metrics and Capital Formation*. Productivity Press, Boca Raton, FL, 2013.

Collins, A: *Rethinking Education in the Age of Technology: The Digital Revolution and Schooling in America (Technology, Education—Connections) (Technology, Education-Connections, the Tec Series)*. Teacher College Press, New York, 2011.

Cook, K: *Online Education 2.0: Evolving, Adapting, and Reinventing Online Technical Communication (Paperback)*. Baywood Publishing Company Inc, Amityville, NY. 2013.

Kitces, M: Are financial planners experiencing a crisis of differentiation? http://www.Kitces.com, August 5, 2013.

Kitces, M: What comes after CFP® certification? Finding your niche or specialization with post-CFP® designations, http://www.Kitces.com, March 27, 2014.

Marcinko, DE and Hetico, HR: *The Business of Medical Practice: Transformation Health 2.0 Skills for Doctors*. Springer Publishing, New York, 2000, 2005 and 2010.

Marcinko, DE and Hetico, HR: *Financial Planner's Library on CD-ROM*. Aspen Publishers, New York, 2001, 2002, and 2003.

Marcinko, DE and Hetico, HR: *Financial Planning for Physicians*. JB Publishers, Sudburry, MA, 2006.

Marcinko, DE and Hetico, HR: *Dictionary of Health Insurance and Managed Care*. Springer Publishing, New York, 2007.

Marcinko, DE and Hetico, HR: *Dictionary of Health Economics and Finance*. Springer Publishing, New York, 2008.

Marcinko, DE and Hetico, HR: *Dictionary of Health Information Technology and Security*. Springer Publishing, New York, 2008.

Marcinko, DE and Hetico, HR: *Insurance and Risk Management Strategies for Physicians and Advisors*. JB Publishing, Sudbury, MA, 2008.

Marcinko, DE and Hetico, HR: *Hospitals & Healthcare Organizations: Management Strategies, Operational Techniques, Tools, Templates, and Case Studies*. Productivity Press, Boca Raton, FL, 2013.

Marcinko, DE and Hetico, HR: *Financial Management Strategies for Hospitals and Healthcare Organizations: Tools, Techniques, Checklists and Case Studies*. Productivity Press, Boca Raton, FL, 2014.

Marcinko, DE and Hetico, HR: *Comprehensive Financial Planning Strategies for Doctors and Advisors: Best Practices from Leading Consultants and Certified Medical Planners™*. Productivity Press, Boca Raton, FL, 2015.

Moore, M: *Distance Education*. Cengage Learning, New York, 2011.

Shattuck, K: *Assuring Quality in Online Education: Practices and Processes at the Teaching, Resource, and Program Levels (Online Learning and Distance Education)*. Stylus Publishing, Sterling, VA, 2014.

Vai, M: *Essentials of Online Course Design: A Standards-Based Guide (Essentials of Online Learning)*. Routledge Press, New York, 2011.

The informed voice of a new generation of fiduciary advisors for healthcare
www.CertifiedMedicalPlanner.org

Appendix 2: Risk Management, Liability Insurance, and Asset Protection Terminology

GLOSSARY OF IMPORTANT DEFINITIONS

Much has been written and much has been opined on the topic of medical risk management, insurance, asset protection, and professional liability for physicians and health-care providers in this textbook. But occasionally, we all still get lost in a wide array of acronyms, jargons, and terms that are constantly changing in this ecosystem. And so, this glossary serves as a ready reference for those who want to know about these definitions in a quick and ready fashion.

Accreditation: A professional status given to a health-care provider by an organization in exchange for meeting a specific set of standards.

Accrete: Medicare term for adding new enrollees in a health plan.

Actual acquisition cost: Net payment, after expenses, for provided medical care or services.

Adjudication: Processing a claim through a series of edits to determine proper payment.

Adjusted community rating: The process of determining a group's premium rate in which an HMO adjusts the standard or pure community rate premium by adding or subtracting an amount that reflects the group's past claims experience.

Adjusted coverage per capita cost: Estimate of average monthly benefits cost, after certain adjustments.

Administrative costs: The costs assumed by a managed care plan for administrative services such as claims processing, billing, and overhead costs.

Administrative services only (ASO): A self-insured plan contract with an insurance company for services such as claims processing and stop-loss coverage.

Admitted carrier: An insurance company that is licensed and regulated by a State Department of Insurance is known as an *admitted* carrier in that state; because the company is *admitted*, its policy holders are protected by the admitting state's *guarantee fund*. This fund affords policyholders some protection against the insurance company becoming *insolvent*.

Admitting physician: A licensed practitioner who has the necessary privileges at a hospital to admit patients for care/treatment (in a group practice setting, there are often hospital-based physicians, usually internal medicine, that do all admitting and treatment planning).

Adverse selection: A particular health plan, whether indemnity or managed care, is selected against by the enrollee, and thus an inequitable proportion of enrollees requiring more medical services are found in that plan. For example, low enrollee out-of-pocket costs might lure those individuals requiring more health services into an HMO rather than an indemnity plan because the former does not have a deductible. Therefore, the HMO would have a greater proportion of less-healthy enrollees, thereby driving up costs and increasing financial risks.

Allowable charge: The maximum fee that a third party will reimburse a provider for a given service.

Allowable costs: Items or elements of an institution's costs that are reimbursable under a payment formula. Allowable costs may exclude, for example, uncovered services, luxury accommodations, costs that are not reasonable, and unnecessary expenditures.

Ambulatory care: Outpatient medical services.

Ambulatory surgery: Surgery performed on a nonhospitalized patient; patient goes home the same day as the surgery.

Ambulatory visit group (AVG): Similar to diagnosis-related groups (DRGs), except outpatient rather than inpatient hospital care.

Ancillary care: Additional health-care services performed, such as lab work and x-rays.

Authorization: As it applies to managed care, authorization is the approval of care, such as hospitalization. For example, pre-authorization may be required before admission takes place or care is given by non-HMO providers.

Basic benefits: A set of *basic health services* specified in the member's certificate and those services required under applicable federal and state laws and regulations.

Bed days: A measurement used by managed care plans to indicate the total number of days of hospital care provided to a member of a health plan.

Benefit package: The list of covered services an insurance company, HMO, or PPO offers to a group or individual.

Board certification: A doctor who is board-certified has pursued advanced training in his or her specialty and has passed a qualifying examination; a doctor who is board-eligible has received the training but has not taken or passed the exam.

Cafeteria plan: A corporate benefits plan under which employees are permitted to choose between two or more benefits that consist of cash and certain qualified benefits. Cafeteria plans are also called flexible benefit plans or flex plans.

California Relative Value Studies (CRVS): A coded listing of physician's services with unit values to indicate the relativity of charges to the median.

Capitation: A per-member, monthly payment to a provider that covers contracted services, paid in advance of the delivery of the service. In essence, a provider agrees to provide specified services to HMO members for this fixed, predetermined payment for a specified length of time (usually a year), regardless of how many times the member uses the service.

Carve out: To separately purchase services that are typically part of a managed care package. For example, an HMO may *carve out* the vision care benefit and select a specialized vendor to supply these services on a stand-alone basis.

Case management: The process by which patients with extensive, complex, or serious medical conditions can receive planned treatment that is both cost effective and of high quality; early intervention and a systematic coordination of care among multiple providers are elements of this approach.

Catastrophic case: A catastrophic case is any medical condition where total cost of treatment (regardless of payment source) is expected to exceed an amount designated by the HMO contract with the medical group.

Causation: The incorrect actions of the health-care provider probably led to or contributed to the injuries and damages suffered. For example, if an emergency room doctor did not quickly examine a patient, it could be a life-or-death situation. However, if the patient would have died, regardless of anything a doctor might have done, then there would be no *causation*, even if the doctor delayed his or her examination. Another example of *no causation* would be a person who receives an incorrect prescription from the pharmacist and realizes the mistake before he or she takes the medicine. However, if the medicine was actually taken, and harm resulted, there is *causation*. To prove a medical malpractice case, it must be probable that the incorrect treatment caused the harm. In this context, *probability* means that it is *more likely than not* that the treatment caused the harm. The plaintiff must prove that there was more than a *50%* likelihood that the harm was caused by the negligence. For example, in a case involving the negligent failure to diagnose cancer, if there was less than a 50% chance that earlier diagnosis would have affected the outcome, there is only a *possibility* and not a probability. The law does not permit recovery of damages based on a *possibility*.

Centers for Medicare and Medicaid Services (CMS): Formerly the Health Care Financing Administration (HCFA).

Claims made: A claims made insurance policy covers events that

- Occur during the policy period (on or after the retroactive date).
- Are reported while the policy is still in force. If you would like the company that you have claims-made coverage through to cover your claims after the policy is no longer in force, tail coverage is required.

Closed-panel HMO: A type of HMO in which physicians either must belong to a special group of physicians that has contracted with the HMO or must be employees of the HMO. Generally, medical services are delivered in an HMO-owned health center. Also known as a *staff model*.

Coinsurance: The percentage of costs of medical care that a patient pays. Coinsurance rates generally hover in the 10–20% range. Coinsurance and deductibles are most commonly found in indemnity, fee-for-service insurance and the PPO market. Their absence in the HMO arena is one of the strong marketing appeals of HMOs.

Commercial plan: Refers to the benefit package an insurance company, HMO, or PPO offers to employers. This is distinguished from a senior plan, which is offered to Medicare beneficiaries.

Community rating: The process of determining a group's premium rate in which the HMO sets premium rates based on the average cost of providing care to the HMO's enrollees. This rating method is required of federally qualified HMOs.

Concurrent review: A method of reviewing patient care, during hospital confinement, to validate the necessity of current care and to explore alternatives to inpatient care.

Consent to settle: The best interests of the insurance company are not always the same as the individual doctor's best interests. You should try to obtain a policy with a *consent to settle* clause, which requires the carrier to obtain your written permission to settle a claim against you. If not, the carrier can settle a claim that you believe is very defensible without your permission. A *hammer* clause is one in which the insurance company must obtain your written permission to settle a claim against you but you are responsible for all costs exceeding the amount of the settlement proposed by your carrier if you will not agree to that settlement. If you push the case to trial and you win, you avoid having the proposed settlement becoming a permanent part of your claims history. But if you lose, you will have to pay the difference between the amount of money the case could have been settled for and the actual costs of awards and extra defense.

Consolidated Omnibus Budget Reconciliation Act (COBRA): A federal law that permits many people who lose eligibility under a group health plan to continue that coverage without lapse.

Continuity of care: The degree to which the care of a patient from the onset of illness until its completion is continuous, that is, without interruption.

Continuum of care: A range of medical, nursing treatments, and social services in a variety of settings that provides services most appropriate to the level of care required. For example, a hospital may offer services ranging from nursery to a hospice.

Conversion factor: A dollar amount for one base unit in the relative value scale (RVS). The price to be paid to the provider for a given service equals the relative value of the service multiplied by the dollar amount of the conversion factor. For example, a blood sugar determination might have a relative value of 5.0, and the conversion factor might be $5. The *price* of the blood sugar determination would therefore be $25.

Conversion plan: If a member's group plan is canceled, the member can opt to continue coverage under an individual plan.

Coordination of benefits: A process wherein if an individual has two group health plans, the amount payable is divided between the plans so that the combined coverage amounts to, but does not exceed, 100% of the charges.

Copayment: A supplemental cost-sharing arrangement in which the HMO enrollee pays, to the provider, a specified amount for a specific service—for example, $5 or $10—that must be paid at the time of service for certain medical services. This is the patient's out-of-pocket expense for health-care treatment.

Corporate practice of medicine: State laws prohibiting lay people, organizations, and corporations from directly or indirectly practicing medicine. They are designed to ensure that those making decisions about the provision of medical services will not be subject to commercial exploitation.

Credentialing: The process of determining eligibility for hospital, PHO, or other medical staff membership, and privileges to be granted to physicians. Credentials and performance are periodically reviewed, which could result in a doctor's privileges being denied, modified, or withdrawn. The process of reviewing a provider's qualifications to be sure they meet the criteria established by a managed care organization.

Custodial care: Care provided primarily to assist a patient in meeting the activities of daily living, but not care requiring skilled nursing services.

Customary and reasonable: Refers to a fee that falls within a common range of community fees.

Damages: Damages are divided into two categories: economic and noneconomic. Economic damages include out-of-pocket losses that have ascertainable monetary value, such as lost earnings and medical bills. If the loss can be replaced with money, it is *economic*. Noneconomic damages are typically known as *pain and suffering* damages. It is compensation for physical impairment or disability, or the diminished enjoyment of life caused by the malpractice. If malpractice resulted in a patient's death, the damages include compensation for the lost financial support that the spouse and family would have received, and compensation for the loss of the decedent's care, comfort, and love.

Days per thousand (per 1000): A measurement of the number of days of hospital care used in a year per 1000 HMO members.

Deductible: A set dollar amount that a person must pay before insurance coverage for medical expenses can begin.

Defense costs: If a malpractice insurance policy pays defense costs *outside* the limits of liability, then defense costs do not erode the limits of liability of the policy. As an example, if your policy limits are $1 million per occurrence and $3 million aggregate and your defense costs for a case are $100,000, you would still have $1 million to cover a potential award for that claim. If your policy pays defense costs *inside* the limits of liability, then you would have only $900,000 left to cover a potential award in the previous example. Clearly, it is preferable to purchase a policy with defense costs *outside* the limits of liability.

Direct contract HMO: Individual, self-insured, employers, or business coalitions contract directly with providers for health-care services with no HMO or PPO intermediary. This enables employers to include in the plan the specific services preferred by their employees.

Discounted fee-for-services: A payment structure in which physicians are paid a certain percentage of their normal fee.

Disease management: A philosophy toward the treatment of the patient with an illness (usually chronic in nature) that seeks to prevent recurrence of symptoms, maintain high quality of life, and prevent future need for medical resources by using an integrated, comprehensive approach to health care. Pharmaceutical care, continuous quality improvement, practice guidelines, and case management all play key roles in this effort that (in theory) will result in decreased health-care costs.

Durable medical equipment: Defined as equipment that meets the following criteria: (1) can withstand repeated use; (2) is primarily and customarily used to serve a medical purpose; (3) generally is not useful to a person in the absence of illness/injury; and (4) is appropriate for home use.

Economic credentialing: This means taking a physician's economic behavior into account (e.g., tests ordered, hospital bed days, outcomes) in deciding upon medical staff appointment or reappointment.

Effective date: The date on which the health plan agreement goes into effect.

Eligibility guarantee: An assurance of reimbursement to the medical group for services or goods provided to a member who subsequently is found to be ineligible for benefits.

Emergency services: Services provided in connection with an unforeseen acute illness or injury requiring immediate medical attention.

Encounter: A member visit to the medical group with the intent of seeing a health-care provider. There may be a variety of services performed at an encounter, including a brief office visit, electrocardiogram (EKG), lab test, or an immunization.

Enrollee: Synonymous with member. A person eligible to receive, or receiving, benefits from an HMO or insurance policy; includes both those who have enrolled (subscribed) and their eligible dependents.

Enrollment: The number of members in an HMO. The number of members assigned to a physician or medical group providing care under contract with an HMO; also, the process by which a health plan signs up individuals or groups as subscribers.

Enrollment area: The geographic area within a designated radius (varies by HMO) of the Primary Medical Group (PMG) selected by the subscriber.

Enrollment protection: The practice of an HMO to protect its contracted medical groups against part or all losses incurred for physician services above a specified dollar amount while caring for the HMO's enrollees; also referred to as stop-loss or reinsurance.

Exclusions: The exclusions of an insurance policy state what the policy will not cover. For example, most individual practitioner's policies specifically exclude coverage for duties as a *medical director.* You should study very carefully the exclusions of your current and any future medical malpractice insurance policy.

Exclusive provider organization (EPO): A health plan in which patients must go to a participating provider or receive no benefit. This is a cross between an HMO and a PPO. Like a PPO, doctors typically are paid on a fee-for-service basis and aren't at risk. However, patients have less freedom to go out of an EPO network than with a PPO. Also, it is a managed care organization usually made up of a group of physicians, one or more hospitals, and other providers who contract with an insurer, employer, or other sponsoring group to provide discounted medical services to enrollees. It is similar to a PPO in that it allows the patient to go out of network for care; however, the patient will not be reimbursed if he or she does so.

Experience rating: The rating method used by most traditional indemnity insurers, which uses the group's claims experience to establish premium rates.

Expert witness: If the subject matter is not commonly understood by ordinary people, then evidence may be offered by someone with specialized knowledge and experience. This person is called an *expert witness.* In most medical malpractice cases, the plaintiff cannot prove the case unless an *expert* testifies regarding the issues of *standard of care* and *causation.*

Federal Employees Health Benefits Program (FEHBP): The health benefits program for federal employees that is administered through the U.S. Office of Personnel Management.

Federally qualified: An accreditation for HMOs that can be obtained from the Office of Prepaid Health Care (OPHC).

Federally qualified HMO: An HMO that meets certain federally stipulated provisions aimed at protecting consumers (e.g., providing a broad range of basic health services, assuring financial solvency, and monitoring the quality of care). HMOs must apply to the federal government for qualification. The process is administered by the Centers for Medicare and Medicaid Services (CMS) and Department of Health and Human Services (DHHS).

Fee: A charge or price for professional services.

Fee-for-service (FFS): A system of payment for health care whereby a fee is rendered for each service delivered. This traditional method contrasts with that used in the prepaid sector where services are covered by a fixed payment made in advance that is independent of the number of services rendered.

Fee schedule: A listing of charges or benefits for specified medical or dental procedures.

Formulary: A list containing the names of certain prescription drugs that an HMO covers when dispensed to its members who have drug coverage.

Fully insured plan: A group health-care plan funding arrangement in which the group policyholder makes monthly premium payments to the organization that provides the health-care coverage, and the insurer bears the responsibility of guaranteeing claims payments.

Global capitation: Providers are paid a single per-member-per-month rate to cover all care (professionals, facilities, and technical services) for a population of people.

Global case rates: Providers are paid a lump sum upon referral to cover all care (professionals, facilities, and technical services) specific to a defined episode.

Group model HMO: This type of closed-panel HMO generally is made up of one or more doctor group practices that are not owned by the HMO but operate as independent partnerships or professional corporations. Instead of employing the Medical Doctor/Doctor of Osteopathy (MD/DOs) and paying them salaries, the HMO contracts with the group practice to provide or arrange covered services for each HMO member who is a patient of the group.

Group practice without walls: A legal entity formed by a network of physicians who maintain their individual practices.

Health Care Financing Administration (HCFA): The agency within the Department of Health and Human Services that administers federal health financing and related regulatory programs, principally the Medicare, Medicaid, and Peer Review Organization. This Administration was renamed the Centers for Medicare and Medicaid Services (CMS) on June 14, 2001.

Health maintenance organization (HMO): A legal corporation that offers health insurance and medical care; a health-care delivery system that provides comprehensive services for subscribing members in a particular geographic area. Most HMO care is provided through a managed network made up of MDs/DOs/DPMs, etc., hospitals, and other allopathic/osteopathic professionals selected by the HMO. HMO enrollees are required to obtain care from this network of providers in order for their care to be covered, except in cases of emergency. All the care the members may need is paid for by the single monthly fee, plus nominal copayments. HMOs typically offer a range of health-care services at a fixed price (see *Capitation*). The types of HMOs are

- Staff model: Organization owns its clinics and employs its doctors.
- Group model: Contract with medical groups for services.
- Independent physician association (IPA) model: IPA contract that in turn contracts with individual physicians.
- Direct contract or network model: Contracts directly with individual physicians.
- Mixed model: Members get options ranging from staff to IPA models.
- Open-panel model: A managed care plan or HMO where members can see any provider for an extra premium cost.

Health plan: A generic term to refer to a specific benefit package offered by an insurer. Also used to pertain to the insurance company (e.g., "I signed up for the Blue Cross health plan").

Health Plan Employer Data and Information Set (HEDIS): The National Committee for Quality Assurance's (NCQA's) standardized set of performance measures for HMOs.

Hospice services: Services to provide care to the terminally ill and their families.

Hospital day: A term to describe any 24-hour period commencing at 12:00 a.m. or 12:00 p.m., whichever is used by a hospital to determine a hospital day, during which a patient receives hospital services at the hospital.

Incident malpractice reporting: How each insurance company defines a *claim* is another important consideration when comparing policies. *Incident reporting* allows the physician to report an adverse outcome to the carrier as a potential claim. This is important because for a claim to be covered under a claims-made policy, the incident must *both* happen *and* be reported as a claim while the policy is in force. If an insurance company requires that the insured receive a *written demand for damages* in order to consider a claim to be reported, then the physician must wait to be sued before the claim is recognized! This can be a real problem for physicians wishing to change professional liability carriers: most insurance companies would decline to offer a policy to prospective clients who can expect to be sued in the future for past adverse outcomes. The carriers often consider such a situation to be the same as *buying future claims*.

Incurred but not reported (IBNR) expenses: This term refers to a financial accounting of all services that have been performed but, as a result of a short period of time, have not yet been invoiced or recorded. A cash reserve set up by a payer to cover claims that have been filed but not officially reported as paid.

Indemnity insurance: Also known as a traditional health insurance, it pays a certain percentage of the charges billed by the provider, and the patient is responsible for the balance.

Independent Physician or Practice Association (IPA): A confederation of physicians and other providers assembled for the purpose of contracting with payers. Participating providers accept the fee schedules negotiated by the IPA, but typically may continue to see patients covered by other plans. An IPA contracts with individual physicians who see HMO members, as well as their own patients, in their own private offices. It is the ability of IPA physicians to see both HMO and private patients in their own offices that principally differentiates an IPA from a group or staff HMO. Physicians in an IPA are paid either on a capitation or a modified fee-for-service basis.

Integrated Delivery System (IDS): A network of hospitals, physicians, and other medical services, along with an HMO or insurance plan, formed to provide a population with a full, cost-effective continuum of care—from prevention through checkups, tests, surgery, rehabilitation, long-term, and home care—and is accountable for costs, quality of care, and customer satisfaction.

International Classification of Diseases, Ninth Revision, Clinical Modification (ICD-9-M): The World Health Organization's (WHO's) ninth edition of its book is used widely for hospital diagnoses. A tenth version has been released.

IPA model HMO: A type of open-panel HMO that typically includes large numbers of individual private practice physicians. Under this structure, physicians practice in their own offices.

Length of stay: The number of consecutive days a patient is hospitalized.

Limits of Malpractice Insurance Liability: What the insurance company will pay on your behalf in the event of a claim. If your limits of liability are $1,000,000/$3,000,000, it would mean that the insurance company would pay a maximum of $1 million per occurrence and $3 million per year for claims. For further clarification, refer to the examples below and assume limits of liability of $1,000,000/$3,000,000:

- In 1 year you have 4 lawsuits each for $800,000:
  The insurance company pays $3,000,000 and you are responsible for $200,000.
- In 1 year you have 2 lawsuits each for $2,000,000:
  The insurance company pays $2,000,000 ($1 million each), and you are responsible for $2,000,000 ($1 million each).
- In 1 year you have 9 lawsuits each for $20,000:
  The insurance company would pay everything.

So, depending on your individual risk, there are a wide variety of limits of liability available that may be an attractive option. However, most states have minimum requirements for limits of liability should you have hospital privileges.

Managed care: A relatively older term coined originally to refer to the prepaid health-care sector (e.g., HMOs) where care is provided under a fixed budget, and costs are therein capable of being *managed*. Increasingly, the term is being used by many analysts to include Preferred Provider Organizations (PPOs) and even forms of indemnity insurance coverage that incorporate preadmission certification and other utilization controls.

Managed care organization (MCO): Refers to any type of organizational entity providing managed care, such as an HMO, PPO, etc.

Management services organization (MSO): A management entity often owned by a hospital, physician organization, or third party. The MSO contracts with payers and hospitals/physicians to provide administrative and practice-management services such as negotiating fee schedules, handling administrative functions, and billing and collections.

Mandated benefits: State legislatures have passed statutes requiring any health plans being offered in the state to include certain treatments for coverage. These treatments may include chiropractic care, mental and nervous disorder coverage, routine mammograms, and organ transplants.

Medically necessary: A term used to describe the supplies and services provided to diagnose and treat a medical condition in accordance with the standards of good medical practice.

Medically unnecessary days (MUD): A term used to describe that part of a stay in a facility, as determined by a case manager, as excessive to diagnose and treat a medical condition in accordance with the standards of good medical practice. A hospital stay may be deemed excessive because it was too long, or because more appropriate care is available in a less costly or more efficient setting.

Medical loss ration: The difference between premiums collected and claims paid out.

Medical standard of care: Health-care providers are required to use that degree of learning and skill ordinarily used under similar circumstances by reputable and careful members of the profession. If, for example, a surgeon's actions are questioned, another surgeon must testify that the doctor being sued failed to do something that he or she should have done, or did something that he or she should not have done.

Medicare: The federally financed hospital insurance system (part A) and supplementary medical insurance (part B) for patients aged 65 and older, created by the 1965 amendment to the Social Security Act.

Medicare select: A type of Medicare supplement insurance that has lower premiums in return for a limited choice of beneficiaries: they will use only providers who have been selected by the insurer as *preferred providers.* Also covers emergency care outside the preferred provider network.

Medicare supplement insurance or Medigap: It provides additional individual benefits under Medicare. There are 10 standardized Medigap plans with specific packages of benefits.

Member: A person eligible to receive, or receiving, benefits from an HMO or insurance policy; includes both those who have enrolled (subscribed) and their eligible dependents.

Messenger model: A method of setting fees for loose, nonrisk bearing MCOs such as IPAs or PHOs. A designated agent must act as a *messenger*, shuttling individual physician information to the payer and vice versa. This method meets the criteria of antitrust laws that bar physicians from sharing any practice data or fee information.

Mixed model HMO: A type of HMO that combines certain characteristics of two or more HMO models.

National Committee for Quality Assurance (NCQA): An independent, nonprofit organization that assesses and reports on HMO quality.

National Practitioner Data Bank (NPDB): Each entity that makes a payment on behalf of a physician, dentist, or other health practitioner in settlement of, or in satisfaction in whole or in part of a claim or judgment against that practitioner must report the payment to the NPDB. Medical malpractice payments are limited to exchanges of money and must be the result of a written complaint or claim demanding monetary payment for damages.

Network model HMO: A type of HMO that contracts with a number of IPAs and/or medical groups to form a doctor network; this allows an HMO to market its services in a broader geographic area.

Non-admitted carrier: Often, a physician simply cannot obtain coverage from an admitted carrier because of past claims history, licensing issues, or high-risk procedures in the doctor's practice. For example, in some states, bariatric surgeons may be declined coverage from every admitted carrier. Excess & Surplus Lines (non-admitted) Carriers usually become the best option for so-called *higher-risk* practitioners. An E&S carrier is not regulated by the state's Department of Insurance and therefore is not subject to the *guarantee* fund. However, each state's Department of Insurance must approve the Excess & Surplus Lines Company for it to be a viable option.

Occurrence policy: An occurrence policy covers events that occur during the policy period regardless of when they are reported as claims. Because it is nearly impossible to predict the cost of future claims in today's medical malpractice environment, occurrence policies have become nearly extinct for medical malpractice coverage.

Office of Prepaid Health Care (OPHC): OPHC ensures that an HMO meets certain requirements by conducting an extensive review of its operations and financial strength.

Open access: Open access arrangements allow members to see participating providers, usually specialists, without referral from the health plan's gatekeeper. These types of arrangements are most often found in IPA model HMOs.

Open enrollment: The annual period during which people in a *dual choice* health benefits program can choose among the two (or more) plans being offered. Also, the period during which a federally qualified HMO must make its plan available without restrictions to individuals who are not part of a group.

Open-panel HMO: A type of HMO in which any doctor or provider who meets the HMO's specific standards can contract with the HMO to provide services to the members.

Outcomes measurement: This process measures the results of specific medical treatments in an effort to pinpoint a pattern and develop reliable practice patterns for providers to follow that keep care quality high, while delivering cost-effective medicine.

Per diem cost: Cost per day; hospital or other institutional cost for a day of care.

Per member per month (PMPM): Generally used by HMOs and their medical providers as an indicator of revenue, expenses, or utilization of services per member per one month period (e.g., "We receive a capitation payment of $30 per member per month").

Per member per year (PMPY): Generally used by HMOs and their medical providers as an indicator of revenue, expenses, or utilization of services per member per year (e.g., "Our patients come in to see the doctor on an average of 3.7 times per member per year").

Physician–hospital organization (PHO): An organization created jointly by a hospital and a physician group. The PHO, in turn, contracts with hospitals and physicians for the delivery of services to payers under contract to the PHO. It can also provide management services and perform other services typically associated with a Management Services Organization (MSO).

Physician organization (PO): A group of physicians banding together, usually for the purpose of contracting with managed care entities or to represent the physician component in a PHO. The PO is a managed care contracting entity owned by and composed exclusively of physicians. The PO tends to be more tightly controlled in terms of members and adherence to treatment protocols than an IPA. POs typically share information systems, claims-processing procedures, financial data, medical records, and other technical support functions.

Physician Practice Management Corporation (PPMC): A firm that purchases physicians' practices in exchange for a percentage of the gross receivables. The PPM leases the office back to the doctor or employs the doctor on a salaried basis. The PPM then contracts with the area MCOs.

Point of service plan (POSP): A type of managed care plan that allows members to choose whether to seek medical care within the plan's network or seek medical care out of network at the point of service (i.e., at the time services are rendered). It allows members to pay little or nothing if they stay within the established HMO delivery system, but permits members to choose and receive services from an outside doctor, any time, if they are willing to pay higher copayments, deductibles, and possibly monthly premiums; also called an open-ended plan.

Preferred provider organization (PPO): A select, approved panel of physicians, hospitals, and other providers who agree to accept a discounted fee schedule for patients and to follow utilization review and pre-authorization protocols for certain treatments. A system in which a payer negotiates lower prices with certain doctors and hospitals; patients who go to a preferred provider get a higher benefit—for example, 90% or 100% coverage of their costs—than patients who go outside the network.

Premium: A predetermined monthly membership fee that a subscriber or employer pays for the HMO coverage.

Primary care physician (PCP): A physician who serves as a group member's personal physician and first contact in a managed care system. PCPs include family/general practitioners, internists, pediatricians, and OB/GYNs.

Private pay patient: Patients who are financially responsible for their own care and are not covered by a third-party payor program.

Prospective review: A method of reviewing possible hospitalization, prior to admission, to determine necessity of confinement, outpatient alternatives, and estimated reasonable length of stay.

Provider sponsored network (PSN): These networks range from loose alliances between physicians to legal entities formed between hospitals and physicians for the purposes of managed care contracting.

Provider sponsored organization (PSO): A term used in Medicare reform legislation to define a provider sponsored health plan that would be licensed to provide coverage of the Medicare benefits package.

Providers: Institutions and individuals that are licensed to provide health-care services (e.g., hospitals, physicians, pharmacists, etc.).

Quality management: A formal set of activities to assure the quality of services provided. Quality management includes quality assessment and corrective actions taken to remedy any deficiencies identified through the assessment process.

Referral authorization: A verbal or written approval of a request for a member to receive medical services or supplies outside of the participating medical group.

Referral physician: A physician who has a patient referred to him by another source for examination or surgery, or to have specific procedures performed on the patient, usually because the referring source is not prepared or qualified to provide the needed service.

Referring physician: A physician who sends a patient to another source for examination or surgery, or to have specific procedures performed on the patient, usually because the referring physician is not prepared or qualified to provide the needed service.

Reinsurance: The practice of an HMO or insurance company of purchasing insurance from another company to protect itself against part or all the losses incurred in the process of honoring the claims of policyholders; also referred to as stop-loss or risk control insurance.

Relative value scale (RVS): RVS is the compiled table of relative value units (RVUs), that is, a value given to each procedure or unit of service. As a payment system, RVS is used to determine a formula that multiplies the RVU by a dollar amount, called a converter.

Resource-based relative value scale (RBRVS): A method of determining physicians' fees based on the time, training, skill, and other factors required to deliver various services.

Retrospective review: A method of reviewing patient care, after hospital discharge, to determine quality, necessity, and appropriateness of care.

Risk: Refers to finances used for providing patient care. For example, an HMO that offers prepaid care for a given premium is *at risk* because it must provide care within the premium funds available.

Risk sharing: The process whereby an HMO and contracted provider each accepts partial responsibility for the financial risk and rewards involved in cost-effectively caring for the members enrolled in the plan and assigned to a specific provider.

Self-funded or self-insured plan: A group health-care plan funding arrangement in which the organization sponsoring the plan takes complete financial responsibility for making all claims payments and paying all related expenses.

Senior plan: Refers to a benefit package offer by an HMO or other insurer to beneficiaries eligible for Medicare parts A and B.

Service area: The geographic area served by an insurer or health-care provider.

Silent PPOs: These plans act like brokers by selling health-care discounts to physicians that do not guarantee patient volume. For example, a contracted PPO sells discounts to an insurer, which applies the discounts to medical bills and claims; also called voluntary PPOs, wrap-around PPOs, faux PPOs, or blind PPOs.

Staff model HMO: A type of closed-panel HMO in which the physicians are salaried employees of the HMO. Medical services in staff models are delivered at HMO-owned health centers.

Stop-loss: The practice of an HMO or insurance company of protecting itself or its contracted medical groups against part or all losses above a specified dollar amount incurred in the process of caring for its policyholders. This usually involves the HMO or insurance company purchasing insurance from another company to protect itself; also referred to as *reinsurance*.

Subscriber: Any individual meeting a health plan's eligibility requirement, and who enrolls in the health plan and accepts the financial responsibility for any premiums, copayments, or deductibles.

Supplemental benefits: Benefits contracted for by an employer group, which is outside of, or in addition to, the basic health plan.

Tail coverage: The *tail* (extended reporting endorsement) provisions are among the most important variables between malpractice insurance policies to consider. Because a claims-made policy will only cover you if the event happened while the policy was in force (after your *retroactive* date) *and* was reported to the carrier while the policy was still in force, you cannot just leave your current carrier and start over with a new insurer! You need to either purchase the extended reporting endorsement (*tail*) from your current carrier *or* purchase prior acts (*nose*) coverage from the new insurance carrier. Purchasing tail coverage from your present carrier effectively converts your claims-made policy into an occurrence policy because it allows you to report claims in the future to that carrier even though the policy period has ended. If you purchase tail coverage from your current insurer and start over with a new insurance company, you will have new retroactive date.

Prior acts (or *nose*) coverage allows you to transfer your existing retroactive date to your new insurance carrier—eliminating the need to purchase tail coverage from your last carrier. It is usually less expensive to obtain prior acts coverage from the new company than to buy tail coverage from the old carrier and then purchase a first-year claims-made policy from the new company. The retroactive date is the first day you became insured by a claims-made policy. That date will follow you for the rest of your medical career in most cases.

Many insurance companies offer free tail coverage if a physician has been continuously insured by that carrier for 5 years and is at least 55 years of age upon permanently retiring from the practice of medicine—or has been continuously insured with the company for 10 or 15 years and is younger than 55 when he/she retires.

Tertiary care: Medical care requiring a setting outside of the routine, community standard; care to be provided within a regional medical center having comprehensive training, specialists, and research training.

Third-party administrator (TPA): An administrative organization, other than the employee benefit plan or health-care provider, that collects premiums, pays claims, and/or provides administrative services.

Third-party payer: A public or private organization that pays for or underwrites coverage for health-care expenses.

Third-party payment: A term used to describe the monetary reimbursement for medical services from someone other than the member or the member's insurance plan.

Treating physician: The licensed practitioner that actually provides care to the patient while hospitalized (e.g., a specialist or hospital-based physician). The primary care provider is not always the admitting or treating physician, but will make *social rounds* on their patients, thus freeing them up to do more in office work.

Utilization: The frequency with which a benefit is used (e.g., 3200 doctor's office visits per 1000 HMO members per a year). Utilization experience multiplied by the average cost per unit of service delivered equals capitated costs.

Utilization review: Evaluation of the necessity, appropriateness, and efficiency of the use of medical services and facilities. Helps ensure proper use of health-care resources by providing for the regular review of such areas as admission of patients, length of stay, services performed, and referrals.

Virtual integration: A pattern of strategic alliances designed to win the cost advantages of affiliation without the overhead disadvantages of ownership.

Withhold: The portion of the monthly capitation payment to physicians withheld by the HMO until the end of the year or other time period to create an incentive for efficient care. The withhold is at risk (i.e., if the physician exceeds utilization norms, he or she does not receive it). It serves as a financial incentive for lower utilization.

Further Readings

Marcinko, DE and Hetico, RN: *Dictionary of Health Insurance and Managed Care.* Springer Publishing, New York, 2007.

Marcinko, DE and Hetico, RN: *Dictionary of Health Economics and Finance*. Springer Publishing, New York, 2008.

Marcinko, DE and Hetico, RN: *Dictionary of Health Information Technology and Security.* Springer Publishing, New York, 2009.

Hospital Administrator Blogs

- *Christina's Considerations*: Christina Thielst is a hospital and health-care administrator and entrepreneur with a deep desire for improving community health.

- *Healing Hospitals (Ask a Hospital President)*: This blog is maintained by Nick Jacobs, who answers questions about health care using his knowledge as a former hospital president.
- *Hospital Life*: Marty Bonick is the president and CEO of Jewish Hospital, and he shares his insights on running a health-care facility.
- *Leading the Way to Medical Excellence*: The president of McLeod Health offers insight into the changing world of medicine and the business of health care.
- *Life as a Healthcare CIO*: Dr. John D. Halamka talks about supporting an entire hospital system, as well as other relevant topics, in this blog.
- *MCDH CEO Forum*: The Mendocino Coast District Hospital offers a blog that focuses on hospital and regional issues.
- *More Than Medicine*: Tom Quinn, CEO of Community General Hospital in Syracuse, New York, offers his insights on medicine and life.
- *Roper on Health*: Dr. William L. Roper of the University of North Carolina Health Care System offers his take on various health issues.
- *Running a Hospital*: This blog is maintained by the CEO of Beth Israel Deaconess Medical Center in Boston and offers insight into hospital administration.
- *St. Joseph Medical Center*: The CEO of St. Joseph Medical Center in Kansas City, Missouri, shares his insight into hospital administration.
- *Todd's Perspective*: Grinnell Regional Medical Center in Grinnell, Iowa, offers up a blog by the CEO Todd Linden. He shares his thoughts on running a nonprofit hospital.
- *Wachter's World*: Dr. Robert M. Wachter is a professor and the associate chairman of the Department of Medicine at the University of California, San Francisco.
- *WakeMed Voices*: WakeMed Health & Hospitals discuss health-care issues nationwide and in the community in this blog.

Health Law and Policy Blogs

- *Drug and Device Law*: This blog is about topics that arise in the defense of pharmaceutical and medical device product liability litigation.
- *FDA Law Blog*: This blog is maintained by Hyman, Phelps & McNamara, P.C., the largest dedicated food and drug law firm in the country.
- *Health Care Renewal*: This blog addresses threats to health care's core values, especially those stemming from concentration and abuse of power.
- *Health Commentary*: This blog is hosted by veteran health-care leader and advocate Mike Magee, MD, who brings the concept of *health populism* to the web.
- *Health Impact Assessment Blog*: This blog is intended as a mechanism to encourage information sharing between HIA practitioners and those with an interest in HIA.
- *Health Populi*: Jane Sarasohn-Kahn is a health economist and management consultant who covers strategic planning, qualitative market research, forecasting, and health policy analysis.

- *IH BLOG*: IH members are professionals who are engaged in international health and they comprise a pool of expertise in a field that covers a full range of international health activities.
- *Life Sciences Legal Update*: Content on this blog is published by Reed Smith to keep clients and friends informed of legal developments affecting the life sciences and health-care industries.
- *Managed Care Matters*: This is Joe Paduda's blog on managed care, covering health-care cost containment, health policy, health research, and medical news for insurers, employers, and health-care providers.
- *The Health Care Blog*: No list about health or hospital care can be complete without this blog. It is "everything you always wanted to know about the Health Care system…but were afraid to ask."

Health It Blogs

- *Chilmark Research*: Chilmark Research is a health-care industry analyst firm performing market research and analysis on health-care information technology (HIT) adoption and use.
- *Crossover Health*: If you are interested in health care, technology, and business, take a look at this blog, an ongoing conversation about those topics.
- *davidrothman.net*: David Rothman is the Information Services Specialist at the Community General Hospital Medical Library of Greater Syracuse.
- *e-CareManagement blog*: Vince Kuraitis, owner of Better Health Technologies, LLC, writes about EHRs, PHRs, health policy and reform, ICT, and much more.
- *Found In Cache*: Ed Bennett follows a different path, discussing social media resources for health-care professionals.
- *Health Business Blog*: Co-founder of MedPharma Partners LLC, David E. Williams provides a background in technology-enabled health-care services.
- *Healthcare & Technology*: This blog covers Health IT, reform, EHRs, EMRs, Internet resources, and more.
- *Healthcare Technology News*: If you crave news and opinion about health-care technology, this blog will support your addiction.
- *HealthNex*: Follow this blog only if you want the most up-to-date information about EHR, clinical transformation, and biobanking from IBM.
- *Informaticopia*: UK-based, international perspective on health informatics and elearning.
- *Medical Devices Today*: Follow strategy, regulations, innovations, and investment coverage from one of the industry's top publications.
- *Neil Versel's Healthcare IT Blog*: Follow this health-care journalist's views on the major segment of the industry he covers.
- *Schwartz Healthcare IT Blog*: Schwartz Communications provides insights into ways to use IT effectively within health-care facilities.
- *The Health IT Channel*: It's a blog, a video, a way to learn about health IT from across the spectrum.
- *The Healthcare IT Guy*: Shahid N. Shah is the CEO of Netspective Communications, which is a software consultancy.

Health Insurance and Disease Management Blogs

- *Disease Management Care Blog*: This is a vast and ongoing resource from the world of disease management including informatics, pay-for-performance, health insurance, and much more.
- *Health Insurance*: This About.com column, written by Michael Bihari, MD, provides updated health insurance information.
- *Health Insurance Blog*: This health resources, which enables consumers to compare health insurance companies, offers a blog filled with health insurance–related news.
- *Insure.com Blog*: This link takes you to the *health* portion of this insurance site, filled with interesting commentary and news.
- *InsureBlog*: This blog covers insurance issues, principles, and solutions.
- *Medicare Update*: This blog covers Medicare compliance, reimbursement, and enforcement.
- *Piper Report*: This blog is about Medicare, Medicaid, pharma, biotech, health reform, and more.
- *Q1Medicare*: This blog is powered by the Q1Group LLC, which supplies education and decision support tools for the Medicare community.
- *Terms + Conditions Insurance Blog*: This insurance industry blog aims to provide timely information and discussion on contemporary insurance topics.
- *The Alan Katz Health Care Reform Blog*: Alan Katz is a past president of both the National and the California Associations of Health Underwriters.
- *Workers' Comp Insider*: This is Lynch Ryan's blog about risk management, business insurance, workplace health and safety, and related topics.

Health Policy and Management Blogs

- *Health Affairs*: The staff of the policy journal *Health Affairs* offers their insights and provide a venue for guest bloggers as well.
- *Health Care Organizational Ethics*: Use this blog to discuss and debate the ethics within today's health-care organizations and within the wider health system.
- *Health Care Policy and Marketplace Review*: This blog provides an ongoing review of health-care policy activity in Washington, District of Columbia and in the marketplace.
- *Health Care Renewal*: This blog, provided by a number of health-care professionals, focuses on "threats to health care's core values, especially those stemming from concentration and abuse of power."
- *Health Policy and Communications Blog*: This blog was created to foster discussion and analysis about how health policy and communications issues affect clinical and economic outcomes.
- *Health Wonk Review*: A handy place to find the best in health-care policy blogs gathered biweekly.
- *Mayo Clinic Health Policy Blog*: The Mayo Clinic Health Policy Center (HPC) blog provides updates about HPC activities, viewpoints, and news, and is an open forum intended to foster a rigorous discussion about health-care reform topics.
- *Medicare News Blog*: This blog provides an easy way to stay on top of Medicare news.

- *The Alan Katz Health Care Reform Blog*: One agent's perspective on health-care reform and other health-care policy issues.
- *The New Health Dialogue*: The New America Foundation provides a health-care policy blog based upon their policy program.

ACKNOWLEDGMENTS

To Dr. Charles F. Fenton III, JD, Atlanta, District of Columbia; Mackenzie H. Marcinko of iMBA Inc.; and Sean G. Todd, Esq., CPA, MTax, CFP®, Roswell, Georgia.

Appendix 3: Risk Management, Liability Insurance, and Asset Protection Abbreviations

GLOSSARY OF IMPORTANT ACRONYMS

Much has been written and much has been opined on the topic of medical risk management, insurance, asset protection, and professional liability for physicians and health-care providers in this textbook, and elsewhere. But occasionally, we all still get lost in a wide array of abbreviations, acronyms, and initialisms that are constantly changing in this ecosystem. And so, this glossary serves as a ready reference for those who want to know about these medical risk-management acronyms in a quick and ready fashion.

ACRONYMS AND ABBREVIATIONS

AAASC	American Association of Ambulatory Surgery Centers
AAHP	American Association of Health Plans
ABN	advance beneficiary notice
ABQAUR	American Board of Quality Assurance and Utilization Review
ACE	acute care episode
ACHCE	American College of Health Care Executives
ACS	American College of Surgeons
ADA	Americans with Disabilities Act
ADC	average daily census
ADL	activities of daily living
ADT	Admission/discharge/transfer
AHA	American Hospital Association
AHIMA	American Health Information Management Association
AHRQ	Agency for Healthcare Research and Quality
AI	average inventory
AIMR	Association for Investment Management and Research
AIR	assumed interest rate
ALE	annualized loss expectancy
ALF	assisted living facility
ALOS	average length of stay
AMA	American Medical Association
AMBAC	AMBAC Indemnity Corporation

AMGA	American Medical Group Association
ANSI	American National Standards Institute
AP	accounts payable
APA	American Psychiatric Association
APC	ambulatory payment classification
APG	ambulatory payment group
APR	annual percentage rate
AR	accounts receivable
ASA	American Society of Appraisers
ASC	ambulatory surgery centers; also Accredited Standards Committee
ASHA	American Surgical Hospital Association
ASO	administrative services only
ASTC	ancillary service technical component
ATM	asynchronous transfer mode
AVG	ambulatory visit group
BANTA	best alternative to negotiated agreement
BBA	Balanced Budget Act (1997)
BBRA	Balanced Budget Refinement Act (1999)
BCP	business continuity planning
BEA	breakeven analysis
BEP	breakeven point
BIPA	Benefits Improvement and Protection Act (2000)
BLS	Bureau of Labor Statistics
BPD	border protection device
BS	balance sheet
BSA	Bank Secrecy Act
BVS	business valuation standard
CA	certificate authority
CAC	Carrier Advisory Committee
CAS	cost accounting standards
CASB	Cost Accounting Standards Board
CC	Common Criteria (for IT Security Evaluation—ISO/IEC 15408); complication or comorbidity (for MS-DRGs)
CCA	certified cost accountant
CCC	cash conversion cycle
CCEVS	Common Criteria Evaluation and Validation Scheme
CCHIT	Certification Commission for Healthcare Information Technology
CCU	critical care unit
CDC	Centers for Disease Control and Prevention
CDH	consumer-directed health care
CDHP	consumer-directed health-care plan
CDPM	clinical data project manager
CDSS	clinical decision support system
CEO	chief executive officer
CF	conversion factor
CFA®	Chartered Financial Analyst®
CFO	chief financial officer

CFR	Code of Federal Regulations
CHAMP	Children's Health and Medicare Protection Act (2007)
CHAMPUS	Civilian Health and Medical Program of the Uniformed Services
CHE	certified health-care executive
CHIPS	Center for Healthcare Industry Performance Studies
CIA	corporate integrity agreement
CIO	chief information officer
CIP	Customer Identification Program
CIS	computer information systems
CLIA	Clinical Laboratory Improvement Act
CLT	capitation liability theory
CME	continuing medical education
CMI	case mix index
CMIO	chief medical information officer
CMIS	contribution margin income statement
CMN	Certificate of Medical Necessity
CMP™	Certified Medical Planner™
CMS	Centers for Medicare and Medicaid Services (formerly HCFA)
COD	cash on delivery
COGME	Council of Graduate Medical Education
COH	cash on hand
COLA	cost-of-living allowance
CON	certificate of need
COO	chief operating officer
COSO	Committee of Sponsoring Organizations
COTS	commercial off the shelf
CPHQ	certified physician in health-care quality
CPIM	certificate in production and inventory management
CPI-U	consumer price index—urban
CPM	critical (clinical) path method
CPOE	computerized physician order entry (system)
CPR	computer-based patient record
CPT	Current Procedural Terminology
CQI	continuous quality improvement
CRL	certification revocation list
CRM	customer relationship management
CRVS	California Relative Value Studies
CSO	chief security officer
CT scan	computed tomography scan (also called CAT scan)
CUSIP	Committee on Uniform Security Identification Procedures
CVE	common vulnerabilities and exposures
CVPA	cost–volume–profit analysis
CY	calendar year
DAC	discretionary access control
DBMS	database management system
DCF	discounted (net) cash flow
DEA	Drug Enforcement Agency

DES disease-specific care
DHHS Department of Health and Human Services
DHMR Designated Healthcare Management Representative
DIO days inventory outstanding
DLH doctor labor hour
DME durable medical equipment
DNFB discharged, not finally billed
D&O directors' and officers'
DO doctor of osteopathy
DOA dead on arrival
DoD Department of Defense
DOJ Department of Justice
DOT Department of Transportation
DPH Department of Public Health
DPM doctor of podiatric medicine
DPO days payable outstanding
DPP direct participation program
DRA Deficit Reduction Act (2005)
DRG diagnosis-related group
DSH disproportionate share hospital (adjustment)
DSO days sales outstanding
DSS decision support system
DVP delivery versus payment
DWC days working capital
EAP employee assistance program
EBDIT earnings before depreciation, interest, and taxes
EBM evidence-based medicine
ECP exposure control plan
ED emergency department
EDI electronic data interchange
EDSS executive decision support system
EEOC Equal Employment Opportunity Commission
EHCR Efficient Healthcare Consumer Response Report
EHO emerging health-care organization
EHR electronic health record
EIN employer identification number
E&M evaluation and management
EMR electronic medical record(s)
EMTALA Emergency Medical Treatment and Active Labor Act
EOB explanation of benefits
EOMB explanation of Medicare benefits
EOQ economic order quantity
EOQC economic order quantity cost (analysis)
EPA Environmental Protection Agency
ePHI electronic personal health information
EPO exclusive provider organization
EPR electronic patient record

EPRI	Emergency Preparedness Resource Inventory
ERISA	Employee Retirement Income Security Act
ERP	enterprise resource planning
FACT Act	Fair and Accurate Credit Transactions Act (2003)
FAR	federal acquisition regulation
FASB	Financial Accounting Standards Board
FBCA	Federal Bridge Certification Authority
FC	fixed cost
FCA	False Claims Act
FDA	Food and Drug Administration
FEHBP	Federal Employees Health Benefits Program
FF&E	furniture, fixtures, and equipment
FFS	fee for service
FGIC	Financial Guaranty Insurance Company
FHA	Federal Housing Administration
FIFO	first in, first out
FIPS	Federal Information Processing Standard
FMAP	Federal Medical Assistance Percentage
FMLA	Family Medical Leave Act
FMV	fair market value
FTP	file transfer protocol
FV	fair value
FY	fiscal year
GAAP	generally accepted accounting principles
GAO	(U.S.) Government Accountability Office (name changed in 2004 from *General Accounting Office*)
GDP	gross domestic product
GIGO	garbage in, garbage out
GMC	guaranteed mortgage certificate
GNMA	Government National Mortgage Association
GNP	gross national product
GPWW	group practice without walls
GSA	General Services Administration
HARA	Healthcare Accounts Receivable Analysis (report)
HCCM	hierarchical condition category management
HCFA	(former) Health Care Financing Administration
HCFAC	Healthcare Fraud and Abuse Control (program)
HCFMA	Health Care Financial Management Association
HCPCS	Healthcare Common Procedure Coding System
HCSS	Health-care staffing service
HD-HCP	high-deductible health-care plan
HEDIS	Health Plan Employer Data and Information Set
HFMA	Healthcare Financial Management Association
HH	home health
HHA	home health agency
HHCA	home health-care agency
HHRG	home health resource group

(D)HHS	(Department of) Health and Human Services
HIM	health information management
HIMSS	Health Information and Management Systems Society
HIPAA	Health Insurance Portability and Accountability Act (1996)
HIPDB	Healthcare Integrity and Protection Data Bank
HIPPS	health insurance prospective payment system
HIS	hospital information system
HISAC	Healthcare Information Sharing and Analysis Center
HIT	health-care information technology
HMMIS	hospital materials management information system
HMO	health maintenance organization
HOPPS	hospital outpatient prospective payment system
HR	human resources
HSA	health systems agency; also health savings account
HSG	hospital service group
HSRV	hospital-specific relative value
I&A	identification and authentication
IBA	Institute of Business Appraisers
IBNR	incurred but not reported (expenses)
ICD-9-CM	International Classification of Diseases, Ninth Revision, Clinical Modification (10-CM)
ICP	inventory conversion period
ICSI	Institute for Clinical Systems Improvement
IDS	integrated delivery system; also intrusion detection system
IDTF	independent diagnostic testing facility
IHS	Indian Health Services
IME	indirect medical education (adjustment)
IOM	Institute of Medicine
IPA	Independent Physician Association; also Independent Practice Association
IPPS	(Medicare) inpatient prospective payment system
IRB	institutional review board
IRC	Internal Revenue Code
IRR	internal rate of return
IRS	Internal Revenue Service
ISAC	Information Sharing and Analysis Center
ISMS	information security management system
ISO	International Standards Organization
ISP	Internet service provider
I-SPY Act	Internet Spyware Prevention Act
IT	information technology
ITL	Information Technology Laboratory
ITR	inventory turnover ratio
JAMA	*Journal of the American Medical Association*
JCAHO	(former) Joint Commission on Accreditation of Healthcare Organizations (now known as the *Joint Commission* [TJC])
JIT	just in time (inventory management)

LAN	local area network
LCC	life-cycle cost
LEP	limited English proficiency
LIFO	last in, first out
LIS	laboratory information systems
LISW	licensed independent social worker
LLC	limited liability company
LLP	limited liability partnership
LMFT	licensed marriage and family therapist
LOS	length of stay
LPCC	licensed professional clinical (mental health) counselor
LPN	licensed practical nurse
LRAC	long-range average cost
LRRA	Liability Risk Retention Act
LSP	limited service provider
LTCPP	long-term care pharmacy provider
LVN	licensed vocational nurse
MABC	medical activity-based costing
MAC	monitored anesthesia care; also mandatory access control
MB	marginal benefit
MBT	Mechanical Biological Treatment (organization)
MC	marginal cost
MCC	major complication or comorbidity
MCM	mixed-cost method
MCO	managed care organization
MCS	Monte Carlo simulation
MD	medical doctor
MDC	major diagnostic category
MEC	modified endowment contract
MedPAC	Medicare Payment Advisory Commission
MGMA	Medical Group Management Association
MI	medical informatics
MIS	management information services
MLIC	malpractice liability insurance component
MMA	Medicare Prescription Drug, Modernization, and Improvement Act (2003)
MMCO	Medicare managed care organization
MOE	maximum office efficiency
MPCA	medical practice cost analysis
MPT	modern portfolio theory
MR	medical records; also marginal revenue
MSA	medical savings account
MSCI	Metals Service Center Institute
MS-DRG	Medicare Severity DRG
MSDS	material safety data sheet
MSO	management services organization
MUD	medically unnecessary day
MVO	mean variance optimization

NACVA	National Association of Certified Valuation Analysts
NAHC	National Association of Healthcare Consultants
NAICS	North American Industry Classification System
NAIP	National Association of Inpatient Physicians
NASD	National Association of Securities Dealers
NASDAQ	National Association of Securities Dealers Automated Quotations
NAT	network address translation
NAV	net asset value
NBER	National Bureau of Economic Research
NCFFR	National Commission on Fraudulent Financial Reporting
NCPDP	National Council for Prescription Drug Programs
NCQA	National Committee for Quality Assurance
NCUA	National Credit Union Administration
NCVHS	National Committee on Vital and Health Statistics
NDC	National Drug Code
NEJM	*New England Journal of Medicine*
NGC	National Guideline Clearinghouse
NIAP	National Information Assurance Partnership
NIC	net interest cost
NIOSH	National Institute of Occupational Safety and Health
NIS	net income statement
NISAC	National Infrastructure Simulation and Analysis Center
NIST	National Institute of Standards and Technology
NOW	negotiable order of withdrawal account
NPDB	National Practitioner Data Bank
NPI	National Provider Identification (number)
NPP	notice of privacy practices
NPS	national provider system
NPV	net present value
NQF	National Quality Forum
NRC	National Research Council
NRV	net realized accounts-receivable value
NSA	National Security Agency
NTFS	new technology file system
NTPA	net target profit analysis
NYSE	New York Stock Exchange
OBO	order book official
OBRA	Omnibus Budget Reconciliation Act (1989)
OCC	Option Clearing Corporation
OCR	optical character recognition; also Office of Civil Rights
OFAC	Office of Foreign Assets Control
OFPP	Office of Federal Procurement Policy
OID	original issue discount
OIG	Office of the Inspector General (U.S. Department of Health and Human Services)
OMB	Office of Management and Budget
OPHC	Office of Prepaid Health Care

OPIM	other potentially infectious material
OPPS	outpatient prospective payment system
OR	operating room
OS	operating system
OSHA	Occupational Safety and Health Administration
OSI	open systems interconnect
OSJ	Office of Supervisory Jurisdiction
OTC	over the counter
P4P	pay for performance
P/E	price to earnings (ratio)
P/R	price to revenue (ratio)
PAC	planned amortization certificate
PAY	postacquisition year
PC	(mortgage) participation certificate; also personal computer
PCC	project cost of capital
PCMCIA	Personal Computer Memory Card International Association
PCP	primary care physician
PDA	personal digital assistant
PDX	patient data exchange
PE(C)	practice expense (component)
PEO	professional employer organization
PFS	patient financial services
PG	purchasing group
PHA	public housing authority
PHI	protected health information
PHN	private health network
PHO	physician–hospital organization
PHR	patient health record
PIN	personal identification number
PIO	public information office
PKI	public/private key informatics/infrastructure
PKIX	public key infrastructure for X.509 certificates
PLIC	(mal)practice liability insurance component
PMG	primary medical group
PM/PM	per member per month
PO	purchase order
POC	point of care
POL	physician office laboratory
POS	point of service
POSP	point-of-service plan
PP	projection profile
PP&E	property, plant, and equipment
PPE	personal protective equipment
PPMC	physician practice management company
PPO	preferred provider organization
PPS	(Medicare) prospective payment system
PR	pregnancy and related conditions

PROM	programmable read-only memory
PSI	patient safety indicator
PSN	provider-sponsored network
PSO	provider-sponsored organization
Pt	patient
PTO	paid time off
PWC	physician work component
PY	projected year
QA	quality assurance
QI	quality improvement
RA	registration authority
RADIUS	remote authentication dial-in user service
RAN	revenue anticipation note
RBAC	role-based access control
RBRVG	resource-based relative value group
RBRVS	resource-based relative value scale
RBRVU	resource-based relative value unit
RDBMS	regional database management system
REIT	real-estate investment trust
RERVU	resource-based relative value unit
REV/PP	revenue per patient
RFI	request for information
RFID	radio-frequency identification device (scanner)
RFP	request for payment
RHIO	regional health information organization
RN	registered nurse
RNANS	Registered Nurses Association of Nova Scotia
ROE	return on equity
ROI	return on investment
ROM	read-only memory
ROP	reorder point
RRG	risk-retention group
RSNA	Radiological Society of North America
RUG-III	Resource Utilization Group III
RVS	relative value scale
RVUm	relative value unit—malpractice
RVUpe	relative value unit—practice expenses
RVUw	relative value unit—work
rWACC	relative weighted average cost of capital
S&P	Standard and Poor's
SaaS	Software as a Service
SAMHSA	Substance Abuse and Mental Health Services Administration
SAN	storage area network
SARS	severe acute respiratory syndrome
SBBI	Stocks, Bonds, Bills, and Inflation (Yearbook)
SCF	statement of cash flows
SCIM	supply-chain inventory management

SCM	supply-chain management
SCP	standard cost profile
SD	standard deviation
SDLC	system development life cycle
SDN	specially designated nationals
SDO	standards development organization
SEC	Securities and Exchange Commission
SERP	supplemental extended reporting policy
SESIP	sharps with engineered sharps injury protection
SHM	Society of Hospital Medicine
SIC	standard industrial code
SIPC	Securities Investor Protection Corporation
SLA	service-level agreement
SMA	special miscellaneous account
SMD	Society of Medical Dental Management Consultants
SMS	socioeconomic monitoring system
SMTP	simple mail transfer protocol
SNF	skilled nursing facility
SNMP	simple network management protocol
SP	special publication
SSH	single-specialty hospital
SSL	Secure Socket Layer
STP	standard treatment protocol
SVPN	secure virtual private network
TEL	Terror Exclusion List
TFC	total fixed cost
TIC	true interest cost
TIN	tax identification number
TLS	Transport Layer Security
TPA	third-party administrator
TQIM	total quality and improvement management
TQM	total quality management
UCC	Uniform Commercial Code
UCSF	University of California at San Francisco
UDP	user datagram protocol
UFS	Unix file system
UIIRC	University of Iowa Injury Prevention Research Center
UM	utilization management
UPIN	Unique Provider Identification Number
UR	utilization review
USPAP	Uniform Standards of Professional Appraisal Practices
v	variance
VA	Veterans Affairs
VAR	value at risk
VC	variable cost
VOC	volatile organic chemicals
VPN	virtual private network

WACC	weighted average cost of capital
WAN	wide area network
WHO	World Health Organization
WIA	weighted industry average
WORM	write once, read many

ACKNOWLEDGMENTS

To Mackenzie H. Marcinko of iMBA Inc.; Perry D'Alessio, CPA, CMP (Hon.), New York; and Daniel B. Moisand, CFP®, principal for Moisand Fitzgerald Tamayo, Melbourne, Florida.

FURTHER READINGS

Marcinko, DE and Hetico, RN: *Dictionary of Health Insurance and Managed Care*. Springer Publishing, New York, 2007.

Marcinko, DE and Hetico, RN: *Dictionary of Health Economics and Finance*. Springer Publishing, New York, 2008.

Marcinko, DE and Hetico, RN: *Dictionary of Health Information Technology and Security*. Springer Publishing, New York, 2009.

HEALTH-CARE ADMINISTRATION BLOGS

- *Candid CIO*: Will Weider, CIO of Ministry Health Care and Affinity Health System, offers his perspectives on administration issues in this blog.
- *Christina's Considerations*: Christina Thielst is a hospital and health-care administrator and entrepreneur with a deep desire for continually improving the health of the community being served. This is her blog.
- *Healing Hospitals—Formerly Ask a Hospital President:* F. Nicholas "Nick" Jacobs has more than 20 years' experience in hospital management, with an acknowledged reputation for innovation and consumer-centered leadership.
- *Hospital Impact*: Part of the Fierce network of health sites, this site is becoming popular among health-care administrators for its news updates, tips, and opinions on health-care matters.
- *Leading the Way to Medical Excellence*: The president of McLeod Health nonprofit institutions provides weekly insights into his facilities and health care in general.
- *Let's Talk Health Care*: Bruce Bullen, interim chief executive officer at Harvard Pilgrim in Massachusetts, provides and open and ongoing conversation about health-care administration.
- *Life as a Healthcare CIO*: Dr. John Halamka records his experiences with infrastructure, applications, policies, management, and governance as he supports 3000 doctors, 18,000 faculty, and about 3 million patients.
- *Managed Care Matters*: Joe Paduda shares his knowledge on managed care for group health, health policy, health research, and medical news for insurers, employers, and health-care providers.
- *More than Medicine*: Tom Quinn, president and CEO of Community General Hospital in Syracuse, New York, began his career as a hospital kitchen worker. His

perspective on administration reflects his knowledge on how hospitals work from every angle.

- *Regis University Health Services Administration Blog*: Learn more about a college health service through the blog provided by its health administrator, Michael Jackson.
- *Running a Hospital*: A CEO of a large Boston hospital shares thoughts on hospitals, medicine, and health-care issues.
- *St. Joseph Medical Center*: Chief executive officer at St. Joseph Medical Center in Missouri, Mr. Kashman, provides personal insight into administrative matters and general topics.
- *Todd's Perspective*: Todd Linden, president and CEO of Grinnell Regional Medical Center, offers insights into medical administration, and guest bloggers provide insight into various departments.
- *Wachter's World*: This blog focuses on hospitals, hospitalists, quality, safety, policy, and much more from Robert M. Wachter, MD, professor and associate chairman of the Department of Medicine at the University of California, San Francisco.

Legal Matters

- *Drug and Device Law*: This blog contains an attorney's personal views (and those of several other Dechert attorneys) on topics that arise in the defense of pharmaceutical and medical device product liability litigation.
- *Drug Injury Watch*: Learn more about drug injury lawsuits from an attorney who represents patients and their families.
- *FDA Law Blog*: Hyman, Phelps & McNamara, PC, is the largest dedicated food and drug law firm in the country. Their knowledge about laws and regulations governing drugs, medical devices, foods, dietary supplements, and cosmetics is helpful to anyone interested in these topics.
- *Health Care Law Blog*: Bob Coffield's expertise lies in helping businesses and health-care providers weave through a variety of state and federal health-care regulations and assisting them in business transactions.
- *Health Plan Law*: This site contains information about group health plans, claims administration, and related ERISA fiduciary issues. This site also contains tutorials.
- *HealthBlawg*: This is David Harlow's popular health-care law blog, offering expert insights and easy-to-understand analysis.
- *Healthcare Law Blog*: Holland & Hart's health-care practice provides insight into this arena, including HIPAA, Stark law, the Anti-Kickback Statute, and more.
- *HIPAA Blog*: Join in on this discussion of medical privacy issues often buried in "political arcana."
- *HIPAA, HiTech & HIT*: This updated blog brings insight into legal issues, developments, and other pertinent information that relates to the creation, use, and exchange of electronic health records.
- *HIT Blawg*: This blog is focused on national health information technology legal trends and current news on this topic.
- *Home Care Law Blog*: Learn more about legal and policy issues in the home health care, private duty, and hospice industries from Gilliland & Markette LLP.

- *Med Law Blog*: This law blog focuses on topics that range from compliance to contracts and from employee benefits to HIPAA and HIT.
- *Physician Law*: This blog provides an easy way to stay on top of current news, updates, and useful tips relating to legal issues that affect physicians and noninstitutional providers.

E-Health and Health IT

- *Chilmark Research*: This blog provides perspectives on key IT trends in the health-care sector.
- *davidrothman.net*: David is the information services specialist at the Community General Hospital Medical Library, but he also provides great ideas for 2.0 tools and tips for health-care industry professionals on this blog.
- *e-CareManagement blog*: Vince Kuraitis, owner of Better Health Technologies, LLC, has a passion for disease management and care coordination that dates back to 1995.
- *e-HealthExpert*: A nonprofit organization provides a free and open forum to support the development of expertise in the field of e-health, healthcare information systems, and health IT (clinical IT).
- *eHealth*: John Sharp is an IT manager for a major medical center in Northeast Ohio, with a focus on e-health, personal health records, Web 2.0 technologies, Windows Sharepoint Services, and project management.
- *Found In Cache*: If you would prefer a professional's take on social media matters, websites, and all things technological, then follow Ed Bennett, a technology expert for a Maryland medical care system.
- *Future Health IT*: A health IT and EPR advocate from the United Kingdom provides a format to discuss the future of health care and IT.
- *Informaticopia*: This UK blogger provides eclectic news and views on health informatics and e-learning.
- *MedGadget*: Stay ahead of the gadget curve with this site, which offers information about the newest health-care gadgets on the market as well as emerging medical technologies.
- *Neil Versel's health-care IT blog*: A health-care journalist provides his views on the major segment of the industry he covers—and, he provides a ton of links to other sites as well.
- *Schwartz health-care IT blog*: A variety of authors from Schwartz Communications provide insights into ways to use IT effectively within health-care facilities.
- *The Health IT Channel*: For a different perspective on IT and EHR as well as other health-care issues, watch a few videos at this site.
- *The Healthcare IT Guy*: The CEO of Netspective, a Java/.NET consultancy that specializes in health-care IT with an emphasis on e-health, EMRs, data integration, and legacy modernization, supplies tips and information for physicians and health-care administrators.

Appendix 4: Glossary of Health Information Technology and Security Terms

GLOSSARY OF IMPORTANT DEFINITIONS

Much has been written and much has been opined on the topic of health information technology, electronic health records, and medical security liability for physicians and health-care providers in this textbook. But occasionally, we all still get lost in a wide array of acronyms, jargons, and terms that are constantly changing in this ecosystem. And so, this glossary serves as a ready reference for those who want to know about these definitions in a quick and ready fashion.

Access control: The process of controlling the access of a user.

Access level authorization: Establishes a procedure to determine the computer or network access level granted to individuals working on or near protected health information, medical data, or secure health data.

Access security: To allow computer or health-care network entry using ID/password/secure socket layer (SSL) encryption/biometrics, etc.; unique identification and password assignments are usually made to medical staff members for access to medical information on a need-to-know basis, and only upon written authority of the owner of the data.

Accountability: The security goal that generates the requirement for actions of an entity to be traced uniquely to that entity. This supports nonrepudiation, deterrence, fault isolation, intrusion detection and prevention, and after-action recovery and legal action.

Accounting: Creating a historical record of who was authenticated, at what time, and how long they accessed the computer system.

Accredited standards committee: Organization that helps develop American National Standards (ANS) for computer and health information technology; accredited by ANSI for the development of American National Standards; ASC X12N develops medical electronic business exchange controls like 835-Health Care Claim Payment/Advice and 837-Health Care Claim.

Administrative simplification: The use of electronic standard code sets for health information exchange; Title II, Subtitle F of Health Insurance Portability and Accountability Act (HIPAA) gives HHS the authority to mandate the use of standards for the electronic exchange of health-care data; to specify what medical and administrative code sets should be used within those standards; to require the use of national identification systems for health-care patients, providers, payers (or plans), and employers (or sponsors); and to specify the types of measures required to protect the security and privacy of personally identifiable health-care and medical information.

Alternative backup sites: Off-site locations that are used for transferring computer operations in the event of an emergency.

American Health Information Management Association: A large trade association of health information and medical data management professionals.

American Medical Informatics Association: An organization that promotes the use of electronic medical management and health-care informatics for clinical and administrative endeavors.

American Telemedicine Association: Established in 1993 as a leading resource and advocate promoting access to medical care for patients and health professionals via telecommunications technology; membership open to individuals, companies, and other organizations with an interest in promoting the deployment of telemedicine throughout the world.

Antivirus software: A software package or subscription service used to thwart malicious computer or network attacks, such as Symantec, McAfee, Trend Micro, Panda Software, Sunbelt Software, Computer Associates, AVG, MS-FF, etc.

Antiworm: A software patch, fix; glitch repairer; do-gooder virus; slang term.

ASC X12N: HIPAA transmission standards, specifications, and implementation guides from the Washington Publishing Company; or the National Council of Prescription Drug Programs.

Assurance: Grounds for confidence that the other four security goals (integrity, availability, confidentiality, and accountability) have been adequately met by a specific implementation. *Adequately met* includes (1) functionality that performs correctly, (2) sufficient protection against unintentional errors (by users or software), and (3) sufficient resistance to intentional penetration or bypass.

Asymmetric cryptology: The use of two different but mathematically related electronic keys for secure health data and medical information storage, transmission, and manipulation.

Asymmetric encryption: Encryption and decryption performed using two different keys, one of which is referred to as the public key and the other one referred to as the private key; also known as public-key encryption.

Asymmetric key: A half of a key pair used in an asymmetric *public-key* encryption system with two important properties: (1) the key used for encryption is different from the one used for decryption; (2) neither key can feasibly be derived from the other.

Attack tree: An inverted tree diagram that provides a visual image of the attacks that may occur against an asset.

Audio teleconferencing: A multisimultaneous dual voice communications between two parties at remote locations; two-way communications between physician and patient at various locations.

Authentication: The process of verifying and confirming the identity of a user.

Availability: The security goal that generates the requirement for protection against intentional or accidental attempts to (1) perform unauthorized deletion of data or (2) otherwise cause a denial of service or data.

Back door: A means to access a computer program that bypasses security mechanisms, sometimes installed by a programmer so that the program can be accessed for troubleshooting or other purposes.

Back-door Trojans or BOTs: Currently, the biggest threat to health care and all PC users worldwide according to the MSFT Corporation.

Bandwidth: The amount of information that can be carried over a communications link.

Bar coding systems: Final FDA ruling issued in February 2004 that required bar codes on most prescription and nonprescription medications used in hospitals and dispensed based on a physician's order; the bar code must contain at least the National Drug Code (NDC) number, which specifically identifies the drug. Although hospitals are not required at this time to have a bar code reading system on the wards, this ruling has heightened the priority of implementing hospital-wide systems for patient–drug matching using bar codes.

Baud: A unit of digital transmission that indicates the speed of information flow. The rate indicates the number of events able to be processed in 1 second and is expressed as bits per second (bps). The baud rate is the standard unit of measure for data transmission capability; typical older rates were 1200, 2400, 9600, and 14,400 baud; the signaling rate of a telephone line in the number of transitions made in a second; 1/300 second = 300 baud.

Beta test: The secondary or final stress examination of newly developed computer hardware, software, or peripheral devices, site, etc.

Bibliographic database: Indexed computer or printed source of citations of journal articles and other reports in the literature; typically includes author, title, source, abstract, and/or related information; MEDLINE and EMBASE.

Bioinformatics: The application of medical and biological science to the health information management field.

Biological information technology: Cross-industry alliance of the Microsoft Corporation to enhance the ability to use and share digital health and biomedical data.

Biometric: Personal security identity characteristics, such as a signature, fingerprints, voice, iris or retinal scan, hand or foot vein geometry, facial characteristics, hair analysis, eye, blood vessel, or DNA; uses the unique human characteristics of a person as a means of authenticating.

Biometric identification: Secure identification using biometrics that identifies a human from a measurement of a physical feature or repeatable action of the individual (for example, hand geometry, retinal scan, iris scan, fingerprint patterns, facial characteristics, DNA sequence characteristics, voice prints, and handwritten signature).

Biopassword: Start-up health-care IT security pioneer of keyboarding patterns to boost online security through neural network patterns.

Bluetooth device: Machines, like cell phone with headset, transmitting across communications channels 1–14, over time.

Bluetooth technology: Wireless mobile technology standard built into millions of mobile phones, headsets, portable computers, desktops, and notebooks; named after Harold Bluetooth, a 10th-century Viking king; health-care telemetry and rural data transmissions; the Bluetooth Special Interest Group (BSIG) advocates measures aimed at pushing health-care interoperability for wireless devices and other computers designed for use in the medical field; other wireless stands include Wi-Fi, ZigBee, IrDA, and RFID.

Buffer: A temporary storage area.

Buffer overflow: A security breach that occurs when a computer program attempts to stuff more data into a temporary storage area than it can hold.

Business continuity plan: A plan that outlines the procedures to follow after a business experiences an attack on its security.

California Database Security Breach Act: A state act that requires disclosure to California residents if a breach of personal information has or is believed to have occurred.

Certification authority: An independent third-party organization that assigns digital certificates.

Chain of custody: A process that documents everyone who has had contact with or direct possession of the evidence.

Chain of trust: Suggestion that each and every covered entity and business associate share responsibility and accountability for confidential protected health information (PHI).

Chain of trust agreement: Contract entered into by two business partners in which it is agreed to exchange data and that the first party will transmit information to the second party, where the data transmitted are agreed to be protected between the partners; sender and receiver depend upon each other to maintain the integrity and confidentiality of the transmitted information; multiple two-party contracts may be involved in moving information from the originator to the ultimate recipient; for example, a provider may contract with a clearing house to transmit claims to the clearing house; the clearing house, in turn, may contract with another clearing house or with a payer for the further transmittal of those same claims.

Children's Online Privacy Protection Act: A federal act that requires operators of online services or websites directed at children under the age of 13 to obtain parental consent prior to the collection, use, disclosure, or display of a child's personal information.

Cipher lock: A combination lock that uses buttons that must be pushed in the proper sequence in order to open the door.

Clearing house: HIPAA medical invoice, health-care data transaction exchange, and medical data implementation service center that meets or exceeds federally mandated standardized Electronic Data Interchange (EDI) transaction requirements.

Clinger–Cohen Act: Public Law 104-106; Information Technology Management Reform Act (ITMRA) of 1996.

Clinical data: PHI from patient, physician, laboratory, clinic, hospital and/or payer, etc.; identifiable patient medical information.

Clinical data information systems: Automatic and securely connected system of integrated computers, central severs, and the Internet that transmits PHI from patient, physician, laboratory, clinic, hospital and/or payer, etc.

Clinical data repository: Electronic storehouse of encrypted patient medical information; clinical data storage.

Clinical informatics: The management of medical and clinical data; the use of computers, networks, and IT for patient care and health administration.

Clinical information: All the related medical information about a patient; PHI from patients, providers, laboratories, clinics, hospitals and/or payers or other stakeholders, etc.

Clinical information system: A computer network system that supports patient care; relating exclusively to the information regarding the care of a patient, rather than administrative data, this hospital-based information system is designed to collect and organize data.

Clinical regional health information system: Electronic entity committed to securely share private patient health information among entities like medical providers, clinics, laboratories, hospitals, outpatient centers, hospice and other health-care facilities; Community Health Management Information Systems (CHMIS), Enterprise Information Networks (EINs), Regional Health Information Networks (RHINs), and Health Information Networks (HINs).

Cold site: An alternative backup site that provides the basic computing infrastructure, such as wiring and ventilation, but very little equipment.

Compact disc-read-only memory (CD-ROM): A computer drive that can read CD-R and CD-RW discs.

Compact disc-recordable (CD-R): An optical disc that contains up to 650 megabytes of data and cannot be changed once recorded.

Compact disc-rewriteable (CD-RW): An optical disc that can be used to record data, erase it, and rerecord again.

Computer security: A computer or network that is free from threats against it.

Computerized physician order entry system: Automatic medical provider electronic medical chart ordering system that usually includes seven features: medication analysis, system order clarity, increased work efficiency, point of care utilization, benchmarking and performance tracking, online alerts, and regulatory reporting.

Confidential health information: PHI that is prohibited from free use and secured from unauthorized dissemination or use; patient-specific medical data.

Counter signature: The ability to prove the order of application of signatures; analogous to the normal business practice of signing a document that has already been signed by another party (ASTM E 1762-95); part of a digital signature.

Covered entity: 42 CFR § 164.504(e)(2)(i)(B). Any of three broadly defined entities that deal with PHI: providers, individuals or group health plans, and clearinghouses.

Cracker: A person who breaks into or otherwise violates the system security with a malicious intent.

Cryptography: The science of transforming information so that it is secure while it is being transmitted or stored.

Cyber-terrorism: Attacks by a terrorist group using computer technology and the Internet to cripple or disable a nation's electronic infrastructure.

Data backup: The process of copying data to another media and storing them in a secure location.

Data encryption standard: An older health or medical data private key cryptology federal protocol for secure information exchange; replaced by AES.

Data interchange standard: X12 HIPAA health data transmission standard format.

Data Interchange Standard Association: The organization that provides X12 HIPAA transmission standards and formats.

Deadbolt lock: A lock that extends a solid metal bar into the door frame for extra security.

Decision support system: Computer tools or applications to assist physicians in clinical decisions by providing evidence-based knowledge in the context of patient-specific data; examples include drug interaction alerts at the time medication is prescribed and reminders for specific guideline-based interventions during the care of patients with chronic disease; information should be presented in a patient-centric view of individual care and also in a population or aggregate view to support population management and quality improvement.

Decryption: Changing an encrypted message back to its original form.

Definition files: Files that contain updated antivirus information.

De-identified health information: Protected health information that is no longer individually identifiable health information; a covered entity may determine that health information is not individually identifiable health information only if (1) a person with appropriate knowledge of and experience with generally accepted statistical and scientific principles and methods for rendering information not individually identifiable determines that the risk is very small that the information could be used, alone or in combination with other available information, to identify an individual, and documents the methods and results of the analysis; or (2) the following identifiers of the individual, relatives, employers, or household members of the individual are removed.

Denial of service: The prevention of authorized access to resources or the delaying of time critical operations.

Designated record set: Contains medical and billing records and any other records that a physician and/or medical practice utilizes for making decisions about a patient; a hospital, emerging health-care organization, or other health-care organization is to define which set of information comprises *protected health information* and which set does not; contains medical or mixed billing records, and any other information that a physician and/or medical practice utilizes for making decisions about a patient. It is up to the hospital, EHO, or health-care organization to define which set of information comprises *protected health information* and which does not, though logically this should not differ from locale to locale. The patient has the right to know who in the lengthy data chain has seen their PHI. This sets up an audit challenge for the medical organization, especially if the accountability is programmed, and other examiners view the document without cause.

Designated standard: HIPAA standard as assigned by the department of HHS.

Device lock: A steel cable and a lock used to secure a notebook computer.

Digital certificate: A certificate that binds a specific person to a public key.

Digital imaging and communications in medicine: Technology broadband transmission imaging standards for x-rays, MRIs, CT and PET scans, etc.; health IT standard transmissions platform aimed at enabling different computing platforms to share image data without compatibility problems; a set of protocols describing how radiology images are identified and formatted that is vendor-independent and developed by the American College of Radiology and the National Electronic Manufacturers Association.

Digital radiology: Medical digital imaging applied to x-rays, CT, PET scans, and related noninvasive and invasive technology; broadband intensive imaging telemedicine.

Digital rights management: The control and protection of digital intellectual property.

Digital signature: Encrypted electronic authorization with verification and security protection; private and public key infrastructure; based upon cryptographic methods of originator authentication, computed by using a set of rules and a set of parameters so that the identity of the signer and the integrity of medical or other data can be verified.

Digital signature standard: Encryption technology to ensure electronic medical data transmission integrity and authentication of both the sender and the receiver; date and time stamps; public and private key infrastructure.

Digital versatile disc (DVD): A technology that permits large amounts of data to be stored on an optical disc.

Digital versatile disc-recordable (DVD-R): An optical disc technology that can record once up to 3.95 GB of data on a single-sided disc and 7.9 GB on a double-sided disc.

Digital versatile disc-rewriteable (DVD-RAM): An optical disc technology that can record, erase, and rerecord data and has a capacity of 2.6 GB (single side) or 5.2 GB (double side).

Disaster recovery plan: A process to restore vital health and/or critical health-care technology systems in the event of a medical practice, clinic, hospital, or health-care business interruption from human, technical, or natural causes; focuses mainly on technology systems, encompassing critical hardware, operating and application software, and any tertiary elements required to support the operating environment; must support the process requirements to restore vital company data inside the defined business requirements; does not take into consideration the overall operating environment; an emergency mode operation plan is still necessary.

Disc-rewriteable (DVD-RW): An optical disc technology that allows data to be recorded, erased, and rerecorded.

Disclosure: Release of PHI outside a covered entity or business agreement space, under HIPAA; the release, transfer, provision of access to or divulging of medical information outside the entity holding the information.

Due care: Managers and their organizations have a duty to provide for information security to ensure that the type of control, the cost of control, and the deployment of control are appropriate for the system being managed.

e-Health: Emerging field in the intersection of medical informatics, public health, and business, referring to health services and information delivered or enhanced through the Internet and related technologies; characterizes not only a technical development but also a state of mind, attitude, and a commitment for networked global thinking to improve health-care worldwide by using information and communication technology.

Electronic data interchange (EDI): Interhealth-care organization computer-to-computer transmission of business or health information in a standard format; direct transmission from the originating application program to the receiving, or processing, application program; an EDI transmission consists only of business or health data, not any accompanying verbiage or free-form messages; a standard format is one that is approved by a national or international standards organization, as opposed to formats developed by health industry groups, medical practices, clinics, or companies; the electronic transmission of secure medical and financial data in the health-care industrial complex; X12 and similar variable-length formats for the electronic exchange of structured health data. The Centers for Medicare and Medicaid Services (CMS) regulates security and EDI.

Electronic data interchange standards: The American National Standards Institute (ANSI) set of EDI standards known as the X12 standards. These standards have been developed by private sector standards development organizations (SDOs) and are maintained by the Accredited Standards Committee (ASC) X12. ANSI ASC X12N standards, Version 4010, were chosen for all of the transactions except retail pharmacy transactions, which continue to use the standard maintained by the National Council for Prescription Drug Programs (NCPDP) because it is already in widespread use. The NCPDP Telecommunications Standard Format Version 5.1 and equivalent NCPDP Batch Standard Version 1.0 have been adopted in this rule (health plans will be required to support one of these two NCPDP formats). The standards are designed to work across industry and company boundaries. Changes and updates to the standards are made by consensus, reflecting the needs of the entire base of standards users, rather than those of a single organization or business sector. Specifically, the following nine healthcare transactions were required to use X12N standard electronic claim formats by October 16, 2003.

Electronic health record: A real-time patient health record with access to evidence-based decision support tools that can be used to aid clinicians in decision making; the EHR can automate and streamline a clinician's workflow, ensuring that all clinical information is communicated; prevents delays in response that result in gaps in care; can also support the collection of data for uses other than clinical care, such as billing, quality management, outcome reporting, and public health disease surveillance and reporting; electronic medical record.

Electronic medical (MEDIA) claims: Usually refers to a flat file format used to transmit or transport medical claims, such as the 192-byte UB-92 Institutional EMC format and the 320-byte Professional EMC-NSF.

Electronic medication administrative record: Electrical file keeping computerized system for tracking clinical medication dispensation and use; integrated with TPAs, PBMs, robotic dispensing devices and CPOEs, etc.

Electronic prescribing: A type of computer technology whereby physicians use handheld or personal computer devices to review drug and formulary coverage and to transmit prescriptions to a printer or to a local pharmacy; e-prescribing software can be integrated into existing clinical information systems to allow physician access to patient-specific information to screen for drug interactions and allergies.

Electronic preventive services selector: A digital tool for primary care clinicians to use when recommending preventive services for their patients unveiled by the Department of Health and Human Services' Agency for Healthcare Research and Quality (AHRQ) in November 2006; designed for use on a personal digital assistant (PDA) or desktop computer to allow clinicians to access the latest recommendations from the AHRQ-sponsored U.S. Preventive Services Task Force; designed to serve as an aid to clinical decision making at the point of care and contains 110 recommendations for specific populations covering 59 separate preventive services topics; a real-time search function allows a clinician to input a patient's age, gender, and selected behavioral risk factors, such as whether or not they smoke, in the appropriate fields, while the software cross-references the patient characteristics entered with the applicable Task Force recommendations and generates a report specifically tailored for that patient.

Electronic signature: Various date and time-stamped electronic security verification systems, such as passwords, encryption, ID numbers, biometrics identifiers, etc.; electrical transmission and authentication of real signatories; signatory attribute that is affixed to an electronic health document to bind it to a particular entity; an electronic signature process secures the user authentication (proof of claimed health identity, such as by biometrics [fingerprints, retinal scans, handwritten signature verification, etc.], tokens, or passwords) at the time the signature is generated; creates the logical manifestation of signature (including the possibility for multiple parties to sign a medical document and have the order of application recognized and proven) and supplies additional information such as time stamp and signature purpose specific to that user; and ensures the integrity of the signed document to enable transportability, interoperability, independent verifiability, and continuity of signature capability; verifying a signature on a document verifies the integrity of the document and associated attributes and verifies the identity of the signer; there are several technologies available for user authentication, including passwords, cryptography, and biometrics (ASTM 1762-95).

Encryption: Changing the original text to a secret message.

Gigabytes (GB): Billions of bytes of data.

Gramm–Leach–Bliley Act: A federal act that requires private data be protected by banks and financial institutions.

Hacker: A person who possesses advanced computer skills and is adept at exploring computers and networks in order to break into them.

Health 1.0: This is the dying health-care system of yesterday and today. Information is communicated from doctors to patients. It is a basic business-to-consumer (B2C) website as the Internet became one big encyclopedia by aggregating knowledge silos. Some doctors maintain websites; others do not. Nevertheless, Health 1.0 has a command and control hierarchy; doctors on top of the pyramid, patients on the bottom.

Health 2.0: According to Matthew Holt (personal communication), Healthcare 2.0 may be defined as follows: "The foundation of Healthcare 2.0 is information exchange plus technology. It employs user-generated content, social networks, and decision support tools to address the problems of inaccessible, fragmentary or unusable health care information. Healthcare 2.0 connects users to new kinds of information, fundamentally changing the consumer experience (e.g., buying insurance or deciding on/managing treatment), clinical decision-making (e.g., risk identification or use of best practices), and business processes (e.g., supply-chain management or business analytics)."

And so, if Health 1.0 was a static book, Health 2.0 is a dynamic discussion.

Example: The power of the Internet is illustrated in the phenomenon of *crowdsourcing*. In this context, the term means to harvest the reach of social networking (wisdom of crowds) to solve a problem. A knowledge seeker asks a question and participants respond. For example, readers can participate on the http://www.MedicalExecutivePost.com site to improve the administration of any medical practice. And, http://www.PodiatryPrep.com is an example of how podiatrists connect for global board certification assistance.

Health 2.0 Plus: The *Dictionary of Health Insurance and Managed Care* defines this emerging hybrid as a bridge uniting the philosophy of contemporary Health 2.0 with futuristic Health 3.0 technologies. Cisco System's HealthPresence is one example developed in 2010 by Dr. T. Warner Hudson. Using the network as a platform, HealthPresence combines video, audio, and information to create an environment similar to what patients experience when they visit their own doctor.

Health 3.0: Soon, patients will be seeking not only information but also actionable intelligence—whether it is artificial or real. Patients will communicate almost as with another patient or doctor. The Internet won't just blindly do what we tell it to do—it will think and represent some amazing opportunities. For example, imagine your toilet running a SMAC 20 and then being instantly notified of the results by your smartphone? Or use your iPhone to send pictures and streaming videos of conditions for a second opinion (http://www.KnockingLive.com).

Health information technology: The application of information processing involving both computer hardware and software that deals with the storage, retrieval, sharing, and use of health-care information, medical data, and knowledge for communication and decision making.

Health information technology auditor: An expert who evaluates a health organization's computer systems to ensure the proper safeguards are in place to protect and maintain the integrity of the firm's data. While the position has existed since the mid-1960s, companies that previously employed just a handful of HIT auditors are now significantly adding to their ranks, sometimes doubling, tripling, or quadrupling current staff levels; much current demand is due to the Sarbanes–Oxley Act and other legislation aimed at improving corporate governance in the wake of major accounting scandals earlier in the decade; publicly traded hospital systems require the expertise of HIT auditors to meet ongoing compliance requirements; the Gramm–Leach–Bliley Act and the HIPAA, among other regulations, also are fueling the need for HIT auditors. Health IT auditors must have a general understanding of accounting principles and the strategic vision to ensure a health organization's HIT systems allow it to achieve its short- and long-term objectives. Many hospitals promote from within for this role. Health facilities that look outside the organization for these professionals usually seek candidates with experience, knowledge of health care of emerging technologies and issues, and increasingly certifications such as the certified information systems auditor (CISA) designation.

Health Information Technology Promotion Act: Legislation to accelerate the adoption of interoperable electronic health records by ensuring uniform standards, championed by Rep. Nancy Johnson, R-Conn. (H.R. 4157), which would codify the Office of the National Coordinator for Health Information Technology in statute and delineate its ongoing responsibilities; create exceptions to the fraud and abuse statutes to allow certain providers to fund health information technology equipment and services for other providers; and provide for a study of federal and state health privacy policies.

Health Insurance Portability and Accountability Act: A federal act that requires enterprises in the health sector to guard protected health information and implement policies and procedures to safeguard it.

Health Level Seven: An international community of health-care subject matter experts and information technology physicians and scientists collaborating to create standards for the exchange, management, and integration of protected electronic health-care information; the Ann Arbor, Michigan–based Health Level Seven (HL7) standards developing organization has evolved Version 3 of its standard, which includes the Reference Information Model (RIM) and Data Type Specification (both ANSI standards); HL7 Version 3 is the only standard that specifically deals with creation of semantically interoperable health-care information, essential to building the national infrastructure; HL7 promotes the use of standards within and among health-care organizations to increase the effectiveness and efficiency of health-care delivery for the benefit of all patients, payers, and third parties; uses an Open System Interconnection (OSI) and high level seven health-care electronic communication protocol that is unique in the medical information management technology space and modeled after the International Standards Organization (ISO) and American National Standards Institute (ANSI); each has a particular health-care domain such as pharmacy, medical devices, imaging, or insurance (claims processing) transactions. Health Level Seven's domain is clinical and administrative data.

Hot site: An alternative backup site that contains the same equipment as found in the organization's actual IT center.

Human firewall: An employee who practices good security techniques to prevent any security attacks from passing through them.

Incident response team: An employee team charged with gathering and handling the digital evidence of an attack.

Individually identifiable health information: Medical information that is created or received by a covered entity; relates to the physical or mental health condition of an individual, provision of health care or the payment for the provision of health care; identifies the individual or there is reasonable belief that the information can be used to identify the individual.

Information security: A computer or network that is free from threats against it.

Integrity: The security goal that generates the requirement for protection against either intentional or accidental attempts to violate data integrity (the property that data have when they have not been altered in an unauthorized manner) or system integrity (the quality that a system has when it performs its intended function in an unimpaired manner, free from unauthorized manipulation).

Intellectual property: Works created by others such as books, music, plays, paintings, and photographs.

IT-related risk: The net mission impact considering (1) the probability that a particular threat source will exercise (accidentally trigger or intentionally exploit) system vulnerability and (2) the resulting impact if this should occur. IT-related risks arise from legal liability or mission loss due to

- Unauthorized (malicious or accidental) disclosure, modification, or destruction of information
- Unintentional errors and omissions
- IT disruptions due to natural or manmade disasters
- Failure to exercise due care and diligence in the implementation and operation of the IT system

Key-in-knob lock: A basic lock that has the lock mechanism embedded in the knob or handle.

Keystroke logger: A type of hardware spyware that captures keystrokes as they are typed.

Logic bombs: A computer program that lies dormant until it is triggered by a specific event.

Lossless: To compress electronic digital data.

Malicious code: Programs that are intentionally created to break into secure computers or to create havoc after the computers are accessed.

Master patient index: Health-care facility composite that links and assists in tracking patient, person, or member activity within an organization (or health enterprise) and across patient care settings; hardcopy or electronic identification of all patients treated in a facility or enterprise and lists the medical record or identification number associated with the name; can be maintained manually or as part of a computerized system; typically, those for health-care facilities are retained permanently, while those for insurers, registries, or others may have different retention periods; a database of all the patients ever registered (within reason) at a facility; name, demographics, insurance, next of kin, spouse, etc.

Medically unbelievable event: Implemented on January 1, 2007, the CMS blockage of payments for medical services that make no sense based on *anatomic considerations* or medical reasonableness when the same patient, date of service, HCPCS code, or provider is involved; unlike other National Correct Coding Initiative (NCCI) edits, MUEs can't be overridden by a modifier because there will never be a scenario where the physician had a good reason to submit a claim for removing a second appendix from the same person; etc.

Megabytes (MB): Millions of bytes of storage.

Memory stick: USB flash or nonvolatile storage device; Sony CompactFlash, pen, or minidrive; flash card, smart media, slang terms.

Mesh: Medical Subject Headings, the controlled vocabulary of about 16,000 terms used for MEDLINE and certain other MEDLARS databases.

Minimum necessary: The amount of protected health information shared among internal or external parties determined to be the smallest amount needed to accomplish its purpose for use or disclosure; the amount of health information or medical data needed to accomplish a purpose varies by job title, CE, or job classification.

Minimum necessary rule: HIPAA regulation that suggests any PHI used to identify a patient, such as a social security number, home address, or phone number; divulge only essential elements for use in transferring information from patient record to anyone else that requires the information; especially important with financial information; changes the way software is written and vendor access is provided. The *minimum necessary* rule states the minimum use of PHI that can be used to identify a person, such as a social security number, home address, or phone number. Only the essential elements are to be used in transferring information from the patient record to anyone else that needs this information. This is especially important when financial information is being addressed. Only the minimum codes necessary to determine the cost should be provided to the financial department. No other information should be accessed by that department. Many institutions have systems where a registration or accounting clerk can pull up as much information as a doctor or nurse, but this is now against HIPAA policy and subject to penalties. The *minimum necessary* rule is also changing the way software is set up and vendor access is provided.

Mirror site: A secondary location identical to the primary IT site that constantly receives a copy of data from the primary site.

National health information network: The technologies, standards, laws, policies, programs, and practices that enable health information to be shared among health decision makers, including consumers and patients, to promote improvements in health and health care; vision for the NHII began more than a decade ago with publication of an Institute of Medicine report, The Computer-Based Patient Record.

The path to a national network of health-care information is through the successful establishment of regional health information organizations (RHIO).

National provider identifier (NPI): Originally was an eight-digit alphanumeric identifier. However, the health-care industry widely criticized this format, claiming that major information systems incompatibilities would make it too expensive and difficult to implement. DHHS therefore revised its recommendation, instead specifying a 10-position numeric identifier with a check digit in the last position to help detect keying errors. The NPI carries no intelligence; in other words, its characters will not in themselves provide information about the provider. More recently, CMS announced that HIPAA-covered entities such as providers completing electronic transactions, health-care clearinghouses, and large health plans must use only the NPI to identify covered health-care providers in standard transactions by May 23, 2007. Small health plans must use only the NPI since May 23, 2008. The proposal for a Standard Unique National Health Plan (Payer) Identifier was withdrawn on February 2006. (According to CMS, *withdrawn* simply means that there is not a specific publication date at this time. Development of the rule has been delayed; however, when the exact date is determined, the rule will be put back on the agenda.)

Network: A group of interconnected computers.

Notebook safe: A special safe secured to a wall or the trunk of a car used for storing a notebook computer.

Operating system hardening: Steps that can be taken to make a personal computer operating system more secure.

Optical disc: A disc that uses laser technology to record data.

Password: A secret combination of words or numbers that authenticates or identifies the user.

Patch: A software update to correct a problem.

Patch management: Tools, utilities, and processes for keeping computers up to date with new software updates that are developed after a software product is released.

Pharmacy information system: Drug tracking and dispensation-related health management information system for hospitals and health-care organizations.

Phishing: An attempt to fraudulently gather confidential information by masquerading as a trustworthy entity, person, or business in an apparently official e-mail, text message, or website; carding or spoofing; video vishing; phish-tank; vish-tank; slang terms.

Physical security: The process of protecting the computer itself.

Port scanning: Sending a flood of information to all of the possible network connections on a computer.

Ports: The network connections on a computer.

Preset lock: A basic lock that has the lock mechanism embedded in the knob or handle.

Privacy: The quality or state of being hidden, encrypted, obscure, or undisclosed; especially medical data or PHI.

Privacy act: Federal legislature of 1974, which required giving patient some control over their PHI.

Privacy enhanced mail: E-mail message standard protocol for enhanced medical, health data, or other security.

Privacy officer: A medical entity's protected client information and security officer; required by each covered entity to be responsible for "the development and implementation of the policies and procedures" necessary for compliance.

Privacy rule: The federal privacy regulations promulgated under the HIPAA of 1996 that created national standards to protect medical records and other protected health information. The Office of Civil Rights (OCR) within the Department of Health and Human Services (DHHS) regulates the privacy rules.

Privacy standards: Any protocol to ensure the confidentiality of PHI.

Private key system: A means of cryptography where the same key is used to both encrypt and decrypt a message.

Public key system: A means of cryptography where two keys are used.

Records, medical: 20 U.S.C. 1232g(a)(4)(B)(iv), all

- Psychotherapy notes recorded (in any medium) by a health-care provider who is a mental health professional documenting or analyzing the contents of conversation during a private counseling session or a group, joint, or family counseling session and that are separated from the rest of the individual's medical record; excludes medication prescription and monitoring, counseling session start and stop times, the modalities and frequencies of treatment furnished, results of clinical tests, and any summary of the following items: diagnosis, functional status, the treatment plan, symptoms, prognosis, and progress to date.
- Public health authority means an agency or authority of the United States, a state, a territory, a political subdivision of a state or territory, or an Indian tribe, or a person or entity acting under a grant of authority from or contract with such public agency, including the employees or agents of such public agency or its contractors or persons or entities to whom it has granted authority, that is responsible for public health matters as part of its official mandate.
- Required by law means a mandate contained in law that compels a covered entity to make a use or disclosure of protected health information and that is enforceable in a court of law. Includes but is not limited to court orders and court-ordered warrants; subpoenas or summons issued by a court, grand jury, a governmental or tribal inspector general, or an administrative body authorized to require the production of information; a civil or an authorized investigative demand; Medicare conditions of participation with respect to health-care providers participating in the program; and statutes or regulations that require the production of information, including statutes or regulations that require such information if payment is sought under a government program providing public benefits.

Regional health information organization: A multistakeholder organization that enables the exchange and use of health information, in a secure manner, for the purpose of promoting the improvement of health quality, safety, and efficiency; the U.S. Department of Health and Human Services sees RHIOs as the building blocks for the national health information network (NHIN) that will provide universal access to electronic health records; other experts maintain that RHIOs will help eliminate some administrative costs associated with paper-based patient records, provide quick access to automated test results, and offer a consolidated view of a patient's history.

Risk assessment: The process of identifying the risks to system security and determining the probability of occurrence, the resulting impact, and additional safeguards that would mitigate this impact.

Risk management: The total process of identifying, controlling, and mitigating information system–related risks. It includes risk assessment; cost–benefit analysis; and the selection, implementation, test, and security evaluation of safeguards. This overall system security review considers both effectiveness and efficiency, including impact on the mission and constraints due to policy, regulations, and laws.

Royalties: Payment to the owner or creator of intellectual property for their work.

Sarbanes–Oxley Act (SARBOX): A federal act that enforces reporting requirements and internal controls on electronic financial reporting systems.

Scanning: Locating a computer that can be broken into.

Script kiddies: Younger and less sophisticated users who break into a computer with malicious intent.

Secure virtual private network: Cryptographic tunneling protocols to provide the necessary health data confidentiality (preventing snooping), sender authentication (preventing identity spoofing), and message integrity (preventing message alteration) to achieve the medical privacy intended. When properly chosen, implemented, and used, such techniques can provide secure communications over unsecured networks.

Security: A set of health-care information technology system characteristic and mechanisms that span the system both logically and physically; electronic access control against unauthorized intervention, both friendly or malicious; encompasses all of the safeguards in an information system, including hardware, software, personnel policies, information practice policies, disaster preparedness, and the oversight of all these areas; the purpose of health information security is to protect both the system and the information it contains from unauthorized access from without and from misuse from within; through various security measures, a health information system can shield confidential information from unauthorized access, disclosure, and misuse, thus protecting privacy of the individuals who are the subjects of the stored data; security life cycle.

Security administration: The physical and electrical protection features of an IT health system needed to be managed in order to meet the needs of a specific installation and to account for changes in the health-care entities operational environment.

Security compromise: Physical or electronic data, file, program, or transmission error due to malicious miscreants or software interventions; health data confidentiality breach.

Security configuration: Measures, practices, and procedures for the safety of information systems that must be coordinated and integrated with each other and other methods, practices, and procedures of the organization established in order to credential safekeeping policy; provides written security plans, rules, procedures, and instructions concerning all components of a health-care entity's security; procedures must give instructions on how to report breaches and how those breaches are to be handled within the organization.

Security configuration management: The measurement of practices and procedures for the security of information systems that is coordinated and integrated with each other and other measures, practices, and procedures of the organization so as to create a coherent system of health data security (NIST Pub 800-14).

Security domain: A set of subjects, their information objects, and a common security policy; foundation for IT security is the concept of security domains and enforcement of data and process flow restrictions within and between these domains.

Security goals: The five security goals are integrity, availability, confidentiality, accountability, and assurance.

Security information system: Security is a system characteristic and a set of mechanisms that span the system both logically and physically.

Security policy: A formal written policy that outlines the importance of security to the organization and establishes how the security program is organized.

Share: An object that is shared with others over a computer network.

Signature files: Files that contain updated antivirus information.

Smart card: A device that contains a chip that stores the user's private key, login information, and public key digital certificate.

Sniffing: Listening to the traffic on a computer network and then analyzing it.

Social engineering: Relying on trickery and deceit to break security and gain access to computers.

Spam: Unsolicited e-mail messages.

Spy: A person who has been hired to break into a computer and steal data.

Spyware: Hardware or software that *spies* on what the user is doing and captures that activity without their knowledge.

Stealth signal transmitter: Software installed on a notebook computer that sends a signal that can be traced.

Threat: The potential for a threat source to exercise (accidentally trigger or intentionally exploit) a specific vulnerability.

Threat analysis: The examination of threat sources against system vulnerabilities to determine the threats for a particular system in a particular operational environment.

Threat modeling: A process of constructing scenarios of the types of threats that assets face.

Threat source: Either (1) intent and method targeted at the intentional exploitation of a vulnerability or (2) a situation and method that may accidentally trigger a vulnerability.

Token: A security device used to authenticate the user by having the appropriate permission (like a password) embedded into the device.

USA Patriot Act: A federal act designed to broaden the surveillance of law enforcement agencies to enhance the detection and suppression of terrorism.

Username: A unique identifier of a person used to access a computer system.

Virus: A program that secretly attaches itself to other programs and when executed causes harm to a computer.

Vulnerability: A flaw or weakness in system security procedures, design, implementation, or internal controls that could be exercised (accidentally triggered or intentionally exploited) and result in a security breach or a violation of the system's security policy.

Vulnerability assessment: A process to determine what vulnerabilities exist in the current system against these attacks.

Vulnerability assessment managed services: Agencies that use scanning devices connected to probe an organization's security to look for vulnerabilities.

War driving: A technique used to locate wireless local area networks (WLANs).

WiMAX: A more powerful version of Wi-Fi that can provide wireless Internet access over a wider geographic location such as a city; an acronym that stands for Worldwide Interoperability for Microwave Access and is a certification mark for products that pass conformity and interoperability tests for the IEEE 802.16 standards.

IEEE 802.16 is working group number 16 of IEEE 802, specializing in point-to-multipoint broadband wireless access.

Wireless hot spot: Specific geographic location in which an access point provides public wireless broadband network services; security is risky for PHI; hotspot.

Wireless local area networks: A computer network that uses radio waves instead of wires to connect computers.

Worm: A program that does not attach itself to other programs or need user intervention to execute.

ACKNOWLEDGMENTS

To Richard J. Mata, MD, MS, MI-CIS, CMP™ (Hon); Mackenzie H. Marcinko of iMBA Inc.; and Shahid N. Shah, MS, Washington, District of Columbia (http://www.healthcareguy.com).

Appendix 5: Sources of Medical Risk Management, Insurance Agent, Business, and Asset Protection Consulting Information

DEEP SUBJECT-MATTER SPECIFICITY REQUIRED

Hiring the right insurance agent, forensic accountant, and/or medical risk-management professional puts the physician in the position of providing a solid foundation on which to build a medical practice business entity, comprehensive and integrated financial plan, and economically successful life. Furthermore, the insurance agent, accountant, or risk manager may plug up risky need gaps not even known to exist. Hiring a good agent or manager also leverages time.

A5.1 INSURANCE COMPANY SELECTION

The physician may have heard of Standard & Poor's, Moody's, and A.M. Best, possibly as a result of doing research for an investment. These are companies that monitor the strengths and weaknesses of the thousands of insurance companies that conduct business in the United States (and around the world). For example, a company that specializes in selling life insurance will be rated according to their ability to pay outstanding death benefit obligations. A property and casualty (P&C) company, on the other hand, is rated on their ability to pay claims associated with property damages or losses. Independently, these rating services assign a rating to the insurance carrier based on their in-depth research.

A5.1.1 Financial Ratings

What do the financial strength ratings mean? It depends on the rating service. From our earlier example, Standard & Poor's rates companies from AAA (extremely strong) to CC (extremely weak). Within those ratings, they may also assign a subrating of a plus (+) or a minus (–), which reflects the company's strength or weakness within the corresponding strength rating. Here is a summary of the three ratings companies mentioned above. The categories are grouped to reflect the similar ratings classes for each company but may not show the actual wording used by the rating service.

	A.M. Best	Standard & Poor's	Moody's
Superior/excellent/strong	A++/A+/A/A−	AAA/AA+/AA/AA− A+/A/A−	Aaa/Aa 1–3
Very good/good	B++/B+/B/B−	BBB+/BBB/BBB−	A 1–3/Baa 1–3
Fair/moderate/marginal	C++/C+	BB+/BB/BB−	Ba 1–3
Weak/vulnerable	C/C−	B+/B/B− CCC+/CCC/CCC−	B 1–3
Poor/very poor/extremely weak	D	CC	Caa/Ca/C
State supervision/regulatory action	E	R	
Liquidation	F		

How important is the financial strength of an insurance company? Well, how important is it for a patient to be treated in one of the best-rated hospitals in America? The answer to these questions will likely vary with each physician-consumer. If someone is shopping for the least expensive insurance product, he/she may be willing to overlook a poor financial strength rating in order to get the least expensive price. On the other hand, if physician-consumers want a company that has an exceptional financial strength rating, they should be willing to pay a little more for the security of knowing that the company they have chosen has a good chance of being there to pay any future claims. For many doctors, it is worth a few extra dollars to get a little more peace of mind.

A5.1.2 Bankruptcy

What would happen if an insurance company goes bankrupt? Although a relatively rare occurrence, the bankruptcy of an insurance company is still a very real and frightening possibility. Think American International Group (AIG), circa the 2007–2008 financial meltdown. Normally, most cases of insolvency can be blamed on one of three circumstances: poor business decisions, corruption, or catastrophe.

Poor business decisions refer to how well a company invests its assets. Much like any business, a few bad economic cycles, coupled with mismanagement, can force an insurance company to declare bankruptcy. According to the National Organization of Life and Health Insurers Guaranty Associations (NOLHGA), only two companies were declared insolvent in 2000 due to poor investment-related business decisions and only one in 2001.

Unfortunately, corruption and embezzlement may occur. A recent case involved the loss of $950 million, included nine insurance companies, and spread through six southern states. This loss occurred when a company that was supposed to invest money for the nine insurers instead transferred it into a variety of untraceable accounts. As a result, over 100,000 policyholders were affected.

Catastrophes cannot be controlled or predicted. In the P&C industry, one natural disaster can wipe out a small company. According to the National Conference of Insurance Guaranty Funds, Hurricane Andrew alone caused 12 insolvencies.

So now that we know that the improbable can happen, what happens to the policyholder? The good news is that it is highly likely that a policyholder would receive insurance coverage, thanks to the state laws.

Every state has a *guaranty fund* or *guaranty association* created by law. This law assures that any insurance company bankruptcy will be *insured*, much like the Federal Deposit Insurance Corporation (FDIC) insures the potential insolvency of banks. Also similar to the FDIC, state guaranty funds will only protect a consumer's insurance interests up to a specified monetary limit, usually $300,000 for auto, home, and life policies. NOLHGA estimates that upward of 90% of all insurance policyholders affected by a bankruptcy will be fully protected.

In many instances, a financially stable insurance company may take advantage of an industry bankruptcy and purchase all or part of the financially troubled company, for a bargain price. The acquiring insurance company would then assume financial responsibility for the insolvent company's policyholders.

What should the medical professionals do if their insurance carrier becomes insolvent? Usually, no action is needed. Policyholders are usually contacted by the company, state guaranty association, or insurance department.

A5.1.3 Lawsuits

It seems we live in an age where lawsuits are very common and a natural cost of doing business—and unfortunately, the insurance industry is no exception. Lawsuits against insurance companies have lately involved misleading sales practices and improper compliance procedures.

The good news is that the industry is working at improving their reputation and increasing their collective commitment to compliance and sales practices. Not only are most companies more active in regulating themselves through various internal and external safeguards, but also, the states' insurance departments and court systems have taken a more active role in protecting the consumer in recent years.

A5.1.4 Insurance Agent Law and Types

Insurance agents work for the company and not the customer. Unlike doctors, attorneys, certified public accountants (CPAs), and the clergy, they are not fiduciaries acting in the best interest of the customer.

A *fiduciary* is defined as a legal or ethical relationship of trust between two or more parties. Typically, a fiduciary prudently takes care of life (physician), religion (clergy), or money (CPA) for another person. In a fiduciary relationship, one person, in a position of vulnerability, justifiably vests confidence, good faith, reliance, and trust in another whose aid, advice, or protection is sought in some matter. In such a relation, good conscience requires the fiduciary to act at all times for the sole benefit and interest of the one who trusts. A fiduciary duty is the highest standard of care, by either equity or law. A fiduciary (abbreviation *fid*) is expected to be extremely loyal to the person to whom he/she owes the duty (the *principal*), such that there must be no conflict of duty (i.e., sales commission or other nondisclosed fees) between fiduciary and principal, and the fiduciary must not profit from his/her position as a fiduciary (unless the principal consents). When a fiduciary duty is imposed, equity requires a different, arguably stricter, standard of behavior than the comparable tortuous duty of care by common law. It is said the fiduciary has a duty not to be in a situation where personal interests and fiduciary duty conflict, a duty not to be in a situation where his/her fiduciary duty conflicts with another fiduciary duty, and a duty not to profit from his/her fiduciary position without knowledge and consent. A fiduciary ideally would not have a conflict of interest.

On the other hand, the *law of agency* deals with a set of contractual relationships that involve a person, called the agent, that is authorized to act on behalf of another (called the principal) to create legal relations with a third party. Succinctly, it may be referred to as the equal relationship between a principal and an agent whereby the principal, expressly or implicitly, authorizes the agent to work under his/her control and on his/her behalf. The agent is thus required to negotiate on behalf of the principal or bring him/her and third parties into contractual a relationship. This branch of law separates and regulates the relationships between

- Agents and principals (internal relationship), known as the principal–agent relationship
- Agents and the third parties with whom they deal on their principals' behalf (external relationship)
- Principals and the third parties when the agents deal

Thus, the word *client* is not appropriate for insurance agent salesman. Their insureds are not clients; they are customers and nothing more. And, insurance agents are generally not consultants or advisors; they are (sales) agents.

A5.1.5 Insurance Agent Group Types

Insurance agents can be divided into groups based on the type of insurance that they sell and on their relationship to the firms that underwrite the policies that they sell. Agents often specialize in one particular field of insurance, such as homeowner's, life, car, health, disability, or malpractice insurance. Some agents work for just one insurer, while others sell products from a number of firms or are hired by the buyers of insurance to shop for policies on their behalf. Agents are also increasingly split between those who work as part of large agent pools and those who operate primarily as individuals.

Each type of insurance product has unique characteristics. The division between types of insurance makes it advantageous for a given agent to specialize in one or two types of insurance coverage. Health insurance is a particularly complicated product post Patient Protection and Affordable Care Act (PPACA), and insurance agents, or "navigators" selling this type of coverage, are apt to be less than precise and/or specialize in individualize policies. Agents in smaller communities or smaller agencies are more likely to sell products in different areas, as specialization makes less sense in those settings. All types of agents may sell secondary products as well, such as annuities or other investments.

A crucial distinction between different types of insurance agents stems from their relationship with the corporations underwriting the policies being sold. Some agents have exclusive relationships with one particular company. These agents may have access to preferential rates but are limited in the variety of products that they can sell. Such *captive* or *exclusive* agents represent a single insurance company or a specified group of insurance companies, meaning they can only offer you one quote, or price, for an insurance policy. These agents are easily identified, as the sign in front of their building is typically the name of a large insurer. These large insurance companies are typically advertised nationally on television. Captive agents are generally not employees of the insurance company they represent. These agents are paid a commission (or percentage) of the total price of your policy by the insurance company they place you with. Well-known examples of captive or exclusive insurance agents include Allstate, Farmers, and State Farm.

Independent agents represent as few as one insurance company or up to several dozen insurers. Independent agents are able to shop your insurance rate with all of the insurance companies they represent, similar to how a mortgage broker can shop your loan around with multiple lenders. Independent agents do not generally advertise nationally, nor do the companies they represent. Independent agents are not employees of the companies they represent. These agents are also paid a commission (or percentage) of the total price of your policy by the insurance company they place you with. There aren't any specific examples of these types of agents you would be aware of by name recognition, as they can be as unique as an individual agent's name. So you may see something like *John Davidson Insurance Agency*, *Mark One Insurance*, or *National Insurance Company of Georgia*. For the record, don't let a ".com" at the end of a name confuse you. Some independent agents sell only via the Internet.

Insurance brokers—Brokers represent the customer rather than the insurance companies. The difference between a broker and an independent agent is minimal. As with independent agencies, these companies can be named after an individual person or by any number of other names.

Insurance counselors (ICs)—ICs provide information and advice on insurance policies for clients. Counselors may become certified insurance counselors (CICs) and may act as agents or brokers for insurance products, which often requires holding a license from a regulatory agency. In addition, they may have a certification from a professional organization that promotes insurance counseling as a profession. This certification indicates that someone has met standards set by the organization, such as taking courses and demonstrating thorough knowledge of relevant topics on an examination. When clients meet with an IC, the counselor can read a policy or offer of coverage over to extract key information. This can be presented in a format the client clearly understands, making it easier to compare policies or select the best insurance. ICs may produce a written document with the key information about coverage and limits highlighted, and can also go over the material orally. Clients can ask questions about specific clauses to get more information about them. Another service offered by an IC can be suggestions on how to save money on insurance or get more complete coverage. This can include bundling insurance services, switching providers to take advantage of incentives, or taking a less publicized policy that offers better services. Clients working with an IC may be able to obtain policies more suitable for their needs for less money, depending on the specifics of the situation.

Fee-only approach—Almost every decision that you make affects the agent's commission, so how can you be sure that you are getting advice that is in your best interests rather than the agent's? But, a fee-only approach to life insurance planning and policy analysis, or other insurance products, is a unique alternative to astute physician clients who have lost confidence in commission-motivated insurance agent salesmen. Fee-only insurance advisors help clients answer questions like these:

- Is my agent recommending a good life insurance policy for me?
- Should I keep this policy that I own?
- Is life insurance a good investment?
- Should I buy an annuity?

Unlike commission-based agents, fee-only insurance advisors have no financial incentive to convince you to do something. They don't sell insurance products. They help clients make informed decisions about insurance, and clients pay them to give a complete picture of options. They have no incentive to downplay risks or to avoid discussing a better alternative. For example, some insurance policies don't pay a commission. Some policies let the agent decide what the commission will be; if the agent gets more, you get less. Some policies have a design that makes it foolish to pay more than the minimum premium in the first year. Fee-only insurance advisors work with your other financial advisors, including your agent, to help you make decisions that are right for you.

Direct writing system—This insurance option does not involve an agent. The people you work with are salespeople for the insurance company, whose duty is to sell insurance only for the company for which they work. Some examples of this type of insurance channel are GEICO and Progressive Direct. It's worth noting that Progressive also sells insurance through independent insurance agents (and they actually have two different rate classes).

Direct response—This system involves no agents or salespeople. Customers are solicited via direct mail, phone, or the Internet.

A5.2 INSURANCE AGENT SELECTION

More than half the nation's 3.25 million insurance agents are independent. That means they are not regularly audited or reviewed by the companies whose products they sell. And state regulators don't have the resources to chase after any more than the most outrageous agents. Unfortunately, it's the bad agents that have been in the news a lot in the past few years. Among the misdeeds, according to insurance and financial journalist Liz Pulliam Weston, are the following:

A5.2.1 Affinity Fraud

In April 2013, a Kansas insurance agent pleaded guilty to fraud charges after convincing at least 10 investors, including members of his church, to invest nearly $200,000 with him. The agent used the money to pay personal expenses, including payments in a bankruptcy plan. Targeting members of a religion, social, recreational, or ethnic group is known as *affinity fraud.*

A5.2.2 Promissory Note Scams

Hundreds of insurance agents were caught up in enforcement actions by 28 states, the Securities and Exchange Commission (SEC), and the North American Securities Administrators Association in recent years for selling so-called promissory notes to investors. Typically touted as low risk and conservative, the investments were actually high risk and often fraudulent. Regulators estimate that investors lost hundreds of millions of dollars.

A5.2.3 Illegal Investment Sales

Arizona regulators accused nine insurance agents in 2010 of selling unregistered securities, including promissory notes, viatical settlement policies, and interests in ATMs. Investor losses were estimated at more than $12 million. The Arizona Corporation Commission's

Securities Division suggested that the sweep was prompted by growing concerns about crossover abuses in the insurance and securities industries. In another action, Florida regulators levied similar charges against eight insurance agents who sold "certificates of grantor" contracts issued by a company that promised returns of 9.25–15% for 1- to 10-year investments. A related SEC filing charged that money from new investors was used to pay bogus returns to earlier investors in a classic Ponzi scheme. Investors lost an estimated $17 million.

The examples above don't include more routine insurance frauds, such as selling phony policies or pocketing policyholders' premiums. And they don't even touch on sales of legal but unsuitable investments—such as saddling elderly physicians and investors with high-risk, high-cost annuities.

A5.3 WHY REGULATORS TARGET INSURANCE AGENTS

A5.3.1 Insurance Agents Have a Built-In Customer Base (Book of Business)

Scam artists have figured out that many agents have large, loyal customer bases and that these agents can be lured to tap these customers when the commissions being offered are high enough. Insurance agents typically know details about their customers' financial lives that allow them to tailor their sales pitches, and they may have built up trust and rapport with these clients over many years.

A5.3.2 Many Physicians and Investors Are Looking for Yield and Safety

At the same time, the incomes and wealth of the most vulnerable people, senior citizens and mature doctors, have climbed in recent years. Because of the huge drop in interest rates since 2000, lower yields on legitimate investments have left many seniors and mature doctors vulnerable to pitches for *safe, high-return* alternatives. Unfortunately, the vast majority of insurance agents lack training in evaluating investments. That is apparently why so many couldn't figure out that *safe* and *high return* are mutually exclusive. Regulators and insurance insiders say that such a lack of financial sophistication means the agent is sometimes a victim along with the client. Many of the agents involved in the promissory note scam, regulators say, believed that the investments were legitimate and lost their own money as well as that of their customers.

So how can you avoid getting scammed? The easiest course is not to buy investments from an insurance agent. If approached about an investment, keep these things in mind:

- *Don't buy investments from someone who isn't licensed to sell them.* Fraudsters often erroneously claim that their investments aren't really securities. At the very least, your agent should have securities licenses if he/she is selling anything but insurance, and the investment itself should be registered with the SEC or your state's securities regulator. As the role of financial planning increases, many insurance agents are choosing to gain the proper licensing and certification to sell securities and other financial products. This includes passing an additional examination. Before agents can qualify as securities representatives, they must pass the General Securities Registered Representative Examination (Series 7 exam), administered by the National Association of Securities Dealers (NASD).

- *Call your state insurance and securities regulators.* Describe the investment to them and ask if they've heard of it. Regulators won't have heard of every new scam, of course, but you might avoid getting bitten by one that's been around awhile.
- *Ask what the agent will get paid and how that compensation compares to the other products he/she sells.* A reputable agent will talk to you about his/her commissions. Evasiveness on this issue should be a warning sign. When insurance agents or stockbrokers deliberately try to bury their fees, commissions, or expenses, it is known as "hiding the weenie."
- *Make sure your agent has some credentials.* If your agent is offering "advice," and you're not getting a second opinion from an independent agent, then make sure your agent has some designations to show he/she has done more than study a sales brochure. Credentials aren't a necessity, but they are a way in which good agents typically distinguish themselves. Because insurers tend to set prices uniformly, you can't really play one advisor against the next. If they both quote policies from XYZ American Life, your costs should be nearly identical; it will only be by searching for more and different providers that an agent may be able to create an edge. Since you will pay roughly the same regardless of the agent working with you, choosing someone with a high degree of professional achievement whose expertise might help you find ways to make your coverage more efficient helps to ensure you'll get the most for your money. The other key reason to pursue agents with credentials is the codes of conduct and ethics that generally go with membership in these groups. Insurance agents are dual agents, working on your behalf while representing the insurer; they are supposed to serve the best interests of both masters. Professional standards certainly give them perspective that makes it easier to walk that tightrope. For life insurance agents, the Chartered Life Underwriter® (CLU®) and Chartered Financial Consultant® (ChFC®) designations are generally considered the top credentials. Both are administered by the American College, with the ChFC being the financial services add-on to the insurance-oriented CLU mark. Agents who have one or both of these credentials agree to abide by the college's code of ethics and conduct. A Chartered Property Casualty Underwriter® (CPCU®) has completed property and liability coverage education requirements from the American Institute for Chartered Property Casualty Underwriters, a group that has a strict code of professional ethics. Insurance is one area where advisors often have subspecialties, and there seems to be an association for each of those groups. There's the Association of Health Insurance Advisors or the Association for Advanced Life Underwriting. That said, the overarching group for many of these niche specializations is the National Association of Insurance and Financial Advisors. Membership does not require the same kind of training as some of the other programs, but there is a code of conduct to follow. Beyond the credentials, insurance agents frequently pursue financial planning designations, such as the Certified Financial Planner® (CFP®) mark. This is helpful, but you need to make sure that the agent understands the role you expect him/her to play, especially if you already have a financial planner to oversee your personal finance needs.
- *Demand to know the downside.* Agents know that dwelling on an investment's drawbacks can kill a sale, so they might not even bring up negatives, even when they're supposed to. So you have to ask, and keep asking until you get answers that

make sense. Every investment has its risks and its drawbacks. Know those specifics before you invest.

- *Look for the deep-pocketed third party.* Any investment should be backed by a bank, brokerage, or insurance company. Of course, this won't eliminate all possibility of fraud; well-known banks and brokerages can scammed, too. But at least you'll have somebody with deep pockets to sue.

A5.4 MAKING THE RIGHT INSURANCE AGENT HIRE

Besides deciding on an insurance company, another important decisions to be made when considering the purchase or review of insurance is choosing the agent, broker, or insurance licensed financial planner to work with. There are a number of issues to keep in mind when considering an insurance advisor:

- *Titles*: Beware of misleading titles. There are many "agents" using fancy titles. Don't be afraid to ask about what the titles (or sometimes just initials) mean and how they were earned or awarded. Most meaningful designations are awarded following the completion of a series of courses and exams. There are, however, some that are used after the agent merely pays a fee and joins an organization.
- *Experience*: Ask the prospective agent or broker about his/her background. How long has he/she been in the insurance or financial services industry? If he/she was a car salesman 3 months ago, it's reasonable to consider getting a second opinion on any recommendation. This would be especially true if the deal sounds too good to be true.
- *Education*: Agents and brokers are both encouraged and required to continue their insurance and financial planning education, not only to keep their various state insurance licenses but also to maintain certain designations. For example, to maintain the right to use the designations of CLU, ChFC, CFP, and Certified Medical Planner™ (CMP™), the bearer must periodically report that the required number of *continuing-education* course hours have been completed.

A5.4.1 Brokers versus Agents

Simply put, a broker is a representative of the consumer. Brokers are supposed to have the best interest of their clients in mind when making a recommendation for insurance protection. They normally have a number of different companies and products to choose from in order to meet their clients' needs.

A traditional agent represents the company for which he/she works, although he/she should also have the best interests of the client in mind. Many P&C insurance companies still have what are referred to as *captive* agents, and they are usually restricted as to which company's products they can offer for sale to clients. As a whole, the life insurance industry is moving away from having a large number of captive agents. Most insurance transactions today are conducted by agents with no real allegiance to a particular company. The exception is possibly for the few agents that seem to gravitate toward the companies that pay the most commissions.

A5.4.2 Commissions

It would be impossible to cover all of the variations of compensation schedules and payment arrangements within the insurance industry. There are, however, a few general rules that may be worth thinking about.

Some insurance companies have begun providing a base salary to their agents with incentive bonuses for superior performance. This is intended to remove the perceived evil of a commission-oriented recommendation. This cutting-edge concept has not yet been embraced by a large percentage of the career insurance industry. The top insurance professionals normally prefer a pure commission structure for the unlimited potential income.

Another attempt by life insurance companies to keep the size of the commission from influencing any recommendation for coverage is that of *levelized* commissions. Here, rather than the insurance company paying 80–110% of the first-year premium as a commission, the agent receives a level 10–15% for the first 10 policy years. Although this is common practice in P&C companies, it has not been universally accepted by life insurance companies.

As a general rule, agents are paid a lower commission in exchange for the insurance company providing office space, training, resource equipment, administrative help, and so on. Although this has been the preferred manner of distribution for many large insurance companies in the past, many companies are beginning to abandon this structure in favor of the less costly brokerage distribution system.

Brokers are truly independent salespeople. Unlike agents, they will usually receive a larger commission because of their anticipated expense of being independent. They must pay for office space, administrative support, and equipment, from their commissions.

A5.4.3 The State Corporation Commission—Insurance Department

What do the various states' insurance departments do? The states' insurance departments have the primary responsibility of providing protection for policyholders due to the insolvency of an insurance company. Beyond that, they have a number of other responsibilities, including

- Regulating the licensing of and the continuing education of insurance professionals. As discussed earlier, insurance brokers and agents are typically required to continue their education. Each state insurance department sets those requirements that must be met in order for agents or brokers to keep their licenses.
- Protecting the consumer from fraud and deceptive sales practices. State insurance departments have the job of protecting consumers from being harmed by insurance companies and their representatives. This includes policing the business practices of those insurance companies that are incorporated within their boundaries, along with keeping a watchful eye on how insurance products are presented to consumers by insurance professionals.
- Approval of products sold by an insurance company. When a company wants to begin sales in a state, they must begin with having each product for sale approved by the state insurance department. This includes the insurance contract and any application or supplemental forms related to each product. Getting a product approved in all 50 states can be quite a project as many state insurance departments have

different agendas and requirements. And simply because a product is *approved for sale* in a particular state does not mean it is a quality product.
- Punishment of companies and insurance professionals, including revocation of licenses and assessment of fines. It is also not uncommon for insurance companies to be fined for the unfair sales practices of their representatives. Agents and brokers can also be individually held responsible for breaking the insurance regulations of a particular state. Such punishment can include removal of state licenses.

A5.5 INSURANCE AGENT SPECIALIZATION

In the insurance world, there is no magic license that shows the world that a particular insurance agent is a good one, and nobody likes to pay insurance premiums. Inadequate coverage, however, can completely devastate a family by quickly wiping out a lifetime of asset accumulation. Buying and maintaining the right amount and type of coverage from solid insurance companies at a reasonable price eliminates these risks in a very efficient manner. Unfortunately, an essential and relatively simple concept like this risk transfer has evolved into an area that makes many people downright queasy. The saying goes "insurance is sold by agents, not bought by consumers." Nevertheless, there are two basic types of agents (personal and property).

A5.5.1 The Life Insurance Agent

Life insurance agents specialize in selling policies that pay beneficiaries when a policyholder dies. As we have seen, depending on the policyholder's circumstances, a cash-value policy can be designed to provide retirement income, funds for the education of children, or other benefits. Other times, a term policy may be more helpful. There are many other policy variations. Some life insurance agents also sell annuities that promise a retirement income. Health insurance agents sell health insurance policies that cover the costs of medical care and loss of income due to illness or injury. They may also sell dental insurance and short- and long-term disability insurance policies.

A5.5.2 The Property and Casualty Agent

Some insurance agents sell P&C insurance. P&C agents sell policies that protect doctors and their practices from financial loss resulting from automobile accidents, fire, theft, storms, and other events that can damage property. For private practitioners, P&C insurance can also cover injured workers' compensation, product liability claims, or medical malpractice claims.

A good P&C agent is needed to protect your home and medical practice. The P&C agent should have an array of carriers with which the business can be placed. One should not hesitate to place different types of coverage with different insurers. Most insurance companies will offer a discount if you place multiple coverages with them. However, this may not be as beneficial as insuring each need with a specialist.

There is a plethora of insurance designations that are narrow in scope and drift away from life and P&C insurance, irrelevant to most physician families' needs, or thin on quality content. Credentials and verification can be obtained from

The American College
(The American College of Financial Service Professionals)
270 S Bryn Mawr Avenue
Bryn Mawr, PA 19010
Phone: 610-526-1000
http://www.theamericancollege.edu

These include Certified Employee Benefits Specialist (CEBS), Registered Health Underwriter® (RHU®), and Certified Insurance Counselor (CIC), and a host of others like ChHC, REBC, CASL, ChSNC, RICP, FSCP, MSFS, and PhD.

For more information about life insurance credentials, contact

- National Alliance for Insurance Education and Research, PO Box 27027, Austin, TX 78755
- LIMRA International, PO Box 203, Hartford, CT 06141
- Independent Insurance Agents of America, 127 S Peyton St., Alexandria, VA 22314; Internet: http://www.iiaa.org
- Insurance Vocational Education Student Training (InVEST), 127 S Peyton St., Alexandria, VA 22314
- National Association of Professional Insurance Agents, 400 N Washington St., Alexandria, VA 22314

For more information about health insurance credentials, contact

- National Association of Health Underwriters, 2000 N 14th St., Suite 450, Arlington, VA 22201; Internet: http://www.nahu.org
- Health Insurance Association of America, 555 13th St. NW, Suite 600 East, Washington, DC 20004; Internet: http://www.hiaa.org

For more information on P&C insurance credentials, contact

- Insurance Information Institute, 110 William St., New York, NY 10038; Internet: http://www.iii.org

For more information on fee-only, and unbiased, insurance advisors who sell no products and accept no commissions, contact

Glenn S. Daily
New York, NY
http://www.glenndaily.com

Peter Katt
Katt & Company
Mattawan, MI

A5.5.2.1 List of Insurance Commissioners by State

Alabama
State Insurance Commissioner's Office
Alabama Department of Insurance
135 S Union St.
Montgomery, AL 36130
Main phone: 334-269-3550
Fax: 334-241-4192

Alaska
State Insurance Commissioner's Office
Alaska Department of Commerce and Economics
PO Box 110805
Juneau, AK 99811-0805
Main phone: 907-465-2515
Fax: 907-465-3422

Arizona
State Insurance Commissioner's Office
Arizona Department of Insurance
2910 N 44th St.
Suite 210
Phoenix, AZ 85018-7256
Main phone: 602-912-8400
Fax: 602-912-8452

Arkansas
State Insurance Commissioner's Office
2100 W 3rd St.
Little Rock, AR 72201-1904
Main phone: 501-371-2600
Fax: 501-371-2618

California
State Insurance Commissioner's Office
California Department of Insurance
300 Capital Mall
Suite 1500
Sacramento, CA 95814
Main phone: 916-492-3500
Fax: 916-445-4280

Colorado
State Insurance Commissioner's Office
Colorado Department of Insurance
Colorado Division of Insurance
1560 Broadway
Suite 850
Denver, CO 80202
Main phone: 303-894-7499
Alternate phone: 800-930-3745
Fax: 303-894-7455

Connecticut
State Insurance Commissioner's Office
Connecticut Department of Insurance
PO Box 816
Hartford, CT 06142-0816
Main phone: 860-297-3802
Fax: 860-566-7410

Delaware
State Insurance Commissioner's Office
PO Box 7007
841 Silver Lake Blvd.
Rodney Building
Dover, DE 19903
Main phone: 302-739-4251
Fax: 302-739-5280

District of Columbia
District of Columbia Department of Insurance
Insurance Administration
441 Fourth St., NW
8th Floor North
Washington, DC 20001
Main phone: 202-727-8000 ext. 3018
Fax: 202-535-1196

Florida
State Insurance Commissioner's Office
Florida Department of Financial Services
200 East Gaines Street
Tallahassee, FL 32399
1-877-MY-FL-CFO (1-877-693-5236)
Out of State: (850) 413-3089

Georgia
State Insurance Commissioner's Office
2 Martin Luther King Jr. Dr.
Floyd Memorial Building
Atlanta, GA 30334
Main phone: 404-656-2056
Fax: 404-657-8542

Hawaii
State Insurance Commissioner's Office
Hawaii Department of Insurance
Department of Commerce and Consumer Affairs
250 S King St.
5th Floor
Honolulu, HI 96813
Main phone: 808-586-2790
Fax: 808-586-2806

Idaho
Idaho Department of Insurance
PO Box 83720
Boise, ID 83720-0043
Main phone: 800-721-3272

Illinois
State Insurance Commissioner's Office
Illinois Department of Insurance
320 W Washington St.
4th Floor
Springfield, IL 62767
Main phone: 217-785-4515
Fax: 217-782-5020

Indiana
State Insurance Commissioner's Office
Indiana Department of Insurance
311 W Washington St.
Suite 300
Indianapolis, IN 46204-2787
Main phone: 317-232-2385
Fax: 317-232-5251

Iowa
State Insurance Commissioner's Office
Iowa Division of Insurance
Lucas State Office Building
6th Floor
Des Moines, IA 50319
Main phone: 515-281-5705
Fax: 515-281-3059

Kansas
State Insurance Commissioner's Office
Kansas Department of Insurance
420 SW 9th St.
Topeka, KS 66612-1678
Main phone: 785-296-7801
Fax: 785-296-2283

Kentucky
State Insurance Commissioner's Office
PO Box 517
215 W Main St.
Frankfort, KY 40602-0517
Main phone: 502-564-6027
Fax: 502-564-6090

Louisiana
State Insurance Commissioner's Office
Louisiana Department of Insurance
950 N 5th St.
Baton Rouge, LA 70804-9214
Main phone: 225-343-4834

Maine
State Insurance Commissioner's Office
Department of Professional and Financing Regulations
State Office Building
Station 34
Augusta, ME 04333-0034
Main phone: 207-624-8475
Fax: 207-624-8599

Maryland
State Insurance Commissioner's Office
Maryland Bureau of Insurance
501 St. Paul Place
Stanbalt Building
7th Floor South
Baltimore, MD 21202-2272
Main phone: 410-468-2000

Massachusetts
State Insurance Commissioner's Office
Massachusetts Department of Insurance
470 Atlantic Ave.
Boston, MA 02210-2223
Main phone: 617-521-7794
Fax: 617-521-7772

Michigan
State Insurance Commissioner's Office
Michigan Insurance Bureau, Department of Commerce
611 W Ottawa St.
2nd Floor North
Lansing, MI 48933-1020
Main phone: 517-373-9273
Fax: 517-373-9273

Minnesota
State Insurance Commissioner's Office
Minnesota Department of Commerce
133 E 7th St.
St. Paul, MN 55101
Main phone: 651-296-6025
Fax: 651-282-2568

Mississippi
State Insurance Commissioner's Office
Mississippi Department of Insurance
1804 Walter Sillers Building
Jackson, MS 39205
Main phone: 601-359-3569
Fax: 601-359-2474

Missouri
State Insurance Commissioner's Office
Missouri Department of Insurance
301 W High St.
6th Floor North
Jefferson City, MO 65102-0690
Main phone: 573-751-4126
Fax: 573-751-1165

Montana
State Insurance Commissioner's Office
126 N Sanders St.
270 Mitchell Building
Helena, MT 59601
Main phone: 406-444-2040

Nebraska
State Insurance Commissioner's Office
Terminal Building
941 O St.
Lincoln, NE 68509-8920
Main phone: 402-471-2201
Fax: 402-471-4610

Nevada
State Insurance Commissioner's Office
1665 Hot Springs Rd.
Carson City, NV 89710
Main phone: 775-687-4270
Fax: 775-687-3937

New Hampshire
State Insurance Commissioner's Office
56 Old Suncook Rd.
Concord, NH 03301-7317
Main phone: 800-852-3416 -or- 603-271-2261
Fax: 603-271-1406

New Jersey
State Insurance Commissioner's Office
New Jersey Department of Insurance
20 W State St.
CN325
Trenton, NJ 08625
Main phone: 609-292-7272
Fax: 609-984-5273

New Mexico
State Insurance Commissioner's Office
New Mexico Department of Insurance
PO Box Drawer 1269
Santa Fe, NM 87504-1269
Main phone: 505-827-4601
Fax: 505-827-4734

New York
State Insurance Commissioner's Office
160 W Broadway
New York, NY 10013
Main phone: 212-480-6400

North Carolina
State Insurance Commissioner's Office
North Carolina Department of Insurance
PO Box 26387
4140 Dobbs Building
Raleigh, NC 27611
Main phone: 919-733-7349
Fax: 919-733-0085

North Dakota
State Insurance Commissioner's Office
600 E Boulevard Ave.
Bismarck, ND 58505-0320
Main phone: 701-328-2440
Fax: 701-328-4880

Ohio
State Insurance Commissioner's Office
Ohio Department of Commerce and Economics
2100 Stella Court
Columbus, OH 43215
Main phone: 614-644-2658
Fax: 614-644-3744

Oklahoma
State Insurance Commissioner's Office
Oklahoma Department of Insurance
3814 N Santa Fe
Oklahoma City, OK 73118
Main phone: 405-521-2686
Fax: 405-521-6635

Oregon
State Insurance Commissioner's Office
Department of Consumer and Business Services
350 Winter St. NE
Room 200
Salem, OR 97310-0700
Main phone: 503-947-7980

Pennsylvania
State Insurance Commissioner's Office
Pennsylvania Department of Insurance
1326 Strawberry Square
13th Floor
Harrisburg, PA 17120
Main phone: 717-787-7000
Fax: 717-772-1969

Puerto Rico
State Insurance Commissioner's Office
Puerto Rico Department of Insurance
1607 Ponce de Leon Ave.
Cobian's Plaza Building
Santurce, PR 00909
Main phone: 787-722-8686

Rhode Island
State Insurance Commissioner's Office
Department of Business Regulation
233 Richmond St.
Suite 233
Providence, RI 02903-4233
Main phone: 401-456-9100
Fax: 401-456-9284

South Carolina
State Insurance Commissioner's Office
South Carolina Department of Insurance
PO Box 100105
1612 Marion St.
Columbia, SC 29202-3105
Main phone: 803-737-6212
Fax: 803-737-6231

South Dakota
State Insurance Commissioner's Office
Department of Commerce and Regulation
500 E Capitol
Pierre, SD 57501
Main phone: 605-773-3563
Fax: 605-773-5369

Tennessee
State Insurance Commissioner's Office
Department of Commerce and Insurance
500 James Robertson Parkway
4th Floor
Nashville, TN 37243-0574
Main phone: 800-342-4029 (toll-free)
Alternate phone: 615-741-2218

Texas
State Insurance Commissioner's Office
Texas Department of Insurance
PO Box 149104
333 Guadeloupe St.
Austin, TX 78714-9104
Main phone: 512-463-6464
Fax: 512-475-2005

Utah
State Insurance Commissioner's Office
Utah Department of Insurance
3110 State Office Building
Salt Lake City, UT 84114-1201
Main phone: 801-538-3800
Fax: 801-538-3829

Vermont
State Insurance Commissioner's Office
Vermont Division of Insurance
Department of Banking, Insurance, and Securities
89 Main St., Drawer 20
Montpelier, VT 05620-3101
Main phone: 802-828-3301
Fax: 802-828-3306

Virginia
State Insurance Commissioner's Office
Virginia Bureau of Insurance
State Corporation
1300 E Main St.
Richmond, VA 23219
Main phone: 804-371-9694
Fax: 804-371-9873

Washington
State Insurance Commissioner's Office
Washington Office of the Insurance
PO Box 40255
14th Ave. & Water Sts.
Olympia, WA 40255
Main phone: 360-753-7301
Fax: 360-586-3535

West Virginia
State Insurance Commissioner's Office
West Virginia Department of Insurance
PO Box 50540
Charleston, WV 25305-0540
Main phone: 800-642-9004
Alternate phone: 304-558-3386
Fax: 304-558-4965

Wisconsin
State Insurance Commissioner's Office
Office of the Commissioner of Insurance
State of Wisconsin
121 E Wilson
Madison, WI 53707-7873
Main phone: 608-266-0102

Wyoming
State Insurance Commissioner's Office
Wyoming Department of Insurance
122 W 25th St.
3rd Floor East
Herschier Building
Cheyenne, WY 82002-0440
Main phone: 307-777-7401
Fax: 307-777-5895

A5.6 THE PURPOSE OF RISK MANAGEMENT IN MEDICAL PRACTICE AND HEALTH CARE

Risks to doctors, patients, staff, and organizations are increasingly prevalent in health care today. It is necessary for a physician, medical practice, clinic, health-care entity, hospital, or organization to have qualified risk managers to assess, develop, implement, and monitor risk-management plans with the goal of minimizing exposure. And, there are many priorities to a health-care organization, such as doctors, medical staff, finance, safety, and most importantly, patient care, etc.

A5.6.1 The Role of Health-Care Risk Managers

Risk managers are trained to handle various issues in multiple settings. The duties a risk manager undertakes are ultimately determined by the specific organization. These professionals typically work in the following areas of medical administration:

- Physician and medical staff advocacy
- Financing, accounting, insurance, and health-care claims management
- Contemporary event and emerging incident management
- Patient care and clinical research

- Psychological and human health care
- Emergency preparedness and workplace violence awareness
- Governmental and federal legislation

Health-care managers identify and evaluate risks as a means to reduce injury to patients, staff members, and visitors within an organization. Risk managers work proactively and reactively to either prevent incidents or to minimize the damages following an event.

A5.6.2 What Is Risk?

According to the *Dictionary of Health Insurance and Managed Care*, "Risk, in insurance terms, is the possibility of a loss or other adverse event that has the potential to interfere with an organization's ability to fulfill its mandate." Examples of adverse events in health care are unexpected death, failure to diagnose or treat disease, surgical mistakes, or accidents. All of those can interfere with a provider's delivery of medical care. Some can result in litigation.

A5.6.3 Kinds of Risk Management

The Joint Commission (TJC), which accredits and certifies more than 17,000 health-care organizations and programs in the United States, defines risk management in health care as "(c)linical and administrative activities undertaken to identify, evaluate, and reduce the risk of injury to patients, staff, and visitors and the risk of loss to the organization itself."

Risk management is proactive or reactive. Proactive is avoiding/preventing risk. Reactive is minimizing loss or damage after an adverse/bad event. Medical care delivery is art based in science. Good results cannot be guaranteed. Every surgery has the potential for an undesirable outcome. Sometimes, regardless of medical intervention, patients die. Applying common sense can prevent bad results or accidents. For example, slippery floors in high-traffic areas can cause accidents. Washing floors at low-traffic times and diverting traffic away from wet floors until dry is a proactive means of risk avoidance.

A5.6.4 Measuring Risk

Potential for some adverse events can be mathematically measured. Treatment choices for a particular patient with a particular disease depend on the reliability of available options, the nature of the disease, whether the patient is hospitalized, the ease of care delivery, side effects, cure rates, and other factors. Statistical data regarding the effectiveness of medications, as well as the kinds and rates of potential side effects, help physicians decide what to prescribe.

A5.6.5 Managing Risk

After the potential for adverse events is identified and measured, a plan is designed and implemented to avoid risk(s) and/or minimize damage and loss. Risk management does not have recipes, although specific plans can be developed. Occasionally, a plan to prevent risk can create new risks.

For example, the introduction of electronic medical records (EMRs) can make more efficient use of providers' time and ease access to information about patients' prescriptions and medical histories. At the same time, EMRs can invade patients' privacy or cause physicians and nurses to rely too much on technology, instead of customizing diagnosis and treatment. Breaches of privacy and diagnostic or treatment mistakes can result in litigation.

A5.6.6 Management Plan

Risk management must be designed for each organization. An organization's purpose, mandate, size, facility construction, nature of business, location, patient populations, demographics, and other factors must be considered.

Health-care risk management can benefit from already available practice guidelines and principles. National standards for delivered care also help to prevent medical mistakes. Making quality of delivered medical care a top priority can avoid unnecessary treatments, undesirable side effects, and unfortunate outcomes.

A5.7 RISK-MANAGEMENT SOCIETIES AND SPECIALISTS

Medical risk-management societies:

- American Risk Management Association
- Medical Risk Management, Inc.
- Property Risk Management Association
- Risk Management Medical Office Association
- *Risk Management Association Journal*
- Health Care Risk Management Association
- American Society for Healthcare Risk Management

ABQAURP
(American Board of Quality Assurance and Utilization Review Physicians)
6640 Congress St.
New Port Richey, FL 34653
Toll-free: 800-998-6030
Telephone: 727-569-0190
Fax: 727-569-0195

The American Board of Quality Assurance and Utilization Review Physicians was established in 1977 and has evolved to become the nation's largest organization of interdisciplinary risk management, case management, peer review, and worker's comp administration professionals.

Employers from all facets of the health-care industry recognize the value of the ABQAURP credential when seeking qualified health-care professionals to meet their consulting needs. Diplomates are distinguished by their level of skill in analysis and review and in the multifaceted health-care quality and management field. The ABQAURP credential offers opportunity, fellowship, networking, and the prestige associated with recognition of its diplomates as experts in the field. Each year, ABQAURP provides live conferences at geographically convenient locations throughout the United States as well as independent study options.

A5.7.1 Financial Risk Management

Certified risk manager (CRM) is a professional designation in finance. It is for those working in risk management and related fields, such as finance, insurance, loss control, and accounting, and claims specialists. The CRM program is conducted by the National Alliance for Insurance Education and Research. As of December 2012, there were 3349 active CRM designees. The CRM is earned after the completion of five practically oriented courses; approximately 70 courses are scheduled in cities across the United States every year. Once the designation is achieved, annual updates are required by attending a related 2 ½-day course, an annual continuing-education requirement. To earn the CRM designation, participants must complete five courses as below and pass the examinations within 5 calendar years. Each 2 ½-day course incorporates the use of case studies and integrates the direct application of risk-management techniques. Each of these five courses concludes with an optional 2-hour essay examination, which is required for those interested in achieving the designation:

- *Principles of Risk Management* is usually the first course participants take. It gives an overall knowledge of the risk-management process.
- *Analysis of Risk* teaches participants to analyze and measure exposures and loss data.
- *Control of Risk* builds proficiency in safety, alternative dispute resolution, employment practice liability, and crisis management.
- *Financing of Risk* compares and studies various financing options and helps attendees learn to deliver the message to management in present-value dollars.
- *Practice of Risk Management* consolidates all aspects of risk management, including implementing and monitoring the risk-management process in an organization.

The *certified fraud examiner* (CFE) title can be obtained with a rigorous application process followed by a comprehensive board exam. CFE certificants are thoroughly trained to investigate, identify, and prevent both legal and financial crime and fraud. They are subject to periodic continuing-education requirements.

A *certified management accountant* (CMA) overlaps with the competencies of a CPA, but CPAs may be better equipped for compliance, accounting for transactions, tax, and controls. CMAs, as the moniker implies, lean toward financial analysis, organizational performance measurement, budgeting, strategic assessment, and ongoing stewardship of the company. The exam is administered by the Institute of Management Accountants (IMA), which has more than 70,000 members.

The *certified internal auditor* (CIA) examination is offered to accountants who conduct internal audits. CIAs must meet several requirements to obtain this designation, such as passing a four-part exam that covers all issues, risks, and remedies that pertain to internal audits. The CIA designation is conferred by the Institute of Internal Auditors (IIA) and is the only such credential that is accepted worldwide.

A5.7.2 Other Accounting Certifications

There are other niche accounting designations out there that are suited for job- and industry-specific roles. These include

- Certified payroll professional (CPP)
- Fundamental payroll certificate (FPC)
- Accredited business accountant
- Accredited financial examiner (AFE)
- Accredited tax advisor (ATA)
- Accredited tax preparer (ATP)
- Certified bookkeeper (CB)
- Certified Financial Services Auditor® (CFSA®)
- Certified forensic accountant (CrFA)
- Certified professional environmental auditor (CPEA)
- Certified quality auditor (CQA)
- Forensic certified public accountant (FCPA)

A5.7.3 Accounting, Business, Insurance, and Medical Risk-Management Degree Programs

Another way to reengineer your practice into a business and integrate risk-management concepts with insurance and financial planning is through education. Online master's degree programs, for medical professionals, like those offered at Regis University (303-964-5447), the University of Tennessee (423-974-1768), Washington University (Olin) in St. Louis (888-273-6820), and the University of Wisconsin (608-263-4889), may help. More traditional, MBA programs are listed below:

Auburn University, Auburn, Alabama
http://www.pemba.business.auburn.edu

University of South Florida, Tampa
http://www.coba.usf.edu/programs/docs

University of Tennessee, Knoxville
http://www.pemba.utk.edu

University of Colorado, Denver
http://www.colorado.edu/execed

University of California, Irvine
http://www.gsm.uci.edu/programs/index.asp

University of Massachusetts, Amherst
http://www.intra.som.umass.edu/mba/acpe/

University of St. Thomas, Minneapolis
http://www.stthomas.edu/chma

Carnegie Mellon University, Pittsburgh, Pennsylvania
http://www.heinz.cmu.edu/mmm

Tulane University, New Orleans, Louisiana
http://www.hsm.tulane.edu

University of Southern California, Los Angeles
http://www.marshall.use.edu/web/execdev.cfm?doc_id=1325

Oregon Health & Services University, Portland
http://www.ohsu.edu

University of Utah, Salt Lake City
http://www.uuhsc.utah.edu/medinfo

A5.8 THE ROLE OF ADVISOR–AGENT TEAMWORK

The major insurance and risk-management players have been assembled. Will the team function together well enough to win the game? Getting all of the players on your advisory team to function well together may seem like a daunting task. In reality, it should be the easiest part of the process.

After taking the time to select insurance agents and risk managers, one now should have a team comprised of competent ethical professionals, such as financial and medical planners, accountants, and attorneys, who have shown they communicate effectively. It is likely that, if these people are as good as they seem, they may already know each other and may have worked with each other. Moreover, good advisors want to learn more. They feed off good interaction with other advisors because it makes them better able to identify and address issues with their clients. This is not to say that merely hiring people adept in their particular field is all that is necessary for the development of good teamwork. The sports world is full of teams with loads of individual talent but no championship rings. There are steps that can be taken to help foster an appropriate level of teamwork.

1. Designate the quarterback. Only the fully licensed CMP has the professional mandate to coordinate a doctor client's financial and practice affairs from the big-picture perspective, as a fiduciary at all times. The planner, however, must hand the ball off to the other players to get the job done properly.
2. Make sure the players know about each other.
3. Define everyone's role and communicate your wishes to all the advisors.
4. Meet as a group on occasion.
5. Tolerate no arguments.
6. Make the advisors clarify confusing issues.
7. Always remember, and remind if necessary, that the doctor client is the boss.

The core of the team is the CMP and/or fiduciary-bound CFP. From time to time, however, other people will be needed. Bankers, actuaries, MBAs, and real-estate agents are the most common. To assemble these other players, one should get feedback from the core advisors.

All other things being equal, an independent provider is usually better, the exception being the banker.

A5.8.1 The Banker

As we have seen, doctors carry notoriously heavy debt loads. Beyond the costs of a medical education are substantial costs for equipping and staffing a practice. Technology changes fast these days, and capital is required frequently.

Unfortunately, bankers are very conservative by nature. It may be increasingly difficult to borrow money, especially since modern bankers know that a medical degree is no longer the guarantee of a steady and high income that it once was in the past. As more than one banker has often opined, "We don't usually loan money to doctors who really need it." They may also not have a clue about what the practitioner can do to better compete in the managed care arena. Bankers do have a good concept of local community politics, however, for those not familiar with a practice venue. They frequently can provide references to advisors (their own internal profit generation). Bankers generally do not charge a fee for their "bank advice," but they do for products. The more business one does with a bank, the better the terms that can be obtained. But, bankers are not fiduciaries.

A5.8.2 The Real-Estate Agent

Real-estate agents come in all sorts of forms. A good one shortens the sales cycle immensely. The choice of agent should consider both the size of the real-estate agency and the experience of the agent. The agent desired is not a part-timer, nor someone with only a couple of years' experience. Further, the agent should be focused on the price range and type of property in question. A good agent asks lots of questions in order to try to keep buyers from looking at properties that do not match what is wanted. But, like bankers, real-estate agents are not fiduciaries.

When choosing a *listing agent*, the size and number of listings an agency maintains is an important consideration: the more, the better. When interviewing an agent to sell a piece of property, ask about how they get and handle potential buyers. The essential question is would someone buy from this person? The lure of investing in a tangible asset like real estate is enticing for high-risk-tolerant physician-investors who need a sense of control and interaction with their investments. If you are among them, here are a few guidelines that may keep you on a profitable path.

1. Don't attempt to purchase investment real estate without the help of a commercial real-estate specialist who is a fiduciary bound to look out for your best interest. Engage a *Certified Commercial Investment Member* (CCIM) with years of training and experience in analyzing and acquiring investment real estate. To find a CCIM near you, go to http://www.ccim.com.
2. You will sign a disclosure agreement that will tell you who the realtor represents. Be sure the realtor you engage represents you and not the seller, both parties, or neither party.
3. Never trust the income and expense data provided by the seller's realtor. While a seller represented by a CCIM will have a greater chance of supplying you with accurate data, most will significantly understate expenses and overstate the

capitalization rate. Selling realtors often understate the average annual cost of repairs and maintenance. We estimate this annual expense at 10%.

4. Another often understated expense is management. Many owners manage their own properties, so the selling broker doesn't include an estimate for management expenses. They should. Real estate doesn't manage itself, ever. You will either need to hire professional management or do your own management (always a scary proposition). Even if you do it yourself, you have an opportunity cost of your time, so you must include a management fee in the expenses. Most small residential apartments and single-family homes will pay 10% of their rents to a manager.
5. You must verify all the costs presented to you by the seller's realtor. Demand copies of at least the last 3 and preferably 5 years of tax returns. Research items like utility bills, property taxes, legal fees, insurance costs and repairs, maintenance costs, replacement reserves, tax preparation, and all management fees. As a rule of thumb, expenses will average 40% of rental income on average-aged properties where the tenants pay for all utilities except water. Newer properties may have expenses as low as 35%, while in older properties, expenses can be as high as 50%.
6. By subtracting the vacancy rate and stabilized expenses from the rent, you will find the net operating income. This is the income you will put in your pocket—assuming the property is paid for. By dividing the net operating income by the purchase price, you will find the return you will receive on your investment, called the capitalization or "cap" rate. In Rapid City, South Dakota, for example, the cap rate tends to be 4% for single-family homes, 5–8% for duplexes to eight-plexes, and 8–12% for larger residential and commercial properties.

Always remember, real estate is not a quick or easy path to riches.

A5.8.3 More on the Property and Casualty Agent

A good P&C agent is needed to protect your home and business. The P&C agent should have an array of carriers with which the business can be placed. One should not hesitate to place different types of coverage with different insurers. Most insurance companies will offer a discount if you place multiple coverages with them. However, this may not be as beneficial as insuring each need with a specialist. Again, the P&C agent is not a fiduciary.

The easiest way to handle this issue is to get consensus agreement from the core team members as to the amount and types of insurance coverage. Once that is accomplished, appropriate agents can be contacted. In addition to the usual questioning regarding competence and a background check, the agent should be made aware that the core team will be reviewing all proposals. Proposals should include what is known as a *ledger statement*.

Ultimately, physician-focused medical practice risk management and insurance planning is about helping some very smart people change their behavior for the better. But, one can't help doctors choose which opportunities to take advantage of along the way unless there is a sound base of technical knowledge to apply the best skills, tools, and techniques to achieve their goals in the first place. Most of the harms inflicted on consumers by insurance agents and risk managers occur not due to malice or greed but ignorance; as a result, better consumer protections require not only a fiduciary standard for advice, but also a higher standard for competency.

Being a risk manager, insurance agent, or CMP entails lifelong learning (LLL). People should not be allowed to hold themselves out as an advisor, consultant, or planner unless they are held to a fiduciary standard, period. Corollary—there's nothing wrong with an agency standard, but those in sales should be required to hold themselves out as salespersons, not advisor.

The real distinction is between advisors and salespeople. And, fiduciary standards can accommodate both fee and commission compensation mechanisms. However, there must be clear standards and a process to which advisors can be held accountable to affirm that a recommendation met the fiduciary obligation despite the compensation involved. Ultimately, being a fiduciary is about process, not compensation.

A5.9 HEALTH INFORMATION TECHNOLOGY AND DIGITAL HEALTH JOB OPPORTUNITIES, QUALIFICATIONS, AND CERTIFICATION BENEFITS

We've written a number of blog articles and done a few video interviews on job opportunities in digital health recently and have received a steady stream of questions since then. Given health-care information technology (IT) professionals can make $90,000 or more annually, there has been growing interest in the industry. To help separate fact from fiction and dive a little deeper in to the realities of these opportunities, we've reached out to Beth Kelly, a freelance writer from Chicago, Illinois, to summarize the projected outlook for specialized positions within the field of health IT (HIT). Careers in HIT are appealing whether your preference lies within the computer or medical sciences; what's clear, though, is that to succeed, you'll need to have your passion fit somewhere between both. As positions in the industry are constantly evolving, the ability to adapt to new technology is also crucial—whatever is cool today will be different tomorrow. As health-care providers and physicians strive to implement new technology systems, the expertise of HIT professionals will guide the industry into the future, so knowing the Outcome-Driven Innovation (ODI) and jobs to be done of clinical professionals will be a differentiator for those who possess such skills. The market for HIT continues to show enormous growth potential—with no signs of slowing down any time soon. Here's what Beth thinks the outlook is:

A5.9.1 General Qualifications and Useful Certifications

It's clear that the expanding field of HIT affords plenty of opportunities. But of course, making the move into this field isn't as simple as picking up the phone and interviewing. Qualifications are important—in a recent salary survey report completed by http://www.healthitjobs.com, it was noted that certified workers are, on average, making $10,000+ more than those without certifications. If you are an IT worker currently, CISSP, CCNA, and PMP are a few technical certifications that are in high demand in HIT. But beyond the classroom, HIT requires a unique set of skills, and not all of them are related to technology. In health care, the right applicant needs to understand more than codes and processes. Many hiring managers look for applicants with "soft skills" who are willing to work in a highly collaborative environment. Applicants for HIT positions need to be aware that in a hospital environment, their position is not the star of the show. Ultimately, the health-care world revolves around the patient, and IT roles provide supportive care. In many cases when hiring, institutions prefer applications with a combination of IT and clinical skills.

Optimizing opportunities afforded by the changing health-care landscape requires a lot of hard work and insight into the diverse nature of the HIT job market. Whether you are transitioning to IT from a clinician position or you have an IT background already but are new to health care, challenges are inevitable. But in an increasingly digital world, where people use technology in more ways perhaps than they even realize, an HIT skill set is almost guaranteed to pay off.

The health-care sector of IT is as diverse as the industry itself. There are numerous areas in which to specialize, the following domains being several of the most promising.

A5.9.2 Mobile Health Care

Looking purely at the numbers, Americans are inseparable from their phones. And with nearly one-third of all mobile applications being health related, the opportunity to access and utilize vast amounts of health data is there, also. As Silicon Valley tech companies take a greater interest in mobile health devices, advances in analytic software now make it possible to capture illuminating data about our daily lives. The sum of this information is aimed to transform medicine. Even as privacy concerns loom, the ubiquity of smartphones and tablets promises career opportunities in the realm of HIT.

Joseph Hobbs, chief information officer (CIO) at Community Hospital Anderson located in Anderson, Indiana, had this to say about mobile technologies: "This is a huge topic for any organization. Whether it is a mobile cart, a tablet or a smartphone, you need to give caregivers access at their fingertips. The [other] challenge in health care is that it's not a one-size-fits-all initiative. Beyond just finding a solution—you then have to worry about security and application presentation to all of these types of devices."

Many health professionals agree that the data from medical devices and data from modern electronic health record (EHR) solutions should be integrated. When mobile devices are capable of being linked to EHRs, physicians can provide patients with appointment alerts and medication reminders, as well as additional medical assistance. In the remote patient monitoring space, cell service provider Verizon represents the Converged Health Management solution, one of the first products that hopes to bridge the gap between monitoring devices and EHRs. Partnering with Ideal Life, a medical device company, Verizon's platform is capable of measuring blood pressure, oxygen saturation, glucose levels, and weight.

The market for mobile health-care apps promises many new opportunities with room for tremendous growth and earning potential. According to German market research firm research2guidance, the worldwide market for mobile health applications and their corresponding services reached $2.4 billion in revenue in 2013 and will grow to $26 billion by the end of 2017.

Mobile apps are becoming increasingly significant in the health-care community, their influence extending throughout both the medical and insurance industries. Mobile app developer positions are in extremely high demand. With medical health app growth ahead of the general mobile market, there are a tremendous number of opportunities for people interested in these positions. According to the U.S. Bureau of Labor Statistics (BLS), from the years 2010–2020, there is a projected growth rate of 57.4% for software application developers. For software systems developers, there is a projected growth rate of 71.7%. It's estimated that overall employment in the industry will continue to grow rapidly.

A5.9.3 Clinical Informatics

Clinical analytics are a top priority for two reasons: data mined by those with analytic skill can be used to understand population health, helping better identify infectious disease outbreaks and other population health trends, and can also be used to help a hospital's bottom line. Big data allows providers to better see how their resources are spent and where they can trim the fat. The recent deal between Apple and IBM only promises to fuel the market for data analyst positions.

In the current market, an advanced degree in health informatics is very useful. Because of the move toward EHRs, hospitals and health systems need qualified people to undertake complex projects. A degree opens the door to working for a hospital, a health system, or a vendor that sells electronic records or computer software, or as a professional consultant. From 2010 to 2020, the U.S. Bureau of Labor has said that employment of computer systems analysts in computer systems design and related services will grow 43%. Businesses will typically hire them to reorganize IT departments to operate more efficiently.

A5.9.4 The Health Insurance Portability and Accountability Act, Meaningful Use, and ICD-10 Project Managers

Now that both the Health Insurance Portability and Accountability Act (HIPAA) and HITECH are being fully enforced, affected entities can be audited for compliance at any time. At Stage 2–3 of the HITECH Act, a certain percentage of a provider's patients must use and interact with patient portals. Navigating HIPAA privacy regulations and the proprietary nature of the portal software is a convoluted process. And the transition from International Classification of Diseases, Ninth Revision, Clinical Modification (ICD-9-CM) to ICD-10-CM is a hefty task as well; ICD-9-CM contains 13,000 three- to five-character alphanumeric diagnosis codes with 855 code categories. ICD-10-CM contains 68,000 three- to seven-character alphanumeric diagnosis codes with 2033 code categories. In the transition to greater coding specificity, hospitals typically look for someone who has worked as a coder and in health information management roles.

As health organizations strive toward integrating ICD-10 throughout every aspect of their business, there is an enormous need for medical coding and billing specialists capable of working with the updated diagnostic coding system. ICD-10 skills will make you a front-runner for an in-demand position such as project manager, ICD-10 coding specialist, or even ICD-10 educator.

Skills in HIPAA compliance qualify you for a high-level HIPAA privacy officer position, a role that typically pays over $60,000 annually. Meaningful-use director positions, a recent addition to the health-care landscape, can pay anywhere between $35,000 and $80,000 each year.

A5.9.5 Privacy and Data Breach Prevention Specialists

Health information privacy specialists are in extremely high demand. EHR applications, particularly when accessed on mobile devices, require enhanced security access and monitoring. Data breaches are expensive, embarrassing, and damaging to health groups, but many physicians still neglect to encrypt the patient information they've stored on various devices. Health-care organizations need to take security seriously and bring on IT professionals to ensure they are doing everything they can to reduce instances of identity theft.

Information security spending is expected to increase nationwide, especially within industries that deal with sensitive information, such as hospitals. New security measures are added and reconfigured constantly, and as a result, the demand for privacy and data protection specialists is always high. Job growth for this title is projected to grow upward of 25% within the next 5–10 years.

Pharmaceutical companies, naturally interested in joining the digital health movement as well, have found it more difficult to gain traction. A 2013 Deloitte survey found that, while people trust doctors and medical professionals the most, they trust companies like WedMD next and then Internet search results. Big pharma companies come in dead last. Health-care organizations and pharma companies are competing, not within their respective sectors but against one another. Digital pharma is only now beginning to take off. According to M2i2's chief medical information and innovation officer Sachin Jain in a May 2015 interview, "[T]he ultimate incentive is that we as a company are gradually finding our way into the outcomes improvement business, as opposed to the pill and vaccine business, and as we do that, I think we realize that data and technology and HIT is going to be a critical enabler."

Getting started in HIT is not as intimidating as it may seem. For new job seekers, however, it is important to research the different types of positions available and where you may be most helpful. Additionally, for those without a background in health, learning clinical work flows and the other processes that go into health care is imperative. Experience, if it's outside the realm of health care, can be transferable, but you will need to be sure to tailor your resume and cover letter around the language of the health industry. If possible, volunteer in a hospital or similar HIT setting to obtain hands-on experience.

Unlike humans, who can handle diversity, computers hate variations. Hospitals and physicians have experienced work flow disruptions and productivity loss as they adopt more advanced EHR systems. HIT workers, cogs in the digital health machine, fulfill hybrid roles that blend the skills of clinicians and traditional IT workers. As the nature of the health-care industry continues to evolve, the future for HIT continues to look very bright.

A5.10 FINDING QUALIFIED BUSINESS APPRAISAL AND VALUATION PROFESSIONALS

One landmark case in the business-valuation industry was *The Estate of Edgar A. Berg v. Commissioner* (T.C. Memo 1991-279). The court criticized its two CPAs for not being qualified and for failing to provide an analysis of the appropriate discount. The court observed that both CPAs made only general references to a prior court decision to justify their opinion of value. In rejecting the CPAs, the court accepted the Internal Revenue Service's (IRS's) expert because of his advanced education and demonstration of the discounting process.

This case marked the beginning of the Tax Court's tendency to lean toward the side with the most comprehensive appraisal. Previously, it had a tendency to split the difference. Some experts think that the Berg case launched the business-valuation profession. Since the Berg case, the corpus of knowledge for the valuation profession has grown exponentially. Valuation professionals include those with advanced degrees and designations by professional accrediting bodies.

Therefore, hire local or regional professionals with publishing, teaching, or academic experience—not commissioned agents. Medical specificity is paramount. Physician valuators with experience and deep subject-matter expertise are ideal. But, finding a qualified medical practice appraiser is not always an easy task in a health-care environment with increasing levels of state and federal scrutiny regarding transactions and compensation related to medical practices. So, consider the following guidelines:

- Make sure appraisers use generally accepted IRS methods and have a proven track record with the government for medical appraisals.
- Make sure the valuation is written, substantiates medical practice value, provides detail to support conclusions, and is signed by the appraiser.
- Avoid conflict of interest or self-dealings. Seek an unbiased and independent viewpoint.
- Make sure the appraiser will qualify as an expert witness and is presentable on the witness stand, if needed.
- Request references and examples for previous medical practice appraisals.
- Inquire about experience in publishing, speaking, and teaching medical practice valuations techniques.

Organizations that accredit business appraisers (but not necessarily medical practice appraisers) include the following:

- Health Capital Consultants (HCC), LLC (http://www.healthcapital.com, 1-800 FYI VALU), specializes in health-care valuation, litigation support and expert testimony, financial analysis, and industry research services for hospitals and medical practices.
- The American Society of Appraisers (ASA) (http://www.appraisers.org) offers the ASA designation for business appraisers.
- The American Institute of Certified Public Accountants (http://www.aicpa.org) provides the accredited in business valuation (ABV) for CPAs only.
- The Institute of Business Appraisers (http://www.go-iba.org) awards the certifications of certified business appraiser (CBA), master certified business appraiser (MCBA), and business valuators accredited in valuation (BVAL).
- The National Association of Certified Valuation Analysts (NACVA) (http://www.nacva.com) awards the designations of certified valuation analyst (CVA), accredited valuation analyst (AVA), and certified forensic financial analyst (CFA).
- Fellow of the Royal Institution of Chartered Surveyors (FRICS—Royal Institution of Chartered Surveyors) and certified merger & acquisition advisor (CM&AA—Alliance of Merger & Acquisition Advisors).
- Institute of Medical Business Advisors, Inc., Atlanta, Georgia (770-448-0769, contact: Ann Miller, RN, MHA).

Since some appraisers feel that certain organizations set the bar for certification significantly higher than others, the NACVA website at http://www.nacva.com offers a comparison of the accreditation criteria required by all four major organizations.

A5.11 ASSESSMENT*

A medical practice should be run as a humane business. Profit margins matter even when operating a patient-centric practice, as they may represent better patient sustainability and are economically healthier for all parties. Yet, Harvard University physician-ethicist Linda Emmanuel, MD/PhD, noted that "health professionals are now accountable to business values (such as efficiency and cost effectiveness); so business persons should be accountable to professional values including kindness and compassion."

A5.12 CONCLUSION

In other words, you don't have to impoverish yourself as a doctor to protect your practice or yourself. Thus, we share the philosophy that a fiduciary standard, profitable medical practice, and personal financial success are not mutually exclusive. The information in this chapter will assist in the pursuit of this noble endeavor.

ACKNOWLEDGMENTS

To Robert James Cimasi, MHA, ASA, ASA, FRICS, MCBA, CM&AA, CMP; Todd A. Zigrang, MBA/MHA, ASA, FACHE; and Anne P. Sharamitaro, Esq., executive vice president and general counsel at Health Capital Consultants (HCC), LLC, St. Louis, Missouri (http://www.healthcapital.com).

FURTHER READINGS

Bethel, D: Real Estate Investing: Diversification Beyond Paper Assets. In Marcinko, DE and Hetico, HR (editors): *Comprehensive Financial Planning Strategies for Doctors and Advisors: Best Practices from Leading Consultants and Certified Medical Planners™*. Taylor & Francis Group, Productivity Press, Florence, KY, 2015.

Cimasi, RJ, Alexander, T and Zigrang, TA: Update on Research and Financial Benchmarking in the Healthcare Industry. In Marcinko, DE and Hetico, HR (editors): *Financial Management Strategies for Hospitals and Healthcare Organizations: Tools, Techniques, Checklists and Case Studies*. Specialty Technical Publishers, Blaine, WA, 2014.

Firebaugh, JW and Marcinko, DE: Hospital Endowment Fund Management. In Marcinko, DE (editor): *Healthcare Organizations: Financial Management Strategies*. Specialty Technical Publishers, Blaine, WA, 2010.

Marcinko, DE and Hetico, HR: *Dictionary of Health Economics and Finance*. Springer Publishing, New York, 2007.

Marcinko, DE and Hetico, HR: Selecting a Healthcare Focused Financial Advisory Team: Providing Physician Centric—Not Advisor Centric—Holistic Financial Planning. In Marcinko, DE and Hetico, HR (editors): *Comprehensive Financial Planning Strategies for Doctors and Advisors: Best Practices from Leading Consultants and Certified Medical Planners™*. Taylor & Francis Group, Productivity Press, Florence, KY, 2015.

* Available at http://www.medpagetoday.com/Columns/ConversationsWith/35291.

A5.11 ASSESSMENT

FURTHER READINGS

Epilogue

In his dictionary, Webster defines the word visionary as, "one who is able to see into the future." Unlike some pundits, prescience is not a quality we claim to possess. To the purveyors of economic gloom and doom however, the future for physicians is a bleak *fait accompli*. If you were of this same philosophical ilk prior to reading this book, we hope that you now realize the bulk of medical risk management, asset protection, financial and insurance advisory activity may take place at the physician-executive level, as doctors take back their rightful place as leaders of their own fate.

For this self migration to occur, doctors and their consulting advisors will need to consider the example of our contributing authors to re-engineer their personal situations and medical practices with the tools of the new millennium. Hopefully, *Risk Management, Liability Insurance, and Asset Protection Strategies for Doctors and Advisors: Best Practices from Leading Consultants and Certified Medical Planners*™ will prove useful in this regard; and serve as a valuable resource for all involved in the often chaotic modern ecosystem of the health-care industrial complex.

Do not be complacent, for as onerous as it seems, we may not survive autonomously as a profession without utilizing this sort of information. A new level of practice liability, danger surveillance and risk management has been reached. Although, many will still need professional advice on an as needed basis, some believe that astute physicians will look back on the release of this book and recognize it as the turning point in the current risk management imbroglio as this growing sea-change becomes transparent to all concerned.

Therefore, please realize that our contributing authors face many of the same issues as you. And, although the multi-degreed experts of this book may have a particular expertise, all consultants should never lose sight of the fact that, *above all else*, risk management, insurance planning and asset protection advice should be delivered in an informed manner; with client interest, rather than self-interest, as a guiding standard.

Omnia pro medicus-clientis; or "all for the doctor-client."

Fraternally,

David Edward Marcinko
Hope Rachel Hetico
Mackenzie Hope Marcinko
Ann Marie Miller

BOOK TESTIMONIALS

Physicians who don't understand modern risk management, insurance, business and asset protection principles are sitting ducks waiting to be taken advantage of by unscrupulous insurance agents and financial advisors; and even their own prospective employers or partners. This comprehensive volume from Dr. David Marcinko, and his co-authors, will go a long way toward educating physicians on these critical subjects that were never taught in medical school or residency training.

Dr. James M. Dahle, MD, FACEP
Editor, The White Coat Investor
Salt Lake City, Utah

With time at a premium, and so much vital information packed into one well organized resource, this comprehensive textbook should be on the desk of everyone serving in the healthcare ecosystem. The time you spend reading this frank and compelling book will be richly rewarded.

Dr. J. Wesley Boyd, MD, PhD, MA
Harvard Medical School
Boston, Massachusetts

Physicians have more complex liability challenges to overcome in their lifetime, and less time to do it, than other professionals. Combined with a focus on practicing their discipline, many sadly fail to plan for their own future. They need trustworthy advice on how to effectively protect themselves, families and practice, from the many overt and covert risks that could potentially disrupt years of hard work.

Fortunately, this advice is contained within *Risk Management, Liability Insurance, and Asset Protection Strategies for Doctors and Advisors: Best Practices from Leading Consultants and Certified Medical Planners*™. Written by Dr. David Edward Marcinko, Nurse Hope Rachel Hetico and their team of risk managers, accountants, insurance agents, attorneys and physicians, it is uniquely positioned as an integration of applied, academic and peer-reviewed strategies and research, with case studies, from top consultants and Certified Medical Planners™. It contains the latest principles of risk management and asset protection strategies for the specific challenges of modern physicians. My belief is that any doctor who reads and applies even just a portion of this collective wisdom will be fiscally rewarded. The Institute of Medical Business Advisors has produced another outstanding reference for physicians that provide peace of mind in this unique marketplace! In my opinion, it is a mandatory read for all medical professionals.

David K. Luke, MS-PFP, MIM, CMP™
Net Worth Advisory Group, Inc.
Sandy, Utah

This book is a well-constructed, comprehensive and experiential view of risk management throughout the entire medical practice life-cycle. It is organized in an accessible, high-yield style that is familiar to doctors. Each chapter has case models, examples and insider tips and useful pearls. I was pleased to see multi-degreed physicians sharing their professional experiences in a textbook on something other than clinical medicine.

I can't decide if this book is right on—over the top—or just plain prescient. Now, after a re-read, I conclude it is all of the above; and much more.

Dr. Peter P. Sidoriak
Pottsville, Pennsylvania

When a practicing physician thinks about their risk exposure resulting from providing patient care, medical malpractice risk immediately comes to mind. But, malpractice and liability risk is barely the tip of the iceberg, and likely not even the biggest risk in the daily practice of medicine. There are risks from having medical records to keep private, risks related to proper billing and collections, risks from patients tripping on your office steps, risks from medical board actions, risk arising from divorce, and the list goes on and on.

These liabilities put a doctor's hard earned assets and career in a very vulnerable position. This new book from Dr. David Marcinko and Professor Hope Hetico shows doctors the multiple types of risk they face and provides examples of steps to take to minimize them. It is written clearly and to the point, and is a valuable reference for any well-managed practice. Every doctor who wants to take preventive action against the risks coming at them from all sides needs to read this book.

Richard Berning, MD, FACC
New Haven, Connecticut

This is an excellent companion book to Dr. Marcinko's *Comprehensive Financial Planning Strategies for Doctors and Advisors: Best Practices from Leading Consultants and Certified Medical Planners*™. It is all inclusive yet easy to read with current citations, references and much frightening information. I highly recommend this text. It is a fine educational and risk management tool for all doctors and medical professionals.

Dr. David B. Lumsden, MD, MS, MA
Orthopedic Surgeon
Baltimore, Maryland

This comprehensive text book provides an in-depth presentation of the cybersecurity and real risk management, asset protection and insurance issues facing all medical profession today. It is far beyond the mere medical malpractice concerns I faced when originally entering practice decades ago.

Dr. Barbara S. Schlefman, DPM, MS
Family Foot Care, Pennsylvania
Tucker, Georgia

Am I over-insured and thus wasting money? Am I under-insured and thus at risk for a liability or other disaster? I never really had the means of answering these questions; until now.

Dr. Lloyd M. Krieger, MD, MBA
Rodeo Drive Plastic Surgery
Beverly Hills, California

I read and use this book, and several others, from Dr. David Edward Marcinko and his team of advisors.

Dr. John Kelley, DO
Orthopedic Surgeon
Tucker, Georgia

An important step in the risk management, insurance planning and asset protection process is the assessment of needs. One can create a strong foundation for success only after all needs have been analyzed so that a plan can be constructed and then implemented. This book does an excellent job of recognizing those needs and addressing strategies to reduce them.

Shikha Mittra, MBA, CFP®, CRPS®, CMFC®, AIF®
President, Retire Smart Consulting LLC
Princeton, New Jersey

The Certified Medical Planner™ professional designation and education program was created by the Institute of Medical Business Advisors Inc., and Dr. David Edward Marcinko and his team (who wrote this book). It is intended for financial advisors who aim specifically to serve physicians and the medical community. Content focuses not only on the insurance and professional liability issues relevant to physicians, but also provides an understanding of the risky business of medical practice so advisors can help work more successfully with their doctor-clients.

Michael E. Kitces, MSFS, MTAX, CFP®,
CLU, ChFC, RHU, REBC, CASL
www.Kitecs.com
Virginia, Reston

I have read this text and used consulting services from the Institute of Medical Business of Advisors Inc. on several occasions.

Dr. Marsha Lee, DO
Radiologists
Norcross, Georgia

The medical education system is grueling and designed to produce excellence in medical knowledge and patient care. What it doesn't prepare us for is the slings and arrows that come our way once we actually start practicing medicine. Successfully avoiding these land mines can make all the difference in the world when it comes to having a fulfilling practice. Given the importance of risk management and mitigation, you would think these subjects would be front and center in both medical school and residency—"they aren't." Thankfully, the brain trust over at iMBA Inc. has compiled this comprehensive guide designed to help you navigate these mine fields so that you can focus on what really matters—patient care.

Dennis Bethel, MD
Emergency Medicine Physician

Index

Page numbers followed by f and t indicate figures and tables, respectively.

I

M

N

O

P

Q

R

S

T

For Product Safety Concerns and Information please contact our
EU representative GPSR@taylorandfrancis.com Taylor & Francis
Verlag GmbH, Kaufingerstraße 24, 80331 München, Germany